DANCE AND DRAMA IN FRENCH BAROQUE OPE

Since its inception, French opera has embraced dance, yet all too often operatic dancing is treated as mere decoration. *Dance and Drama in French Baroque Opera* exposes the multiple and meaningful roles dance has played, starting from Jean-Baptiste Lully's first opera in 1672. It counters prevailing notions in operatic historiography that dance was parenthetical and presents compelling evidence that the divertissement – present in every act of every opera – is essential to understanding the work. The book considers the operas of Lully – his lighter works as well as his tragedies – and the 46-year period between the death of Lully and the arrival of Rameau, when influences from the commedia dell'arte and other theatres began to inflect French operatic practices. It explores the intersections of musical, textual, choreographic, and staging practices at a complex institution – the Académie Royale de Musique – which upheld as a fundamental aesthetic principle the integration of dance into opera.

REBECCA HARRIS-WARRICK is Professor of Music at Cornell University in Ithaca, NY. She has published widely on French baroque music and dance, with excursions into nineteenth-century opera, and has prepared critical editions of ballets by Lully and of Donizetti's opera, *La Favorite*. Much of her scholarly work has been informed by her interests in performance; she has studied early dance and performed as a baroque flutist. She serves on the editorial boards for *Les Œuvres complètes de Jean-Baptiste Lully* and the *Journal of the Society for Seventeenth-Century Music*. Her research has been supported by fellowships from the National Endowment for the Humanities, the Mellon Foundation, and the Guggenheim Foundation.

CAMBRIDGE STUDIES IN OPERA

Series Editor: Arthur Groos, Cornell University

Volumes for *Cambridge Studies in Opera* explore the cultural, political and social influences of the genre. As a cultural art form, opera is not produced in a vacuum. Rather, it is influenced, whether directly or in more subtle ways, by its social and political environment. In turn, opera leaves its mark on society and contributes to shaping the cultural climate. Studies to be included in the series will look at these various relationships including the politics and economics of opera, the operatic representation of women or the singers who portrayed them, the history of opera as theatre, and the evolution of the opera house.

Published Titles

Opera Buffa in Mozart's Vienna
Edited by Mary Hunter and James Webster

German Opera: From the Beginnings to Wagner
John Warrack

Johann Strauss and Vienna: Operatta and the Politics of Popular Culture
Camille Crittenden

Opera and Drama in Eighteenth-Century London: The King's Theatre, Garrick and the Business of Performance
Ian Woodfield

Opera Liberalism, and Antisemitism in Nineteenth-Century France: The Politics of Halévy's *La Juive*
Diana R. Hallman

Three Modes of Perception in Mozart: The Philosophical, Pastoral, and Comic in *Così fan tutte*
Edmund J. Goehring

Landscape and Gender in Italian Opera: The Alpine Virgin from Bellini to Puccini
Emanuele Senici

Aesthetics of Opera in the *Ancien Régime*, 1647–1785
Downing A. Thomas

The Puccini Problem: Opera, Nationalism, and Modernity
Alexandra Wilson

The Prima Donna and Opera, 1815–1930
Susan Rutherford

Opera and Society in Italy and France from Monteverdi to Bourdieu
Edited by Victoria Johnson, Jane F. Fulcher, and Thomas Ertman

Wagner's Ring Cycle and the Greeks
Daniel H. Foster

When Opera Meets Film
Marcia J. Citron

Situating Opera: Period, Genre, Reception
Herbert Lindenberger

Rossini in Restoration Paris: The Sound of Modern Life
Benjamin Walton

Italian Opera in the Age of the American Revolution
Pierpaolo Polzonetti

Opera in the Novel from Balzac to Proust
Cormac Newark

Opera in the Age of Rousseau: Music, Confrontation, Realism
David Charlton

The Sounds of Paris in Verdi's *La traviata*
Emilio Sala

The Rival Sirens: Performance and Identity on Handel's Operatic Stage
Suzanne Aspden

Sentimental Opera: Questions of Genre in the Age of Bourgeois Drama
Stefano Castelvecchi

Verdi, Opera, Women
Susan Rutherford

Rounding Wagner's Mountain: Richard Strauss and Modern German Opera
Bryan Gilliam

Opera and Modern Spectatorship in Late Nineteenth-Century Italy
Alessandra Campana

Opera Acts: Singers and Performance in the Late Nineteenth Century
Karen Henson

Foreign Opera at the London Playhouses: From Mozart to Bellini
Christina Fuhrmann

Dance and Drama in French Baroque Opera: A History
Rebecca Harris-Warrick

Dance and Drama in French Baroque Opera

A History

Rebecca Harris-Warrick

CAMBRIDGE
UNIVERSITY PRESS

CAMBRIDGE
UNIVERSITY PRESS

University Printing House, Cambridge CB2 8BS, United Kingdom

One Liberty Plaza, 20th Floor, New York, NY 10006, USA

477 Williamstown Road, Port Melbourne, VIC 3207, Australia

314-321, 3rd Floor, Plot 3, Splendor Forum, Jasola District Centre, New Delhi - 110025, India

79 Anson Road, #06-04/06, Singapore 079906

Cambridge University Press is part of the University of Cambridge.

It furthers the University's mission by disseminating knowledge in the pursuit of education, learning and research at the highest international levels of excellence.

www.cambridge.org
Information on this title: www.cambridge.org/9781316502785

First published 2016
First paperback edition 2018

A catalogue record for this publication is available from the British Library

Library of Congress Cataloging in Publication data
Harris-Warrick, Rebecca, author.
Dance and drama in French baroque opera / Rebecca Harris-Warrick.
New York : Cambridge University Press, 2016. | Series: Cambridge studies in opera | Includes bibliographical references and index.
LCCN 2016023675 | ISBN 9781107137899
LCSH: Dance in opera – France – History – 17th century. | Dance in opera – France – History – 18th century. | Opera – Dramaturgy. | Opera – France – 17th century. | Opera – France – 18th century. | Lully, Jean-Baptiste, 1632–1687. Operas.
LCC ML1727.2 .H37 2016 | DDC 782.10944/09032–dc23
LC record available at https://lccn.loc.gov/2016023675

ISBN 978-1-107-13789-9 Hardback
ISBN 978-1-316-50278-5 Paperback

For Ron

my partner on the dance floor and in life

CONTENTS

FIGURES

ACKNOWLEDGEMENTS

I am profoundly grateful for the support I have received from institutions and individuals alike over the long gestation of this book. The reading room of the Bibliothèque de l'Opéra has come to feel like a second home and I have spent many fruitful hours in the Département de la Musique of the Bibliothèque nationale de France as well. Other branches of the BnF house materials that were important for this study: Tolbiac, les Arts du Spectacle, Manuscrits, Estampes, and the Arsenal. The BnF's online library, Gallica, has become indispensable for those of us who do not live in Paris. I owe special thanks to Pascal Denécheau at the Institut de Recherche en Musicologie (IReMus, formerly IRPMF) who generously helped me locate materials and even signaled scores and documents he encountered that he knew would interest me. The library system at my home institution, Cornell University, has a substantial collection of materials on opera that has been thoughtfully nourished during my time at Cornell by the late Lenore Coral and her successor at the helm of the music library, Bonna Boettcher. They and their staffs have aided me in ways far too numerous to detail. Other libraries where I have worked on this project include the National Library of Sweden, particularly its music collection (where the late Anders Lönn welcomed me), the Harvard Theatre Collection, the Music and Dance Collections of the New York Public Library, and the Library of Congress, particularly its website of early dance treatises, curated by Elizabeth Aldrich. To the librarians and staffs of all these collections I offer my thanks for their welcome and assistance. I am very grateful to the National Endowment for the Humanities and the Guggenheim Foundation for their support of my research. I would also like to thank the James R. Anthony Endowment of the American Musicological Society, funded in part by the National Endowment for the Humanities and the Andrew W. Mellon Foundation, for subvening production expenses of the book.

My interest in baroque dance was first awakened by Wendy Hilton, with whom I studied while a graduate student at Stanford University. Ingrid Brainard further nourished both my scholarly and practical interests in early dance. Neither they nor James R. Anthony, who helped guide my early explorations into the music of Jean-Baptiste Lully, lived to see this project develop, but their guidance and encouragement remain models for me. Scholars whose work in French baroque opera undergirds several portions of this study include Lois Rosow, Jérôme de La Gorce, and Nathalie Lecomte. All of them have stimulated my thinking and supported my work in many important ways. I am particularly grateful to Nathalie Lecomte, who generously allowed me to consult her unpublished work about the dancers at the Opéra and answered countless questions, large and small. The sections about the dance troupe owe an enormous debt to her research.

The experience of working with Carol Marsh on *Le Mariage de la grosse Cathos* transformed the nature of the questions that I could ask about dance in opera. Carol has been a companion every step of the way in the development of this book, from its earliest beginnings to its final stages. Over the years she has acted as a sounding board, read drafts of chapters, corrected my errors, and guided me in how to organize data visually; I could not have done the tables without her help. Other colleagues who have generously assisted me include Antonia Banducci, Bruce Alan Brown, Marian Smith, and Arthur Groos, my colleague at Cornell and series editor of Cambridge Studies in Opera. I am grateful to the anonymous readers for CUP whose insightful comments improved the manuscript. I would also like to thank Mickaël Bouffard, Damien Mahiet, and Andrew Zhou for their assistance with the book's production.

One of the most rewarding parts of working on this book has been the exchanges it has fostered with scholar-performers on both sides of the Atlantic. These have run the gamut from informal conversations to sustained correspondence to collaborative presentations at workshops and conferences, and even to staged performances. Some of those working on the intersections between scholarship and performance from whose perspectives I have benefitted include Julie Andrijeski, Christine Bayle, Marie-Françoise Bouchon, Caroline Copeland, Sarah Edgar, Jane Gingell, Irène Ginger, Moira Goff, Guillaume Jablonka, Edith Lalonger, Jean-Noël Laurenti, Marie-Thérèse Mourey, Laura Naudeix, Eugénia Roucher, Stephanie Schroedter, Linda Tomko, Catherine Turocy, Jed Wentz, and, at the Boston Early Music Festival, Gilbert Blin, Steven Stubbs, and Paul O'Dette. I owe particular debts to three dancer-scholars – Hubert Hazebroucq, Ken Pierce, and Jennifer Thorp – who have repeatedly helped me think through thorny questions regarding baroque dance practices. Performances I organized at Cornell allowed me to try out some of my research on stage, most notably Lully's *Carnaval mascarade*, done in 2003 in collaboration with the Eastman School of Music, with Paul O'Dette, music director, and Ken Pierce, choreographer; *Harlequin's Capers*, choreographed by Catherine Turocy with the New York Baroque Dance Company in 2007; and, in 2012, *Les Voyages de l'Amour,* a pastiche of works by Campra, Clérambault, and Rameau, choreographed and directed by Catherine Turocy. I offer my grateful thanks to all those involved in those productions. Countless other dancers and musicians have opened my eyes and ears by bringing new life to works that had been sitting silently on library shelves. When I began the research for this book only a handful of operas by Lully had been performed or recorded and almost no others before Rameau; now the landscape is undergoing transformation. I hope that this book repays some of my debts to the dancers and musicians whose performances have enriched it.

This book could not have been written without the ongoing support of my family, particularly of my parents, who led me to love opera, and of my husband Ron, an extraordinary neurobiologist who learned – and even taught – baroque dance at my side and who has been steadfast in his encouragement ever since.

NOTES TO THE TEXT

All translations are mine, unless noted otherwise. Quotations from French, of titles and citations, have been modernized and the spelling of proper names standardized.

Music examples are transcribed into modern notation, but retain their original time and key signatures. In most examples of orchestral music only the treble and bass lines have been transcribed. Trio textures, however, adhere to the sources.

In this book, the word "score" refers to a musical score; the term is not applied to dance notations.

I have published some of the observations made in this book in earlier versions. These are generally identified in the relevant chapters; see also the Bibliography.

Appendix 3 is online at www.cambridge.org/9781107137890

ABBREVIATIONS

ARM	Académie Royale de Musique
B.C.	basse continue
BnF	Bibliothèque nationale de France
FL	Francine Lancelot, *La Belle Dance: Catalogue raisonné fait en l'an 1995* (Paris: Van Dieren Éditeur, 1996).
HW&M	Rebecca Harris-Warrick and Carol G. Marsh, *Musical Theatre at the Court of Louis XIV: Le Mariage de la Grosse Cathos* (Cambridge University Press, 1994).
LLC	Carl B. Schmidt, *The Livrets of Jean-Baptiste Lully's* Tragédies Lyriques*: A Catalogue Raisonné* (New York: Performers' Editions, 1995).
LMC	Meredith Ellis Little and Carol G. Marsh, *La Danse Noble: An Inventory of Dances and Sources* (Williamstown, MA: Broude Bros., 1992).
LWV	Herbert Schneider, *Chronologisch-thematisches Verzeichnis sämtlicher Werke von Jean-Baptiste Lully* (Tutzing: Hans Schneider, 1981).
MF	*Mercure de France*
NGO	*New Grove Dictionary of Opera*
PG	partition générale (full score)
PR	partition réduite (reduced score)

Library Sigla adhere to those given in *The New Grove Dictionary of Music and Musicians*.

Introduction

"Opera is a spectacle made as much for the eyes as for the ears."

Durey de Noinville, *Histoire du Théâtre de l'Opéra en France* (Paris, 1753), I, 6.

Since its inception, French opera has embraced dance – a reality that operatic historiography has not yet fully fathomed. Up until the eve of the Revolution, dance figured in every act of every opera, yet all too often operatic dancing is treated as if it were merely decorative. The few music historians who recognize that dance matters to French opera have tended to endorse such a view implicitly, studying the music in isolation using formalist tools (dance types, rhythmic profiles, key structures, and so forth). Dance historians, on the other hand, are obliged to locate the roots of ballet in its operatic history, but tell the story as a struggle for ballet to free itself from opera's shackles. The viewpoints of the two disciplines may differ, but the result is the same: few music or dance historians have taken an interest in how dance participates dramatically within operatic works. Now that opera studies have broadened to acknowledge that opera incorporates multiple discourses and multiple systems of meaning, the time seems ripe for an integrative model for French opera that includes the dancing instead of marginalizing it.

My premise that dance matters deeply to the operas created at the Paris Opéra during its first 80 years has grown out of the process of taking individual works and investigating what dance is doing inside each of them. My research thus rests on librettos, scores, and – where they exist – choreographic notations, more than on theoretical writings, past or present. The single most important lesson that emerges from such a work-centered approach is that dance is so thoroughly woven into the fabric of the opera that it cannot be considered in isolation. The so-called "divertissement," the part of every act in which crowds of singing and dancing characters flood the stage, must be understood as a unit, and because every divertissement is so substantial, its function within the act and the opera also begs for interpretation. Every moment of dancing thus has a double frame: the immediate surroundings and the larger dramatic context. The framing of divertissements has generated a modest amount of scholarly attention, but most writers operate from a narrow perspective: they assume that librettists and composers were obliged to work divertissements into every act, whether they wanted to or not, and that success is measured by how well librettists managed to concoct rationales for their inclusion. By this standard, the village wedding in the fourth act of Lully's *Roland* is much admired because it sets off, by way of contrast, the hero's misery and impending madness. But, by this point of view, the choices made within a divertissement are insignificant – any reasonably appropriate music and text could serve the purpose.

Such a perspective – based on twin assumptions that divertissements are, with few exceptions, parenthetical, and that what happens within them rarely matters – has had the unfortunate effect of deflecting attention away from what is often some of the most beautiful music in an opera. In Lully's day, the lushest and most expansive music occurs in the divertissements; in the next century Rameau raised dance music to new expressive heights. Clearly more is at stake in these scenes than choreographed display alone. The Italians loved ballet as well, but since they usually relegated it to entr'acte entertainment, its existence does not impinge on our conception of the operatic object. In French opera, however, dancing occurs within the acts and is interwoven with vocal music. Such an aesthetic choice cries out for investigation.

This book covers the period from the birth of the Académie Royale de Musique until 1735; a second book will start from the ground-breaking works of Jean-Philippe Rameau. I have based this study on the works performed at the Opéra's public theater, although I have sometimes looked to court performances when they supply evidence otherwise lacking. I have also taken into account performances at other public theaters in Paris, since the Opéra did not function in isolation. My study starts not in 1669, the date enshrined above the proscenium of the Palais Garnier, but in 1672, when Jean-Baptiste Lully wrested the *privilège* for composing opera in French from Pierre Perrin and began writing the works that defined the new genre. The institution Lully founded incorporated the first permanent, professional dance troupe – one that exists to this day. This integrated institutional structure was of a piece with an integrated artistic vision that allowed ballet to flourish and develop; within the framework of opera as a genre and the Opéra as an institution, dance achieved a prominence and an artistic range that set the standard for all of Europe. Even when free-standing ballets came into existence, the old ties between the arts were not severed and reciprocities between the two genres continued to shape them both.

As a more ephemeral art than poetry or music, dance is notoriously difficult to recapture. However, thanks to Louis XIV's desire to include dance in his artistic legacy, he ordered his court choreographer, Pierre Beauchamps, to develop a system of dance notation; as a result we know more about the dance of this era than of most periods before or after. But the notation only transmits individual dances, not entire works, and, like all systems of notation, is incomplete. Even so, its existence has enabled dancers to recover hundreds of choreographies and give today's audiences glimpses of what made French dancing so enthralling in its own time. Moreover, the fact that a number of the choreographies originated on the stage of the Académie Royale de Musique, where they were performed by specific members of the troupe, provides crucial information about the dancing itself that also helps interpret other primary sources. I have sought to give readers a sense of what the dances might have looked like, and to contextualize these movements as they were used on stage. This book is not, however, about dance technique in the baroque era; rather, it aims to put what can be learned from choreographies in the service of broader questions regarding the styles of dancing at the Opéra and operatic dramaturgy. Since moving dancers around the stage makes it necessary to ask what the other people sharing the space with them were doing, I have attempted in a limited way to deal with questions of staging.

Part I starts of necessity with Jean-Baptiste Lully, whose operas gave dance a dramatic centrality that set the pattern for many generations to come. It does not, however, limit itself to the *tragédie en musique*, as do most studies, since Lully himself composed other types of opera that shaped, and were shaped by, dance in ways other than in the *tragédies*. Of the six chapters devoted to Lully, the first provides brief divertissement-centric readings of three of his best-known *tragédies*, by way of illustrating what can be learned when the divertissements are accorded full dramatic standing. Chapter 2 lays out the conventions that Lully and his main librettist, Philippe Quinault, established for operatic divertissements, and then moves from mechanics to broader questions of dramaturgy. Chapter 3 surveys the basic principles of baroque dance and provides information about Lully's dance troupe. Chapter 4 focuses on the staging and styles of operatic dancing, including musical characterization. Chapters 5 and 6 turn to less familiar portions of Lully's operatic output – prologues and works with comic elements – where dance functions differently from the *tragédies*. These works, too, produced offspring; Lully's example remained powerful even when he was composing in less lofty styles.

Part II is devoted to the 46-year period between the death of Lully and the arrival of Rameau, when the proportion of operas that were not *tragédies* began to grow. Works set not in mythological realms but in contemporary locations broadened the styles of dancing and singing, while competition from the fair theaters and the Théâtre Italien even induced the Opéra to borrow from its rivals. The jockeying for position implicit in the variety of works performed at the Académie Royale de Musique becomes explicit in prologues that stage competitions for ascendancy among the Muses, and I have appropriated the librettists' conceit as a structure for the second part of this book. Chapters 8 through 10 cover the works governed by Thalie, Muse of comedy, who was first allowed onto the stage of the Académie Royale de Musique in an Italian guise. But as Chapters 11 and 12 show, her sister Melpomène, Muse of tragedy, remained a powerful rival, even as the divertissements in *tragédies en musique* began to show the impact of practices developed within the lighter genres. When operas were revived, the divertissements, more than any other part of the opera, became the site of revisions and updatings. Terpsichore, Muse of the dance, had an ever-increasing influence that is discussed in Chapters 13 and 14; her power may be seen in alterations to divertissement architecture, the growing roster of dancers in the troupe, and the emergence of star dancers, around whom entire scenes were composed. This is also the period for which

47 choreographies from the stage of the Opéra survive, and during which an increased interest in pantomime led to the introduction of innovative danced sequences to the Opéra, both within and as appendages to full-length works. The varied – or even contradictory – tendencies that the divertissements of this era exhibit do not support a tidy teleology for either dance or music; the variety is refreshing, and many worthwhile operas are now emerging from the general obscurity in which this period of operatic history used to languish.

The impetus for this book has grown out of my experiences in playing, dancing, researching, and editing French music of this period, coupled with a lifelong love for opera. Learning about French dance through my own body was transformative, and as a baroque flutist I also had the valuable experience of accompanying dancers. The artists with whom I have worked or whom I have watched instilled in me both a love of the art and a desire to advance the collective knowledge about it. The historian in me was curious about what such beautiful dances meant to their original audiences, while my editorial work gave me the tools essential for grappling with the complex primary materials. Over the long gestation of this book it has been gratifying to hear so much music that used to be imprisoned in scores transformed into sound, and even into performances on stage, as more and more performers have brought portions of this repertoire back to life. I hope to participate in this continuing revival by offering the fruits of my labor to performers, scholars, and opera lovers alike.

PART I

Lully

1 | The Dramaturgy of Lully's Divertissements

> Mêlons aux plus aimables chants
> Les danses les plus belles.
>
> *Les Fêtes de l'Amour et de Bacchus*, prologue
>
> (Let us mingle our loveliest songs with the most beautiful dances.)

These words, sung by three of the Muses at the end of the prologue to Jean-Baptiste Lully's first opera, invite the members of the audience into the world of the spectacle they are about to watch. At the same time they articulate a statement of aesthetic purpose: the new art was to unite song and dance. This fundamental principle had already surfaced earlier, when Quinault introduced Polymnie as the Muse "who has discovered the means of ushering onto the stage characters who through actions and dances express what others explain in words." Words, music, and dance – their alliance lies at the heart of the operatic world that Lully and Quinault were to create together.

Eighty years later, Louis de Cahusac, himself a librettist and dance historian, was still pondering this type of opera:

> What was Quinault's goal? It was [. . .] to use dance to advance the action, to animate it, to embellish it, to lead it by progressive stages to its perfect development [. . .] Is it possible that he would have introduced dance into his work as a principal component, if dance were not always supposed to act, to paint – to conserve, in a word, the character of imitation and representation that everything placed on the stage must have?[1]

Cahusac's eagerness to enlist Quinault on behalf of his own reformist agenda challenges us to identify the qualities that made Quinault's divertissements so successful. His words further remind us that even in the middle of the eighteenth century, Lully's operas were a touchstone. Not only were many of them still in the repertoire, they remained a powerful model for newly created works. The basic template could be manipulated, but it could not be abandoned.

In the operas of Lully and Quinault the dancing is so thoroughly intertwined with the vocal music that the two arts must be viewed together: dance cannot be separated from its dramatic underpinnings. This chapter uses three of Lully's most familiar operas to sample some of the interpretive options that open up when operatic divertissements are taken seriously; it places the librettos and scores of the operas at the center of the study. Other contemporary sources supplement, but cannot replace, close attention to the works themselves.

[1] Cahusac, *La Danse ancienne et moderne* (1754), III, 75–76. Cahusac wrote many of the dance articles in Diderot's *Encyclopédie* and several librettos for Rameau.

In general, the dancing occurred during the part of every act that came to be called the "divertissement," when groups of performers flooded the stage in a musically and visually sumptuous display that became one of the hallmarks of French opera. The term itself implies a diversion from the main action of the opera, and some historians apply it only to celebratory scenes – at the time often called "fêtes" – not to ceremonies, battles, or other actions.[2] I have chosen, however, to use "divertissement" as a structural term, which refers to a conventionally circumscribed portion of every act, regardless of its contents; its multiple forms are described in Chapter 2. A divertissement generally constitutes a single scene, but may spill over into others or even occupy most of an act. Within all, however, the dances are treated with restraint, in keeping with Lully's overall aesthetic, which eschewed excess. In fact, Lully's divertissements typically include only two or three instrumental dances, each usually quite short. No one in Lully's day would have complained about dancing drowning the opera.[3]

This is not to say that dancing was restricted to instrumental music; dancers were also set in motion during some of the choruses, and the structures that Quinault and Lully crafted are what made the integration of the arts of song and dance possible. The two Cavalli operas performed in Paris – *Xerse* in 1660 and *Ercole amante* in 1662 – may have served as important musical models for Lully, but their relegation of dancing to between the acts, in line with contemporary Venetian practices, partook of an entirely different aesthetic – and this notwithstanding the fact that Lully had supplied the dance music for Cavalli.[4] The fundamental fact that dance in Lully's *tragédies* is embedded within a vocal framework, regardless of whether the dance piece is instrumental or sung, has crucial implications; it impacts how we hear both vocal and instrumental music, interpret the sung texts, think about staging practices, and conceptualize Lully's musical architecture.

Lully's stage is crowded. One or two of the main characters may give their names to the opera, but inside it they are never treated in isolation. On the contrary, the worlds in which they participate are visible and audible in every act (see Figure 1-1). This insistence on the social webs within which protagonists function is what distinguishes French opera the most from its Italian counterpart – even more than the much emphasized differences in vocal writing.[5] As if the stage weren't crowded enough by the beings ready to break into song or dance at a moment's notice, Quinault may also provide silent followers for personages of stature: in *Atys*, the goddess Cybèle is generally surrounded by a troupe of priestesses who, with the exception of her confidante, Mélisse, remain seen but not heard. King Célénus, too, has his own silent

[2] See, for example, Fajon, *L'Opéra à Paris*, 26.

[3] This critique was levelled against Campra's last opera; see the Epilogue.

[4] Only in the last act might dancing be integrated into the action; see Alm, "Winged feet," 223.

[5] By 1672, when Lully began composing opera, Venetian opera had almost eliminated the chorus and relegated dancing to entr'acte entertainment. Exceptions, most notably some operas of the 1690s, may exhibit French influence. See Alm, *ibid.*, esp. 263–64, and Hansell, "Theatrical ballet," esp. 178–82.

Figure I-1: The end of Lully's *Triomphe de l'Amour*, with Jupiter and other gods in the heavens, Amour on his throne, and Flore, Arcas, Pan, nymphs, shepherds, and zephyrs in the foreground. (Photo BnF)

retinue.[6] And then there are allegorical and mythological characters who participate in spectacular acts of stagecraft: personified winds that whip up a tempest to conclude the first act of *Alceste*, or the demonic zephyrs who whisk Armide and Renaud to her hideaway after she cannot bring herself to kill him. Even if supernatural beings or

6 "Suivants de Célénus" figure in seven scenes; at the opening of Act II, Célénus even sends them away. Only in his most private moments does Célénus appear alone.

people in crowds were sometimes supplemented by figures painted on the scenery,[7] there is no escaping their presence in French opera.

Dancers are heavily implicated in the functioning of these social worlds, but they do not act alone. Almost always the dancing characters belong to a collective entity in conjunction with singers; within this group the dancers provide the movement, the singers the voices. Since unity of place was not held by French theorists to apply to opera, these collective characters represent different beings from act to act. More often than not, the groups are at the beck and call of a powerful being, human or divine; the libretto often makes this explicit by identifying them as someone's "followers." In other cases the group may have a leader from among its number – or even two, as happens in the mourning scene in *Alceste* – or it may occasionally act spontaneously. In all three cases the question arises as to who, within the world of the opera, controls these groups and what generates their words and actions. The ability to set bodies in motion provides a visual sign of a leader's power, but even when there is no single agent in command, the mere presence of a group may reveal something crucial about a protagonist or about the surrounding social networks. The question of who exercises power leads naturally to asking what kind of power is being exercised and to what ends. At this point it becomes important to look not only at how the group scenes in the opera are framed, but what happens within them. In *Alceste* – Lully's second *tragédie en musique* – the crowds show that they have a real stake in what happens to their rulers.

ALCESTE (1674)

As Act I opens, Alceste is about to marry Admète, king of Thessaly; the populace rejoices with repeated cries of "Long live the happy couple." In fact, the first utterance of the opera comes not from an individual, but from the chorus – a dramaturgical choice that emphasizes the Thessalians' collective interest in the orderly succession of their rulers. These short choral outbursts, which are *not* accompanied by dancing, also highlight the distress the wedding is causing in some quarters. Alceste has two disappointed suitors: Hercules (here called Alcide) and Licomède, king of the island of Scyros. Alcide struggles to control his feelings for Alceste in order not to betray his friend Admète, but the duplicitous Licomède calls upon a group of sailors to offer a fête in celebration of the wedding, during which he kidnaps the unsuspecting Alceste. The loyal Thessalians come to her aid, but the goddess Thétis, Licomède's sister, calls upon the Aquilons to make a storm that slows their attempts to get to their ships. In Act II Admète comes to the rescue of his bride, and with the help of Alcide lays siege to Scyros. The battle takes place on stage, complete with battering rams; the besiegers win, but Admète is mortally wounded. Apollon announces that Admète's life can be

[7] Swedish architect Nicodemus Tessin so reported in 1687; see Ch. 2, n. 26.

saved only if someone offers to die in his place; Alceste alone is willing to sacrifice her life, and in Act III weeping men and women mourn her untimely death. In Act IV Alcide braves Pluton's demons in the Underworld and, when Proserpine intercedes with her husband, is allowed to leave with Alceste. His motivation, however, is selfish, as he plans to keep her for himself. But upon returning to earth, where he witnesses Alceste and Admète's reunion, he overcomes his baser instincts. Act V concludes with celebrations of the double victory: Alceste's return from the dead and the victory of Alcide over himself (the opera's subtitle is *Le Triomphe d'Alcide*). The words of the double chorus make this explicit: "Triomphez, généreux Alcide," sings one group, while the other responds, "Vivez en paix, heureux époux." A resolution that achieves moral advancement as well as the restoration of order draws not only the population of Thessaly to the celebrations, but people from all over Greece, plus Apollon and the Muses.

The dancers animate the crowd scenes in every act: in the first they are sailors, who dance ostensibly in honor of the wedding, but in actuality as a screen for the abduction; in the second they battle each other as besiegers and besieged; when Alceste dies, they mourn her death; in the Underworld, dancers help evoke the atmosphere of Pluton's realm; and when the opera ends happily, their joyous movements embody the resolution of the preceding four acts. They even help wrap up the opera's subplot. In a loose parallel to the main storyline, there is a comic love triangle among the protagonists' confidants: Céphise, who is attached to Alceste, is courted both by Straton, a follower of Licomède, and by Lychas, Alcide's confidant. Quinault was severely criticized for diluting the main storyline with a frivolous subplot, and after his next opera, *Thésée*, he abandoned overt humor and went back to the single plot line prescribed for classical French drama.[8] But having introduced these three lightweight characters, he was obliged to tie up the loose ends, which he did through a humorous confrontation in V/3 (when Céphise rejects both suitors) and in the concluding divertissement. Among the various peoples of Greece are two groups of rustic dancers: shepherds and shepherdesses, who attach themselves to Céphise, and herdsmen (*pâtres*) who join Straton. These two troupes then join to dance during the chorus that concludes the opera. The words of this double chorus, which celebrate Alcide on the one hand and Alceste and Admète on the other, return to the main plot of the opera, but through a non-verbal medium – the bodies of the dancers associated with the minor characters – the chorus absorbs the subplot as well.[9]

With the exception of the battle in Act II, where the dancers' movements were undoubtedly mimetic, the divertissements engage them in social rituals that resonate outside the fictional world of the opera as well as inside it. The roles the various groups

[8] *Alceste* excited a series of polemics about which much has been written. See, *inter alia*, Couvreur, *Lully*, 292–302, and Norman, *Touched by the Graces*, 99ff. Lully's contemporary Charles Perrault defended these comic characters; see Norman, 108 and Couvreur, 385.

[9] A similar phenomenon occurs at the end of *Cadmus et Hermione*, which has an even more overtly comic subplot.

assume seem very much of a piece with the ones Louis XIV's subjects were assigned in the ritualized world of his court. Celebrations marked important milestones in the French monarchy – Louis XIV's wedding in 1660, for example, or the birth of the Dauphin the following year – in which the public was invited to participate via processions, firework displays, and fountains of wine. The outdoor fête Licomède stages at the end of Act I to honor the newlyweds is reminiscent of the pageantry that marked the multi-day spectaculars the king hosted in the gardens of Versailles in 1664 and 1668. In fact, *Alceste* itself participated in yet another series of elaborate festivities in 1674, when it was performed before the king in the marble courtyard of the royal château, as part of the celebrations marking France's second conquest of Franche-Comté. Similarly, the pomp with which Alceste's death is memorialized reflects the theatricalized mourning rituals that marked the passing of court notables; Jean Berain, who designed most of the sets and costumes for Lully's operas, also designed the decors for a number of court funerals, including the queen's in 1683, just as Lully provided the music.[10] This is by no means to say that the divertissements in an opera such as *Alceste* were intended to imitate specific court practices, but rather that the audience for Lully's operas would have found the public expressions evoked there familiar and uncontrived.

In *Alceste*, then, the social groups function unproblematically to uphold the established order. All act either in obedience to powerful beings, or in spontaneous displays of loyalty to their rulers. Yet for all their loyalty as subjects, groups may nonetheless serve to reflect on the protagonists in telling – and not always flattering – ways. As Buford Norman points out, "*Alceste* raises questions about the nature of kingship," because the actual king, Admète, is portrayed as much weaker than Alcide, the hero who is willing to brave the Underworld.[11] Admète, far from resolving on any course of action, faints when he learns that Alceste has died; the scene in which his subjects mourn the death of their queen takes place around his unconscious body. At the end of the opera Admète shares the glory with Alcide, but the fact that Alcide has gone from a curmudgeonly loner to someone celebrated by Apollon, the Muses, and the assembled multitudes casts him into the brighter light. Even when the crowds behave in conventional ways, the construction of their interactions with the protagonists is not necessarily neutral.

The kinds of social rituals built into an opera such as *Alceste* would have required music in real life, so they provide easy vehicles for staging sumptuous music. At the start of Lully's festive divertissements there is almost always some kind of cue that the discursive frame has shifted from a realm in which singing represents speech to one in which the characters on stage experience what they are doing as musical. In the last act of *Alceste*, the singing characters tell us so themselves: "Chantons, chantons, faisons entendre / Nos

[10] See some of Berain's funeral designs in La Gorce, *Berain*, 104 and 128–35. Beaussant, *Lully*, 537–40 and 773–84, draws analogies between the funeral ceremonies for Chancellor Séguier in 1672 (at which a *Miserere* by Lully was performed) and the funeral rites depicted in *Alceste*.

[11] Norman, *Touched by the Graces*, 105–06; see also 33–36.

chansons jusques dans les cieux," sings Apollon, echoed by the chorus. ("Let us sing, and may our songs reach the heavens.") Another signaling device is the one Quinault used in I/5, when Licomède announces, "It is now time for the fête to start. Let everyone advance and get ready." A third mechanism was to make the music-making visible by putting instrumentalists on stage, as in the dream sequence in Act III of *Atys*. Such insistence on the musicality of the divertissement seems rooted in French uneasiness with the whole concept of opera. For decades the French, who had a long and distinguished tradition of spoken theater, were unconvinced that a drama could plausibly be sung throughout; when at last they themselves succumbed to the allure of opera, the style that emerged eschewed vocal display in favor of a flexible yet restrained recitative, accompanied only by continuo, that set the text with almost no repetition in something akin to real time.[12] But opera cannot survive on heightened speech alone; places where time relaxes and music takes precedence over words were needed to expand the sound world. The divertissements, which drew upon the full resources of the orchestra and introduced structures such as strophic dance-songs and extended choruses, allowed for musical and visual indulgence. In order to justify such radical changes in sonority and in text delivery, these scenes had to be framed, one way or another, as diegetic.

One rationale was situational. Weddings and other festivities plausibly involve music, as do sacred ceremonies. The participation of dance was justified as a natural part of music-making, but also by appeals to ancient authorities, as in the following by dance-theorist Claude-François Menestrier:

> From this discourse by Lucian we learn that the Ancients believed that the gods danced and that they wanted one to dance to honor them [. . .] Virgil has Diana dance on the banks of the Eurotas and on Mount Cynthus with the mountain nymphs [. . .] Apuleius has Venus dance at the wedding of Psyche, and Horace depicts her dancing by moonlight with the nymphs and Graces [. . .] Bacchus danced in the Indies [. . .] The Persians did not believe anyone could be initiated into the mysteries without dance and music. At Delos no sacrifices were performed without both [. . .] The Romans had dancing priests dedicated to Mars [. . .] There is no reason to be surprised that Virgil has departed souls and spirits dance in the Elysian Fields in the sixth book of the *Aeneid*.[13]

This passage reads almost like a list of dancing roles from Lully's operas – which is no accident, as Menestrier goes on to point out (p. 53) that the subjects of ballets are taken from "myth and history"; such types passed easily from court ballets onto the operatic stage. In addition, this list hints at a related justification for dancing, which is that certain character types were defined as beings who by their very nature expressed themselves through dance and song. Thus supernatural beings such as demons or

[12] Starting with *Bellérophon* (1679) Lully sometimes used the orchestra to accompany solo singers, but even in his latest operas his practice was marked by restraint.

[13] Menestrier, *Des Ballets* (1682), 18–29.

dreams danced, as did the earth-bound nymphs and shepherds who inhabited Arcadian landscapes and whom venerable literary tradition defined as natural singers and dancers.[14] In order to satisfy the demands of verisimilitude, characters either had to be dancers by nature, or, if they were ordinary mortals, had to find themselves in situations that made dancing plausible. The celebrations at the end of *Alceste* are doubly acceptable, because royal weddings always have dancing, and because the pastoral characters invited by Apollon are dancers by nature.

Such punctiliousness about verisimilitude may seem out of place within an operatic world that accords such a prominent role to the supernatural. But as Catherine Kintzler has persuasively argued, the *merveilleux* has its own kind of logic, one that both acknowledges and inverts the strict precepts of French classical spoken tragedy:

> Let's take [French] classical spoken tragedy and turn it inside-out like a glove. Reverse the agents, the plot, the means, the effect; pass from the ordinary world to the world of myth or of the *merveilleux* [. . .] Once these inversions have been made, the fundamental laws of classical theater go into effect; this is what makes the *tragédie lyrique* the exact and playful homologue of its dramatic correspondent; this is what places it at the poetic opposite to Italian opera. These laws are reducible to three: necessity, appropriateness, and verisimilitude. They are applied *mutatis mutandis*, but with rigor. In this way one obtains deliciously sophisticated concepts such as "the necessity of dance" or "the verisimilitude of the *merveilleux*."[15]

Once the realm of the *merveilleux* has been accepted as a fundamental part of opera, a set of conventions governing it falls into place, of which its musicality is one. "Music and dance find in the *merveilleux* a favorable terrain that is almost natural. [. . .] It is by nature, therefore, and by virtue of a sort of automatic conformity that demons, furies, naiads, fauns, and wood gods sing and dance; everything that arises from the extraordinary finds a justifiable form of expression in music. At the opera, the *merveilleux* takes the place of nature and gives a foundation to the rationality of the extraordinary."[16] Jean-François Marmontel, *encyclopédiste* and a librettist for Rameau, Grétry, and Piccinni, put the case for French opera succinctly when he wrote that "la musique y fait le charme du merveilleux, le merveilleux y fait la vraisemblance de la musique." ("The music gives enchantment to the *merveilleux* and the *merveilleux* gives verisimilitude to the music.")[17]

Kintzler's insight about "the rationality of the extraordinary" is key to interpreting the divertissements, which, notwithstanding the change in mode from "speech" to

[14] Pierre Perrin, who before Lully tried and failed to get opera established in France, described as prone to singing "poets, musicians, lovers, shepherds, rustics, drunkards, women, and children." Letter quoted in Auld, "'Dealing in shepherds,'" 68.

[15] Kintzler, "La tragédie lyrique," 54. These ideas are more fully developed in her *Poétique de l'opéra français*.

[16] *Ibid.*, 59.

[17] From Marmontel's article "Opéra" in *Eléments de littérature* (1777), cited in Masson, *L'Opéra de Rameau*, 11.

a musical realm, always have a logic that attaches them firmly to the main threads of the opera. In *Alceste* four out of the five divertissements are grounded in the practices of a monarchical society, and the fifth, for all that it is set in the Underworld, presents an orderly foreign kingdom with which one can negotiate. Other operas introduce the *merveilleux* more often than does *Alceste*, but Quinault controls the plotting so tightly that there never seems to be a disruption in the fabric of the work. Lully's fourth tragédie, *Atys*, provides a case in point. One of the main characters, Cybèle, is a goddess, yet the supernatural and human realms blend in an almost seamless manner. Moreover, the divertissements, far from offering distraction from the tensions within the opera, serve to intensify them.

ATYS (1676)

The central conflict within Atys – both the opera and the hero alike – concerns the dissonance between his private desires and his public duties. Atys feigns indifference to love, but the real explanation for his reticence is his love for someone unattainable: Sangaride is, on that very day, to marry Célénus, king of Phrygia and Atys's friend. As the opera opens Atys is preparing for the imminent arrival of the goddess Cybèle, whose visit to Phrygia is a sign of her favor and who is expected to name Célénus as her *grand sacrificateur*. Atys's first words show him in his public role as organizer of the rites in her honor, notwithstanding the fact that he is alone on stage.

Atys: Allons, allons, accourez tous,
Cybèle va descendre.
Trop heureux Phrygiens, venez ici l'attendre.
Mille peuples seront jaloux
Des faveurs que sur nous
Sa bonté va répandre.

("Come, hasten, Cybèle is about to descend. Fortunate Phrygians, come wait for her here. A thousand nations will be jealous of the favors her goodness will bestow upon us." *Atys* 1/1)

The Phrygians he calls do not appear until the end of the act, but they are repeatedly invoked by the refrain (the first two lines above), which from a solo utterance becomes a duet, then a duet for different characters, and finally a quartet, as more and more of the main characters enter the stage. Although in this part of the act the protagonists operate in private, their public selves impinge on their conversations; we learn, for instance, that Sangaride shares responsibility for the honors to be shown Cybèle. (1/6, "*Atys*: Sangaride, ce jour est un grand jour pour vous. *Sangaride*: Nous ordonnons tous deux la fête de Cybèle, / L'honneur est égal entre nous.") Finally, with the Phrygians reported to be in sight, Atys and Sangaride find themselves alone together; their self-imposed silence breaks down and each confesses to loving the other. But just as they are reveling in this discovery, their private moment is shattered by the arrival of the crowds. Instantly Atys and Sangaride must assume their social duties, as they lead the invocation urging Cybèle to favor them with her presence. The larger society now becomes palpably real, as the Phrygians sing and dance to welcome the goddess.

In Act II Cybèle surprises everyone by announcing that her choice of high priest for her cult is not Célénus, but Atys. Atys unenthusiastically accepts his new role and cannot avoid participating in celebrations in his honor. As a sign that both the heavens and the earth pay homage to Cybèle, people from "the two ends of the universe" come to her fête, along with Zephyrs dancing in a *gloire* above the stage.

Earlier in Act II, Cybèle had revealed to her confidant that she chose Atys for this signal honor because she is in love with him. Notwithstanding her great power – or perhaps because of it – she cannot bring herself to tell him so directly. Instead, in Act III, she sends him two sets of dreams while he is asleep on stage: first, happy dreams who reveal the joys that await him if he returns her love, then nightmares, who threaten him with dire consequences should he reject her. Atys awakes with a start, only to be confronted by Cybèle, who tells him to heed the dreams she has sent, and then, left alone, confronts her own loss of hope for the realization of her love.

The jolly divertissement in Act IV ("Que l'on chante, que l'on danse") transports us to the watery realm of Sangaride's father – Sangar, the river god – who is blissfully unaware that his daughter is miserable in the face of her impending wedding. The celebrations among the gathered divinities of rivers, streams, and fountains, which go on at great length, make us realize how impossible it is for Sangaride to escape the roles that are being imposed on her, even as they simultaneously provide needed relief for the audience from the tensions mounting within the opera.

Act V brings on the inevitable tragedy: after Atys and Sangaride attempt to defy Cybèle, she temporarily maddens Atys, who takes Sangaride for a horrible monster and kills her. Brought back to his senses, he turns the knife on himself. The remorseful Cybèle transforms the dead Atys into a tree sacred to her cult. Any sense of resolution is undermined by the opposing words of the double chorus in the concluding divertissement, which go back and forth between pain and rage ("Quelle douleur!" sing the woodland gods, while the Corybantes reply, "Ah, quelle rage!") and by the remarkable set of three instrumental dances that make visible this emotional division.[18] In this opera the social fabric has been torn asunder; the thunder and earthquakes that

[18] See Ch. 4, p. 117.

accompany the concluding chorus tell us that the tragedy is not individual but universal, and the key word in the chorus's last utterance is "horror."[19]

In Quinault's carefully crafted libretto we do not merely hear about the obstacles the protagonists confront, we see them in action. This opera, shorn of its divertissements, would make little sense. The fact that no single individual governs all the group scenes illustrates for the audience how broadly distributed are the social forces with which Atys and Sangaride have to contend.

ARMIDE (1686)

The strictures of society so vividly illustrated in *Atys* are completely lacking in *Armide*. In this opera the central conflict takes place entirely inside the heroine; outside society may be relevant for the hero, Renaud, who in the end returns to the pursuit of military glory, but it means nothing to her and just barely figures inside the world of the opera. The warrior princess Armide, leader of the forces fighting the Crusaders, declares that she has no interest in love, despite her uncle's urging that she marry. She lays a trap for her bitterest enemy, Renaud, but when she stands over his sleeping figure, knife upraised, she finds herself incapable of killing him. Instead she whisks him off to her magic realm, where she alternately tries to drive the love she feels for him from her heart and uses magic to renew the power she has over him. Renaud's commander sends two knights to rescue him; they succeed in breaking the charm, although Renaud leaves Armide with reluctance. In a despairing rage, Armide destroys her enchanted palace and departs on a flying chariot.

In what might seem like a paradox, the divertissements become one of the most effective means of focusing attention on the heroine's struggles with herself. Here are the group characters who sing and dance in *Armide*:

- Act I: the populace of the kingdom of Damascus, celebrating the success Armide's beauty has had in defeating the Christian knights;
- Act II: demons conjured by Armide, disguised as shepherds and shepherdesses, who enchant Renaud;
- Act III: Hatred accompanied by the Furies and the Passions, whom Armide has summoned in a vain attempt to drive the love for Renaud from her heart;
- Act IV: demons transformed by Armide into rustic inhabitants of the island where Armide is holding Renaud captive – here they try to distract the two knights coming to rescue Renaud;
- Act V: demons disguised as Fortunate Lovers and Pleasures, who entertain Renaud while Armide is away.

[19] The opera ends with the words, "Que tout sente, icy bas, / L'horreur d'un si cruel trépas." ("May everyone on earth feel the horror of such a cruel death.")

Already in Act 1, the only time when an actual human society is represented, the chorus focuses our attention on Armide's powers, which have just won her a major victory over Godefroy's knights.

Hidraot et le Chœur: Armide est encor plus aimable
Qu'elle n'est redoutable.
Que son triomphe est glorieux!
Ses charmes les plus forts sont ceux de ses beaux yeux.
Phénice et le Chœur: Suivons Armide et chantons sa victoire.
Tout l'univers retentit de sa gloire.

(*Hidraot and Chorus*: Armide is even more beloved than she is fearsome. How glorious is her triumph! Her strongest charms are the ones that come from her eyes. *Phénice and Chorus*: Let us follow Armide and sing of her victory. The entire universe resounds with her glory.)

In the subsequent four acts, the key word of this passage, "charm," moves from the figurative to the literal. These lengthy and musically rich scenes all arise from Armide's magical powers; within her realm no one else – least of all the putative hero Renaud – has any control over other beings. Armide, however, has an apparently infinite supply of demons ready to assume any human form at her slightest command. Moreover, via a mechanism of displacement, Armide's seductiveness gets activated more through the singing and dancing bodies of her followers than it does through her own utterances. If it were not for the divertissements that Armide conjures up, we would have a very different understanding of both her person and her powers. This is most overt in the last act, the only time in the entire opera when the two lovers have a scene together. Their love duet lasts a mere seven minutes, whereas the famous passacaille that follows, sung and danced by Fortunate Lovers vaunting the pleasures of Love, goes on for over twice as long and warms up the emotional temperature considerably – this despite the fact that Armide herself leaves before it starts. Dance, then as now, was a powerful vehicle for evoking erotic love; it is presumably no accident that the three surviving Baroque choreographies set to this passacaille are all for women.[20] Yet Armide's conjurations ultimately serve only to externalize the struggles going on in her own heart. She succeeds in gaining power over her enemy, but, much to her shame, falls in love with him. She summons Hatred only to drive it away, when she cannot face the consequences of her action. After that fatal moment, she uses her charms to keep Renaud in thrall, knowing full well that his love for her is a product of magic. The creatures she conjures up have nothing to do

[20] Two come from early eighteenth-century English sources. The third, choreographed by Pécour, Beauchamp's successor at the Opéra, was not designed for that stage, but *was* performed by Mlle Subligny – who had been one of the dancers in Act 5 of *Armide* during the 1703 revival.

with the social worlds of *Atys*, even if, on the level of divertissement mechanics, they behave according to similar conventions. No matter how crowded the stage, everywhere we see only Armide.

The same divertissements that show off Armide's powers also serve to underscore Renaud's weakness. Armide herself calls Renaud "the most valiant of all" ("Le plus vaillant de tous," I/1), but the audience has to take her word for his prowess, since it is never exhibited inside the opera. One measure of Renaud's weakness is his failure to control any groups in any of the divertissements; instead, he is the passive recipient of two of them (Acts II and V). The ostensible theme of *Armide* is the classic conflict between love and duty, as the prologue itself states,[21] but in the opera the emphasis lies elsewhere, and the divertissements share the responsibility for shifting the dramatic weight away from Renaud and onto Armide.

INSIDE AND OUTSIDE THE DIVERTISSEMENT

Armide shows the divertissement at its most pointedly focused: the heroine's obsessive love finds expression as much in the group scenes as it does in her own utterances. In *Alceste*, the divertissements highlight power relationships among individuals, and those in *Atys* intensify the progression of the drama by working back and forth across the private and public spheres. Such reciprocities between the main characters and the worlds they inhabit are a fundamental feature of the operatic style that Quinault and Lully created together.

Armide and *Atys* are only two of the operas where group characters represent words or actions that the principals cannot or will not express for themselves. Sometimes the libretto even makes the substitution explicit. In I/2 of *Cadmus et Hermione*, Cadmus arranges a divertissement as a subterfuge for communicating with the captive Hermione: "If I am not allowed to speak to her myself, or to dare say that I love her, at least my Africans will use their sweet songs to tell her about the strength of my love, despite a jealous rival."[22] This effort does not succeed as planned, because the amorous giant and four of his fellows arrive uninvited. The sung texts, which on the surface could just as easily speak for the giant as for Cadmus ("Suivons l'amour, laissons nous enflâmer"), nonetheless carry a subtext intended for Hermione's ears: "Two lovers may dissemble when they are in agreement; the more love has to fear, the more it makes an effort."[23]

[21] "We will see Renaud, notwithstanding sensual pleasure, follow wise and faithful council . . . and fly to where glory calls him." ("Nous y verrons Renaud, malgré la volupté, / Suivre un conseil fidèle et sage; / . . . / Et voler où la gloire appelle son courage.")

[22] "S'il ne m'est permis de lui parler moi-même, / Et d'oser dire que je l'aime; / Du moins nos Afriquains par leurs chants les plus doux, / Pourront l'entretenir de mon amour extrême, / En dépit d'un rival jaloux."

[23] "Deux amants peuvent feindre / Quand ils sont d'accord; / Plus l'Amour trouve à craindre, / Plus il fait d'effort."

In this instance the substitution of surrogates for the hero derives from demands of the plot, but often it has to do with what is appropriate behavior for a high-born character operating within a rigidly hierarchical social system. As Kintzler points out regarding the law of *propriété* (appropriateness), one of the three she sees as applying to both spoken tragedy and *tragédie en musique*, "Someone cannot say or do just anything. A god of first rank will not act directly, as that would be unworthy of his majesty. Instead, he will send an intermediary who, within the hierarchy of the mythological realm, occupies a lower rank, or else he will send dreams to make his intentions known."[24] Kintzler's point about appropriate behavior applies to humans as well. The main characters in Lully's operas generally display a kind of reserve, both textual and musical, that has led some commentators to criticize the operas' emotional temperature. But at least some of what the protagonists do *not* do or say gets displaced onto the bodies of their followers, in scenes that allow for greater musical and visual expressiveness. Most obvious are the celebrations that conclude operas after the hero has conquered adversity and won the hand of his beloved. There the lovers utter at most a few words before their joy is taken over by the chorus and dancers to express at great length. More interesting still are the places where a divertissement externalizes a protagonist's internal state (as when we see Atys's dreams), offers a scene of seduction (*Armide* v/2), or fulfills the function a love duet would have in a different type of opera (*Roland* ii/6).[25]

A divertissement may also objectify the tensions in an opera by deflecting them away from the character who is really their object, thus providing a safe outlet for topics that might appear unseemly if addressed directly. The divertissement in *Thésée* ii/7, in which the Athenian populace celebrates Thésée's latest military victory and urges that he be named King Égée's successor, has as its surprising centerpiece a song and dance for old folks – two old men who sing, and, according to the libretto from the production in 1675 at Saint-Germain, two old couples who dance. With an implicit wink, the text urges oldsters to enjoy their remaining years; an engraving of the dancer Magny as one of the old men provides a sense of the tone (see Figure 1-2).[26] This disruption is not, however, arbitrary. At the start of the act, the aging sorceress Médée has revealed that she loves the young hero; the elderly king of Athens, although sworn to Médée, has not managed to hide the fact that he is in love with beautiful young Aeglé, Thésée's beloved. In other words, two inappropriate, intergenerational, love attractions that are central to the plot have just been acknowledged. The king, warned in advance, does not remain on stage to see the populace offer a triumphal entry to Thésée or to hear their desire to have him as their king. Nor does the king witness the

[24] Kintzler, "La Tragédie lyrique," 56. [25] See my "Reading *Roland*," par. 5.1–5.3.

[26] In the 1707 revival the old men were danced by François and Pierre Dumoulin, who specialized in comic roles; see Ch. 13.

Figure 1-2: "Magny costumed as an old man dancing in the opera *Thésée*."

cavorting of the old folks that holds him and Médée up for ridicule. His absence preserves – just barely – the strictures of social decorum. By the end of the opera his dignity is restored and the right couple comes together, after the king has recognized Thésée as his son and Médée has fled. Mocking lustful oldsters was stock-in-trade of the *comédie italienne*, and *Thésée* provides but one instance of how a more respectful variant on the theme might impinge even upon the *tragédie en musique*.[27]

When divertissements are viewed only in isolation, they often come under attack as a kind of graft onto the opera; Lecerf's much-cited claim that Lully composed the music of the dance-songs first, with Quinault having to fit the words to his rhythms afterwards, has been invoked, explicitly or implicitly, as yet another rationale for dismissing the divertissements:

> When it came to the divertissements, Lully wrote the melodies first, to his own design and in his own style. Words were then needed. In order to get these exactly right, Lully sketched out the lines of verse, and did the same for some *airs de mouvement*. For these *airs de mouvement* and divertissements, Lully added verse whose principal merit was to fit the music perfectly, and he sent this outline to Quinault who made his own adjustments. That is how this free verse (*petites paroles*) . . . came to fit the melodic line so neatly and smoothly.[28]

Such a working arrangement between Lully and Quinault – which seems plausible for the dance-songs, if not necessarily for the large-scale choruses – does not automatically mean that the resultant texts will be trivial and meaningless. What this anecdote does suggest is that Lully may have had more responsibility in setting the affect and structure of the divertissements than did Quinault.[29] Surely the order of composition should not serve as a measure of value; the verses and the music deserve evaluation on their own merits.[30] In fact, Lecerf's last sentence conveys an admiration for Quinault's versifying that was expressed even more strongly by Charles Perrault, who wrote that Quinault's words for dance-songs "were every bit as appropriate, and often even more so, than if they had been composed first."[31]

[27] The same congruence of elements shows up in *Télèphe* (1713), a *tragédie* by Campra and Danchet, which also involves an old king who wishes to marry the young heroine. The divertissement in III/6 opposes an old man, still interested in love, to a young girl singing that winter has no flowers to offer; the dancers included two old and two young couples. Couvreur, citing Charles Perrault, makes a useful distinction between dramatic and thematic links within operas (*Lully*, 385).

[28] Lecerf, *Comparaison*, III, 218, trans. Wood and Sadler, *French Baroque Opera*, 143.

[29] Lecerf (*ibid.*, 212–16, trans. Wood and Sadler, 142–43) reports in a much-quoted passage that after Quinault had given him a scenario for a new opera, Lully went to work on the divertissements, while Quinault drafted the verses for the rest of the opera. Lully reportedly sent multiple drafts back to Quinault for revisions.

[30] Laurenti's study of the philosophical and religious values projected by French opera is based on attentive reading of all the texts, including those inside divertissements; see his *Valeurs morales et religieuses*.

[31] Cited in Norman, *Touched by the Graces*, 41 n.

Given that the divertissements offer the most sumptuous moments in Lully's operas, where the pacing of the music expands, the orchestra is given fuller voice, and the dancers are in motion, they invite analogy with the most striking musical moments in Italian operas – the arias. Cahusac brought the following dance-centric perspective to the question of operatic verisimilitude: "The charm of such a song makes one forget its enormous lack of appropriateness. It is nonetheless all the more inexcusable that an *aria* is almost always an isolated piece that is attached without skill to the end of each scene and that could be removed without damaging the plot; if it were suppressed, the plot would almost always benefit."[32] We certainly are not accustomed to thinking of arias in opera seria as dramatically superfluous; Cahusac's startling perspective asks us to reconsider where in opera the drama resides.

The issue of how well a divertissement is introduced into the act is important, but discussion should not end there. Once the question broadens to what it means for an opera when crowds come together in every act – how the specific choices Quinault and Lully made signify – then a myriad of interpretive possibilities becomes available. A divertissement may or may not further the action, but by virtue of its salience within the act it always participates in the drama.

[32] Cahusac, *La Danse*, III, 60.

2 | Constructing the Divertissement

Just as the larger dramaturgy of divertissements is very carefully controlled, so too is their construction. Lully's notational practices emphasize connectedness, as when the last measure of a recitative changes to the meter of the entrance music for the divertissement, which starts on beat 3 (Figure 2-1). This is not an operatic style that lends itself to interruption by applause; the sense of continuity is far too great. Yet even the most basic questions – such as who danced where – rarely have easy answers, and it is only after comparing every one of Lully's divertissements to its fellows that I have come to identify his conventions. Because some of these have been misunderstood by both scholars and performers, I have felt compelled to lay out the evidence for my conclusions in some detail. This chapter explores the conventions Quinault and Lully developed that allowed for the integration of dance and song within dramatic structures that favor coherence and continuity.

PRIMARY SOURCES

There is no single source to consult for establishing the mechanics of a divertissement. The two most basic are the librettos and scores associated with performances at the Opéra during Lully's lifetime: a libretto was printed for each premiere, and, for every opera starting with *Bellérophon* (1679), a full score was printed by Christophe Ballard, under the supervision of Lully himself.[1] *Isis* was published in partbooks in the year of its premiere (1677), and for two earlier operas, *Atys* and *Thésée*, Ballard published full scores within two years of Lully's death.[2] This means that, for ten out of Lully's thirteen *tragédies en musique*, there are important contemporary sources for both the text and music. The eighteenth-century full scores for *Cadmus et Hermione*, *Isis* (both from 1719) and *Psyché* (1720) are less reliable than the earlier Ballard prints, as are the reduced scores published starting with *Alceste* in 1708 by Henri Baussen or the Ballard family.[3] But even the best of Ballard's scores and librettos have ambiguities and errors; several problematic instances are discussed below.

[1] See Rosow, "The principal sources for Lully's *Armide*," esp. 249–59.

[2] Most of Ballard's scores of Lully's operas have been reprinted in facsimile (by Broude International) or are consultable online via Gallica, the BnF's digital collection.

[3] For the publication history of Lully's operas, see Sadler, "The *basse continue*," 387.

Figure 2-1: Metrical connection between recitative and dance in Lully's *Persée* 1/4.

To date, three operas have appeared in the new critical edition of Lully's *Œuvres complètes: Armide, Thésée,* and *Isis.*[4] The two earliest *tragédies, Cadmus et Hermione* and *Alceste,* were published in the old edition of Lully's works, as was the late opera *Amadis.* These three volumes are not without problems, but are nonetheless works of serious scholarship.[5] The piano-vocal scores published between 1876 and 1892 as part of the

[4] Edited by Rosow, Denécheau, and Sawkins, respectively in Lully, *Œuvres complètes* (2001–).

[5] Lully, *Œuvres complètes,* general editor Prunières (1930–39).

series *Chefs d'œuvre classiques de l'opéra français* cannot be considered reliable. Some extant copies of the Ballard prints were marked up for performance, although most of the annotations appear to date from the middle of the eighteenth century.[6] Numerous manuscripts of Lully's operas survive; some are copies of the printed scores, others are commercial copies made by workshops such as the one established in Paris by Foucault; still others have unique pedigrees.[7] In addition, there are some performing parts for a few of Lully's works preserved in Paris at the Bibliothèque de l'Opéra, almost all of them from the eighteenth century.[8] It is far beyond the scope of this book to take into account this mass of disparate and dispersed source material, even though some of it might contain useful information. I have thus relied on the original layer of Ballard's full scores, librettos published during Lully's lifetime, the librettos collected in the *Recueil général des opéra*,[9] and the available critical editions.

One subgroup of librettos are particularly useful: those that contain the names of the performers and thus combine the functions of libretto and program. These may reveal how the singing and dancing roles were distributed, how many performers of each there were, and whether there were any solo dancers. Such librettos generally list the performers in the prologue separately, the cast of the *tragédie* on pages just before the start of Act I, and the performers in the divertissements at the start of the relevant scene; see Figure 2-2, for Act III of *Atys*. During Lully's lifetime such librettos were printed only for court performances, but Lully did not mount all of his operas at court and not all such productions generated their own librettos.[10] There are no personnel records from the Académie Royale de Musique during Lully's tenure and the extent to which the court and Palais-Royal productions had performers and staging practices in common can be only partially reconstructed. That said, the court librettos do represent performances done under Lully's direction, and presumably represent practices he endorsed or initiated. When it comes to the dancers in particular divertissements, the numbers of performers are similar in the court librettos to those for revivals in Paris starting in 1699. This stability suggests that the differences between Paris and Saint-

6 In the introduction to her edition of *Armide*, n. 36, Rosow identifies five first editions of Ballard scores in F-Po that were marked up for revivals. See also her "From Destouches to Berton," esp. 296–305; Schneider, *Rezeption*, 75–100, and Denécheau, "*Thésée* de Lully et Quinault," 424–25, 433–41, and 619–31.

7 The printed and manuscript sources are listed in *LWV*.

8 See La Gorce, "L'orchestre de l'Opéra," and Rosow, "Paris Opéra orchestration."

9 Published by Ballard 1703–46, this includes all the operas created between 1669 and 1737. Quinault's librettos have been edited by Norman as *Philippe Quinault: Livrets d'opéra*, 2 vols. The published texts of Lully's operas were remarkably stable, with few variants among different printings; see Norman's vol. I, xxix–xxxii.

10 The seven *tragédies* for which court librettos were printed (sometimes more than one) are: *Cadmus et Hermione* (revival of 1678), *Alceste* (revival of 1677), *Thésée* (premiere of 1675 and revival of 1677), *Atys* (premiere of 1676, revivals of 1677 and 1682), *Isis* (premiere of 1677), *Bellérophon* (revival of 1680), and *Proserpine* (premiere of 1680), all described in *LLC*. Unfortunately Schmidt did not preserve the distinction between soloist and group dancers visible in the layout of the libretto.

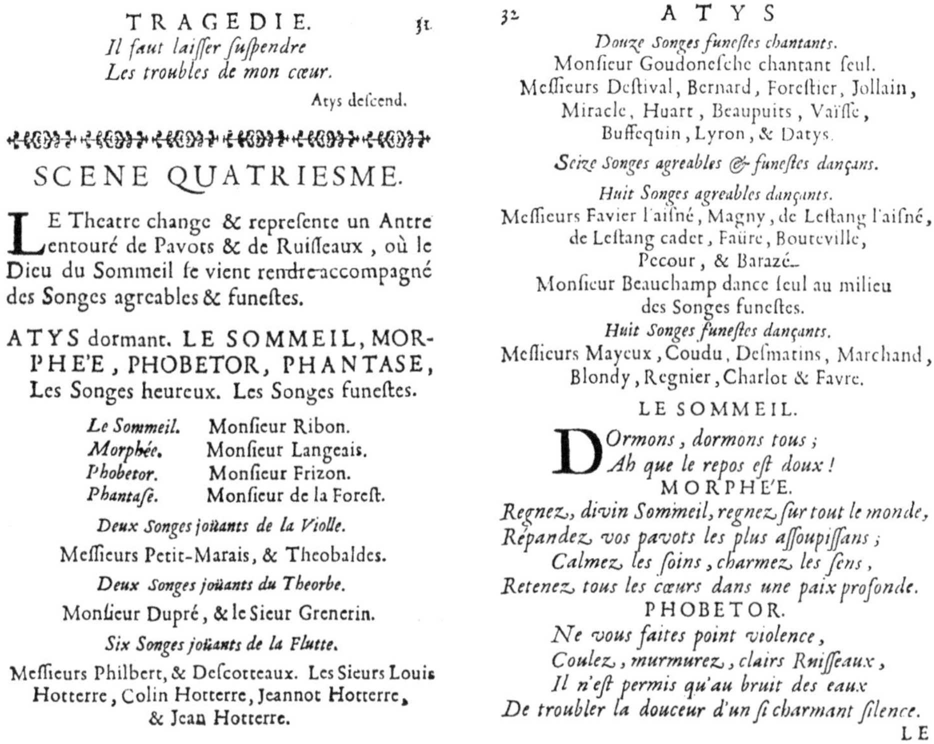

TRAGEDIE. 31

Il faut laiſſer ſuſpendre
Les troubles de mon cœur.

Atys deſcend.

SCENE QUATRIESME.

LE Theatre change & repreſente un Antre entouré de Pavots & de Ruiſſeaux, où le Dieu du Sommeil ſe vient rendre accompagné des Songes agreables & funeſtes.

ATYS dormant. LE SOMMEIL, MORPHE'E, PHOBETOR, PHANTASE, Les Songes heureux. Les Songes funeſtes.

Le Sommeil. Monſieur Ribon.
Morphée. Monſieur Langeais.
Phobetor. Monſieur Frizon.
Phantaſe. Monſieur de la Foreſt.

Deux Songes joüants de la Violle.
Meſſieurs Petit-Marais, & Theobaldes.
Deux Songes joüants du Theorbe.
Monſieur Dupré, & le Sieur Grenerin.
Six Songes joüants de la Flutte.
Meſſieurs Philbert, & Deſcotteaux. Les Sieurs Louis Hotterre, Colin Hotterre, Jeannot Hotterre, & Jean Hotterre.

32 ATYS

Douze Songes funeſtes chantants.
Monſieur Goudoneſche chantant ſeul.
Meſſieurs Deſtival, Bernard, Foreſtier, Jollain, Miracle, Huart, Beaupuits, Vaïſſe, Buffequin, Lyron, & Datys.
Seize Songes agreables & funeſtes dançans.
Huit Songes agreables dançants.
Meſſieurs Favier l'aiſné, Magny, de Leſtang l'aiſné, de Leſtang cadet, Faüre, Bouteville, Pecour, & Barazé.
Monſieur Beauchamp dance ſeul au milieu des Songes funeſtes.
Huit Songes funeſtes dançants.
Meſſieurs Mayeux, Coudu, Deſmatins, Marchand, Blondy, Regnier, Charlot & Favre.

LE SOMMEIL.

DOrmons, dormons tous;
Ah que le repos eſt doux!

MORPHE'E.

Regnez, divin Sommeil, regnez ſur tout le monde,
Repandez vos pavots les plus aſſoupiſſans;
Calmez les ſoins, charmez les ſens,
Retenez tous les cœurs dans une paix profonde.

PHOBETOR.

Ne vous faites point violence,
Coulez, murmurez, clairs Ruiſſeaux,
Il n'eſt permis qu'au bruit des eaux
De troubler la douceur d'un ſi charmant ſilence.

LE

Figure 2-2: The cast for *Atys* III/4 in performances at the royal château of Saint-Germain-en-Laye, 1676.

Germain performances during the 1670s as to how the dancers were deployed may not have been great.

In general, scores tend to have only rudimentary headings (Premier Air, Chœur de Nymphes), whereas librettos include more information about the characters appearing in a given scene. However, librettos focus on the sung texts and only rarely mention the dance pieces. It would be easy to infer from the Parisian libretto of *Atys* that Act V has no dancing at all, whereas the score includes three instrumental dances. But scores have their own limitations: they offer little guidance as to which characters do the dancing, and the sequence of events may sometimes be unclear.[11] Cases of ambiguity are signaled in the discussions that follow.

Because the librettos and scores do not provide sufficient information for reconstructing a divertissement, additional guidance must come from Lully's contemporaries. The choreographies in Beauchamps-Feuillet notation that can be linked to the Paris Opéra would seem a likely place to start, but none originated during Lully's

[11] One all-too-frequent discrepancy concerns the numbering of scenes. Where the libretto and score differ, I have generally followed the libretto.

lifetime, nor do they ever preserve more than one or two isolated dance pieces from an opera. There is, however, one fully choreographed stage work dating from 1688, the year after Lully's death, the comic mascarade *Le Mariage de la grosse Cathos*; it conveys enormous amounts of information about how a work of musical theater was put together, notwithstanding its differences in genre and scale from Lully's *tragédies en musique*. The mascarade, which was performed privately at Versailles in a large room, involves nine singers, eight dancers, and an on-stage, eight-member oboe band. Its composer, André Danican Phildor *l'aîné*, and choreographer, Jean Favier *l'aîné*, had both performed for years under Lully's direction; Favier had almost certainly been a regular member of the Paris Opéra's dance troupe since its inception. The dance notation (which uses Favier's own system), preserves not only the ten choreographies that appear in the course of the approximately 45-minute work, but also shows some of the floor patterns traced by the singers and the on-stage instrumentalists.[12] This little work does not answer all the questions raised by a Lullian *tragédie en musique*, but the staging conventions it evinces prove valuable as a lens for examining Lully's own practices. Another useful source is Marc-Antoine Charpentier's autograph score for *Circé*, a machine play written by Thomas Corneille and Donneau de Visée in 1675.[13] Charpentier's autograph includes annotations showing where the dancers do and do not dance; its practices in this regard are entirely consistent with those seen thirteen years later in *Le Mariage de la grosse Cathos*.

Some additional information about dance practices comes from seventeenth-century writings. However, during this period eyewitness accounts of performances are both rare and vague. And whereas dance theorists and aestheticians do offer important perspectives that are discussed in later chapters, they rarely deal with practicalities. Moreover, many writers from this period copy from each other without acknowledgement, a phenomenon that makes evaluating their remarks more difficult. The *encyclopédistes* delve into greater detail about useful musical and choreographic matters, but they were writing in the middle of the eighteenth century after more than one major aesthetic shift had occurred. The foundation for this chapter thus remains a close reading of the librettos and scores.

INTERPRETING THE *DIDASCALIES*

Generally speaking, the librettos supply more information about staging than do the scores. This comes in the form of *didascalies*; I have chosen to adopt the French word

12 This manuscript is reproduced in facsimile and thoroughly discussed in Harris-Warrick and Marsh, *Musical Theatre at the Court of Louis XIV* (hereafter HW&M).

13 Charpentier, *Meslanges autographes*, fols. 1^r – 17^r. On this work see Hitchcock, *Les Œuvres de Marc-Antoine Charpentier*, 369–71; Cessac, "Charpentier et les pièces à machines," 118–21; and Powell, *Music and Theatre*, 278–92.

rather than the English "stage directions" because of its broader meanings. In Quinault's librettos, the *didascalies* are of three types:

(1) identification of where the action takes place;
  (*Atys* II/1: "*Le théâtre représente le temple de* CYBÈLE")
(2) the names of the characters who appear in a scene;
  (*Atys* II/2: "CYBELE, CELENUS, MELISSE, *Troupe* DE PRETRESSES DE CYBELE")
(3) an indication of what the characters are doing.
  (*Atys* I/8: "Cybèle, carried by her flying chariot, enters her temple, all the Phrygians hasten to go there, and they repeat the last four lines that the goddess has pronounced.")

Categories 2 and 3 are particularly useful, even if not as extensive as one would like. Convention dictated a change of scene number whenever characters entered or left the stage. Quinault's *didascalies* note the presence of characters who remain silent as well as of the singers. In the second example above, three individuals and a group of priestesses are shown to be on stage, but as the scene develops only two of them – Cybèle and Célénus – sing. Melisse is given lines in the next scene, but the priestesses never open their mouths; in fact, they remain mute for the entire opera, even though they have quite a bit of stage time. Given that dancers are also silent characters, a system of enumeration that includes everyone who makes a physical appearance is extremely helpful.[14]

On the surface the third category looks intended to tell the actors what to do. In practice, however, Quinault's *didascalies* function quite differently. In this example the first two of the three clauses could be read as instructions for the performers, but the third is superfluous: the four lines of Cybèle's text that the chorus repeats are written out twice in the libretto, once for her and again for them (see Figure 2-3). Perhaps the second two-thirds of the *didascalie* were intended to insist on the Phrygians' urgency, to give a sense of the emotional climate, rather than to offer instructions for movement. In fact, category 3 *didascalies* often seem aimed at the armchair reader, as a means of enabling someone who is *not* in the theater to form a mental picture of the stage or to get a sense of a scene's overall affect. At the conclusion of *Proserpine*, "The heavens open and Jupiter appears, accompanied by celestial divinities. Pluton and Proserpine come out of the Underworld, seated on a throne, and Cérès takes a place near her daughter." This is not a set of staging instructions for a singer or for a director (a position that did not yet exist). Moreover, Lully's operas were proprietary; there was

[14] *Didascalies* listing the characters are sometimes incorrect. In the 1675 court libretto for *Thésée*, the names of on-stage trumpet players figure as part of the *didascalie* introducing I/9, whereas the trumpeters' entrance almost certainly did not take place until the following scene.

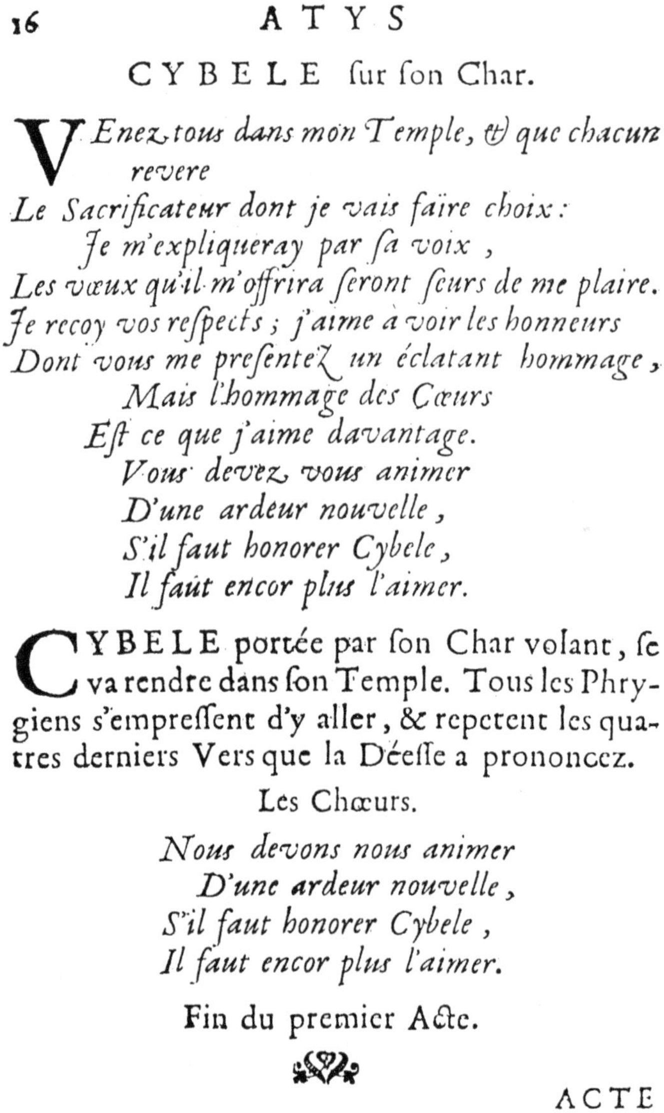

16 ATYS

CYBELE ſur ſon Char.

VEnez tous dans mon Temple, & que chacun revere
Le Sacrificateur dont je vais faire choix :
Je m'expliqueray par ſa voix ,
Les vœux qu'il m'offrira ſeront ſeurs de me plaire.
Je recoy vos reſpects ; j'aime à voir les honneurs
Dont vous me preſentez un éclatant hommage ,
Mais l'hommage des Cœurs
Eſt ce que j'aime davantage.
Vous devez vous animer
D'une ardeur nouvelle ,
S'il faut honorer Cybele ,
Il faut encor plus l'aimer.

CYBELE portée par ſon Char volant, ſe va rendre dans ſon Temple. Tous les Phrygiens s'empreſſent d'y aller, & repetent les quatres derniers Vers que la Déeſſe a prononcez.

Les Chœurs.

Nous devons nous animer
D'une ardeur nouvelle ,
S'il faut honorer Cybele ,
Il faut encor plus l'aimer.

Fin du premier Acte.

ACTE

Figure 2-3: The end of Act 1 of *Atys*.

no reason to write *didascalies* with future performers in mind.[15] It is worth remembering that librettos were often read for pleasure at home.

Another *didascalie* that seems aimed at the armchair reader comes from *Roland* III/5: "Angélique leaves to find Roland, in order to keep him away from the port from where she plans to embark with Médor." If this were a true stage direction, it could end after

[15] Not until 1685 did an opera house open in France outside of Paris – in Marseille, authorized by Lully. See Schneider, *Rezeption*, 69–74 and 354–57.

the first two words, but instead Quinault reveals Angélique's intentions, which have no impact at all on the stage, since Angélique's planned encounter with Roland does not figure inside the opera. Even when *didascalies* do appear to describe a set of events, the temporal frame may be difficult to pin down. In the following instance are the actions simultaneous or consecutive? "The nymphs and woodland gods hide, Alphée and Aréthuse descend to the Underworld, Cérès's flying chariot stops, and the goddess gets out" (*Proserpine* III/3). *Didascalies* often seem to offer a snapshot of an entire scene, one in which time is collapsed and dancing is implied only in the vaguest terms, such as the following from *Atys* II/4: "The Zephyrs appear in an elevated, brilliant glory. The different peoples who have come to the fête for Cybèle go into the temple and try together to honor Atys, and they acknowledge him as the high priest for Cybèle." This kind of *didascalie* seems akin to the engravings from the period that collapse several events into a single, impossible moment.[16]

Sometimes Quinault's *didascalies* do appear to describe the action, as in the dream sequence in *Atys* III/4: "The nightmares approach Atys and threaten him with Cybèle's vengeance if he scorns her love and does not love her faithfully." This, however, paraphrases the sung texts rather than offering instructions for on-stage movement. Moreover, it applies to all the Songes funestes, without discriminating between dancers and singers. Such a *didascalie* makes a significant aesthetic statement about how group characters are conceived, but it does not help much with questions of staging.

Every now and then a *didascalie* offers a bit of information about the dancing, as in *Thésée* I/10: "A combat in the manner of the Ancients is formed," or *Roland* I/6: "The chorus of Insulaires sings [...] and the other Insulaires dance in the manner of their country." These two have the virtue of giving a hint, however vague, about the movement style. More often, however, the *didascalies* allude to the emotion the scene is supposed to convey, without mentioning through what kinds of movements the emotion is to be expressed: "The fairies and the shades of the heroes show, through their dances, the joy they feel at Roland's return to health" (*Roland* V/3); or "The followers of Hatred show that she is making ready with pleasure to triumph over Love" (*Armide* III/4). A few appear to offer help as to where in a scene the dancing occurs ("The Arts, disguised as gallant shepherds [...] are the first to start dancing" (*Psyché* V/4)), but matching such remarks with the score often proves a challenge.[17] Yet even with their limitations, *didascalies* offer a crucial tool for envisaging the dances within an opera.

[16] In "Lully's orchestra," 541–45, Zaslaw discusses this type of compression in the well-known engraving by Le Pautre of *Alceste* performed in the Marble Courtyard.

[17] It is not uncommon for a *didascalie* of the snapshot type to be printed in the libretto at the end of the previous scene (e.g., the ends of IV/2 and V/3 in *Roland*). This has the effect of emphasizing the continuity from scene to scene, but it poses problems when it comes to locating the *didascalie* in a critical edition of the score (where special notation should make clear that it comes from the libretto and that the choice of location is editorial).

THE MECHANICS OF LULLY'S DIVERTISSEMENTS

The Characters

The "verisimilitude of the *merveilleux*" identified by Kintzler allowed for human and divine characters to mingle freely throughout the opera, and the structure of the divertissement promoted a free exchange between individuals – including the main characters – and groups. But as a practical matter, the functions of singing and dancing were supplied by different people, whether they represented gods or humans, individuals or collective characters. A division of labor is explicit throughout the librettos, where in divertissement after divertissement the lists of roles distinguish between those who sing and those who dance. Occasionally a semantic distinction is even made between a *chœur* (singers) and a *troupe* (dancers), even when the characters are members of the same group: "Chœur de Phrygiens chantants, Chœur de Phrygiennes chantantes, Troupe de Phyrigens dansants, Troupe de Phrygiennes dansantes" (*Atys* I/7). The librettos that provide the performers' names are even more explicit: the 1677 libretto of *Alceste* identifies sixteen of the attacking soldiers in Act II as singers and four of them as dancers, while among the defending combatants there are only six singers, but still four dancers.

Even if functionally distinct, such characters were conceptually unified, subsumed into a single group. A typical *didascalie* identifies the performers in *Alceste* V/6 as "a troupe of shepherds and shepherdesses, some of whom sing, the others of whom dance." Furthermore, the collective characters are all engaged in the same enterprise: "The people of the kingdom of Damascus show, through their dances and their songs, their joy about the advantage that the princess's beauty has won over Godefroy's knights" (*Armide* I/3); or "the shepherds and silvans, dancing and singing, come to offer presents of fruit and flowers to the nymph Syrinx, and they attempt to persuade her not to go hunting, and to submit herself to Cupid's laws" (*Isis*, III/6). In this division of labor, one group supplies the text, the other the movement; the dancers serve, in a sense, as surrogates for the singers. Another way of conceptualizing this type of casting is to see every role as being assigned two sets of bodies, although the number of singers and dancers need not be equal for the principle to apply. The modes of discourse may be different, but the expressive goals are the same.

This amalgamation of singers and dancers into a single entity is also implicit in the writings of aestheticians, who locate its roots in the chorus of ancient Greek tragedy, which they understood to have been danced as well as sung:

> It is permissible to mix ballets into musical representations, because the two are made for each other and this blend is both pleasing and natural – not at all freakish. Tragedies may also have ballet interludes, because such ballets are to the tragedy what the choruses of the Ancients were, where one sang and danced.[18]

[18] Menestrier, *Des Ballets*, 290.

> Barring a few infidelities made to verisimilitude, opera is almost a tragedy such as the Greeks had. For if we have introduced into our operas some things that they would have repudiated and that they certainly would not have wanted, in recompense we have retained their choruses, which our [spoken] French tragedies have rejected. By that means, I argue, opera makes up for some of its defects and has acquired a great advantage over tragedy.[19]

One important distinction emerges not along functional lines, but on the basis of gender. Quinault and the librettists who followed him were scrupulous in distinguishing between male and female roles: in most cases a scene will have both Bergers and Bergères, Phrygiens and Phrygiennes. The one exception is with troupes of "peuples," where it is understood that the populace includes both men and women. Quinault's syntactical distinction was not pedantic; Lully often composed passages or even entire numbers for the male or female subgroups, be they singers or dancers. Some divertissements may involve characters of a single gender only, as when Proserpine sings with her nymphs in Act II of the eponymous opera; demons, in Lully's operatic world, are always male. The French language easily allows for this distinction, but sometimes a libretto may attribute different names to groups who nonetheless function together. There is, for instance, no such being as a male Amazon, so in *Bellérophon* I/5 the corresponding male roles are for Solymes, a warlike people from Lycia in Asia Minor whom the mythological Bellerophon is reputed to have conquered. (The distinction is one of role, not of the gender of the performer; the singing Amazons in *Bellérophon* were performed by six men and six women, and all of the dancers, both Amazons and Solymes, were men.[20]) Shepherds might be paired with either shepherdesses or nymphs; in both cases all are treated as members of a single group. There are, however, some cases where there are genuinely distinct groups on stage at the same time, often set up in opposition to each other. Two groups react in song and dance to the tragic death of Atys; a group of female Corybantes (followers of the goddess Cybèle) expresses rage, while a mixed chorus of wood and water divinities expresses sorrow (*Atys* V/7). Such divisions of the chorus and dancers into distinguishable groups, often the followers of separate gods, are likelier to occur at one end or the other of the opera – either in concluding celebratory divertissements or in prologues.

Very occasionally a chorus and a group of dancers may have different roles. In Act I of *Persée*, Queen Cassiope attempts to appease the wrath of the goddess Junon by offering games in her honor. The chorus is identified as spectators, whereas the dancers are "young persons chosen for the games." In Act II of *Atys*, the dancing Zephyrs have no choral counterpart, although there are also Zephyrs on stage playing instruments. More often, particularly in celebratory divertissements, the dancers may be a special subset of the population represented by the choral singers. In the last act of *Phaéton* the

[19] Saint-Mard, *Réflexions*, 21–22.

[20] *Bellérophon* was created in 1679, two years before the first appearance of women dancers at the Opéra.

chorus is made up of diverse people – Egyptians, Indians, and Ethiopians – whereas the dancers are Egyptian shepherds and shepherdesses.

Rarer still than divertissements where the chorus and dancers have different roles are those that have dancers, but no chorus at all. In *Phaéton* I/7, "Triton comes out of the sea accompanied by a troupe of followers, of whom one group plays instruments and the other group dances." Here the chorus has been replaced by on-stage instrumentalists; the only singers in this scene, during which Proteus transforms himself into several different shapes, are the two soloists: Proteus himself and Triton. In *Cadmus et Hermione* II/6, Amour, the only singer in the divertissement, animates a group of golden statues, who jump off their pedestals and dance. Yet even here dancing is in close contact with singing. The vocal forces may sometimes be reduced, but in no Lully opera does dancing ever occur without some kind of vocal framework.

The instrumentalists on stage in Act II of *Atys* are not unique: eleven court librettos for seven different operas provide the names of the instrumentalists who appeared on stage, and the example of *Phaéton* shows that such practices were not confined to court performances.[21] In other operas their presence is implicit; the *didascalie* in *Amadis* I/4 does not mention the trumpets that the score calls for, but as the scene staged a combat, military instruments would be natural. By bringing instrumentalists on stage Quinault and Lully could signal to the audience that a shift had occurred from the world of "speech" to a realm in which music is the medium of discourse; the opening of the dream sequence in *Atys* III/4 is marked by the arrival of dreams playing viols, flutes, and theorbos (see Figure 2-2). On-stage musicians, like the singers and dancers, were assigned roles and costumed appropriately; there is a costume design by Berain for a priestess playing the "flute" in *Thésée*.[22] If the functioning of the on-stage oboe band in *Le Mariage de la grosse Cathos* bears a relationship to Lully's practices (and its composer, Philidor, was an on-stage oboist in many of Lully's operas), then Lully's musicians may well have participated in the overall choreography, and not just remained fixed in place.[23]

Other moving bodies beside dancers and musicians – supernumeraries or acrobats – were sometimes called upon to provide special effects. In *Alceste*, at the end of Act I, personifications of the winds are conjured up by Thétis and Aeolus: first the Aquilons cause a storm, then the Zéphyrs calm it;[24] the cast list for Act III calls for "followers of

21 Because scores indicate orchestration only partially, historians have investigated the information about on-stage musicians to learn more about Lully's orchestra. See, in particular, La Gorce, "Some notes." Regarding the dramatic impact of on-stage instrumentalists, see my "Magnificence in motion."

22 Reproduced in La Gorce, "Some notes," 101.

23 Regarding the oboe band's movements, see HW&M, 48–52, 56–59, and 63.

24 That these winds were not dancers can be seen from the fact that they are listed as characters in the *didascalie* for Scenes 8 and 9, but not among the dancing roles in the librettos that transmit names. Winds could, however, be represented by dancers, as they were in 1678 in the prologue to *Cadmus et Hermione*.

Pluton, singing, dancing, and flying." At the end of Act IV in *Atys*, flying Zephyrs whisk Sangaride and Atys away from her father's horrified courtiers.[25] Also in *Atys* V/3, Alecton, a silent character, "comes out of the Underworld, holding a torch in her hand, which she shakes over Atys's head," driving him temporarily mad. Such characters are rarely identified by name in the librettos. One exception was the famous acrobat Allard, who played the role of a flying phantom in *Thésée* at Saint-Germain-en-Laye in 1675 and 1677. Spectacular special effects such as these appear to have been carried out by non-dancing personnel with the help of stage machinery.[26]

One carryover from the conceptualizing of singers and dancers as all members of the chorus is the terminology, still in use at the Paris Opéra today, of "coryphée." In the ancient Greek theater, the *coryphæus* meant the individual in a chorus delegated to speak individually, and at the Opéra, since 1779 if not earlier, *coryphée* has designated a rank for dancers who sometimes step out of the *corps de ballet* to do a solo or perform in a small ensemble. Similarly, in a Lullian divertissement an individual may step out of the chorus or the dance troupe, but still share the collective identity. In the scene of mourning in *Alceste* one of the singing Femmes affligées leads the group in its rituals, but leadership may also be entrusted to a dancer: in the first act of *Proserpine*, one of the dancing Sicilians has a solo role as the Conducteur de la fête. This particular role is mentioned in the main body of the libretto, but more often solo roles for dancers are only discernible from the lists of performers included in court librettos. The 1676 court libretto for *Atys*, for example, identifies Beauchamps as a soloist among the eight other dancing Songes funestes (see Figure 2-2). Whether in such an instance the soloist functioned as a leader of the group is unclear, but should be considered a possibility.

Solo turns inside divertissements are not confined to anonymous characters; singers of secondary roles may participate. This is the case with Céphise and Straton, confidants of Alceste and Licomède, who each sing a dance-song in Act V of *Alceste*; in Act I of *Armide* it is Hidraot, Armide's uncle, who leads the celebrations in her honor. However, some of the characters who have names are episodic, appearing only in one act, even though their role may be crucial. Pluton and Proserpine in Act IV of *Alceste* are two such, as are Le Sommeil, Morphée, Phobétor, and Phantase – the fantastic beings who populate Atys's dreams. In this scene the dancing analogues of these four singers are the Songes agréables.

The roles protagonists play in divertissements may be either active or passive. (Excluded from consideration are the *fêtes* where a protagonist does nothing but

[25] The 1676 court libretto reads, "Les Zéphyrs volent, et enlèvent Atys et Sangaride." The libretto in the *Recueil général* omits the word "volent," which suggests that flying might not have been a part of every production.

[26] Swedish architect Nicodemus Tessin, following a visit to the Opéra in 1687, reported on machinery that enabled fourteen children dressed as cupids to fly above the stage; see Wood and Sadler, *French Baroque Opera*, 124.

watch.) The dream sequence in *Atys* III/4 is of the passive variety: Atys falls asleep on stage and the audience sees and hears what passes through his mind. In *Persée* II/8–10 the hero is armed in a solemn ceremony by a series of divinities, so that he will be prepared to battle Medusa. On the active side of the ledger are divertissements ranging from *fêtes* to battles. Atys and Sangaride lead the ceremonies that honor the arrival of the goddess Cybèle (*Atys* I/7). It is within a sumptuous celebration that Médor and Angélique give full expression to their love (*Roland* II/5). Proserpine frolics with her nymphs; the hidden Pluton is so taken with her charms that he interrupts the festivities to kidnap her (*Proserpine* II/8–9). In the following act (III/8) her mother, Cérès, and her equally enraged followers set fire to the earth.

The converse of placing protagonists within divertissements is giving voice to group characters in other parts of an act. *Alceste* opens with a sequence of brief choral interjections that wish happiness to the newlyweds. The chorus is listed in the *didascalie*, so is presumably on stage, but in other instances the chorus is either invisible (*Amadis* V/4) or sings from off stage (*Bellérophon* IV/2–3) and no dancers function in conjunction with their voices. Such spots are dramatically effective, but they do not figure in this study.

Staging the Dancers and the Chorus

A system that assigns function based on a specific skill set solves a practical problem of finding high-quality performers in both domains. Lully's dancers were highly trained professionals. If they had an additional skill, it was usually playing the violin; many, among them such luminaries as Pierre Beauchamps and Jean Favier, came from families of violinists. Only occasionally was a performer good enough at singing and dancing to be hired to do both. Marie-Louise Desmâtins made her debut in *Persée* (1682) as both a singer and dancer, and her name appears in librettos in both capacities until 1703; thereafter, until her death in 1708, she sang only.[27]

This division of labor impacts not only Lully's musical constructions, but also the staging. If dancers are to provide actions on behalf of the chorus, they need space. Evidence from the eighteenth century suggests an arrangement of the stage with the chorus in two rows on its perimeter; as early as 1700 librettos listed the choristers according to which of two rows they stood in, and later in the century the choristers were identified as standing either on the queen's side (stage right) or the king's (stage left).[28] This arrangement was mocked by Fuzelier in a parody of Lully's *Persée* done at

[27] Mlle Desmâtins sang virtually all the lead female roles in Lully's operas; see the performance personnel index in *LLC*.

[28] The seventeenth-century evidence, although less precise, suggests the same kind of arrangement: *didascalies* for *Le Triomphe de l'Amour* (1681) state that the members of the singing chorus are "placés autour du théâtre." The earliest libretto to list choristers by row is Collasse's *Canente* (1700); the practice of listing them by king's side or queen's side began in 1717 with Mouret's *Ariane*. In both

the Théâtre Italien in 1722: "[the nymphs] take their places with the cyclopes along the two sides of the stage, like the chorus at the Opéra."[29] In three Lully revivals between 1699 and 1705, chosen by way of example, the chorus constituted a substantial group: 35, 28, and 31 singers respectively.[30] According to mid-century writers such as Cahusac who complained about it, the chorus, once it had entered and taken up its positions, did not move, no matter what the text.[31] The chorus may not have been quite so immobile in Lully's day as it was 75 years later: some of Quinault's *didascalies* suggest movement, most notably one in *Cadmus et Hermione* III/6, in which singing *sacrificateurs* prostrate themselves while other *sacrificateurs* dance; after the dance those who had been prostrated stand up and sing. But even in this scene the choristers might not have to do more than bow down and stand up in place; they still would need to be out of the way of the dancers, who perform between their moments of song. Figure 2-4 shows one such division of the stage: the concluding divertissement in *Isis*, with the chorus of Egyptians in two rows on the sides, the dancers surrounding the altar, and Jupiter and Junon, joined by other gods, welcoming Isis to the heavens.

The one contemporary document to show placement for the singers – the choreographic notation for *Le Mariage de la grosse Cathos* – does not have as rigid a use of space as the eighteenth-century evidence suggests, but it does show a concern with keeping the performers on the periphery until they become the focus of attention. Each of the different groups – singers, dancers, and instrumentalists – has a home position around the perimeter of the stage, from which individuals venture into the center when needed, only to retreat after their moment in the limelight.[32] In this modest work it is the oboists who occupy the sides of the stage, but in their use of space they seem somewhat analogous to the chorus in an opera.

A relatively static approach to staging the chorus seems consistent with what can be gleaned from Lully's librettos. In some scenes the chorus was even seated, as in the last act of *Alceste*: "the stage changes and represents a triumphal arch between two amphitheaters, where are seen a multitude of different peoples from Greece, assembled to welcome Alcide who has returned triumphant from the Underworld." This strategic positioning leaves the center of the stage open. The libretto for *Bellérophon*, which has a similarly grandiose finale, describes the space as "the courtyard of a palace which appears elevated in the Glory. It is approached by two large steps [...] which are enclosed by two large architectural structures of extraordinary height. The two steps

systems, the fact that the names appear in a similar order in every libretto suggests that individual choristers tended to stand in roughly the same positions for each opera. For further discussion, including a 1773 diagram showing the position of the choristers, see Rosow, "Performing a choral dialogue," esp. 329–30.

29 *Arlequin Persée*, in *Parodies du nouveau théâtre italien*, II, 119.

30 *Proserpine* (1699), *Acis et Galatée* (1702), and *Bellérophon* (1705).

31 Cahusac, "Chœurs," *Encyclopédie*. 32 HW&M, 48–59.

Figure 2-4: The concluding divertissement of *Isis*.

and the surrounding galleries are filled with the people of Lycia." The chorus of twelve Hours that sang in the Sun's palace in Act IV of *Phaéton* was seated behind a cloud-enclosed balustrade in the 1721 revival, if not before.[33] The stage might have looked

[33] *MF* (November 1721), 119: "Au septième chassis de chaque côté, on voit deux colonnes isolées sur le devant, qui terminent une estrade élevée de six degrés, avec une balustrade qui semble être envelopée

Figure 2-5: Jean Berain, scene showing a seated chorus, probably from the last act of *Proserpine*. (Photo by the Archives Nationales)

something like the one seen in Figure 2-5; in grandiose scenes such as these, the visual impression might have been increased by figures painted on the scenery, as Tessin reported in 1687.[34]

It has been claimed that in French baroque opera the chorus generally remained on stage during the course of an entire act, but this assertion cannot be supported.[35] Lully's librettists were scrupulous about listing the characters in every scene, to the point of mentioning characters who are present but do not sing. In the librettos the chorus and the dancers are generally shown to arrive together at the start of a divertissement, and Lully often composed music for their entrance. Moreover, their arrival is often

de nuées, où sont assises douze actrices représentant les douze heures du jour. " (See Ch. 10, p. 288, for a chorus that makes a ceremonial entrance before taking its seats.)

34 Tessin (see n. 26) wrote about *Achille et Polixène*: "Another set is to be made to represent a number of people watching the spectacle. Below, living people will be seated on either side, while above the tiers of seats they will be represented, painted in white, between large grey columns topped with a domed ceiling, multicoloured. One remarkable feature is that at the moment when the lower spectators exit, the painted ones above will also disappear … " Trans. Wood and Sadler, *French Baroque Opera*, 124.

35 "The *chœur* usually remained on stage throughout each act […] the chorus seemed particularly conspicuous during a long scene in which they were not required to sing." Cyr, "The dramatic role of the chorus," 105 and 107. However, Cyr's only piece of evidence does not stand up to scrutiny; see Banducci, "Staging and its dramatic effect," 19, n. 44.

preceded by some kind of invitation or anticipation. Roland hears shepherds arriving before he sees them ("J'entends un bruit de musique champêtre" (*Roland* IV/2)) and Atys, at the opening of the opera, repeatedly invites the Phyrigians to come honor Cybèle, before they finally arrive in Scene 7; he even offers a progress report in Scene 5. Prompt notes for mid-eighteenth-century performances of French operas call for entrances and exits of the chorus in expected places.[36] A case could be made that when the chorus appears without the dancers early in the act and then sings again a few scenes later, as in the last act of *Alceste*, it might have remained visible the entire time.[37] But acts constructed in this manner are considerably less frequent than ones where the libretto identifies the divertissement, which is usually well into the act, as the place where the chorus appears for the first time. It makes much more sense to conclude that the chorus, involving both dancers and singers, enters and leaves where the libretto says it does.

Once the two groups were on stage, how did they interact? At first glance the answer might seem straightforward: vocal pieces would be sung and instrumental pieces danced. But this begs the question of what vocal pieces that use dance rhythms might imply about movement on stage. Straton's air in the last act of *Alceste* ("A quoi bon") shares key, meter, gavotte rhythms, and overall affect with the dance that precedes it; the musical connections are so strong that the audience perceives this pair of pieces as a single unit. Would both have been danced? The available evidence suggests that the conventions were different for choruses than they were for solo songs or small ensembles. Whereas choruses could sometimes, within specific parameters, be danced, songs by soloists, no matter how danceable in affect, were not – at least not in Lully's day. The next sections explore the separate conventions in turn.

Dance Inside of Choruses

Lully's choruses come in many musical guises. But when it comes to how the singers and dancers behave relative to each other, the choruses reduce to four types: ones that have intermittent dancing; ones danced throughout; ones that involve some kind of movement other than dancing; and ones that have no dancing at all. It is not always a simple matter to identify the category to which a chorus may belong. However, models from Lully's contemporaries provide enough data to offer a point of entry into the practices of the day.

Many of Lully's choruses are celebratory and these often call attention to their own musicality: "Chantons tous, en ce jour, la gloire de l'amour," sings the chorus at the conclusion of *Amadis*. The texts not infrequently also invite dancing: "Que l'on chante,

[36] See Banducci, "Staging and its dramatic effect," and her "Staging a *tragédie en musique*," 180–90.

[37] The chorus sings in Sc. 1, but is not mentioned again until Sc. 4; the dancers enter in Sc. 6.

que l'on danse," sing Sangar and the chorus in *Atys* IV/5. Just this kind of text is found in Thomas Corneille's machine play *Circé*, which was first performed by Molière's troupe in 1675:

> *Chœur des Divinités des Forets*:
> Les plaisirs sont de tous les âges / Les plaisirs sont de toutes les saisons. / Pour les rendre permis on sait que les plus sages / Ont souvent trouvé des raisons. / Rions, chantons, / Folâtrons, sautons. / Les plaisirs sont de tous les âges / Les plaisirs sont de toutes les saisons.
> (*Chorus of woodland gods*: The pleasures are always in season. Wise men have often found reasons for justifying them. Let's laugh and sing and have fun and jump around. The pleasures are always in season.)

Charpentier's music survives in his own hand; his annotations show not only that dancers were involved, but where.[38] This particular piece has three different textures: vocal trio, chorus, and four-part instrumental ensemble. The dancers' participation is a function of the texture, as Table 2-1 shows. (Here and in subsequent tables, the instrumental sections are shaded.)

The dancers apparently remain still during the first instrumental phrase (unless Charpentier neglected to write an instruction), but thereafter they appear in every instrumental interlude, no matter how short. They do not, however, move when the chorus is singing, until the last twelve bars of the piece. The rapidity with which the

Table 2-1: Charpentier, *Circé*: chorus "Les plaisirs sont de tous les âges".

Bars	No. of bars	Texture	Charpentier's annotations
1–7	7	Two vocal trios alternate	
8–20	13	Chorus	
21–28	8	Instrumental	
29–40	12	Chorus and vocal trio alternate	
41–48	8	Instrumental	"danseurs"
49–59	11	Vocal trio	
60–62	3	Instrumental	"danseurs"
63–77	15	Chorus and vocal trio alternate	
78–79	2	Instrumental	"danseurs"
80–81	2	Chorus	"sans danseurs" (without dancers)
82–89	8	Instrumental	"danseurs"
90–101	12	Chorus	"ici les danseurs figurent sur la fin de ce chœur" (the dancers move at the end of this chorus)

[38] *Meslanges autographes*, fols. 13^r–15^r.

Table 2-2: Philidor, *Le Mariage de la grosse Cathos*: chorus "Passons toujours la vie".

Bars	No. of bars	Texture	Choreography
1–8	8	Chorus	No dancing
9–16	8	Instrumental	Danced by the four women
17–24	8	Chorus	No dancing
25–32	8	Instrumental	Danced a8
33–40	8	Chorus	No dancing
41–48	8	Instrumental	Danced by a solo man
49–56	8	Chorus	Danced a8

dancers alternate between movement and stasis in response to the musical texture can be startling. Whereas most of the dance phrases are eight bars long, one lasts only three, and starting at m. 78 the dancers spring into action for a mere two bars before stopping out for another two.

The same pattern of alternation can be observed in *Le Mariage de la grosse Cathos*. In one of its choruses, whose four-line text celebrates the pleasures of life, Favier's notation shows not only that this chorus was danced, but with what steps and to which phrases of the music. This simple piece consists of seven phrases, of which the four sung ones frame the three purely instrumental ones. The dancing occurs only during the instrumental sections, until the last choral refrain (see Table 2-2).[39]

Neither Philidor nor Charpentier wanted dancers to move while singing was going on – *except* during the concluding phrase. The general rule appears to be that only one thing should happen at a time, so that the two systems of discourse – textual and choreographic – do not compete for the audience's attention. The music is the glue that holds the two systems together, and once the text has become familiar after multiple repetitions and the piece builds toward a conclusion, both singing and dancing are allowed to happen simultaneously. Thus the chorus ends with satisfaction for the eyes as well as the ears.

This pattern – identical in these two choruses, which between them frame Lully's operatic career – has far-reaching implications. Many of Lully's choruses are constructed along similar lines, with changes of texture from the vocal to the instrumental, sometimes even with further textural changes within the two basic divisions. Example 2-1 shows the end of a chorus from *Armide* IV/2, whose text invites participation by the dancers and whose musical construction allows for it. More importantly, the principle

[39] HW&M, 171–77.

Example 2-1: *Armide* IV/2, end of the chorus "Voici la charmante retraite" (Paris: Ballard, 1686), 176–79. The orchestra accompanies the four-part chorus.

of alternation – of a single focus for the audience's attention – turns out to have wide application, as the section below on dance-songs shows.

A second type of chorus is danced throughout – or almost so. The model, from *Le Mariage de la grosse Cathos*, again circumscribes where the dancing appears. This chorus repeats an astonishing announcement that has already been sung as a solo and a duet: "Allons, accourons tous / La grosse Cathos se marie." (Come on, let's all hasten, Fat Kate is getting married!") Philidor's chorus is sung throughout, with the brief text repeated three times. On the words "Allons, accourons tous" the dancers rush forward from either side of the stage, then freeze for two bars while they listen to the news. This pattern happens twice; on the third and last iteration of the text, the dancers move throughout the phrase and end by taking up positions that free the center of the stage for the approaching solo singers.[40] Would the dancers have moved throughout the entire chorus if its text had been different? With a sample of one only, we cannot know. But the impulse to end this chorus with movement as well as song seems to be one shared with the earlier choreographed chorus, as it serves to round out the number visually as well as aurally. This model suggests that choruses in Lully operas with action words might also be susceptible to choreographic treatment, whether or not they contain purely instrumental passages.

The third type of chorus involves a violent and frightening event, such as the earthquake that destroys part of Cérès's palace at the end of Act I of *Proserpine*, while the members of the chorus comment on what they are watching. The chorus may either be sung throughout or else may have instrumental interludes that provide a convenient place for the action to take place. In *Alceste* II/3–4, a battle wages between the soldiers attacking the city of Scyros and those defending it. A march brings the attackers on stage and the battle takes place during this double chorus; there is no other music available. Its action may be traced in the texts: after the dancing attackers bring in battering rams, their comrades sing "Let each of us eagerly fight; let us break down the towers and ramparts." The response of the defenders suggests that their group of dancers shot arrows down upon the attackers: "May the enemy shudder under the hail of our arrows and spears." The chorus is punctuated by instrumental phrases that feature trumpets and drums, and the meter changes as the battle progresses. Whether the dancers gestured while dancing or simply mimed is impossible to know, but in all performances for which librettos with the performers' names exist, dancers, not supernumeraries, supplied the movement.[41]

The battle in *Persée* IV/5–7, on the other hand, relies upon special effects, as the hero, using Mercure's winged sandals to fly through the air, defeats the sea monster and rescues Andromède. The commentary sung by the two rival groups of spectators – Andromède's fearful countrymen on the one hand, the water deities rooting for the

[40] *Ibid.*, 52 and 132–35. [41] These date from 1677, 1706, 1716, 1728, and 1739.

monster on the other – is continuous, so the action has to take place while the chorus is singing. In *Bellérophon* IV/7, the hero battles with the Chimera that is ravaging Ethiopia. In what must have been a spectacular piece of stagecraft, Bellérophon, mounted on Pegasus, swoops down three times from the heavens, succeeds in killing the Chimera on the third pass, flies around the stage three more times, then rises through the clouds. An off-stage chorus describes the action as it happens, urges the hero on, and applauds his ultimate victory; their words are punctuated by vigorous instrumental passages. Such choruses provide plenty of visual stimulation, but require no dancers.

The fourth – and perhaps most common – treatment for choruses is no dancing at all. Here again *Le Mariage de la grosse Cathos* provides a useful model: of its five choruses only two are choreographed; the three that lack dancing also lack instrumental interludes. Moreover, none of them has the kind of text that invites physical movement. In many instances, it would appear, choruses are to be heard, not watched. Any dancers on stage (which in most instances there would be) simply stand in place. The proportion observable in Philidor's masacarade – slightly more than half of the choruses are not danced – seems in line with Lully's practices. In view of later practices, when composers made a point of identifying a chorus that was intended to be danced by labeling it a "chœur dansé,"[42] it would appear that the default was for choruses *not* to be danced, unless the structural or textual criteria were met. Nonetheless, every chorus should be considered as a possible candidate for choreographic treatment, the evaluation being made on the basis of its structure, text, location within the divertissement, dramatic context, and musical surroundings.

The Choreographic Treatment of Dance-Songs

One of Lully's most reproducible conventions inside divertissements, especially those framed as fêtes, is the dance-song – a vocal piece with the structure of a dance (binary or rondeau), clear phrasing, and set to texts with short poetic lines that are more metrically regular than those in recitative, even if not every line has the same number of syllables (see the example from *Phaéton* on p. 71). Dance-songs may be set as solos, duets, trios, or choruses.[43] Solo singers are generally anonymous members of the choral collective (e.g., a shepherd), but sometimes are named secondary characters. The text may be strophic – in which case there are never more than two strophes – or it may have a single strophe only. Dance-songs are the property of divertissements; they are not found in other parts of the opera. This is another point of difference between

42 See Betzwieser, "Musical setting."

43 A trio texture, or even a duet, may sometimes be sung by groups, in which case the score generally calls it a chorus; see in *Armide* II/4 the "Chœur de Bergers et Bergères héroïques."

Lully's practices and Venetian opera, where strophic structures were one of the main ways for defining arias.[44] For the French, strophic structures called attention to themselves as music and had to be used diegetically. These pieces are certainly danceable – but were they in fact danced?

A dance-song never stands alone. Lully always pairs it with an instrumental dance piece that precedes or follows it (sometimes both) and that may carry a genre designation such as menuet or gavotte, but more often does not. In many instances the dance piece and the song are identical, except for the change in performing medium (see Figure 2-6). Alternatively, the song and the dance may be similar rather than identical, being related by key, meter, rhythmic patterns, phrase structures, and overall affect, as is the case with the two back-to-back dance-songs in the last act of *Alceste*. In each pair the text has only a single verse, and the dance comes first (see Example 2-2). There may even be no double bar between the two pieces, such that the notation alone encourages a continuous performance.

Example 2-2: *Alceste* v/6 (Baussen PR, 1708), 189–90. (a) "Troisième Air"; (b) the song for Céphise that follows it.

On musical grounds, there is no reason why dancing begun in the instrumental section could not continue on into the vocal one. Furthermore, some of the *didascalies* that Quinault wrote into his librettos might seem to suggest simultaneity of song and dance, including the ones for this very spot in *Alceste*: "Straton sings in the middle of the dancing herdsmen" and "Céphise sings in the middle of the shepherds and shepherdesses who dance" ("Straton chante au milieu des Pâtres dansants"; "Céphise chante au milieu des Bergers et des Bergères qui dansent"). Nonetheless, there are compelling

[44] See Rosand, *Opera in Seventeenth-Century Venice*, 281ff.

Table 2-3: Charpentier, *Circé*: outline of the dance-song "Mes soupirs."

Musical unit	Key, meter	Annotations
Trio, strophe 1: "Mes soupirs"	B♭, $\frac{6}{4}$	
Rondeau	B♭, $\frac{6}{4}$	"danseurs"
Trio, strophe 2: "Craignez-vous"	B♭, $\frac{6}{4}$	
Rondeau repeated	B♭, $\frac{6}{4}$	[danseurs]

reasons for concluding that the meaning of such *didascalies* is not transparent.[45] Rather, the general rule appears to be, yet again, that the dancing and singing occur in alternation. Moreover, Lully turns out to have had a blueprint for strophic dance-songs (see Table 2-5). The next several paragraphs lay out the evidence for these conclusions. The discussion of necessity becomes intertwined with notational conventions that Ballard used, as some of the ambiguity derives from space-saving shortcuts.

The aesthetic rationale implicit in the construction of choruses – one that shifts the focus back and forth between singing and dancing – would seem to apply even more strongly to solo songs, where the words are repeated much less than in choruses and therefore require more attention from the audience. In fact, not one of the solo songs or duets in *Le Mariage de la grosse Cathos* is choreographed, no matter how danceable the music. Charpentier's *Circé* corroborates this pattern, in a strophic complex very similar in construction to many units found in Lully operas.[46]

Charpentier made a point of the continuity from vocal trio to dance by omitting a double bar between them and by writing, "Go on without interruption to the following rondeau." As he had in the chorus already cited (see p. 41), Charpentier annotated his score to show that he wanted the dancers to figure *only* during instrumental passages. Further annotations reveal that the dancers – or rather, acrobats (*sauteurs*) – run to get themselves into fixed positions, then move to another pose. The second strophe of the trio is said to follow the rondeau without interruption, after which "the rondeau is played again while the acrobats form three other figures, after which the play concludes with a chorus mixed with dances and dangerous leaps."

The practice of alternation can be documented within Lully's own operas, thanks primarily to explicit *didascalies* in the two librettos written by Thomas Corneille and Bernard le Bovier de Fontenelle – *Psyché* and *Bellérophon*. Whereas Quinault was economical in his use of *didascalies*, Corneille and Fontenelle's more generous

45 Performers and historians alike have often taken this type of *didascalie* at face value. La Gorce, for example, has written (*Lully*, 633) that in *Bellérophon* the menuet in the prologue, the bourrée in III/5 (Fig. 2-8), and the canarie at the end of the opera are danced while the chorus sings.

46 *Meslanges autographes*, fols. 16^r–17^r.

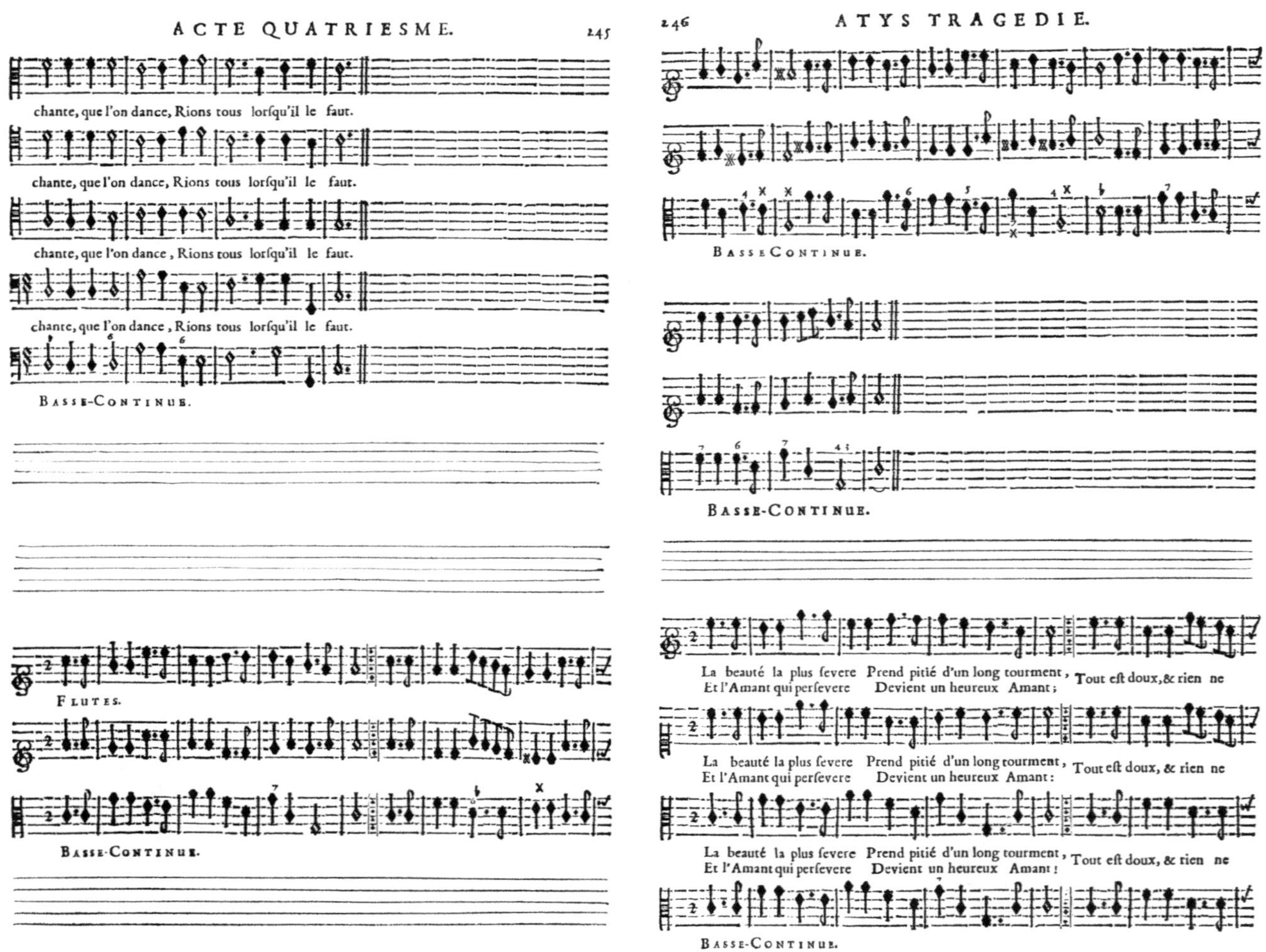

Figure 2-6: Dance-song from *Atys* IV/5 in which the dance and song have identical music.

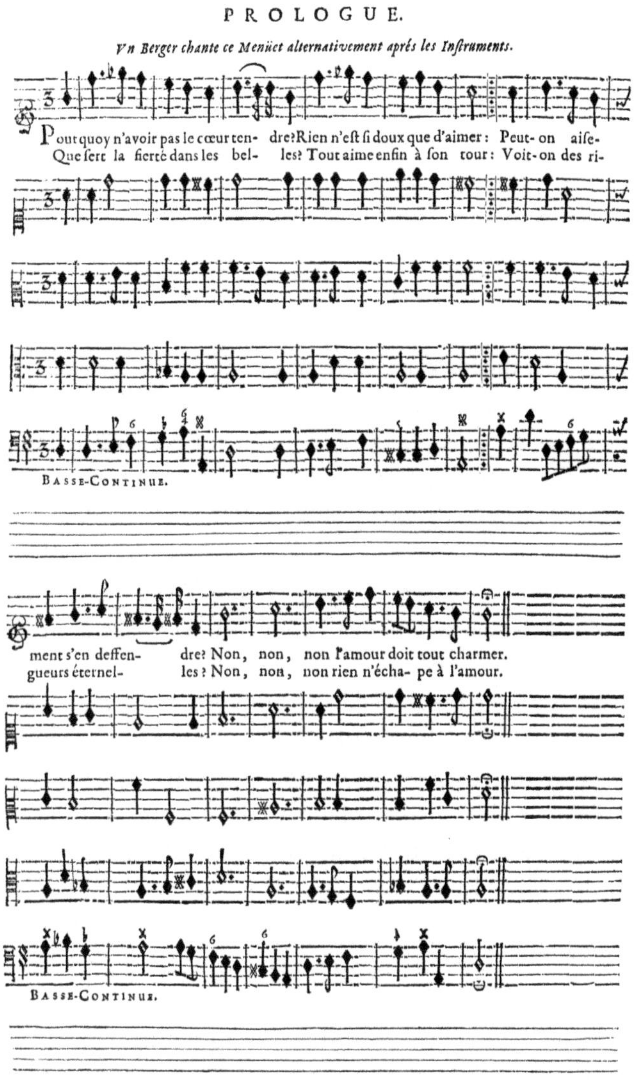

Figure 2-7: Strophic dance-song from the prologue to *Bellérophon*. "A shepherd sings this menuet in alternation after the instruments." I.e., this single page generates two instrumental playings of the menuet interleaved with two strophes sung by voice and B.C.

approach helps clarify the order of events. In the prologue of *Bellérophon* three groups of characters are on stage: Apollon and the Muses; Pan with shepherds and shepherdesses; and Bacchus with Aegipans and Mænades. After a large chorus involving the followers of all three gods, the score presents three short binary pieces in a row, starting with a vocal minuet (Figure 2-7). This single page presents the entire piece: a *didascalie* above

Table 2-4: *Bellérophon*, prologue: outline of dance-song "Pourquoi n'avoir pas le cœur tendre?"

Musical Unit	Texture	Comments
Menuet	strings a5	danced by shepherds and shepherdesses
Sung menuet, strophe 1, "Pourquoi"	solo voice, B.C.	no dancing
Menuet, repeated	strings a5	danced
Sung menuet, strophe 2, "Que sert"	solo voice, B.C.	no dancing

the music indicates that the instrumental and vocal music alternate, whereas a longer *didascalie* in the libretto insists that the shepherd sings *after* the first dance and that dance and song are interleaved. ("Les Bergers et les Bergères commencent ici une entrée, après laquelle un Berger chante les deux couplets suivants, qui sont entremêlés de danses.") Table 2-4 outlines the order of events when the libretto and score are read together.[47]

The identical structure appears in *Bellérophon* III/5.[48] This complex divertissement, rich with *didascalies*, depicts a ceremonial sacrifice at the oracle of Apollon. It includes no fewer than three choral dance-songs, all exhibiting the same structure. In the second one the people dance around the fire and sing "Montrons notre allegresse." Like many dance-songs it is binary and has short, clear phrases (Figure 2-8). Its strophic structure is discernible not only in the parallel construction of the two strophes, but is mentioned explicitly in the libretto, which makes a point of insisting that the *didascalies* belong in specific places relative to the sung texts. Two key words, "ici" and "ensuite," anchor the sequence: "*here* the people dance around the fire, and *then* sing the first verse." The libretto then writes out the first verse in full, followed by the instruction, "the people continue their dance, and [then] sing the second verse." ("Then" is implicit in the "alternativement" written into the score.) Notwithstanding the alternation in performance, these *didascalies* further demonstrate the conceptual unity of the singing and dancing characters, who are treated as a single group ("le peuple"), even though their modes of communicating with the audience are not the same. The instructions are also valuable because Ballard did not print the dance separately from the chorus; the two are conflated into the choral version. It is obvious that the way to derive the instrumental version is simply to omit the voices; the orchestra part stands perfectly well on its own.

47 Although the notation looks as if the orchestra accompanies the singer, the convention was for the soloist to sing with B.C. only, as a similarly notated passage in *Phaéton* IV/1 makes explicit (Ballard score, 182): "One of the Hours sings alone the chorus that follows, and the chorus responds to her with the strings."

48 The *Recueil général* identifies this as Scene 4, but it has two consecutive Scenes 3.

Figure 2-8: Strophic dance-song from *Bellérophon* III/5. "The strings play the chorus in alternation with the voices."

After a brief intervention by the Sacrificateur, there is another strophic chorus from which the alternating instrumental version must be derived. This one has a very different affect; the text begs Apollon for deliverance from the sorrows caused by the ravages of the monster. The music is in G minor, in (a presumably slow) triple meter, with an orchestral accompaniment that intersperses strings and trio passages for flutes. Yet notwithstanding the musical differences, the overall structure is the same.

Thanks to the *didascalies*, we can be sure that its four-part structure consisted of dance – chorus strophe 1 – dance repeated – chorus strophe 2. The march that opens the divertissement also turns out to function in an identical way. It is a binary piece in gavotte rhythm and is followed by a chorus with the same rhythmic profile and the same structure. There is no verbal instruction in the score to repeat the march, but the libretto is clear : "here a second entrée is done, after which the people sing the second verse." Not only is the march the only available instrumental piece, its close musical relationship to the chorus makes it the only piece that could possibly fulfill the function.

The principle of alternation seems to apply to the rest of this divertissement as well: every time action is required, such as when the bull is sacrificed or the Pythie emerges from her cave, instrumental music is supplied. The same principle applies to I/5 of this opera: "The Amazons and Solymes begin their dances here and then sing the following words, *of which each verse is sung after a dance.*" (Emphasis added.) This particular divertissement offers a slightly expanded variant on the pattern: a dance that is independent of the vocal music ("Premier Air") opens the sequence, but thereafter comes a four-part choral dance-song, initiated by the dance piece (the "Second Air").

The sources for *Bellérophon* thus reveal two important principles: (1) the norm is for singing and dancing to alternate; and (2) dance-songs with a strophic construction adhere more often than not to the blueprint shown in Table 2-5. This structure applies whether the song is choral, solo, or for a small ensemble. Ballard's notational practices often obscure the order of events[49] – perhaps because it was too obvious to need spelling out – but thanks to the more generous *didascalies* in the libretto for *Bellérophon*, the structure of the convention emerges.

After studying the informative *didascalies* in *Bellérophon*, one returns to Quinault's librettos with a different eye. Occasionally Quinault does make the same kind of distinction, as when in *Thésée* IV/7 the inhabitants of the enchanted island dance "to

Table 2-5: Lully's dominant blueprint for strophic dance-songs.

Instrumental piece	[danced]
Song, strophe 1	
Instrumental piece, repeated	[danced]
Song, strophe 2	

[49] Some copies of Ballard's scores have manuscript annotations that clarify the order of the pieces; see Denécheau, "*Thésée* de Lully," 274.

the tune of the shepherdess's song," which is played by rustic instruments. But the question remains whether or not *didascalies* such as the ones in the last act of *Alceste*, where Céphise sings "in the middle of" (*au milieu de*) shepherds and shepherdesses who dance, or the one from *Isis* III/3, in which "one part of the nymphs dances during the time that the others sing" ("Une partie des Nymphes dansent dans le temps que les autres chantent") can be read as calling for the simultaneity of song and dance. If one chooses to read such *didascalies* literally, one would be obliged to conclude that Lully staged dance-songs differently when Corneille was the librettist than when Quinault did the writing – that the dancing and singing are interleaved in *Bellérophon* and *Psyché*, whereas in Quinault's operas, they are simultaneous. That explanation does not pass the test of Occam's razor. Quinault's *didascalies* cannot be read as if they had been written in the nineteenth or twentieth century. Rather, they rely on verbal formulas that give a global overview of several minutes of a scene, in which time is collapsed.

A passage from Menestrier supports a sequential interpretation of dancing "in the middle of" singing:

> Just as musical performances are sometimes interrupted by ballet entrées, it is also possible to interrupt ballet entrées with songs. In the ballet entitled *Le Triomphe de l'Amour*, which was danced for the king and queen last winter, [the goddess] Diana sang in the middle of dances by her nymphs, and an Indian man and two Indian women sang in the middle of another entrée. A nymph among the followers of Youth sang in the middle of another entrée.[50]

Menestrier's examples are of one art "interrupting" the other; his "in the middle of" means "in between parts of."[51] Quinault's formulaic language makes much more sense interpreted in this vein, as a shorthand, rather than as a descriptor.[52] The practice of alternating song and dance is observable on other stages as well: at the Théâtre Italien, the fair theaters, and in ballets done at Jesuit colleges.[53] The practice seems to have been widely observed, not confined to the stage of the Académie Royale de Musique.

50 Menestrier, *Des Ballets*, 207–08.

51 For additional instances of this usage, see Desmarest's *tragédie en musique Vénus et Adonis* (1697), where, in the prologue and I/3, characters sing "in the middle of" a danced entrée: libretto, 6 and 16; score, xxviii–xxxi and 23–26.

52 Even in *Bellérophon* Corneille uses a formulation suggesting simultaneity that is patently impossible: "The altar that had appeared sinks and the Pythie comes out of her cave, her hair wild. *At the same time* loud thunderclaps are heard. The temple shakes and everything is lit up by lightning." (III/5, emphasis added.) Lully's vivid music makes it clear that these events are sequential, not simultaneous.

53 See, for example, the Jesuit ballet *La Conquête de la toison d'or* (Rouen, 1701), Entrée I, where, after a song, "the shepherds resume their dances" (similar annotations occur elsewhere); the concluding divertissement in *Les Deux Arlequins* (Gherardi, *Théâtre italien*, III, 340), where "in the pauses between the dancing and the charivari a voice sings a song with two strophes in praise of old age"; or many scores by Mouret for the later Théâtre Italien with markings such as "This tune is danced before it is sung" (*La Descente d'Arlequin aux enfers*).

Yet even once we recognize alternation as a governing principle, the order of events may appear ambiguous. Although many Ballard scores do supply instructions (e.g., *Roland* I/6, 68: "On reprend l'air et la chanson encore une fois"), many strophic songs have none. In unmarked cases should we assume that, following the dance, the two strophes are sung one directly after the other? I think not. Among Lully's dance-songs, the strophic construction outlined in Table 2-5 is by far the dominant model. The dance and the song may either be identical or closely connected; the strophes may have a refrain or lack one;[54] the form of each strophe may be either binary or rondeau; the song may be sung by an individual, an ensemble, or a chorus. But however those parameters may vary, the four-section unfolding of the piece, starting with the dance, is the most common construction.[55]

A tiny number of four-section structures reverse the order and put the vocal part first; in *Thésée* III/7 a chorus of shades ("On nous tourmente / Sans cesse aux Enfers") is followed by a dance ("Second Air"), the second verse of the chorus, and a repeat of the dance – all of them fully written out in the Ballard score. The basic dance-song structure may be expanded by including both a soloist and a chorus (see Table 2-6 for an example from *Phaéton*). Another type of expansion, although rare, consists of adding a third iteration of the dance after the second verse of the song.[56]

Not all of Lully's dance-songs are strophic. When the song has only one verse, it is often embedded in the center of an ABA structure, with a dance to which it is closely related on both sides. Another formal option presents the dance and the related song only once each, in which case it is more common for the dance to go first, as with the back-to-back dance-songs in Act V of *Alceste*, sung by Straton and Céphise. When the order is reversed and the vocal piece is heard first, the context generally carries extreme emotion, as in *Armide* III/4, when the followers of Hatred insist in rapid and forceful homorhythms that nothing causes so much suffering as Love ("Tu fais trop souffrir sous ta loi. / Non, tout l'Enfer n'a rien de si cruel que toi"). The dance that follows ("Second Air," marked "Vite") interposes jagged hemiolas into the rapid $\frac{6}{4}$ meter. According to the *didascalie*, "the followers of Hatred show that she is preparing with

[54] Approximately half of Lully's strophic dance-songs, including those for chorus, have refrains.

[55] It is only from looking at all of Lully's divertissements that this convention has become clear to me. An individual divertissement with ambiguous instructions in the score or libretto has the potential to mislead. In writing about Act IV of *Persée*, Rosow hesitated, then proposed that the menuet to be repeated in the third slot of such a structure was not the one that preceded the first strophe of the chorus, but a menuet in the parallel major from earlier in the divertissement ("Lully's musical architecture," par. 6.1). Given the overwhelming preponderance of the four-part structure described here, her solution seems unlikely.

[56] See, for example, the prologue to *Persée* (Ballard score, xiii). The instructions state clearly that the oboes play last ("Les hautbois reprennent le même air, Mégathyme et Phronime chantent le second couplet, et les hautbois le rejouent encore une fois"). The modulatory tag that moves from the A minor of this unit to the C major of what follows is erroneously notated at the end of the vocal duet.

pleasure to conquer Love." The cumulative threat of chorus and dance so horrifies Armide that she abruptly changes her mind and renounces Hatred's help. In a similarly charged scene, *Atys* III/5, the chorus of nightmares is followed by a vigorous dance in the same meter ($\frac{3}{2}$); Atys wakes up terrified.

A strophic dance-song, juxtaposed with a related dance piece, offers a clear structure for the alternation of song and dance. However, there may be some instances in which such units would seem to invite participation by dancers at the end of the second strophe. It is hard to imagine that the celebrations that conclude an opera such as *Bellérophon*, which ends with a strophic choral dance-song, would leave the dancers standing still during the final measures, no matter how the chorus is constructed (see the outline in Table 2-6). In this instance the sung canarie has a refrain, so a likely spot for the dancers to join the singers would be the B section of the second strophe, when the refrain is sung for the second time. This would respect the principle of not having dance compete with new text, yet would still allow the opera to end in spectacular fashion, with all the characters on stage taking part.

Structures in which an instrumental piece is related to a song or chorus in one of the ways discussed above account for approximately two-thirds of the instrumental dance pieces in Lully's operas. This close correspondence between the vocal, text-bearing realm and the world of physical movement is one of the hallmarks of French opera, but the aesthetic principle of a single focus that governs how the two realms interact may seem counterintuitive to today's opera spectators, who are used to seeing many activities happening on stage at once. Rosow has extended the principle of a single focus to argue that whereas Lully and Quinault generally separated dancing and singing in real time, within the realm of the opera, which operates according to different rules than does the outside world, the two happen, in a sense, simultaneously:

> A corollary of this principle of single focus is its implication of continuous behavior that the audience neither sees nor hears. While we watch the dancing Ethiopians, the singing Ethiopians continue to celebrate, but we do not hear them; while we hear the singers, the dancing Ethiopians continue to celebrate, but we do not see them [...] Lully and Quinault want us to understand these activities to occur simultaneously as we focus on them successively. The conventional code for presenting such a structure involved symmetrical patterning: an apparently static tableau.[57]

Independent Instrumental Dances

Whereas most of Lully's instrumental dance pieces are intimately connected to a vocal piece, approximately one third of them have no musical relationship to the rest of the divertissement other than key, and, perhaps, meter. One independent type is the

[57] Rosow, "Lully's musical architecture," par. 6.3.

marche, which often provides the entrance music in ceremonial contexts. Marches that involve military processions, as in the battle scenes in Act II of *Alceste* and Act I of *Thésée*, are in rondeau form with trumpets and drums playing during the refrains. The triumph in honor of Bellérophon in I/5 receives the military musical treatment, even though those processing are not soldiers but the hero's prisoners from a campaign conducted before the opera starts. Armide's triumph in Act I, however, has no trumpets and drums, perhaps because those entering, the people of Damascus, are civilians, even if they are celebrating her military successes – or is it because she is a woman and only men merit trumpets? The fact that marches are not usually anchored to vocal pieces seems unsurprising,[58] and they are generally followed by something sung, often an announcement in recitative, setting the scene for what is to come.

Other ceremonial processions may be set to marches, such as the entrance of people offering gifts to the goddess Isis in *Phaéton* III/4. The libretto specifies that "the young male and female Egyptians who carry the offerings approach the temple of Isis while dancing."[59] A possible model for performing such a piece is offered by the single extant march choreography, the opening number in *Le Mariage de la grosse Cathos*. There the through-composed music is played twice, first as a processional for the entire cast, the second time as a dance for eight. During the procession everyone takes one step per measure, whereas the choreography assigns the dancers a varied step vocabulary.[60] Given the large number of people entering the stage in *Phaéton* III/4 and the relatively short music available (a binary piece of 18 notated bars – or 36, if both repeats are made), the option of playing the entire piece twice so that the entrance can be made with due pomp is attractive. An extension of the amount of music also offers the possibility of highlighting the gift-giving by making the dancing subsequent to, rather than simultaneous with the procession.

One other category of instrumental dance does not have a vocal analogue – the *entrée grave*. This is a slow dance in duple meter characterized by dotted quarter-note/eighth-note patterns, rather like the opening portion of an overture. The adjective "grave" is found in the headings for choreographies (see Chapter 3, pp. 94–95); in scores such a piece is generally identified simply as an entrée or an air. Nor do scores often say to which group of dancers a piece may be assigned, but in choreographic sources *entrées graves* are always danced by men, and in the divertissements that include one there are always male characters – or nasty creatures that are coded male – available to dance it. One such instance is the first dance for the nightmares in *Atys* (Example 2-3).

In divertissements where they are used, *entrées graves* tend to be the first purely instrumental dance, perhaps following a chorus. They are often followed by another

58 The march in III/5 of *Bellérophon* is exceptional, being part of a four-part unit with a chorus.

59 The score confirms this: "Marche où dansent les Peuples qui portent des présents à Isis."

60 HW&M, 46–7 and 126–32.

Example 2-3: *Atys* III/4, "Entrée des Songes funestes" (Paris: Ballard, 1689), 192.

instrumental dance in a contrasting character, but one that is part of a dance-song complex. This is the case in *Phaéton* IV/2, which takes place in the palace of the Sun, where the next dance is in a light triple meter and tied both to a solo vocal air and to a chorus on the same text. Similarly, in the celebrations that end *Bellérophon* the *entrée grave* is followed by two canaries, the first instrumental, the second sung by the chorus. In both of these cases, the second unit adheres to Lully's normal blueprint for dance-songs, with the one difference that the unit in *Phaéton* uses an expanded version, involving both a soloist and the chorus (see Table 2-6).[61]

Table 2-6: Comparison of sequences from *Phaéton* and *Bellérophon*.

Phaéton IV/2	Bellérophon V/3
Spring and his followers dance to the following airs.	*Nine Lyciens separate from the group and here perform an entrée, after which the People sing.*
Premier Air [*entrée grave* in g, **2**]	Premier Air [*entrée grave* in C, **2**]
Second Air [g, **3**]	Second Air (also labeled "Fanfare" or "Canaries"[a]) [C, $\frac{6}{4}$]
1st strophe of song, sung by une Heure ("Dans ce palais") [g, **3**]	1st strophe of song, sung by chorus ("Les plaisirs nous préparent leurs charmes") [C, $\frac{6}{4}$]
Chorus repeats 1st strophe	–
Second Air, repeated	Second Air, repeated
Second strophe of solo vocal air	Second strophe, sung by chorus
Second strophe repeated by chorus	–

[a] Although not so labeled in the Ballard score, this piece and the chorus that follow are called "canaries" in several musical sources (see LWV 57/69-70) and in a notated choreography (see Ch. 4, p. 112).

[61] The *Phaéton* divertissement contains one further piece, another chorus in triple meter. In *Bellérophon* the four-part dance-song ends the divertissement (and the opera).

The dream sequence in *Atys* III/4 is organized differently. After the Songes heureux have been dispatched by a bass Songe funeste, who warns Atys in recitative that if he refuses Cybèle's love, she will take revenge, the dancing nightmares embody the warning in the *entrée grave* shown above in Example 2-3. Next a pair of related pieces – chorus and dance – reinforce the threat. (See Section III in Table 2-11, p. 64.) Here, as in the other two operas, the *entrée grave* makes a strong statement on its own through music and movement. Yet Lully does not often present dance pieces in isolation, and in all three of these cases, the very next dance returns to the orbit of vocal music and a sung text. This phenomenon is not limited to cases that involve *entrées graves*. In *Phaéton* V/4 a bourrée is the musically independent piece, but it is immediately followed by a strophic dance-song.

It occasionally happens that Lully places two – or once even three – independent dances in a row,[62] but he nonetheless integrates them into a dramatic whole. In Act IV of *Armide* the Chevalier danois and Ubalde have come looking for Renaud, intending to rescue him from the sorceress's clutches. Armide tries to distract them by conjuring up false images of their own sweethearts; the first such temptation, aimed at the Chevalier danois, constitutes the divertissement proper (IV/2). First, his beloved Lucinde, seconded by a chorus of rustic folk, tries to charm him ("Voici la charmante retraite"). Next come a gavotte and a canarie that have no musical connection either with each other or with the choruses on either side. The second chorus, however, follows the same pattern as the first (Lucinde's words and music are repeated by her followers) and it quickly transforms into a repeat of "Voici la charmante retraite." Thus even though the two dances are musically independent, they are enfolded within a structure that circles back on itself.

Chaconnes and Passacailles

Chaconnes and passacailles, the largest of all the dance types, have affinities with both the independent dances and the dance-songs, in that of the six such dances in Lully's *tragédies*, two of them are purely instrumental (the chaconne in *Phaéton* II/5 and the passacaille in *Persée* V/8), whereas the other four incorporate vocal sections (the chaconnes in *Cadmus et Hermione* I/4, *Roland* III/6, and *Amadis* V/5, and the passacaille in *Armide* V/2). Of these the only one to end the opera is the enormous chaconne in *Amadis*; the oft-repeated claim that Lully's *tragédies* end with chaconnes is not accurate.[63]

[62] The remarkable three-dance sequence from *Atys* is discussed in Ch. 4, p. 117.

[63] *Acis et Galatée*, a three-act pastorale, also ends with a passacaille. La Gorce has pointed out that Lully became particularly interested in large-scale ground-bass constructions toward the end of his life (*Lully*, 641–42 and 710–12); his last six works for the Opéra all incorporate at least one.

Table 2-7: Outline of the passacaille in *Armide* v/2.

No. of bars	Scoring
149	Instrumental passacaille
16	Premier Récit, by an Amant fortuné, "Les plaisirs ont choisi"
16	Premier Couplet du chœur, "Les plaisirs ont choisi"
8 + 8	Instrumental trio, then a5 texture
24	Amant fortuné, "C'est l'amour"
24	Chorus, "C'est l'amour"
8 + 8	Instrumental trio, then a5 texture
24	Amant fortuné, "Jeunes cœurs"
24	Chorus, "Jeunes cœurs"
16	Premier Récit, repeated
16	Pr. Couplet du chœur, repeated
149	Repeat of instrumental passacaille*
16	Premier Récit, repeated*
16	Premier Couplet du chœur, repeated *

The passacaille from *Armide* illustrates how Lully interweaves vocal and instrumental sections into a gigantic construction (see Table 2-7). If all the repeats the Ballard score calls for are taken, the piece lasts approximately fifteen minutes and has 522 measures. The chaconnes from *Amadis* and *Roland* are longer still, each having over 800 bars. (It is not unusual for these long pieces to have internal repeats, although many are through-composed. When repeats are indicated by sign or by verbal instructions, how much music to repeat is sometimes ambiguous.)

In her critical edition of *Armide*, Rosow chose to adhere to the sequence of the piece copied into the two instrumental parts remaining from the premiere, which do not repeat the last three sections (marked in the table with asterisks). Even in this shorter form, the passacaille has 341 measures.[64] In both versions the passacaille is marked by an alternation between instrumental and vocal sections, a construction that lends itself to alternating dancing and singing; presumably the last sixteen measures, sung by the chorus to a now thoroughly familiar text, would also have been danced.

Whereas the chaconne and passacaille are both structured as unfolding variations above either a ground bass or a repeating harmonic pattern, they differ from each other both in their music and in the dramatic uses to which they were put. The passacailles in French opera tend to be in a minor mode and to start on the downbeat; whereas chaconnes are usually in a major mode and tend to begin on the second beat of the bar. Passacailles have a slower tempo than chaconnes[65] and narrower uses; they are often

[64] Rosow edition, xxvi and 292n. [65] See Legrand, "Chaconnes et passacailles," 160.

found in association with women, not infrequently when seduction is involved. Chaconnes have broader dramatic uses (and sometimes an exotic flavor); a substantial subgroup of them is comic.[66] Because their great length and exceptional construction color any divertissement in which they appear, chaconnes and passacailles are discussed in several parts of this book.

Divertissement Architecture

Lully's divertissements vary enormously in length and structural complexity, but the most common elements are the close connections between vocal and dance music and the use of repetition as a structural device. The principle of expansion via repetition, built into dance-songs, appears at larger organizational levels as well and even extends beyond the divertissement into other parts of the act.[67] The divertissements are also unified by key: most remain in the same key throughout, unless they occupy more than a single scene; excursions away are limited to the parallel major or minor, or, if the mode is minor, to the relative major. The examples that follow lay out a few of Lully's varied structures.[68]

The organizing principle in *Persée* 1/5 is a palindrome. When the opera opens Junon is angry with Cassiope, queen of Ethiopia, because she dared compare herself to the goddess. Junon has sent a monster, Méduse, to ravage the land. In an attempt to appease Junon, Cassiope leads a set of religious games, whose centerpiece is a dance contest (Table 2-8).[69] The *jeux junoniens* fail to calm Junon's wrath and the news that Méduse is approaching sends everyone fleeing.

The "Premier Air" fulfills the function of the marches found in so many ceremonial scenes, and, like them, is musically independent. It may well have been danced, especially given that some of the people entering the stage have been designated to

66 Burgess has argued that "more than any other dance form the chaconne exemplifies [the representation of sovereign power]," and that its ground bass can be seen "as an emblem for the hidden restrictions submerged beneath the glitter of the courtier's life" ("The chaconne," 81 and 84). His insightful conclusions do not exhaust the dramatic uses to which chaconnes were put. Rosow has found that for Lully and Charpentier the descending minor tetrachord, which often figures in passacailles and chaconnes, signifies not necessarily lament, but "profound emotion" and that "while its affective power and association with love are matters of convention, only poetry and context can clarify its particular meaning." ("The descending minor tetrachord," 86–87.)

67 See Rosow, "Lully's musical architecture," and "The articulation of Lully's dramatic dialogue." For an overview of Lully's divertissement structures and those of his successors, see Wood, *Music and Drama*, 256–63.

68 This discussion is based on the scores as published by Ballard, not on annotated copies or manuscript scores, both of which may show changes in order, additions, or deletions. Regarding revisions made to Lully's operas during revivals, see Ch. 12, pp. 371ff.

69 For a more extended discussion, see Pierce and Thorp, "The dances in Lully's *Persée*," pars. 3.11–3.12 and 4.1–4.5.

Table 2-8: *Persée* 1/5: Cassiope, Andromède, Mérope, Phinée, followers of Cassiope carrying the prizes, young people chosen for the contest, chorus of spectators.
Games in honor of Junon, where young people compete in dancing.

	Musical Unit	Key, meter	Comments
	Premier Air [rondeau]	G, **3**	Probably served as entrance music (only Andromède, Mérope, and Phinée were already on stage), but could also be danced. Musically independent.
	Ritournelle, then recitative by Cassiope	g, **3**	Cassiope begs for clemency from Junon.
A	Chœur de Spectateurs, "Laissez calmer votre colère, / O Junon, exaucez nos vœux!"	g, $\frac{3}{8}$	Long, with five instrumental interludes, two of them 20 bars long. Related to dance that follows.
B	Second Air. *On commence les jeux, en disputant le prix de la danse.*	g, $\frac{3}{8}$	Binary. ("The games begin with a competition for the prize in dance.")
C	Troisième Air	g, **2**	Binary. Musically independent.
B	Repeat of Second Air	g, $\frac{3}{8}$	
A	Repeat of chorus, "Laissez calmer"	g, $\frac{3}{8}$	Probably danced.

participate in the dance contest. Cassiope probably enters last, as she has her own ritournelle before she addresses Junon; she explains that she has assembled young couples about to be married to demonstrate their skill in dance, and that she herself acknowledges her guilt and wishes to make amends. The chorus that follows, entreating Junon to heed the country's pleas, represents the first of the five pieces in the palindrome. It is followed by three instrumental pieces: a dance in $\frac{3}{8}$ that is related to the chorus; a musically independent piece that may be a bourrée; and a repeat of the dance in $\frac{3}{8}$. This central sequence, where the dance contest must have taken place, is rounded off by a repeat of the chorus. The connection made via the music between the dancers and the chorus of spectators, who beg Junon for mercy, reminds us that the dance contest is a serious matter. If the chorus did not involve dancing in its first iteration, it must surely have done so the second time, as both its position at the end of the divertissement and its construction invite dance: of its 113 measures, 58 are choral and 55 instrumental, in a lopsided alternating pattern that becomes more instrumental as the piece progresses (Table 2-9).

The chorus's ritualistic text repetition begins to sound almost desperate when, after the opening prayer, which uses all four lines of text, the group thereafter repeats only the words, "If we could please you, how happy we would be!" ("Si nous pouvions vous plaire, / Que nous serions heureux"). It is worth noting that the chorus, for all that its members are identified as spectators, shows more initiative than do most of Quinault's

Table 2-9: *Persée* 1/5: chorus "Laissez calmer votre colère".
White = choral; shaded = instrumental

28	5	6	7	6	20	6	3	6	20	6

choruses: the text they sing is their own, not a repetition of Cassiope's words. Their independence from her, both textual and formal (Cassiope's recitative stands outside the palindrome), serves to emphasize the enormity of their queen's transgression, which has put her at odds with her subjects and threatened the survival of Ethiopia.

The divertissement in the following act operates on a different principle, one that uses parallel structures to cumulative effect. After the failure of the games honoring Junon, Persée has volunteered to try to kill Méduse. Mercure ascends from the Underworld to tell him that Jupiter, Persée's father, along with all the other gods except Junon, is on his side. (As a god, Mercure would normally descend from the heavens, but his quest for material aid has taken him to the Underworld.) In a series of three parallel scenes different demigods arm Persée: the cyclopes bring winged sandals and a sword made by Vulcain, warrior nymphs provide a diamond shield given by Pallas (Athena), and Underworld divinities give him Pluton's helmet (Table 2-10). Each scene involves dancers (plural, although their number is not indicated in the libretto) plus a single singer from the same group of demigods, and each has the same tripartite structure. The three scenes have a symmetrical key scheme: the outer ones are in major, the central one in the relative minor.

Table 2-10: *Persée* II/8–10: cumulative divertissement in which the gods arm the hero.

Scene	Musical units	Key, meter	Gift
8. Cyclops			
	Entrée	B♭, **2**	
	Recitative/air	B♭, **3**	Winged sandals, sword made by Vulcain
	Entrée repeated	B♭, **2**	
9. Warrior nymphs			
	Entrée	g, **2**	
	Recitative/air	g, **2**	Diamond shield from Pallas
	Entrée repeated	G, **2**	
10. Underworld divinities			
	Entrée	B♭, $\frac{6}{4}$	
	Recitative/air	B♭, **3**	Pluton's helmet
	Entrée repeated	B♭, $\frac{6}{4}$	

After Persée is solemnly and progressively armed from his heels to his head, Mercure sings an air that is taken up by the chorus: "May the Underworld, the earth, and the heavens, may the entire universe favor your generous undertaking." This chorus, which crowns the divertissement, offers its own three-part structure: two extended choral passages surrounding an instrumental section of approximately equal length. The sequence offers the necessary opportunity for "the entire universe" to be represented visually as well as textually: the libretto indicates that each group of demigods has remained on stage when the new one arrives. Thus all three groups of dancers are available to end the act in a grand choreographic image of unity, as Mercure and Persée fly off together.[70]

The dream sequence in *Atys* has a complex three-part structure (Table 2-11).[71] The first section evokes the world of sleep in a long instrumental prelude that is extended vocally by the personified figure of Sommeil and his companions, who extol the peace that sleep provides above a continuation of the bass line from the prelude. In the second section, the sweet dreams (dancers), aided by Sommeil's three companions, reveal Cybèle's love to Atys. In the third, nightmares (both singers and dancers) threaten Atys with the consequences if he does not return Cybèle's affections. The two happier sections involve structural repetitions: the first has a large ABA form, with the A section instrumental and the B vocal;[72] the second expands the vocal portion of Lully's standard strophic dance-song unit. In the third section, the nightmares' avoidance of formal constructions magnifies the disruption their arrival causes.

The *Atys* dream sequence is long and sumptuous, but a few divertissements are very lean, with only one instrumental piece. This is the case in IV/2 of *Cadmus et Hermione*, Lully's first *tragédie*, which draws upon one of the ancient Greek origin myths: Cadmus kills a dragon, and then distributes its teeth over a ploughed field as if they were seeds. Here is Quinault's version of what happens (in this case all of the characters except Cadmus are dancers; the 1678 court libretto calls for eight): "Cadmus sows the dragon's teeth and the land produces armed soldiers, who at first turn their weapons against Cadmus. He, however, throws into their midst a kind of grenade that Amour has given him. It breaks into many pieces, which force the soldiers to fight and slaughter each other. The five who remain alive at the end of the battle deposit their weapons at Cadmus's feet." The fanfare-dominated music for the battle, a binary "Air pour les Combattants," is not associated with any vocal

70 Two other cumulative divertissements are the celebrations offered by Sangar in *Atys* IV/5 and the pleasures of the enchanted island depicted in *Thésée* IV/7.

71 For a detailed analysis of this divertissement, plus a discussion of its operatic progeny, see Wood, "Orchestra and spectacle," 34–40.

72 The repeat of the prelude after the vocal section is called for by a verbal indication in the Ballard 1689 score.

Table 2-11: *Atys* III/4: outline of the dream divertissement.

I	*The stage changes and represents a cave surrounded by poppies and streams where the god of sleep arrives, accompanied by sweet dreams and nightmares.*		
	Prelude (also called Le Sommeil)	g, **2**	Alternates trio of flutes w. strings, 57m
	Sommeil, "Dormons tous"		Sung by *haute-contre*, functions as refrain
	Morphée, "Regnez, divin Sommeil"		Second *haute-contre*
	Phobétor, "Ne vous faites point violence"		Bass air texture, flutes play treble lines
			Repeat of refrain
	Sommeil, "Dormons tous"		Expansion of refrain, texturally and in length
	All three, "Dormons tous"		
	Prelude		Repeat of instrumental Prelude
II	*The sweet dreams approach Atys and by their dances reveal to him Cybèle's love and the happiness he should expect from it.*		
	Recitative Morphée, "Ecoute, Atys"	g, —	Tells Atys of honor Cybèle is bestowing on him
	Trio Morphée, Phantase, Phobétor, "Mais souviens-toi"	g, **2**	Reminds Atys that an immortal goddess demands truly eternal fidelity
	Song Phantase, first strophe, "Que l'Amour a d'attraits"	g, **3**	Extols the pleasures of new love
	Entrée des Songes agréables	g, **3**	Gentle in character, similar to song, binary
	Air Phobétor, "Goute en paix"	g, ¢	Bass air texture, flutes play treble lines
	Trio Morphée, Phantase, Phobétor	g, **2**	Repeat of trio, text and music
	Song Phantase, second strophe, "Trop heureux un Amant"	g, **3**	Music repeats, words new: a lover exempted from a long wait is fortunate
	Entrée des Songes agréables	g, **3**	Repeat of dance
III	*The nightmares approach Atys and threaten him with Cybèle's vengeance if he disdains her and does not love her faithfully.*		
	Recitative Songe funeste, "Garde-toi d'offenser un amour glorieux"	B♭, —	Warns Atys that if he does not reciprocate Cybèle's love, her revenge may fall on him
	Entrée des Songes funestes	B♭, ¢	Entrée grave, independent of vocal music
	Chœur des Songes funestes, "L'amour qu'on outrage"	B♭, $\frac{3}{2}$	Warns Atys that he will suffer and even perish if he does not love Cybèle
	[Second Air des Songes funestes]	B♭, $\frac{3}{2}$	In same key and meter as chorus, binary
	Terrified by the nightmares, Atys awakes with a start. Le Sommeil and the dreams disappear along with the cave, and Atys finds himself back in the palace where he fell asleep.		

music; in fact, it is introduced only by an exchange in recitative between Cadmus and Amour, who brings him the grenade, and an eight-bar duet for the two of them. These three little pieces constitute the entire divertissement. The dance's status as action cannot account for its brevity, as can be seen by a comparison with the divertissement in Act II of *Alceste*, in which Alcide and Admète's troops attack the walls of Scyros, only to meet sufficient resistance that the battle rages for quite some time. But these are both special cases where the usual conventions governing divertissement structures do not apply.

In Act IV of *Bellérophon*, the hero's battle with the Chimera, which is set against a single chorus punctuated by instrumental phrases, fulfills the function of a divertissement. At the opposite extreme stands Act III of *Persée*, where it makes little sense to try to define the divertissement as something separate from the rest of the act. As it opens, the Gorgon Méduse is with her two hideous sisters, mourning her lost beauty. They hear sweet music as Mercure appears. He enchants them to sleep, then summons Persée, who decapitates Méduse. Her two sisters try to attack, but, thanks to Pluton's helmet, Persée is invisible. Méduse's blood produces monsters, who fly, crawl, or run in search of the invisible Persée; this, the "Entrée des Fantômes," is the only "official" dance piece in the entire act (Example 2-4a). The sisters urge the monsters to take revenge, and the rushing sixteenth notes of the dance reappear in their duet, suggesting that the monsters continue their threatening gestures in alternation with the Gorgons' exhortations (Example 2-4b); the duet ends with monster music. At Mercure's bidding, Persée flies off with Méduse's head, as chasms open and the two remaining Gorgons fall into the Underworld.

Isis has two divertissements that not only drive the story, but exhibit architectural fluidity. In III/4 the audience learns that the nymphs and shepherds are actors in a play that retells the story of Pan and Syrinx, produced by Mercure with the goal of making Argus fall asleep. Mercure is acting on behalf of Jupiter, who is trying to rescue his latest love-interest, Io, from the prison in which his jealous wife has enclosed her, with Argus as guard. This effort fails, and for all of Act IV a Fury drags poor Io around the globe from one torment to another.

Even in more conventional constructions the boundary between the divertissement and the rest of the act may blur. In *Armide* II/3, after his famous monologue, "Plus j'observe ces lieux, et plus je les admire," Renaud is lulled to sleep to the same rocking motions of muted strings that had punctuated his words. While he sleeps, demons disguised as nymphs and shepherds tempt him to yield to love, in vocal and instrumental music that is similar to the lullaby. The chorus, dancers and singers alike, must sneak onto the stage, as there is no obvious point for their entry. Trying to define one particular spot as the start of this divertissement seems artificial – although on its other side it does come to an abrupt and dramatic end when Armide arrives, dagger at the ready. The fuzziness around the edges of many divertissements – or within them – is a significant feature of Lully's style, as is the fuzzy line between recitative and air. In both cases, attempts to delineate separable units may serve useful analytical purposes but run the risk of over-codyfing Lully's actual practices. Moreover, even when the musical boundaries seem clear, the visual ones may be less so. It often happens that the chorus remains on stage after a divertissement ends and a new scene begins; this is the case in Act I of *Armide* when the celebrations in her honor are interrupted by the arrival of a messenger bearing bad news. A dramatic rupture has occurred, but from the audience's perspective, the stage looks just as crowded as before. The movements of masses of people on and off stage may belong to a different category of architecture than do musical structures, but they nonetheless have an enormous impact on how the operas are experienced in the theater.

THE DRAMATURGICAL IMPLICATIONS OF MECHANICS

Before going on, it seems useful to summarize the main points already made about the mechanics of Lully's divertissements. After his death these practices underwent modifications, although the basic templates remained in place, especially in *tragédies*, through the time of Rameau – and even beyond.

- Dance in Lully's operas functions within a primarily vocal context. Instrumental dance pieces are either musically related to adjacent vocal pieces, or, if they are musically independent, are in close proximity to vocal pieces to which they have dramatic connections.
- Two categories of instrumental pieces account for many of the dances that are musically independent of the vocal music: marches and *entrées graves*. The former are not restricted to military contexts, but serve when ceremonial entrance music is in order. The latter, which also tend to come toward the beginning of divertissements, are in a slow duple meter with dotted figures and seem to be intended for male characters.
- Approximately two-thirds of Lully's instrumental dance music is closely related – or sometimes even identical – to a vocal piece with which it alternates. Many of these dance-songs are strophic, with two strophes (only); in most such cases the dance piece initiates the unit, yielding dance – first strophe of song or chorus – repeat of dance – second strophe. (In Ballard's scores such structures are rarely written out in full; more frequently verbal instructions reveal the order of events, although these may sometimes be incomplete or even missing. It is essential to read the librettos in conjunction with the scores for help in establishing the proper sequence.)
- A corollary is that whereas some instrumental dances lack a vocal correlate, virtually all solo songs or duets in Lully's divertissements are part of a larger structure. Either they are linked to a chorus, usually on the same text and with closely related music, or they are paired with an instrumental dance.[73] (This observation applies only to

[73] The few exceptions are found in unusual divertissements such as the scenes of mourning in *Alceste* III and *Psyché* I or the extended vocal sequence in the first section of the dream scene in Act III of *Atys* (see Table 2-11). *Armide* II/4 (also a sleep scene) opens with a ternary air by the Nymphe des Eaux that is not paired with a dance piece, but is in the same key and meter as the prélude it follows (which is part of its own larger structure).

Example 2-4: *Persée* III/4 (Paris: Ballard, 1682), 166 and 169. (a) "Entrée des Fantômes"; (b) the duet for Euryale and Sténone.

(a)

(b)

songs in closed forms, not to passages of recitative. Choruses may also be paired with dances, but do not have to be.)

- The dancers are, in a sense, "body doubles" for the members of the chorus or for the minor characters who sing in the divertissements; the dancers supply the movement, the singers the voices. When the roles of the dancers and singers within the chorus are not fully congruent, it is usually because the dancers represent a subgroup. (In *Bellérophon* v/3 the singing chorus represents peoples from different nations, the dancers a group of nine lords.) The numbers of singing bodies and dancing bodies do not need to be equal; the singing chorus is always more numerous than the dancers, and even when the dance is juxtaposed with solo singing or a small ensemble, the numbers of singers and dancers are not necessarily identical.
- This functional division finds its analogue in structures that favor alternation between dancing and singing over simultaneity. The basic principle seems to be that there should be a single focus for the audience's attention, either on song or on dance, but that the two should not compete with each other.
- The principle of alternation can be seen in other parts of the operas as well: in the instrumental music provided to cover entrances and exits or changes of scenery, so these movements do not have to happen while someone is singing, or in vocal pieces (mostly choruses) describing action that takes place in instrumental phrases strategically structured into them. Any instrumental piece, or instrumental passage within a sung piece, should be considered as a potential site for movement of some kind.
- Dancing does not take place during solo singing, but may within some (not all) choruses. Conventions govern where the dancing occurs:
  - Choruses that have a "let's sing and dance" kind of text invite the dancers to participate. Other choruses may be preceded by a *didascalie* suggesting dancing, or operate within a dramatic context where dancing seems appropriate.
  - Lully's choruses often interleave instrumental phrases with the vocal ones. In those choruses where dancing seems dramatically plausible, the instrumental phrases, no matter how short, offer sites for dancing; during the vocal phrases, the dancers remain still. Toward the end of the chorus, once multiple repetitions of the text have made it familiar, the dancers may move during the vocal phrases. Involving everyone on stage seems particularly appropriate for choruses that end divertissements.
  - Choruses that are structured as dance-song complexes with the instrumental dance coming first may have been danced at the end of the second strophe – particularly if the chorus has a refrain and if it concludes the divertissement. There is no clear evidence as to this practice, but it seems to follow from the general pattern of inviting participation by the entire on-stage group at the end of a divertissement.

   - Choruses that have texts invoking action on the part of the group may have been danced (or mimed) throughout, even if there are no instrumental phrases within the chorus. If, however, the chorus is adjoined by an instrumental piece available to absorb the actions, the dancing might have occurred there rather than during the chorus.
- Lully and Quinault's divertissements come in many different overall shapes, but most of them rely on some kind of structural repetition – of a chorus (all or in part), of an instrumental dance, or of a dance-song. When something danced is repeated, the choreography was probably varied (see discussion in Chapter 14, pp. 440ff).
- The structure of divertissements as a whole shows that dance functions within a continuous texture that connects pieces to each other. Dance is presented not as an interruption or as a parenthesis within the action, but as part of a natural continuum that incorporates multiple modes of expression.

These findings impact both performance and interpretation. Once we understand the structural conventions of Lully's divertissements, we acquire tools for resolving thorny practical questions such as who dances where and how such scenes might be staged. Furthermore, this type of understanding becomes crucial for those preparing critical editions, in view of the notational ambiguities found in the Ballard scores. Once we realize how much can be learned by examining how the parts work with the whole, we position ourselves to address questions of meaning. The remaining sections explore case studies where this wider angle of vision allows for interpretive possibilities that are unavailable if the dance music is taken in isolation.

Reading the Texts

Operatic historiography has tended to dismiss divertissement texts as trivial or even immoral.[74] However, once we pay attention to the words sung by supposedly minor characters, we discover that they offer hermeneutic tools and that Quinault carefully crafted them for their particular location.

In Act IV of *Phaéton* the deeply ambitious title character, who is angling to become the next king of Egypt, comes to the palace of his father, the Sun. He has been insulted by his rival, Epaphus, son of Jupiter, and wants to restore his honor by dispelling all doubts about his lineage. The Sun, surrounded by the Hours of the day and the four Seasons, welcomes him in style. After the festivities, Phaéton asks his father for a sign that will

[74] Boileau's famous condemnation – "And what of all those clichés of lewd morality / Which Lully rekindled with the sounds of his music?" – takes aim at the little aphorisms about love that tend to be enunciated by confidants, but surely includes many divertissement texts as well. For a longer excerpt from Boileau, see Wood and Sadler, *French Baroque Opera*, 39. For the broader context of French value judgments about opera, see Laurenti, *Valeurs morales et religieuses*, 29ff.

prove his parentage to the world. The Sun rashly assents before asking what sign Phaéton has in mind. When he learns that Phaéton wishes to drive the Sun's chariot across the sky, he instantly foresees the consequences, but cannot go back on his word. The inevitable catastrophe occurs in the last act. However, during the happy period before Phaéton requests the favor, the festivities in the Sun's palace extend over two scenes, one in the presence of the Sun, the other after Phaéton joins him. In Scene 1 a chorus of Hours and the personified Autumn praise the benefits the Sun brings. Although it is constructed as a gigantic rondeau, with the chorus singing a refrain to danceable music in triple meter, this scene appears to be devoted to *singing* the Sun's praises; it is only after Phaéton arrives that dancers embellish the festivities. Quinault aligned the two personified seasons who participate in this divertissement with the two main characters: the older figure, Autumn, sings for the Sun and the youthful Spring dances for Phaéton.

The welcome extended to Phaéton is initially expressed through movement: Scene 2 opens with a musically independent *entrée grave* (the Premier Air), but the Second Air initiates a four-part, strophic dance-song complex whose text is addressed to Phaéton (outlined in Table 2-6). Each verse is sung first by one of the Hours (soprano) and then by the chorus. The exceptionally square, triple-meter music is called a menuet in some secondary Lully sources.[75] Beyond Spring, who probably danced a solo during the *entrée grave*,[76] the number and gender of the dancers are unknown for the 1683 premiere; in 1702 Spring's followers included four men and four women.

Scène Seconde:[77] *Le Printemps et sa suite dansent, et les autres Saisons chantent avec les Heures, pour témoigner qu'ils se réjouissent de l'arrivée du fils du Soleil, dans le palais de son père.*

	Premier Air
	Second Air
	Une des Heures et les Choeurs, qui lui répondent
[First strophe:]	Dans ce palais

[75] See *LWV* 61/58; these include various arrangements of music by Lully.

[76] In 2012 a choreography by Beauchamps for a solo man, set to the music of the *entrée grave*, was discovered in a private collection; see Marsh and Hazebroucq, "Revisiting" (forthcoming).

[77] The score and libretto locate the start of Scene 2 in different places, but the libretto (followed here) seems correct; not only does a new character (Phaéton) enter, but Lully marks the spot by a modulatory tag in the bass to a new key. The order of events within the dance-song is indicated by an annotation in the score following the Second Air: "Une des Heures chante seule le choeur qui suit, et tous les chœurs lui répondent avec les violons, et l'on reprend le Second Air page 181, alternativement avec les chœurs." The annotation does not reveal whether the entirety of each strophe should be sung by the soloist and then again by the chorus, or whether the order should be A section (solo), A section (chorus), B section (solo), B section (chorus).

(Cont.)

Bravez l'envie,
Dans ce palais,
Vivez en paix.
Soyez content, tout vous y convie;
Goûtez toujours les biens les plus parfaits,
L'honneur qui suit une illustre vie,
Est un bonheur qui ne finit jamais.

Repeat of Second Air

Une des Heures et les Choeurs

[Second strophe:]
Ne tardez pas,
La Gloire est belle,
Ne tardez pas,
Suivez ses pas.
Vous la cherchez, sa voix vous appelle,
Vous êtes fait pour aimer ses appas,
L'amour constant que l'on a pour elle,
Porte un grand nom au-delà du trépas.

Les Choeurs

Dans cette demeure charmante,
Venez jouir d'une gloire éclatante;
Jeunes héros, tout répond à vos vœux,
Venez jouir d'un sort heureux.

(*Spring and his followers dance; the other Seasons sing with the Hours, to show their joy about the arrival of the son of the Sun at his father's palace.*

One of the Hours and the chorus, which repeats her words: In this palace defy envy and live in peace. Be happy; everything invites you. Always enjoy the best. The honor that attaches to an illustrious life brings unending happiness. *[Second verse:]* Do not wait; Glory is beautiful, follow her steps. You search for her, her voice is calling you; you love her attractions. A constant love for Glory carries a great name beyond death. *[Chorus:]* In this charming domain come enjoy a brilliant glory. Young hero, everything responds to your wishes; come enjoy your happy fate.)

Both the first strophe of the dance-song and the chorus that concludes the divertissement allude to the happiness, glory, and honor Phaéton can find in his father's palace. The second strophe, while not breaking the joyous mood, is more pointed: whereas the first quatrain exhorts Phaéton to seek glory (encouragement he does not need), the second puts a finger on his psychological state and, in a double-edged aphorism, prefigures the outcome of the opera, in which a love of glory carries an illustrious person beyond death. Whether this degree of subtlety could have been conveyed in the dancing cannot be known, but it is nonetheless built into the unit as a whole.

Table 2-12: *Atys* IV/5 as it appears in the Ballard full score of 1689.

Musical units	Key, meter	Scoring, comments
Introduction		
Prelude	C, ¢	Orchestra a5
Recitative, Sangar	C, —	With choral interjections
Bass air, Sangar, "Que l'on chante, que l'on danse"	C, $\frac{6}{4}$	Strings a3
Chorus, "Que l'on chante"	C, $\frac{6}{4}$	Male chorus a4, B.C., very similar to air
Dance-Song 1[a]		
[Gavotte]	C, **2**	Flute trio: G^1, G^1, C^3
"La beauté la plus sévère"	C, **2**	3 vocal parts (G^2, C^1, C^3), B.C. in C^3
Dance-Song 3		
[Menuet]	C, **3**	Flute trio: G^1, G^1, C^3
"L'Hymen seul"	C, **3**	3 vocal parts (G^2, C^1, C^3), B.C. in C^3
Dance-Song 3		
[Menuet]	a, **3**	Orchestra a5
"D'une constance extrême"	a, **3**	2 vocal parts (G^2, C^3), B.C. in F^4
Dance-Song 4		
[Gavotte]	a, ¢	Orchestra a5
"Un grand calme"	a, ¢	Chorus a4, orchestra a5

[a] Reproduced in Fig. 2-6, p. 48.

The divertissement texts in Act IV of *Atys* also reward attentive reading. The scene is the palace of Sangar, father of the opera's heroine, Sangaride. He and his followers – river gods of various types – have come together to celebrate the imminent wedding of Sangaride to Célénus, king of Phrygia. In the preceding scene, Sangaride and Atys have vowed eternal faith to each other, even if their love must remain secret. Atys leaves, aiming to use the power the goddess Cybèle has granted him to help resolve their dilemma, but Sangaride remains behind, obliged to participate with Célénus in the unwelcome festivities her father is hosting. On one level this divertissement, which consists of an invitation to sing and dance, followed by no fewer than four dance-songs in a row (see Table 2-12), offers a much needed respite from the untenable situation in which Sangaride and Atys find themselves. The jolly dance music Lully provided, which alternates menuets and gavottes, seems joyous and unproblematic.[78]

Quinault, however, appears to have had a more subtle conception, one that sets up a dialogue between two competing views of love and marriage, one naïve, the other cynical. The arguments are laid out over six strophes, set as three songs, that conclude

[78] In the 1987 production of *Atys*, choreographer Francine Lancelot treated this series as line dances, in the manner of Renaissance branles.

Table 2-13: *Atys* IV/5: Quinault's interleaving of two of the strophic songs.

	Text	Form	Music
Song 1, strophe 1	"La beauté la plus sevère"	10-line strophe, 6-line refrain	[Gavotte]
Song 2, strophe 1	"L'Hymen seul ne saurait plaire"	8-line strophe, 4-line refrain	[Menuet]
Song 1, strophe 2	"Il n'est point de résistance"	10-line strophe, 6-line refrain	[Gavotte]
Song 2, strophe 2	"L'Amour trouble tout le monde"	8-line strophe, 4-line refrain	[Menuet]

in a single-strophe chorus ending the divertissement with the statement, shocking under the festive circumstances, that "A great calm is too boring, we prefer storms." ("Un grand calme est trop facheux, / Nous aimons mieux la tourmente.") Storms and upheaval are certainly what the rest of the opera provides, starting with the next scene in which Atys returns, refusing to perform the marriage ceremony on the untrue grounds that Cybèle won't allow it, and departs with Sangaride. The chorus reacts with anger to end the act: "Quelle injustice!"

An interpretation of the divertissement as promoting the kind of conversation that might have graced the salon of a Précieuse[79] hinges on close attention to the libretto. The Ballard full score, published thirteen years after the opera went on the stage, includes the order of events outlined in Table 2-12.[80] Whereas the score makes it appear that all four of these dance-songs have only one strophe, the libretto gives two strophes to each of the first three. However, Quinault interleaved the texts of the first two songs, rather than presenting them sequentially, as is apparent in the libretto from their structural characteristics alone (see Table 2-13). That the interleaving was purposeful is confirmed in a parody of *Atys*, whose texts follow the same pattern.[81]

This order of events – assuming it is preserved in performance[82] – turns the sequence into a back-and-forth dispute about love. The first song argues that a

[79] As a young poet, Quinault frequented the salons of the Précieuses, some of whose verbal mannerisms may be seen in his plays and librettos. See Rosow, "Quinault," *NGO*, and Howard, "The influence of the Précieuses."

[80] The 1720 reduced score follows the same order and also omits the second strophes, but identifies dances 3 and 4 as menuet and gavotte respectively.

[81] Mouret's score for a parody of *Atys* (Théâtre Italien, 1726) includes two vaudevilles parodying these very texts, with the instruction that they are to be sung "alternativement." In order to remove all ambiguity, Mouret numbered each strophe: Vaudeville 1, strophe 1; vaudeville 2, strophe 1; vaudeville 1, strophe 2; vaudeville 2, strophe 2. *Divertissements du Nouveau Théâtre Italien*, III, 226–27.

[82] The recording by Les Arts Florissants (HM 901257.59) does give each song its second strophe, but sings the two strophes in succession before going to the next song. Moreover, the same performers are used for both songs, another decision that makes the dialogue hard to notice.

persevering lover will succeed in the end, just as water, falling drop by drop, can pierce the hardest stone. The second song claims that marriage alone cannot please, that love is what matters. But love cannot be controlled: Hymen (the god of marriage) comes when he is called, but Love comes when he pleases. The second strophe of the first song responds that fidelity triumphs in the long run, to which the second strophe of the second song replies that Love is a perpetual trouble-maker. The third song disputes the cynical view, saying in its first strophe that the singer plans to love the same person forever and in the second warning that a fickle heart that strays from the safe harbor is sure to encounter a storm. The concluding chorus continues the weather imagery of the third song, but rejects calm waters as boring, in favor of meteorological excitement. For the Parfaict brothers, this divertissement, with its equivocal tone, "verges on base ridiculousness."[83]

The perspectives in these texts are so distinctive that the performance must have assigned the different points of view to different groups. The 1676 court libretto, which lists the 41 performers (Table 2-14), reinforces this impression. The rivers are male roles, the fountains female; the little streams were performed by children. The qualification "grands" applied to some of the river gods means they are adults – to distinguish them from the little streams and also from the old rivers and fountains who dance. Given that river gods appear in various places on the list in the libretto, the separation must be functional, between larger groups and those who appear in small ensembles.

Table 2-14: Roles in the Act IV divertissement in *Atys*, as listed in the 1676 court libretto.

12 big river gods, singing [men, those who form the male chorus]
5 river gods playing the flute
4 fountain divinities, singing [women]
2 river gods [men, presumably singers in the small ensembles]
2 river gods, dancing together [men]
2 little gods of streams, singing and dancing [boys]
4 little gods of streams, dancing [boys]
6 big river gods, dancing [men]
2 old rivers gods, dancing [men]
2 old fountain nymphs, dancing [men in women's roles]

[83] Parfaict, *Histoire*, 36: "Dans les endroits qu'on a critiqué de cette piéce [*Atys*], je n'ai point remarqué qu'on ait parlé de la scène du fleuve Sangar, qui frise le bas ridicule." The last four words are crossed out and replaced in the margin by "qui est d'un ton trop différent du reste du poème."

This setting apart of the groups in the list suggests that these distinctions were discernible on stage. But how they map onto the various musical numbers inside the divertissement is less than clear, not least because the headings are vague in the libretto and in the score almost non-existent. The only unambiguous piece is the chorus "Que l'on chante," labeled "Choeur des Fleuves" and scored for male chorus; this must have been sung by the twelve adult river gods. The final chorus calls for all four voice types and probably involved the entire group of singers and dancers. For the remaining pieces, various hypotheses can be imagined, but there is no clear solution. And where, in all of this disputation, should the two old couples dance? As in *Thésée*, a dance for old folks seems intended to ridicule, or at the very least to raise a smile. The oldsters have no vocal counterparts, and the *didascalies* do not mention them; they would, nonetheless, seem likely to share the jaundiced view of songs two and four – or perhaps their dancing could be used to undercut the greeting-card sentiments of song three. Wherever they may have danced, their presence in this divertissement is not a fluke: danced roles for old rivers and old fountains remained in revivals of *Atys* until 1725.[84]

A director today would have to decide who does what where, but an ideal performance would make visible and audible the questions about marriage the texts present. After all, the bridal couple, Sangaride and Célénus, are on stage to witness these debates; these words – less than reassuring – matter to them.

Text and Action

In most of Lully's dance-songs, as in the sequence just discussed, the dancers and instrumentalists first present the idea, then the singers put into words what the audience has just seen and heard. In such structures the audience receives the visual sign before it gets the textual one. This progression is not so different from what happens elsewhere in Lully's operas, where a prelude or ritournelle may serve not only as entrance music for a main character, but also as a means of introducing a mood that is given voice when the character begins to sing. In his divertissements it is dance that usually initiates the expressive unit.

In pieces where the librettist, composer, and choreographer have done their jobs effectively, there exists a built-in reciprocity between the text, the music, and the movements of the dancers. However, the relative representational weight on the different components may shift depending on the order of events. In those sequences where a dance *follows* a related vocal piece, the sung text sets up the movements of the dancers, and their interpretation is more transparent. When, however, the chorus that precedes a dance is one of high passion and alludes to actions, then the question re-

[84] Starting with the 1738 revival the oldsters disappear.

emerges of whether the members of the chorus are expected to act. In such cases differences in the way the libretto presents the text have the potential to impact our interpretations of how scenes were staged. In III/4 of *Armide* Hatred and her followers, whom Armide has summoned in an effort to destroy the love she feels for Renaud, sing energetically of their desire to destroy the power of Love: "Let's break his bowstring, tear up his blindfold, burn his arrows, and extinguish his torch." Their text invites action, but who performs it – the choristers while they sing, or the dancers, to the fiendish instrumental air that follows?[85] In the libretto the *didascalie* that describes the action *follows* the text of the chorus: "The followers of Hatred hasten to break and burn the weapons used by Love." Should the location of the *didascalie* lead us to conclude that these words apply only to the dance piece and thus represent another instance where the singing and the dancing were sequential?

A similar question emerges in *Alceste* III/5, during the mourning for Alceste's sacrifice of her own life to save her husband's. After an extended and complex choral scene that honors Alceste's memory and deplores her death, there is a vigorous chorus ("Let us smash the sad remnants of these superfluous ornaments") followed by a musically similar dance piece, with which it overlaps (Example 4-6) – but this time the *didascalie* is located in the libretto *before* the text of the chorus:[86]

> A spasm of pain overcomes the two troupes of mourners. Some of them rend their clothes, others tear their hair, and all of them break the ornaments they have been carrying at the feet of the image of Alceste.

The "two troupes of mourners" allude to men and women, so the *didascalie* does not answer the questions of whether the dancers, choristers, or both are the ones carrying out the actions or of where within the two pieces of music (one choral, one instrumental) the violent actions would have been represented. Could this chorus have been danced throughout? Or would the movements of the dancers have been deferred until the instrumental piece, the only dance in the entire divertissement? It may be coincidence, but this brief chorus (20 bars) has an identical structure to the action chorus in *Le Mariage de la grosse Cathos*: the text is sung three times in a row to slightly different music, without any instrumental interludes. More significantly, the sorrowing woman who leads the ritual has already introduced the text slightly earlier in the scene, singing it three times herself, so that it is already familiar to the audience.[87] Under these circumstances, it seems conceivable that the chorus itself could have provided a site for

[85] This unlabeled binary instrumental dance is filled with dotted notes, tirades, and rushing sixteenth notes in a style typical of Lully's music for nasty characters; see Ch. 4, pp. 136–37.

[86] This ordering of chorus and *didascalie* follows the libretto in the *Recueil général,* but also conforms to Norman's edition, which is based on the libretto for the premiere; see his *Livrets d'opéra,* I, 90.

[87] This reading follows the score in the Prunières Lully edition, 216–20; not all manuscript sources present the pieces in the same order.

action, and that the movement could have continued on into the dance piece that follows.

If this possibility can be admitted, it is worth looking at *Armide* again and asking whether the chorus about breaking Love's weapons, which directly follows Hatred's utterance of the same words, could also have accompanied movement. The difference between the two scenes is the location of the *didascalie* in the libretto: in *Armide* the *didascalie* follows, rather than precedes the text of the chorus, whereas in *Alceste* it comes before the chorus sings. Should a distinction in staging be based on this typographical difference? In my view, both options for performance – action deferred until the instrumental dance or action during both the chorus and the dance – can be supported by the evidence we have, which is only partial. The one point that does seem clear is that no matter where the action occurred, the dancers would have been the ones performing it. Whether the chorus also gestured, we cannot know, but surely the burden of the physical expression was on the dancers.[88]

Other scenes pose the question of whether a specific action that appears to be assigned to a singer might also, in practice, have been performed by dancers. In *Roland* I/6 Angélique is presented with a valuable gift on behalf of her suitor Roland, who is away battling his enemies. In Act IV the bracelet becomes a symbol of Angélique's betrayal, when Roland learns that she has given it away. The gift is thus central to the plot and the gift-giving must be done in a suitably ceremonial manner. The transaction happens during the Act I divertissement, when one of Roland's companions, the prince Ziliante, and his followers pay Angélique homage. The only pertinent *didascalie* reports that "The chorus sings the last few lines while Ziliante presents the bracelet to Angélique." Notwithstanding what sounds like a clear stage direction, it seems likelier that Ziliante's followers – the dancers among them – were the ones who made the actual presentation. First, the social hierarchies visible both within the opera itself and within the society that gave it birth support such an inference. Ziliante is a prince; he is *not* the type who does work himself, rather he orders other people to carry it out. (See Kintzler's observation [Chapter I] that the laws of verisimilitude demand that lofty characters behave in a manner worthy of their rank.) The last few lines of the chorus represent a classic spot where the dancers are already likely to be in motion; it is not difficult to imagine the ceremonial presentation of the bracelet as part of the choreography. This type of surrogacy seems completely in line with Lully's aesthetic and was to remain in place in subsequent decades.[89]

The phenomenon of singers as explainers, dancers as their active agents may even occur outside of divertissements. At the end of *Phaéton*, during which the arrogant

[88] Dubos was to cite this scene as one with "scarce any dancing movements"; see Ch. 4, p. 122.

[89] See my "Ballet, pantomime," esp. 55–60.

young man loses control of the Sun god's chariot as it careens across the sky, the Egyptian shepherds who had prematurely celebrated Phaéton's success remain on stage during the last four scenes and are therefore available to carry out the frantic movements of the populace as it tries to escape the fires scorching the earth. The alternations between choral supplications and frenzied instrumental passages that Lully constructed into the choruses in Scenes 5 and 7 call for a vigorous physical response.

Celebrations

Of all the divertissement types in Lully's operas, the celebrations that conclude most of them are the least examined, probably because they can be dismissed as nothing more than joyous tags onto a work whose plot has already been resolved.[90] Whereas these scenes may seem hard places to argue that a divertissement really matters to an opera, it turns out that happy celebrations are not all alike. The endings of *Alceste*, *Bellérophon*, and *Persée* have in common that the protagonist's heroic deeds have restored order to society, a royal marriage is being celebrated, and at least one god participates in the festivities. On one level all three reinforce the monarchical status quo, by showing the populace joyously endorsing the deeds of their rulers, in an ending punctuated by a rousing chorus. Yet the individual features of each divertissement impact the audience's perception of what is being celebrated and offer a retrospective commentary on the entire opera.

Of the three, the ending of *Alceste* is the most complex. As we have already seen (Chapter 1), the celebration has a dual basis: Alcide's triumph over his baser desires and the reunion of Alceste and Admète. The singing and the dancing choruses involve both male and female roles, and the presence of Apollon and the Muses signifies that knowledge and the arts have added their blessings to those of the populace. Alcide, a loner at the start of the opera, now shares in the general adulation. But the divertissement also embraces the two comic characters, Céphise and Straton, who each sing a dance-song while surrounded by their rustic followers. These two groups of dancers then participate in the double chorus that ends the opera, thus signaling that the harmony now reigning includes not only the noble characters, whose merits are celebrated in the sung texts, but the lowly ones, whose movements animate the opera's final moments. No one person dominates this scene; the entire social order from the gods to the herdsmen is celebrated.

In *Bellérophon* the hero has overcome the magical forces arrayed against him, killed the Chimera, and earned the hand of the king's daughter. Yet again joyous crowds gather (peoples of different nations) and the goddess Pallas Athena, who had lent

[90] Only *Atys*, *Phaéton*, and *Armide* do not end with celebrations.

Bellérophon a hand earlier in the opera, escorts him to the festivities in her flying chariot. Since a wedding is being celebrated, a mixed group of dancers would seem to be appropriate, in keeping with the mixed chorus. But, instead, there are nine Lords, one of whom dances alone, plus the eight who compose his retinue. Four on-stage trumpeters accompany them.[91] This choice casts an entirely different character over the proceedings, especially when the first dance is a virtuoso, noble-style *entrée grave*. (See Table 2-6, p. 57.) This dance puts not social harmony but manly vigor and prowess on display – all the more since the dancing roles call for a leader and a group of followers. The object of the celebrations, the dancers seem to be saying, is Bellérophon the hero, not Bellérophon the bridegroom. This heroic impression is reinforced by the words of the choruses that surround this dance, which mention love only obliquely and attribute the cause for joy to the unnamed hero's acts. The trumpets and drums that play during the first chorus as well as in the canarie (also labeled "fanfare"), the dance that alternates with the concluding chorus, further add to the luster. In this militarized environment love seems beside the point.

Of all Lully's heroes, Persée is by far the most visibly heroic. Inside the opera alone, before the eyes of the audience, he kills Méduse, rescues Andromède by killing a sea serpent, and fights off an armed attack by the troops of his rival, Phinée. If ever a hero deserved magnificent celebrations, featuring a god or two, Persée would be the one. Yet the celebrations that conclude *Persée* have a very different cast from those in *Bellérophon*. There are actually three places in this act where dancers appear: first, during the wedding ceremony in Scene 3, where the singing priest of the god Hyménée is supported by dancing followers; second, during the battle that interrupts the wedding; and third, as part of the concluding celebrations. A god does put in an appearance at the appropriate moment, but it is not Persée's father, Jupiter, or any of the gods who had armed Persée in Act II. Rather, it is Vénus, the goddess of love, accompanied by Amour, Hyménée, the Graces, the Jeux, and cherubs. Their descent from the heavens is announced by Persée himself, just after he has petrified his enemies:

> La tête de Méduse a fait leur châtiment.
> Cessons de redouter la fortune cruelle;
> Le ciel nous promet d'heureux jours.
> Vénus vient à notre secours,
> Elle amène l'Amour, et l'Hymen avec elle.
> *Le palais de Vénus descend.*

[91] This information comes from the *didascalie* in Scene I ("quatre Trompettes, un Seigneur seul dansant, huit autres Seigneurs de sa suite dansants"); later in the act the nine dancers are identified simply as "Lyciens."

(Méduse's head has punished them. Let us cease fearing cruel fortune; heaven promises us happy days. Vénus is coming to our aid, bringing Love and Marriage with her. *Vénus's palace descends.*)

Persée's air ("Cessons de redouter") is preceded by an unlabeled instrumental piece that is identical to his extended binary air in structure, melody, and bass line.[92] The function of the prelude may well have been to accompany the descent of Vénus's palace, notwithstanding the location of the *didascalie* in the libretto. Although it is not built over a ground bass, the triple meter of this unit leads seamlessly into the passacaille that follows; there is even a modulatory descent (from C major to a minor) written into the last measure of the song to smooth the connection. The passacaille, which is 99 measures long and purely instrumental, is to be understood as operating within the realm of Vénus, who is clearly the one controlling the divertissement. Her recitative, telling Cassiope, Céphée, Andromède, and Persée that they are about to be elevated into the heavens as constellations, follows this dance. Given her dominion over the passacaille, it is no wonder that a choreography from the stage of the Opéra, which probably dates from the 1703 revival, is one of the most tender and romantic dances for a couple Pécour ever composed.[93] As Vénus, her followers, and the two apotheosized couples rise to the heavens, the Ethiopians pay homage both to the marriage and to the heroic Persée:

Héros victorieux, Andromède est à vous.
Votre valeur, et l'Hymen vous la donnent.
La Gloire et l'Amour vous couronnent.
Fut-il jamais un triomphe plus doux?
Héros victorieux, Andromède est à vous.

(Victorious hero, Andromède is yours. Your valor and Marriage give her to you.
Glory and Love crown you. Was there ever a sweeter triumph?)

Given the broadened emphasis it is not surprising to see that a dance piece, simply called "Air" in the score but with the rhythmic characteristics of an *entrée grave*, appears within two iterations of the chorus. This provides an opportunity for virtuoso male dancing to be put on display, so that Persée's heroic side can be highlighted.[94] Yet the

92 In Persée's vocal air, the A section is repeated, yielding AABb; the instrumental piece, however, is notated in the Ballard score without a repeat of the A section, even though it is otherwise identical to the song.

93 Pierce and Thorp, "The dances in Lully's *Persée*," pars. 3.26 and 4.6–4.10, report that "the dancers move in axial symmetry – that is, around one another – for roughly half the dance and only occasionally do they direct their attention toward the public."

94 The choreographic purpose of this dance is my inference; neither the score nor libretto indicates who danced it.

triple-meter chorus, connected to the passacaille and to Vénus both musically and textually (Vénus, Amour, and Hyménée all have solos within it) returns to end the opera on the words "Andromède is yours." The heroic moment is subsumed within a paean to love.

This chapter has argued that the mechanics of operatic divertissements reward study because they help us understand operatic staging and offer hermeneutic tools to historians and performers alike. It is a challenge to tease out seventeenth-century performing practices from the incomplete and dispersed evidence available, but if we learn from the process that even celebratory fêtes can project strikingly different affects, we begin to understand how great are the potential rewards. The principle of alternation, in which dance and solo singing are reserved for separate moments, is so far removed from our own conceptions of theatrical performances, that the evidence for it has generally passed unnoticed or even been misread. The conclusions presented in this chapter rest upon examination of all Lully's divertissements; it is only through a broad view that patterns have emerged.

In 1704, the eminent choreographer Pierre Beauchamps, then approaching the end of his life, claimed in a legal deposition that about 30 years earlier Louis XIV had ordered him to "discover the means of making the art of dance comprehensible on paper" and that he had "applied himself to shaping and disposing characters and notes in the form of tablature in order to represent the steps of the dances and ballets performed before the king and at the Opéra" in such a way that the dances could be learned "without need for personal instruction."[1] Beauchamps's own notations for the Opéra, originating during Lully's directorship, appear not to have survived;[2] thus, reprehensible as it appears today, Raoul Anger Feuillet's act of intellectual property theft resulted in the preservation of hundreds of dance notations. In the 106-page book Feuillet published in 1700, *Chorégraphie, ou l'art de décrire la danse*, in which he claimed the invention of the elaborate system of dance notation as his own, Feuillet simultaneously initiated publication of individual choreographies, both theatrical and social, more than 350 of which have been located to date.[3] These dances, most of which date from between 1700 and 1725, form the principal basis for our understanding of baroque style. They also mean that we know more about dance of this period than about many later styles.

Beauchamps retired when Lully died in 1687, but the troupe he founded remains one of the most important ballet companies in the world. Its membership under his leadership is surveyed at the end of this chapter.

BASIC PRINCIPLES OF BAROQUE DANCE

The surviving choreographies in Beauchamps-Feuillet notation, valuable as they are, nonetheless have limitations. First, the notation focuses primarily on floor patterns and steps, and conveys little about the many other features that characterize a dance.

1 F-Pan V^6 796, document n° 10.

2 Among the items Beauchamps submitted as part of his suit were five notebooks of notational symbols and a "cahier de tablature de la chaconne de Phaéton de l'année 1684." Until recently, his only known dances were a ballroom rigaudon and a theatrical sarabande for a solo man, but in 2012 a choreography from *Phaéton* attributed to Beauchamps – not the chaconne, but the "Entrée du Printemps" from Act IV – was discovered in a private collection; see Marsh and Hazebroucq, "Revisiting."

3 Two catalogues exist of the fully notated dances: Little and Marsh, *La Danse Noble*, which aims to include all such dances; and Lancelot, *La Belle Dance*, which includes primarily dances by French choreographers. Since their publication, a few more dances have come to light.

Second – a particularly unfortunate limitation for the purposes of this study – the theatrical notations only preserve individual dances, not sequences of dances, let alone all the choreographies from any given opera. Third, with a single exception, the theatrical notations are for a soloist or a couple, whereas much of the dancing in operas was for groups. Nonetheless, we can be grateful that 47 choreographies done on the stage of the Paris Opéra between 1693 and 1713 are among those published; see the discussion and figures in Chapter 14. There were at least two other notational systems developed during the 1680s, although never published: one, by André Lorin, preserves thirteen country dances that he had brought from England and adapted to French style; the other, by Jean Favier, preserves the only known complete work from the period, the mascarade *Le Mariage de la grosse Cathos* (see Chapter 2, p. 28).[4] In addition, several books about dance, published in France, England, and Germany during the early eighteenth century, help us interpret the notation and provide contextual information;[5] these are complemented by a good deal of iconography. The cumulative evidence makes it clear that France led Europe in the development of ballet: French dancing masters held positions all over Europe and French was the lingua franca in dance vocabulary. This dominance was to undergo inroads from Italy starting in the second quarter of the eighteenth century, but during Lully's tenure at the Paris Opéra, his dancers and choreographers set the standard for all of Europe.

The sophistication of the system and the enormous movement vocabulary it records demonstrate that this style of dance had existed for many years prior to the publication of *Chorégraphie*. The ten dances from 1688 preserved in Favier notation belong to the same stylistic world. The general principles enunciated below should thus be seen as applicable to a longer period than from 1688 to 1725, when most of the surviving notations originated. Some of these principles still applied as late as 1782, date of a manuscript by Auguste Ferrère which preserves the choreography of several short pantomime ballets.[6] Moreover, a number of basic stylistic principles – not to mention dance terms – have been handed down over the generations as part of the technique of classical ballet. In fact, the term "baroque dance" is problematical, both because the style itself has significant classical elements and because it is questionable whether the term "baroque" is at all appropriate for arts arising in France during the reign of

4 The Lorin manuscript is available in facsimile as *Dances for the Sun King* (ed. Sutton). On the development of dance notation, see HW&M, 82–92 and Pierce, "Dance notation systems." Some of the symbols of Favier notation may be seen at the bottom of Figure 10-1, p. 305.

5 The two most consulted by those translating Beauchamps-Feuillet notation into movement are Pierre Rameau, *Le Maître à danser* (Paris, 1725) and Kellom Tomlinson, *The Art of Dancing* (London, 1735). Other important writers from the early eighteenth century include Louis Bonin, Gregorio Lambranzi, Gottfried Taubert, and John Weaver. For further writings see Schwartz and Schlundt, *French Court Dance*.

6 See Marsh and Harris-Warrick, "Putting together a pantomime ballet."

Louis XIV. That said, this nomenclature is so entrenched that it has been retained here as a convenience.

The account that follows is not designed to teach dance notation or to explain how to perform the steps.[7] Rather, it aims to outline the general principles of this style of dance and to lay the conceptual groundwork for the discussions in later chapters of how dance functioned in its operatic contexts.

Movement Vocabulary

Any baroque dance involves multiple parameters. The steps and the floor patterns ("figures," as the choreographers of the period called them) traced by the dancers may be preserved in notation, but there are many other features that affect the quality of the movement and the audience's response, which are rarely, if ever, notated. These include the carriage of the upper body,[8] shifts in weight, movements of the arms and hands, the angle of the head, or eye contact between dancers. Whereas dance notation represents the foundations of the art, it does not answer all the questions involved in reconstructing dances.

The technique of baroque dance is advanced and demanding. Whereas ballroom dances of the type to which amateurs could aspire used the same basic step vocabulary and structural principles, the theatrical dances were much more difficult, requiring long and specialized training.[9] Some amateur dancers, such as Louis XIV himself and, in the next generation, his daughter the Princesse de Conti, took their dancing seriously enough to hold their own alongside professionals; moreover some of the dances published for the ballroom originated on the stage of the Opéra. This continuum shows that social dancers aspired to a remarkably high level of expertise (even learning to do a dance as simple as the minuet required a minimum of six months of study, according to Italian dancing master Gennaro Magri[10]); more importantly for this study, it means that audience members at the Opéra brought muscle memory and a trained eye with them to the theater.

Baroque dance technique is based on the five basic positions of the feet still in use in ballet today (which were codified by Beauchamps, according to Pierre Rameau[11]), although the degree of turnout of the feet has been considerably enlarged from the approximately 90 degrees it was in Beauchamps's day. Both men and women wore shoes with heels (whose heights seem to have varied) and flexible soles; they made their rising steps onto partial toe, moving through the instep.[12] The basic technique,

[7] Regarding the practice of baroque dance, see Hilton, *Dance of Court and Theater*. For a succinct explanation of the notation, see Whitley-Bauguess, "Reading baroque dance notation."
[8] Favier notation includes a symbol for the bending of the upper body; see HW&M, 104.
[9] See Fairfax, *The Styles of Eighteenth-Century Ballet*.
[10] *Trattato* (1779), 52; trans. Skeaping, 87. [11] *Le Maître à danser*, ch. 3.
[12] Regarding dancers' shoes in the eighteenth century, see Fairfax, *Styles*, 339–44. Pointe work did not become a regular part of ballet technique until the nineteenth century.

with its normal degree of turnout, can be transgressed for expressive purposes; demons, for example, seem to have used false positions of the feet and arms. Even within the parameters of the noble style, steps can be done in multiple ways – big or small, fast or slow, or with different expressive content; these decisions impact how a choreography is perceived by the audience, even when the dancer adheres to the notation.

The step vocabulary of baroque dance is rich and varied. Feuillet's numerous step-tables in *Chorégraphie* show that dance was based upon a limited number of fundamental movements, each of which could be modified in many ways. For example, one of the most basic movements, a *demi-coupé* (a bend on one foot followed by a rise onto the other), may be done *en avant, en arrière, ouvert en arrière, ouvert en arrière avec un rond de jambe par devant,* and so on for 54 more ways. More important than the variety, however, is the concept of the individual unit: the movements of the dance are conceived as a series of fundamental building blocks that can then be assembled at will into *pas composés* (step-units). The *contretemps de gavotte,* for example, consists of a hop on one foot followed by two *pas marchés* (walking steps). Like the smaller units, *pas composés* can be done in different directions or ornamented in multiple ways; Figure 3-1 shows variations on the *contretemps de gavotte* that include beats and turns. Some theatrical dance notations include complex *pas composés* that may not have a name in *Chorégraphie,* but that can nonetheless be broken down into nameable units – in other words, the active step vocabulary was even larger than the approximately 530 step permutations that Feuillet identified.[13]

The general rule of thumb is that one step-unit occupies one measure of music, whether in duple or triple time. This means that a basic step-unit such as the *fleuret* (three forward steps preceded by a *plié*) can be adjusted to the meter of the music, whether it is duple, triple, or compound. The rhythm of the step-unit may change (or there may be more than one possible rhythm for it within some meters), but the basic movements composing the step-unit remain the same. Every step-unit has a preparatory *plié,* the landing from which (either a step or the arrival of a jump) corresponds to the downbeat of the measure; this point of arrival occurs on the downbeat even when the music has an anacrusis, as in the passepied, bourrée, and gavotte.[14]

Exceptions to this general rule do exist. First, the basic step-unit for both the menuet and the passepied, the *pas de menuet,* occupies six beats of music; thus if the menuet is

[13] This number, which Pierce has calculated from Feuillet's tables in *Chorégraphie,* does not exhaust all the possible combinations, nor does it include all the composite steps found in notated choreographies. See his "Dance vocabulary" and "Choreographic structure," 184–90.

[14] The single exception is the courante, whose basic step-unit, the *pas de courante,* starts on beat three of a three-beat measure. Very rarely a choreographer may notate steps across the barline; for one such passage in a ballroom dance, see Witherell, *Louis Pécour's 1700 Recueil,* 96 and 100.

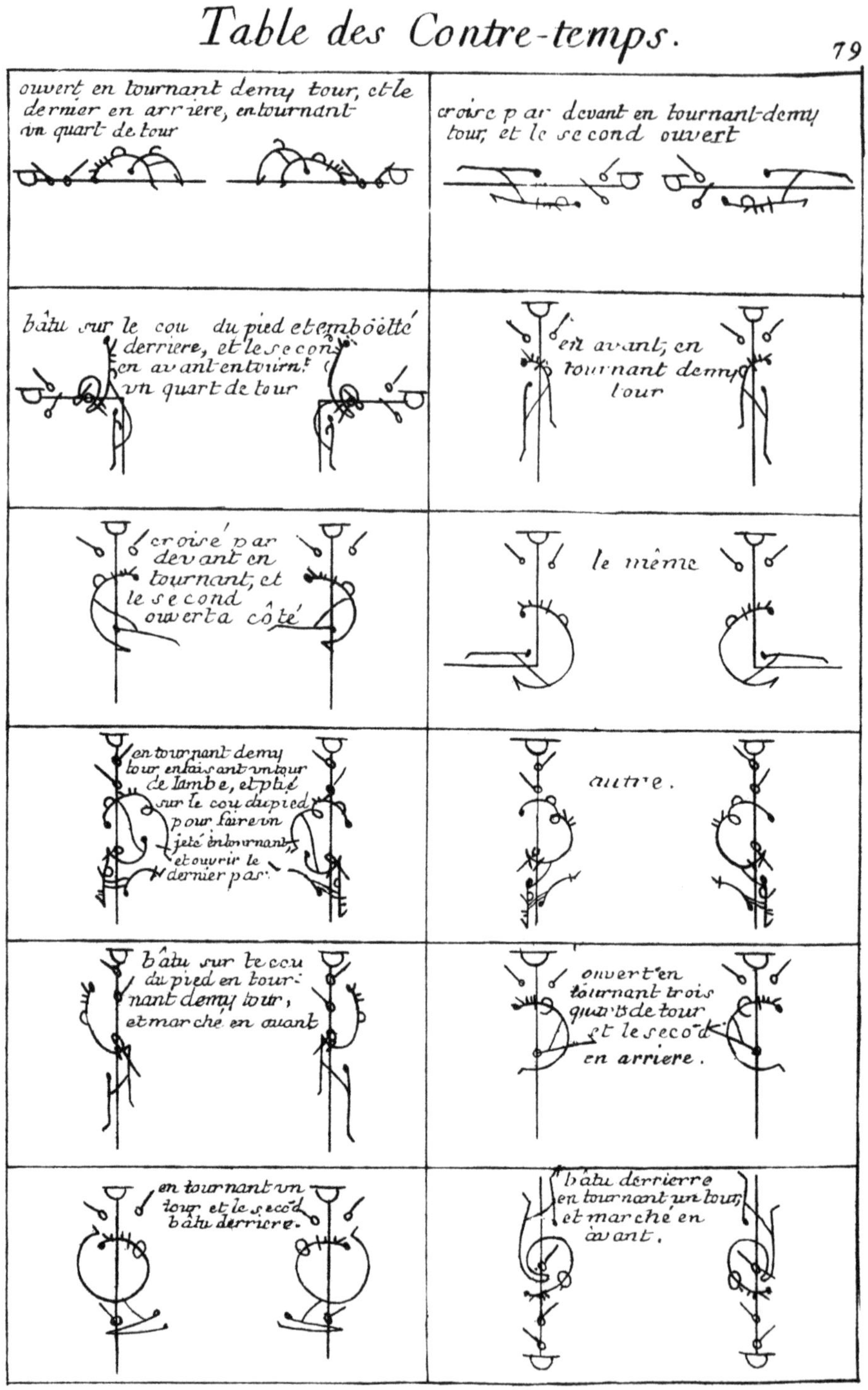

Figure 3-1: Some of the variations on the *contretemps de gavotte* from Feuillet's *Chorégraphie.*

notated in **3** or $\frac{3}{4}$, or a passepied in $\frac{3}{8}$, the step-unit requires two measures. This applies to all the variations on the basic step-unit.[15]

Second, some theatrical dances in a slow tempo have two step-units per measure, each of which occupies one half of the bar. This may occur in the loure or other dances in $\frac{6}{4}$, and also in duple meter, in dances such as the *entrée grave* or in some gavottes. The presence of two step-units within a duple measure imposes a slow tempo, all the more so since such dances tend to contain difficult, complex steps. Thus recognizing that a dance has two step-units per bar provides tempo information that the music may lack. In $\frac{6}{4}$, however, which amounts to the same thing as two measures of $\frac{3}{4}$ time, the tempo range is more varied.

The general rule that in most dances a step-unit is coterminous with a measure of music means that, contrary to received opinion among musicians, dance steps do *not* impose any particular phrase structure on the music. Many composers of dance music did write in four-bar phrases, but this was a compositional choice and they used other phrase-lengths as well. In fact, in Lully's dance music, regular four-bar phrase structures are the exception, not the rule. Even his menuets often have an uneven number of measures and phrases of unequal lengths (see Chapter 4, p. 135). Dancers adapt easily to the variety.

Most Baroque dances contain a variety of step-units. In fact, in theatrical dances it is rare for more than two of the same step-unit to be done in a row; rather, steps are combined in myriad ways. The only dance-types that can be considered "generic," in that they are based on a limited step-vocabulary that repeats in predictable or easily controlled ways, are the most popular social dances: the courante (in the seventeenth century); the menuet (which succeeded the courante as the pre-eminent ballroom dance); and the passepied (which also uses menuet steps). But even in the ballroom, the floor pattern of these dances may vary even if the steps repeat.[16] All other dances were choreographed individually to specific pieces of music. There is thus no such thing as a generic bourrée, but only the "Bourrée d'Achille" or the "Bourrée Dauphine," each to its own piece of music. Even though some of the step-units mention dance-types in their names (*pas de bourrée, contretemps de gavotte, pas de rigaudon*, etc.), such steps are neither limited to that particular dance-type nor found in greater numbers therein.

A corollary to this variety is that almost all extant choreographies are through-choreographed: when the music of a binary dance or a rondeau repeats, the dance does something new. Even the simplest of choreographies, such as the "Gavotte du roi à quatre" composed by Claude Balon for Louis XV when he was six years old, varies the

[15] Menuets, especially those for the theater, are not restricted to the *pas de menuet* and its variants; see Ch. 14, pp. 431–32. Step-units using only a single measure of music are also found.

[16] The repetition of a single step over and over as a feat of virtuosity, as seen in nineteenth-century ballet, is not found in this period, but does occur in the late eighteenth century; see Marsh and Harris-Warrick, "Putting together a pantomime ballet," 248 and 250.

figures when the music repeats. It is not uncommon, even in theatrical dances, for there to be some near repetition of phrases within a dance, in correspondence with the music. For instance, the first four measures may build a phrase that is then repeated in the next four on the other foot, or to a different side, or with only minor differences in the steps. But the repetition always carries some element of change, and more often than not, especially in theatrical dances, the dance phrases are new as the music unfolds.[17]

The rhythm of a given step-unit within measures is somewhat variable, although operating within a set of conventions. Beauchamps-Feuillet notation shows the correspondence between a measure of music and a measure of dance, but is less precise when it comes to indicating on which beats within the measure the movements occur. (Feuillet did develop a system for notating step rhythms, but it was not consistently applied in choreographies, nor does it resolve all ambiguities.) Favier notation, on the other hand, does indicate step-rhythms precisely, and some dancing masters, most notably Tomlinson, discuss the rhythm of steps.[18] From such indications it is possible to see, for example, that a *fleuret* done in triple meter would normally have changes of weight on beats 1, 2, and 3: ♩♩♩. It could also be done, however, twice as fast at the start, with the second change of weight occurring on the eighth note between beats 1 and 2: ♪♪𝅗𝅥. Dancers reconstructing notated choreographies can draw upon these conventions when setting the rhythm of the step, but may need to make decisions about rhythm in cases where there are options; choices may be governed by their ideas about phrasing, affect, or other expressive goals.

Step-units are composed of different components and types of movement that offer varied possibilities for surface rhythms and accentuation. Changes of weight, rises onto partial-toe, landings from a hop or a leap, or movements such as gestures with the free leg define the rhythms of the dancer's movements and generally correspond to countable beats within a measure. Most step-units have either two or three pulses within a measure, but some have more and some only one. Some motions carry stronger feelings of accentuation than others (e.g., the rise onto the ball of the foot when it corresponds with the downbeat of a measure), but shaping the phrase into coherent units of stress and release, within the general guidance provided by the steps, is as much a duty for the dancer as is the art of shaping a musical phrase for the musician. All theatrical choreographies, and most ballroom dances – even menuets – have abundant variety in the rhythms of the dance steps that may or may not correspond to the surface rhythms of the music. Sarabandes, for example, do not necessarily favor dance steps that stress the second beat of the bar. Step rhythm is a

17 See Pierce's articles on choreographic structures.

18 Regarding notated step-rhythms, see HW&M, esp. 113, and Pierce, "Dance notation systems," 291–93.

significant part of the affect of a step, but it is only one of the elements that govern the character of a dance.

When dancers perform together, either as a couple or in a group, they almost always perform the same steps in unison. This practice applies to mixed as well as same-sex groups. Thus the radical differentiation between male and female movements characteristic of later ballet did not apply when men and women danced together in this era. In a few dances a man may have, for a measure or two, an ornamental version of a step that the women does in simpler fashion, or there may be a brief echo passage, in which first one dancer does a series of steps while the other watches, with the roles reversed immediately after. Or there might be a slightly longer passage in which the man may circle around the woman, who performs pirouettes. Such differences, however, are so short-lived that they barely impact the overwhelming impression of unison dancing. A *pas de deux* from this period thus highlights a sense of equality between the couple, rather than casting one person in a starring role, the other supporting.

The most salient hint that there may have sometimes been exceptions to what otherwise seems the dominant unison practice comes from the rigaudon in *Le Mariage de la grosse Cathos*. This is a dance for five, a man surrounded by four women.[19] For many measures, particularly toward the start of the dance, his steps represent a more vigorous version of theirs; as he is in the center, he is also set off by his position on the stage. If this sample size of one shows that dancers could sometimes break out of unison movements for more than a few measures, it also suggests that at least in 1688 the circumstances permitting such choreographic choices were circumscribed and the differences subtle. According to Menestrier, different things could happen simultaneously in the same entrée, provided the movements are reciprocal. His examples are all mimetic:

> Within a single entrée it is possible to make different movements, provided that they relate to each other. Some [dancers] might make thrusts with a sabre or a club, while others receive the blows on their shields. A magician might call up ghosts and make circles with his wand, while the ghosts take various positions. Some might dig up the earth, while others put it into baskets and still others take it away.[20]

In single-sex dances the step vocabulary for men and women was quite distinguishable. Dances for men alone allowed for more virtuosity; there was a noticeable difference in technique, involving more leaps and hops ("la danse haute"), and more ornamental steps such as *pas battus, entrechats*, or *ronds de jambe*.[21] For example, one virtuoso move, then as now, was to have the dancer balance on one leg for a long stretch of time, while the other leg performs complex gestures. Solo choreographies for women also pose

[19] See HW&M, 55–56 and 153–61. [20] Menestrier, *Des Ballets*, 167.

[21] French dancing master Louis Bonin, who spent most of his professional life in Germany, thought it was not appropriate for women to do jumps and caprioles (*Die neueste Art*, 174–75 and 188).

technical challenges, although in different ways.[22] The only surviving choreographies assigned to female characters but danced by men come from *Le Mariage de la grosse Cathos*; there a "female" movement vocabulary was assigned to them. When Mlle Camargo, a brilliant technician, made her impression on the dance world starting in the 1720s, she was often said to dance like a man.

In comparison with later classical ballet, the steps of baroque dance are relatively small, for men and women both. In addition, theatrical dancers had to deal with limited space. The stage of the Académie Royale de Musique was deep and narrow, i.e., the opposite of most stages today, and measured approximately 17 meters deep by 9 meters wide at the front, narrower in the back, with six flats on either side; it was also raked.[23] The dancers probably performed mostly downstage, as going upstage would make them appear disproportionately large relative to the vanishing-point perspective of the scenery. Given that the chorus was generally on stage along with the dancers and that there also might be solo singers about, the dancers did not have much room to maneuver.

With very few exceptions, dance notations do not include symbols for movements of the upper body, head, or arms. This does not mean there were no such movements. In fact, dance sources show that there were general principles of arm movements based on the idea of opposition – the observation that when someone walks, the left arm naturally swings forward when the right foot steps out. In dance terms, this translates into raising the hand on the other side of the body from the foot in front (see Figure 3-2), but the principle was not applied in a mechanical way; conventions were established for certain kinds of arm movements in conjunction with specified steps, and one page of *Chorégraphie* gives a sample sixteen-bar passage showing how to co-ordinate arms and feet.[24] A few choreographies have notations for special kinds of arm movements, such as the hands-on-hips and interlaced arms for a dance in the German style.[25] Pierre Rameau's instructions always maintain the hand no higher than the shoulder, but his book applies to ball dances, and some iconography from the theater shows higher positions of hands and arms. Moreover, a considerable latitude seems to have been left the dancer to use arm movements for expressive ends. Differences in arm movements, are, in fact, one of the most distinguishing features among today's baroque dancers.

Dance-Types

The word "dance-type" – if it implies a stereotypical and recognizable set of movements used in conjunction with music of distinct profile – is problematic in this context.

22 See Goff, "Surprising monsters." 23 Coeyman, "Theatres," 31–34.

24 *Chorégraphie*, 93, a choreography set to the "Folies d'Espagne" tune that shows steps, arm gestures, and castanet rhythms. Rameau devoted all sixteen chapters in part II of *Le Maître à danser* to arm movements.

25 Pécour, "L'Allemande," published by Feuillet in 1702.

Figure 3-2: "Mr Balon dancing at the Opéra," in the noble style, with arms in opposition to his feet. (Photo BnF)

Whereas it is possible that earlier in the seventeenth century, and perhaps even during part of Lully's working life, dances such as the bourrée may have relied upon the steps of the same name, by the era of notated choreographies the step vocabulary used in the dance-types that appeared on the stage was so mixed as to have limited value as a marker of a dance's identity. The menuet and passepied are the most recognizable, because they always involve at least some menuet steps, even on the stage.[26] The bourrée and the gavotte, on the other hand, have distinguishable musical profiles, but few if any differences in the range of steps. Dancer and choreographer Francine Lancelot, who made a systematic study of the notated choreographies by dance-type on the basis of their steps, reluctantly came to conclusions such as "the identification of a sarabande is more precise through the music than the choreography."[27] The choreographic differences she *was* able to discern came from ballroom dances. Any study of the distinctions among theatrical dances on the basis of their choreography will need to draw not just upon step vocabulary, but upon more subtle parameters such as the combinations in which steps are used, their location relative to the phrase, the figures the dancers trace in the space, and other interlocking features that dancers feel in their bodies, and which are (by their own admission) heavily influenced by the music to which the dance is set. With the exception of the menuet and passepied, the question of whether choreographic, as separable from musical, "types" exist remains open.

Whatever the basis for the distinction – musical, choreographic, or both – Lully did label some of the dances in his scores as to type. The following list includes only those dance-types so labeled in his opera scores; these account for approximately one third to one half of the dances in any opera.[28] Lully's operatic dance-types are:

bourrée
canarie
chaconne
gavotte
gigue
loure
marche
menuet
passacaille
passepied
sarabande

[26] See Ch. 14, pp. 431–33, regarding theatrical menuets and passepieds. The courante is also recognizable by its steps, but it was not used on the operatic stage (except occasionally in the eighteenth century, when satirized as out-of-date).

[27] Lancelot, *La Belle Dance*, xlii and lii.

[28] The list (with incipits) Meredith Ellis [Little] published in her "Inventory of the dances of Jean-Baptiste Lully," 21–55, includes dances from the ballets and other works as well. However, Little chose to omit those dance pieces found in Lully's scores that do not fit into an identifiable dance-type (e.g., the "airs" or "entrées"), nor did she include the march.

The allemande was no longer danced in this era[29]; the courante and the various types of branles belonged to the ballroom[30]; and the Folies d'Espagne, for which four theatrical choreographies survive, do not appear in any of Lully's scores. Although the contredanse and the rigaudon already existed in France, they only appeared in operas with the next generation of composers.[31] (These various lists show that dances used in actual practice overlap, but are not congruent with, dances found in instrumental suites, particularly those for solo instruments. Orchestral suites are likelier to contain dances found on the stage, including some for character types, but the history of all types of instrumental suites is sufficiently separate from operatic practices that this study cannot take it into account.)

The dance-types in the above list do not begin to account for all the dances found in Lully's operatic scores. Most are simply called "entrée" or "air," sometimes followed by the name of the characters performing them, such as the "Air pour les nymphes de Flore" from the prologue to *Atys*.[32] The music for such dances aims to express the essence of the characters dancing. Sometimes a piece that Ballard labels "air" or "entrée" may be identified as a dance-type in a secondary musical source, but many such identifications come from sources outside of Lully's orbit, such as arrangements of dances for solo instruments, and they may disagree in their designations; one dance from *Acis et Galatée* (II/6) that Ballard identifies as a gigue is called a loure in a choreographic source.[33] Whereas it can sometimes be useful to identify a dance piece as to type, attempts to shoehorn every dance into a category seem counterproductive and unnecessary. The more important question for dances on the stage is what types of characters are dancing.

[29] The allemande in slow quadruple meter, familiar from harpsichord suites, was not used for dancing. After 1700, a different kind of allemande, a German character dance, appeared occasionally on the French stage (see n. 25).

[30] By the time Lully began composing operas, the courante was being replaced by the menuet. In the comedy-ballet *Le Mariage forcé* (1664) the dancing master who gives a lesson to Sganarelle tries to teach him a courante; in 1670, in the *Bourgeois gentilhomme*, Monsieur Joudain attempts a menuet. Branles appear only in scenes set in ballrooms; see Ch. 9, pp. 273–75.

[31] The rigaudon was in existence by 1688, when it appeared in the prologue to *Zéphire et Flore* by Lully's sons. A manuscript ballroom choreography notated in the eighteenth century, entitled "Le vieux rigaudon" was set to two back-to-back tunes from the prologue to *Acis et Galatée* (1686), where they are simply called "Airs."

[32] In her "Inventory of the dances of Jean-Baptiste Lully," 21, Ellis [Little] estimates that "pieces with specific dance titles" (gavotte, menuet, etc.) probably constitute "eighty per cent of the dance music," but this proportion is far from accurate. For example, Little lists the five dance pieces from *Proserpine* designated in the score as to dance-type, but this opera has fourteen dances in all. Similarly, only five of the sixteen dances in *Psyché* figure in her inventory.

[33] See Ellis [Little], "Inventory," 28. Little derived some of her identifications as to type from secondary sources, many of which were produced after Lully's death; this choice impacts not the dance-types per se, but her statistics as to their relative frequency. For more details, see her unpublished thesis, "The dances of J.-B. Lully."

It has been claimed that the menuet "is the Lully dance *par excellence*: the most frequently used dance in his operas."[34] There are, indeed, quite a few menuets – approximately 30 in his thirteen *tragédies* – but a blanket statement about numbers masks the fact that menuets are much likelier to appear in Lully's prologues than elsewhere in his operas. *Armide*, for example, has three menuets in the prologue and none thereafter. (When menuets do appear outside of prologues, they figure as part of celebrations, such as the party given by Sangaride's father for his fellow river gods in Act IV of *Atys*.) One hypothesis for the prologue–menuet connection has to do with the menuet's status as the pre-eminent ballroom dance of the day, one danced frequently at court. Its use in the prologue, a paean to the king, may have favored associations between the dance and the monarch.[35]

The geographic origins imputed to some dance-types (e.g., the bourrée d'Auvergne, passepied de Bretagne, menuet de Poitou) have no discernible impact on how the dances are used in Lully's operas, for the simple reason that characters from these French regions do not show up in his mythologically based tragedies. However, Lully did make use of such associations in other contexts: the Spaniards in the "Ballet des nations" that closes the *Bourgeois gentilhomme* dance a sarabande and the Breton characters in *Le Temple de la Paix*, a ballet put on at court, dance passepieds. In his operas, Lully does occasionally seem to invoke an association between a dance-type and certain characters, such as the chaconne danced by Africans playing guitars in *Cadmus et Hermione* (I/4)[36] or the two sarabandes in rondeau form in *Armide* I/3, which are musically akin to the Spanish sarabande from the *Bourgeois gentilhomme*. In fact, the choice of this variant on the sarabande for a divertissement offered to Armide by the people of Damascus may be a means of marking her kingdom, and by extension herself, as exotic.[37]

In the generation of composers following Lully, when works set in existing locales were put on the stage, geographic associations grew stronger.

One dance-type that does not get discussed as such in musicological writings, but that is nonetheless identifiable in choreographies, is the *entrée grave*. It has a musical affinity to the opening section of a French overture, in that it is in duple meter and characterized by dotted figures (see Example 2-3, p. 57); the tempo has to be slow

[34] Wood, *Music and Drama*, 184. This and similar claims are based upon Little's work. Given the ambiguities within the primary sources, it seems prudent to avoid specific counts and to view proportions as approximate. My numbers are lower than Little's, because I rely primarily on the scores of the operas, not secondary sources.

[35] By the time Lully began composing operas, Louis XIV had stopped dancing: he retired from the stage in 1669 and his last known participation in a ball is in 1679; see my "Ballroom dancing," 44.

[36] Lully had earlier used the chaconne as a dance for Moors in the *Ballet d'Alcidiane* (1658).

[37] Regarding Lully's "Spanish" sarabandes, see Ch. 6, p. 170.

Example 3-1: *Armide* prologue, "Entrée" for the followers of Glory (Paris: Ballard, 1686), xlvii–xlviii. The opening bars of (a) the first strain, and (b) the second strain.

because there are two – often technically demanding – step-units per measure. There are several *entrée grave* choreographies in Beauchamps-Feuillet notation, all of them assigned to men, whether as a solo, duet, or group dance (see Chapter 14, p. 428ff).

Most *entrées graves* have the same musical features throughout both sections, but there is a subgroup in which the second strain retains the same meter, but moves the dotted figure to the next smallest note values. This can be seen in the "Entrée" for the followers of Glory in the prologue to *Armide* (Example 3-1). Another variant that also increases the level of rhythmic activity either uses smaller note values in the B section (see the "Air pour la suite de Melpomène" in Example 5-1, p. 148) or assigns it a faster tempo, as when the second strain of the "Premier air" for the followers of Hatred in *Armide* III/4 is marked "Vite," an alternative notation that produces much the same result.

Construction of Choreographies

Beauchamps-Feuillet notation has the virtue of showing the floor pattern for each figure of a dance. The choreographies for more than one person show that the principle underlying any dance's construction is symmetry: the dancing space is oriented around an invisible axis running front to back through the center of the stage (see Figures 14-1 and 14-2). When there is an even number of dancers, half are on each side of the stage; with an odd number, one dancer occupies the center axis while the others are arranged symmetrically on either side (Figure 3-3). Dancers in a couple start on opposite feet and move in mirror image as they go through figures such as coming downstage, separating from each other, and coming back together. If the figure changes to, say, a circling

Figure 3-3: Jean Berain, a symmetrical grouping of six couples dancing with a soloist.

pattern, the dancers move onto the same foot, an adjustment that maintains symmetry from the audience's perspective.[38]

When a man and a woman dance together, the convention is for the man to start on the left (facing downstage), the woman on his right. Most dances end with a retreat

[38] Marsh, "'Regular and irregular figures'"; see also the discussion of symmetry in Thorp and Pierce, "Taste and ingenuity."

back to the same relative positions. *Danses à deux* do not have to be for a mixed couple – many were for pairs of men or of women – but all notated couple dances start with the two dancers standing side-by-side facing the audience.

Although some dances may include figures in which the dancers trace a diagonal path – the middle of the Z figure in the ballroom menuet being the most obvious example – never does a dance begin or end in an upstage corner and orient itself along the diagonal, as was to become common in nineteenth-century ballet. No matter what shape the various figures may take, the central vertical axis remains the one that defines the space.[39]

Many dances are presentational, in that the dancers start upstage and move toward the audience, before going into various floor patterns, which may also face forward. On the other hand, a choreography may favor figures in which the dancers relate more to each other than to the audience. Some dances even open with a turn of the dancers to face toward each other. Variety is the rule in the composition of figures, just as it is in the choice of steps, although symmetry still reigns. The use of space has an enormous impact on the affect that a choreography projects.

In couple dances the only exceptions to the principle of symmetry are found in menuets and passepieds, which make use of what Feuillet called a *figure irrégulière*.[40] In such a figure the dancers move in parallel – for example, both moving first to the right and then to the left. But even though the dancers may move off center for a while, there is always a reciprocal movement that restores balance.[41]

It is hard to generalize about the figures used in group theatrical choreographies because the sample is small, consisting of Feuillet's "Ballet de neuf danseurs" (published in 1700) and seven of the ten dances from *Le Mariage de la grosse Cathos*.[42] Whereas the "Ballet de neuf danseurs" is rigidly symmetrical and, in fact, never has all nine dancers in motion simultaneously, some of the dances in the mascarade include other kinds of figures: the entrance and exit marches snake around the stage; the opening danced march has a brief asymmetrical figure; part of the passepied is a line dance; and the rigaudon has a brief hey figure.[43] Nonetheless, in the mascarade overall mirror-image symmetry dominates the use of space.

There is a close relationship between a piece of music and its choreography, but this does not mean a literal kind of imitation of one medium through the other. The surface

[39] Orientation around a vertical axis remains apparent in the dances transmitted by Ferrère in 1782; see Marsh and Harris-Warrick, "Putting together a pantomime ballet," 269–72.

[40] Feuillet, *Chorégraphie*, 92.

[41] Marsh has dubbed this kind of motion "translational symmetry"; see n. 38.

[42] Two later sources of theatrical choreographies include several dances for groups: *Ludus pastoralis*, a ballet danced at the Jesuit college of Metz in 1734, and the Ferrère manuscript, dated 1782 (see n. 39.) Both use Beauchamps-Feuillet notation, either all or in part.

[43] HW&M, 49ff.

rhythms of the music may or may not be paralleled by the step rhythms, although the downbeat of most measures generally receives accentuation of some kind via the body of the dancer. A musical cadence may sometimes correspond to a point of stillness in the dance, but often the dancers keep moving at cadences, albeit in ways that seem coherent with the phrasing.[44] A change of direction, for example, may provide the means for articulating the conjunction of two phrases.

The number of performers may vary within a given dance, but only in ways that respect the musical structure. The "Ballet de neuf danseurs" and five of the ten dances from *Le Mariage de la grosse Cathos* offer models of how the number of dancers may be varied within a single choreography (see Chapter 4). In every case a change in the number of dancers occurs either when the entire piece is repeated or at the start of a new strain of music (e.g., at the start of the B section in a binary construction or when an instrumental phrase within a chorus begins). The choreographers appear to have taken their cue for changes to the visible structure from the musical structure.

A given choreography may require more than one repetition of the music, a phenomenon that is rarely apparent in the score. Yet since the dance is through-choreographed, it is possible to see how much music it involves. A number of dances in Beauchamps-Feuillet notation require that the music be played twice in a row (AABBAABB)[45]; in cases where more than one choreography exists for the same tune, the repeat structures may not be identical (see Chapter 4, p. 132). It is possible that repeating a dance piece more than once was part of the performance practice of Lully's operas; Dubos, writing after Lully's death, believed as much.[46] Musical repetition would not only extend the divertissement, but also offer the opportunity to vary a choreography. Although the choreographies in Beauchamps-Feuillet notation that require more than an AABB playing of the music involve the same dancers throughout, the four choreographies in *Le Mariage de la grosse Cathos* that repeat the entire piece of music adhere to a different model: a musical repeat is accompanied by a related but new choreography using a different number of dancers. These extended dances balance the familiar with the new.

LULLY'S DANCE TROUPE

The troupe assembled for the Académie Royale de Musique was the first standing professional dance company and, as the Ballet de l'Opéra de Paris, is still in existence.[47]

[44] In the article "Saut" in his *Dictionnaire universel* (1690) Furetière noted that jumps often punctuated the ends of phrases in theatrical dances. Ken Pierce confirms that this practice can be found in notated solos for men (personal communication).

[45] Of the 73 choreographies whose repeat structures Little studied, seven require two full repetitions of the music; see her "Problems of repetition and continuity," 429–30.

[46] See discussion of this issue in Ch. 12, p. 352.

[47] For its history see Guest, *The Paris Opéra Ballet*.

Since no personnel records survive from its first three decades, it is not clear whether Lully hired the same dancers that Pierre Perrin had assembled for his short-lived Académie d'Opéra (1669–1672), and dance histories vary in dating the birth of the troupe from 1669 (the granting of the privilège to Perrin), 1671 (*Pomone*, the first production), or 1672, when Lully took over and changed the name of the institution to the Académie Royale de Musique.[48] Before turning to opera, Lully had composed ballets for the court, and had also collaborated with the great playwright Molière on a series of works that included danced and sung interludes; the best known is the *Bourgeois gentilhomme* (1670); the last of them the tragedy-ballet *Psyché* (1671). Lully thus had long-standing professional relationships with many dancers and singers, and at least some of those he had directed at court joined his new operatic enterprise.

Pierre Beauchamps (1631–1705), the king's *Surintendant des ballets*, became the choreographer at the Opéra and one of its lead dancers, although perhaps not for Lully's first production. The preface to the first volume of the *Recueil général des opéra* (pp. [iv–v]) reports that Beauchamps choreographed both of Perrin's operas, but that Desbrosses and Lully himself shared the choreographic duties for Lully's first opera, *Les Fêtes de l'Amour et de Bacchus*, which premiered 11 November 1672. A plausible explanation for the hiatus in Beauchamps's service is that when Lully and Molière broke off their collaboration, which had happened by the spring of 1672, Beauchamps remained with Molière.[49] If so, he did not sever all ties with Lully, as he was probably working with him again by the time *Cadmus et Hermione* premiered in April of 1673, two months after Molière's sudden death. Beauchamps retired from the Opéra when Lully died in 1687, although he remained active as a choreographer at Jesuit colleges.[50]

In the absence of personnel records, the only way to get an idea of which dancers might have belonged to Lully's troupe is to draw inferences from the names published in librettos. Those used for court performances of Lully's *tragédies* between 1675 and 1680 contain eight names that reappear in 1699, when the librettos for the Opéra started naming the performers on a regular basis.[51] As only family names are given, with an occasional marker such as "le cadet" (the younger), it is rarely possible to tell whether

48 Some histories have attributed the origins of the troupe to the formation of the Académie Royale de Danse in 1661, but the dance academy was a separate entity and, moreover, not a performing organization.

49 See Powell, "Pierre Beauchamps," n. 54, for documentary evidence that Desbrosses choreographed *Pomone* and that Beauchamps was hired to replace him only toward the end of the run. Regarding the opposition Lully encountered when he took over the Opéra, see La Gorce, *Lully*, 180–90.

50 Astier, "Pierre Beauchamps."

51 The lists of possible members have been generated by comparing the names appearing in librettos for court performances of Lully's operas with names of the dancers in the earlier court ballets, and those for the first three years (1699–1701) of Parisian opera librettos that include names – as based on my own examination of librettos; on Schmidt, *LLC*; and, especially for the later period, on Lecomte's "Danseuses and danseurs." Dancers named in only one or two librettos from Lully's lifetime are excluded, since they were probably not regular members of the troupe. It is beyond the scope of this book to sort out the familial and professional relationships among these dancers.

these are the same individuals or other members of the family; the gap of 20 to 25 years could easily mean a generation gap, but on the other hand, some dancers, Pierre Beauchamps among them, had remarkably long careers.[52] These eight names appear in alphabetical order, with spelling variants noted; names in italics indicate dancers mentioned in the preface to Volume 1 of the *Recueil général* as having performed in Lully operas:[53]

Barazé (Barasé)
Blondy[54]
Bouteville (Boutville, Boutteville)
Dumirail (Du Mirail)[55]
Germain
La Pierre (Lapierre)
Lestang (L'Estang)[56]
Pécour (Pecourt, Pecoul).

Other names that appear in at least three court librettos and from among whom Lully may have drawn for performances in Paris are:

Arnal
Beauchamps (Beauchamp)
Bonnard (Bonard, Bonnart)
Charlot
Chicanneau (Chicaneau)
Des-Airs (Deserts, Dezerts)
Desmatins
Dolivet (d'Olivet)[57]
Faure (Favre)
Favier l'aîné (Jean)
Favier *le cadet* (Bernard-Henri)[58]
Foignard (Foignart, Foignac)[59]

52 According to one anecdote (*Mercure galant*, December 1701, 300–01), Beauchamps was still dancing vigorously at the age of 66.

53 The preface provides a brief history of the Académie Royale de Musique, but does not distinguish fully between performances at court and in Paris.

54 Parfaict, *Histoire*, 84, reveals that the Blondy of the 1670s was the father of the Blondy who joined the troupe in 1691. The younger Blondy was to have a brilliant career (see Ch. 13, p. 379).

55 There were at least two dancers with this family name.

56 There were at least two dancers in this family, *l'aîné* and *le cadet*.

57 There were at least three dancers in this family.

58 For the Favier brothers' careers, see HW&M, 21–29.

59 There were two dancers by this name. According to La Gorce, *L'Opéra à Paris*, 42–43, dancer Pierre Foignard killed the Opéra's hairdresser following a quarrel and had to appeal to the king for mercy.

Joubert
Lechantre (Le Chantre)
Le Doux (Ledoux)
Magny[60]
Mayeux
Noblet
Pezan (Pesan, Pesant, Pezant, Paysan)[61]
Vagnard (Vaignard, Vaignac)

Most of the dancers on this list had already performed in ballets at court during the 1660s.[62] Two additional dancers mentioned in the preface to the *Recueil général* as having danced at the Opéra under Lully are Saint-André and Le Basque (qualified as "homme très léger").[63] The court librettos single out five dancers as soloists: Beauchamps himself (by far the most times), Dolivet, Favier *l'aîné*, Lestang, and Pécour. All five are known to have choreographed as well; Guillaume-Louis Pécour was to succeed Beauchamps as the official choreographer at the Opéra after Lully's death.[64]

All of the names listed above are of men. This is because only men danced in public performances at the Opéra until 1681, and between 1681 and 1699 the librettos do not list performers' names. It is not clear why no women danced at the Opéra in its early years. Female singers had been employed there from the start, and many women, mostly aristocrats, but also a few professionals, had danced for decades in court ballets.[65] But whatever the reason, the performances of *Le Triomphe de l'Amour* in 1681 marked a watershed. The work had premiered at Saint-Germain-en-Laye on 21 January, with several of the king's children among the dancing cast, and when in May it moved to the Palais-Royal for public performance, Lully gave the roles previously danced by court ladies to professional women dancers. The Parfaict brothers report that "among the *danseuses* who appeared for the first time in this ballet, Mlles La Fontaine, Pesant, Carré, and *la petite* Le Clerc stood out," and that these same four also danced in the revival of *Proserpine* in November of that year.[66] Mlle La Fontaine was singled out in the preface to the *Recueil général* as "shining" in *Le Triomphe de l'Amour*; she was to dance solos in

[60] Regarding the members of this family, see Antoine, "Les Magny."

[61] There was probably more than one dancer by this name.

[62] See Christout, *Le Ballet de cour*, 253–56.

[63] Writing in 1725, Pierre Rameau (*Le Maître à danser*, xiii) supplied many of the same names as having danced under Lully "in Paris and at the court": St. André, Favier *l'aîné*, Favre, Bouteville, Dumirail, Germain, Lestang, and Pécour.

[64] La Gorce, *Lully*, 190–95, contains useful information about the formation of Lully's troupe.

[65] See, for example, the roles performed by Mlle Vertpré, daughter of a dancing master, including in the *Ballet royal de l'impatience* (1661).

[66] The Parfaict brothers further report (*Histoire*, 48) that Mlle Le Clerc distinguished herself dancing in subsequent Lully operas and that Mlles Pesant and Carré withdrew from the Opéra before 1700.

subsequent operas, and even to choreograph her own entrées. The next soloist to attract attention was Mlle Subligny. She is usually said to have joined the troupe around 1690,[67] but already in 1687 the Swedish architect Tessin reported that Subligny and La Fontaine were the best female dancers at the Opéra, L'Estang and Pécour the best among the men.[68]

The fact that women did not dance on the stage of the Opéra before 1681 does not mean that there were no female dancing roles. *Atys* calls for Phyrgiennes as well as Phrygiens, *Thésée* for both shepherds and shepherdesses. Dancers were trained to perform both male and female roles, although the listings in the librettos suggest that some of them were more frequently cast as females than others, namely Arnal, Bonnard, Bouteville, one member of the Dumirail family, Favier *le cadet*, Lestang *le cadet*, and Noblet.[69] Perhaps younger (adolescent?) dancers were assigned the female roles and graduated to dancing as men as they aged.[70] Or perhaps the ones who performed regularly as women were among the smaller dancers. However the assignments were made, once women professional dancers became available, the number of female roles in Lully's operas increased. *Alceste*, as it was performed at court in 1677, had female dancing roles only in the prologue (two nymphs) and in Act v (two shepherdesses, performed by the same two men as the nymphs); for the rest of the opera the danced roles were all male.[71] In *Persée*, on the other hand, the first *tragédie* written with women dancers among the cast, there are female roles in the prologue, in Act i (mixed couples in the dance contest), Act ii (warrior nymphs), Act iv (wives of sailors), and Act v (Éthiopiennes). Only in Act iii, where the dancers embody horrible monsters born of Medusa's blood, were there no roles for women. Since it must have taken time to build up the troupe's female personnel, men probably still danced some female roles, especially those of a grotesque or masculine cast: the warrior nymphs in *Persée* seem like good candidates.[72] Nonetheless, it is clear that the availability of women to dance on the stage changed the character of the divertissements Lully and Quinault wrote into their operas.

When Lully died in 1687, the dance troupe still had more men in it than women; this can be inferred from the lists of performers found in three librettos of works performed by the Académie Royale de Musique at court during the first decade after his death. Lorenzani's *Orontée* of only one year later has dancing roles for 20 men or boys and for

67 Parfaict, *Histoire*, 73. 68 Wood and Sadler, *French Baroque Opera*, 125–26.

69 Several of these names also appear on Powell's list of dancers in court performances of comedy-ballets who "seemed to have made a specialty of performing female roles." See his *Music and Theatre*, 410, n. 67.

70 La Gorce believes this to have been the case with Pécour, who danced several female roles starting from 1671, but from 1677 onwards was no longer so cast. See his "Guillaume-Louis Pecour," 5 and 19.

71 When *Alceste* was revived in 1706 (and perhaps in 1682), the sailors in Act i acquired wives.

72 In 1688 in the *Ballet de Villeneuve-Saint-Georges*, the Bacchantes in Act iii were danced by men.

11 women. The *Ballet de Villeneuve-Saint-Georges*, a shorter work, requires 18 male and 9 female dancers, a proportion that is similar in *Issé*, performed for the wedding of the Duc de Bourgogne in 1697. By 1704, however, the first year for which there are personnel records at the Opéra, the proportions were almost equal: of the 21 dancers officially on the rolls, 11 were men and 10 women.[73]

Children also danced. Their roles can be discerned when a libretto describes the dancers as "little," as in Act IV of *Atys*, where "little streams" dance alongside the (adult) rivers. The same young dancers named in this scene in 1676 also appeared as Zephyrs in the Glory in Act II, dancing in a machine that hovered above the stage. Some children went on to become stars. Claude Balon danced as a little faun and a little Cupid in *Orontée* in 1688, when he was twelve, along with Michel Blondy who was approximately the same age.

The dancers in Lully's troupe were very versatile. The two Favier brothers danced both male and female roles, and in serious, comic, pastoral, and exotic styles.[74] Similarly, their younger colleague, Pécour, had operatic roles as varied as a Songe agréable and a nymph in *Atys*, a demon in *Proserpine*, or a follower of Bacchus in *Bellérophon*.[75] A few anecdotes attribute differing qualities to some of the dancers: "Pécour and Lestang danced, the one with the beautiful arms and majestic steps that even at the end of his career made him a dancer almost without peer; the other with the air of a high-born man that is so rare for a dancer to acquire."[76] By the early eighteenth century dancers were beginning to specialize, although most of them still performed a variety of roles.

Whereas Beauchamps was the main person responsible for the choreography, Dolivet was apparently the one Lully charged with the mimed divertissements, such as the dreams in *Atys*, the *trembleurs* in *Isis*, the mourners in *Alceste*, and the old men in *Thésée*;[77] the preface to the *Recueil général* qualifies Dolivet as a "grand pantomime." Lully himself also choreographed. According to Lecerf:

> Lully involved himself in dance almost as much as he did in everything else. "Part of the ballet *Les Fêtes de l'Amour et de Bacchus* was devised by him, the remainder by Desbrosses." (This according to the preface to the *Recueil des opéra* in the Ballard edition, notes Lecerf in a footnote.) And Lully had almost as much part in the ballets in the operas which followed as Beauchamps. He reformed the entrées, devised expressive steps which suited the subject, and when necessary danced in front of his performers himself to give them a better idea of what he wanted. However, he had certainly not studied dancing, and he only performed in this way on a whim and by chance; but the experience of watching ballet and his extraordinary

[73] See Ch. 13, p. 379ff, for this later period.

[74] HW&M, 21–23. Regarding the training of dancers, see Astier, "La vie quotidienne."

[75] See the list of Pécour's roles in La Gorce, "Pecour," 19–22.

[76] Lecerf, *Comparaison*, II, 12, in regard to a revival of *Armide*.

[77] Dubos, *Réflexions critiques*, I, 534–35.

> ability in every aspect of stagecraft (*spectacles*) gave him the ability to dance, if not with any great elegance, at least with a delightful vivacity.[78]

Lully may or may not have had formal dance training, but he did have practical experience. Starting from 1652, when he danced in the *Mascarade de la foire Saint-Germain* as a vendor of cheese tarts,[79] Lully appeared repeatedly on stage in court ballets, mostly as a dancer or mime, but sometimes as a singer. He specialized in comic roles, such as Scaramouche in *L'Amour malade* (1657), one of the earliest ballets for which he also wrote the music. However, he did occasionally give himself serious roles, as when he sang as Orpheus in the *Ballet des Muses* (1666). His most famous characterization was as the Mufti in the *Bourgeois gentilhomme*, which he performed at Chambord in 1670, and again at court in 1681, by request of the king. Lully did not appear in his own operas, but his long experience on stage, combined with his domineering personality, lend credence to Lecerf's testimony that Lully had a major hand in shaping the choreography of his operatic divertissements.

[78] Lecerf, *Comparaison*, II, 228–29; trans. Wood and Sadler, *French Baroque Opera*, 69.

[79] La Gorce, *Lully*, 51–55.

4 | Dance Practices on Stage

Even if dance is the most ephemeral of the arts, tools do exist for identifying some of the practices on the stage of the Opéra in Lully's day. This chapter starts with practical issues about the dancing forces, laying out the evidence from librettos and scores, then moves to questions of movement styles. Beauchamps's choreographies are not recoverable, but the writings of aestheticians offer insights as to the expressive range available to him, and these can be read against the divertissements themselves. The last section of the chapter aims to identify compositional conventions Lully used in the service of characterization.

THE DANCING FORCES

Counting the Dancers

In a Lully libretto there are three possible forms that information about the dancing cast may take. First, librettos generally contain two cast lists, the usual formulation being "Personnages du prologue" and "Acteurs de la tragédie." The lists include both singers and dancers, and whereas the group characters are sometimes assigned specific functions ("the followers of Pluton, singing, dancing, and flying"), more often than not they are subsumed along with the members of the chorus into a single group (a troupe of shepherds and shepherdesses). Even the "grand Seigneur de la cour d'Égée" in the cast list for *Thésée* is not distinguished by function, but must be a dancer because there is no such singing role.[1] Second, the heading for each scene lists the performers that figure within it, and may single out the dancing roles, although groups are generally understood to include both singers and dancers. Third, *didascalies* that are internal to scenes, assuming they exist at all, may mention the dancers. All three of these sometimes state how many dancers, or even group singers, there are; the cast list for the prologue to *Bellérophon* calls for ten singing fauns, ten singing shepherds, two dancing shepherdesses, four dancing shepherds, and four dancing followers of Bacchus. In addition, the court librettos that name the performers thereby reveal the numbers playing each role. This information dates only from between 1675 and 1680, but the groupings of dancers are quite consistent

[1] This function is confirmed in court librettos that provide the performers' names.

with the practices seen in the librettos from 1699 onwards, when the Opéra began providing casting information for its public performances.

Several patterns emerge from the librettos dating from Lully's lifetime. First, with very few exceptions dancers come in even-numbered groups. Second, the most common group by far consists of eight dancers. Either all eight filled the same role (the sailors in *Alceste* I) or they were subdivided by gender (the four female and four male followers of the goddess Cérès in the prologue to *Thésée*). In the latter case, they were presumably still conceived as a single group. The unique case of a group of individuals comes in the prologue to *Atys*, where Melpomène is followed by eight ancient heroes who revive their old quarrels ("Hercules fights against Antée, Castor and Pollux against Lyncée and Idas, Ethéocle against his brother Polynice"). In this case the dancers were undoubtedly dressed to be recognizable as individuals – Hercules with his emblematic club and lion skin – in distinction to most dancers in groups, who all wore the same costume.

Dancers may also appear in groups of four, such as the Ombres heureuses in *Proserpine* IV/5. But in many such scenes, there are parallel groups; four Divinités infernales join the four Ombres heureuses in paying homage to Proserpine. The assembled group may be larger still; in *Isis* V/3 the people who celebrate Io's apotheosis consist (according to the 1677 court libretto) of four Egyptiennes and eight Peuples d'Egypte. In Act I of the same opera, three groups of four divinities each pay homage to Jupiter. A group of four that stands on its own may be subdivided into two couples, as is the case for the two old men and two old women in II/7 of *Thésée*.

Groups of six are less common, but still found in significant numbers, e.g., the shiverers in *Isis* IV/1 in 1677, the priestesses in *Thésée* I/10, and the *sacrificateurs* in *Cadmus et Hermione* III/6. In one case groups of six were subdivided unequally: in the prologue of *Bellérophon*, the suite of Bacchus consisted of two Bacchantes and four male followers of Bacchus, while the suite of Pan had two shepherdesses and four shepherds. Inside the prologue these two troupes first appear separately and then join together. There are a few other instances of groups this large – e.g., the twelve Lutins (goblins) who dance in *Thésée* III/7 – but this does not happen often and twelve is the largest number to appear in any single troupe in the Lully librettos. A larger number of dancers may nonetheless be on stage at the same time, such as the eight followers of Cérès who join the eight followers of Bacchus in rounding off the prologue to *Thésée*.

Uneven numbers of dancers in uniform groups are rare – not a surprising finding in a style that places so much emphasis on symmetry. The two identifiable instances of three dancers occur in the same divertissement (*Atys* V/7); these are probably the male and female members of a single larger group of six – woodland gods and nymphs. Also in *Atys* (II/4), five little Zephyrs danced in a *gloire* above the stage. The three Graces, a mythological grouping that was to become familiar to eighteenth-century audiences, appear in Lully's works only in the first entrée of *Le Triomphe de l'Amour*.

It is primarily when a soloist is attached to a group, or set off against it, that an uneven number of dancers is generated. At the end of *Cadmus et Hermione* (V/3) Comus arrives with four (male) followers and four (female) Hamadryads. "Comus begins to dance alone [. . .] Cupids bring down from the heavens, under a kind of little pavilion, gifts from the gods, attached to pleasing chains. The Hamadryads and the followers of Comus carry them to the bride and groom and form a dance, into which Charite mingles a song." This description does not reveal whether the group of nine ever danced simultaneously. Other instances include the Lord and the four male courtiers who dance in the last act of *Thésée* or the seven Liberal Arts in the prologue to *Isis*, one of whom was identified as a soloist.

Because the librettos that include performers' names all date from before 1681, the year women entered the troupe, it is not possible to identify where female soloists might have figured. The Parfaict brothers claimed, much after the fact, that Mlle La Fontaine appeared as a solo Ethiopian in *Persée*[2] (1682, in IV/7); this spot makes sense for a solo woman, since it celebrates the hero's having saved Andromède from the sea monster. The passacaille in Act V of *Armide* is a place where in eighteenth-century revivals a solo woman danced; perhaps the tradition started at the premiere. Another likely place for a solo by a woman is *Amadis* II/7, in which the hero is enchanted into thinking that one of the demons disguised as nymphs is his beloved Oriane.

In the librettos for Lully's *tragédies* there are no places where a dance for a couple, be it mixed or same sex, is unambiguously required. The strongest hint of couple dancing comes in *Persée* I/5, the *jeux junoniens*, where Cassiope alludes to the participants in the dance contest as "these lovely young people whom the torch of Hymen will soon shine upon." This comment suggests that the dancers would be organized in mixed couples, but it does not answer the question of whether they danced two at a time or in groups. However, a lack of positive evidence within Lully's *tragédies* in favor of duets does not mean that there were none. The ballets Lully wrote before he turned to opera include some dances for a couple, and *Le Carnaval*, which was performed at the Opéra in 1675, has a dance for a bride and groom in the sixth entrée. The village wedding scene in IV/3 of *Roland* also seems a strong candidate for a dance by a couple, although it may not have had one until the revival of 1690, when a piece of music borrowed from an earlier Lully ballet was added to the divertissement to fulfill just such a purpose.[3] But the ballroom tradition in France, during which one couple at a time danced while everyone else watched, was so entrenched, that an operatic style that relied upon an understanding of social rituals must have incorporated *danses à deux*. By the start of the

[2] Parfaict, *Dictionnaire*, IV, 105.

[3] See Ch. 12, p. 373. Starting in 1705, the first revival of *Roland* after librettos began incorporating performers' names, dancing roles are indicated for the bride and groom.

eighteenth century there were many danced duets on the stage of the Opéra; in Lully's period the question is where they might have taken place.

Distributing the Dancers

Identifying the number of dancers in a scene does not reveal how many of them danced at any given moment. Once again, *Le Mariage de la grosse Cathos* offers more information about deploying dancers than any other seventeenth-century source. As a comic mascarade it does not provide an exact parallel to Lully's operas, but in one of its most basic parameters it adheres to Lullian models: it requires eight dancers. As in Lully's early operas, all were men, even though four of the roles were female. In addition, one of the vocal soloists (the bridegroom, La Couture) danced in two of the musical numbers, in one of them as a soloist; he thus conforms to the Lullian pattern of the individual added to an even-numbered group (although he differed from Lully's performers in that he sang as well as danced). The ten dances exhibit a number of different combinations.[4]

Table 4-1: Group dances in *Le Mariage de la grosse Cathos*.

No. of dancers	No. of dances
4 men, 4 women[a]	5
1 man, 4 women	1
2 men, 2 women	1
2 men	2
2 women	1

[a] Part of the passepied involves 5 men and 4 women.

Here group dances are favored over couple dances by a ratio of 7:3 and half are for the troupe of eight. These data reinforce the impression given by Lully's librettos that groups of four and of eight provide a fundamental scaffold for choreographies. However, that blanket observation masks the varying configurations that may occur within a single piece of music. A closer look reveals that variety in the number of dancers is a feature of the choreographic structure.

Three of the dances form a sequential unit of their own. First comes an entrée in duple meter for two Garçons de la noce, then a gigue for two Filles de la noce, and, last, a menuet for all four, arranged as mixed couples. This unit of three recalls some of Lully's structures, in which two groups start out separately, then come together.

The remaining dance for a single couple functions in a way that is visually analogous to one of Lully's dance-songs, although the musical construction is different. The Swiss character, who sings with a thick accent, consoles himself through drink for his lack of

[4] See HW&M, 46–48, and discussion of the individual dances in Chs. 3 and 5.

love. His self-pitying air is followed by a dance for two drunks – a parody of the noble *entrée grave* that requires exquisite control on the part of the dancers in its imitation of drunkenness. Although the song and the dance are musically independent (as expected, when the instrumental dance is an *entrée grave*), the two pieces work together.

The dance for five may provide a model of what could happen in the not-uncommon Lullian arrangement that involves a group of four dancers plus a soloist. Four of the dancers are the female wedding guests; the fifth is the bridegroom himself. The music, a rigaudon, is performed twice: first as a dance for five, the second time as a solo for La Couture. Within the first iteration of the music, La Couture's movements also have soloistic characteristics: he is located in the center of a square formation, with the women positioned in each of the corners, and his steps offer more vigorous variants on theirs. This choreography thus provides two crucial insights: first, that the same piece of music can serve two different choreographic configurations, and second, that a soloist may simultaneously be integrated into a group and yet retain some independence from it.

La Couture participates in the passepied as well, this time with all eight other dancers. It, too, requires two repetitions of the music. The first section functions as a line dance for nine, led by La Couture, which snakes around the oboe band standing in the center of the stage. The single step-unit is the *pas de menuet*, but in its figures this part of the passepied recalls the Renaissance branle. This choreography is the only notated instance of a line dance for the theater; whereas it is not surprising that such a basic dance figure would be used on the stage, it is reassuring that a model exists for figures besides the symmetrical. However, symmetry does return in the second part: La Couture leaves the line and the eight remaining dancers perform more varied steps, weaving in and out among the members of the oboe band, who by this time are standing in parallel lines on either side of the stage. Notwithstanding its cast of four men and four women, this choreography is *not* about coupleness. At one point the four women briefly dance together, and then the four men – an interesting sequence that shows that not all dancers have to be in motion all the time. But no one has a partner; group formations govern the movement.

The chorus "Passons toujours la vie," which alternates dancing and singing, has already been discussed (Chapter 2, p. 42). But it also shows how the number of dancers may change within a single dance; the third column of Table 2-2 indicates the three different configurations: four women, solo man, or all eight dancers. Each dance phrase lasts only eight measures; the two phrases danced by the whole group have different steps and figures. The chorus ends with full participation by the cast, singers and dancers alike.

The remaining three dances of the mascarade keep all the eight dancers in motion, without any variation as to their number. One is the action chorus discussed in Chapter 2, p. 44, in which the words "Allons, accourons tous" are transformed by the dancers into physical movement. The other two come at either end of the mascarade, when the procession of the entire cast is interrupted by a dance for eight; here, unlike the passepied, the dancers *do* group themselves as couples. Both these dances provide further instances of repetitions of the same music serving different purposes: a march for the entire cast on the one hand, a choreography for eight on the other.

If only the music of *Le Mariage de la grosse Cathos* had survived, we would have no idea how much choreographic variety was available within a single short work. This one offers so many insights into how dancers function on stage, that it is worth extracting its general features.

- Purely instrumental pieces are choreographed, but solo vocal numbers and duets are not, even if they have danceable rhythms.
- Some choruses may be danced, under specific conditions. Whereas an instrumental piece is choreographed throughout, in a chorus the dancing may be intermittent.
- The core group consists of eight dancers, out of which subgroups may form. An additional dancer (one of the singers) twice turns the group into an odd number of dancers, but the majority of the dances use an even number.
- The mascarade includes dances, or parts of dances, for one, two, four, five, eight, and nine. Half of the dances are for the full group; three are duets.
- A single piece of music, when performed more than once in succession, may encompass more than one choreography. This happens in four of the instrumental dances in the mascarade; in each of these there is always overlap in the personnel – a repeat of the music never involves a complete change of dancers.[5]
- Inside group dances one choreographic option is to vary the number of dancers from section to section or from phrase to phrase. This phenomenon can be observed within two of the five group dances: the chorus "Passons toujours la vie" and the passepied.
- Duets for couples of the same sex are common – in this work, all three couple dances are for same-sex pairs.
- Within group choreographies that have an equal number of men and women, the dancers may be treated as mixed couples, may be choreographed as same-sex subgroups, or may be treated as a mass of undifferentiated people.
- As in the choreographies in Beauchamps-Feuillet notation, the dance figures favor symmetry. The brief exceptions – line figures, a hey, and one brief moment when more dancers are on one side of the stage than on the other – suggest that a non-symmetrical choreographic figure was an option, but that it was rare.

[5] In Lalande's *Ballet de l'Inconnu* (1720), there are some examples of complete changes in dancing personnel upon repeat of the music; see Ch. 14, pp. 440–41.

- In processions all those entering or leaving move in time to the music and in unison with each other; in this work they take one walking step per measure. Moreover, they enter as part of a cohort: first the oboe band, next the dancers, then the singers.
- On-stage instrumentalists may be incorporated into the choreography of a dance, not just of a procession. This happens in the passepied, when the oboes form a circle in the center of the stage and the dancers weave among them.
- Each group of performers has its own home position around the perimeter of the stage, from which individuals or groups emerge when they perform. The notation shows that as one group retreats at the end of a number, the next group starts moving into the performing space. The emphasis is on continuity.
- The dancers do not appear to go off stage between their dances; rather, they retreat to their home positions until they are again involved in the stage movement. This seems in keeping with the integrity of the scene, which in French drama was defined by entrances or exits of characters.
- Step vocabulary for male and for female characters is different, with the two duets for men using a more technically demanding set of steps than the duet for women. Conventions regarding representation of gender thus trump the dancers' own capabilities, since in this work all the performers were men.
- Soloists may be entrusted with their own choreography; that, at least, is one reasonable inference from the fact that the two solos called for in this work are not notated.[6]
- The two solos are not set to independent pieces of music, but are part of larger choreographic structures. One is done to a repeat of the music for a group dance, the other consists of a solo phrase within a choreographed chorus. In this work, at least, solo dances are not given special prominence and occupy only a small fraction of the overall choreography.

No other seventeenth-century work provides anything like this much information, but there is one theatrical choreography in Beauchamps-Feuillet notation that offers an additional look at how soloists functioned relative to a group: the "Ballet de neuf danseurs," choreographed by Feuillet himself and published in 1700, which is set to three consecutive pieces of music from the last act of *Bellérophon*. Even though there is no reason to think that this particularly choreography would have been danced on the stage of the Opéra, it does use the number and configuration of dancers called for by the libretto of *Bellérophon*: "a solo dancing lord and eight other dancing lords in his retinue." Moreover, it demands a professional level of technical expertise. In Table 4-2, the letters refer to the musical structure; each of the three pieces is binary, with both sections repeated.

The choreography's most notable feature is that the soloist and the group never dance simultaneously. Inside the *entrée grave* the soloist alternates phrases with

[6] For more on this topic, see Ch. 14, p. 421.

Table 4-2: Feuillet, "Ballet de neuf danseurs": distribution of dancers. *Recueil de Dances, Composées par M. Feuillet* (Paris, 1700), 67–84.

Dance Notation	Score	Form	Dancers
Entrée grave	Premier Air	A	solo
		A	a4
		B	solo
		B	a4 (same four)
Canarie	Second Air/Fanfare	CCDD	solo
Seconde Canarie	Chœur de peuples, "Les plaisirs nous préparent leurs charmes"	EEFF	solo
[Canarie repeated]	[Second Air repeated]	CCDD	a8
[Seconde Canarie repeated]	Second strophe of chorus, "Que la paix"	EEFF	a8

a subgroup of four dancers; he then performs two dances in a row by himself, whose music is then danced by the remaining eight. This sequence gives the soloist more prominence than do the dances in *Le Mariage de la grosse Cathos*, but he still is not given a piece of music of his own. In other words, the soloist is treated as part of a group, not as an independent character. This relationship is reinforced in yet another aspect of the dance notation: those who are not dancing, including the soloist, do not leave the stage, but remain in place on its perimeter.

It seems decidedly odd that at the very end of an opera, one dancer could remain motionless, but we must remember that Feuillet gives no hint that this choreography has anything to do with an opera; it is only by identifying the source of the music that the connection can be made. Nor does the dance notation reveal that the second canarie would have been sung in the opera, so this choreography has limited applicability. The important point is how the dancers alternate within and across the three pieces of music. This choreography and the ones in *Le Mariage de la grosse Cathos* offer possible models when we turn to the more complicated structures found in Lully's operas.

Deploying the Dancers Across a Divertissement

The librettos and scores for Lully's operas never reveal precisely who dances to which music. Moreover, Ballard's scores can be misleading or even wrong in their headings for individual dances. In order to develop plausible hypotheses about conventions governing the deployment of the dancers, we need to look carefully at representative divertissements, comparing structural, textual, and musical clues with what can be learned from related repertoires and bearing in mind that variety seems to have been cultivated, even within a single piece of music. Practical considerations clearly matter for someone putting an opera on the stage, but they also matter for those engaged in interpreting what the opera means.

Some divertissements are relatively unproblematic to work out; one such is the dream sequence in *Atys* III/4 (for an outline see Table 2-11, p. 64). Even if the structure of the score did not clarify which set of dreams dances where, it is not possible to mistake nightmare music for sweet dreams music. The 1676 libretto calls for eight Songes agréables and nine Songes funestes, the ninth being a soloist. That imbalance gives the nightmares slightly more visual presence, which may partially compensate for the fact that the sweet dreams' music last for much longer than does theirs. Nonetheless, questions do emerge.

First, the *didascalie* at the start of the scene suggests that the entire cast, sweet dreams and nightmares alike, entered the stage together: "The stage changes and represents a cave surrounded by poppies and streams, where the god of sleep arrives, accompanied by sweet dreams and nightmares." Should a director take this literally? Simultaneous entrance would give an entirely different character to this scene than a sequential one, even if the nightmares withdrew to spots on the periphery while they awaited their turn. Or, could this *didascalie* represent yet another instance where the temporal frame is collapsed? A second question is whether the prelude for Sommeil, which at 57 bars is exceptionally long for such a piece, would have been danced. In the Saint-Germain performances most of the musicians playing this prelude (on recorders, viols, and theorbos) were brought onto the stage, as one means of showing the move from ordinary reality to the realm of sleep. The prelude is played twice, both before and after the first vocal section of the divertissement. If it were to have been danced, it would probably have been so during its second iteration.[7] Third, beyond this possibly danced prelude, there is only one instrumental piece for the Songes agréables, but it is played twice – not in succession, but interleaved with vocal music. How might the eight dancers of 1676 have been distributed? Here we enter the realm of speculation, but at the very least it seems unlikely, given the evidence discussed above, that the dance would have used the same choreography twice, or even had the same group of dancers both times. Two out of the three vocal sections that precede each iteration of the dance piece are varied (only the trio, "Mais souviens-toi" is the same both times), which would give added impetus to varying the choreography, by changing either the steps and figures or the number of dancers or both.

The Songes funestes are assigned two dances, one on each side of a chorus that seems unlikely to have been danced. First, the words it sings are crucial: they tell Atys that if he does not return Cybèle's love, he will die. Moreover, the chorus is short and has very little repetition of the words. When the sung text is this important, competition from the dancers for attention would run counter to aesthetic norms. In that case,

[7] For other examples of through-composed pieces used for dancing, see below, p. 131.

the question remains the same as for the sweet dreams: who dances during the instrumental pieces? In 1676 there was a solo Songe funeste, performed by Beauchamps. If the "Ballet de neuf danseurs" could serve as a model, then Beauchamps might have alternated strains with the group during either of the two dances, rather than having one entire dance for himself. Or an entire dance piece could have been played twice, for different choreographic settings. It does seem likely, though, that the whole group (or the eight without Beauchamps?) would have danced the end of the "Second Air des Songes funestes," in order to invoke maximum fear in Atys. The last bit of dance music may also be needed to get the dreams off stage and for the set to disappear, since the *didascalie* that concludes the divertissement suggests that this all happens very rapidly – one of the instantaneous transformations that made baroque theater so spectacular.

Another divertissement whose workings seem amenable to solution is the celebratory conclusion to *Alceste* (see Chapter 1, p. 11). The score assigns all three instrumental dances to *pâtres*,[8] an attribution that does not make sense with the libretto, which calls for *two* troupes, one of shepherds and shepherdesses, the other of herdsmen (*pâtres*).[9] In 1677 these groups were divided as two shepherdesses and two shepherds supplemented by a solo shepherd, and four (male) herdsmen, thus yielding a pool of nine dancers. The statement in the last *didascalie* that the two troupes dance together in a grand show of unity, implies that earlier on the two troupes had danced separately; the cues as to where must come from the musical characteristics of each dance and from the vocal music with which it is associated.

Within the social hierarchy of the pastoral world, *pâtres* (herdsmen) occupy a lower rank than do *bergers* (shepherds). This class of character was also called a *paysan* (peasant), in contradistinction to the *bergers*, who, as in *Armide* II/4, were sometimes qualified as "héroïques." In the early eighteenth century, dances for *paysans* or *pâtres* were to become a shtick (see Chapter 12, p. 360ff), and even in Lully's era their character seems to have been that of the country bumpkin; Menestrier (1681) said their dancing should be "loutish and rustic." Herdsmen make sense as companions for the boorish Straton; they probably would dance the "Deuxième Air," which is musically connected to Straton's song ("A quoi bon"). The dances on either side of Straton's unit offer musical contrast. The "Premier Air" bears some of the hallmarks of the *entrée grave*, so seems both masculine in character and a likely spot for a soloist, which would suggest assigning it to the three male shepherds. The dance associated with Céphise is a menuet (see Example 2-2, p. 46), which in choreographic notations is always assigned either to

8 This is how the dances are assigned in the score edited by Prunières for the old collected works. Prunières based his edition on manuscript sources; his critical notes do not reveal whether there are variants among the headings of the dances.

9 The *Dictionnaire de l'Académie Française* (1694) defines *pâtre* as "Qui garde des troupeaux de bœufs, de vaches, et chèvres, etc."

women or to a mixed group. That means that the shepherdesses need to be involved, and given that Céphise's text advocates love, a mixed group that also includes the shepherds seems appropriate. The concluding chorus would then become the site where the shepherds/shepherdesses and the herdsmen finally join together. Moreover, the construction of the music – which not only alternates instrumental and vocal phrases, but involves two choruses, vocal soloists, and two different instrumental textures – would favor a choreography that alternates the two groups. All the dancers would surely have joined together during the final full statement of the sung text, to bring the opera to a rousing conclusion.

There are some instances where the headings in Ballard's scores misidentify the dancers. Act III of *Isis*, most of which presents the story of Pan and Syrinx as a play within the opera, has two sets of group characters: Syrinx's nymphs, and a united group of male Bergers, Sylvains, and Satyres. In Ballard's 1719 score (p. 177) the dance identified as "Air des Sylvains et Satyres" must actually belong to the nymphs. In the first place, it is the only instrumental dance piece available, and the libretto tells us that the nymphs dance as well as sing. Second, this dance follows a chorus for the nymphs to which it is connected in key, meter, and rhythm. Third, immediately following this dance the score presents a "Marche des Bergers et Satyres" that serves to bring the male troupe on stage; the *didascalie* tells us that they enter and offer presents to Syrinx. In other words, the sylvans and satyrs aren't even on stage when the dance attributed to them is played. Ballard should have labeled this piece "Air des Nymphes."

Much more common than errors, however, are places where a score labels the pieces "Premier Air" or "Second Air" without further indication. As we have seen, one convention divided the dancers by gender. Quinault's practice of so identifying the dancers does not require separate dances by each subgroup, but does allow for them. In cases where a division between male and female dancers seems appropriate to the particular divertissement, the style of the music can help. In *Atys* I/7 the chorus and dancers represent Phrygiens and Phrygiennes; the 1676 libretto points out that the men were led by Atys, the women by Sangaride, something that suggests even more than usual that the two subgroups be perceived separately. The headings for the two instrumental dances, "Entrée des Phrygiens" and "Second Air des Phrygiens," do not make a distinction by gender, but the music does: the first dance is not a classic *entrée grave*, but with its prominent dotted rhythms, duple meter, and independence from any of the vocal music it looks like a piece for men. The "Second Air," a gigue-like rondeau, uses music appropriate either for women or for a mixed group, but given the libretto's insistence on a distinction by gender, a dance by the women alone seems likelier. Many divertissements make similar kinds of musical suggestions, even when the libretto is not as informative as the court libretto for *Atys* – and as the dances in *Le Mariage de la grosse Cathos* show, breaking men and women into separate groups, both for short phrases and for entire dances, seems to have been a common practice.

Musical texture may provide another clue. In vocal ensembles, Lully distinguishes a female chorus by setting it as a high vocal trio, usually notated in treble, soprano, and alto clefs. This texture can be found in *Proserpine* II/8, where the heroine frolics with her nymphs.[10] The dance pieces in the same divertissement use two instrumental textures: either a trio of two oboes and bassoon or the full five orchestral parts. The use here of a bass line in a low range shows that differences in texture do not necessarily translate in literal fashion onto the bodies of the dancers: women alone can dance to pieces that have a true bass line, and, conversely, a piece in a five-part texture does not require male dancers. Still, the high trio texture is so often assigned to female singing characters that it seems worth considering whether whatever dance pieces it may be associated with might also be coded female.[11]

This possibility then begs the question of what the choreographic implications might be when there are textural changes *within* an instrumental dance piece. Whereas Lully often sets up dialogues between groups of singers (and sometimes also groups of instrumentalists) within his big choruses,[12] changes of texture may also occur – albeit less often – inside dance music. A visual analogue to a change in texture would be a change in the number of dancers. Is such a literal connection between the visible and aural realms plausible? *Atys* has two divertissements where this question emerges.

The divertissement in II/4 honors Cybèle's choice of Atys as her Grand Sacrificateur. The celebrations involve both the heavens and the earth: Zephyrs suspended in a Glory above the stage (five of whom danced and eight of whom played the oboe, according to the 1676 court libretto) and, down below, people of different nationalities (six each of Indians and Egyptians). The 1689 Ballard score has two instrumental dances, whose titles suggest that each group gets one dance: first comes an "Entrée des Nations," then an "Entrée des Zéphyrs." However, the second piece has two different instrumental textures; five-part strings alternate phrases with a four-part oboe band. Since the oboists are identified as Zephyrs, the music provided by the strings probably belongs to the earth-bound people, which would suggest that two groups of dancers alternate. The rapidity of the exchange is no greater here than in the choruses from Charpentier's *Circé* (see Table 2-1, p. 41), where the alternation for the dancers was between movement and stasis; on the mechanical level, then, there is no impediment to this solution.

By the last scene of the opera Atys has committed suicide out of remorse for having killed Sangaride, and Cybèle has transformed him into a tree. She is surrounded by two

10 A part notated in alto clef was sung by male *hautes-contre*, who in this instance would have been costumed as women.

11 A high vocal trio may occasionally involve male roles. In *Armide* II/4, when demons in disguise try to seduce the sleeping Renaud away from the pursuit of glory, the high trio is labeled "Choeur de Bergers et de Bergères héroïques."

12 See Rosow, "Performing a choral dialogue."

groups: Corybantes (worshipers in the cult of Cybèle, here coded female) and a mixed group consisting of nymphs and woodland gods; according to the 1676 court libretto there were twelve singers and six dancers in the pastoral group, fourteen singers and eight dancers among the Corybantes.[13]

Cybèle: Sous une nouvelle figure,
Atys est ranimé, par mon pouvoir divin;
Célébrez son nouveau destin,
Pleurez sa funeste aventure.

(Through my divine power, Atys is brought back to life in a new form.
Celebrate his new destiny; weep for his tragic fate.)

The two emotional poles evoked by Cybèle, celebration and weeping, evolve in a subsequent chorus into two stronger emotions – sorrow and rage ("Ah! quel malheur! Ah! quelle rage!") – and, as the opera closes, into affliction and horror: "May the misfortune of Atys afflict the entire world; may everyone on earth feel the horror of such a cruel death" ("Que le malheur d'Atys afflige tout le monde. / Que tout sente, ici bas, / L'horreur d'un si cruel trépas"). Between these two choruses come three instrumental dances, none of which is musically connected to any of the vocal music. They nonetheless portray the emotional divisions expressed in the texts through their musical characterizations. The first dance, the "Entrée des Nymphes" is in a slow triple meter and a minor mode, with chromatic inflections in both treble and bass.[14] The sorrow the nymphs express (and perhaps the woodland gods with them?) is opposed by the vigorous $\frac{6}{4}$ of the "Première Entrée des Corybantes," in a major mode with triadic figures and pounding repeated notes that map onto the singing Corybantes' rage. The third dance (Example 4-1) goes back and forth between these two emotional poles (major mode, duple meter, aggressive repeated notes vs. a tender and slow triple meter) that must have been choreographed for the two opposing groups of dancers; in this remarkable piece rage has the last word.

Alternation between groups of dancers also seems implicit in the longest dances of the period, chaconnes and passacailles. For pieces such as the passacaille in *Armide* that interweave instrumental and vocal sections (see Table 2-7, p. 59), it seems likely that the

[13] In Book IV of Ovid's *Fasti*, one of Quinault's sources for this libretto, the unnamed Atys figure castrates rather than kills himself. Ever since, Ovid's narrator goes on to explain, Cybèle's " effeminate" followers have disfigured themselves in the same way. (See excerpts from the 1660 translation into French by Michel de Marolles in the issue devoted to *Atys* of *L'Avant-Scène Opéra* (No. 94, 1987), 26–27.) One wonders if this background had any impact on Quinault's choice of making the Corybantes female, or in how they were interpreted on stage.

[14] Exceptionally, this piece is notated in only two voices – treble and figured bass – in Ballard's full score, rather than in a trio or five-part texture.

Example 4-1: *Atys* v/7, "Seconde Entrée," first strain (Paris: Ballard 1689), 304.

number of dancers would have varied across the sections. For the two such dances that are purely instrumental (the chaconne in *Phaéton* ii/5 and the passacaille in *Persée* v/8), or for the long instrumental sections within the complexes that also include singing (such as the 149-bar opening to the *Armide* passacaille), varying the number of dancers may also have been an option, especially given the stamina required of the dancers for these very long dances. The evidence suggests a variety of approaches. The few surviving chaconne and passacaille choreographies, all for soloist or a couple and all set only to instrumental music, keep the same dancers throughout, even when there are changes in instrumental texture. Only one of these choreographies, however, originated on the stage of the Opéra, in the 1703 revival of *Persée*; it is a dance for a mixed couple.[15] On the other hand, a *didascalie* in the Ballard score of *Phaéton* assigns the chaconne in ii/5 to three troupes – Egyptians, Ethiopians, and Indians – who must have danced both separately and together, since the purpose of the divertissement is to unite the various peoples in Egypt around the choice the king has made of his successor. In the eighteenth century, the evidence favors variety in the deployment of dancers (see Chapter 14, p. 437ff).

Although pinpointing exactly where within a given divertissement a soloist may have danced is generally not possible, the court librettos do give a sense of how often soloists were featured: approximately two or three divertissements per opera explicitly mention a soloist, who is always a part of a larger group. In the 1679 court performances of *Bellérophon*, for example, Pécour danced as a solo Solyme in Act i, Beauchamps as a sorcerer in Act ii, and Lestang as a lord in Act v. In *Cadmus et Hermione* in 1678 Beauchamps had two solos: as an African in Act i and as Comus in Act v. There are no

[15] See the discussion of this divertissement in Ch. 2, p. 80. In their article "The dances in Lully's *Persée*," table 2, Pierce and Thorp offer a hypothetical reconstruction of how Pécour's couple dance might be turned into a dance for a group, with the couple as intermittent soloists.

court librettos after 1680, and only the occasional Parisian libretto has *didascalies* specific enough to demonstrate the unambiguous presence of a soloist; one such is *Phaéton* IV/2, where Spring dances with his followers. Nonetheless, it seems unlikely that there would have been any fewer solo dances in this period than before; if anything, there might have been more, since the women such as Mlle La Fontaine now in the troupe are also reported to have performed alone. If the surviving choreographies discussed above (pp. 108–12) are representative of how soloists related to the group dancers in the period up to 1700, then the soloists were not treated in isolation, but were integrated into complexes that emphasized the group over its individual members. Nor do the librettos or scores suggest that the divertissements in Lully's era engaged in the kind of star-driven display that was to become a feature of certain operatic divertissements in the eighteenth century.

STYLE AND EXPRESSION

Choreographies in Beauchamps-Feuillet or Favier notation show dancers what to do with their feet and the trajectories they trace through space, but rarely convey more subtle distinctions regarding style and expression. Partly this is because most of the 350+ surviving choreographies belong to what is generally called the "noble style" or "la belle danse," which emphasizes technical precision and abstract movements. The noble style embraces many different movement characteristics and may be inflected in multiple ways, but it does not represent the full expressive range that Quinault and Lully wrote into their divertissements. This section thus explores stylistic and expressive possibilities that existed in Lully's era, including the extent to which they may have involved miming. What emerges for this era is not the three-part categorization of movement styles that classical ballet was to institutionalize (noble, demi-caractère, and grotesque), but a continuum, based primarily on notions of character types and inflected by the dramatic context.

"Ballet is mute poetry that speaks, in that without saying anything it expresses itself through gestures and movements. That is, it speaks to the eyes." Dance theorist Menestrier may have drawn upon Plutarch for authority, but he had in mind the ballets of his own era, which he believed should imitate nature.[16] For him a distinction was to be made between ballet and social dances, "which are simple carryings of the body, adjusted to the rhythms and sounds of the instruments [. . .] without any expression." Ballet, on the other hand, "imitates not only actions, it imitates, according to Aristotle, passions and manners [*mœurs*], which is more difficult than the expression of actions. It is thus necessary to express in ballets the movements of the heart and the affections of the soul, which is the pinnacle of the art, because it is essential to have

[16] *Des Ballets*, 153–54.

a profound knowledge of nature in order to imitate them."[17] Menestrier's lofty goals for the art of dance inspire us to ask whether Lully shared these aesthetic concerns.

Menestrier's book was published in 1682, a decade after Lully turned his attention to opera, but its frame of reference was the *ballet de cour*. Nonetheless, much of what he had to say about dance was supported by writers who did take opera into account; passages from Menestrier's book were borrowed without acknowledgement by Jacques Bonnet in his 1723 *Histoire générale de la danse sacrée et profane*. In fact, Bonnet praised the choreographers at the Opéra, from Beauchamps through Pécour and Blondy, for their attention to the expressive potential of ballet.[18] Some of what he thought relevant finds echoes in the writings of other theorists of the period.

In his influential book on aesthetics, *Critical Reflections on Poetry, Painting and Music*, the Abbé Dubos claimed that there were sixteen different stylistic categories for theatrical dances:

> About threescore years ago [*c.* 1660], the Fauns, Shepherds, Peasants, Cyclops, and Tritons danced pretty near in the same manner; but now the dance is divided into several characters. The artists, if I am not mistaken, reckon sixteen, and each of these characters has its proper steps, attitudes, and figures upon the stage. Even the very women have entered by degrees into these characters, and render them perceptible at present in their dance as well as men.[19]

Whereas Dubos's claim that such stylistic differences were recent developments is dubious, his two larger points are crucial: different character types have different movement vocabularies, and the number of theatrical characters subject to differentiation is very large. His high number of styles underscores the assertion, repeated over and over in seventeenth-century writings about dance, that the movements of the dancer must express the character of the role.[20] Dubos does not provide particulars, but Menestrier and Bonnet explain how some of these styles should look:

> The dance of the winds must be light and quick, one by blacksmiths requires the beats and intervals for banging on the anvil. A dance by crazy people or drunks must be irregular, as is one for blind people, who must search about, wobble, and feel their way. A dance by peasants must be loutish and rustic [. . .] Love requires zeal and tenderness and a sweet and serene face that nonetheless sometimes shows concern and which takes as many forms as there are feelings in the heart capable of altering it. [The dancer] must show constraint when love is new, boldness as it progresses, and great enthusiasm at its success [. . .] Anger is

[17] *Ibid.*, 158–59 and 160. [18] *Histoire générale*, 65.

[19] Dubos, *Réflexions critiques* (1719); trans. Nugent (1748), III, 130.

[20] See, for example, Saint-Hubert, *La Manière de composer . . . les ballets* (1641), esp. "De la danse," 12ff., and Pure, *Idée des spectacles*, 250: "C'est là où gist l'habilité du Maistre de Dance, d'accorder ce mouvement du dancer [*sic*] avec son idée, avec la cadance de l'air, & d'en faire en sorte qu'il ne contrarie ny l'un ny l'autre . . . " He goes on to discuss the different qualities dancers need to express anger, love, sickness, sadness, and joy.

> passionate, impetuous; it has nothing measured about it, all its movements are violent, and to express this passion the steps must be rapid, with falls and irregular rhythms. The dancer must stamp the foot, engage in sudden movements, make menacing gestures with the head, eyes, and hand, and throw wild and furious looks. Fear uses slow steps in the approach and rapid ones in retreat, a trembling and hesitant demeanor, an uneasy look, and awkward arms. Those who are afflicted lower their heads, cross their arms, and appear enveloped in sorrow.[21]

Michel de Pure confirms that this kind of expressiveness involves the whole body, not just the feet:

> A dance in a ballet does not only consist of subtle movements of the feet, or of various movements in the body. It requires both and includes everything that a dexterous and trained body may have by way of gesture or action in order to express something without speaking [. . .] But the principal and most important rule is to make the dance expressive, so that the head, shoulders, arms, and hands communicate what the dancer does not say.[22]

It is worth noting that de Pure and Bonnet mention the face as one of the sites for expression, since it is commonly assumed that dancers wore masks. (To Bonnet's "sweet and serene face" may be added de Pure's rather oblique comment that a dancer should paint the expressions "that love, infirmity, sorrow, or joy may cause on the face or on the other parts [of the body]."[23]) A remark made in 1699 about one of the dancers at the Opéra implies that she danced unmasked: "People say that she has never been seen to laugh or to smile while dancing."[24] But at the same time, de Pure seems to take the use of the mask as a given, saying that it helps make the role intelligible to the audience and even offering advice as to where to buy one.[25] Menestrier also alludes to masks as part of the characterization of roles, along with the costume and the movements.[26] The iconography of theatrical dancers shows them both with and without masks, but only occasionally does a costume design call attention to the mask as part of the costume; actual stage usage in Lully's day is difficult to assess.[27] But one of de Pure's points seems

[21] Menestrier's original passages from *Des Ballets*, 159 and 161–62 were somewhat rewritten by Bonnet in his *Histoire générale*, 63–65. Bonnet transfers the wobbly movement ("chancellante") from the blind people to the drunks; he also adds, "thus everyone in his own style [*genre*] or in his own manner must have different movements." In regard to a person in love, Bonnet adds, "in short he must have all the colors that the Naturalists have identified; everything must speak in him; his eyes, his gestures, his steps, his demeanor, his movements must reveal who he is and what he feels."

[22] Pure, *Idée*, 248–49. [23] *Ibid.*, 251.

[24] Bordelon, *Diversités curieuses*, cited in Ladvocat, *Lettres* (ed. La Gorce), 113.

[25] Pure, *Idée*, "Des Masques," 291–96.

[26] " . . . Ce qui se fait par les habits, les symboles, les masques, et certains gestes ou movements qui sont propres ou particuliers à certaines personnes; comme Vulcain étoit boiteux, Esope étoit bossu, Tiresias étoit aveugle." Menestrier, *Des Ballets*, 139.

[27] In his influential *Lettres sur la danse* (1760), Letter IX, 195–260, Noverre railed against the use of masks, which he found a barrier to expression. Whether the practice was as ubiquitous as he claims is not known.

particularly pertinent: for him, the mask served theatrical illusion, as a means of making the audience think about the role, not about the person playing it.

When we turn to Lully's librettos and scores, we see that the two kinds of imitation described by Menestrier – imitation of action and imitation of passions – do indeed appear. An extreme example of action comes from Lully's *Cadmus et Hermione* IV/2, where Cadmus kills the dragon and then distributes its teeth over a ploughed field as if they were seeds:

> The land produces armed soldiers, who at first turn their weapons against Cadmus. He, however, throws into their midst a kind of grenade that Amour has given him. It breaks into many pieces, which force the soldiers to fight and slaughter each other. The five who remain alive at the end of the battle deposit their weapons at Cadmus's feet.

All of the characters in this scene besides Cadmus may have been dancers by profession, but their movements seem unlikely to have drawn upon a regular step-vocabulary and symmetrical structures. Similarly, the battle scene in *Alceste* II/4 was enacted by the dancers, whose movements may have been stylized, but who, according the libretto, engaged in specific actions associated with making war.

The next act of the same opera (III/5) displays the other kind of imitation, not of action but of a passion – grief – over the death of Alceste:

> A spasm of pain overcomes the two troupes of mourners. Some of them rend their clothes, others tear their hair, and all of them break the ornaments they have been carrying at the feet of the image of Alceste.

This particular scene, along with four others from Lully's operas, was cited by the Abbé Dubos as an example of ballet with "scarce any dancing movements":

> In fine, we have seen a chorus, which without speaking imitated only the mute action of the chorus of the ancient tragedy, meet with great success and applause at the opera, when they were executed with some attention. I mean those balets which had scarce any dancing movements, but were only composed of gestures, external signs, and in a word, of a dumb shew; which Lulli placed in the funeral pomp of Psyche, and in that of Alcestes, as well as in the second act of Theseus, where the poet introduces some old men a dancing; as also the balet of the fourth act of Atys [*recte* third], and in the first scene of the fourth act of Isis, where Quinault brings on the stage the inhabitants of the *Hyperborean* regions. [. . .] Lulli had so great an attention to these balets, that in composing them he employed a particular dancing-master, whose name was Olivet. This was the person (and not Des Brosses or Beauchamps, whom Lulli commonly made use of) that composed the balets of the funeral pomp of Psyche, and Alcestes, and likewise those of the old men of Theseus, of the melancholy dreams of Atys, and the quakers and shiverers of Isis. The latter was composed intirely of gestures and external signs of people shivering with cold; and had not so much as a single step of our ordinary dance.[28]

[28] Dubos, *Réflexions critiques*, trans. Nugent, III, 187–88.

It is useful to juxtapose Dubos's remarks with the descriptions of these scenes in the librettos. Whereas the brief *didascalie* for the shiverers in *Isis* might suggest action, especially when taken in conjunction with the heading for the dance in the score ("Les Trembleurs"), and the mourners in *Alceste* are said to rend their clothes and hair, the *didascalies* for the other scenes do not communicate much about the movement. The one for *Atys* mentions the ideas the dreams are trying to communicate, but not how they do so. The *didascalie* in *Psyché* makes it sound as if the dancers do nothing but carry torches around, and the libretto of *Thésée* supplies no *didascalie* at all for the dancing old men. Without the hint from Dubos, it is not clear that anyone would conclude that these scenes favored some other kind of movement over dancing:

> The scene changes and represents the coldest place in Scythia. The people appear numb with cold. (*Isis* IV/1)
>
> A troupe of mourners approaches the mountain to lament the misfortune of Psyché. Their laments are expressed by a grieving woman and two grieving men. They are followed by six people playing the flute, and eight others who bear torches in the same manner as the Ancients for their funeral ceremonies. (*Psyché* I/2)
>
> The pleasant dreams approach Atys and by their songs and dances tell him of Cybèle's love and the happiness he may hope for from it. [. . .] The frightful dreams approach Atys and threaten him with Cybèle's vengeance if he scorns her love and does not love her faithfully. (*Atys* III/4)
>
> Thésée appears, accompanied by the populace of Athens, who rejoice over the victory won by the prince's valor and want to proclaim him as the successor to king Égée. (*Thésée* II/7)

Other divertissements suggestive of actions could be added to Dubos's list, the following among them:

> Four of the *sacrificateurs* erect an altar and the four others carry military trophies above the Grand Sacrificateur as he walks to the center of the stage. (*Cadmus et Hermione* III/6)
>
> Four male and four female magicians appear and show, while dancing, the enthusiasm with which they are preparing to assist Amisodar. (*Bellérophon* II/6)

Dubos's observations invite us to imagine how Menestrier's remarks about movement might be applied. Certainly the two scenes of mourning could incorporate the gestures he invokes for expressions of sorrow. The Zephyrs that dance in *Atys* II/4 are but one example among several roles for winds in Lully's operas.[29] Act II of *Psyché* seems right in line with Menestrier's characterization of blacksmiths. The scene is a palace that the god Vulcain is constructing with the help of his cyclopes. "His forge is visible in the background and the decor overflows with anvils and other tools proper to blacksmiths." The next *didascalie* only hints that the blacksmiths might bang on their anvils, as Menestrier describes – "the cyclopes prepare to work and music is heard that excites

[29] According to Bonin, in dances for winds, figures and speed matter more than steps, which are mostly *pas de bourrée*; see *Die neueste Art*, 197.

Example 4-2: *Psyché* II/2, "Les Forgerons," second strain (Paris: Ballard, 1720), 64–65.

them to the task" – but Lully's music makes it clear that they do so. An instrumental piece called "Les Forgerons" is marked by repetitions of pitch and rhythm that must match the hammer blows the cyclopes deliver to their forges (see Example 4-2). *Isis* also has an extended scene for blacksmiths (IV/3), who are eagerly engaged in forging various types of weapons, and whose repeated self-encouragements to work rapidly ("Tôt, tôt, tôt") also invite the dancing Chalybes to hammer away as they "pass by Io, with pieces of half-forged swords, lances, and hatchets."[30]

Did divertissements such as these separate imitative gestures from dancing? The only choreographic source for dancing blacksmiths – Gregorio Lambranzi – makes the two types of movement sequential: the first time through the music the two dancers bang on the anvil in time with the beat, then to its repetition they dance individually and together, using named dance steps (see Figure 4-1). Yet it is clear in the middle of the eighteenth century that the use of pantomimic gestures was not seen as incompatible with the simultaneous use of dance steps,[31] and Dubos's own "scarce any dancing movements" leaves the door open to a blend of movement styles in the scenes he cites from Lully's operas. It is telling that in his category of dances without dance steps Dubos mentions only the "melancholy dreams" in *Atys*, not the sweet ones; he must have considered that the movements by the Songes agréables did not constitute action. Yet their function was to communicate a crucial message to Atys; that they were perceived to be "dancing" does not preclude the possibility that they were also miming.[32]

[30] For more on this scene, see Ch. 6, pp. 175–77.

[31] See in Harris-Warrick and Brown, *The Grotesque Dancer*, chs. 8, 217–25 and 9, 258–65.

[32] In their article about the dances in *Persée*, Pierce and Thorp conclude (par. 3.23) that "though it appears from comments by Dubos and Bonnet that 'imitative' dance was generally 'almost without steps,' we must consider the possibility that [. . .] the notated steps of an 'imitative' dance could sometimes be indistinguishable from those of an 'ordinary' dance."

Figure 4-1: "Two blacksmiths hammer a nail in time to the beat." Lambranzi, *Neue und curieuse theatrialische Tantz-Schul* (1716).

I have deliberately avoided the term "pantomime" in this discussion of movement styles. Today its uses are culturally specific: "pantomime" does not mean the same thing in the US as it does in England, and in France it has still different resonances. More importantly, over most of the period covered in this book the word referred not to a genre but to a person, a particular type of actor with forebears in ancient Greece and Rome. According to the first edition of the *Dictionnaire de l'Académie Française* (1694) a pantomime is "a type of actor, a mute character who performs, who expresses himself through gestures"; Menestrier and de Pure use the term only in this sense. Lully's comedy-ballet, *Les Amants magnifiques* (1670), has three dances for characters called Pantomimes, "that is, who explain by their gestures all sorts of things."[33] This usage was still in place in 1745, when the *Mercure de France* reported, "By the word *pantomime* they [dancing masters] normally understand a mere comic dancer, worthy of exercising his talents only at the Fair Theatres [. . .] The *pantomimes* themselves [. . .] share this unfair misconception with the serious dancers who despise them."[34]

By 1729, however, if not before, the word was also used as an adjective referring to wordless movement, as in the term "ballet pantomime," a type of spectacle then becoming frequent at the fair theaters,[35] and by 1739 the word could stand alone as a noun, referring to a style as well as a person. In the following passage the word is used in both its old and new senses (emphasis added): "Demoiselle Barbarina always dances in a very brilliant manner, as does Sieur Rainaldy [*sic*], a Neapolitan who has the reputation of the most excellent *pantomime* ever seen in France. Together they perform several entrées in different types of *pantomime*, which no one ever tires of seeing."[36] By that time "pantomime" as a style or a genre had begun to project narratives through dance, an aesthetic shift that was promoted by practitioners such as Dehesse and reformers such as Cahusac. But in Lully's day, that use of the term did not yet exist. Its retrospective application clouds our ability to envisage Lully's stage.

For all that Cahusac advocated for reforms to the operatic dancing of his day, he saw Quinault as a kindred spirit: "There is not a single opera by Quinault that cannot furnish dance with a large number of noble and stageworthy actions, that lend themselves to the loveliest realization."[37] One of the scenes he admired concerned the false Oriane in *Amadis* II/7:

> Several demons, disguised as terrible monsters, try in vain to astonish and stop Amadis. Other demons, disguised as nymphs, shepherds, and shepherdesses, replace the monsters and

33 *Les Amants magnifiques*, second and fifth intermèdes.

34 *MF* (February 1745), trans. Wood and Sadler, *French Baroque Opera*, 71.

35 See announcements in the *MF*, e.g., August 1729, 1844: "Le même Opéra-Comique donna le 16 un nouveau ballet pantomime [. . .] intitulé la *Noce anglaise*."

36 *MF* (September 1739), 2245, reporting on performances at the Opéra of Royer's *Zaïde*.

37 Cahusac, *La Danse*, III, 153.

enchant Amadis [. . .] The enchanted Amadis thinks he sees [his beloved] Oriane [. . .] He places his sword at the feet of the nymph he takes to be Oriane and follows her eagerly.

This *didascalie* applies to the whole scene. In this long sequence, the music for the monsters is exclusively instrumental – which means that they communicate through movement alone – whereas the pastoral demons both sing and dance. It could be argued that the sung texts and the explanatory *didascalies* might have removed the need for imitation of actions and allowed the choreographer to make the dancers' movements more abstract. On the other hand, Beauchamps and Dolivet might have taken the sung text as a spur toward greater mimesis in the choreography, encouraging them to engage in a kind of madrigalistic text painting through movement. Cahusac's admiration for Quinault suggests that he envisaged the latter.[38]

The scene from *Amadis* involves both of Menestrier's two types of imitation – of actions and of emotions – and seems to demand gestures as well as dance steps. Yet dance that imitates action does not necessarily mean that it narrates. The shiverers in *Isis* may not use identifiable dance steps, but their shivering shows us only that they are cold; it does not advance the plot. The false Oriane, on the other hand, probably did use orthodox steps while she enticed Amadis to follow. In other words, the nature of a dancer's movements is independent of the question of how those movements relate to narration.

In the scenes discussed so far dance represents either action or a strong emotion, but many of Lully's divertissements present dance as celebration. In *Amadis* v/5 "the heroes and heroines show their joy [at the union of Amadis and Oriane] through dances intermingled with songs." Even Cahusac described joy as the principal emotional state that gives rise to dancing, on the stage as in life.[39] Thus celebratory scenes were viewed not only as opportunities for diegetic dancing, but also as fulfilling demands for dramatic verisimilitude. But even though joy is a recognizable human emotion, Menestrier, perhaps, would not have seen this kind of dance as imitative, but rather in the category of those "figured dances that have beautiful steps without representing anything."[40] Such a dance would indeed have drawn from a recognizable step vocabulary, all the more so since the chorus of heroes and heroines makes a point of calling attention to its own musicality: "Chantons tous, en ce jour, / La gloire de l'amour."

Menestrier – like other theorists both earlier and later – saw physical movement as part of a network of signs that worked together in communicating both the subject and character. Costuming was another crucial element: "since ballet has only mute actors, their clothes must speak for them and make them just as recognizable as do their

[38] "The enchantment of the false Oriane in Amadis is an episodic *action de danse* [. . .] this action will remain, when it is well performed, one of the most piquant beauties of the operatic stage." *Ibid.*, 152–53.

[39] Cahusac, *La Danse*, III, 116–17. [40] Menestrier, *Des Ballets*, 301.

movements." He continues that in a group everyone should be dressed in the same way and in the same colors.[41] Even a partial list of the dancing characters in Lully's *tragédies* goes well beyond Dubos's sixteen types: soldiers, sailors, ancient heroes, amazons, prisoners, mourners, blacksmiths, giants, cyclopes, phantoms, dreams, fairies, magicians, cupids, priests of various gods from the ancient pantheon, other types of followers of gods, followers of allegorical characters such as Abundance or Glory, hours, seasons, pleasures, games, statues, fortunate lovers, shepherds and shepherdesses, herdsmen, fauns, satyrs, maenads, bacchantes, nymphs, dryads, naiads, woodland divinities, river gods, tritons, corybantes, demons, goblins, monsters, furies, winds, zephyrs, Polichinelles, matassins, lords, and peoples of many different regions and countries (Egypt, Phrygia, Sicily, Greece, Ethiopia, Cathay . . .). The situations in which these characters find themselves range from the solemn to the frivolous, from the joyous to the frightening.

It is not possible that so many characters would have been distinguishable on the basis of movement alone. Probably the creators of the operas relied on a combination of movement, music, costume, and attributes (the blacksmith's tools, the shepherd's crook), which they inflected in response to the situation and emotional climate of the scene. At the same time, however, if movement codes were in fact differentiated to the extent that Dubos suggests, such that even fauns, shepherds, and peasants – all of them inhabitants of the pastoral realm – had different step vocabularies and used different figures, it behooves us to try to figure out how these various character-types moved and what it is that distinguishes "demon-ness" from "shepherd-ness" and "shepherd-ness" from "peasant-ness."

The various categorization systems proposed by the published dance theorists of this period are not very helpful, in that they tend to draw upon what they understood to be the practices of the ancients, as well as both the social and theatrical dances of their own age; no two systems were identical.[42] The only seventeenth-century source that bases a system uniquely on contemporary theatrical practice is an anonymous manuscript written about the *ballet de cour*, which mentions something akin to the tripart division that was to become standardized later in the eighteenth century: "I call these three genres, in the ballets, first the heroic, second the agreeable or gallant, and third the burlesque."[43] The author adds that this classification is useful when one wishes to indicate what the preponderant affect is in a particular ballet; in other words, this is a descriptive tool, not a prescription of movement codes. It is easier to envisage movement styles for the era after Lully, when some theatrical choreographies survive. Judging from the pastoral dances preserved in Beauchamps-Feuillet

[41] *Ibid.*, 250–51 and 253. [42] See Schroedter, *Vom "Affect" zur "Action,"* esp. ch. III.1.

[43] F-Po C. 4844, *Règles pour faire des ballets*, 16. A penciled annotation on the flyleaf suggests the author might be Menestrier.

Figure 4-2: Design by Jean Berain for a demonic scene, probably a revival of *Thésée*.

notation, shepherds used steps from "la belle danse," whereas the iconography of furies and demons (there are no demon choreographies) suggests that they showed their nastiness by transgressing the rules of the noble style – using false positions of the feet, raising the same arm and leg simultaneously, and making extravagant gestures (see Figure 4-2). Other hints come from writers such as Cahusac: "In a specific entrée, Furies, for example, could undoubtedly depict the rage that excites them via rapid steps, sudden jumps, and violent whirling."[44] But what happens when, as in *Thésée* III/7–8, the demons "express the sweetness they find in the orders Médée has given them of scaring people and making Aeglé suffer"? What choreographic form does "expressing sweetness" take when the character is a demon? Which matters more for the choreographer, the sweetness or the demon-ness?

Music can help answer such a question, and the scores reinforce the other evidence that in Lully's day a continuum of dance styles was recognized, from the comic and grotesque at one end to the noble and heroic at the other, with many overlapping gradations in between. The space between dance that imitates action and diegetic dance – which the characters within the opera would themselves have identified as dancing – also operates along a continuum; there is a large representational middle

[44] Cahusac, *La Danse*, III, 48–49.

ground between the soldiers who emerge from the earth and kill each other in *Cadmus et Hermione* IV/2 and the shepherds dancing at a wedding in *Roland*. My own sense is that the extant choreographic sources do not give us anything like the full range of steps and gestures that would have appeared in one evening at the Académie Royale de Musique.

MUSICAL CHARACTERIZATION

The variety Lully composed into his dance music reveals his adherence to the principles of composition articulated by de Pure:

> The first and most essential beauty of an *air de ballet* is appropriateness – that is, the correct relation that the air must have to the thing represented [. . .] If a woman mourning the loss of her husband or children is represented, one must use lugubrious sounds, piercing accents, and slow rhythms [. . .] When a prince appears, one must give the air majesty. If a lover, one will favor the tender or passionate. Finally, one must choose from among the variety of tones and modes whatever is necessary to provide airs for the different subjects [of the ballet] and to appropriately set the melodies and composition to the steps that the entrée or the subject requires.[45]

The partnership between Lully and his choreographer was so successful on these very grounds that it came in for extravagant praise from no less a person than François Raguenet, a partisan of Italian music:

> There are no dancers in Europe who can touch the French; even the Italians agree. The combatants and cyclopes in *Persée*, the tremblers and blacksmiths in *Isis*, the night-mares in *Atys* and their other ballet entrées are truly original, both for the music Lully composed and for the steps that Beauchamps set to his music. Nothing comparable had been seen on stage before these two great men. They are the inventors and they brought these pieces to such a high degree of perfection, that no one in Italy, or in any other place on earth, has been able to achieve it since – nor, perhaps, will ever be able to achieve it.[46]

The continuum of characters and situations in Lully's divertissements means that his dance music does not lend itself to easy categorization. The fact that so few of his dance pieces have generic dance titles (menuet, gavotte, etc.; see Chapter 3, pp. 92–93) is a choice; the expressive requirements of the stage were broader than the palette of dance types permitted. In a musical style that favors variety over predictability, characterization depends on subtle interactions among all the parameters of a piece: form, key, harmony, melody, meter, rhythm, tempo, phrase structure, texture, and orchestration. It is thus more fruitful to study individual pieces *in situ* than to

[45] Pure, *Idée*, 260–62. [46] Raguenet, *Parallèle*, 19–21.

generalize, and pertinent discussions may be found in several places within Part I.[47] The remarks that follow touch on some of the parameters that are germane to the realization of an instrumental piece in dance. Dubos's reaction to the Underworld music in *Alceste* challenges us to listen more broadly for affects as subtle as what he heard there:

> As we have already observed, there is a probability or seeming truth even in this imaginary music. Tho' we never heard Pluto's music, yet we find a kind of probability in those airs, to which Lulli makes the retinue of the infernal Monarch dance in the fourth act of the opera of Alcestes, because these airs breathe a tranquil and serious contentment, and as Lulli himself expressed it, a *veiled joy*.[48]

Key

Lully's divertissements have a home key in which they remain, unless they occupy more than one scene. Harmonic excursions are limited to the parallel major or minor, or, if the mode is minor, to the relative major. If Lully had thoughts about the affects associated with keys, he did not write them down, as did a few of his contemporaries. But as Rosow points out, "The subjectivity of these systems is clear from the lack of agreement regarding individual keys – for instance, G minor is 'sad' (Jean Rousseau, 1691), 'serious and magnificent' (Charpentier, *c.* 1692), or 'sweet and tender' (Charles Masson, 1697). It seems ill-advised to apply these characterizations to the work of Lully, who left us none of his own."[49] To date, no study has been made concerning the choices of keys Lully made for different character types.

Form

The vast majority of Lully's instrumental dances fall into one of three formal categories – binary, rondeau (generally either ABACA or ABA), or continuing variation (chaconnes and passacailles). There are a few formal exceptions: the village wedding in *Roland* IV/3 includes a fourteen-bar through-composed piece labeled simply "Hautbois" that falls between two dance pieces and seems likely to have been danced. The "Troupe d'Astrée dansante" that opens the prologue to *Phaéton* – in triple meter with a menuet-like profile – is built around three eight-bar phrases, each of which falls into two very square halves, but there is no double bar or other sign of internal repeat (a sign does call for the piece to be repeated in its entirety). Occasionally a single piece incorporates sung and instrumental passages that are both substantial; chaconnes and passacailles are the most common, but in *Roland* V/2, Logistille and her fairy followers use both

47 See in particular the discussions and music examples in Ch. 6.

48 Dubos, *Réflexions critiques*, trans. Nugent, III, 129.

49 Rosow, "The descending minor tetrachord," n. 9.

song and dance to restore the hero to reason – this to a single long piece that intersperses extensive instrumental passages among the solos and choruses.

One ambiguity concerns the repeat structures within binary pieces: was AABB the norm? Ballard's practice – and that of most music copyists as well – was to indicate repeats via a double bar with dots in all the spaces between the two lines; sometimes a notation more akin to our modern repeat sign is found. The convention of the day was to use such a symbol only in the middle of a binary piece and to place a simple double bar at the end (see Figure 2-6, p. 48). When the sources supply first and second endings in the second strain, the repeat scheme is clear, but the absence of dots at the final double bar has led many editors and performers to interpret Lully's intent for repetitions within a binary piece as AAB.[50] Yet as theorists Saint-Lambert and Montéclair explained, in 1702 and 1736 respectively, the dotted bar in the middle meant that *both* strains of the piece were to be repeated.[51] As a matter of editorial policy, it seems prudent to translate this practice into modern notation and thus to add dots to the final barline of a binary piece; this has the advantage of allowing for a repeat of the second strain without imposing one, whereas when dots are omitted, modern performers will not take a repeat.

The variants in notation found among manuscript sources and Ballard's prints suggest that repeat structures were not standardized – and notated choreographies, which show how much music is required, present binary pieces in several different patterns ("p" indicates a *petite reprise*): AABB (the most numerous), AAB, AABp, AABBp, AABBAABB, etc.[52] The "Air pour les Amours et les Guerriers" in *Le Triomphe de l'Amour* (LWV 59/13) has a structure of AABpBp in Ballard's score. The sarabande from IV/2 of Destouches's opera *Issé* generated three choreographies, each choreographed by Pécour for the Opéra, yet set to different structures: AABB (1708), AB, and ABB (both 1720).[53] This last situation confirms what common sense suggests: choreography has the potential to impact musical structures. Rondeaux also exhibit variations in repetition: AABACA, ABACAA, ABACABACA, etc. It is important to remember in this context that dances were through-choreographed, regardless of how much the music repeated. Modern scores whose notation imposes a single pattern do not give their users access to the variety that prevailed in Lully's day.

Lully rarely places two dances of the same type back-to-back and when he does, as in the prologue to *Armide* where there are two successive menuets, he does not call for the

50 AAB can be heard on many recordings and seen in many modern editions. In *La Belle Dance*, Lancelot identifies the repeat structure of both the score and the dance notation; many pieces are listed as AAB for the music, AABB for the choreography.

51 Saint-Lambert, *Les Principes du clavecin*, 33 (trans., 56) and Montéclair, *Principes de musique*, 36.

52 See Little's study of repeat structures in 73 choreographies in "Problems of repetition," 429.

53 The first was danced by Dumoulin *l'aîné* and Mlle Chaillou at the premiere. For the other pair see Le Roussau, *A Collection*, 81–91, and 117.

first to be repeated after the second. That performance convention seems not to have developed until well into the eighteenth century; see Chapter 14, p. 439.

Texture and Orchestration

Lully wrote most of his dance pieces in a five-part string texture, structured around a treble-bass duet with three sizes of viola playing the inner parts; oboes and bassoons frequently double the outer voices, although their participation may not always be indicated in the score.[54] During the first seven years of his opera career, Lully called upon the resources of the full five-part orchestra only in the overture, the divertissements (dances and choruses), and the entr'actes; it was not until *Bellérophon* (1679) that Lully began to accompany solo singers orchestrally, and even then he did so sparingly. This pattern of usage meant that the beginning of a divertissement was marked by aural as well as visual sumptuousness.

Lully's next most frequent texture is a trio – either two treble instruments and bass, or a high trio in which the "bass line" is also written in a treble range. A trio texture – standard for ritournelles – may also be used for dance pieces, as in *Atys* IV/5 (see Figure 2-6). Trios may be assigned to members of the same family of instruments (string and double-reed trios are both common) or, less frequently, may mix strings and winds. An entire piece may be in trio texture, or a trio may alternate within a single piece with the five-part orchestra (see Example 5-2, p. 152). Occasionally Lully wrote instrumental pieces – all or in sectional alternation – in four parts; this texture seems to have been used primarily or exclusively by wind instruments.[55] Changes in texture within a piece coincide with structural points or with the ends of phrases. Lully did not write soloistic pieces, or even sections that featured a single instrument; rather, he used sound in blocks.

Lully used his orchestra emblematically. Trumpets and drums appear alongside soldiers; members of the oboe family feature in pastoral scenes; flutes (recorders) in religious ceremonies. These general categories of usage are nuanced, depending on the particularities of the dramatic contex; his orchestrations are not always fully indicated in Ballard's scores.[56] Nonetheless it *is* clear that orchestration was a fundamental part of characterization, an aural form of costuming. When Roland hears the sounds of rustic music, he knows that shepherds are about to appear. Similarly, the trumpets and drums

[54] Much has been written about Lully's orchestration. See, *inter alia*, Eppelsheim, *Das Orchester*; Rosow, "Paris Opéra orchestration"; and Zaslaw, "Lully's orchestra."

[55] See my "A few thoughts," 101–02.

[56] The only percussion instrument notated in Lully's scores is the *timballes*, which played with the trumpets. Whereas there is some evidence for the broader use of percussion in Lully's day (see Eppelsheim, *Das Orchester*, 168–72), the colorful percussion heard in many recent performances represents the performers' choice.

do as much to characterize the soldiers in Act II of *Alceste* as does their armor. It was not rare for players of emblematic instruments to appear on stage.[57]

In a dance piece where instrumental textures alternate, the textural changes may signal that different groups of dancers do so as well. This possibility seems most appropriate when an opposition between groups has already been structured into the divertissement. In the prologue to *Armide*, the confrontation between the followers of Wisdom and the followers of Glory plays out in the orchestral writing (and the accompanying dancing) as well as in the chorus (see Chapter 5, p. 150). On the other hand, structural alternation of instrumentation may not always serve as such a signal. The marches that have a military context and involve trumpets and drums are always in rondeau form: trumpets and drums fill out the orchestra on the refrain, but the intervening episodes are always played only by strings. The march in I/10 of *Thesée* serves as entrance music for *sacrificateurs* and combatants, "who carry standards and the spoils of their vanquished enemies" and add to a stage already crowded with the King and his retinue, Aeglé, Cléone, the High Priestess and a group of priestesses. Nothing in the dramatic context would make an alternation between the combatants and the priestesses (the two available groups of dancers) salient. Chaconnes and passacailles always incorporate changes in texture between five and three parts, and here as well it seems rash to assume that a textural change would always be matched by one in the dancing personnel, even if that could sometimes be the case. To be plausible, a choreographic response to textural changes should be based on the number of different groups available to dance, their relationship to each other, and the musical features of the particular piece.

Phrase Structure

Irregularity of phrase lengths is a fundamental part of Lully's style; he avoids square phrases even for benign pastoral characters who dance menuets. Others among the dance types Lully used – the gavotte, for instance, and even more so a dance such as the gigue – also defy stereotypes about the square phrasing commonly attributed to dance music. Not even the march is reliably regular: the processional that brings on the priests preparing for a sacrifice in *Cadmus et Hermione* III/6 has seven measures in the first strain, nine in the second. Of the dances that lack generic labels and are identified in the score as an "Air" or "Entrée," only about 15 percent have consistent four-bar phrases, with pieces in an even number of bars (but not multiples of four) constituting another 15%. The remaining two-thirds either have phrase lengths that vary within a single piece, or are constructed so as to avoid clearly defining a phrase until the end of a strain. Irregular phrase lengths are central to Lully's approach to composition, not a special effect, a fact that complicates their interpretation as a measure of characterization.[58]

57 See my "Magnificence in motion."

58 A more developed version of this section may be found in my "The phrase structures of Lully's dance music."

Example 4-3: *Atys* prologue, "Gavotte en rondeau. Air pour la suite de Flore," refrain (Paris: Ballard, 1689), 24.

Irregularity takes different shapes, however, some of them quite balanced. Lully may have constructed the refrain of the rondeau in Example 4-3 in five bars, but he did so by extending the second of two almost parallel subunits. The graceful, melodic lilt seems perfectly appropriate for followers of the goddess of spring.

Example 4-4 shows two consecutive menuets from the prologue to *Roland*, where they are danced in celebration of peace by spirits and fairies. The first has consistent five-bar phrases that are melodically parallel within each strain. The second menuet has six bars in the first strain, and eight in the second, neither of which breaks down easily into subunits. Cadential motion in the bass of bars 3 and 10 is overridden by the insistent repetition in the melody of a triadic figure that confounds any attempts to hear either strain as divided neatly in the middle.

The second menuet may surprise ears accustomed to antecedent–consequent phrases, but it does not move too far away from the balanced irregularity that characterizes many of Lully's celebratory dances, especially the generic ones. Enough other positive characters dance to music that is still less regular to suggest that phrase lengths per se do not impose a single affect on a dance. In *Phaéton* v/4 the "Second Air" danced by joyful, undisguised Egyptian shepherds and shepherdesses (F major, in $\frac{6}{4}$ time) has phrases of four and six bars in the first strain, and of 5+4+6+5 in the second. Here the quirky phrase lengths are held in balance by the repetitiveness of the rhythm and melody. The competitors in the dance contest in Act I of *Persée* dance first to an air in $\frac{3}{8}$ that has, in the first strain, eleven bars in a single phrase and in the second twenty-nine bars that may be parsed as 9+6+14. In this case the irregularity is balanced by simple rhythms and harmony that lessen the impact of the phrasing. Their second dance has surface rhythms in the melody that suggest both bourrée and gavotte, and whose phrasing mixes the regular with the irregular. The long-winded phrases of both are more typical of dances labeled "air" or "entrée" than of generic types. It might be tempting to link the irregularity of both dances to the dramatic context – the *jeux junoniens* represent Queen Cassiope's vain attempt to appease the angry Junon – except for the fact that such irregularity appears in less fraught circumstances as well. The "Air pour les sacrificateurs" in *Persée* v/3, a solemn triple-meter piece in A minor, comes in the middle of the wedding

Example 4-4: *Roland* prologue, two consecutive menuets (Paris: Ballard, 1689), xix–xx. (a) first strain of the first menuet; (b) the entire second menuet.

ceremonies for Andromède and Persée. The melodic phrase end in m. 3 is deflected by a deceptive cadence, and a real harmonic arrival, on C, does not occur until m. 7. The phrase is then extended another four bars to the cadence on E at the double bar. The second strain also has three phrases, of three, four, and five bars respectively. The followers of Glory in the prologue to *Armide* dance to music whose first strain is ten and a half bars, because the starts of phrases switch from the downbeat to the middle of the bar (Example 3-1, p. 95; see also Example 5-1, p. 148).

For certain types, such as demons and other nasty characters, irregularity is the norm. The "Entrée des Furies" from the third act of *Phaéton* (Example 4-5) accompanies not only movement by the dancers, but a scenic transformation: "The doors of the temple open, and this place, which had formerly appeared magnificent, turns into a frightful abyss that vomits flames and from which emerge furies and terrifying

Example 4-5: *Phaéton* III/5, "Entrée des Furies" (Paris: Ballard, 1683), 147.

phantoms who overturn and break the offerings and who threaten and chase away the assembled people." The meter sign of ¢ and the predominant sixteenth-note motion suggest a fast tempo. The two strains have seven and eleven measures respectively and the overall affect is one of frenzied activity.

Lully also drew upon irregularity when characters are seen to be engaging more in action than dance. In *Alceste* III/5, two troupes of mourners rend their clothes, tear their hair, and break ornaments at the foot of the effigy of Alceste; this is one of the dances mentioned by Dubos as having no dance steps. The physicality of their rage is represented musically by a rapid binary dance that grows out of the "Rompons, brisons" chorus. Whereas the melody uses only quarter and eighth notes, variety in the surface rhythms joins with the harmonic structure in delaying cadences to the end of each strain – which last seven and ten bars respectively (Example 4-6). However, the *entrée grave*, a dance type which is consistently irregular in its phrasings,[59] neither represents action nor are the characters necessarily nasty; it is more often used in the celebratory scenes that end operas than in the Underworld.

Lully's dance pieces do nonetheless exhibit a few general trends regarding how phrase structure relates to musical characterization. Demons, furies, and other threatening creatures move to irregular, long-winded phrases; their music becomes regular only if, as in Act II of *Amadis*, they are disguised as something benign. Similarly, characters engaged in some kind of miming dance, either serious or grotesque (e.g., blacksmiths, *sacrificateurs*, or magicians) generally get irregular phrases, although this pattern is not absolute: the famous shiverers in *Isis*, for example, have music built on four-bar phrases, with one five-bar phrase thrown in. Pastoral characters – shepherds, nymphs, dryads, silvans, and the like – have dances in both irregular and regular

[59] Examples include the entrée for Le Printemps in *Phaéton* IV/2 (eleven bars in the first strain, nineteen in the second) or the first dance for the Lyciens in *Bellérophon* V/3 (eleven bars in each strain).

Example 4-6: *Alceste* III/5, dance for the mourners (Paris: Baussen, 1708), 126.

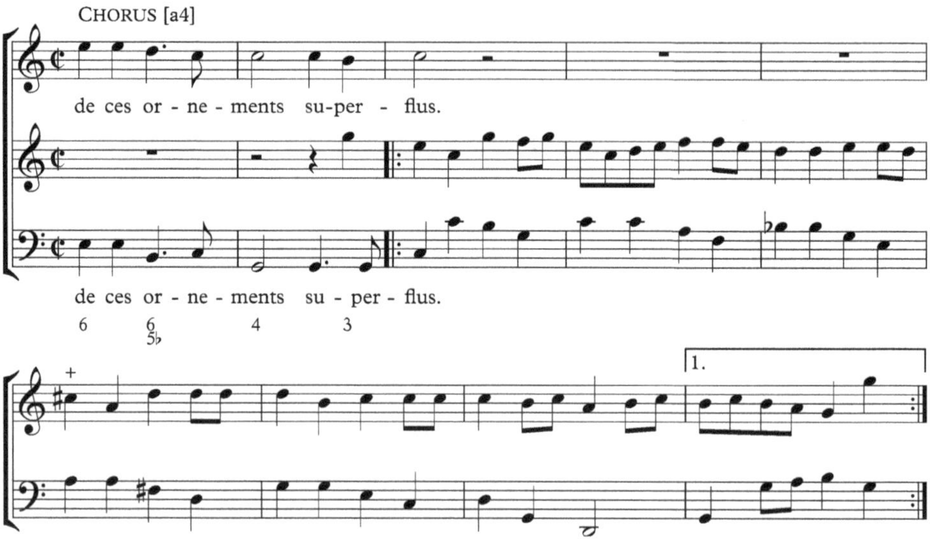

phrasings, although both types of phrase tend to adhere to short, melodically well-defined units. Celebratory characters, whether humans or divinities, have a fairly high proportion of dances that are either square or reasonably regular – that is, dances that either have a regular number of odd-numbered phrases or that only once or twice deviate from a basically four-bar pattern. But the "hedging" adverbs in the previous sentence show how unstable this category is.[60] Lully's style does not rest on a template of regular antecedent–consequent phrases that can then be manipulated to expressive ends; for Lully no such template exists.

INSTRUMENTAL MUSIC AND MOVEMENT

In this context it is useful to ask whether dance pieces offer analogies to the other types of instrumental music inside operas: perhaps all of it invites movement, whether for people or stage machinery. The entr'acte music definitely served this function; the curtain remained up and the scene transformations between acts were done in full view

60 It is interesting to compare another body of theatrical dances, those found in Lambranzi's *Neue und curieuse theatralische Tantz-Schul*, most of which are comic or burlesque. The elegantly dressed couple dancing a sarabande moves to simple, square phrases, but so do ridiculous old women scratching where they itch or Mezzetin and his wife. On the other hand, the Swiss soldier performing fancy maneuvers with his pike has three seven-bar phrases and Scaramuzza performs his antics to phrases of eleven and fifteen bars. But in this collection the tunes with irregular phrase lengths actually occupy a smaller proportion of the total than in Lully's works, their comic intent notwithstanding.

of the audience.[61] The same music might also be used to accompany action that ends the act – at least so it seems at the end of Act III of *Thésée*, where the heroine, Aeglé, is chased off stage by malevolent demons. The entr'acte music, which repeats a dance for demons that has already been heard twice, must have been available to extend the brief choral outburst ("Quelle douceur de voir souffrir!") whose mere nine measures of rapid triple meter seem insufficient to cover all the action. Other through-composed instrumental pieces were designed to accompany more vigorous movement; a particularly spectacular effect is found in *Alceste* I/8–9, where Aquilons create a tempest that prevents the boats from leaving the harbor, then are forced into the sea by flying Zephyrs.

Inside the acts there are, besides the dances, two main categories of instrumental pieces: ritournelles and préludes. Notwithstanding the suggestive names, the differences concern not function but texture; with few exceptions, ritournelles are composed as trios, préludes in five parts. Both are through-composed, although they may have brief repeated internal phrases that do not add up to a regular form, and generally speaking, they serve as introductions to vocal pieces to which they often have musical similarities.[62] Preludes and ritournelles are usually quite short, at least when they provide entrance music for an individual singer. Occasionally, however, a piece labeled "prélude" may initiate a divertissement, in which case it is correspondingly more substantial. There are two such in *Thésée*: in I/8 the piece called "Le Sacrifice," as well as "prélude," ushers a troupe of priestesses onto the stage; and in V/8 a 50-bar prélude accompanies the arrival of Minerva in a Glory. The musical construction of a piece like this last one, which is not only very long but has several changes of texture, suggests that more must be going on than the arrival of one goddess in a machine. Another long prélude (57 bars) opens the dream sequence in Act III of *Atys* (outlined in Table 2-11), where it accompanies a scenic transformation and the arrival of the characters of the realm of sleep (singers, dancers, and instrumentalists). Exceptionally, the prelude is repeated later in the scene, after everyone is on stage. Surely something worth watching must have been happening.[63]

If the default position is that an instrumental piece invites movement, the question then becomes what kind of movement is right for the context. This same question could also be applied to the instrumental passages inside choruses, which range in length from a single measure to passages that are longer than some independent dances. Any instrumental intervention, wherever it occurs, should provoke us to ask if it might accompany some kind of movement.

[61] See Rosow, "Making connections."

[62] For an overview, see Wood, *Music and Drama*, 173–78.

[63] The Arts Florissants production of *Atys* in 1987 treated the first iteration of the prélude as entrance music for Sommeil and his followers, and used its repetition for a dance by a solo Songe agréable.

Even the overture might serve as a site for action. A *didascalie* in the libretto for *Cadmus et Hermione* reveals that the curtain went up to reveal a lovely countryside at dawn followed by a brilliant sunrise "during the time that the instruments finish playing the overture."[64] In the next generation, at least one opera made use of the overture for mimed action. The prologue to Rebel's tragedy *Ulysse* (1703) centers around Orpheus, who offers his voice and his lyre to sing the praises of the king. According to the first *didascalie* in the libretto, "the scene represents a lovely forest [. . .] Orpheus, pensive, arrives toward the middle of the overture and goes to sit on a grassy knoll at the foot of the largest tree. There he readies his lyre and when the overture is over, a few measures are heard of the tender *symphonie* that precedes his first song."

I do not mean to suggest that every time Lully writes purely instrumental music something has to happen. Nor do I mean to imply as a corollary that anything sung would require the performers to remain still; Armide's dramatic monologue in which she attempts to kill Renaud is but the most famous example of operatic acting that requires movement while singing. Moreover, we have seen that choruses could be danced under certain circumstances and there are many places where the characters in a divertissement have to make their entrances or exits while someone is singing, simply because Lully did not provide any instrumental music to cover their movements. Nonetheless when thinking about the visual side of the opera, paying attention to the instrumental music seems like a fundamental tool. Dance, by this perspective, does not occupy a category of its own, but falls at one end of a continuum of movement.

64 The curtain normally went up at the start of the overture, according to Tessin (quoted in Rosow's introduction to her edition of *Armide*, xxx).

5 | Prologues

In *The Fabrication of Louis XIV*, historian Peter Burke discusses the mechanisms by which Louis XIV carefully cultivated his image throughout his long reign: the creation of royal academies for the arts and sciences; patronage of artists, writers, and scholars; and the creation of administrative structures to oversee the enterprise of his glorification. The products included paintings, sculptures, medallions, sermons, poems, dedications to the king in all French publications of note – and the operatic prologue. In Lully's day a libretto's writing was overseen by the so-called "Petite Académie," of which Quinault was a member.[1] The prologue as a genre was not new – it had been used upon occasion in the spoken theatre as well as in ballets – but as Quinault developed it for an operatic environment, it acquired its own textual, musical, and choreographic conventions.

Dramatically, the prologue almost always stands outside the plot of the opera, being built around allegorical or mythological characters who do not reappear in the five acts of the *tragédie*,[2] and whose job is to praise the king. Wood describes the prologue as "an extension of the fawning dedication to the king with which the composer prefaced his score,"[3] and the verses can indeed be heavy handed. The prologue of *Armide* opens with the following extravagant hyperbole.

La Gloire: Tout doit céder dans l'univers
À l'auguste héros que j'aime.
L'effort des ennemis, les glaces des hivers,
Les rochers, les fleuves, les mers,
Rien n'arrête l'ardeur de sa valeur extrême.

La Sagesse: Tout doit céder dans l'univers
À l'auguste héros que j'aime.
Il sait l'art de tenir tous les monstres aux fers;
Il est maître absolu de cent peuples divers,
Et plus maître encore de lui-même.

[1] Formed by Colbert in 1663 and dedicated to "la seule gloire du roi," the Petite Académie adopted the name Académie Royale des Inscriptions et Médailles in 1701. Regarding its functioning, see Couvreur, *Lully*, 43–63.

[2] Only in *Psyché* and *Amadis* does a character from the prologue reappear in the opera.

[3] Wood, *Music and Drama*, 193.

> (*Glory*: Everything in the universe must yield to the august hero whom I love. His enemies' efforts, the frozen winters, rocks, rivers, seas – nothing stops the ardor of his extreme valor. *Wisdom*: Everything in the universe must yield to the august hero whom I love. He knows how to keep all monsters enchained; he is absolute master of a hundred different peoples; he is a greater master still over himself.)

There is, however, more to prologues than sycophancy. For Couvreur, one feature is that they kept Louis XIV on stage even after he had given up dancing. "For all that he had renounced appearing on the stage of the Académie Royale de Musique in flesh and blood, Louis XIV nonetheless expected to be praised in all the entertainments he offered to his court. Quinault made His Majesty the main character of his prologues [. . .] Most often Louis XIV is the 'hero,' the 'conqueror' or, in all simplicity, 'the greatest king in the world.' King, hero, or conqueror are words that return in the tragedy proper; by the imprecision of his terminology Quinault facilitated the identification of mythological or chivalric characters with Louis XIV."[4] Dance, an art at which the king had excelled, is woven throughout every prologue, even if its use is not as blatantly encomiastic as the sung texts.

But beyond its function as a "performed dedication,"[5] the prologue serves to set up the opera that follows as a theatrical spectacle. In *Les Fêtes de l'Amour et de Bacchus* the satirical *donneur de livres* scene stages its own theatricality (see Chapter 6, p. 157ff), but in the *tragédies* the transition between the realm of the prologue and the world of the opera is treated with appropriate seriousness. The prologue to *Bellérophon* ends with an exhortation by Apollon to the Muses and the pastoral beings that form his entourage: "Leave off your trivial songs. We must through more noble means honor today the hero of France. Let us now transform ourselves, and in a charming spectacle celebrate before his eyes the fortunate event that in former times gave birth to Parnassus.[6] For this great king, come, redouble your efforts; prepare your sweetest music."[7] In other words, the characters of the prologue are the ones who will perform the opera, or, as Cornic has phrased it, "the prologue engenders the *tragédie*."[8] The prologue thus serves to justify the musicality of the entire five-act opera, and in a sense serves an analogous function, on a higher level, to the sung texts that frame the divertissements within acts as "stage music." In some cases the reference to the spectacle to follow may be indirect – in *Thésée* it takes the form of a choral refrain, "In the midst of war, let us enjoy the pleasures of peace" – but in the prologue to *Atys* Quinault makes an unambiguous statement regarding the primacy of

[4] Couvreur, *Lully*, 325. [5] Burgess, "Revisiting *Atys*," 466.

[6] This type of trope, common in prologues, presents the king as protector – or even creator – of the arts.

[7] "Quittez de si vaines chansons. / Il faut par de plus nobles sons / Honorer en ce jour le héros de la France. / Transformons-nous en ce moment, / Et dans un spectacle charmant, / Célébrons à ses yeux, l'heureux évènement, / Qui jadis au Parnasse a donné la naissance. / Allons, pour ce grand roi, redoublez vos efforts; / Préparez vos plus doux accords." This libretto was written by Thomas Corneille, but adheres to the conventions Quinault had established.

[8] Cornic, "Ad limina templi Polymniae," 54.

tragedy over the pastoral in the opera to follow, when Melpomène wrests control over the proceedings from Flore, the goddess of spring: "May the rustic ornaments of Flore and her pleasures give way to the magnificent trappings of the tragic Muse and her solemn spectacles."[9] Although Quinault did not return to this kind of statement of artistic principles in his later operas, the prologue to *Atys* lays the groundwork for the aesthetic debates that were to feature in operatic prologues in the coming generations.

The "hero" himself never appears, but is alluded to by the characters who make it their business to celebrate him – or sometimes to chide him gently for devoting so much attention to war. These allegorical/mythological individuals are singers who have groups of followers. In prologues the followers are always obedient; they serve to magnify through movement and sound whatever their leaders say. In two operas only (*Cadmus et Hermione* and *Proserpine*) is there a true enemy with a set of nasty followers; all the other followers are benign. There is no single model for the structure of the prologue, but Wood has identified two main types: one in which "action unfolds as a sequence of events leading to a logical conclusion and a triumphant celebration" and one that "unfolds without conflict or change of mood" in which "the structure [. . .] is a cumulative one."[10] Her study extends to 1715; within Lully's operas, the structural distinction she makes maps onto the political. Even though the prologues only allude to outside events in oblique ways, it is nonetheless possible to trace within them the broad strokes of France's military engagements.[11] War and peace on the diplomatic front play out differently inside Lully's prologues on the level of structure.

Lully's first four *tragédies* – *Cadmus et Hermione* (1673), *Alceste* (1674), *Thésée* (1675), and *Atys* (1676) – were all composed while the French were at war with the Dutch; hostilites had broken out in April 1672. In *Cadmus* the conflict is reflected in a staging of the epic battle between the Sun and Python; as the libretto's preface points out, the allegory is too clear to require explanation. The other three reveal their wartime origins by mourning the hero's absence because he is off at the front. In *Alceste* the Nymphe de la Seine opens the prologue by asking – in a much-repeated refrain – "Le héros que j'attends ne reviendra-t-il pas?" ("Will the hero I await ever return?") She accuses Glory of being responsible for his absence: "He follows you all too often into the horror of combat." This is not the only reference in a prologue to the horrors of war: in *Thésée* Mars sends Bellone off with orders to bring the hero's enemies "everything horrible war has to offer." Buford Norman states that "there is an undeniable element of criticism" in the brief lines such as these with which Quinault sprinkles his prologues. Norman adds that "this 'criticism' is perhaps best understood in the context of the

9 "Que l'agrément rustique / De Flore et de ses jeux, / Cède à l'appareil magnifique / De la Muse tragique, / Et de ses spectacles pompeurx." See the stimulating discussions of this prologue in Cornic, "Ad limina," and Burgess, "Revisiting *Atys*."

10 Wood, *Music and Drama*, 197–200.

11 Regarding the content of Quinault's prologues, see Gros, *Quinault*, 526–40.

long-standing debate about the relative benefits of war and peace for a kingdom. Reservations about the excessive devotion of a king to war are common not only in sermons, but also in the harangues in the presence of the king by Quinault and other members of the Petite Académie."[12] In this period of war, the hero's court is portrayed as a place of refuge from the brutal realities of the outside world; the prologue to *Thésée* ends with the words, "May the rest of the world envy the good fortune of these attractive places. In the middle of war, let us enjoy the pleasures of peace."[13] This theme was to become central to the prologues late in the reign, when France's fortunes were at an ebb.

The conflicts alluded to in these early prologues find an analogue in their construction, which is built around some kind of opposition that plays out in dance or action as well as song. The most dramatic instance is found in *Cadmus et Hermione*, in the violent battle that takes place on stage between the Sun and Python, complete with spectacular visual effects, and in which dancers figure as whirlwinds accompanying Envy. The other prologues set up rhetorical rather than physical disputes – between the Nymphe de la Seine and Gloire in *Alceste*, between Vénus (love) and Mars (war) in *Thésée*. In each case the dispute is resolved, and the restoration of harmony is enacted through sequences of songs and dances for two troupes who are at first separate and then unite. The resolution takes various forms and is not necessarily acted out by the followers of the original disputants. In *Thésée*, after Mars and Vénus decide to "join the songs of victory to the sweet songs of love," they call upon Cérès and Bacchus, who arrive not only with their own followers, but bring back the Amours, Grâces, Plaisirs, and Jeux (i.e., the chorus) who had left near the start of the prologue in despair over the hero's absence. First Cérès's harvesters dance, then comes the turn of the Silvains and Bacchantes who follow Bacchus. Finally, "the troupe that follows Cérès and the troupe of Bacchus's followers unite and together express their joy by a dance." The union of the two troupes provides a visual as well as an aural resolution to the conflicts.

By the time *Isis* was composed in 1677, the tide of war was turning to favor the French, and Neptune himself announced naval successes: "My empire has served as the war theater; announce new exploits. The same conquerer who is so famous on land has now triumphed on the seas."[14] Following the treaties of Nijmwegen between France and the Netherlands in 1678–79, the next few prologues celebrate the making of peace. The libretto for *Bellérophon* (1679) even has a preface explaining that "since the king has given peace to Europe, the Académie Royale de Musique thought it should participate in the expressions of public joy by giving a spectacle in which it could show its zeal for

[12] Norman, *Touched by the Graces*, 53.

[13] "Que tout le reste de la terre / Porte envie au bonheur de ces lieux pleins d'attraits. / Au milieu de la guerre, / Goûtons les plaisirs de la paix."

[14] "Mon Empire a servi de théâtre à la guerre; / Publiez des exploits nouveaux: / C'est le même vainqueur si fameux sur la terre, / Qui triomphe encore sur les eaux."

the glory of this august monarch." The Opéra's zeal is built into the prologue: "Thanks to this august king Discord has been banished," announces Apollon. "After having sung the furors of war, let us now sing the sweetness of peace."[15] In the next opera, *Proserpine*, Peace has been captured by Discord, but is freed by Victory and restored to union with Abundance and Happiness: "We have put down our weapons; now is the happy time of pleasures filled with charms; now is the happy time of pleasures and games,"[16] concludes the final chorus.

Starting with *Persée* in 1682, internal conflicts have vanished from the prologues; France is at peace and so are the prologues' dancers and singers. These peacetime prologues fall into Wood's second category, in which the mood is positive throughout, with only the tiniest of competitive spats between some of the allegorical figures as to who gets to honor the hero the most. The arrival of peace to France happened to coincide with the arrival of professional women dancers at the Opéra, and from 1682 on, the only divisions among troupes in the prologues are between those made up of men and those made up of women. Sometimes these are followers of different deities, at other times members of a single troupe. So not only are the peacetime and wartime prologues very different in tone, they also differ in structure. The prologues to *Atys* and *Armide* may serve to show how these differences play out in practice.

ATYS

The prologue to *Atys* is more complex than most, in that it involves five solo singers and three sets of followers; it is structured into four sections and dances are sprinkled throughout three of them (see Table 5-1). It opens in the palace of Time, who is surrounded by the twelve Hours of the day and the twelve Hours of the night; these form the core of the chorus. Time explains that whereas he respects the memory of the ancient heroes, a new one has eclipsed them all. His choral followers highlight the qualities that bring glory to the new hero: a trio mentions his just laws and a four-part group his great exploits. Because Time's followers are not said to be dancers, there is no reason to think this chorus would have been danced. However, following it a troupe that does include dancers arrives: Flore, the goddess of spring, and her followers. ("La déesse Flore conduite par un des Zéphyrs s'avance avec une troupe de Nymphes qui portent divers ornements de fleurs.") They enter to a graceful rondeau in triple meter whose refrain consists of a five-bar phrase. Whereas the *didascalie* mentions only nymphs, the 1676 court libretto gives Flore six singing nymphs, two dancing nymphs, and four dancing followers. The flowers they carry prompt Time to ask how Flore can

[15] "Par cet auguste roi la Discorde est bannie." [. . .] "Après avoir chanté les fureurs de la guerre, / Chantons les douceurs de la paix."

[16] "On a quitté les armes / Voici le temps heureux / Des plaisirs pleins de charmes, / Voici le temps heureux / Des plaisirs et des jeux."

Table 5-1: *Atys*: outline of the prologue.

	Musical Unit	Character(s)	Key, meter	Comments
I	Recitative	Le Temps	g, —	A new hero has almost erased the memory of the old ones.
	Chorus, "Ses justes loix"	Chœur des Heures	g, **3**	The hero's exploits and just laws make his glory immortal.
II	Air [rondeau]	Nymphes de Flore	g, **3**	Dance bringing in Flore and her followers
	Recitative	Le Temps, Flore	g, —	Flore explains she has arrived during winter to make sure the hero has not yet left.
	Duo	Le Temps, Flore	g, **3**	Both sing that nothing can stop him when Glory [i.e., battlefield] calls.
	Chorus, "Rien ne peut l'arrêter"	Chœur des Heures	g, **3**	Chorus repeats text of 2nd part of duo to similar music.
	Air [gavotte en rondeau]	Suite de Flore	G, ¢	Dance for Flore's followers
	Air	Un Zéphyr	G, **3**	Warns that spring comes at a cost [the hero's departure]; winter is the time when pleasures assemble.
	Repeat of gavotte	Suite de Flore	G, ¢	Flore's followers dance again.
III	Prélude pour Melpomène	Melpomène, suite de Melpomène	C, ¢	Melpomène, Muse of tragedy, enters.
	Recitative	Melpomène	C, —	She tells the others to withdraw, that Cybèle has ordered her to honor the memory of Atys in a "spectacle pompeux."
	Air [binary]	Suite de Melpomène	C, **2**	Dance [mock battle] for the ancient heroes
IV	Ritournelle		G, ¢	
	Recitative	Iris	G, —	Iris arrives to say that Cybèle wants
	Duo	Flore, Melpomène	G, **3**	Flore and Melpomène to join in honoring the "new Mars"; they acquiesce.
	Chorus, "Préparez de nouvelles fêtes"	Chœur des Heures, Flore, Melpomène, le Temps	G, ¢	All wish to take advantage of the hero's current leisure for festivities; he uses this period for contemplating new conquests.
	Menuet	[Suite de Flore, suite de Melpomène]	G, **3**	Dance for all the followers

appear in the middle of winter. She explains that if she were to wait for spring, she would miss the hero, who always leaves for the front when the weather warms: "As soon as he sees Bellone [goddess of war], he abandons everything for her. Nothing can stop him when Glory calls."[17] Despite the fact that a group of dancers is now available, this does not look like the kind of chorus that invites dance: it is sung throughout and the text concerns the hero's rejection of pleasures. However, it is followed by an instrumental "Air pour la Suite de Flore" in gavotte rhythms (Example 4-3, p. 135), which allows Flore's followers to evoke the pleasures the hero is in danger of missing. A Zephyr warns that "spring is sometimes less sweet than it seems; its pleasant days come at a cost. It chases away pleasure and love, and it is winter that reassembles them."[18] Flore's followers offer their choreographic pleasures a second time.[19]

The mood changes abruptly when Melpomène, Muse of tragedy, and a troupe of eight ancient heroes enter to a pompous prélude. After she announces that the goddess Cybèle (who is to figure as a main character in the opera) has instructed her to honor Atys by recounting his story, "the heroes take up their ancient quarrels. Hercule fights and wrestles with Antée; Castor and Pollux battle against Lyncée and Idas; and Ethéocle fights against his brother Polynice" – a rare example of dancing characters with individual identities. The music available for these combats is a single binary "Air pour la suite de Melpomène" (Example 5-1): it is in duple meter with, in its first strain, the rhythms of an *entrée grave* and a harmonic rhythm that changes only once per bar. The second strain increases the level of rhythmic activity and doubles the rate of the harmonic rhythm, a change in musical rhetoric that probably signals a change in the teams of combatants and perhaps in the level of their own physical activity; the piece may have been played more than once. Menestrier's brief comments about staged battles (cited in Chapter 3, p. 89) allow for the combatants to break away from identical movement provided their actions are reciprocal: "Some may deliver blows with a sword or club, and the others parry them with shields." It is interesting to note that the deployment of dancers does not depart from the norm of eight, even though here they seem to be arranged in one group of four and two groups of two. By virtue of its character and its location within the divertissement, this dance does triple duty: to invoke the wars that plague societies, both ancient and modern; to support the claim that the absent hero surpasses even the greatest heroes of antiquity; and to set up the opera to come as a genuine tragedy, one based on conflicts that end in bloodshed.

But the tone changes once again: in the fourth section Iris, the messenger of the gods, appears by order of Cybèle to insist that Melpomène and Flore join forces. A gesture of reconciliation is typical of prologues, but as Cornic has pointed out, Iris's

[17] "Sitôt qu'il voit Bellone, il quitte tout pour elle; / Rien ne peut l'arrêter, / Quand la Gloire l'appelle."

[18] "Le printemps quelquefois est moins doux qu'il ne semble, / Il fait trop payer ses beaux jours; / Il vient pour écarter les Jeux et les Amours, / Et c'est l'hiver qui les rassemble."

[19] Choreographies exist for both dances for Flore's nymphs; see Appendix 3.

Example 5-1: *Atys* prologue, "Air pour la suite de Melpomène" (Paris: Ballard, 1689), 29–30.

words constitute a statement of poetics, an acknowledgement that the pastoral realm is to be allowed into the operatic enterprise, albeit in a subordinate position.[20] As in the prologue to *Thésée*, the court is depicted as a refuge from war where the arts flourish:

Iris: Cybèle veut que Flore aujourd'hui vous seconde,
Il faut que les Plaisirs viennent de toutes parts,
Dans l'empire puissant, où regne un nouveau Mars,
Ils n'ont plus d'autre asile au monde.
Rendez-vous, s'il se peut, dignes de ses regards,
Joignez la beauté vive et pure
Dont brille la Nature,
Aux ornements des plus beaux Arts.

(Today Cybèle wants Flore to assist you. The Pleasures must come from everywhere to this powerful empire where a new Mars rules; they have no other refuge in the world. Make yourself, if possible, worthy of his esteem; join the pure lively beauty with which Nature shines to the most beautiful ornaments of the Arts.)

Melpomène and Flore dutifully join their voices to indicate compliance and their two troupes follow their lead, first in a chorus in which Time, Flore, and Melpomène also sing ("Préparez/Préparons de nouvelles fêtes") and then in an instrumental menuet. Although neither the score nor the libretto makes the function of this piece explicit, it is the only unambiguous place where the heroes attached to Melpomène and Flore's followers can join in dance.

In this prologue, then, it would appear that the dancing was confined to the four instrumental pieces: two for the followers of Flore, which are separated from each other by vocal music; one for the ancient heroes; and the menuet where the two groups

20 Cornic, "Ad limina," 61–62.

join. The dances thus provide visual reinforcement for the conventional narrative arc of a prologue – two groups in opposition who are brought together in admiration of the hero – and their musical differences serve to heighten the sense of separation that the eventual reconciliation overcomes. These instrumental dances do not exhibit the same degree of musical connection to the adjacent vocal pieces as do the dances inside the five acts of an opera. The *entrée-grave* type piece for the heroes would not be expected to have such a connection, but of the remaining three, none is part of a dance-song unit. The two triple-meter dances are adjacent to triple-meter choruses, but overall the connections between vocal music and the dances seem relatively attenuated. Whereas dance-songs can be found in prologues (see Figure 2-7, from *Bellérophon*), the greater independence that dance music tends to be accorded in them seems to be a product of how the various troupes of performers are defined. In the prologue to *Atys*, the singing chorus, consisting of the Hours of the day and night, does not dance. The two troupes that do dance – Flore's followers and the ancient heroes – may not sing.[21] This greater separation between singing and dancing group characters might be due to practical staging considerations. Whereas in the main body of the opera the chorus goes off stage every act and can change costumes, variety in choral roles in a prologue would require more choral singers. But whatever the reason, prologues overall exhibit a looser connection between dance and vocal music than do the divertissements within the operas.

ARMIDE

The prologue to *Armide* was composed during a period in which France was engaged in no foreign wars. Two allegorical figures, Glory and Wisdom, enumerate the hero's virtues (see their encomiastic verses above, p. 141), and each champions one of the same two attributes the prologue to *Atys* evokes: his laws and his exploits. However, they are in agreement from the start ("We love the same conqueror with equal tenderness"); the only question is which loves him better. Presumably because peace reigns, Quinault gives Wisdom more to say than Glory; it is she who points out that the hero has defeated a monster that had been thought invincible – an allusion to Louis XIV's decision of the preceding year (12 October 1685) to revoke the Edict of Nantes in which king Henri IV had declared a policy of tolerance towards Protestants. By the time *Armide* was first performed, in February of 1686, thousands of Huguenot "heretics" had left France for more tolerant shores.

[21] The cast list in the libretto (as printed in the *Recueil général*) does indicate that some of Flore's nymphs sing, and the 1676 court libretto calls for six singing heroes in addition to the eight who dance. But the *didascalies* in the prologue proper allude to the chorus consistently as the Chœur des Heures. Perhaps both indications are historically accurate and the performances at court involved a larger singing cast than did those in Paris.

Both Glory and Wisdom, the only two solo singers in the prologue, are on stage with their followers from the start, which means that the kinds of structures Quinault set up in *Atys* to pit an arriving figure against one already present do not pertain. Instead, a distinction into troupes plays out only as differences in gender. Whereas both allegorical figures are portrayed as women, the followers of Glory are defined as heroes, those of Wisdom as nymphs. This dichotomy allowed Lully to set the groups off musically and choreographically. The first chorus, which picks up the words uttered by the two soloists, consists of a double chorus in which the followers of Wisdom, set as a high trio, alternate with a four-part vocal texture representing the followers of Glory. ("Let us sing of the mildness of his laws," "Let us sing of his glorious exploits."[22]) Shortly before the end of the chorus (mm. 121–29) there is an instrumental passage that also alternates textures, a high trio that is set against Lully's usual five-part orchestral texture. If the textures can be taken as a cue, then the dancing nymphs may well have traded phrases with the dancing heroes, and probably continued to do so during the last singing of the text. The introduction of dance at the earliest possible moment is a harbinger of things to come: this prologue, notwithstanding the small number of troupes and their high degree of agreement, has much more dance in it than does the prologue to *Atys* (see Table 5-2).

After Wisdom and Glory's tiny spat as to which one of them loves the hero more ("Disputons seulement à qui sait mieux l'aimer") – an expression of disagreement that is completely undermined by the fact that they sing it in parallel thirds – their followers similarly move closer to full agreement. The chorus that grows out of the duet still alternates vocal textures, but the two groups share the key text, "Can one know him and not love him?" ("Peut-on le connaître / Et ne l'aimer pas?") Likewise, the three instrumental dances that follow seem designed to showcase a developing sense of unity: "The followers of Glory and the followers of Wisdom, show, through their dances, the joy they feel at seeing these two divinities in perfect agreement."

As is so often the case, clues as to who dances what have to come from the musical rhetoric. The first dance, entitled simply "Entrée," starts off like a majestic *entrée grave* and is notated in the usual five parts; however, on a half cadence after four and a half measures it switches to a trio of flutes that maintains some dotted rhythms but has a much gentler character. The alternation of textures and affect continues throughout this binary piece: each group plays twice in each strain (see Example 5-2.) It is hard not to hear this compositional choice as designed to accompany choreographic alternation between the male followers of Glory and the female followers of Wisdom. No two musical phrases are identical until the end of the second strain, when a seven-bar descending sequence played by the flutes is repeated by the full orchestra. If we once

[22] "Chantons, chantons la douceur de ses loix," "Chantons, chantons ses glorieux exploits." See Rosow, "Performing a choral dialogue."

Table 5-2: *Armide*: outline of the prologue.

	Musical Unit	Characters	Key, meter	Paraphrase of sung texts/ comments
I	Airs, duo	La Gloire, la Sagesse	C, **3**	The hero's virtues are enumerated.
	Chorus, "Chantons, chantons la douceur de ses loix"	Suite de la Sagesse, suite de la Gloire	C, **3**	The double chorus praises the hero's laws on the one hand, his exploits on the other.
	Duos, recitative	La Gloire, la Sagesse	C→a	Wisdom and Glory disagree only as to who loves the hero more.
	Chorus, "Dès qu'on le voit paraître"	Suite de la Sagesse, suite de la Gloire	a, **3**	Those who see the hero love him.
	Entrée Menuet Gavotte	[Suite de la Sagesse, suite de la Gloire]	a, **2** a, **3** a, **2**	First two dances probably danced by the two troupes in alternation, the third all together.
II	Prélude, airs, then chorus, "Que l'éclat de son nom"	La Sagesse, la Gloire, followers of both	C, **3**	This large unit, which introduces the subject of the opera to follow, eventually returns to the chorus "Chantons la douceur de ses loix."
	Entrée Premier Menuet Second Menuet	[Suite de la Sagesse, suite de la Gloire]	C, **2** C, **3** C, **3**	"The followers of Glory and those of Wisdom continue their celebrations."
	Duo → Chorus "C'est à lui"	Two male members of chorus, then tutti	C, **3**	The hero has united Wisdom and Glory.

again take our cue from the music, this mixing of the melody from one group with the texture associated with the other suggests that this is the place where the two troupes join for the first time.

The next dance, identified as a menuet, alternates the same two textures. The binary structure is fully written out, but the only real difference is the texture; melody and harmony are the same.

A	a3
A′	a5
B	a3
B′	a5

This dance, where textures alternate but the music is the same, seems similar in idea to the earlier chorus "Peut-on le connaître," where the two groups singing began to downplay their differences. Perhaps here the followers of Wisdom danced the a3

Example 5-2: *Armide* prologue, "Entrée" (Paris: Ballard, 1681), xxvi.

sections, but both groups participated when the full orchestra played. Certainly by the third dance in this group, a gavotte en rondeau, the two groups must have become one: the texture is a5 throughout.

Following this visual expression of unity, Wisdom lays out the moral of the opera that is to follow: "We will see Renaud, in spite of sensuality, follow sage advice and escape from the enchanted palace where, through love, Armide had held him prisoner, and fly to where Glory calls him."[23] The on-stage Glory then summons everyone to join their voices in celebrating the king who is sponsoring this spectacle; her words are picked up by a chorus that transforms itself back into the earlier double chorus, "Chantons, chantons." The two groups of singers and dancers re-enact their separation

[23] "Nous y verrons Renaud, malgré la volupté, / Suivre un conseil fidèle et sage; / Nous le verrons sortir du palais enchanté / Où, par l'amour d'Armide, il était arrêté, / Et voler où la Gloire appelle son courage."

and coming together, and a *didascalie* reveals that "the followers of Glory and the followers of Wisdom continue their celebrations." Here follow three more instrumental dances, a male duet that is akin to the menuets (voices provided by singers from the chorus), and a related chorus that seems designed to end the prologue with full participation by everyone on stage:

Que dans le temple de Mémoire
Son nom soit pour jamais gravé,
C'est à lui qu'il est reservé
D'unir la Sagesse et la Gloire.

(In the temple of memory may his name be engraved forever; it is he alone who unites Wisdom and Glory.)

In these and other prologues, dance has a more circumscribed niche than it does in the five acts of a *tragédie*. Its most common role is to amplify the words of allegorical figures who represent essences and who do not develop or change. Their followers thus have little particularity and are mostly called upon to celebrate.[24] The range of character types is relatively narrow (followers of Victory do not differ much from followers of Glory), especially when compared with the enormous variety of roles Lully calls upon in the divertissements. Given that dancers in prologues mostly engage in diegetic dancing – "The followers of Peace show their joy by dancing and singing," reports the libretto to *Proserpine* – it is unsurprising to find that prologues have a higher percentage of generic dance types than do the divertissements. Gavottes and menuets are particularly in evidence: there are three menuets and one gavotte in the prologue to *Armide*, and the instrumental dances in the prologue to *Roland* consist entirely of a gigue, two menuets, and a gavotte. These two dance types were central to ballroom practices; during the time that Lully was composing his stage works the gavotte separated itself from the suite of branles that opened every formal ball and the menuet was pushing aside the courante as the ballroom dance par excellence. Virtually everyone in the audience at the Opéra would have known how to dance gavottes and menuets; they would thus have been lifted onto the stage, into participating in the encomiastic celebrations, by the muscle-memory of their own bodies.

In their trope of setting up a dialectic that achieves a resolution enacted in both song and dance, Lully's prologues bear similarities to the operas' conclusions. Final choruses may collapse the distinction between the honoree of the prologue and the male protagonist of the opera by once again invoking an unnamed "hero." This is the case in *Bellérophon*, which ends with choruses whose texts would be perfectly at home in the

24 Exceptions include the prologues to *Cadmus et Hermione*, where some of the dancers embody whirlwinds, and *Proserpine*, where demons, the followers of Discord, are routed by the followers of Victory.

prologue: "The greatest of heroes has returned peace to the earth . . . During the beautiful days that a hero has given us, let us enjoy laughter, games, and pleasures."[25] The ends of prologues and the ends of Lully's operas must have looked similar as well, with an enormous cast crowded onto the stage and a large group of dancers in motion.

25 "Le plus grand des héros rend le calme à la terre . . . "; the opera concludes with the words, "Dans les beaux jours qu'un héros nous ramène, / Cherchons les ris, les jeux et les plaisirs."

6 | The Lighter Side of Lully

When the curtain rose at the Académie Royale de Musique in 1672 for the performance of Lully's very first opera, the pastorale *Les Fêtes de l'Amour et de Bacchus*, the audience saw a caricatured mirror image of itself: in a beautiful theater, several pushy provincials, seated in the balconies, compete with each other for the attention of the man distributing librettos. A Swiss complains bitterly in his thick accent that he is losing his voice from shouting for attention, an aging bourgeoise whines that it is shameful to neglect a woman who was once the ornament of the Palais-Royal quarter, while the couple with social pretensions argue that their status should give them precedence. Just as the man with the librettos has succeeded in satisfying his customers, a cloud descends from the heavens to reveal Polymnie, the Muse "who presides over the arts dependent upon geometry."[1] "Elevate your music-making above ordinary song," she preaches, "and remember that you are here to please the greatest king in the universe." Her appeal provokes the arrival of two other Muses: Melpomène ("who presides over tragedy") and Euterpe ("who invented pastoral harmony"). Suddenly the scene has shifted from the realm of comedy to the exalted reaches of Mount Parnassus. But Melpomène and Euterpe begin to quarrel about which one of them will control the opera to follow. Polymnie decides in favor of Euterpe – the still-visible theater audience will see a pastorale – and tells Melpomène that tragedy's turn will come soon.[2] The three Muses agree to join forces. The audience that had earlier been competing for librettos now expresses the collective wish to please the greatest of kings.

In one sense, this peculiar prologue, in which ordinary workmen rub elbows with the Muses, roughly traces the trajectory of Lully's own career, from the low comedy of his early ballets to the *tragédie en musique* to come, from the biting social satire of Molière (for it was he who had penned the *donneur de livres* scene[3]) to the more judicious versifying of his new collaborator, Quinault. The sterner Muses do, after all, push aside their sister Thalie, Muse of comedy, who, though absent, presides in

[1] The characterization for each Muse comes from *didascalies* in the libretto. Quinault shaded the definitions to suit his own purposes; Polymnie is further characterized as the Muse "who has discovered the means of ushering onto the stage characters who through actions and dances express what others explain in words." In Classical antiquity Polyhymnia was the Muse of the sublime hymn, Euterpe of lyric poetry.

[2] *Cadmus et Hermione* was already in preparation; see La Gorce, *Lully*, 580.

[3] Molière had written it two years earlier, as the prologue to the "Ballet des nations" that concludes the *Bourgeois gentilhomme*. By the time Lully reused it in *Les Fêtes de l'Amour et de Bacchus*, their partnership had ended.

spirit over the opening scene.[4] Yet as the prologue also spells out, the operas that Quinault and Lully were to write would be a mixed genre, one that would unite tragedy with the pastorale – and even, sometimes, with the comic. Couvreur reads the second part of this prologue as Quinault's *art poétique*, the expression of his aesthetic vision for opera that he did not otherwise commit to paper. Couvreur perceptively points out that "Polymnie does not denounce either comedy or the pastoral. She invites them to raise the tone and to fit themselves into the mold for tragedy. This was to become the aesthetic basis for *Cadmus et Hermione*, *Alceste*, and *Thésée*."[5] Yet even after Quinault eschewed the overt comic elements that color his first three *tragédies en musique*, humor maintained a presence on the stage of the Académie Royale de Musique. Just as the on-stage audience modified its attitude but did not leave when the Muses arrived, so Lully kept Thalie within confines, but never abandoned her.

Lully's thirteen *tragédies en musique* have so dominated the historiography of his works for the Opéra that it is easy to ignore the ones with a very different character. Whereas the *tragédies* garnered more attention in their own day, not just in ours, the other works were successful enough to get revived, in whole or in part, on into the eighteenth century. The generic labels attached to these six works include pastorale, ballet, mascarade, and divertissement; the works themselves are lighter in character than the *tragédies*, or, in places, comic. Even some of the *tragédies* have comic moments, particularly the ones written before Quinault was pressured by his critics to maintain an elevated tone throughout. But although Quinault mostly complied in his subsequent works, the suspect operas were revived without rewriting. Moreover, Lully's operatic career ended as it had opened, with a three-act pastorale. Ariane Ducrot has hypothesized that before Lully died, he was moving in the direction of a repertoire that would alternate *tragédies* with lighter works.[6] Lully's own audience (and those who attended the Académie Royale de Musique in the eighteenth century) had a much broader view of his compositional output than we do today. Below is a list of the works Lully put on the stage of the Opéra that either belong to a genre other than the *tragédie en musique*, or are *tragédies* that include comic elements.[7]

1672: *Les Fêtes de l'Amour et de Bacchus* (pastorale)
1673: *Cadmus et Hermione* (tragédie en musique)
1674: *Alceste* (tragédie en musique)
1675: *Thésée* (tragédie en musique)
1675: *Le Carnaval* (mascarade)
1677: revival of *Thésée*

[4] In his discussion of a poster advertising this opera, La Gorce concludes that the allegorical figures on the lower edge are Euterpe and Thalie; see his "Lully's first opera."

[5] Couvreur, *Lully*, 286–90. [6] Ducrot, "Les représentations," 35.

[7] This list includes only works performed on the Opéra's public stage in Paris.

1678: revivals of *Cadmus et Hermione* and *Thésée*
1678: *Psyché* (tragédie en musique)
1681: *Le Triomphe de l'Amour* (ballet)
1682: revivals of *Alceste* and *Le Triomphe de l'Amour*
1685: *L'Idylle sur la paix* (divertissement) and *Le Temple de la paix* (ballet)
1686: *Acis et Galatée* (pastorale)

Whereas the category of works that are not *tragédies* defines itself, identifying which among the *tragédies* have enough comic elements to be singled out is a slipperier proposition. *Cadmus et Hermione* and *Alceste* both show vestiges of Venetian operatic traditions in their inclusion of comic characters (such as the randy old nurse played by a man) and frivolous subplots among servants. *Thésée* also has a subplot, but one that involves characters of higher social standing who behave themselves with more decorum; whereas there is some frivolous dialogue that attracted opprobrium, the plainest element of humor comes in the Act II divertissement, which includes a song and a dance for ridiculous old folks. This deflection of the comic into the divertissements was to become frequent in the next generation, but it can be seen (or argued) in some of Lully's other works as well. The divertissement in Act IV of *Atys*, set in the palace of the river god Sangar, is one possible candidate; the vignette of people shivering from cold in Act IV of *Isis* is another, and an unambiguous case can be found in the divertissement that concludes *Psyché*, which introduces Momus (the god of mockery), a troupe of Polichinelles, and a drunken Bacchus.

Both categories of works – *tragédies* with comic elements and ones belonging to other genres – are worth examining, because they use dance in different ways and invite varied styles of movement. The following section highlights points of particular interest and ones where Lully's practices opened up possibilities for his successors.

LES FÊTES DE L'AMOUR ET DE BACCHUS

It is perhaps indicative of the central place dance was to acquire in Lully's operas that the first person the audience saw moving around the stage in his first operatic work was a dancer:[8]

> The stage represents a large room where the most superb ornaments that architecture and painting can furnish are seen. It is set up for a magnificent spectacle and in the background is

[8] *Les Fêtes de l'Amour et de Bacchus* premiered on 11 November 1672. Any conclusions drawn about this opera – a pastiche of scenes from Lully's ballets and comedy-ballets, with some new text and music – must be provisional until a critical edition has been prepared. The score published by Ballard is very late (1717), after revivals in 1689, 1696, and 1706. My remarks are based on the 1717 score.

> seen a large vestibule opened to reveal a superb palace in the middle of a garden.[9] A multitude of people from different provinces are seated in balconies along the two sides of the stage. A man charged with distributing librettos to the spectators starts to dance as soon as the curtain rises. The entire crowd in the balconies shouts out in music, demanding librettos, but he is prevented from distributing them by four irksome individuals who follow and surround him.

The first key point is that the Donneur de livres does not just dance, but mimes, as he attempts fruitlessly to hand out librettos to the overeager provincials.[10] Second, the people calling out "À moi, Monsieur" are not the ones grasping for the librettos; the singers uttering those words are seated in the balconies on either side of the stage – gesturing, perhaps, but fixed to one spot[11] – and the people actively pestering the poor man with the librettos are four other dancers, the "Importuns." This is not precisely the same type of double-casting of chorus and dancers that was to become the norm, but the staging does rely on a division of labor between those who move and those who sing. Third, the cries of the individuals and the attempts by the Donneur to ward off the Importuns might be happening simultaneously. Whereas there is a brief instrumental introduction – a binary "Symphonie" with eleven bars in the first strain and ten in the second – before the eager spectators start shouting for their books, it seems short for all the action, which has to cover what has been described above plus the Donneur's withdrawal, exhausted, after the first round of strident demands. After the members of the on-stage audience have been given a chance to complain about the poor service, the Donneur de livres returns, with the Importuns still trailing him, which sets off another round of "À moi, Monsieur" from the singers. This time, however, the Importuns decide to help, and set to work to the strains of a sprightly piece in triple meter:

> The Importuns, having taken librettos from the hands of the person giving them out, distribute them to the spectators demanding them. Meanwhile the Donneur de livres dances; the Importuns join him and together they form the first entrée.

The *didascalie* implies that there are two sets of events: first, the Importuns finish distributing the librettos, and next they dance with the Donneur de livres. In this case, then, mimed action and dance seem to have been done consecutively. There is, however, only one piece of music available to absorb both – the otherwise unlabeled "Air" that constitutes the "Première Entrée" – a lively but very square binary piece with

9 Could this detail, which does not appear in the *Bourgeois gentilhomme*, represent yet another instance of self-reflexivity? Lully's first opera house was a converted *jeu de paume* court on the Rue de Vaugirard, very near the Palais du Luxembourg – a superb palace in the middle of a garden.

10 Over the years, this role was performed by some of the troupe's leading dancers, including Beauchamps, Pécour, and Blondy.

11 See Ch. 2, pp. 37–39 and Figs. 2-5 and 9-1 for other examples of seated choruses.

consistent rhythms throughout that has the profile of a canarie.[12] Nothing in the music corresponds to the probable change in movement style that must have occurred either within the piece or upon its repeat. The question of musical rhetoric for a comic dance – the extent to which the music does or does not reflect the choreographic highjinks – thus emerges in Lully's very first opera.

Even after three Muses arrive ceremoniously on cloud machines and Polymnie insists that the tone be raised, in order to honor "the greatest king in the universe," humor is not kept completely at bay. It returns in a gentle mode, in the ludicrous comingling of three disparate groups – four each of heroes, shepherds, and workmen – who join in preparing for the upcoming performance. Although the libretto does not label the dancers as "followers," each group belongs to one of the Muses: the heroes are there to support Melpomène, Muse of tragedy; the shepherds Euterpe, the pastoral Muse; and the workmen Polymnie, whose emblems in this prologue are "several ornaments of painting and architecture." (These twelve are unambiguously dancers; the chorus remains the on-stage audience):

> Heroes, herdsmen, and workmen obey the orders from the Muses. The heroes engage in a kind of combat with their weapons; the herdsmen play with their sticks, and the workmen work on the sets for the pastorale to follow, and synchronize the sound of their hammers, saws, and planes with the music of the violins and oboes.

Here again, only one piece of music is available, but this one has textural, metric, and rhythmic changes that suggest that the groups danced separately (see Example 6-1). The first strain, governed by majestic dotted rhythms, must belong to the heroes. At the double bar simultaneous changes from duple to triple meter and from a five- to a four-part texture signal that the shepherds take over.[13] When, after eight bars, the full five-part texture returns but the meter stays triple, the workmen must pick up their tools, also to an eight-bar phrase. Further alternations in texture suggest more back-and-forth between the shepherds and the workmen, who perhaps dance simultaneously to conclude the strain. Nothing in the concluding bars hints that the heroes would have joined them there, although a grand reunion is not out of the question. On one level it makes sense for the heroes to drop out visually, since Polymnie has just told Melpomène that she will have to wait her turn. On the other hand, all three groups of dancers and all three Muses do figure as part of the chorus that concludes the prologue. An engraving by Le Pautre for the prologue appears to show this dance – or a conflated version of it – with the heroes in the foreground, the herdsmen behind them, and the workmen in the rear.[14]

12 The piece, which replaces a duple-meter piece Lully had used in the *Bourgeois gentilhomme*, is identified as a canarie in two manuscript sources; see *LWV* 47/3.

13 In Lully's stage works, four-part textures are generally intended for wind instruments; see Ch. 4, p. 133.

14 See La Gorce, "Lully's first opera," fig. 2.

Example 6-1: *Les Fêtes de l'Amour et de Bacchus* prologue, "Quatre Héros, quatre Pâtres et quatre Ouvriers forment la seconde entrée. Premier Air" (Paris: Ballard, 1717), 29–30.

It is perhaps a measure of the comic character of the pastorale proper (most of which can be attributed to Molière[15]) that the two title gods never appear; they exist only through the imaginations of their adherents, who live firmly on earth. The other key word in the title, "Fêtes," would seem to mean that the work is framed as festivities, which might make the dancing diegetic and frequent. Yet the amount of dancing is restrained and the three acts continue the two functions exhibited in the prologue: dancing and miming. These movement styles largely divide along the lines of the two sets of group characters: the shepherds who are in Love's camp and the satyrs who follow Bacchus. At the end of Act I, fauns are invited by the shepherds to "join your steps with our sounds and trace upon the grass the image of our songs." This purely diegetic dancing is performed by four fauns and four dryades, starting with a piece in triple meter comprising some of Lully's most regular seven- and five-bar phrases. In the next act, however, which takes place in the realm of the satyrs, the dancers, disguised as demons, participate in a fake magic ceremony that the ugly Forestan thinks will make him handsome. To two appropriately distinct instrumental airs, interspersed with ludicrous songs by the witches, they engage in hocus-pocus and dress him "in a ridiculous and bizarre manner" (II/2). When Forestan realizes he has been duped, he decides to get drunk (II/4–5). In Act III, when the shepherds' love intrigues have been happily resolved, the pastoral characters join in a fête to honor Love, framed as a series of dance-songs. The celebratory but languorous party is suddenly interrupted by a rival fête in honor of Bacchus, whose followers arrive riding wine barrels and playing instruments. Each side proclaims its own god as "le plus grand des dieux." Fisticuffs ensue among the dancers, while the singers take sides: "Ah! quel plaisir d'aimer!" sing Love's supporters, while the others respond, "Ah! quel plaisir de boire!" Inevitably, the combatants reconcile; their unanimity is expressed in a dance for four each of shepherds, shepherdesses, satyrs, and bacchantes and in a chorus:

> Mêlons donc leurs douceurs aimables,
> Mêlons nos voix, dans ces lieux agréables,
> Et faisons répéter aux échos d'alentour,
> Qu'il n'est rien de plus doux que Bacchus et l'Amour.
>
> ("Let us mingle their pleasing pleasures, / Let us mingle our voices in these agreeable places, / And let us make the echoes repeat / That nothing is sweeter than Bacchus and Love.")

CADMUS ET HERMIONE, ALCESTE, AND *THÉSÉE*

By the next year, when Lully and Quinault readied their first *tragédie en musique* for the stage, they had considerably raised the tone for their new theater. Yet in both *Cadmus et Hermione* and *Alceste,* comic elements figured within the sung text, among them the

[15] See La Gorce, *Lully*, 563–64, for the origins of each scene.

cowardly servant Arbas and the randy old nurse (sung by a man) in *Cadmus et Hermione*, or, in *Alceste*, Charon insisting upon a gratuity before he will ferry souls across the River Styx. The comic also played out in at least one divertissement per opera. In *Cadmus et Hermione* I/4 the Africans dancing for Hermione at Cadmus's behest are joined by some unwelcome giants, who probably galumph around the stage.[16] In *Alceste*, the comic attaches to the bumpkin herdsmen who surround Straton in the final divertissement. The old Athenians in *Thésée* II/7 intend to kick up their heels for whatever time remains to them ("Life holds charms right up to the end"; see Figure 1-2, p. 21). Whereas from one angle these vignettes seem superfluous, or, from a perspective of generic purity, even pernicious, a case can be made that Quinault conceptualized them as part of the whole.[17] He and Lully did nonetheless feel compelled to eschew the comic in their later *tragédies*. The Abbé Dubos pointed out that "no sooner had Quinault written two operas than he realized that roles for buffoons – essential in Italian opera – were not appropriate in operas designed for the French. *Thésée* was the last opera in which Quinault introduced buffoons ... "[18] As Mme de Sévigné put it, the comic was eschewed "in order to erase Venice."[19]

Discussions of Lully's abandonment of the comic, however, overlook the fact that all three of his early *tragédies* stayed in the repertoire on into the eighteenth century. *Cadmus et Hermione* was revived eight times between its premiere and 1737, complete with the comic role for the nurse, always sung by a man. The basso buffo Charon, forever holding out his hand for bribes, never disappeared from the much-revived *Alceste*, nor did the comic old men from *Thésée* (eleven revivals, the last in 1779).[20] These humorous scenes occupy only a small proportion of the elapsed time of the operas, and are less ribald than comparable scenes in Venetian operas. Nonetheless, their decades-long presence on the stage of the Opéra means that Parisian audiences received a multifaceted image of what Lully's *tragédies en musique* could encompass.

[16] There is a discrepancy between the *didascalie* in the main text of the libretto, which calls for giants as well as Africans, and the cast list for the court libretto of 1678, which names nine dancers performing as Africans but no giants; see my article "La danse dans *Cadmus et Hermione*," 239–41.

[17] See Ch. 1, pp. 11 and 20.

[18] Dubos, *Réflexions critiques*, I, 178, as cited in Couvreur, *Lully*, 292. Cahusac was later to argue that Quinault had courted trouble by calling his operas "tragédies," a designation that made comparison with spoken tragedy inevitable: *La Danse*, III, 94–96; trans, Wood and Sadler, *French Baroque Opera*, 46.

[19] Letter of 24 November 1673, cited in Couvreur, *Lully*, 291.

[20] Parfaict, *Histoire*, names a handful of dancers who attracted attention in the 1707 revival, but the only dancing roles mentioned are the two old couples, who were performed by four of the best dancers in the troupe (cited in Denécheau, "*Thésée* de Lully, " 390). In 1765, the Opéra's director, Berton, tried to cut the vocal duet for the two old men, but reinstated it by popular demand, and although in 1766 the Act II divertissement was transformed into a massive scene for Athenians of all ages, the vocal duet remained, as it did through the last revival. See Denécheau, 440, 445, 455, and 619–20.

LE CARNAVAL

Carnival, the season of pre-Lent gaiety, disguise, and amorous intrigue, supplies the governing affect for this plotless work. Qualified as a mascarade – a word that sometimes is subsumed into its title – *Le Carnaval* harks back in its structure to Lully's court ballets, which comprise a series of entrées for different sets of characters. But in distinction to the ballets, where dance is the dominant art, the framework for each of these little vignettes is vocal.[21] The true novelty of the work, however, is not that most of the entrées were comic, but that the characters within them were people from the contemporary world. There is not a mythological character, or even a pastoral one, to be found in *Le Carnaval*. This is not to say that the characters are naturalistic, but rather that they are grounded in the world of the comic theater, not of the *tragédie en musique* or the pastorale.[22] The singers and dancers incarnate Italians, Spaniards, gypsies, Arlequins, Basques, and Turks. The musical and choreographic styles arising from these characterizations were not all new, but they were new to the Académie Royale de Musique, whose prestigious stage accorded them a public presence that had enormous implications for the future. The range of expressive possibilities at the Opéra was broadened in a single stroke.

Like *Les Fêtes de l'Amour et de Bacchus*, *Le Carnaval* is a pastiche, but with some new music. *Le Carnaval* is framed as a party and requires only a single set: "the theater represents a *salle de spectacle*, where all sorts of masked figures may be received." After an introduction by Carnival personified, eight groups appear in turn, each performing songs and dances appropriate to the roles they have adopted. This is very much like what would have happened at a Carnival ball at court, where it was not uncommon for guests costumed all alike to perform set pieces they had prepared in advance.[23] The masked ball that is theatricalized in *Le Carnaval* features a parade of characters from Lully's ballets and comedy-ballets. Lully probably selected those scenes that not only worked within the festive framework but that had known the most success; this pastiche thus gives us a sense of what audiences of the day found appealing. The various characters sing in four different languages, but readers of the libretto were not provided with translations;[24] perhaps the dancers had to help put the texts across even more than they usually did.

21 The word "entrée" acquired a broadened meaning here, in that a single set of characters could generate a much longer scene than the dance or two of an "entrée" in a court ballet. This meaning broadened still further in the genre of opera-ballet, where an entrée becomes the equivalent of an act; see Ch. 7, p. 209.

22 In the revival of 1700 a pastoral entrée ("Bergerie") was added; it appears in the 1720 Ballard score as Entrée IV.

23 See my "Ballroom dancing," 46–48. It is curious, given the season for Carnival (which generally fell during January and February), that this work probably premiered in October; see La Gorce, *Lully*, 566.

24 Some librettos do translate foreign texts; in the operatic *Psyché* the "Plainte italienne" receives a verse translation.

The modular construction of *Le Carnaval* means that entrées could be slotted in or out – which they were, in the revivals of 1692 and 1700. As a result of the complicated performance history, the sources for *Le Carnaval* are very messy. For the purposes of this discussion I have relied on the libretto in the *Recueil général*, which adheres to the one published by Baudry at the work's first performance, and on the full score published by Ballard in 1720, which stays fairly close to this libretto. In 1675 the work included the sections outlined in Table 6-1.

The many Italianisms in *Le Carnaval* expose not only Lully's own roots, but the long interpenetration of commedia dell'arte into French theater. Italian comedians had resided in Paris more often than not since the middle of the sixteenth century, but the troupe that established itself there in 1661 was soon given the status of "comédiens du roi," which meant that it was subsidized by the royal treasury. Even before then the Italians had performed frequently at court, both on their own and in joint productions with other actors, musicians, or dancers.[25] *L'Amour malade* (1657), for example, consisted of a burlesque play in Italian, for which Lully composed extensive music for the French dancers. Conversely, Lully's French ballet and comedy-ballet scores are sprinkled with songs in Italian – such as the lament that survived into the operatic version of *Psyché* – and he himself created some of the comic bass roles, such as that of Barbacola, which got recycled in *Le Carnaval*. In the imported Italian troupe, the actors were better known by the roles they played than by their own names. The two stars of the Italian troupe during Lully's early career were Scaramouche (Tiberio Fiorelli) – whose role derived from the blustering *capitan* and whose costume was entirely black – and Trivelin (Domenico Locatelli) – a valet type whose costume and demeanor were similar to Arlequin's. Both were known for their agile bodies; Scaramouche was famous for generating laughter by his movements alone. Perhaps the dancing Scaramouches and Trivelins that appear on the stage of the Opéra from *Le Carnaval* onwards – usually in groups – represent a tribute by way of imitation of these two magisterial performers.

In 1675 both character types were called upon to dance in the fourth entrée, "Italiens," whose two singers represent another category of characters, the *innamorati* (lovers). Since Carnival balls brought in professional performers from time to time, the implicit conceit here is that actors from the Théâtre Italien (see Figure 6-1) are making a guest appearance.[26] The entrée has no plot; rather it samples what this theater has to offer. First to appear is a Musicienne italienne; her strophic song reveals that she had once resisted love, but now is reveling in its sweet torments.[27] Next

[25] See Mazouer, "Les Comédiens italiens."

[26] Several of Lully's court ballets – the *Ballet des Muses*, for example – intersperse little plays by either the French or Italian comedians. Perhaps the Italian entrée in *Le Carnaval* alludes to that tradition, since performing a spoken scene was not admissible on the stage of the Opéra.

[27] The text was appropriated by von Hofmannsthal for the Italian tenor who performs in Act I of *Der Rosenkavalier*.

Table 6-1: Outline of *Le Carnaval* as it was performed in 1675.

	Source	Language	Synopsis
[Prol.]	*Le Carnaval, mascarade* (1668)	French	Carnival calls upon his followers to use the pleasures of the season to amuse "the greatest king in the world." The chorus agrees that the time for pleasure is now, since spring means a return to warfare.
Entrée I	"Ballet des nations," *Bourgeois gentilhomme* (1670)	Spanish	A Spaniard complains about the pains of love; two other Spaniards attempt to console him, as do the six dancers.
II	*Les Noces de village* (1663)	Italian	A village school master named Barbacola boasts of his exploits, rebukes, consoles, and then dances with his four pupils.
III	*Monsieur de Pourceaugnac*[a] (1669)	French and Italian	Pourceaugnac, an Italian bourgeois accused of bigamy, appeals for help from two lawyers, both of whom tell him repeatedly that polygamy is a capital offense. Next two quack doctors try to cheer him up, first by suggesting wine and tobacco, then by urging an enema upon him, as they chase him around the stage.
IV	"Ballet des nations," *Bourgeois gentilhomme* (1670)	Italian	Scene mixing serious and comic songs and dances "in the manner of the Italian comedians" and involving dancing commedia characters such as Arlequin, Scaramouches, and Trivelins.
V	*Bourgeois gentilhomme* (1670)	"Turkish" = lingua franca[b]	The famous Turkish ceremony during which Monsieur Jourdain is duped by a phony Mufti into thinking he is being inducted into a secret Turkish society.
VI	*Ballet royal de Flore* (1669)	French	A double-edged serenade for a bride and groom (dancing roles), warning them that Love is not always invited to weddings.
VII	*La Pastorale comique* (1667)	French	An Egyptienne (gypsy), who both sings about unrequited love and dances, is accompanied by Bohémiens playing guitars, Basques playing castanets, and Egyptiens playing nakers.
VIII	*Le Carnaval, mascarade* (1668)	French	Gallantry, personified and accompanied by two Basques and five Polichinelles (dancers), offers maxims about love to both men and women.
IX	*Le Carnaval, mascarade* (1668)	French	Carnival joins Gallantry and together they urge their followers, who show up from all the previous entrées, to sing and dance, while the season lasts.

[a] All the music sung by the title character is new; Molière's original character, a speaking role, was a Limousin who goes to Paris to get married and is the victim of a series of hoaxes.

[b] Lingua franca was a trading language used in the Mediterranean basin.

Figure 6-1: "The royal troupe of Italian comedians performing at the Hôtel de Bourgogne all kinds of plays on subjects both ancient and modern, serious and comic." On the left: Aurelio, Isabelle, the Doctor, Colombine, Diamantine (?), Gradelin (?), Polichinelle. Center: Mezzetin, with Arlequin on a pedestal in the background. On the right: Pasquariel, Scaramouche, Pierrot, Monsieur Fréquet, Pantalone, Spezzafer. (Photo BnF)

comes a complete change of mood: "four Scaramouches, four Trivelins and one Arlequin represent a night in the manner of the Italian comedians, in time to the music." This number probably calls more for mime than dance, presumably of the type in which the characters fall prey to surprises arising from their inability to see each other, and perhaps including *lazzi* of fright – a type of routine for which the real Scaramouche was famous.[28] That their movements are timed to the music acknowledges the translation required when one type of theater becomes another. The music, which starts in a solemn duple meter, lends itself to variation in the actions by changing character at the midpoint, then changing meter part way into the second strain. Next, a duet between the Musicienne and her male counterpart voices the bromide that love needs to be enjoyed before youth fades away. To close the entrée there is a return to zaniness, as "the Scaramouches and Trivelins make merry" ("dansent une réjouissance"). Since the duet is strophic, this appears to be an instance where the dance is interleaved with it, and so performed twice.

The music for the *réjouissance*, a chaconne (Example 6-2), was on its way to becoming iconic, this being the third time Lully had put it on the stage.[29] Whereas the bass line makes intermittent use of the descending major tetrachord, the regularity expected from a chaconne fails to materialize; the first phrase, for example, is ten bars long. The seesaw melodic figures that begin thereafter and the empty downbeats in parts of the melody are only two of this chaconne's quirks. The three dances for Arlequin in Beauchamps-Feuillet notation, two of them set to this tune, draw upon a frankly comic movement vocabulary (see Chapter 14, pp. 425–27); even if they have no claims to performance at the Opéra, they reveal a set of conventions for a dancing Arlequin.[30] Moreover, this piece

Example 6-2: *Le Carnaval*, "Chaconne d'Arlequin" (Paris: Ballard, 1720), 68–69.

[28] Scott, *The Commedia dell'arte in Paris*, 68.

[29] After composing this Italian scene for the *Bourgeois gentilhomme*, Lully reused it in 1671 in the *Ballet des ballets*.

[30] La Montagne, choreographer of one of the dances set to this tune, performed this scene at court in *Le Ballet des Ballets*, so did have professional connections to Lully.

stands as the first in a line of chaconnes for commedia characters to appear on the stage of the Opéra.

It is unfortunate that the names of the performers in *Le Carnaval* in 1675 are not known. In 1670, when the *Bourgeois gentilhomme* premiered at Chambord, Arlequin was performed by the Arlequin of the Italian troupe, Domenico Biancolelli (known as Dominique), who on this occasion must have been doing a star turn, as all the other dancers were French. But this was during the time when the theatrical troupes were still collaborating with each other. When Lully took over the Académie Royale de Musique in 1672, he immediately set to work to hobble his competition: both the French and the Italian companies were forbidden to use more than two singers and six instrumentalists or to employ any of the dancers on the royal payroll. The musical portions of Molière's comedy-ballets thus became unperformable in his own theater.[31] By the time Lully constructed *Le Carnaval*, Molière had died and both the French and Italian troupes had been obliged to find new quarters, thanks to Lully's takeover of the theater in the Palais-Royal that they had formerly shared. The performance of *Le Carnaval* at the Opéra in 1675 was not innocent: what had been a collaborative effort only a few years earlier was now an act of appropriation.

How much the dancer in the role of Arlequin in 1675 appropriated from Dominique cannot be known. But merely admitting Arlequin to the circle of allowable operatic types is remarkable – especially since this happened during a time when Lully was retreating from the comic in his *tragédies*. Perhaps mindful of the new pressures, Lully himself did not call upon Arlequin again; it was not until the revival of *Le Carnaval* in 1692, five years after Lully's death, that Arlequin made his next appearance at the Opéra, part of the advance-guard of a second wave of Italianisms (see Chapter 8). In later operas Arlequin was treated as an individual, even if he was made mute;[32] the other commedia masks, on the other hand, transmogrified from individuals who spoke into group characters who danced – witness the Trivelins and Scaramouches in *Le Carnaval* and the Polichinelles in *Psyché*. Their costumes must have resembled their models in the Théâtre Italien (see Figures 6-1 and 6-2), and they must have had a movement vocabulary that both set them apart from the more serious dancing roles and distinguished them from each other. So at the same time that the Opéra appropriated other theatrical traditions, it also transformed them.

The performance of *Le Carnaval* on the public stage in Paris opened the door to other new characters. These can loosely be categorized as national types (Spaniards, Turks,

[31] La Gorce has pointed out (*Lully*, 182–83) that Lully had his own grievances: Molière had put on performances of *Psyché* in Paris in 1671 for which Lully, the composer of the score, received no compensation.

[32] The single exception occurs in one of the less frequently performed entrées of Campra's *Fêtes vénitiennes*; see Ch. 8, p. 232.

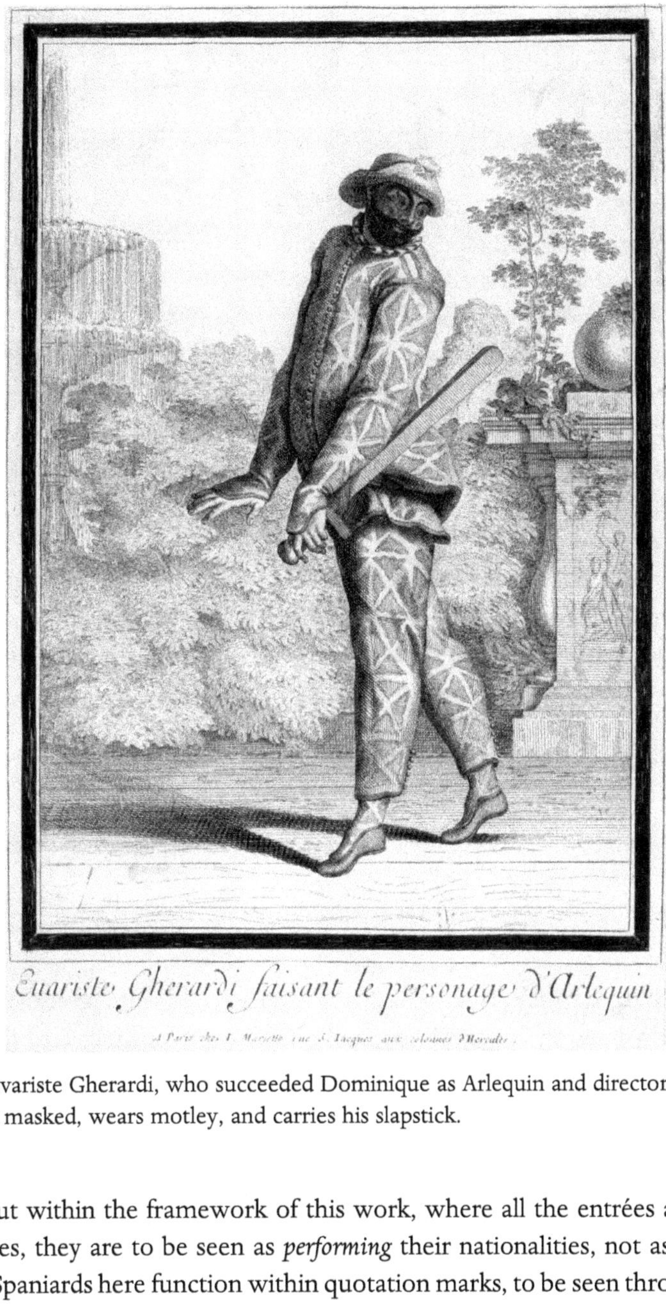

Figure 6-2: Evariste Gherardi, who succeeded Dominique as Arlequin and director of the Italian troupe. He is masked, wears motley, and carries his slapstick.

Basques), but within the framework of this work, where all the entrées are set up as performances, they are to be seen as *performing* their nationalities, not as incarnating them. The Spaniards here function within quotation marks, to be seen through the lens of masquerade, as if they were performing a set piece at a masked ball at Versailles. In 1670, when Lully composed the music for this scene, he did give it distinctive features; whether these can be traced to Spanish models seems less important than the larger question of whether these dances communicated "Spanishness" to their French

Example 6-3: *Le Carnaval*, "Sarabande pour les Espagnols," first two strains (Paris: Ballard, 1720), 16.

audience. One measure of Lully's efforts is that his successors imitated many of his musical characterizations in their own "Spanish" dances. This entrée is but one of the many by Lully that spawned musical offspring.

In its early years in Spain, the sarabande had a lively tempo and a lascivious character;[33] when adopted in France, it became respectable and its tempo slowed. But an association with Spain remained in the public imagination, even if the sarabande found uses in various dramatic contexts. Lully differentiated this particular piece from his sarabandes in French style: the melody starts on the second beat, moves mostly in quarter notes, and is structured completely in four-bar phrases (see above, Example 6-3). Musicians today tend to choose a moderate tempo, as do the dancers who perform any of the four choreographies set to this piece.[34] Several years later Lully was to compose two similar sarabandes into 1/3 of *Armide*, where their non-French character serves as a subtle marker of Armide's alterity.

Example 6-4: *Le Carnaval*, "Air pour les Espagnols" (Paris: Ballard, 1720), 19.

The second dance for the Spanish characters also has a distinctive profile: it is in a slow $\frac{6}{4}$ with dotted rhythms, an iambic pickup, and a first strain constructed of three two-bar phrases, each ending with a pause in the melody (Example 6-4). That these characteristics were conceptualized as "Spanish" can be seen in the fact that Campra adopted exactly the same profile for one of the dances in "L'Espagne" in *L'Europe galante* (see Chapter 8, p. 238). The $\frac{6}{4}$ meter, dotted rhythms and slow tempo also characterize the dance type known as the loure (sometimes called the gigue lente), which, like the sarabande, figured in various contexts on stage; according to Andrijeski, the two-bar phrases with the melodic pause are

[33] According to Furetière's *Dictionnaire universel* (1690), the sarabande came from the Saracens and was danced to the sound of the guitar or castanets. The article "geste" says it was gay and amorous.

[34] The piece is labeled a sarabande in the Ballard 1720 score of *Le Carnaval*, but most of the *Bourgeois gentilhomme* sources simply call it "Premier Air des Espagnols"; see *LWV* 43/27. The sarabande designation is consistently used in the four choreographies set to this tune.

markers of the loure in its "Spanish" guise.[35] The dancers might have played castanets in one or both of these dances, as do the Basques in the seventh entrée; Lully's scores do not indicate percussion instruments except timpani, but some engravings from the period depict dancers holding castanets (see Figures 6-4 and 6-5), and in *Chorégraphie* Feuillet included instructions for playing them, set to an excerpt from the "Folies d'Espagne."

The Turkish entrée is in a class by itself, because it depends upon sustaining a plausibly "Turkish" world throughout a lengthy ceremony. But removed from its context in the *Bourgeois gentilhomme*, the ceremony is no longer a hoax; instead, it functions here as yet another – and particularly elaborate – masquerade for Carnival, whose "Turks" are, however, every bit as fake: the *didascalie* describes this as a "Turkish ceremony to ennoble a bourgeois[36] in the Turkish manner, carried out in music and dance." The decontextualization – not to mention the replacements necessary for the two starring roles (in 1670 Mr Jourdain was performed by Molière, the Mufti by Lully) – begs the question of how this scene was performed in its new surroundings. The *didascalies* in the *Carnaval* libretto, while much fuller than usual for an opera, do not distinguish between the singers and the dancers, nor do they convey as much about the action as Molière's text supplies. Yet if Lully did maintain something resembling the staging that he and Molière had worked out five years earlier, then the dancers were very busy, but did little dancing.[37]

Example 6-5: *Le Carnaval*, "Premier Air pour les Turcs" (Paris: Ballard, 1720), 93.

[35] Andrijeski, "The elusive loure," 298. It is curious that this tune reappears in Lambranzi's *Neue und curieuse theatrialische Tantz-Schul* as a dance for Scaramouche; see Fig. 8-2, p. 233.

[36] The *didascalies* in the *Carnaval* libretto refer to this character only as "a Bourgeois," but some of the sung texts retain his name – "Giourdina" in lingua franca.

[37] The discussion about staging is based on the critical edition of *Le Bourgeois gentilhomme* by Schneider, *Œuvres complètes*, 183–211, in comparison with the score of *Le Carnaval*.

The famous march that opens the scene (Example 6-5) received elaborate ceremonial treatment. "Six dancing Turks enter gravely two by two, to the sound of all the instruments. They carry three long carpets, with which they make several figures, and at the end of this first ceremony they raise them high. The singing Turks and the instrumentalists pass underneath. Four dervishes, who accompany the Mufti, bring up the rear. Then the Turks spread the carpets on the ground and kneel on them; the Mufti stands in the center." The march – only fifteen bars long – must have been played several times to allow for so much action. Probably all the Turks, not just the dancers, alternately kneeled and stood as the scene progressed. After the Mufti quizzes the bourgeois about whether he is firm in his Muslim beliefs, the Mufti dances off stage as he and the chorus sing nonsense syllables over and over. The second "dance" piece provides music for a mimed "burlesque invocation": the Mufti returns, wearing a turban with lighted candles; the dervishes make the Bourgeois kneel and place the Koran on his back, as a pulpit. There is more kneeling and standing, then the Mufti decides it is time to award the Bourgeois his turban. This happens to a binary dance in triple meter with numerous strong hemiolas; the piece recurs later when the dancing Turks beat the poor Bourgeois, in time to the music. The earlier dance, the burlesque invocation, is played for another round of hocus-pocus, which is mingled with repetitions of the sung incantations. Finally the march returns, while, "to the sound of Turkish instruments," everyone sings and dances their way off stage.

Such a scene may provoke unease today, and the beating, which is a common component of seventeenth-century farces, no longer seems funny – not even if the entire *Bourgeois gentilhomme* is read as a send-up of Colbert, Louis XIV's finance minister.[38] But in *Le Carnaval* the Turkish scene had to stand on its own, and from the perspective of the demands it puts on the dancers it is full of interest. As in Lully's tragedies, the connections between the vocal music and the instrumental pieces are so seamless that the action seems all of a piece – all the more so since some of the dancers' actions have to begin during or grow out of choruses.

The Turkish ceremony reappeared at the Opéra in 1700 when *Le Carnaval* was revived, but that seems to have been its last appearance. However, another exceptional entrée from *Le Carnaval* – "Pourceaugnac" – did have a long career at the Opéra, as a free-standing divertissement put into programs of "fragments" (see Chapter 9, p. 283ff). Its success may perhaps be due to the fact that it hangs together better as a little story than does the Turkish ceremony, notwithstanding its origins in two separate intermèdes in Molière and Lully's comedy-ballet of 1669, *Monsieur de Pourceaugnac*. In

[38] See Schneider's introduction to his edition, xli–xlii. The immediate provocation for the Turkish scene – a visit to France in 1669 by an ambassador of the Turkish Sultan – has been much discussed. See in particular Whaples, "Early exoticism revisited," 11–14, and Betzwieser, *Exotismus*, 125–33, who also discuss the musical features of Lully's "Turkish" style.

distinction to the Turkish ceremony, the role of the dancers is minor, although their character is decidedly comic.

Like Monsieur Jourdain, the title character has ridiculous pretensions and is easily duped. In *Le Carnaval*, Pourceaugnac, an "Italian bourgeois," appeals for justice (crying "Giustizia" eight times over, before he gets another word out), because two women have declared that they are both married to him. He catches sight of two lawyers in turn and eagerly lays out the case, accusing the women of lying about all the little babies they claim are his ("tanti bambini, tanti puttini, piccini, piccini"). The first lawyer tells him, descending a major scale v-e-r-y s-l-o-w-l-y, that polygamy is a hanging offense. The second lawyer, who chatters in a high-pitched patter – and, like the first one, in French – recites all the possible precedents and authorities, all of whom agree . . . that polygamy is a hanging offense. Pourceaugnac rails against them to no avail, his attempts at interruption and their replies culminating in a clever bilingual trio.[39]

In despair, Pourceaugnac complains to Cupid. The humor in his mock-lament resides in the contrast between the refrain, with its heart-felt chromatic inflections, and the exaggerated whining of the middle section. All of a sudden two Italian quack doctors appear, determined to save Pourceaugnac from his melancholy.[40] They come accompanied by six dancing "Matassins," a vague category of jolly, playful maskers,[41] who seem like cousins to the Trivelins and Scaramouches from the Italian entrée. In a lively $\frac{3}{8}$ duet, the doctors recommend singing, dancing, laughing, plus a glass of wine and the occasional tobacco; the dancers prolong the merriment in a closely related dance piece. Pourceaugnac does not respond – at least not in music – so the Opérateurs insist that what he needs is an enema. Syringes in hand, they and the Matassins chase him around the stage, as he tries to escape their clutches ("No, no, no, no, no, non lo voglio pigliare," set to eighth notes almost all on the same pitch). The chase is articulated in song, acted upon in dance, and the two discourses go back and forth in one "chorus," so-called even though it involves only two singers. The chase by the syringe-wielding quacks had such durable comic valence that it was used almost 300 years later to illustrate a children's biography of Lully.[42]

39 No dancers are called for in this part of the entrée, even though in the 1669 original there had been dancing roles for two prosecutors and two sergeants. This scene, as it appears in Molière's play, was another source of inspiration for Hofmannsthal's libretto for *Der Rosenkavalier*, this time for Baron Ochs's predicament in Act III.

40 In 1669 Lully sang the role of the bass doctor.

41 Furetière's dictionary of 1690 defines Matassins as "Espèce de danse folâtre. Ces Masques ont dansé les Matassins. On le dit aussi de ceux qui la dansent." The word, which derives from the Italian "mattaccino," sometimes carried connotations of mock combats, but in *Le Carnaval* and subsequent operatic works these characters do not seem martial.

42 Guillemot-Musitot, *Lully: Petit Violon du Roi* (Paris and Brussels, 1959), 143. This scene also provided the frontispiece for the 1682 edition of Molière's works.

"Pourceaugnac," with its mixture of social satire and scatological humor, occupies a unique niche within *Le Carnaval*. It is very telling that Lully switched the nationality of his title character from the French provincial he had been in the play, to an Italian bourgeois. If Lecerf is correct that Lully himself wrote all the Italian texts in "Pourceaugnac,"[43] then he must have done so for the freedom he could derive from his native language and its comic traditions. The other place in *Le Carnaval* where Lully displays his comic roots is the Barbacola entrée, in which the *basso buffo* has a boasting patter song, one that Lully had composed for himself in *Les Noces de village* (1663). "Pourceaugnac" shows that even after he had begun writing *tragédies en musique*, Lully had not forgotten how to be funny in Italian. All of the music for Pourceaugnac himself – of which there is quite a bit – is new and very different from Lully's French style. Lully even expanded the end of the duet for the two lawyers by giving Pourceaugnac (a *haute-contre*) an independent line between the nattering, high-pitched lawyer and the drawling bass one. In this brief trio, all three characters are independently delineated in both music and in the bilingual text. This was the last music Lully composed in Italian, and in view of his genuine comic gifts, one wonders if he abandoned the style with reluctance. But his comic side was ratified by the eighteenth-century operatic public, which was happy to watch "Pourceaugnac" over and over.[44]

Le Carnaval exhibits a compositional breadth that after 1675 Lully only occasionally exercised. Even though the comic remained a contested category, this work, unique in Lully's operatic output, must have been seen by his successors as a precedent for composing in genres other than the tragic and the pastoral. It cannot be an accident that Campra's *L'Europe galante* put on stage the same four nationalities as Lully did in *Le Carnaval* – French, Spanish, Italian, and Turkish – and that Campra worked a singing and dancing gypsy into *Les Fêtes vénitiennes*. Moreover, the disorderly spirit of Carnival was to reign over a whole series of later works and to offer liberties not just to their protagonists, but to their composers and librettists. The key to this freedom was, once again, Italian.

Lully's *Carnaval* concludes when the personified Gallantry and Carnival invite all those who have appeared in the earlier entrées to return and dance together. The disparate costumes would have provided a brilliant and varied spectacle, one that broke from the more homogeneous groups that figure at the ends of *tragédies*. But the dancers, now mere party guests with no need to stay in character, must have all united in the same dance – perhaps using the gavotte music as the basis for a branle[45] – for even a work this unorthodox needs to end in a grand expression of unity. Here, however, the unity supports nothing but pleasure and we are all invited by the chorus to prolong the merriment.

[43] Lecerf, *Comparaison*, II, 195. [44] See the section on "Fragments" in Ch. 9, p. 284.

[45] Branles, of which the gavotte was originally one, were group social dances; see Ch. 9, pp. 273–74, regarding another staged ball that includes branles.

Chantons et dansons,
Que le plaisir recommence
En mille façons;
Chantons et dansons.

(Let us sing and dance. May pleasure be renewed in a thousand ways. Let us sing and dance.)

PSYCHÉ

When the Abbé Dubos wrote that *Thésée* was the last of Lully's operas to include buffoons, he neglected to mention *Psyché* – perhaps because the work was not entirely new. Based on the *tragédie-ballet* Lully had composed in 1671, it had to undergo massive adaptation in order to become an opera: the spoken dialogue for the main characters was revised and set to music, and what had been intermèdes in the earlier version became the core of the divertissements.[46] Yet *Psyché* lost none of its buffoons – who numbered many more than there were in *Thésée* – even though it follows on the heels of *Atys* (1676) and *Isis* (1677). Why the comic elements were not removed or softened when the new *tragédie en musique* went on the stage of the Académie Royale de Musique in 1678 is a mystery. Perhaps the forces allied against the comic were not as strong as has been thought; or perhaps the fact that the humor was (mostly) confined to divertissements made it acceptable. There are two, quite different, places where it is found – Act II, where dancing cyclopes introduce a grotesque element, and the concluding celebrations, for which Jupiter has drawn up a very peculiar guest list.

Act II opens with the god Vulcain obeying Amour's orders to prepare a magnificent palace for Psyché, whom Amour has just rescued from imminent sacrifice to a monster. Vulcain has eight cyclopes working for him as blacksmiths; the forge is visible at the back of the set and the stage is filled with their anvils and other tools. Since one of the anomalies of this opera is that a singing chorus is required only in the prologue and in Act V, the blacksmiths are dancers only. As the grotesque and cuckolded husband of Venus, Vulcain has been the butt of jokes since time immemorial; no *didascalie* describes what he looks like in this opera, but traditional representations depict him as lame (see Figure 6-3). That he is also capable of crudity becomes clear in the next scene, when Vénus objects to the work he is doing on behalf of her son's beloved. Their marital spat veers dangerously close to the vulgar in its almost everyday language and references to sexual misconduct.

The blacksmithing cyclopes partake of the comic side of the grotesque, and their music lends itself to actions that must have been as much mime as dance. The first "Entrée des Cyclopes" is one of Lully's duple meter pieces where the level of note values doubles in the second strain; the impression created is that the cyclopes switch

[46] See La Gorce, *Lully*, 568–71 for a list of the new portions of the score.

Figure 6-3: Nicolas Bonnart, "The Vulcain of the Opéra."

abruptly from deliberate actions to something much livelier. Their second binary dance also changes character abruptly, switching at the double bar after seven bars in $\frac{3}{2}$ to a rapid **3** in which the repeated quarter notes evoke the banging of the blacksmiths on their forges – in time with the music, if Lambranzi's instructions for such characters apply here (Example 4-2, p. 124 shows the second strain of this piece, Figure 4-1 a dancing blacksmith). Next comes a remarkable dialogue between Vulcain and his workers: as annotations in the score show, he exhorts them in song and they respond in movement (Example 6-6). The blacksmiths even anticipate his orders: see mm. 50–55, where the rhythms of his words "Redoublez vos coups" and "Frappez" are anticipated

Example 6-6: *Psyché*, II/2, part of the dialogue between Vulcain and the blacksmiths (Paris: Ballard, 1720), 71–72. (*Vulcain*: "May the ardor [you feel] for pleasing [Amour] make your tasks sweeter. Redouble your blows! Strike!")

in the orchestra. This close back-and-forth recalls the chorus in Charpentier's *Circé* (see Table 2-1, p. 41) where the dancers and singers alternate, only here – very exceptionally – there is not a chorus, but only one singer.

The opera concludes with a grandiose celebration that dwarfs any other in Lully's output; in the libretto the texts go on for eight pages. But first Vénus must be induced to give up her opera-long persecution of Psyché, which she does under pressure from Mercure and Jupiter. Amour and Psyché are restored to each other and take up positions next to Vénus at the feet of Jupiter, who is seated on his throne. The celebrations begin when four more gods descend on cloud machines. Two of them – Apollon and Mars – were regulars on the operatic stage, but two novel guests – Bacchus and Momus – send the festivities off in unconventional directions. Bacchus extols the benefits to be derived from drinking and Momus promises to spare no one, not even the gods, from his mockery. In this irreverent environment, even the Olympians relax: Apollon sings a bourée-ish strophic dance-song whose refrain reminds us that night time is the right time for pleasure and love, and Mars admits that he too has succumbed to love, although he discreetly neglects to mention what Vulcain's presence has reminded us already – that his affair was with the married Vénus, now seated at Jupiter's feet, and that the pair had been caught *in flagrante* by her husband.

As usual, each god has a retinue and each retinue has its own set of dances – although fewer than usual of its own songs, because the chorus, composed of "celestial divinities" participates only at the beginning and end of this massive scene. Instead, the dancers relate to individual singers. The Arts, disguised as shepherds, translate Apollon's words into movement. Two Muses, also backed up by the dancing shepherds, offer a counterweight to Apollon's hedonism by warning young women against love's dangers. Merriment, however, quickly returns. Bacchus, who in *Les Fêtes de l'Amour et de Bacchus* never made an appearance, not only sings his own song in praise of wine, but is seconded by his foster-father Silène, who rides in on his donkey. Wine is wonderful, Silène says, because it makes everyone laugh all day and sleep all night. The portrayals of Bacchus and Silène both carry an extra comic charge because they sing in falsetto – something extremely rare for adult male roles in France.[47] Their dancing counterparts are ménades (bacchantes) and satyrs, whose movements in the two interleaved instrumental pieces may well have demonstrated the effects of "the juice of the vine." Whereas in a *tragédie en musique* their dancing probably did not go as far toward the comic as the only known notated drunk dance, a male duet in *Le Mariage de la grosse Cathos*,[48] the music of the "Premier Air pour les Ménades et les Satyres" conveys wobbliness by being performable in both $\frac{6}{4}$ and $\frac{3}{2}$ and by the abrupt ending of the first strain after seven bars (Example 6-7). The acrobatic satyrs, who in 1671 used Silène's donkey as a vaulting horse, seem to have disappeared from the operatic version.[49] Yet even if this omission represents a move toward greater decorum, the two singing Satyrs still sum up the spirit of the moment: "Do you want perfect joys? Look for them only at the bottom of a jug."[50]

Drunkenness is replaced by hilarity when Momus's followers, a troupe of commedia-style characters, "come to contribute jokes and fooling around to this grand fête."[51] This represents the first appearance of Momus, the god of

Example 6-7: *Psyché* v/5, "Premier Air pour les Ménades et les Satyres" (Paris: Ballard, 1720), 189.

[47] According to Couvreur, *Lully*, 247, Bacchus is typically depicted as effeminate. Here he has a *dessus* range of d' to f''. Silène has a similar range in his solo song, but drops to a *haute-contre* range in the trio he sings with two Satyrs.

[48] HW&M, 149–53.

[49] "Deux autres satyres enlèvent Silène de dessus son âne, qui leur sert à voltiger, et à former des jeux agréables et surprenants." This *didascalie* is absent in the opera libretto.

[50] "Voulez-vous des douceurs parfaites? / Ne les cherchez qu'aux fonds des pots."

[51] "Une troupe de Polichinelles et de Matassins vient joindre leurs plaisanteries et leurs badinages aux divertissements de cette grande fête."

mockery, on the operatic stage, but Momus was to become a frequent visitor starting in the 1690s. Polichinelles and Matassins had already danced at the Opéra three years earlier, in *Le Carnaval*; that they were deemed acceptable within a *tragédie*, however, is novel. Their dance piece, which is loosely related to Momus's strophic air, offers opportunities for different styles of dancing by changing meter from $\frac{6}{4}$ to **2** at the mid-point. These characters, or some of them, may also have danced a comic chaconne, if the inclusion in the 1720 Ballard score of the *Bourgeois gentilhomme*'s Arlequin chaconne is to be believed. (The chaconne does not appear in a manuscript score copied by Philidor; moreover, it is in the wrong key for this section of the divertissement.[52]) But whether they had one dance or two, their shenanigans are brought to an end by Mars, whose military trumpets and flag-throwing soldiers remind us that in 1678 France was still at war with Holland. Peace was, however, on the horizon, and Mars, now fully in his heroic mode, enjoins all the assembled groups to "mingle the image of war among the most charming pastimes." The chorus – dancers and singers alike – take up his call with enthusiasm, and in a chorus punctuated by both trumpet calls and "the sweet sound of musettes," they effect an idealized union between war and peace, within the overarching celebration of love.

Couvreur's insights about the tragédie-ballet *Psyché* apply to the operatic version as well. "Partly tragic, partly pastoral, *Psyché* is also and especially comic [. . .] In order for *Psyché* to be the synthesis of all dramatic genres, only farce was missing; the finale takes care of that oversight."[53] The heterogeneous mingling of styles must have been just as visible as it was audible. Yet as a practical matter, the finale of *Psyché* offers puzzles to today's directors and choreographers over how far to push the physical comedy without exceeding the boundaries of *bienséance* that would have prevailed on the stage of the Opéra in 1678. The comic sections are, after all, contained – bookended by the realms of the pastoral and the martial. The texts that flirt with crudeness or with satire never go to extremes: Momus makes the general claim that mockery is both agreeable and necessary, but he never mocks anyone or anything. Might the dancers have filled the lacuna? Dance does seem to have been a means of working a broader range of affects into a divertissement than the text alone might allow, but how far would this liberty have been pushed in a work such as *Psyché*? Clearly further than in other *tragédies en musique*, and perhaps the movement styles on view here achieved a legitimacy from their use, however limited, that gave them greater purchase for the future.

[52] The Ballard score of *Psyché*, not published until 1720, is problematic in many respects.

[53] Couvreur, *Lully*, 244 and 246.

LE TRIOMPHE DE L'AMOUR

Le Triomphe de l'Amour marks a landmark in ballet history, as the first work in which professional women dancers appeared on the stage of the Académie Royale de Musique. The ballet (so labeled in the libretto) was not written for that stage, however, but for performance at court upon the occasion of the Dauphin's marriage, which took place on 7 March 1680. For an event of this dynastic importance, it was decided to revive the tradition of the *ballet de cour*, which had been quiescent for more than a decade. In *Le Triomphe de l'Amour* the loose structure and the mixture of professional and amateur performers followed tradition, but Lully's experience in composing operas led him to a new type of ballet, one with more vocal music and different frames for dancing. The fact that Quinault, not Benserade, wrote the libretto undoubtedly made a difference.[54] The ballet premiered at Saint-Germain-en-Laye on 21 January 1681, where it received numerous performances;[55] it opened at the Académie Royale de Musique – now with a fully professional cast – in May. The ballet's court origins explain its anomalous structure vis-à-vis the other works Lully put on the stage of the Opéra.

The love that triumphs is both metaphorical and incarnate. In the first sequence of vignettes, gods such as Mars, Borée, and even Diane are shown first resisting and then succumbing to the power of love; a second sequence is organized around gods who had already acknowledged love's power. At the ballet's conclusion, Love himself appears on his throne, and the heavens open to reveal all the celestial divinities, led by Jupiter, "who recognizes Love as the most powerful of gods." The libretto's narrow thematic focus did not hamper Lully's musical creativity; on the contrary, it may have spurred his inventiveness, particularly in exploiting timbres for characterization. Woodwinds in particular are used in striking ways, including the first documentable use of transverse flutes in Lully's œuvre; the one aspect of the score that has attracted scholarly attention is its orchestration.[56]

Accounts of this work, going back to the eighteenth century, usually mention that it is constructed in twenty "entrées." The term derives from the *ballet de cour*, where it refers to a dance, or a sequence of several dances, performed by the same set of characters; the occasional vocal pieces receive a separate heading, such as, in the *Ballet des saisons*, the "Récit de la Nymphe de Fontainebleau." The twenty entrées in *Le Triomphe de l'Amour* each contain from one to three separate dance pieces, but there is also a great deal of vocal music, most of which receives no heading in either the libretto

[54] Benserade had written most of the librettos for Lully's ballets, his farewell work being the *Ballet de Flore* (1669). In 1681 he came out of retirement to write *vers pour les personnages* – the double-edged poems for the noble performers that comment both on the role and on the person playing it. These were printed at the end of the libretto, but not performed; Benserade's authorship of these verses explains why this libretto is sometimes attributed to him as well as to Quinault.

[55] See the *Mercure galant* of December 1680, 317–28 and January 1681, 284–97.

[56] See Eppelsheim, *Das Orchester*, 64ff.

or the score beyond the name of the character singing.[57] The only time the libretto allows for vocal music within an entrée is when Lully composed a dance-song, where the vocal and instrumental music are the same or very similar: this happens, for example, when the Pleasures sing and dance inside Entrée 3.

Table 6-2 redefines the ballet's structure on the basis of the characters who appear in each section. As in earlier court ballets, these characters are episodic and disappear at the end of their scenes, until toward the end of the work (probably from section XI) when they seem to remain, in preparation for the grandiose conclusion. The chorus, however, may have been on stage throughout. There was only a single set, as the opening *didascalie* shows (and a report in the *Mercure* confirms[58]): "The stage represents a magnificently decorated place, that has been arranged for welcoming Love, who is to arrive in triumph. A great number of divinities and a multitude of different peoples have assembled and taken their places, in order to witness the splendid spectacle. Vénus begins this pleasing fête [. . .] " In a ballet framed as a gigantic spectacle, an on-stage audience has a role to play even when it is silent.

These thirteen scenes vary radically in length, dramatic weight, and structure.[59] In most, the division of labor familiar from Lully's operas prevails: the singers occupy the main roles, the dancers subordinate ones; in some, however, dancers play the leads. In fact, three scenes (II, IV, and IX) consist exclusively of dance, much of it pantomimic. Even in some of the sections that involve singing, the lead characters – Bacchus and Ariane, for instance – are dancers. Such assignments may be attributable to the imperative of crafting dancing roles for members of the royal family, but the net result, once the ballet had acquired an all-professional cast, is that from section to section the work features surprisingly varied relationships among the performers. The most surprising of all comes in section V, where the goddess Diane is a singer, her lover Endymion a dancer.

Even though the novelty of women dancers on the public stage made a big impression, it is not known what roles they danced. The introduction to the first volume of the *Recueil général* (1703) singles out Mlle La Fontaine as having "shone" in this work; the Parfaict brothers mention three other women as well – Mlles Carré, Leclerc, and Pesant – but not whether these four constituted the sum total of the women dancing.[60] The Parfaicts' *Dictionnaire* (V, 539) says that "Lully assigned

[57] The layout and typography of the libretto mislead by giving weight only to headings for the entrées.

[58] *Mercure galant* (December 1680), 317: "The decor, which will remain unchanged throughout, will be a unique creation."

[59] There is no known independent libretto for the performances at the Opéra. The score (Ballard, 1681), shows signs of having been expanded, via unnumbered pages in three different places: sections VI (the Cariens) and X, which had originally consisted only of two dances (Entrées 17 and 18). I suspect that these additions – of vocal music only – occurred when the work was transferred to the stage of the Opéra; the sources of *Le Triomphe de l'Amour* await study.

[60] Parfaict, *Histoire*, 48.

Table 6-2: Structure of *Le Triomphe de l'Amour*.
Sections entirely sung are in white, entirely danced light gray, mixed singing and dancing dark gray. An entrée may contain from one to three dance pieces.

	Singers	Dancers	Synopsis	Entrées within the section
[I: Prol.]	Vénus, Chorus of Divinities and Peoples	Graces, Dryads, Naiads, Pleasures	Vénus honors first the peace-making hero, then her own son, "the conqueror of conquerors."	1: Graces, Dryads 2: Naiads 3: Pleasures [All dance in final chorus]
[II]		Mars, Warriors, Cupids	Mars furiously claims he loves only combats, but is disarmed by little Cupids.	4: Mars and Warriors 5: Cupids [plus Mars]
[III]	Amphitrite, Neptune	Marine gods, Nereids	A. at first resists N.'s advances, then succumbs.	6: Marine gods and Nereids
[IV]		Borée, cold Winds, Orythie, Athenian maidens	The cold North Wind sees O., falls in love, and kidnaps her.	7: Borée and the winds 8: Orythie and the Athenian maidens [plus B. and the winds]
[V]	Diane, Night, Mystery, Silence	Diane's Nymphs, Endymion, Dreams	Diane prides herself on her independence, but is attracted to Endymion. She asks Night for help.	9: Diane's Nymphs 10: Endymion 11: Dreams
[VI]	Chorus of Cariens, one Carien	Cariens	The people are afraid because the moon no longer lights up the sky. They beg Diane to return.	12: Cariens

[VII]	an Indian man, two Indian women	Bacchus, Ariane, male Indians, Greek girls	Bacchus, returning from conquering the Indies, has fallen in love with the Greek Ariane.	13: Bacchus and Ariane 14: their followers
[VIII]	Mercure, Chorus of Divinities and Peoples		Mercure invites everyone to submit voluntarily to the power of love.	
[IX]		Apollon, 4 heroic Shepherds	Apollon is eager to place himself among love's captives.	15: Apollon 16: heroic Shepherds
[X]	Arcas, Chorus of Sylvains	Pan, Fauns	Arcas praises love's empire.	17: Pan 18: Fauns
[XI]	A Nymph	Flore, Zéphyr, Nymphs, Zephyrs	F. and Z. are in love; their followers prepare the way for Cupid's arrival	19: Flore, Nymphs, all the Zephyrs
[XII]	Cupid, a Nymph	Youth, *Jeux*, some Zephyrs and Nymphs	Cupid is carried in by the heroes he has conquered; he boasts that even Jupiter has succumbed to him.	20: Youth, *Jeux*, joined by some of Flore's Nymphs and some Zephyrs
[XIII]	Jupiter, Chorus of Divinities in the heavens, Chorus of Divinities and Peoples already present	Apollon, Shepherds, Pan, Fauns, Nymphs, Zephyrs, *Jeux*	The heavens open to reveal Jupiter on his throne surrounded by divinities; Jupiter recognizes Love as the most powerful of the gods.	"Danse générale" [done within the final chorus]

Figure 6-4: Jean Dolivar after Jean Berain, costume for the nymphes, followers of Orythie, in *Le Triomphe de l'Amour*, roles danced by men.

[professional] women dancers to the entrées that had been performed at Saint-Germain by the princesses and ladies of the court." That probably means the solo roles danced by the new Dauphine (Diane's lead nymph in section v and the goddess of spring, Flore, in xii), and by her sisters-in-law, the Princesse de Conti (Ariane) and Mlle de Nantes (Youth). The other solo female role, Orythie in section iv, was danced in the court performances by a male professional, as were her four followers, variously identified as Athenian girls or nymphs (see Figure 6-4). Given the practice since the Opéra's birth of

Figure 6-5: Jean Berain, costume for demons disguised as nymphes in *Armide*, roles danced by women. (Photo BnF)

men dancing *en travesti*, Orythie and her followers probably continued to be danced by men. Moreover, in Paris the dancing cast could not possibly have been as large as it was at Saint-Germain: 43 female roles plus 73 male roles, for a total of 116. Probably each of the five different sets of female characters (in sections I, III, V, VII, and XI–XIII) had fewer dancers than at court; perhaps Vénus had only four nymphs instead of eight. Four women cannot have accounted for all the female roles in *Le Triomphe de l'Amour*; some of the ones danced by noblewomen in January must have been assigned to men in May.

Lully saw immediately that *danseuses* were an asset to his theater. Only a few months later, when *Proserpine* was revived, the *Mercure galant* reported that the entrées had been rendered "more beautiful, by including most of the girls who danced all summer in *Le Triomphe de l'Amour*."[61] Mlle La Fontaine went on to became the leading female soloist at the Opéra, until around 1690 when Mlle de Subligny replaced her.[62] Assuming that the four solo roles in court performances of *Le Triomphe de l'Amour* were taken over by the professional women, we can get at least some sense of what they were dancing. (See Figure 6-5 for a costume worn by a woman dancer.)

The two dances for Diane's nymphs (section v, entrée 9) are both connected to songs in which Diane states her conviction that love is slavery. Her followers reinforce this sentiment: "Diane's nymphs dance and show the joy they feel in being exempt from love's pains and in enjoying the sweetness of liberty." Yet Diane's words, "Away, dangerous Love, away; flee far from these woods!"[63] are undercut by sounding above a descending minor tetrachord, and the lovely phrase is played first, during the ritournelle that opens this sequence, by a solo flute – an extremely rare texture in Lully's output. Diane's insecurity about the strength of her resolve is thus introduced from the start.

Ariane and Bacchus, both dancers, do not enter until three of their followers have told the story of how Bacchus, on his return home from conquering the Indies with thousands of prisoners, caught sight of Ariane and fell instantly in love. Their entrance music sounds designed to foreground Bacchus as a conqueror. (This heroic Bacchus has nothing in common with the drunken reveler in *Psyché*.) Next comes a menuet, perhaps danced as a love duet, however, what follows is a chaconne – a long and particularly complex one that starts with an instrumental section in rondeau form and goes on to a vocal chaconne that is also structured as a rondeau, with a strophic text and many instrumental passages inside the refrain. Ariane probably danced here as well: in its review of the court performances, the *Mercure* praised the Dauphine for learning at the last minute, when the Princesse de Conti fell ill, "a big entrée all filled with figures and in which there are more than twelve *reprises*."[64] This can only mean the chaconne, and Ariane was the Princesse de Conti's most prominent role. The complexity of the music suggests that Ariane is unlikely to have danced alone throughout; moreover, as the texts emphasize the charms to be found in the pains of love, a partner would seem essential for much of the dance. Lully may have chosen to use a chaconne in this particular spot as an exotic marker, a reference to Bacchus's conquest of the Indies: a few years later, in *Le Temple de la Paix* (1685), he wrote a chaconne for Africans celebrating the clemency of their French conqueror.

[61] *Mercure galant* (November 1681), 319–20. [62] See Ch. 3.

[63] "Va, dangereux Amour, va, fui loin de ces bois, / Je veux y conserver la paix et l'innocence."

[64] *Mercure galant* (January 1681), 289.

Zéphyr and Flore form another dancing couple (section XI), but their scene is much shorter than the one for Bacchus and Ariane. It opens with an "Air" that has the profile of a gavotte and follows with an unlabeled bourrée, which alternates with a related song by one of Flore's nymphs. The two lovers each have followers, so as usual, the dancing must have involved both duets and/or solos and group dances. But given how quickly this scene goes by, the choreographic emphasis must have been on charm.

The dance for Youth (Jeunesse) appears to have been a late addition, as the *Mercure*'s write-up during the rehearsal period, which otherwise lists the dancing cast entrée by entrée, does not include it.[65] In the original conception, the last entrées were thus the ones for the bridal couple in the roles of Flore and Zéphyr. But a role for the king's youngest illegitimate daughter, Mlle de Nantes, was added, presumably by order of her doting father; she was seven and a half at the time. She must already have been an accomplished dancer, as she not only danced alone, but played castanets. Her piece, labeled only "Air" in the score, has the identical phrase structure and almost identical rhythms as the Spanish sarabande in *Le Carnaval* (see above Example 6-3). Mlle de Nantes would not have been on stage when *Le Triomphe de l'Amour* moved to the Palais-Royal, but perhaps the castanets and the Spanish accent remained.

Louis XIV, who had been an enthusiastic participant in many court ballets up until 1669, appears symbolically in the role of Apollon, in section IX. Not only was the sun the emblem most strongly associated with the king, Apollon had been one of Louis's signature roles during his ballet-dancing days.[66] Lully made the connection explicit in his dedication to the score:

> I concluded that I needed powerful help and I decided to follow the example of the Muses, who, notwithstanding all their knowledge in the beautiful art of harmony, had recourse to a god who enlightened them and who presided over their concerts. But I recognized from my youngest years that the Apollo who would inspire the songs I intended to compose was neither in my birthplace [Florence] nor on the summits of Parnassus. I thought I could find him in the most flourishing empire on earth and I easily recognized him as soon as I was fortunate enough to lay eyes on Your Majesty.

Lully's Apollon is the source of the arts; the silent Apollon inside the ballet has a different role: "Apollon, followed by a troupe of heroic Shepherds, hastens to appear among the captives who will accompany the triumphant Love." This take on Apollon/Louis is perhaps apt inside a work featuring three of the king's illegitimate children, by two different mothers. But if the two choreographies for a solo man set to the *entrée grave* music Lully wrote for Apollon (entrée 15 in section IX; see Example 6-8) are anything like what Lestang *cadet* performed in 1681, then the image Apollon projected

[65] *Mercure galant* (December 1680), 328.

[66] That said, the king did not restrict himself to noble roles. See Astier, "Louis XIV, 'premier danseur'," and my "Louis XIV et la danse," 117–19.

Example 6-8: *Le Triomphe de l'Amour*, "Entrée d'Apollon" (Paris: Ballard, 1681), 188.

was of nobility, power, and control.[67] The dance music that follows for the Bergers héroïques (entrée 16) maintains a similarly noble air.

Whereas the entrées for Apollon and Pan aim to communicate the essence of the character, two of the purely danced sequences present little stories; even at court, both were performed by professional dancers. The first falls within the section concerning the divinities who once had opposed Love:

> Mars, armed and accompanied by warriors, appears furious and claims to love only combats, blood, and carnage. He is surrounded by a troupe of Cupids, who get rid of the warriors. The little Cupids disarm the terrifying god of war and play with the weapons they take away from him; they enchain him with bonds made of flowers, and dance in celebration of their victory.[68]

This sequence is set to three pieces of music that correspond to entrées 4 and 5 in the libretto:

> Entrée de Mars et de Guerriers. Vite. Air.
> Airs [sic] pour les Amours et les Guerriers. Gai. Air.
> Entrée de Mars et des Amours. Air.

The titles in the score suggest that each dance corresponds to one of the sentences in the *didascalie*. That is, the first air, which has a march-like character, a rapid tempo, and uneven phrase lengths, is where Mars and his warriors express their love for war. The second piece, also fast and in duple meter, but in the parallel minor, accompanies the entrance of the little Cupids who drive away the warriors. The third, a triple-meter rondeau whose seven-bar refrain is partially built over a descending major tetrachord, would then apply to the remaining three bits of action: disarming Mars, enchaining him with flowers, and dancing victory. Whereas this storyline is very simple, the standard binary and rondeau structures do not impede its unfolding through time.

The other of the two narrative dance scenes has somewhat more of a plot:

> Borée, covered in ice and frost and accompanied by cold, frozen winds, claims that he is protected from the fires of love; he hides the winds who follow him and withdraws in order

[67] See Ch. 14, pp. 429–31.

[68] At court Mars was danced by Beauchamps, with eight each of warriors and Cupids.

> to watch Orythie, daughter of the king of Athens, who has come to amuse herself by dancing with a troupe of Athenian maidens. Borée approaches Orythie, and cold as he is, nonetheless feels himself growing warm with love for her. The princess takes fright at the sight of Borée and tries to escape from him; the Athenian maidens surround and defend her; the winds who follow Borée drive off the maidens and allow Borée to kidnap Orythie.[69]

This scene is set to four binary pieces:

> Air pour l'entrée de Borée et des quatre Vents
> Gavotte pour Orythie et ses Nymphes
> [Unlabeled piece]
> Air pour Borée et les quatre Vents qui enlèvent Orythie et les Nymphes. Vite.

During the first piece, a binary air in G minor, in $\frac{6}{4}$ time with rushing, stepwise eighth notes, Borée and his four fellow winds make their entrance. Orythie frolics to a gavotte while Borée hides. The third piece has no heading, but its gentle triple meter and three-bar phrases suggest that this is the place where Borée attempts to express his love. The last piece, which intersperses rushing eighth notes with dotted figures, accompanies the abduction. This little scene looks both forward and backwards: Lully's *Ballet des Amours déguisés* (1664), has a similar sequence across six instrumental pieces, during which Pluton encounters Proserpine while she picks flowers with her nymphs and then abducts her. An expanded version of the same story – complicated by a love triangle between a personified rose and two winds (Borée and Zéphyre) – features in Rameau's opera-ballet *Les Indes galantes* (1735), within the entrée entitled "La Fête persane." The "Ballet des fleurs," which unfolds over nine instrumental pieces, is often seen as an early instance of pantomime-ballet, but the Borée-Orythie scene, composed before Rameau was born, shows that narrative ballet inside of opera had long roots.

The weightiest sequence of *Le Triomphe de l'Amour* (section v) encompasses several vocal numbers and three danced entrées. After Diane, the chaste goddess of the moon, has tried to strengthen her resolve against love, she feels a tenderness awakening in her heart and suddenly loses the ability to speak; in this key scene (entrée 10), built around two consecutive instrumental dances, she and Endymion both resort to mime:

> Endymion approaches Diane and her nymphs. The severe goddess tries to flee with her nymphs, but she cannot prevent herself from gazing at Endymion and she withdraws in confusion at feeling herself touched by love for him.

Lully composed contrasting pieces to set the different parts of the action. The "Premier Air" must be for Endymion's arrival, the second for Diane's confused reaction (Examples 6-9 and 6-10). This fraught encounter sets up the centerpiece of *Le Triomphe de l'Amour*, a long section that in its musical sumptuousness recalls the dream sequence

[69] At court this scene was danced entirely by men; see Fig. 6-4.

Example 6-9: *Le Triomphe de l'Amour*, "Entrée d'Endymion. Premier Air" (Paris: Ballard, 1681).

Example 6-10: *Le Triomphe de l'Amour*, "Deuxième Air pour Endymion" [*sic*, but must have been danced by Diane] (Paris: Ballard, 1681), 84.

in *Atys*. To the sounds of muted strings, the allegorical figures of Night, Mystery, and Silence enter in turn, bringing darkness to the earth in order to further the secrecy favored by lovers. Their slow utterances are punctuated by long instrumental passages – the prelude that initiates the scene is over four minutes long – and when they sing the orchestra accompanies them. No dancers animate the stage; all is still. The continuous sonority of the muted strings draws a sonic curtain that hides Diane's desires even as it furthers them. When the anguished Diane reappears to beg Night to hide her shame, Night decides instead to obey the desires of her heart and calls upon dancing dreams to transport the sleeping Endymion to Diane's abode. This 35-minute sequence is one of the most remarkable in all of Lully's works.[70]

This section, from Diane's first appearance through the Carien's prayers for her return to the sky, constitutes the most sustained dramatic sequence in a work that otherwise consists of brief vignettes. Quinault did provide the ballet with a single governing theme and an overarching shape: the Vénus scene functions as a prologue by both praising the king and setting up the parade of divinities who succomb to love, and the work ends in Love's apotheosis as the most powerful god of all. But within this general arc Quinault left Lully ample opportunity to shape the vignettes in interesting and varied ways – for surely Lully must have had a hand in the general design of this divertissement-driven work. Beauchamps, together with Lully, must have decided how best to play to the strengths and weaknesses of the dancers at his disposal: the sizeable number of menuets and other ballroom dances[71] surely reflects the participation of the courtiers, while the mimed dances remind us of the varied

[70] These timings are based on the recording (2003) by La Simphonie du Marais (Accord 476 1053).

[71] There are five dances labeled "menuet" in the Ballard score and two others that could be so construed, plus two gavottes and an unlabeled bourrée.

abilities needed by professionals. In composing this anomalous work Lully drew upon all sides of his past theatrical experiences: parts of it function like a *ballet de cour*, other sections like operatic divertissements, yet still others escape from either template. As a work in a class by itself, *Le Triomphe de l'Amour* does not fit comfortably into the usual narratives about French operatic history. But it has so much remarkable music and so much choreographic interest that it deserves more attention than it has received.

Le Triomphe de l'Amour, which is so thoroughly grounded in the life of the court, reminds us how much the Académie Royale de Musique, for all that the theater was open to the public, was still attached to the monarchy. Lully was to put two more court-derived works onto his Parisian stage – *L'Idylle sur la paix* ("divertissement") and *Le Temple de la paix* ("ballet") – which appeared as a double bill in November of 1685, after premiering separately at court.[72] Unlike *Le Triomphe de l'Amour*, however, these two are saturated with encomiums of the king that go far beyond anything found in the prologue to a tragedy. *Le Temple de la paix*, the more substantial of the two, stages, in a sequence of entrées, the homage paid in song and dance by various subject peoples to their monarch: after the usual nymphs and shepherds come Basques, Bretons, "savages" from France's New World colonies, and Africans.[73] The single-mindedness of the project further complicates our picture of the repertoire at the Académie Royale de Musique during Lully's lifetime; a comic work such as *Le Carnaval* occupies one extreme, these two works the other.

ACIS ET GALATÉE

With *Acis et Galatée*, Lully's operatic career came full circle, ending, as it had begun, with a three-act pastorale. It should not have been so: Lully was at work on a tragedy, *Achille et Polyxène*, when the accident that was to kill him occurred.[74] Yet Lully's career had already taken a new turn when, after *Armide*, Quinault decided to retire; deprived of his long-standing collaborator, Lully turned to Jean Galbert de Campistron,[75] who had previously written several spoken tragedies. The first fruit of their collaboration, *Acis et Galatée*, was commissioned by the Duc de Vendôme, as part of a fête in honor of the Dauphin held in September 1686. For this venue a

[72] For more about both, see La Gorce, *Lully*, 689–94.

[73] For insights into the "savages" and their music, see Bloechl's chapter "Savage Lully," in her *Native American Song*.

[74] Lully died on 22 March 1687, at the age of 54.

[75] Regarding Quinault's withdrawal from the theater and his replacement by Campistron, see La Gorce, *Lully*, 334–35 and 702–03.

pastorale was preferred; the prologue is set in the gardens of the duke's château at Anet and pays homage to "the son of the most powerful and most just of kings." Because Anet did not have a theater, Campistron could not construct a libretto that required elaborate machinery. Yet even when the new work moved to the Opéra later that month, it retained the trappings of its origins: the prologue in honor of the Dauphin and the relatively simple staging.

Notwithstanding Campistron's qualification of this pastorale as "héroïque," *Acis et Galatée* has a very mixed tone. It does not descend to the low comedy of Lully's other operatic pastorale, *Les Fêtes de l'Amour et de Bacchus*, but within its much more coherent plot, Lully and Campistron play in multiple registers. Right from the start of the prologue we are reminded that the gods' images may be manipulated to less than lofty ends: the Diane who welcomes everyone to Anet is not the chaste goddess of the moon, but her namesake, Diane de Poitiers, mistress of Henri II, for whom the king had built the château – as a footnote on the first page of the libretto points out. Following Diane's reminder of the magnificence that reigned there in her day, Abundance and Comus, the *dieu des festins*, point out how essential the two of them are – especially when it comes to the pleasures of the table. Apollon arrives to approve the proceedings and to express the wish – futile, as it turned out – that the father of the honoree would someday allow himself to be amused by the opera. Nothing in the prologue hints at the sorrows in the story to be performed – Apollon even calls the opera to follow "a sweet amusement." At Anet all is play.

The love triangle of the opera proper involves the two title characters – the shepherd Acis and the sea nymph Galatée – plus the gigantic cyclops Polyphème. (He is called a giant in the cast list and both a giant and a cyclops at various points in the text.) A subplot concerns the lovelorn shepherd, Télème, and his hard-hearted beloved, Scylla. At the start of the opera, Acis is in despair over Galatée, who is also playing hard-to-get, but in Act II she decides to marry him, whereas Scylla remains firm in rejecting love. Even though Act III involves Acis's death at the hands of the jealous Polyphème, who crushes him with a boulder, the work ends happily when Neptune revives Acis and transforms him into a river. The chorus that concludes the opera seems aimed at Scylla: young women are warned that Love will punish those who do not take advantage of their youth.[76] The work careens between tones, from the mopey shepherds and their snippy beloveds, to the simultaneously frightening and ridiculous cyclopes, to Galatée's heartfelt lament upon discovering Acis's body. Much of the dialogue has a cynical edge, as when Télème tells Acis that he is lucky to be in love with Galatée, because goddesses are not the difficult ones (I/2). Many sections of the work could be played in an

[76] Laurenti, *Valeurs morales et religieuses*, 53, points out that Scylla's refusal to accept love was seen within the epicurism reigning in librettos as "a sacrilege toward divinity in general" and that Campistron gestures in more than one place toward the fate Ovid accorded her in *Metamorphoses*, where she is turned first into a monster and then into a rock.

exaggerated, even campy style – one perhaps not out of keeping with the libertine spirit that, from what La Gorce reports, reigned at Anet during the week-long fête of which the premiere was a part.[77]

Acis et Galatée is actually quite light on instrumental dances; in fact, it has fewer per act – only two – than many tragedies. (The one exception is the prologue, which has seven dances, some very short, in three units.[78]) On the other hand, every act has at least one chorus that invites dancing, and the opera closes with a gigantic passacaille that is both instrumental and vocal. All three divertissements turn out to be extraordinarily interesting in their inner workings and dramaturgical centrality, notwithstanding the fact that all three are pastoral and framed as fêtes.

The Act I divertissement comes on the heels of Acis's and Télème's failed attempts at wooing. Galatée finds the shepherds' complaints of mistreatment annoying, while Scylla harshly says they don't matter, because no one listens. These cruel words are interrupted by the sweet sounds of flutes, announcing the arrival of shepherds and shepherdesses who have found happiness in love; Acis hopes that their example will prove persuasive for the recalcitrant Galatée and Scylla. The high trio texture that announces the divertissement turns out to saturate both the instrumental and vocal writing. Not only does the chorus sing only in three high parts (the clefs are G^2, C^1, and C^3), the instrumental passages within the choruses also consist of high trios. Such a texture is surprising in a pastoral divertissement involving, as here, both shepherds and shepherdesses; normally a mixed chorus sings in the expected four parts, and Lully usually reserves high trios for female roles. In Act I of *Acis et Galatée* these high sonorities seem part of a larger plan, in that they match the vocal assignments of the solo singers: the fact that Galatée, Scylla, and Aminte (the shepherdess inside the divertissement) are all sopranos is normal, but it is not to be expected that the three men – Acis, Télème and Tircis (Aminte's lover) – would all be *hautes-contre*. Lully carries this special sound world into Act III, where everyone gathers for the wedding of Acis and Galatée. Even the priest of Junon, who officiates, is a *haute-contre*, and the chorus of his followers adheres to the same sonority Lully gave to the shepherds in Act I, for the voices and orchestra alike.

Against the high, sweet sound-world of the shepherds, Lully sets the low, rough, and awkward music of Polyphème and his fellow cyclopes. Polyphème is a bass; his followers sing in four low parts with *haute-contre* on the top. Even the orchestral music that surrounds these characters has a low tessitura. Once in each act Polyphème forces his presence on the sweet-sounding shepherds. The first time brings the Act I divertissement to an abrupt halt: "the shepherds' concerts are interrupted by a barbarous noise," says

[77] La Gorce, *Lully*, 332–40. Lully himself appears to have enjoyed the freedoms offered by the week in an invitation-only environment. La Gorce believes that Lully's work for Vendôme contributed to the king's disaffection toward him during this period.

[78] This prologue, which contains two menuets, one gavotte-like march and two proto-rigaudons, conforms to the pattern identified in Ch. 5, p. 153, of more generic dances than elsewhere in the opera.

one of the very few *didascalies* in the entire libretto. In Act II Polyphème breaks in on Galatée's reverie, which ends without musical resolution, as he and his followers offer her a grotesque attempt at gallantry. In the last act Polyphème overhears the wedding ceremony getting underway, flies into a rage and murders Acis. Every time he appears, low sonorities envelop him. Such extreme contrast between sound worlds demands musical resolution, and at the very end of the opera Lully provides it. Neptune, who responds to Galatée's pleas to repair the damage wrought by Polyphème, recuperates the bass voice for the side of the good, and in so doing cleanses our ears of the voice of his son. Furthermore, the watery followers he calls upon to celebrate Acis's transformation into an immortal river – in a kind of aquatic pastoral fête – join in a chorus that finally sings properly in all four parts, from *dessus* to *basse*. A transformation of an audible type has been effected, and it finds expression in a huge passacaille in D minor, sung as well as danced: "Sous ses lois l'Amour veut qu'on jouisse / D'un bonheur qui jamais ne finisse." (Love wishes that everyone enjoy unending happiness under his laws.) Yet in this anomalous opera the transformation of the sound worlds is incomplete: the soloists within the vocal portions of the passacaille are two Naiads, that is, two women; male voices sing only from within the chorus. Perhaps this is because the texts seem aimed at least as much at the recalcitrant Scylla (even though she voluntarily banished herself in II/3 and disappeared from the opera) as they are at the rest of us: "Henceforth one must love without fear," a Naiad warns. "What good is unjust constraint? You beauties to whom heaven has given a thousand attractions, Love will punish you, if you don't benefit from them." The tone at the end of this opera is, once again, mixed.

As we saw in Chapter 1, Lully's concluding divertissements often set up oppositions that find both aural and visual resolution. Here Lully engages a similar pattern, but on a larger scale, by resolving oppositions set up across the opera. The D minor passacaille that concludes the opera is anticipated by a D major chaconne in II/5, that is also both vocal and instrumental. But here Galatée is alone on stage, after Acis has left to make preparations for their wedding. In a moment of insight she regrets her former harshness and revels in her new joy – until the sight of Polyphème interrupts her soliloquy.

Galatée: Qu'une injuste fierté nous cause de contrainte,
Et tyrannise nos désirs!
Tandis qu'à mon amant j'ai caché mes soupirs,
J'ai souffert mille maux, dans cette longue feinte;
À peine mon amour s'est expliqué sans crainte,
Que j'ai senti mille plaisirs:
Qu'une injuste fierté nous cause de contrainte,
Et tyrannise nos désirs!
Doux transports d'une âme contente
Que vous êtes charmants!

Mais je vois le Cyclope, il prévient mon attente;
Contraignons-nous quelques moments.

(Unjust pride serves only to constrain us and tyrannize our desires. While I hid my sighs from my lover, I suffered a thousand pangs from this long dissembling. No sooner had I admitted my love than I felt a thousand pleasures. Unjust pride serves only to constrain us and tyrannize our desires. Sweet transports in a happy soul, how charming you are! But I see the Cyclops; he is impeding my waiting [for Acis to return]. Let me restrain myself for a few minutes.)

The initial section of this text has the rounded shape typical of Lully's monologue airs – a two-line refrain that is repeated after several lines of new text – and Lully follows his normal practice of making the refrain a musical as well as textual repetition, but he does so, exceptionally, within the larger structure of a chaconne, which is so labeled in the score. But the chaconne is not exclusively vocal; Galatée's words are introduced and punctuated by long instrumental passages. There are 40 measures of instrumental chaconne, 29 bars in which she sings the first section of her text, another 23 instrumental bars, and 8 more vocal ("Doux transports"), before she breaks off suddenly on the dominant, changing from lyric mode to recitative when she sees Polyphème approaching. That is, almost two-thirds of the chaconne's 90 bars are instrumental, yet there is not the slightest hint that it would have been danced. Not only is Galatée the only person on stage in this scene, the only group characters that figure in this act at all are the followers of Polyphème, who do not arrive until later.

That Galatée herself might have danced does not make sense. There is nothing to motivate her dancing, either in her situation or in the text she sings; if Galatée danced here, the scene would have transgressed all the conventions about dancing Lully had constructed over his years of writing operas. The only possible conclusion is that no one danced during this chaconne.[79] So why might Lully have located a chaconne outside of a divertissement and denied it status as a dance? For one thing, its music gives weight to the self-understanding Galatée has just achieved; much more than the brief love duet that precedes it, the chaconne demonstrates her transformation from a coquette into someone with real depth of feeling. Perhaps Lully also knew that the singer in the role, Marthe Le Rochois, would turn the instrumental sections of the chaconne into something dramatic; after all, she had mesmerized audiences only a few months earlier with both her acting and her singing in the role of Armide.[80]

[79] La Gorce (*Lully*, 710–12) also concludes that this chaconne was not danced; he points out that Lully was obsessed by ground bass pieces toward the end of his life. A copy of the Ballard 1686 score, marked up for performances in the mid-eighteenth century (F-Po A22a), bears the annotation "Cette chaconne n'est point dansée." A choreography for a couple exists to the first instrumental section of this chaconne, played twice, but it was made by L'Abbé for the London stage.

[80] Le Rochois's appearance in *Acis et Galatée* is attested in Parfaict, *Dictionnaire*, I, 12. She was by many accounts a riveting actress.

Polyphème and his fellow Cyclopes burst in upon Galatée's reverie. Polyphème is trying hard to please, but his fête succeeds only in caricaturing the pastoral world evoked in the sweet divertissement in Act I. Like the shepherds, the Cyclopes keep sheep; both flocks are visible in the surrounding woods. In keeping with their description in Ovid's *Metamorphoses*, the Cyclopes also play little flutes or panpipes: the march that brings them on stage, which is exceptionally low in tessitura, is interrupted every four bars by a Papageno-like flute flourish up and down a perfect fifth. These passages are attributed in the score to unison solo flutes, but according to Lecerf de la Viéville, Lully used boilermakers' whistles (*sifflets de chaudronnier*) for this refrain.[81] Perhaps some of the dancing Cyclopes mimed – or even played – the whistles, while the others attempted to bring off a pastoral dance. This little comic flourish continues to punctuate Polyphème's air and the chorus, both built around the same music (Example 6-11). The text reveals how wrapped up in themselves the Cyclopes are in their misguided efforts to make a good impression.

Example 6-11: *Acis et Galatée*, "Chœur. The strings play with the chorus" (Paris: Ballard, 1686), 85. (*Cyclopes*: "Let us vie with each other in following you to this place. To a heart wounded by love every moment is precious. Let us prepare a glorious triumph for the goddess.")

[81] Lecerf, *Comparaison*, II, 206. La Gorce (*Lully*, 709) suggests that Lully had panpipes in mind.

Example 6-12: *Acis et Galatée*, "Entrée des Cyclopes" (Paris: Ballard, 1686), 97.

A second chorus, which at least has the good grace to be addressed to Galatée ("O vous adorable immortelle, / Ecoutez favorablement / Les voeux de votre amant"), is interspersed with instrumental passages whose unexpected harmonic turns invite comic choreographic treatment, and the dance piece that follows, the "Entrée des Cyclopes" has, in addition to its low tessitura, an unbalanced phrase structure and an insistence on repeated notes at ends of phrases (Example 6-12). Its $\frac{6}{4}$ meter and dotted rhythms recall the dances of the shepherds in Act 1, both of which are also in $\frac{6}{4}$; Lully seems to have set up superficial similarities between the two divertissements in the interest of comic exaggeration. (Pastoral dances are not confined to $\frac{6}{4}$ meter; Lully's choice of the same meter and similar rhythms in two divertissements must have been deliberate.) Whereas the shepherds' music is graceful, the cyclopes' is out of kilter. This piece provides the main showcase for the cyclopes' efforts at dancing; they must have been made to look awkward and inept.[82]

[82] There are two choreographies set to the music of the "Entrée des Cyclopes," both for two men and both post-dating Lully. According to Ken Pierce (personal communication), these dances take a quirky approach to the choreography, with familiar male theatrical steps mixed in with sequences

Another point of contact between this divertissement and the one in Act I is that both are interrupted by the socially maladroit Polyphème. In Act I he frightens everyone away; here he is so eager to propose marriage to Galatée that he sends his followers away before they can finish the festivities he has planned. In Act III Polyphème comes across her wedding to Acis while it is in progress; his brutal murder of Acis takes place not off stage, but in full view of the audience. The Cyclops so dominates all the turning points in the opera that it almost seems as if it should be named after him, but what pulls the opera back from the grotesque brink is, first, Galatée's moving lament and, second, the long passacaille in minor mode that constitutes most of the concluding divertissement. As with Galatée's chaconne in Act II, the long instrumental section of the passacaille (166 bars) brings gravity to a scene whose texts could cut more than one way. Yet within it, and even more so within the passacaille's sung sections, the high, sweet sound world of the shepherds keeps intruding, even while the relentless ground contains it. The insistence in the texts on the benefits to be gained from love may represent lack of imagination on Campistron's part, but more probably attempt to recuperate Scylla's angry refusal to accept love; certainly Galatée and Acis do not need any such exhortations. But in distinction to *Cadmus et Hermione* and *Alceste*, where the subplots are resolved within the concluding divertissement, Scylla does not return in Act III and her loose end remains dangling. Notwithstanding the Naiads' efforts to draw her symbolically into the circle, their threats of punishment for those who refuse love are an admission of their failure. This passacaille does not function, as many do, as an act of seduction, but the connection with women is highlighted by the texts and the high vocal trios. The contrast between the solemnity of the music and the lightness of the words makes for an unsettling ending; even here the opera refuses a consistent tone.

Just as the prologue to *Les Fêtes de l'Amour et de Bacchus* announces Lully's operatic enterprise as one that would draw upon many and varied theatrical traditions, so does *Acis et Galatée*, Lully's last complete opera, demonstrate that his career did not have a single linear trajectory with the *tragédie en musique* at its pinnacle. Lully may have devoted more of his energies to the tragic in the second half of his operatic output than he did in the first, but he never fully turned his back on the comic and the grotesque. Rather, he worked these diverse elements into a number of his operatic works, in varying proportions and degrees; the divertissements, with their reliance on the body as a crucial medium of expression, became the most prominent site for this aspect of his creative output.

that seem designed to communicate "essence of cyclops," which are unorthodox but not necessarily clumsy.

It is useless to speculate what Lully might have composed had the pressures from his patrons and critics allowed him more freedom. But it is within our control to redress a historiographic imbalance by paying attention to the works he composed that do not fit into a tragic mold. Lully's output is varied and complexly ambiguous. His successors recognized the breadth of his abilities and did not confine themselves to the *tragédies en musique* in paying him the homage of imitation.

PART II

The Rival Muses in the Age of Campra

7 | The Muses Take the Stage

Lully was scarcely cold in his tomb before there were signs of aesthetic changes at the Académie Royale de Musique. Before his death in March 1687 he had begun work on a new *tragédie, Achille et Polixène*, set to a libretto by Campistron; according to the score, he composed only the first act, the rest being credited to Pascal Collasse.[1] The prologue alone marks a rupture from Quinault's practices, or even from Campistron's encomium to the Dauphin in the prologue to *Acis et Galatée*. This one features an encounter between three of the Muses – Melpomène, the Muse of tragedy, Thalie, the Muse of comedy, and Terpsichore, normally the Muse of dance, but here identified as the Muse of music – set in "a place appropriate for staging spectacles, that could serve either tragedy or comedy." After years of operating on the margins, comedy suddenly finds itself publicly placed on an equal footing with tragedy.[2] But all is not well in this mythic theater. "This place no longer has the magnificence of former times; in fact, it is almost destroyed and ruined," reports the *didascalie* that sets the stage. The three Muses appear alone, without followers, thus without the power to generate art. When Mercure flies down from the heavens to ascertain what has caused this sorry state, Melpomène reports that "the greatest of kings" is no longer coming to the Muses' fêtes. Thalie adds that his absence has robbed their spectacles of their magnificence, and Terpsichore has the most reproachful text of all.

> La tristesse règne en ces lieux,
> Nous rougissons de ne pouvoir lui plaire,
> Hélas! Ne saurions-nous rien faire
> Digne de paraître à ses yeux?
>
> (Sadness reigns here; we blush at our inability to please him. Alas! are we incapable of producing anything worthy of appearing before his eyes?)

The difficulties that the Académie Royale de Musique underwent in the years following Lully's death, as it struggled both to redefine itself without his powerful

[1] La Gorce, *Lully*, 704–05.

[2] Melpomène figures in the prologue to *Atys*, but this was the first time either Terpsichore or Thalie had made any individual statement. In the prologue to *Isis*, Thalie and Melpomène sing among a group of five Muses, while Terpsichore is an instrumentalist. Her identification as Muse of music is exceptional; in Classical mythology no single Muse represented music, but in French librettos, Euterpe, the Muse of lyric poetry, generally has that role.

presence and to secure its funding in the face of the king's declining interest, have often been recounted.[3] But this bald public admission of the institution's problems still shocks,[4] and whereas in this prologue Jupiter does turn up to reinvigorate the Muses, the period *Achille et Polixène* initiated was one of artistic floundering: of the 22 new works, most of them tragedies, performed in the first ten years after Lully's death, only five were ever revived, and only two of these (*Alcide* and *Les Saisons*) more than once.[5] Lully revivals helped keep the institution afloat and it was not until October of 1697 that Campra's first theatrical work, *L'Europe galante*, gave the Opéra a resounding success. As time went on, a new balance established itself among the three Muses: Melpomène retained her prestige, but lost stage time to Thalie and Terpsichore. Whereas *tragédies* had accounted for approximately three-quarters of the repertoire around 1700, by the time Rameau composed his first opera, in 1733, approximately half of the works performed at the Opéra belonged to lighter, more dance-oriented genres.[6] Moreover, even within *tragédies* the proportion of dancing tended to grow, while the ties between vocal music and instrumental dances began to weaken.

The period between the death of Lully and the arrival of Rameau is marked by three tendencies that impact the dancing presented on the stage of the Opéra. First, the infusion of new genres such as the opera-ballet changed the tone of the theater by increasing the number of works with light-hearted, or even comic elements. Second, the *tragédie en musique* came to exist in a state of tension between the Lullian model and the new tendencies; the divertissements, both in newly created works and in revivals, became crucial sites where such tensions played themselves out. Third, the amount of dancing on the stage expanded, in all genres, and the best dancers developed a fan base that came to the theater to see them perform, no matter what the work.

3 See especially La Gorce, *L'Opéra à Paris*.

4 One wonders if Lully saw or approved the text. The text of the five acts must already have been in place before he began composing Act I, but prologues were generally written last. Whatever its timing, this prologue is very different in tone from those in his previous operas. Lully was not in good standing with the king at the end of his life (see La Gorce, *Lully*, ch. 12) and Beaussant reads Lully's dedicatory letter to the king in the score of *Armide* as expressing his anxiety over the king's neglect (*Lully*, 805–07). In that context, perhaps this prologue might have been the same, even if Lully had lived to see the opera onto the stage.

5 The operas are listed in Ducrot, "Les représentations" and in La Gorce, *L'Opéra à Paris*, 197–203. Ducrot, 21, points out that since later operas were generally less successful than Lully's had been, there were both more premieres and more revivals during this period. Barthélemy, *André Campra*, 47, argues, however, that blaming Lully's successors is too simple; the situation was complex and there were several successes. We should also note that failure at the time does not necessarily mean that today we agree with the audiences' judgment: among the works not revived are Charpentier's *Médée* and Jacquet de La Guerre's *Céphale et Procris*.

6 These approximate statistics include premieres and revivals, as based on the librettos published in each year. For figures regarding premieres by genre, 1715–1750, see Lagrave, *Le Théâtre*, 348–49.

Changes this extensive did not happen without anxiety, and librettists increasingly made use of the prologue as a site for airing institutional and aesthetic concerns. Because the framework for opera remained largely within the realm of mythology, the Muses provided convenient mouthpieces; *Achille et Polixène*'s is but the first of many prologues in which they served this function.[7] In one of the most pointed, the prologue to Mouret's opera-ballet *Les Fêtes de Thalie* (1714), Thalie and Melpomène square off over which one of them will control the Opéra, on whose stage the prologue is set. Melpomène vaunts her glorious record: "Armide, Phaéton, Atys, Roland, Bellérophon, Thétis[8] – these give me sovereignty over this brilliant place. Muse, withdraw!" Thalie replies with a tart, "My sister, one tires quickly of weeping. Does anyone ever tire of laughing?" Apollon, who appears to have the early operas of Lully in mind, attempts a compromise. "Could you not," he asks Melpomène, "get together with Thalie in the same work, as you did in the past? This mixture still charms Italy today." Perhaps Melpomène has a more up-to-date understanding of Italian operatic practices than does Apollon, who does not seem to realize that by 1714 Venetian opera's mixture of the high and low was giving way to the strictures of *opera seria*, but whatever the reason, she refuses his offer to share the stage with Thalie. Apollon then decrees that the two will take different seasons, and this being the summer, Thalie gets to start.[9] The chorus applauds: "Triumph, charming Muse; triumph over boredom, tears, and sighs. Crown the triumphant troupe of *Jeux* and Pleasures."

Les Fêtes de Thalie, a thoroughly comic work, was a huge success, but generated criticism. As a means simultaneously of defending and mocking himself, La Font added to the end of the work a new entrée, a "Critique des Fêtes de Thalie," undoubtedly inspired by Molière's "Critique de l'École des femmes."[10] This time Thalie is quibbling with Polymnie over which one of them deserves credit for the success of the opera. Each reproaches the other with weaknesses the critics had pointed out: Polymnie attacks Thalie's "weak and languid verses," while Thalie says that her sister's music has

[7] The Muses appeared in other theaters as well: the prologue of Regnard's *Les Chinois* (Théâtre Italien, 1692), for example, is set on Mount Parnassus and stages a dispute among the Muses, in which Colombine plays the role of Apollon, Arlequin that of Thalie (Gherardi, *Théâtre italien*, IV).

[8] I.e., Collasse's *Thétis et Pélée* (1689), the one opera on this list not by Lully.

[9] New regulations, promulgated in 1713, provided that the winter season would open with a new *tragédie en musique* (replaced, if necessary, by a Lully revival), and that the summer season, which started after Easter, would open with either a new *tragédie* or one by Lully, followed by a ballet (translated in Wood and Sadler, *French Baroque Opera*, 11). In practice, however, ballets were performed at various times of year.

[10] Molière's *School for Wives* (1662) set off a series of polemical attacks; in the *Critique* Molière staged a conversation among spectators who had just seen his play. Similar responses were sometimes staged at the Théâtre Italien as well; see, for example, Regnard's *Arlequin homme à bonne fortune* and the *Critique de l'homme à bonne fortune* (1690; Gherardi, *Théâtre italien*, II).

"a thousand mistakes that shock the most knowledgeable ears." Terpsichore bursts in, claiming that:

> Sans mes pas
> Et sans leurs appas,
> Vos jeux et vos chants ne brilleraient pas.
> Mes figures
> Sont des peintures,
> Dont l'attrait flatteur
> Charme les yeux, séduit le cœur.
>
> (Without my steps and without their charms, your games and songs would not shine. My figures are paintings whose gratifying attractions enchant the eyes and seduce the heart.)

Terpsichore continues to boast about her *pas de deux*, her sailors, her shepherds, until Thalie and Polymnie grudgingly admit that she does have a point – but that she still cannot compare dance to the arts of her sisters. Terpsichore angrily retorts that they are deceiving themselves, and that Apollon had sworn that the honor was hers alone. But Apollon, who is thoroughly annoyed by the Muses' quarrels, sends Momus, the god of mockery, to arbitrate in his place. Momus allows that the music is "aimable," the dance "vive, admirable," but as for the poetry, he's glad he didn't write it. Thalie is outraged, but Momus calms her by saying that all three deserve credit and by quickly calling everyone to "laugh, sing, and dance."

Twenty years later, the Muses have settled their differences. The prologue to Campra's last opera, *Achille et Déidamie* (1735), is structured as a homage to Lully and Quinault, whose statues occupy center stage, at the foot of Mount Parnassus. The Muses, Graces, Pleasures, and followers of Love have all gathered, and the Spirits of the Arts crown the statues with myrtle and laurels. Since the work to follow is a tragedy, Melpomène is one of the hosts; her sister Thalie does not receive individual attention, and Lully's comic side is passed over in silence. Amour, however, makes a point of seeking out Terpsichore from among her sisters, inviting her to dance with the Graces in order to "form the image of our sounds." After their dance, Melpomène calmly remarks that if the Graces do not join with the Muses, "all art languishes without charm." Apollon descends to ask Amour and Melpomène to prepare a spectacle about the young Achille, for whom "Glory was always his most ardent desire." Glory herself then turns to Terpsichore and tells her that her participation is essential.

> *La Gloire*: Votre soin nous est nécessaire,
> Muse, qui dans nos jeux faites briller vos pas:
> C'est quelquefois à vos appas
> Qu'un spectacle nouveau doit le bonheur de plaire.

(Muse, you who dance so brilliantly in our entertainments, your help is necessary for us. It is sometimes thanks to your attractions that a new spectacle has the good fortune of pleasing the audience.)

Here again, a venal financial reality is enshrined in the text of the work. As if to demonstrate how essential she is, Terpsichore dances a solo that shows off many different characters. Melpomène has no more to say; Terpsichore's centrality, even to a *tragédie*, is taken for granted.

The power struggle among the Muses, thematized often by librettists, provides the framework for the chapters that follow. The three devoted to Thalie explore not only the mechanisms by which the comic entered the repertoire, but also the resistance it encountered. The two chapters devoted to Melpomène show that the Lullian template retained its centrality even as it was inflected by the workings of both Thalie and Terpsichore. The Muse of the Dance figures throughout, but the chapters bearing her name concentrate on changes to the dance troupe at the Opéra, contextualize the choreographic notations that originated in that theater, and discuss developments in the treatments of operatic dance. Just as music was represented by no single Muse, since music was understood by the Greeks to permeate the arts of the nine sisters, so music is not assigned its own chapter, but figures in them all.[11]

GENRE TERMINOLOGY

The vast majority of the works performed at the Académie Royale de Musique at this time bore one of three labels on the title page of the libretto: "tragédie," "pastorale" (sometimes "pastorale héroïque"), or "ballet." The "tragédie" designation implied not only loftiness of subject and characters, but also (with very few exceptions) a structure – a prologue and five acts.[12] A *tragédie en musique* could, and often did, have a happy ending. "Pastorale" designated a realm and a type of character; as a genre it also indicated a work with a continuous storyline, but whose structures could vary from one act to five. "Ballet" was the most fluid term; it seems primarily to have meant a work that was something other than the other two, although it might share elements with them. The designation "ballet" does not indicate whether the work is serious or in a light vein, whether the characters come from the realm of mythology or a seraglio in Turkey, nor how it is organized internally.

[11] Although musical characteristics that impinge on the divertissements receive coverage, the major stylistic changes that happened within French opera during this period are beyond the scope of this book.

[12] In the immediate post-Lully period a few *tragédies* have only three acts. A few works designated as *tragédies* should more properly have been labeled something else: *Astrée* (1691) is really a pastorale, and the designations for *La Naissance de Vénus* (1696) hesitate between "tragédie" and "opéra." Regarding the poetics of the post-Lullian tragedies, see Kintzler, *Poétique*, 298ff.

The crucial common point was that singing served to carry the plot, and thus all three genres, including ballets, were often colloquially called "opera," in the eighteenth century as well as now. Dance was no less important to a *tragédie* than to a ballet, and the divertissement structures Lully and Quinault had established for *tragédies* carried over into the other genres, where the divertissements were framed in similar ways. Whereas in ballets the role of dance sometimes expanded beyond a single divertissement per act, it nonetheless remained subordinate, in that the main characters were singers. The one thing "ballet" did *not* mean in France at this time was a work danced throughout, based purely on instrumental music and devoid of singing. What came to be called "ballet pantomime," precisely in order to distinguish it from the broader category, lay in the future.[13]

Some dance historians have applied the term "opera-ballet" to all French operas, from Lully's *tragédies en musique* to all the varied genres of Campra or Rameau. This usage derives from an understandable desire to acknowledge the centrality of dance to them all, but it obscures important distinctions. Musicological writings define opera-ballet more narrowly, as a sub-category of opera in which each unit has a separate cast of characters and its own plot – Campra's *L'Europe galante* of 1697 being the defining example.[14] Since the structural distinction is crucial to the discussions that follow, and because this definition of opera-ballet has been consecrated by long musicological usage, the term has been adopted in this book.[15]

Often, however, an opera-ballet has more unity than its separate plots imply. Not only is there always some kind of overarching idea, but the work may have a logical sequence (youth, adulthood, old age in the *Ballet des âges*), or there may be some kind of epilogue that ties the work together (as in the "Critique" at the end of *Les Fêtes de Thalie*), or the individual entrées may be constructed in a way that distinguishes between internal entrées and ones that could reasonably serve as a finale. Such is the case with *L'Europe galante*, where only "La Turquie" ends with the kind of extended celebrations appropriate to ring down the final curtain. Not all opera-ballets, however, exhibit this kind of conceptual unity, in which case the choice and order of entrées could be manipulated in revivals; Campra's *Fêtes vénitiennes* is the most extreme case in point. This looser type of opera-ballet moves in the direction of yet another genre – "fragments," a term applied to a sequence of entrées of different origins that were nonetheless performed together on the same night.

[13] The court ballets Lully composed in the 1650s and 1660s always had at least one vocal number – and often more.

[14] The *Ballet des saisons* (1695) has the structure of an opera-ballet (prologue and independent entrées), but is set in mythological realms. Its score intermingles pieces recycled from Lully with new ones by Collasse.

[15] This term has some historical grounding (the *Mercure* applied it to *Les Fêtes vénitiennes* in 1731), even if it was not used consistently; see Anthony, "The French opera-ballet," 198–99.

Some "ballets" had continuous plots over several (often three) acts, two examples being Desmarest's *Les Amours de Momus* (1695) and Campra's *Aréthuse* (1701). Sometimes a genre designation might have a modifying word, depending on the nature of the dramatic material; La Barre's *La Vénitienne* (1705) is called a "comédie-ballet,"[16] and Villeneuve's *La Princesse d'Élide* (1728) a "ballet héroïque." Although the term "ballet" did not itself show how the work was constructed, the terms used for its internal parts did: with few exceptions, the units of a ballet with a continuous plot were called "acts," whereas the units of a work in which each has its own set of characters (an opera-ballet) were called "entrées."[17] Ballets of both types provided a more natural home for comic elements than did the *tragédie en musique*, although the latter was not exempt from an infusion of humor from time to time.

Some writers have adopted the term "lyric comedy" for ballets with continuous plots in a comic or romantic vein.[18] This term was not, however, used at the time: two of the works often so dubbed today, Mouret's *Les Amours de Ragonde* and Rameau's *Platée*, were called respectively "comédie en musique" and "ballet bouffon" in their librettos. The fact that both were called "comédie-ballet" in their published scores is but another instance of how loosely genre designations were applied during this period.

SOURCES

The operas written between the eras of Lully and Rameau are finally beginning to receive study, yet a major impediment to their revival is the state of the sources. Whereas Lully's operas from 1679 onwards benefitted from publication in full score under the composer's supervision, Ballard switched in 1695, with few exceptions, to reduced scores.[19] When composers used engravers instead of the Ballard house's moveable type, as did Marais for *Sémélé* (1709), these usually also appeared in reduced format (see Figure 12-3, p. 367). The "partitions réduites" transmit the solo vocal parts, but only the outer voices of the choruses; for orchestral passages they include the treble and bass, and, occasionally, trio textures. Verbal cues for instrumentation are sometimes provided; these help convey to the researcher the emblematic use of instruments, but they do not supply full information for performers. Some published scores do not even transmit the full text of the opera. Desmarest's *Didon* was published in 1693 by

[16] This work bears no structural relationship to the comedy-ballets Molière wrote with Lully, in which a spoken play has interludes of music and dance.

[17] The word "entrée" had three main meanings in seventeenth- and eighteenth-century ballets and operas: (1) a single dance for a given set of characters, not necessarily ones just entering the stage; (2) in the *ballet de cour* of Lully and earlier, a sequence of dances for the same set of characters, who generally enter for the entrée and leave at its end; (3) the equivalent of an act in the genre of opera-ballet.

[18] See, for example, Anthony, *French Baroque Music*, 188–89, following a path laid down by Masson.

[19] For a list of Ballard's scores in both formats, 1672–1715, see Guillo, "L'édition musicale," 96–98.

Ballard in two parts, one containing the vocal music, the other the "symphonies," and his *Iphigénie* appeared in 1704 only as "excerpts." For a few operas, manuscript full scores exist, but even for operas that were not published the manuscript scores may survive only in reduced format. Moreover, manuscript scores, even more than do the prints, raise questions of dating and of their relationship to the composer and to the Opéra.

The researcher and the musician must also confront a lesser degree of congruence between libretto and score than was the case for Lully. Librettos continued to be issued for every opera performed, including for every revival, and, starting in 1703, the Ballard house began issuing collected volumes of librettos under the title *Recueil général des opéra représentés par l'Académie Royale de Musique, depuis son établissement.*[20] But both librettists and composers often revised their works – in response to audience reactions, both positive and negative, as well as to whatever inner compulsions or outside pressures they may have felt. These revisions left their mark in various ways: revised editions of the libretto; a note in the score or libretto explaining that changes had been made; a supplement to the score that was either issued separately or attached to later printings; a new edition of the score; or, when only one libretto and one score exist, discrepancies between them suggesting that changes must have occurred between the publishing of the one and the other. It is not rare to find texts in the libretto for which no music exists in the published score, or vocal pieces in a score for which the text is lacking in the libretto. When massive changes were made, a new libretto and/or a new score might be issued during a single run of performances. Montéclair's *Jephté* generated no fewer than four librettos during its first year (1732–33). The score of Destouches's *Amadis de Grèce* was published by Ballard in 1699, then again the same year in a "second edition, revised, corrected, and enlarged." La Coste's *Philomèle* represents a different approach. The last page of the score Ballard published in 1705 states that "several pieces have been removed from this opera in order not to make the performance too long on the stage. Nonetheless, it seemed desirable not to suppress these pieces when the music was printed." The revival of the opera in 1709 generated a new libretto, but not a new score; these three documents present three different versions of the prologue, among other passages.

Even when an opera was not revived, it might produce more than one libretto. Baptistin Stuck's first for the Opéra, *Méléagre* (1709), had only a moderate success and was never revived. The problems were apparently due to the libretto rather than the score, to the point that the librettist, François-Antoine Jolly, rewrote parts of every act, although not until the run of the opera had finished. His explanations of the changes and the revised libretto were published five years later in the *Recueil général*, which

[20] Paris, 1703–46. Single librettos were published by the Ballard house up to 1713, by Pierre Ribou through May 1716, by Ribou's widow from then until June 1727, and by Jean-Baptiste-Christophe Ballard thereafter.

means that the text as it was *not* performed is the one preserved in the collected edition of the Opéra's repertoire. On the other hand, changes to an opera were often due to success rather than failure. Many scores include a "Supplément" at the back that sometimes replaces existing music but often adds still more, especially to divertissements. Ballard published scores for the popular *L'Europe galante* in 1697, 1698, and 1699, each time with more music in the divertissements.[21] The most dramatic example of how popular success could lead to a publishing frenzy is the opera-ballet *Les Fêtes vénitiennes*, whose premiere in 1710 generated so much enthusiasm that Danchet and Campra wrote more entrées that necessitated the publication of more scores and librettos and spun off numerous manuscript copies. The resulting complex of sources remains to be adequately sorted out.[22] This opera represents an extreme case, but for many works the researcher risks drowning in the details of surviving artifacts before even beginning to consider their content.

Some of the discrepancies may arise from the fact that Ballard appears to have rushed the scores into print so that they would be available for the premiere, thus before changes in response to audience reactions could have been made. Ballard's score for *Les Amours des déesses* (1729) includes the following note: "The prologue and the first two entrées being already printed, we thought it better to make them available by the first performance, so as not to defer satisfying the public. We are working to offer the third entrée without delay." Ballard kept his word: "The printing of this third entrée, which is the last one in *Les Amours des déesses*, was achieved on 13 August 1729. It is thus available to the public for the fourth performance of this ballet."[23] The score of Gervais's *Hypermnestre* was even published one month before the premiere.[24] Sometimes delays occurred, and in a preface to the score of Stuck's *Méléagre*, Ballard begged the public's indulgence for publishing the score almost three weeks after the premiere; he explained that the decision to publish the score at all had been made very late and that the score was longer than usual, so required extra time.[25] The title page for the score of Villeneuve's *Princesse d'Elide* (1728) says that the printing was finished "on the day of the ninth performance, with all the changes."

21 These scores were all in reduced format; in 1724 Ballard published the work again, this time in full score; see Anthony, "Printed editions." Anthony reports (60–62) that in 1703 Ballard sued Campra for breach of contract because he had made so many changes to the *Ballet des Muses* that the work as performed no longer conformed to the score.

22 For an overview of the changes made during its first season, see Masson, "'Fêtes vénitiennes'," esp. 130–32; regarding the reprises, see Pt 2, 218–24. Lütolf's edition (Paris: Heugel, 1971) does not include all the entrées, nor does it deal thoroughly with the sources.

23 Each entrée in this score has separate pagination. Ballard's first note warned his customers not to have the score bound until they had bought the third entrée.

24 The premiere took place on 3 November 1716, according to the title pages of both score and libretto. A copy of the score (F-Po A.95b) bears a note on the last page, dated 3 October 1716 and signed by Gervais and Ballard, indicating that the score had been reviewed and corrected.

25 Ballard's "Avis" promised that future scores would come out on time.

Yet another complication arises within many published sources, both musical and textual: the conflation of more than one edition or issue of the publication within a single surviving copy. Sometimes a new title page with a new date may be put onto a publication that is otherwise identical in content to the original. At other times, pages from various issues or editions may be mixed, or portions of a work originating at different times may be bound into the same volume.[26] This is particularly prone to happen for the category of works called "fragments," although the problem is by no means exclusive to them.

In an ideal world, the myriad source problems surrounding the repertoire between Lully and Rameau would have been solved and critical editions of all the works published before I began writing this book. But only a handful of modern editions in full score have been published to date, not all of them reliable; the most extensive series, the *Chefs d'œuvre de l'opéra français classique*, exhibits too much editorial tampering and cutting to allow its piano-vocal scores to serve as the basis for scholarly study. Reality has obliged me to deal with the primary sources in all their messiness. In order to impose a modicum of consistency on my research, I have chosen to use the first libretto and first published score, when one exists, as the main basis for study; exceptions are signaled in the notes. I have also eschewed, with few exceptions, discussion of the annotations for performance found in some copies of the published scores, many of which date from revivals of the operas during the 1750s and early 1760s; these consist of additions of new music or borrowings from other works, suppressions, annotations regarding tempo, expression, and ornaments, indications of repeats, and, occasionally, of performers' names.[27] These annotations not only generally post-date the limits of this study, they need to be sorted out before they can be used with any claim to authority – another task that is beyond the scope of my own research.

Because so much remains to be learned about the sources from this period, both in general and in regard to individual works, some of my observations may need to be modified in the light of future studies.[28] I have nonetheless tried to confront head-on the problems the sources present, without, however, allowing them to prevent me from looking both for general tendencies and interesting individual scenes. In cases of significant ambiguity I have laid out the problems as part of the discussion, but I have also allowed myself to use my experience in looking at many scores and librettos to draw conclusions, however tentative these may prove. Too much attention to details of the primary sources would have made the book unreadable.

[26] For a succinct discussion of this phenomenon in regard to Lully's librettos, see Schmidt, *LLC*, xvii–xviii.

[27] See Rosow, "From Destouches to Berton," esp. 296–305. For one example, see Fig. 13-1, p. 400.

[28] I find myself speculating about the extent to which our views on French operatic history have been colored by this publishing phenomenon. If, like Lully's works, these operas had been published in full score, we might assess them quite differently.

Yet the sources for this repertoire also present opportunities unavailable for the Lully era. As of 1699 the librettos for performances at the Opéra in Paris began to include the names of the performers, both singers and dancers. These listings are an enormous boon, as they open vistas onto the inner workings of the operas and make it possible to track the professional profiles of individual performers.[29] The period after Lully's death also saw the commercial exploitation of a system of dance notation that preserves over 350 choreographies, of which 47 indicate in their titles that they were "danced at the Opéra" and identify the performers (see Chapter 14); this information makes it possible to establish that they originated in 24 different works from between 1693 and 1713. Another helpful development is that more people began writing about what they were seeing when they went the theater. In particular, the monthly periodical, the *Mercure de France* (its name as of 1724 – through most of its previous history the *Mercure galant*) increased its coverage of theatrical performances in Paris, including of the Opéra. It cannot be said to offer an independent voice (reviews in this period are almost always positive), but its comments about the divertissements often provide information unavailable elsewhere.

READING THE CAST LISTS IN LIBRETTOS

Before 1699 only librettos printed for court performances included the names of the performers. In Lully's day these people were in the king's employ, although a number of them also worked at the Opéra; a few later court librettos that include names, such as Lorenzani's *Orontée* of 1688, also bear the statement that the work was performed "by the Académie Royale de Musique." But as of 31 July 1699 (a revival of Lully's *Proserpine*), the librettos sold at the door of the Opéra started listing the names of the singers and dancers and thus served simultaneously as programs of a sort. Even though cast lists were rarely updated to reflect the inevitable substitutions that must have occurred, the inclusion of names makes it much easier to identify the singing and dancing roles in the divertissements, which in turn allows for a greater understanding of how the divertissements were constructed. But even before 1699 the lists of roles that appear in librettos may convey information that helps interpret the main text.

Two librettos of Campra's opera-ballet *L'Europe galante* – one from the premiere in 1697, the other from the 1706 revival – may serve to illustrate the kinds of information that can be drawn from the two different types of listings. Before 1699, there were

[29] The cast lists have been collated in an unpublished catalogue by Nathalie Lecomte, whom I thank for allowing me to consult her work. Most of the librettos collected in the *Recueil général* do not include the names of the performers. However, starting in volume 7 (1703), Ballard printed the cast list for the first or last opera in each volume, in order, the preface states, "to make known those who are currently appearing on stage."

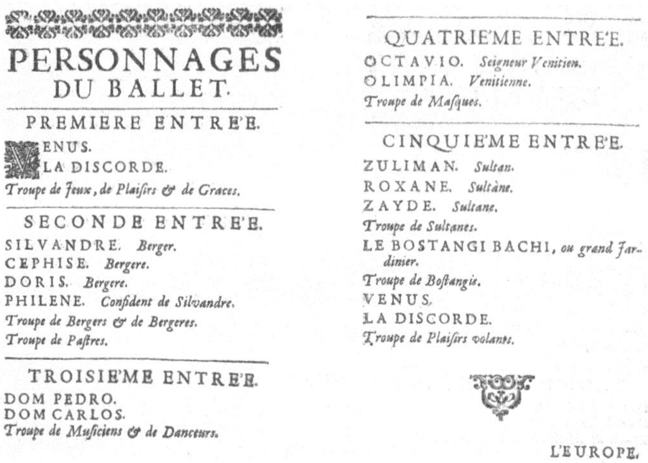

PERSONNAGES
DU BALLET.

PREMIERE ENTRE'E.

VENUS.
LA DISCORDE.
Troupe de Jeux, de Plaisirs & de Graces.

SECONDE ENTRE'E.

SILVANDRE. *Berger.*
CEPHISE. *Bergere.*
DORIS. *Bergere.*
PHILENE. *Confident de Silvandre.*
Troupe de Bergers & de Bergeres.
Troupe de Pastres.

TROISIE'ME ENTRE'E.

DOM PEDRO.
DOM CARLOS.
Troupe de Musiciens & de Danceurs.

QUATRIE'ME ENTRE'E.

OCTAVIO. *Seigneur Venitien.*
OLIMPIA. *Venitienne.*
Troupe de Masques.

CINQUIE'ME ENTRE'E.

ZULIMAN. *Sultan.*
ROXANE. *Sultàne.*
ZAYDE. *Sultane.*
Troupe de Sultanes.
LE BOSTANGI BACHI, *ou grand Jardinier.*
Troupe de Bostangis.
VENUS.
LA DISCORDE.
Troupe de Plaisirs volants.

L'EUROPE.

Figure 7-1: Cast list from the 1697 libretto of *L'Europe galante*.

generally two such lists in a libretto, one for the prologue, the other for the rest of the opera.[30] The 1697 libretto of *L'Europe galante* (see Figure 7-1) does not conform to this pattern because Ballard treated the prologue as the first entrée and provided only a single list, the "Personnages du ballet." As was the norm, this one highlights the solo singing roles, and lumps the chorus and dancers together into "troupes." In the pastoral second entrée ("La France"), for example, it identifies a cast consisting of four solo singers, a troupe of shepherds and shepherdesses, and a troupe of herdsmen (*pâtres*); the function of the group characters is not revealed, but the text proper of the libretto shows that the shepherds and shepherdesses both sing and dance, whereas the herdsmen are not explicitly mentioned. The third entrée ("L'Espagne") lists only two solo singers; the group characters are identified as singers and dancers, who, it turns out, participate in a serenade that includes dance as well as song. Throughout this list the singing roles are succinctly qualified ("Zuliman, Sultan"), whereas in some others, particularly *tragédies*, the qualification is often more detailed (in *Vénus et Adonis*, also from 1697, Adonis is identified as "son of Cyniras, king of Cyprus").

When this list of roles for *L'Europe galante* is compared with the full text of the libretto, it becomes apparent that it is not complete. The serenade in "L'Espagne" is performed not by Don Pedro or Don Carlos, but by a "Musicien" and a "Musicienne." The troupe of maskers in the fourth entrée ("L'Italie") includes at least two solo singers, a Venetian woman and a "Femme du bal." Other singers inside of divertissements are also left out. However, lists of roles do not always neglect this kind of secondary character; a "Bostangi bachi" is listed among the cast in the fifth entrée. Still, even a case

[30] The list for the prologue comes directly after the title page, unless a preface and/or dedication intervenes. The second list is located between the prologue and the rest of the opera.

PERSONNAGES
DU BALLET.

PREMIERE ENTRÉE.

VENUS, Mademoiſelle Pouſſin.
LA DISCORDE, Monſieur Mantienne.
GRACES, Meſdemoiſelles Loignon, & Demerville.
Autre GRACE, Mademoiſelle Cochereau.

LES GRACES,
Meſdemoiſelles Provoſt, Guyot, & Saligny.
PLAISIRS,
Meſſieurs P-Dumoulin, Dangeville-l'aîné, Dumirail, Javilliers, & Marcel.
JEUX,
Meſſieurs Germain, Ferrand, Dumoulin-l'aîné, & Blondy.
AMOURS,
Dupré, Moreau, Pierret, & Sallé
a ij

SECONDE ENTRÉE.

SILVANDRE, Monſieur Thevenard.
PHILENE, Monſieur Boutelou.
CEPHISE, Mademoiſelle Pouſſin.
DORIS, Mademoiſelle Dupeyré.
BERGERES, Meſdemoiſelles Aubert, & Cochereau.
UN BERGER, Monſieur Boutelou-fils.

BERGERS,
Monſieur Blondy,
Meſſieurs Germain, D-Dumoulin, Dangeville-l'aîné, & H-Dumoulin.
BERGERES,
Meſdemoiſelles Lecomte, Saligny, Baſſecour, & la Fargue.
PASTRES,
Monſieur F-Dumoulin.
Meſſieurs, Dangeville-cadet, Javilliers, Marcel, & P-Dumoulin.

TROISIEME ENTRÉE

DOM PEDRO, Monſieur Choplet.
DOM CARLOS, Monſieur Dun.
UN ESPAGNOL chantant *Nuit, ſoyez fidelle.* Monſieur Bourelou.
UNE ESPAGNOLETTE, Mademoiſelle Aubert.

ESPAGNOLS,
&
ESPAGNOLETTES,
Monſieur Balon, & Mademoiſelle Guyot.
Meſſieurs Germain, Dangeville-l'aîné, & H-Dumoulin.
Meſdemoiſelles Saligny, Lecomte, & Baſſecour.

QUATRIEME ENTRÉE.

OCTAVIO, Monſieur Cochereau.
OLIMPIA, Mademoiſelle Journet.
VENITIENNES, Meſdemoiſelles Aubert, & Joubert.

LE BAL.
MORE & MORESSE,
Monſieur Balon, & Mademoiſelle Provoſt.

UN FOL, Monſieur Dangeville-cadet.
UNE FOLLE, Mademoiſelle Carré.
UN SUISSE, Monſieur Ferrand.
UNE SUISSESSE, Mademoiſelle Lecomte.
UN FRANÇOIS, Monſieur H-Dumoulin.
UNE FRANÇOISE, Mademoiſelle Saligny.
UN HOLLANDOIS, Monſieur P-Dumoulin.
UNE HOLLANDOISE, Mademoiſelle Mangot.
UN GREC, Monſieur F-Dumoulin.
UNE GRECQUE, Mademoiſelle Guyot.
CRISPIN, Monſieur Dumirail.
CRISPINE, Mademoiſelle la Fargue.
DEUX PETITS MASQUES,
Le petit Dupré, & la petite Rochecour.

CINQUIEME ENTRÉE.

ZAYDE, Mademoiſelle Journet.
ROXANE, Mademoiſelle Deſmâtins.
ZULIMAN, Monſieur Thevenard.
LE GRAND BOSTANGI. Monſieur Dun.

SULTANES,
Meſdemoiſelles Provoſt, Guyot, Saligny, Lecomte, Baſſecour, & la Fargue.
BOSTANGIS,
Meſſieurs Ferrand, Blondy, Marcel & Javilliers.
GARCONS BOSTANGIS,
Meſſieurs Dangeville-C., Dumirail, & P-Dumoulin.
ICOGLANTS,
Meſſieurs F-Dumoulin, & D-Dumoulin.

Noms des Perſonnages chantants dans tous les Chœurs du Ballet de l'Europe Galante.

MESDEMOISELLES.

Dupeyré.	Baſſet.	Dujardin.	Joubert.
Duval.	Loignon.	Pouſſin.	Cochereau.
Guiller.	Chevalier.	Demerville.	Aubert.

MESSIEURS.

Prunier.	La Coſte.	Dacqueville.	Lebel.
Courteil.	Cadot.	Deſvoys.	Boutelou-fils.
Solé.	Jolain.	Mantienne.	Perere.
Renard.	Bertrand	Le Jeune.	Paris.
Marianval.	Maillard.	Crêté.	

Figure 7-2: Cast list from the 1706 libretto of *L'Europe galante*.

this straightforward serves as a useful reminder that a libretto may not always be internally consistent and that it is important to check all possible places where characters are mentioned.

From July 1699 onwards the inclusion of the performers' names resolves the ambiguity in regard to the number of singing roles and gives the dancers much more prominence. The new convention was to divide the cast into separate lists of singers and dancers, while still maintaining the usual separation between the prologue and the rest of the work.[31] The libretto for the 1706 revival of *L'Europe galante* (Figure 7-2)

[31] This is a different system from the court librettos of the 1670s, in which the dancers' names were listed at the start of the relevant divertissement; see Fig. 2-2, p. 27.

reveals that in the first entrée (i.e., the prologue), the female role of Discord was sung by a man, that there were three dancing Graces as well as three singing Graces (a classic instance of double casting), and that the remaining thirteen dancers were all male (the four Amours may have been children). "L'Espagne" requires, in addition to the two Dons, an "Espagnol" and an "Espagnolette"; similarly there are two Venetian women who sing in "L'Italie," one of them presumably equivalent to the "Femme du bal" mentioned in 1697. It also becomes possible to track how many roles any given performer was assigned; in this revival, most of the solo singers had roles in two of the five entrées, while the dancers tended to appear in three.

Unlike the dancers, the members of the chorus are not identified as to role, but only by name – and once only for the entire work. As a result, the libretto cannot reveal variations in the make-up of the group that may have taken place among acts. The initial convention in Ballard's librettos was for women to be listed first; the chorus for this opera included twelve women and nineteen men.[32] Starting in 1700 the choristers' names are often given by their position on stage – second row and first row, in that order[33] – and from 1717 by location of the singers on either stage right or stage left (*côté de la reine* or *côté du roi*).[34] These listings seem to indicate that the members of the chorus stood symmetrically, in two lines on either side of the stage; other accounts also suggest that they moved little, if at all (see Chapter 2, p. 36ff).

On the dancers' side of the ledger, the way roles and names are laid out on the page is very telling. When a name appears alone on a single line, that person can be taken to have danced as a soloist; the same practice extends to couples. In the third entrée, all eight dancers represent Spaniards, but one mixed couple, Balon and Guyot, are set off from the others; these were among the leading dancers of the troupe and here they must have danced a *pas de deux* and possibly also solos. There must have been group dances as well, likely possibilities being a *pas de six* and/or a *pas de huit*. The fourth entrée takes place at a masked ball. The 1697 libretto identifies the group characters simply as a troupe of maskers, whereas the 1706 libretto groups the dancers as eight couples, each given a distinct national or affective character (a Moorish couple, who are given the greatest prominence; a madman and mad woman; etc.).[35] Even if all these people danced simultaneously, there must have been a visual emphasis on "coupleness." The second entrée, on the other hand, features soloists, first by setting off a single

[32] The women all sang the *dessus*, the men were divided on the other three parts. See Rosow, "Performing a choral dialogue," 326–27.

[33] Between 1700 and 1707 both systems for listing names – by gender and by row – are found in librettos; between 1707 and 1717 the system by row prevailed.

[34] It is curious that the terminology of king's side and queen's side emerged during a decades-long period when there was no queen in France. Louis XIV's wife had died in 1683 and in 1717 Louis XV was only seven years old; he was to marry in 1725.

[35] For another differentiated libretto listing, see Fig. 12-2, p. 364.

shepherd against four other shepherds and four shepherdesses, and then by involving another set of rustic characters – five *pâtres* – of whom one is a soloist. The last entrée shows yet another arrangement of the dancers, in three distinct roles: six female Sultanas; seven gardeners (*Bostangis*, four adults and three boys); and two young male servants (Icoglans). Simply on the level of the number and groupings of dancers, each entrée has a distinct profile.

The visual variety operates not only for its own sake, but makes sense within the fictional world of each entrée. A ball naturally involves couples, and since the one in "L'Italie" takes place during Carnival, the guests wear extravagant costumes. In "L'Espagne" the dancers function as part of the serenade that the two hapless Spanish noblemen offer to women who never appear. The fact that the dancing serenaders are equally divided between men and women and feature a solo couple only emphasizes the fantasy of togetherness that the two noblemen fail to achieve. The women of the Sultan's harem are unlikely to dance with his gardeners; here the dancing groups separate along gender lines. The pastoral realm was so pervasive in French opera that no single model prevails for its inhabitants; this one embraces both the more idealized rustics (the shepherds and shepherdesses) and the less elevated *pâtres*. But whereas the *pâtres* probably functioned as an independent, all male group, the shepherds and shepherdesses must have danced together at least part of the time.

Cast lists also reveal general tendencies in casting. In *L'Europe galante* as performed in 1706 the number of dancers in the divertissements ranges from a low of ten to a high of sixteen. In two of the entrées the number of male and female dancing roles is equal; in the other three, male roles predominate, the greatest disproportion occurring in the first entrée, where there are thirteen men and three women. The stars of the dance troupe, who in this period included Balon and Blondy among the men, Guyot and Prévost (here spelled "Provost") among the women, appear to figure not only as soloists or in couples, but as parts of groups. One cannot draw firm conclusions on the basis of a single libretto, but when this kind of information is put together with the scores, patterns emerge.

8 | Thalie, Muse of Comedy

Thalie had a presence at the Académie Royale de Musique even in Lully's day, but after 1675 she had spent more time in the wings than center stage. Her sister Melpomène dominated the repertoire, both numerically and, more importantly, ideologically: the *tragédie en musique* was the genre that defined French opera. At the turn of the eighteenth century, however, librettists and composers began to call upon Thalie for inspiration with some regularity, and audiences responded with enthusiasm. Over the years Thalie's influence waxed and waned in response to the climate at the Opéra, but the door to the theater was always left open for her.

The works in which Thalie made her presence felt do not necessarily lend themselves to classification as "comedies" by Aristotelian standards; one reason is that many such works were opera-ballets, whose individual entrées could vary considerably in tone. In addition, works with continuous plots that are not *tragédies* do not have consistent genre designations (see Chapter 7, p. 207ff). Kintzler, who has wrestled repeatedly with categorization questions in the French operatic repertoire, has pointed out that the title of a work such as *Les Amours de Momus* (1695) suggests comedy, but that "in reading the text, one discovers a work in which the comic effect is not sought. Rather, it is a pastorale without great originality."[1] Her reaction points to the challenges in categorizing this repertoire; *Les Amours de Momus* is one of several works that self-consciously borrow from multiple theatrical conventions.

On the other hand, the comic as a localized descriptor finds a home in many of the works of this period – primarily in "ballets," but even within some *tragédies*. When a comic plot provides the framework, the divertissement is of a piece with it. But divertissements in general, and the dance in particular, may sometimes introduce a comic element into surroundings of a different cast. In both cases, a comic environment opens up additional possibilities for the dramaturgy of dance beyond the established conventions. New ways of structuring dance into a work come into play, ones that do not necessarily restrict it to the divertissement; the traditional unity of identity between dancers and choristers may not always be maintained; and comic characters who express themselves through the medium of dance and gesture become recognizable types. These innovations occurred first

[1] Kintzler, *Poétique*, 323–24.

in the lighter works of this era, before being adopted, in certain instances, into *tragédies*.

The prefaces that librettists of this era wrote to justify the inclusion of comic elements reveal just how sensitive the issues were for an institution such as the Académie Royale de Musique. As a result of this nervousness, the realm of the comic was circumscribed. Characters and situations borrowed from the *comédie italienne* provided a common framing device, but a second route was the rural, via the peasants who occupy the lower reaches of the pastoral realm. Another, much less common, but increasing in frequency, was the exotic, some of whose denizens (such as the Sultan's gardeners in *L'Europe galante*) could be exploited for humor. All three of these fictional worlds have long roots in French theater, including the Opéra, but came into greater prominence there during the era of Campra. Nonetheless, counter-pressures were also at work; the period of greatest liberty for the comic lasted about two decades, which happened to overlap with the last years of Louis XIV's long reign. Thereafter the comic had to succumb more and more to "circumlocution," as one librettist put it. New works shifted away from Italianisms toward the realms of the "heroic" and the exotic, tendencies explored in the following chapters. The bodies of the dancers, which had the potential for inflecting, or even escaping, the restraints put on language, had crucial roles to play in these aesthetic shifts.

THE DECADE AFTER LULLY

The comic re-emerged only four years after Lully's death, tacked onto the end of an anomalous work where it seems to invite the expansion in the repertoire that was to follow. *Astrée* (1691), with music by Collasse set to a libretto by Jean de La Fontaine (whose famous fables had first been published in 1668), is labeled a *tragédie* on the title page of the libretto, but in character, form (three acts), and ancestry should more appropriately be classified as a pastorale; Barthélemy sees it as something of a parody.[2] The shepherd lovers, Astrée and Céladon, are beset by a jealous suitor who misleads the heroine by forging poison-pen letters, and by a rustic princess who kidnaps the hero after falling in love with him. Their sensible confidants and some magic wrought by a good fairy help untangle the complications and the lovers are finally reunited, at the Fountain of Truth. The tone of the texts is often tongue-in-cheek, even at the opera's end (III/6).

[2] This work borrows its characters from Honoré d'Urfé's eponymous pastoral novel (1607–27). Barthélémy argues that La Fontaine despised operatic heroes, yet was dying to write a libretto (*Métamorphoses*, 47).

Amants, votre persévérance
Du sort surmonte les rigueurs;
Que l'Hymen et l'Amour toujours d'intelligence
Vous comblent à jamais de toutes leurs douceurs.

(Lovers, your perseverance has overcome the rigors of fate. May Love and Marriage – always of the same mind – crown you forever with all their sweetness.)

The opera could have ended with this seemingly benevolent benediction, which is initiated by their good fairy, Ismène, and seconded by the chorus; with the addition of a few dances, it could have become a standard celebratory divertissement. But instead, the Princess of the Forest, now recovered from her crush on Céladon, has arranged a fête in honor of the lovers. The "indiscreet waters" of the Fountain of Truth produce a little *buffo* set-piece, performed by three burlesque Italian characters appearing here for the only time in the opera. Lizetta, who describes herself as young and charming ("Fanciulletta, / Vezzozetta, / Leggiadretta"), but who is sung by a tenor, is desperate for a husband: "Meco più non posso star / Chi per mogl' mi vuol pigliar?" ("I can't be alone any more. Who wants to take me to wife?"). She faces a choice between a self-satisfied old man (Galioffo) and an ignorant oaf (Gambarini). She chooses neither, and all three end by rejecting marriage: "Non voglio tal servitù, / Nè mi maritarò più." ("I'm not interested in servitude; I'll never marry.")

The scene is set by a little dance sequence consisting of a gigue, chaconne, gavotte, and sarabande, all connected to each other and each deliberately irregular in regard to melody, rhythm, and phrasing. The libretto is too early to name the dancers, but their roles must have been assigned to similarly burlesque Italian characters. The chaconne, which mixes simple-minded melodic figures into its irregular phrases and does not use a ground bass until toward the end of its 57 bars, invites comic treatment. But in a nod to French operatic practices, the triple meter of the chaconne structures much of the scene and even returns for 16 bars between the trio in Italian ("Cantiamo, balliamo, ridiamo" ["Let us sing, dance, and laugh"]) and the concluding chorus in French. Ismène's followers take the whole thing as a joke, as this so-called "tragédie" draws to its close in laughter:

Chantons, portons nos voix jusqu'au céleste empire.
Que les plus graves dieux en nous entendant rire
Y soient forcés de rire aussi.

(Let's sing, let's raise our voices all the way to the celestial empire, so that the most serious gods, upon hearing us laugh, will be forced to laugh as well.)

These "serious gods" (did La Fontaine mean the same ones who regularly appeared in the *tragédie en musique*? or their analogues at the court of France?) were implicitly called upon to laugh in the Opéra's next performance as well. This was a double bill that opened in September 1692, consisting of the revived *Carnaval* (this time with Monsieur de Pourceaugnac fleeing from the syringe-wielding apothecaries as its final scene) plus the *Ballet de Villeneuve-Saint-Georges*, a work by Banzi and Collasse consisting of three brief pastorales. The third of these takes an overtly comic turn when the "ridiculous shepherd" Lupin parties with the drunken satyr Silène. It is perhaps no coincidence that both the *Ballet de Villeneuve-Saint-Georges* and *Astrée* were aimed more at the pleasure-loving Dauphin than at the king, who had not attended the opera for several years; the ballet was originally performed privately in the Dauphin's honor before it moved to the stage of the Opéra, and *Astrée*'s prologue, set on the banks of the Seine with Marly in the distance, makes a point of honoring not just the monarch, but his son.[3] But perhaps the powers-that-be disapproved of these irreverent works, if one feels inclined to read the succession of repertoire at the Opéra allegorically: this double-bill lasted only two months before being replaced by Lully's *Phaéton*, in which the son of the Sun falls to his death after daring to drive his father's chariot across the heavens.

Disruptive comedy, having been invited back to the Opéra, however tentatively, did not stay away for long. In 1695 another little manifesto justifying comedy on its stage was written by librettist Duché into the prologue of Desmarest's ballet *Les Amours de Momus*, the first of the many prologues where disputes between the Muses bring aesthetic questions to the surface. Here Melpomène is preparing to put on a spectacle for the "hero" who is going to come that day (by whom she means the Dauphin), when Thalie arrives accompanied by shepherds. Melpomène takes offense at her sister's intrusion; Thalie concedes the point that her sister represents High Art, but claims that the hero will be willing to descend from the heights from time to time.

Melpomène: Vous ne prétendez pas du moins
Que vos jeux sur les miens remportent la victoire?
J'offre à ses yeux des rois vainqueurs de l'univers;
Je le peins à lui-même, en cent tableaux divers,
Où de mille vertus brille un noble assemblage:
Vous combattrez en vain mon pouvoir glorieux,
Il n'est permis qu'à moi de former une image
Si semblable à celles des Dieux.

Thalie: Il descendra de sa grandeur suprême,
Pour prendre part à nos jeux les plus doux:
Sa bonté quelque fois le dérobe à lui-même,
Pour l'abaisser jusques à nous.

3 Quite a few of the operatic prologues in this decade honor the Dauphin; some do not mention the king at all.

(*Melpomène*: Do you really mean to claim that your pleasures take precedence over mine? I place before his eyes the conquering kings of the universe; I portray him in a hundred different pictures where a noble assembly shines with a thousand virtues. You battle my glorious power in vain; it is permitted to me alone to draw a portrait so similar to those of the gods. *Thalie*: He will descend from his supreme elevation to take part in our sweet pleasures. Sometimes his goodness allows him to lower himself to our level.)

Glory descends from the heavens to offer a compromise: today Thalie will provide the entertainment, but Glory will take Melpomène to see the exploits of her hero on the battlefield that will provide material for her future songs.[4] Melpomène climbs into Glory's flying chariot, but leaves her followers behind. Thalie accepts this solution while still claiming novelty for the work that is to follow.

Thalie: Unissons nos accords: Qu'une fête nouvelle
Fasse voir notre zèle
Au plus grand des héros!

(Let us unite our music. May a novel fête reveal our zeal to the greatest of heroes!)

In the three acts that follow, the genres of tragedy and comedy do effect a compromise, mediated by the pastorale. The two main characters are both gods, albeit from the lower reaches of Mount Olympus: Comus, the god of parties ("dieu des festins"), and Momus, god of mockery ("dieu de la raillerie") are both in love, the former with Hébé, goddess of youth, the latter with one of her nymphs.[5] The shape of the acts and much of the language of the libretto ring familiar from the *tragédie en musique*, including little maxim airs, sung back-to-back:

Comus: Un cœur qui semble être indomptable,
Tôt ou tard par l'Amour se laisse désarmer;
Il n'est rien de plus redoubtable,
Qu'un ennemi qui sait charmer.

Momus: L'Amour est moins fort qu'on ne pense
On peut mépriser ses ardeurs:
Mais la faiblesse de nos coeurs
Fait la grandeur de sa puissance. *(Les Amours de Momus, I/1)*

(*Comus*: A heart that seems untameable sooner or later lets itself be disarmed by love. Nothing is more formidable than an enemy who knows how to charm. *Momus*: Love is not as strong as we think; we may spurn his ardor. But the weakness of our hearts is what makes his strength so great.)

[4] During the War of the League of Augsburg the Dauphin served upon occasion on the German and Flemish fronts, without great distinction.

[5] For a study of Momus's presence across theatrical genres, see Quéro, *Momus philosophe*.

Notwithstanding this operatic idiom, the two love objects are not interested; they string their suitors along, then reject them. At the end (III/7) Comus still nourishes hope, but the other three agree that "indifference is the ultimate good" and Bacchus arrives to offer a different kind of oblivion – "Wine makes us forget a faithless lover, and it is in forgetting her that we take our revenge" – while the chorus of Momus's followers cynically concludes that "the true pleasures are made for us. How sweet is our lot!"

The admittance of Momus, Comus, and Thalie to the pantheon of the Académie Royale de Musique marked a turning point that was to have a profound impact on the way dance was used in opera. Whereas during the course of Lully's tenure the Opéra had moved away from the comic toward a higher tone, Francine's administration chose to enlarge the generic range beyond *tragédie*, a tendency that picked up momentum following the first resounding success at the Opéra since Lully's death, *L'Europe galante* (1697), and reached full expression in *Les Fetes de Thalie* (1714).[6] Not everyone appreciated the infusion of comic elements into the repertoire and eventually institutional pressures forced a correction. But for over twenty years the Opéra welcomed creations of works in a comic vein alongside its tragedies.

"ITALY" COMES TO THE OPÉRA

1697 was a watershed year in French operatic history, and not just because a new genre, opera-ballet, gained real definition in the hands of a good composer. Only a few months before *L'Europe galante* premiered, the long-established troupe of Italian comedians was expelled from Paris, leaving an artistic vacuum that the remaining theatrical companies – including the Académie Royale de Musique – rushed to fill. Based on the traditions of the commedia dell'arte, but having adapted its performing traditions to its French home, the *comédie italienne* had been operating under royal protection since 1661.[7] The actors specialized in specific roles, either as *innamorati* (lovers, with names such as Octave, Léandre, Isabelle) or in the comic roles of *zanni* (Arlequin, Pierrot, Columbine), old men (Pantalon or the doctor), or captain (Spezzafer, Scaramouche). In the recent past the troupe had been led by its Arlequin: this role was played by Domenico Biancolelli until his sudden death in 1688, then by Evaristo Gherardi (Figure 6-2). Although the troupe had originally performed in Italian, by the 1680s it incorporated more and more French, and even presented works by French playwrights such as Regnard and Dufresny. By 1692 all the company's plays were in French, with only a few *canevas* still performed in Italian, although physical comedy

6 The trend is visible even before *L'Europe galante*. The work that preceded *Les Amours de Momus* was a revival of *Acis et Galatée*, and the one that followed was the *Ballet des saisons*. These three lighter works were bookended by two tragedies.

7 See Scott, *The Commedia dell'Arte in Paris*, 81ff.

remained fundamental to the acting style.[8] Music and dance were important elements, and much of the repertoire was built around parodies of plays in other theaters and of Lully's operas.[9] The troupe was able to incorporate more spectacle into its plays after 1680 when it moved into the Hôtel de Bourgogne, a theater equipped for special effects. The *comédie italienne*'s mixture of wit, physical comedy, music, and social satire was enormously popular, and the theater seems to have had much the same audience as the troupe of French players and of the Opéra. But during the 1690s, when a more devout climate reigned at the court, the Italians' antics came under more scrutiny, until on 14 May 1697 their theater was suddenly sealed by the police and the troupe banned from further performances.[10]

The fair theaters, which had no official standing and existed on the margins of Parisian theatrical life, rushed to fill the void – taking over much of the Italian theater's repertoire and even hiring some of its performers.[11] Thus between 1697 and 1716 Parisians could still enjoy the antics of the Italians' stock characters by going to the temporary theatres installed every season in the Foire Saint-Germain and the Foire Saint-Laurent, where the resourceful performers came up with ingenious ways around the repressive measures promulgated by the Opéra and the Comédie-Française. This is the origin story of the genre that came to be known as *opéra comique*, and it has been told many times.[12] But it has been pointed out much less often that the Académie Royale de Musique exhibited the same opportunism, as it too co-opted as many features of the Italians' repertoire as it could decently do within the bounds of *bienséance*. Venice, the city of masquerades, provided the Opéra with the ideal platform for working Italian-style comedy into its

8 The balance that obtained between improvisation and recitation of memorized texts remains controversial; see Mazouer's informative introduction to his edition of selected plays from Gherardi, *Théâtre italien* (1, 7–43). Mazouer points out that the term "commedia dell'arte" did not come into use until around 1750, in the writings of Goldoni. For that reason, and also in order to acknowledge how intertwined the Italians' performances were with the theatrical traditions of their adopted homeland, I have chosen to use the seventeenth-century term "comédie italienne" to refer to the style, and "Théâtre Italien" for the institution in Paris (which was referred to at the time in various ways).

9 Gherardi's collection of plays received its definitive edition in 1700. Given that one of its goals was to convince the authorities that the troupe should be allowed to reopen its doors, there is every reason to believe that Gherardi tidied up the plays and toned down their crudities. The 55 plays call for 340 musical numbers, many of which were published at the ends of the volumes, cued to the spots within the plays where they would be performed. Consisting mostly of simple songs in French (vaudevilles), plus some passages excerpted from Lully operas and a few Italian arias, these pieces also show the extent to which the Italian theater had adjusted to its French environment. See Grout, "The music of the Italian theatre."

10 The reasons behind the Italians' expulsion are not entirely clear, but they extend beyond the supposed satire of Mme de Maintenon in a play called *La Fausse Prude*. See Moureau, *De Gherardi à Watteau*, 29–32. Moureau points out that the Italian troupe engaged in social satire, but avoided overt political critique.

11 See Sakhnovskaia, "Sur les traces des Italiens."

12 See, for example, Barthélemy, "L'opéra-comique." Regarding the complex dynamics among the Parisian theaters as to Italian-style repertoire following the expulsion of the Italian troupe, see Moureau, *De Gherardi à Watteau*, 99–119.

highbrow repertoire. The Italian Theatre closed in May; *L'Europe galante* opened in September, and thereafter Arlequin, Colombine, and Scaramouche danced frequently across the stage of the Palais-Royal. Even Elizabeth Gherardi, wife of the director of the banned troupe, was hired to sing at the Opéra.[13] Stories were appropriated as well: the "Sérénade vénitienne" from *Les Fragments de Lully*, not to mention the "Fête marine" and the "Fête des barqueroles" from *Les Fêtes vénitiennes*, all ring variants on the familiar *comédie italienne* plot of the old doctor determined to marry his beautiful young ward, whose plans are thwarted by the young lover and his comic servants.

French fascination with Venice was of long standing. In fact, in 1680 the French writer Saint-Didier had published a long travel book about Venetian customs, among the people termed "the sybarites of Europe."[14] During the same period, the *Mercure galant* also published several reports from Venice, most of them about Carnival seasons, including accounts of operas and balls.[15] French writers were clearly titillated by the sexual license that the Venetian Carnival appeared to offer:

> The Place Saint-Marc provides the stage on which the pomp of Carnival is displayed every day. All the maskers in Venice go there an hour before sunset, and even though the square is huge, it can hardly contain all the costumed people and the spectators. Gentlewomen only put on costumes and come during the final days of Carnival; those who have admirers find a thousand ways to deceive their husbands and their chaperones, for people in costume are allowed virtually everywhere. Thus Carnival is the true harvest for love affairs, when it becomes possible to pluck the fruit of all the intrigues planted during less favorable seasons . . .[16]

For French composers and librettists, the disguises of a Venetian Carnival meant that traditions of the *tragédie en musique*, in which mortals rub elbows with gods, could still function in these "contemporary," often comic, works without transgressing the sacred French rules of verisimilitude. All it required to bring in a god in a machine was to stage him in an opera-within-the-opera, set in one of Venice's numerous opera houses. Another strategy was to make him a costumed guest at a masked ball. Venice conveniently served yet another agenda – the growing taste in certain French quarters for Italian music. The 1690s was the decade during which composers such as François Couperin and Michel de La Barre began writing sonatas in imitation of Corelli, and a pamphlet war between the partisans of French and Italian music began just after the turn of the century.[17] Campra, whose father was Italian, was on the compositional cutting edge.

[13] For instance, she sang the role of an Espagnolette in the *Ballet des saisons* (1700 revival).

[14] Saint-Didier, *La Ville et la République de Venise*. In the preface Saint-Didier says that he spent the years 1672–74 in Venice.

[15] Masson ("Fêtes vénitiennes," 134, n. 15) believes that Danchet knew the article published in the *Mercure galant* in April 1679, 118–48.

[16] Saint-Didier, *La Ville*, 342.

[17] The key documents were Raguenet's *Parallèle* (1702) and Lecerf's *Comparaison* (1704–6). For the wider context, see Sadie, "Paris and Versailles," esp. 131–33, 148–55, and 157–59.

No fewer than eight of the works that premiered between 1697 and 1718 were set, all or in part, in a fantasy contemporary Italy (see Table 8-1 and Figure 8-1). The Place Saint-Marc was *the* iconic spot for evoking Venice.[18] Other scenes evoked gambling in the Ridotte; serenades under palace windows; singing gondoliers; ritual contests between rival groups for possession of a bridge; masked balls; and operatic spectaculars. It is no coincidence that two of the librettists mentioned, Regnard and La Motte, had written for the Théâtre Italien before they turned to opera, and a third, Fuzelier, had written for the fair theaters.[19]

Such dramatic changes to the repertoire could not pass unremarked. The librettists felt compelled to make their case directly to the public: in the prologue to *La Vénitienne* La Motte made an overt acknowledgement of his debt to Italian comic traditions – and to the risks involved in transporting them to the stage of the Opéra. The prologue is set in the gardens of Momus, where statues of the Italian comedians (Arlequin, Pantalon, le Docteur, Spezzafer, Scaramouche, Polichinelle, and Pierrot) decorate the landscape. After lecturing the statues about the misdeeds that led to their silencing, Momus tells them that he will bring them back to life temporarily, so that they can once again make an audience laugh.

Momus: Vous qui sous de libres portraits
Faisiez voir des humains les faiblesses extrêmes,
Et qui par d'agréables traits
Les forciez à rire d'eux-mêmes,
Vous avez abusé des droits
Qu'on laissait prendre à votre badinage,
Et bientôt d'équitables loix
De vos sens indiscrets vous ravirent l'usage.
Pour quelque temps je vais vous ranimer:
Qu'à rire avec vous tout s'apprête;
Mais songez dans les jeux que vous allez former,
Que Momus préside à la fête.

(You whose free likenesses made human foibles visible and who through agreeable sketches obliged people to laugh at themselves, you abused the rights granted to your jesting, and soon just laws deprived you of the use of your indiscreet senses. For a short time I am going to reanimate you; may everyone prepare to laugh with you. But remember in the amusements you are going to create that it is Momus who oversees the fête.)

[18] I have retained the French names in order to emphasize the filter through which Venetian sights were seen by Parisian audiences.

[19] Regnard's seven plays for the Théâtre Italien (1688 to 1694) have been republished in *Gherardi: Théâtre italien*, II, ed. Guichemerre; he co-authored several more plays for the same theater with Dufresny. (See the complete list in Anthony's introduction to the Pendragon facsimile score of *Le Carnaval de Venise*, xvi.) La Motte, who was to supply a number of librettos for the Opéra, wrote *Les Originaux* for the Théâtre Italien in 1693. Fuzelier had been writing for the fair theaters for some years before he wrote his first libretto; he was later to work at the restored Théâtre Italien and the Comédie-Française. Danchet, on the other hand, wrote only librettos; his first, the tragedy *Hésione*, was set to music by Campra in 1700.

Table 8-1: Operas and ballets, 1697–1718, with settings in contemporary Italy.

Date	Title	Composer/ librettist	Genre	Section	Location	Comments
1697	*L'Europe galante*	Campra/ La Motte	opera-ballet	Entrée IV: "L'Italie"	[Venice]	Location not mentioned, but characters are Venetians
1697	*Les Fêtes galantes*	Desmarest/ Duché	ballet	All 3 acts	Naples	
1699	*Le Carnaval de Venise*	Campra/ Regnard	ballet	All 3 acts	Venice	
1702	*Les Fragments de Lully*	Lully and Campra/ Danchet	opera-ballet	Added entrée: "Sérenade vénitienne"	Venice	Plus *divertissement comique* "Cariselli," sung entirely in Italian
1703	*Le Ballet des Muses*	Campra/ Danchet	opera-ballet	Entrée IV: "La Comédie"		Set in Athens, but plot and characters from *comédie italienne*
1705	*La Vénitienne*	La Barre/ La Motte	comédie-ballet	All 3 acts	Venice	
1710	*Les Fêtes vénitiennes*	Campra/ Danchet	opera-ballet	All 9 entrées	Venice	
1718	*Le Ballet des âges*	Campra/ Fuzelier	opera-ballet	Entrée III: "La Vieillesse, ou l'amour enjoué"	Padua	

Figure 8-1: Costumed merrymakers enjoy Carnival in Venice.

The statues jump down from their pedestals and dance merrily. But here the irreverent, quick-tongued, Italian comedians are silent; their bodies (animated by the highly trained French dancers of the Opéra's troupe) are given the right to expression, but not their tongues.[20] Yet as if to further justify the Italian troupe's

[20] No singing characters correspond to these dancers, a phenomenon not uncommon in prologues.

presence on the stage of the Opéra – not to mention the troupe's absorption into a new, purely musical environment – Euterpe, here identified as the Muse of music, arrives; she and her followers are ready to embrace the realm of laughter ("je veux que les Ris me suivent à leur tour").[21]

The Italian comedians are brought back to life not just in the prologue, but in the three-act work that follows, which draws shamelessly upon some of the conventions of the *comédie italienne*, even as it remains within the bounds of propriety. The plot revolves around a love triangle, whose Venetian setting almost guarantees the use of disguises. Isabelle disguises herself as a man in order to spy on her faithless lover, then pays court to her rival, Léonore, as a means of making Octave jealous, but, in a bit of gender-bending, ends up making Léonore fall in love with her. Isabelle next disguises herself as an oracle in an attempt to frighten her lover back into the fold with predictions of what will happen to him if he strays. Two servants participate in the intrigues, and it is in their roles that the taming of the characters for the stage of the Opéra can most succinctly be glimpsed. In Act II, when Zerbin, disguised as his noble master, remains alone to wait for a sorcerer, his fear is stereotypical of the comic servant; however it is couched not in stuttering and crude language but in alexandrines that borrow their rhetoric, not to mention their appeals to the gods, from the *tragédie en musique*, even as Zerbin takes a comforting swig out of his bottle.

> Ciel! il me laisse, il m'abandonne,
> Que je vais payer cher ses nouvelles amours!
> Où suis-je! Malheureux! je tremble, je frissonne,
> Quoi! Bacchus, ai-je en vain imploré ton secours?
> Ne saurais-tu bannir le trouble qui m'étonne?
> Quels funestes objets s'offrent à mes regards?
> Je crois voir s'élever mille spectres terribles;
> Des monstres sous mes pas naissent de toutes parts.
> Quel bruit affreux! Quels cris! Quels hurlements horribles!
> [. . .]
> Lâche, tu ne vois rien, rougis de tes allarmes.
> Bacchus, viens dissiper les erreurs de mes sens;
> Ne m'as-tu donc prêté que d'impuissantes armes?
> Ah! Je te reconnais au calme que je sens.

(Heavens! He is leaving me, abandoning me; I am going to pay dearly for his new loves! Where am I? Unfortunate one! I tremble, I shake. What? Bacchus, have I implored

[21] The person honored in this prologue, the Dauphin, was influential in forwarding the new Italian styles. See La Gorce, *L'Opéra à Paris*, 104, and Fader, "The 'Cabale du Dauphin.'"

help from you in vain? Wouldn't you be willing to banish the state of mind that is disturbing me? / What dreadful objects appear before my eyes? I think I see a thousand terrifying phantoms. Monsters spring up everywhere beneath my steps. What frightful noise! What cries! What horrible howling! [. . .] Coward, there's nothing there to see; blush at your fears. Bacchus, come dispel the errors of my senses. Have you lent me only impotent weapons? Ah! I recognize you from the calm that overcomes me.)

This particular scene has roots not only in the *comédie italienne*, but in Molière; in fact, it calls to mind *Les Fêtes de l'Amour et de Bacchus* II/2, when the grotesque satyr Forestan is the victim of a hoax involving fake sorcerers and demons. The borrowing reminds us that the *comédie italienne* had been in France for so long, that by 1697 it had a complex history of reciprocal penetration with French spoken theater. Molière learned a great deal from his exposure to the Italian theater: he borrowed plots and characters, then transformed them for his own purposes.[22] As we have seen (Chapter 6), the first round of Italianisms at the Opéra derived from arrangements and pastiches of works that Lully and Molière had written together between 1664 and 1671 and that Lully recycled in *Les Fêtes de l'Amour et de Bacchus* and *Le Carnaval.* The Italians in return borrowed from Molière; various plots of *canevas* have been traced to his works and the influence increased when French authors began writing for the Italian theater in the late 1680s, since they, of course, knew their Molière, whose plays remained on the stage of the Comédie-Française.[23]

It was thus a complex mixture of styles and influences from Italian comedy, French spoken theater, and French opera that made up the performances of the Théâtre Italien at the point when the troupe was banned, and this mixture was the point of reference for the Académie Royale de Musique when it started borrowing some of the practices of its enormously popular rival. Whereas the proximate cause of the Opéra's adoption of Italian-inflected works into its repertoire seems to have been the exclusion of the Théâtre Italien from Paris, it did not necessarily follow that such a work had to be set in Italy. (In fact, not even the Théâtre Italien set its plays in Italy; most of those that Gherardi published take place in France.) So whereas Venice provided a useful vehicle for getting a new type of work before the operatic public, composers who were not as interested as Campra in Italian music could still borrow from the *comédie italienne* while setting their works elsewhere.

[22] There is a huge literature on this subject; see the bibliography in Bourqui, *Les Sources de Molière.*

[23] See, *inter alia*, Moureau, *Dufresny*, 208–11, and Guichemerre's introduction to his edition of the *comédies italiennes* of Regnard, (see n. 19), 17–18.

Just as Ovid's *Metamorphoses* served as a wellspring for mythological plots, so did the repertoire of the Théâtre Italien and its imitators in the fair theaters provide a new generation of librettists with ideas. The extent of the borrowings ranges from the structural to the superficial: in *La Vénitienne* the influence is overt and extensive; other works feature commedia masks only as guests in fêtes. In an opera-ballet the Italian elements may be limited to a single entrée. Appendix 1 lists those works up until 1733 where the impact of the *comédie italienne* is explicit; it would have been longer still had the works colored by more traditionally French comic traditions been included. But the number of creations of Italian-inflected works declined after 1718, two years after Louis XIV's death allowed the Regent to invite a new Italian troupe to reopen the theater. Prefaces in librettos from around that time reveal that librettists and composers were under pressure to avoid the comic in their new operas (see Chapter 10, p. 299ff). Nonetheless, comic works already in the repertoire continued to be revived, and in 1729 two genuine Italian works – comic intermezzi – were performed (Chapter 10, p. 311ff). This was, however, an isolated event; no other Italian opera appeared on the stage of the Académie Royale de Musique until the infamous arrival of *La serva padrona* in 1752.[24]

An Italian location offered composers the opportunity to write in an Italian style. Interest in Italian music had been growing in Paris in the years surrounding the turn of the century, marked in the public realm by its increasing availability in music shops and by French composers' fascination with genres such as the sonata and cantata. Not many years later François Couperin was to dub his own blend of French and Italian styles "les goûts réunis."[25] The composers who worked at the Opéra responded in mixed ways to the opening up of the repertoire. In some works the Italian presence is blatant, in the form of da capo arias or Italianate instrumental writing; in other cases, an Italian setting may evoke only the merest hints of Italian musical styles. But no matter how Italianate, French music always maintained its native accent. What Campra wrote in the introduction to his first book of *cantates* (1708) applies just as well to the Italianate music in his operas: "I have tried as much as possible to blend into the delicacy of French music the vivacity of Italian music."

The introduction of Italianisms was not restricted to the various kinds of "ballet"; even *tragédies en musique* could become sites for Italian influences (see Chapter 11). But in all genres these had to be adapted to their new environment; the august Académie Royale de Musique could borrow from the Italian theater, but it had to raise the tone.[26]

[24] *La serva padrona* was, however, performed in Paris before then, at the Théâtre Italien in 1746.

[25] Sonatas were published in Paris starting in 1705, cantatas from 1706, although both genres had circulated in manuscript before then. Couperin's second book of chamber works, *Les Goûts réunis*, was published in 1724.

[26] Cowart sees the Italianate works produced at the Opéra during these years as participating in a cult of subversion aimed at monarchical absolutism; see in particular "Carnival in Venice" and

Prose had to become verse, speech had to become song, and coarse laughs had to change into smiles. In his new environment Arlequin had to fall silent, transformed from an impudent chatterbox into a mute dancer. Only once is he given a voice, in "La Comédie: Le Triomphe de la Folie" from *Les Fêtes vénitiennes*. Here Arlequin is cast as Diogenes, hunting through the Place Saint-Marc, lantern in hand, in search of a wise (rather than honest) mortal. But everyone he encounters has succumbed to the follies of love, even the old doctor, and Arlequin himself loses interest in wisdom as soon as Colombine appears. In this unique entrée, one of the closest in spirit to its Italian models, Arlequin sings without losing his abilities to dance and mime. Yet even when he and his comic cohorts were silenced, their body language allowed them a powerful means of expression that could even descend to low humor. "Monsieur de Pourceaugnac," in the version Lully made part of *Le Carnaval*, remained on the stage of the Opéra for decades, with its protagonist forever running from the dancing apothecaries who want to give him an enema.[27]

The dancers were not called upon often to engage in scatological humor, but the explosion in the number of dancing roles for characters from the *comédie italienne* suggests that the latter's characteristic movement vocabulary must have been translated into dance terms recognizable to audiences that had formerly frequented the Théâtre Italien. After all, the Opéra had an entire troupe of trained bodies in its employ, some of whom now began to specialize in comic roles (see Chapter 13). A handful of dance notations for Arlequin, supplemented by Lambranzi's book of engravings of Italian-style dancers, published in Germany in 1716, provide some idea of what such dances looked like: in Figure 8-2 Scaramouche and his partner adopt positions far removed from the noble French style, and in Figure 8-3 a gondolier and his wife perform a "furlana" in front of a backdrop depicting one of Venice's many bridges.[28] The texts in Lambranzi's book call for steps familiar from French dance manuals, so even if the style at the Opéra was more refined than these engravings suggest, it would have been located along a continuum of movement that drew upon a common

The Triumph of Pleasure esp. chs. 5–7. Whereas an iconoclastic tone is unmistakable in many of these works, one that mocks authority even when it is upheld, whether "subversion" may serve as the governing concept, is, in my view, questionable. I do not find the operatic works of this period as ideologically tidy as Cowart would have them, and I find many of her specific examples, especially of how some opera-ballets supposedly reverse absolutist characterization embodied in court ballets, unpersuasive.

[27] According to Beffara, *Dictionnaire*, "Pourceaugnac" was performed as a free-standing entrée, attached either to fragments or to full-length works, more than a dozen times between 1715 and 1741 – mostly, although not exclusively, during Carnival season.

[28] The commentary below their dance explains that they repeat the dance shown for gondolier alone in the previous plate, a "furlana in the Venetian manner." (Translated in Beaumont's edition of Lambranzi, I, 23–4 and II, 1.) In neither plate does the music say "furlana"; the solo dance is in $\frac{6}{8}$, entitled "Polesana," this one "Schiavona."

Figure 8-2: Scaramuzza (Scaramouche) and a woman. "These two persons jump from the wings and take up the position shown." Lambranzi, *Neue und curieuse theatrialische Tantz-Schul* (1716).

technique. At the Opéra the bodies of the dancers offered a site for introducing an ephemeral humor that left no traces in the texts printed in the libretto and that thus was less open to censure.

Whereas the impact of the *comédie italienne* often extended into the plot lines and role assignments of these new works, the musical and choreographic Italianisms tended to cluster in the divertissements, where their extroverted musicality could be framed as performance. Treating divertissements as diegetic had been central to French operatic

Figure 8-3: A gondolier and his wife. Lambranzi, *Neue und curieuse theatrialische Tantz-Schul* (1716).

aesthetics since Lully, but the expanded emphasis on the act of performing was new; elaborate arias, whether in Italian or in French, were matched by more prominent dancing. The structural relationship that Lully and Quinault had crafted between the dancers and the chorus did not disappear, but it loosened; in the works under the aegis of Thalie the number of dances tended to increase, while the role of the chorus diminished. These new tendencies were not confined to operas and ballets with Italian themes; rather, the blending of Italianisms and long-standing French theatrical traditions played itself out in endless imaginative combinations.

L'Europe galante (1697)

L'Europe galante was not the first opera-ballet – the *Ballet des saisons* preceded it by two years – but it set the standard for those that followed. Cahusac, writing in 1754, credited its librettist, La Motte, with the invention of the new genre:

> [The *tragédie en musique*] as conceived by Quinault is a grand plot which unfolds over the course of five acts. It is a canvas on a huge scale, like those of Raphael or Michelangelo. The entertainment devised by La Motte comprises several different acts, each of which presents a plot interspersed with divertissements, singing and dancing. They are pretty Watteaus, striking miniatures, which need great precision of design, graceful brushstrokes and brilliance of color.[29]

The governing conceit, the styles of love around Europe, is presented in the "Première Entrée," which functions as a prologue;[30] as is so often the case, its allegory is tied to the moment: the wedding of Louis XIV's oldest grandson, the Duc de Bourgogne, to Marie Adélaïde de Savoie, a marriage made possible by the Treaty of Ryswick, which ended the War of the League of Augsburg and thus allied France with a part of northern Italy. Although this opera was not the one commissioned for the wedding,[31] it was performed as part of the festivities. The prologue cleverly uses the circumstances surrounding the wedding both to set up the theme of the opera-ballet and to prepare the audience for its mixed tone. The trope of a dispute between two divinities sets Vénus against Discord, who claims credit for the recent war. At first, it appears as if Vénus has the upper hand, and when Discord claims victory over love, Vénus triumphantly replies:

> Tu t'applaudis d'une fausse victoire,
> L'Amour, a dans l'Europe, une nouvelle gloire.
> Il recueille le fruit de tes noires fureurs;
> Il a triomphé de la guerre,
> Malgré tous tes efforts, il rassemble deux cœurs,
> Qui feront quelque jour le destin de la terre.
> [. . .]
> C'est lui, qui dans l'Europe a ramené la paix,
> Ses peuples, à tes yeux, vont chanter ses attraits [. . .]

> (You are giving yourself credit for a false victory. Love has achieved new glory in Europe. He is plucking the fruit of your black rages; he has triumphed over war. In spite of your efforts, he has joined two hearts who someday will control the world's destiny. [. . .] It is he who has brought peace to Europe; before your eyes, his people are going to sing of his charms . . .)

[29] Cahusac, *La Danse*, 108–09, trans. Wood and Sadler, *French Baroque Opera*, 48.
[30] The sources differ as to whether the prologue is separate or labeled as the first entrée.
[31] The official opera, *Issé*, by La Motte and Destouches, was performed in the Grand Trianon, 17 December 1697, in a three-act version. It was expanded to five acts for the Opéra in 1708.

Discord grimly responds that if she is going to have to watch such a distasteful spectacle, the least she can do is to put her own stamp on it:

> Faisons des inconstants, des jaloux odieux.
> Jetons dans tous les cœurs, les soupçons et les craintes:
> Que l'on connaisse à mille plaintes,
> Que la Discorde est dans ces lieux.

> (Let me create people who are fickle and unbearably jealous. Let me throw suspicions and fear into all hearts. May everyone realize, from a thousand complaints, that Discord is here.)

Love does indeed struggle in the entrées that follow. In "La France" a main character loses her beloved, and the ending of "L'Italie" is downright grim, with the jealous, rejected lover left hesitating between suicide and the desire to plead his case one more time. In "L'Espagne" two men serenade women who never appear. Only "La Turquie" ends in happiness for a pair of lovers, and even there one of the three main characters ends up exiled and embittered. From our perspective of 300 years later we can see that the peace this opera celebrates was of short duration. Whereas La Motte is unlikely to have foreseen the outbreak of the War of Spanish Succession, fought over Louis XIV's claims to put another of his grandsons, the bridegroom's younger brother, on the throne of Spain, the tone of *L'Europe galante* is less celebratory than the occasion of a royal wedding would seem to warrant; when, in a brief epilogue, Discord cedes victory to Vénus on the grounds that "everything escapes my hatred and yields to love," she seems not to have been paying attention to her own successful handiwork.[32] Nonetheless, the work opened a new chapter in the repertoire of the Opéra. In a brief but interesting preface, La Motte admits to upholding cultural stereotypes in the interests of theatricality:

> We have chosen those European nations that are most contrasting and that offer the greatest potential for stage treatment: France, Spain, Italy, and Turkey. We have followed what is normally considered to be characteristic behavior of their inhabitants. The Frenchman is portrayed as fickle, indiscreet and amorous. The Spaniard as faithful and romantic. The Italian as jealous, shrewd and violent. Finally, we have expressed, within the limitations of the stage, the haughtiness and supreme authority of Sultans and the passionate nature of Sultanas.[33]

[32] The mixed tone drew comment 30 years later from Fuzelier in the preface to his libretto for *Les Amours des dieux* (1727): "If we have ballets that have succeeded under the auspices of Thalie, we have others where Melpomène has not disdained to appear and to set up tragic situations. A sword is drawn two times in *L'Europe galante*."

[33] Translation adapted from Anthony, *French Baroque Music*, 171.

These fantasy landscapes allow for musical and textual differentiation within the conventions of the day for local color. "France" is represented via a pastorale, in a timeless Arcadian landscape, but the other three offer something akin to contemporary society. "Spain" is set in a public square at night, "Italy" in a magnificent ballroom in Venice, "Turkey" in the gardens of a seraglio. As in Lully's operas, there is no single structure governing the divertissements. However, since the plot has to be concentrated into such a short period, the divertissement assumes even more prominence than it has in a *tragédie*, and the dancing may spill out into the action. In "France," the divertissement is contained and, at least in 1697, relatively short.[34] The shepherd Silvandre has transferred his affections from Doris to Céphise. The divertissement, performed by shepherds and peasants, is framed as a fête Silvandre offers to his new flame in an attempt to attract her, but it fails completely in its goal. Céphise declares that she is not interested in fickle men. Doris, devastated by Silvandre's betrayal, decides nonetheless to hope that his inconstancy will one day return him to her. In this case the divertissement, a mixture of choruses, solo airs and five instrumental dances (seven for the revival of 1698) falls in the middle of the entrée and has clear boundaries.[35]

In "Spain," on the other hand, there is no plot to speak of, but merely a situation: two Spaniards have come to a public square to serenade their beloveds, who never appear. The serenading continues on and off throughout the entrée, thus there is little distinction between the divertissement and its surroundings. Campra does, nonetheless, use some traditional framing devices, namely the designation of proxies to speak, at least part of the time, for the principals. In Scene 2 Dom Carlos asks the musicians and dancers he has brought along to "try with your tender songs to charm the Beauty who enchants me; let her know the pleasure I feel in loving her." The serenade is expressed through movement as well as song; in fact, it opens with two dances in a row. Next a *haute-contre*, seconded by the chorus, addresses a song not to the invisible Léonore, but to night: "O night, be faithful; Love reveals his secrets only to you." Perhaps this indirectness explains why the serenade fails to work; in any case, Dom Carlos takes over from his singer and berates Léonore for failing to show herself to "the most faithful lover in the world." Dom Pedro claims that he is the one who deserves the title, thanks to his devotion to Lucile, even though she is no more inclined to respond than is Léonore. After a bit of banter between the two of them, Dom Carlos again asks his followers to sing, thus setting off another sequence of songs and dances. This time the sung texts hint

[34] *L'Europe galante* had a complex publication history; see Anthony, "Printed editions."

[35] Regarding the structure of the entrées, with emphasis on "La France," see Barthélemy, *André Campra*, 89–91. Both "La France" and "L'Italie" end with monologues by a main character, in the manner of some *tragédies en musique* from this period.

that the two men may have reason to hope that their sweethearts will eventually yield ("A heart that is always attacked eventually grows tired of resisting"), or perhaps the Spanish woman who sings them represents not the two beloveds but the serenaders' wishful thinking. Whatever the case, the situation remains static: the chorus draws this entrée to a close by expressing hope that their music will succeed someday.[36]

The local color in "L'Espagne" draws upon conventions established by Lully. The first dance shares its time signature $\frac{6}{4}$, rhythmic profile, and overall character with an "Air pour les Espagnols" that Lully had composed for the "Ballet des Nations" in the *Bourgeois gentilhomme*, and which he reused in the Spanish entrée of *Le Carnaval* (see Example 6-4, p. 170). Campra also followed Lully in giving his dancers a sarabande, a dance that the French associated with Spain, and he set one song to a Spanish text. The dancers may well have used castanets, which were enough a part of French dance technique that Feuillet devoted three pages to their use at the end of *Chorégraphie*.[37] An engraving of Lestang shows him in a magnificent Spanish costume, although without castanets (see Figure 8-4).[38]

There are three choreographies from this divertissement that claim to have been danced at the Opéra, which means that they must have originated in the first run of performances.[39] Two are set to the same piece of music, the "Air des Espagnols," but are for different performers: two men in one, a solo woman in the other. This suggests that the music must have been repeated, although the score does not so indicate. The other choreography, set to the rondeau, is for a man and a woman – a visual suggestion that the serenaders may someday succeed. The only other dance, the sarabande, might have been a group dance, particularly as it comes close to the end, adjacent to the concluding chorus. The number of dancers is not known for 1697, but in 1706 there were eight (see Figure 7-2). This is the smallest number of dancers of any entrée in this revival (the others had fourteen to sixteen), a choice that seems entirely in line with the overall torpor of the story.

The entrée set in Turkey also owes debts to Lully – namely to the Turkish ceremony from the *Bourgeois gentilhomme*, which had been seen at the Opéra in performances of *Le Carnaval*. Campra, however, does not invoke the buffoonery of his Lullian model until the end; leading up to it comes a story of love and violent

[36] This synopsis follows the 1697 score; the 1698 and 1699 scores have a somewhat different order.

[37] See *Chorégraphie*, 100–02. The two excerpts notating the castanet part are from the chaconne in *Phaéton* and the *Folies d'Espagne*.

[38] Ladvocat (*Lettres*, 58) described in some detail the similar Spanish costume Pécour wore in the *Ballet des saisons*.

[39] The dances were published two years before the opera's first revival; see Appendix 3.

Figure 8-4: "Monsieur de Lestang in a Spanish costume dancing at the Opéra". (Photo BnF)

jealousy. Zayde has been enslaved and added to the Sultan's harem. At first she was miserable, but now that she has fallen in love with her master, her only goal is to make him love her. Meanwhile Zuliman, the Sultan, is trying to extricate himself from Roxane, his former favorite. Roxane realizes that he has fallen in love with another woman, but doesn't know which one. The Sultanes in the harem dance and sing "in order to please Zuliman," while Roxane jealously eyes them. In this instance there is no proxy singer; Zayde herself leads the singing, and her attempt at seduction works. Zuliman reveals that he has loved her since he first set eyes on her, but before she can reply, Roxane tries to stab her rival. Zuliman wrests away the dagger and sends Roxane into custody. The lovers have a tender duet before Zuliman calls for a fête.

This entrée thus has two divertissements, of very different character. The first, by the harem women, consists of a long passacaille followed by a related vocal complex that intersperses Zayde's words of love with choral responses set for high voices, all purely French in musical style.[40] Its sung texts make the point of the dance unambiguous: "May love give rise in our hearts to a thousand ardors toward our august master. May our tender sighs anticipate his every desire." As in the fifth act of *Armide*, a passacaille functions as an act of seduction on behalf of an exotic woman. The dancers in 1697 remain unknown, although it would be surprising if Mlle Subligny, the leading female dancer of the time, had not been among them.[41] In the 1706 revival there were six Sultanes, two of them, Mlles Prévost and Guyot, among the troupe's stars. In the revival of 1736, another star dancer, Marie Sallé, was to alter the nature of this passacaille by turning it into a miniature pantomime ballet with an unhappy outcome.[42]

The second divertissement in "La Turquie" is noteworthy for the exoticism of its musical language, which is put in the service of good-natured buffoonery. Here the chorus, singers and dancers alike, are the sultan's gardeners (Bostangis); they have rakes[43] and sing in lingua franca, the pidgin Italian used as a trading language around the Mediterranean basin. The lingua franca marks another point of contact with the Turkish Ceremony, and the short, rhymed lines of the two texts are similar. The translation into French (or rather, "sense of the words") provided in the libretto gives a (deliberately?) misleading impression of the actual sung text, by smoothing over its choppy rhymed lines, adding content, and elevating the tone. Here, by way of example, are the first two quatrains of the text, which are sung *alternatim* by the Bachi (the leader of the Bostangis) and the chorus; in the subsequent verses the French departs still more from the lingua franca.

40 In an essay about the Turkish style in late eighteenth-century opera, Hunter points out the same phenomenon: "in opera the venue for *turquerie* is almost always a seraglio," yet the women who inhabit it "are typically identified by no obviously 'exotic' musical topics"; see "The *alla turca* style," 44. Betzwieser (*Exotismus*, 135) hears the Sultan's vocal lines as partaking of exoticizing gestures.

41 According to the choreographies mentioned above, Mlle Subligny danced twice in "L'Espagne," once as a soloist and once with Balon.

42 The anecdote comes from Cahusac, *La Danse*, III, 154–55.

43 The set design by Jean Berain lines the sides of the stage with trees and sheds, from which rakes and other tools protrude. See La Gorce, "De l'opéra-ballet aux fragments," 42.

[Lingua franca]	**Le sens des paroles franques**
Vivir, vivir, gran Sultana.	Vive le Souverain, qui nous donne des loix;
Unir, unir li cantara.	Chantons, chantons, répétons mille fois,
Mille volte exclamara,	Vive le Souverain, qui nous donne des loix.
Vivir, vivir, gran Sultana	
Bello como star un flor;	Qu'il ignore à jamais les peines,
Durar quanto far arbor.	Qu'il éprouve mille douceurs,
All'enemigos su sçiabola,	Qu'il brille autant que les fleurs,
Come a frutas tempesta.	Qu'il dure autant que les chênes.
Translation	***Translation***
Live, live, great Sultan.	Long live the sovereign who gives us laws;
Unite, unite, the song.	Let us sing, let us repeat a thousand times,
Thousand times exclaim,	Long live the sovereign who gives us laws.
Live, live, great Sultan.	May he never know suffering,
Be beautiful like a flower;	May he always experience sweetness,
Last as long as a tree.	May he shine as much as the flowers,
To enemies his saber	May he last as long as the oaks.
Like a tempest to fruits.	

In this divertissement musical novelties are couched within a traditional structure. The scene is introduced by a march, then framed by choruses, within which there is one musically independent dance and one related to the final chorus. But each of the pieces has musical characteristics that take it outside of French norms. The march is made heavy by its low tessitura, repeated half notes, and a slow harmonic rhythm that is reinforced by the imitative opening (see Example 8-1). Each phrase of the Bachi's "Unir, unir li cantara" is punctuated in the orchestra by subito forte octave drops, as a kind of aural exclamation point. The "Premier Air pour les Bostangis" has large leaps in both treble and bass, an imitative opening that calls attention to the leaping dotted half notes in the first bar, and a harmonic rhythm that changes at most every three beats (Example 8-2). The lively second dance and its related chorus worry little rhythmic/melodic cells over and over. Campra may or may not have known real Turkish music, but he knew his Lully: he borrowed the three repeated notes and the irregular phrasing from Lully's Turkish march (see Example 6-5), the iambic rhythm of "Vivir" from the invocation to Allah, and like the Mufti, the Bachi is a bass.[44] Campra's divertissement does not involve a

44 Whaples, "Early exoticism revisited," 125–29, finds that Campra's march is closer to Janissary music than is Lully's and that Destouches's "Air des Américains" in *Issé* v/5 shares some of the same features. Regarding the musical realizations of exoticism, see her "Early exoticism revisited"; Betzwieser, *Exotismus*; and, for later periods that still have points in common with Campra's day, Hunter, "The *alla turca* style," and Locke, "The Turkish style" in his *Musical Exoticism*, 114–23.

Example 8-1: Campra, *L'Europe galante*, "Marche des Bostangis" from "La Turquie" (Paris: Ballard, 1697), 181.

Example 8-2: Campra, *L'Europe galante*, "Premier Air pour les Bostangis," from "La Turquie" (Paris: Ballard, 1697), 194.

ceremony, but within its own idiom it invokes the comic spirit of the earlier scene, even to the point of insisting verbally and musically on the Sultan's turban (the bestowing of the turban having been the high point of Lully's fake ceremony).[45]

A theatrical choreography set to the three instrumental pieces of this divertissement exhibits choreographic analogues to the anomalies of the music: flat-footed stamps, brushes of the foot back and forth, sideways hops, and a startling conclusion with a foot in the air.[46] The "Turkish Dance" originated in England after *L'Europe galante* premiered,

[45] The reference to the turban comes in the third stanza of the text; it is sung three times by the Bachi and twice more by the Bostangis ("may heavenly favor cover his turban"). The French "translation" does not mention the turban.

[46] For a discussion of the choreography and its cultural context, see Tomko, "Framing Turkish dances." L'Abbé's notation runs the three instrumental dances together, whereas in *L'Europe galante* they are separated by vocal pieces.

but its choreographer, Anthony L'Abbé, had been in the Opéra's troupe in the late seventeenth century, before he decided to pursue his career across the Channel; he may even have danced in *L'Europe galante*, given that he performed in *Issé* in the same year. In addition, he is known to have danced the role of a Turk in a court performance of the *Bourgeois gentilhomme* in 1691.[47] Even though his Turkish dance cannot be directly associated with the Opéra, L'Abbé may have drawn upon a set of movement conventions developed over the years for representing Turks. Perhaps, like some of the musical gestures, these went back to 1670 when the *Bourgeois gentilhomme* was created, in which case they may owe their origins to Lully's primary choreographer, Beauchamps, or even to the Mufti – Lully himself.

A practical performance question hovers over this divertissement, one that makes a major difference in how the dancing would have looked: in Paris in 1697 did only the Bostangis dance or did the Sultanes join them? By the norms of the day, a concluding celebratory divertissement – and this one ends the opera[48] – would involve all the dancers and singers on stage, men and women alike; the *didascalie* for this scene does include the Sultanes. But the evidence is ambiguous and the locale, the ludicrous texts, and the exoticizing music differentiate this scene from the usual Lullian expressions of social unity that round off his *tragédies*. The score assigns the dances to the Bostangis – but its failure to mention the Sultanes cannot be taken as definitive. The fact that the chorus includes a treble part allows for women to sing, but does not require it – there exist choruses scored in the usual four parts when the roles are all male. The call and response between the Bachi and the chorus, who sing the same texts in lingua franca, seem to invoke a male fraternity, not one that the Sultanes would have entered. Moreover, it seems unlikely that the women of a Sultan's harem would ever dance with his gardeners. But the Turkey on view is a fantasy. At the end of an opera would Pécour have left the female half of his dance troupe standing around the edges of the stage? Or would French theatrical norms for celebratory divertissements have overridden concerns about verisimilitude? We cannot know. What we can see is that the exoticism on display in the final divertissement has a comic shading lacking in the rest of "La Turquie," one that Campra amplified via allusions to "Turkish" musical gestures originated by Lully. Whether or not the Sultan is to be taken as a stand-in for Louis XIV, as Betzwieser has proposed, the concluding songs and dances spoof as much as they honor.[49]

The third entrée, "L'Italie," offers its own kind of local color, in that it provides a plausible habitat for the first da capo aria to appear in a French opera. "Ad un cuore"

47 Information about L'Abbé's roles comes from Lecomte (private communication).

48 Only a brief conversation between Vénus and Discord follows.

49 Betzwieser, *Exotismus*, 138–39, sees the honoring of the Sultan as aimed at France's sovereign; he does not discuss the dissonance between the French translations of the lingua franca and Campra's musical language.

Example 8-3: Campra, *L'Europe galante*, from "L'Italie" (Paris: Ballard, 1724), 172–75. (a) "Ad un cuore"; (b) "Air pour les Masques."

(a)

(b)

(Example 8-3a) is in $\frac{12}{8}$, a time signature that in France in 1697 signaled an Italian style. It has a motto opening, an obbligato treble part, the rhythmic hallmarks of a *giga*, and even dynamic markings in Italian. This Italianate incursion into French territory was so successful that Campra added two other da capo arias to this scene the following year, one of his own composition and one by Louis Marchand.[50] Eleven years later, in 1708, Campra was the first composer to apply da capo form to an operatic air in French – this

[50] See Anthony, "Air and aria," and La Gorce, "Vogue et influence."

in his tragedy *Hippodamie* – a type that came to be called *ariette*.[51] But what is particularly fascinating is not the mere fact of the conscious and rapid adoption of a foreign style, but the way this new kind of piece functioned in its French context.

Just as Arlequin had to be toned down when he moved from the earthy Italian theater into the rarefied atmosphere of the Opéra, so did Italian music have to be framed in ways that would make it pass in this environment. Given French concern with verisimilitude, the most natural way to insert something foreign was to call attention to its musicality by staging it as a performance for the on-stage audience, not as a personal utterance by one of the main characters.[52] (For an outline of this divertissement, see Table 9-1, p. 269) This aria is, indeed, performed by an anonymous Venetian woman, one of the maskers at a costume ball. The fact that the woman is bilingual – her next utterance, as leader of the chorus, is sung in French – does not seem to pose a problem of verisimilitude, perhaps because audiences had so often seen characters switch back and forth between French and Italian at the Théâtre Italien. Moreover, the text of her aria – "To a jealous heart Love must deny pity" – fits seamlessly into the progression of the divertissement, which starts with a chorus warning against jealousy ("S'il se trouve ici des jaloux, / L'Amour ne les amène / Que pour les tromper tous") and ends by extolling pleasure in a joyous refrain ("Livrons-nous aux plaisirs, il n'est rien de plus doux; / Pour qui seraient-ils faits, si ce n'était pour nous?"). As usual in a French opera, the divertissement directly implicates a protagonist – in this case the violently jealous Octavio, who watches the dancing but fails to heed the sung messages and wishes he had not brought Olympia to the ball at all.

But beyond its thematic connections to the work as a whole, "Ad un cuore" is embedded within a musical structure that could come out of any Lully opera: a strophic song that is interleaved with an instrumental dance (Example 8-3b) to which it has close musical connections. The fact that each strophe consists of a da capo aria adds a new wrinkle to an old practice, but otherwise this is a classic French way of constructing a divertissement, and the remaining vocal pieces are also interwoven with a related dance. (For more regarding the dances Campra chose to use in this divertissement, see in Chapter 9 "The masked ball on stage," pp. 268ff.) The dropping of one or two Italian elements into an otherwise very French scene – even if it is set in Venice – could seem

[51] Masson's brief history of the term "ariette" points out that Brossard's *Dictionnaire de musique* (1703) uses the word in two senses: (1) a little air, simple in style; and (2) an Italian aria of the type found in a cantata. By the time of *Les Fêtes vénitiennes* (1710) the word was also applied to da capo arias sung in French; see Masson, *L'Opéra de Rameau*, 229–30.

[52] In *Le Carnaval de Venise* one of the main characters, Léonore, does sing a da capo aria in Italian, but she does so in response to a serenade and seems to be performing a stage song. Similarly, Iphise, a main character in "Le Bal" from *Les Fêtes vénitiennes*, sings a da capo aria in Italian as a performance at an on-stage party. In *L'Ecole des amants*, Elismène, a French widow, sings an aria in Italian to her jealous Roman suitor in order to show that she loves him enough to have learned his language.

artificial, but from another perspective Campra has very cleverly worked a new, exciting musical style into a familiar environment; it is exotic, but ultimately safe – perhaps like the imaginary Venice herself for the young French adventurers who people so many of these operas.

Les Fêtes vénitiennes (1710)

The triumphant success of *L'Europe galante* allowed Campra to resign his position as *maître de musique* at Notre Dame cathedral and to devote himself thereafter to the stage.[53] Over the next 38 years he composed or arranged nineteen works for the Opéra in a variety of genres, seven of which generated revivals. But without doubt his biggest success came with *Les Fêtes vénitiennes*, which had 66 consecutive performances between June and November of 1710, before being taken up again in January of 1711; in various configurations the work was revived many times up until 1762.[54] The opera-ballet format allowed Campra and his librettist Danchet to add or subtract entrées, and within the first year the two of them wrote two versions of the prologue and eight separate entrées – all of them imbued with the spirit of Carnival in a city imagined by the French as a sexual playground. No fewer than three of the protagonists in the various vignettes are young Frenchmen in search of adventure. As Masson pointed out, "the general impression given by *Les Fêtes vénitiennes*, to which both the libretto and the music contribute, is that it is governed from one end to the other by the spirit of comedy."[55]

The following brief outline gives a sense of how much the work owes to the traditions of the *comédie italienne* and the fair theaters, not only in its storylines and characters, but in its irreverence and its willingness to engage in self-critique; overall the tone is cynical. The synopsis below follows the order of the entrées as they appear in the *Recueil général*, which includes all nine of them, even though only a subset would be seen in a given run of performances.[56] The setting of the entrées in Venice during Carnival gave the two creators a degree of freedom in their handling of the music and the texts that they particularly exploited in the divertissements:

[53] According to Barthélemy, Campra's withdrawal from Notre Dame was a gradual process that was finalized in October 1700; see his *André Campra*, 40–42. Campra did compose some sacred music later in his life, but his primary output henceforth was secular.

[54] See the list of the revivals in the score edited by Lütolf, x–xi.

[55] Masson, "Fêtes vénitiennes," 217–18.

[56] Lütolf's edition includes only what he considers the "definitive" version and omits three of the entrées: "La Fête des barquerolles"; "La Fête marine"; and "Le Triomphe de la Folie, comédie." Because *Les Fêtes vénitiennes* was so subject to revision, its sources are numerous and complex. My discussion rests on Lütolf's edition in consultation with the reduced score published by Ballard in 1714 (3rd ed.).

Prologue, Le Triomphe de la Folie sur la Raison dans le temps du Carnaval. Masked merrymakers from all over arrive in the port of Venice, with personified Carnival at their head. Reason, accompanied by philosophers, urges wisdom and tranquility, but is mocked by Folly, who joins forces with Carnival in singing and dancing. (A later version, "Le Carnaval dans Venise," eliminated Reason and her followers.)

La Fête des barquerolles. The old Doctor moons (in Italian) over the young Lilla, who does not hesitate to treat him with contempt. Her suitor, Damiro, excitedly tells her (in French) that he has just won the mock battle held among the gondoliers; the news provokes her into declaring her love. Gondoliers arrive *en masse* to help him celebrate his double victory.

Les Sérénades et les joueurs. Set outside the Ridotto, where Venetians gather to gamble, the story concerns a young Frenchman, Léandre, who has been toying with the affections of two young Venetians, Isabelle and Lucille. Realizing they have been jilted, the two team up to interrupt a serenade he is offering to his new heartthrob, Irène. (The serenade provides Irène the opportunity for a da capo aria, in Italian, about unfaithful butterflies.) Léandre is saved from having to confront all three by the arrival of a troupe of gamblers, who urge him to pay homage to Fortune: "For the gambler and the lover, Fortune is equally fickle." He decides to seek a new lover.

L'Amour saltimbanque (also entitled "Les Saltimbanques de la Place Saint-Marc"). Another young Frenchman, Éraste, disguised as a Venetian, has fallen in love with Léonore, but since she is always accompanied by her mistrustful chaperone, Nérine (played by a man), he has not yet met her. He enlists the help of a troupe of players (*saltimbanques*), who transform their wagon into a stage, on which Amour and his masked followers provide a distraction while Éraste woos Léonore. Amour sings that fickleness is now in style, but Éraste proposes marriage. Amour wryly warns the young couple not to expect to see him after the wedding.

La Fête marine. The jealous Astolphe is keeping a tight rein on his ward, Céphise. Her lover, Dorante, has disguised himself as a sailor so that he can get close to her during the marine festivities. These provide cover for him to escape with her on board ship; Astolphe is left to rage on the shore, exhorting the sea to swallow them up.

Le Bal. A Polish prince, Alamir, wishes to make sure that the Venetian beauty Iphise loves him for himself, so has exchanged places with his confidant. The disguised Thémir is preparing for a masked ball and has invited two renowned French masters to help with the music and the dance. The two spar with each other over the beauties of their respective professions, but after Iphise has admitted her love and Alamir has revealed his true identity, the two return to lead the ball.

Les Devins de la Place Saint-Marc. Zélie has disguised herself as a gypsy in order to test the affections of her young French lover. She offers to tell his fortune and sees in his hand that he no sooner makes one conquest than he moves on to the next. He tells the "gypsy" that his French birthright makes it impossible for him to remain faithful. She predicts that he is about to fall in love with someone who offers resistance; he welcomes the challenge. She unmasks, saying that now she understands his character, she is no longer interested. He takes the rejection as encouragement, and runs after her.

L'Opéra. A performance is about to start in the Grimani opera house – not, however, of an Italian opera, but of the "Ballet de Flore." A young Neapolitan, Damire, has disguised himself as Borée, with the goal of using the performance as a means of eloping with its heroine under the nose of his rival. In the middle of the performance the stage goes dark and Borée, the North wind, arrives with Aquilons to abduct Flore. When Jupiter fails to come to the rescue, the confused Zéphyr steps out of character to ask the shepherdess what's going on. When she reveals that Léontine has run off, the singer playing Zéphyr abandons his role and the jilted suitor, in a rage, hurries toward the port.

Le Triomphe de la Folie, comédie. Arlequin, dressed as the philosopher Diogenes and carrying a lantern, comes to the Piazza San Marco in search of a wise man. (Diogenes, founder of the philosophical school known as Cynicism, is reputed to have searched Athens, lantern in hand, for an honest man, but to have found only scoundrels.) Folly tempts him with pleasures and games; Arlequin/Diogenes has to admit that, after wisdom, he likes folly best. Resuming his search, he encounters the Doctor, but finds him in thrall to love, even at his advanced age. After similar encounters with a Spaniard and a Frenchman, Arlequin/Diogenes despairs of fulfilling his quest. Colombine, whom he had once loved, appears and before long he succumbs again to her charms. He throws off his philosopher's gown and the two sing a happy duet. Disguised Venetians suddenly arrive, playing guitars and singing. During the ensuing festivities, Colombine rejects the advances of the Doctor and Arlequin mocks him in mime. Everyone agrees to enjoy life to the full.

The level of complexity in these little scenes is uneven; in some, such as the "Fête des Barquerolles," the plot merely provides a skimpy pretext for a divertissement, but in the most interesting ones (which were the most revived), the storyline could not function without the divertissement. This is the case even though every single divertissement is framed as some kind of performance, not as action. A diegetic framework might seem to limit the dramatic possibilities, but because the spirit of Carnival favors disguises and play-acting and allows anyone to fall into song and dance, the opportunities for dramatically pertinent divertissements are wide open.

One sign of the greater freedom provided by the comic frame is that some characters both sing and dance. This practice seems to have come to the Opéra from the fair theaters and the old Théâtre Italien, where it was not rare for a single individual to sing, dance, and act.[57] At the Opéra, however, the roles were structured to separate the functions of singing and dancing – until the advent of opera-ballet and other light

[57] See, for example, Regnard's play *La Coquette*, III/3 (Théâtre Italien, 1691): "Arlequin, dressed as a marquis, enters singing and dancing, giving himself ridiculous airs, and combing his wig."

genres occasionally allowed both talents to be united in the same person.[58] Three of the entrées from *Les Fêtes vénitiennes* make the character's ability to do both part of the plot, and in all cases this promotes flexibility in the handling of divertissement architecture: "Le Triomphe de la Folie" (the entrée, not the prologue), in which Arlequin as Diogenes both sings and dances; "Le Bal," which includes a dancing master who sings; and "Les Devins de la Place Saint-Marc."

In this last entrée, Zélie, a young Venetian who has disguised herself as a gypsy in order to test the fidelity of her French suitor, Léandre, dances as she offers to tell his fortune. This portion of the entrée (Scene 3) is, strictly speaking, outside the divertissement, since no group characters are on stage. The fact of her dancing does not, however, contravene the laws of verisimilitude, in that gypsies are among those characters within the world of French musical theater seen to be dancers by nature. The libretto even tells us that Zélie enters dancing, and the score provides eight measures of a lively duple-meter piece in C major for her entrance, which then returns to punctuate her offer to tell Léandre's fortune. Her short phrases are accompanied by continuo, while the instrumental passages that break up her line are set for orchestra. The texture suggests that she alternates singing and dancing except, perhaps, on the last phrase, where the orchestral accompaniment to her words may indicate that she is also dancing. Table 8-2 shows how the four lines of her text are interleaved with the orchestral passages.

Table 8-2: *Les Fêtes vénitiennes*: "Les Devins de la Place Saint-Marc," Scene 3, Zélie's entrance.

No. of bars	Content
8	Orchestral phrase
5	Voice and continuo: "Jeune étranger, veux-tu savoir / Ta bonne ou mauvaise fortune?"
4	Orchestral phrase
4	Voice and continuo: "Ma science n'est point commune / Dans le grand art de tout prévoir."
3	Voice and orchestra: [danced?] "Dans le grand art de tout prévoir."
4	Orchestral phrase

This truncated orchestral piece is later heard in full, as the entrance music for the gypsies who arrive in the next scene. Zélie, in other words, is borrowing the gypsies' dance as part of her disguise; she puts on their movements along with her mask. Campra uses the same musical construction to a slightly different end a bit later in Scene 3: when Zélie examines Léandre's hand, a "Symphonie" in A minor, marked "Gai," introduces

58 Insofar as it is possible to tell from the surviving evidence, this phenomenon of singing dancers or dancing singers seems to have been limited at the Opéra to a few solo roles.

and then punctuates her describing of Léandre's character to himself: "What do I see?"; (orchestra); "You have promised love to so many beautiful women here!"; (orchestra); "You know how to speak of love"; (orchestra); etc. In this case, the orchestral music would seem to accompany action rather than dance, although the phrases are long enough (usually four to six bars) to allow her to throw in a few dance steps, if she so desired. This piece, too, recurs during the divertissement, as a dance entitled "La Bohémienne." Whether Zélie herself joined the dancing gypsies in the divertissement proper is not something the sources reveal. In 1710, at least, it seems unlikely, as the person cast as Zélie, Mlle Poussin, was a singer, and she would have had to hold her own against two of the leading dancers of the troupe, Balon and Mlle Prévost.[59]

The divertissement proper has an unusual structure, which falls into two distinct parts (see Table 8-3). It opens in a conventional manner with a march followed by a chorus; the introductory section also includes instrumental dances, all performed by the gypsies. Next, however, comes not another chorus or a mixture of songs and dances, but a highly organized set of pieces attributed to a solo singer and labeled "Cantate." In 1710 the *cantate*, modeled on the Italian chamber cantata, was still a young genre in France, one that had grown out of the musical circle surrounding the Italophile Philippe d'Orléans, the king's nephew and future Regent; the first books of *cantates*, composed by Jean-Baptiste Morin, Nicolas Bernier, and Baptistin Stuck, were published in 1706, and Campra published the first of his own three books in 1708.[60] The mere presence of a chamber genre inside an opera is unexpected, and this one adheres to the conventional alternation for a single soloist of recitative and da capo aria. (Most French *cantates* of this period have three recitative-aria pairs, rather than the two Campra provides here.) Campra also follows Italian practices in adopting a time signature of C for the recitative, rather than the changing time signatures characteristic in France, and the instrumental writing in the *ariettes* also borrows from Italy. But in order to fit an Italianate *cantate* into a French operatic context, Campra extends what would normally be the concluding ritornello for each aria into something long enough to serve as a dance, even though it has an unconventional structure. The French penchant for making musical connections between song and dance is thus maintained, even when the musical style owes more to Italy than to France. Campra's solution here is different from how he handled the dances near the da capo aria in *L'Europe galante* (see above, p. 245), but the impulse is the same.

The sources differ as to whether the solo role in the *cantate* is attributed to Zélie or to an unnamed Bohémienne.[61] In effect, the difference between the two alternatives is not

[59] A similar case occurs in the prologue to *Le Carnaval et la Folie* by Destouches and La Motte, where Vénus (singing role) dances briefly with Mars (dancing role), while her husband Vulcain observes them.

[60] See Tunley, *The Eighteenth-Century French Cantata.*

[61] The 1710 libretto, the *Recueil général*, and Lütolf's edition (based on a manuscript score) assign the *cantate* to Zélie, whereas the 1714 Ballard score attributes it to a Bohémienne.

Table 8-3: *Les Fêtes vénitiennes*, "Les Devins de la Place Saint-Marc," Scene 4.

Heading in score	Musical features	Paraphrase of sung text/ comments
Marche	C, ¢; rondeau	[Entrance music for the gypsies, previously heard introducing Zélie]
Choeur, "Venez, empressez-vous"	C, ¢; similar to the march	Lovers, come have your fortunes told, so that you will know what success to expect in love.
Rondeau	C, **3**	[In modern ed. but not in 1714 Ballard scores]
Premier passepied	C, $\frac{3}{8}$	
Deuxième passepied	C, $\frac{3}{8}$	[No indication to repeat first passepied]
	Cantate	
Prelude. Lentement	C, **c**; 4¼ bars long	
[Récitatif], "Sans troubler le repos du ténébreux empire"	C, **c**; 5 bars	We gypsies have the ability to tell fortunes without recourse to the powers of the Underworld.
Ariette, "Amant, si vous êtes content"	C, **3**; da capo, 2 violin parts, motto opening	Lover, if you conduct your wooing properly, it is easy to tell your fortune; no woman could resist.
Danse	Uses melody and instrumentation of *ariette*, ABAC structure (four 6-bar phrases).	
Récitatif, "Venez, fières beautés"	c, **c**; 11 bars	Proud beauties, take heed. If you spurn your lovers now, you will be sorry later.
Ariette, "L'Amour qui vole sur vos traces"	c, **c**, but mostly behaves like $\frac{12}{8}$; marked "Gay," two treble parts for doubled fls and vlns	The love that pursues you now will flee with the spring of your youth. What good will it do you to love when you are no longer lovable?
Danse	17-bar instrumental extension of the *ariette*, ABAC structure	
	[End of *Cantate*]	
La Bohémienne	a, **2**; ABA structure	[Instrumental dance in a new key, but same music as when Zélie told Léandre's fortune]

great, in that a strong musical association has already been made between Zélie and the gypsies. Since the anonymous gypsy can be seen as Zélie's mouthpiece, her words become significant. The first *ariette* is directed at Léandre ("Amant" in the singular), who is told that if he is faithful, his wooing will succeed. Not coincidentally, perhaps, the vocal style is more French than Italian; the Bohémienne speaks to him in a musical language that he understands. The second, more Italianate, *ariette*, is aimed at "young beauties" in the plural, who are told, in the recitative, that if they treat their suitors badly they will be sorry, and, in the aria, that love must be enjoyed while they are young. Given the mixed messages of the two *ariettes*, it is not surprising that Léandre finds reason to hope for success.

This *cantate* is not the only one Campra worked into *Les Fêtes vénitiennes*; he identified the central portion of the divertissement in "L'Amour saltimbanque" in the same way, with the featured soloist none other than Amour. The divertissement within which this *cantate* is embedded is considerably longer than the one in "Les Devins de la Place Saint-Marc," but is also framed as a performance. "A troupe of Saltimbanques [travelling street players] arrives. They bring a cart that opens up into a stage. Amour [a pants role][62] appears in the guise of a Saltimbanque and is characterized only by the bow that he holds in his hand. The Plaisirs and Jeux, dressed as comic figures, surround him." These consist of a motley crew of masks from the *comédie italienne*: Arlequin and Polichinelle, who seem to be the partners of two Espagnolettes; Spezzafer and Scaramouchette; an old couple; a peasant couple; Pantalon and Pantalone; and a Masque galant who has no partner, for a total of thirteen dancers.[63] The group enters to the sounds of a march, after which Filandro, the troupe's leader, tries to draw a crowd by boasting that the show is coming directly from Cythera. His exhortation, taken up by the chorus, is set to music similar to the march and punctuated by instrumental phrases that provide opportunities for action. The warm-up act concludes with a danced "Air pour les Arlequins," a piece independent of any vocal music. Amour then steps forward to make his pitch; he is selling the secret to happiness.

Amour's *cantate* intersperses his three songs with two dance pieces and only one recitative.[64] All the texts are in French, but the vocal and instrumental styles mix French and Italian elements in varying proportions. "Venez tous" has a rondeau structure (ABACA), a syllabic text setting, and a French-style melody in the manner of a loure, but the piece is introduced and concluded by ritornellos for the obbligato flute that punctuates the sections and accompanies the vocal line in the couplets between refrains. The music is surprisingly somber in mood, given the hucksterism of the text, and coming as the piece does on the heels of a dance for Arlequins. In the

62 Casting a woman in the role of the child Amour goes back at least as far as Lully's *Psyché*.

63 The roles come from the cast list in the 1710 libretto, which lists the dancers in two columns, men in one, women in the other, a format that suggests the dancers were, with one exception, paired. That said, the listing may be more a graphic convenience than a representation of groupings on stage, especially in the case of Arlequin, Polichinelle, and the Espagnolettes, who are lined up opposite each other, but seem unlikely partners.

64 Campra also designated Sc. 4 in "Les Sérénades et les joueurs" as a *cantate*; it is sung only, and makes no provision for dances. On the other hand, two later operatic *cantates* feature a solo dancer; see Ch. 13, pp. 398 and 402.

Table 8-4: *Les Fêtes vénitiennes*, the *cantate* sung by Amour in "L'Amour saltimbanque," Scene 3.

Heading in score	Musical features	Paraphrase of sung text/ comments
[Air], "Venez tous, venez faire emplette"	d, **3**; rondeau; simple vocal style, flute obbligato	Amour invites everyone to buy his wares.
Air des Espagnols	d, **3**; binary, similar to preceding vocal air	
[Air], "Effet admirable"	D, ¢; rondeau, Italianate	Amour vaunts his power to improve everyone's lives.
Air des Polichinelles [Ballard PR]; also called Air des Espagnoles [ms. PG]	D, ¢; binary, related to the preceding vocal air	Libretto: "The Pleasures who follow Amour form a comic divertissement."
[Récitatif], "Le prix d'un si grand bien"	Changes meters, but nonetheless Italianate	Amour says the cost of his wares is astonishing: everything is free. He no longer charges a price of sighs and tears.
Ariette, "Ce n'est plus la mode des amants constants"	d, $\frac{6}{8}$; da capo form	Faithful love is no longer in fashion; Amour has adjusted to the temper of the times.

second, much livelier air, Amour vaunts his powers: youth is more enjoyable, old age less bitter, ugliness prettified, and beauty sweeter, all thanks to his art. The structure of his air is, once again, a French rondeau, but the musical style is considerably more Italianate, and the obbligato violin part provides the lively melody for the dance that follows (Example 8-4). In the recitative Amour reveals that, best of all, his offer has no price tag – the secret to happiness is free. "In the days of Amadis," he says – making reference not only to the chivalric Middle Ages, but to Lully's eponymous opera – "I demanded a high price for love: sighs, tears, constancy, a discreet heart that was willing to languish without reward, to burn in secret. [But] Faithful lovers are no longer in style; Amour must adjust to the defect of the times."[65] This cynical sentiment, set to a jolly *ariette* in $\frac{6}{8}$ time in the manner of a *giga*, provokes Éraste into defending fidelity and proposing marriage to Léonore. She replies that she likes his words much better than Amour's. Amour warns them that he cannot be counted on to stay for long; he invites the merrymaking to resume, while he is still in the area. The merrymakers hardly need encouragement; they continue with a dance for Amour's followers, a substantial

[65] Recitative: "Le prix d'un si grand bien, peut-être, vous étonne; / Je ne le vends plus, je le donne. / Au bon vieux temps des Amadis, / Je le mettais à trop haut prix. / J'exigeais des soupirs, des pleurs, de la constance, / Un coeur sincère, un coeur discret, / Et qui même sans récompense, / Fût content de languir, de brûler en secret." Ariette: "Ce n'est plus la mode / Des amants constants; / L'Amour s'accommode / Au défaut du temps."

Example 8-4: Campra, *Les Fêtes vénitiennes*, "Air des Polichinelles" aka "Air des Espagnoles" from "L'Amour saltimbanque" (Paris: Ballard, 1714), 49–50.

chaconne, and conclude the divertissement – and the entrée – with a musically related chorus: "Love supplies the antidote to sadness."[66]

The ambiguities in the sources as to who does the dancing inside this *cantate* highlight a shift in how the dancers and members of the chorus relate to each other. In Lully's operas, the two troupes generally filled the same roles – all cast as shepherds, Athenians, or the like. But in works where the dance pieces are related not to a chorus, but to elaborate *ariettes* sung by a soloist, a different relationship prevails among the roles. In this instance, Amour's followers number thirteen, mostly paired merry-makers, rather than a single group. The scores assign the first dance to Spanish men, which is musically plausible, but the cast list includes no such characters. (Given the serious cast of the music, perhaps it was danced by the Masque galant.[67]) The second dance has conflicting attributions in the sources: to Polichinelles in Ballard's prints, but to Spanish women in the manuscript full score on which the modern edition is based. (The latter are likelier, given choreographic evidence,[68] although it is not impossible that the dance was performed twice, with different sets of characters.) The confusion is probably a source problem, but it does seem symptomatic of two general trends that can be seen emerging in the works of this era.

First, the newly introduced arias in Italian style, which call attention to the act of singing much more than a Lullian dance-song ever did, change the balance within a divertissement by shifting the emphasis away from the chorus and toward solo singers. French-style dance-songs, whether choral or individual, do not disappear from

[66] "Accourez, que chacun s'empresse, / L'Amour présente à vos désirs / L'antidote de la tristesse, / Et la source des vrais plaisirs."

[67] A theatrical-style choreography for a solo man to this music is found in the Gaudrau collection, but the notation does not claim that the dance originated at the Opéra, nor does it say who performed it.

[68] See Ch. 14, p. 419.

divertissements by Campra and his contemporaries, but they decrease in number and prominence (a dance-song takes less time to sing than a da capo aria), and there tend to be fewer choruses of any type. At the same time, the conception of the chorus as a single group that encompasses both singers and dancers starts encountering exceptions. The traveling players who arrive on Cupid's cart in "L'Amour saltimbanque" have a double identity, collectively as Plaisirs and Jeux, but also as thirteen individuals. There are still many examples of the old system to be found in these works; in "La Fête des barquerolles" all the collective characters are gondoliers. But a collective identity is no longer the only possibility, and Carnival, the season of disguises, provides a natural avenue for extravagant individual displays.

The second emerging trend is an increase in the number of musically independent dance pieces. This is not to say that the ties between song and dance were severed; dance-songs still figure frequently in divertissements and Campra found innovative ways to keep vocal pieces and dances connected, even when the music is Italian in style. But in *Les Fêtes vénitiennes* the average number of instrumental dances in a divertissement is six, even without counting possible repeats and even when one of them might be a chaconne. Fewer of these dances have a musical connection to a vocal piece than was the case for Lully. The new emphasis on individual dancing roles may account for some of the additional pieces, in that differentiated characters lend themselves to individualized character dances. An increase in the number of dances does not necessarily dilute the effect of a divertissement; in some of the scenes discussed in the next chapter the large number of dances contributes to making the divertissement dramatically cogent. But the rebalancing marks a step away from the template Lully and Quinault had established. The theatricalizing of Carnival provided a perfect vehicle for opening up previous conventions.

9 | Thalie Visits the Fairs

A self-consciousness about the acts of singing and dancing had always characterized French opera, but the works that Campra and his contemporaries were now writing under the aegis of Thalie shine a spotlight on their own theatricality. The devices of borrowing, parody, and theatricalization of the act of performing reach outside the walls of the Opéra to make contact with practices on other Parisian stages. Whereas meta-theater goes back at least as far as Aristophanes and can be found in the works of Molière and Corneille, the Opéra's impulse in this direction seems to have come in reaction to its rivals, most notably the Théâtre Italien and the fair theaters, where the act of performing was foregrounded and where parody of other theaters lay at the heart of the enterprise.[1] The crossover process was facilitated by movement among the theaters by writers, composers, and performers. The Opéra may have jealously guarded its privileges as the loftiest theater in Paris, but it did not disdain borrowing from the competition.

APPROPRIATED FRAMES

As the ones who set up the framework, the librettists were central to this new phenomenon, and several of them had cut their teeth writing plays. The prologue Regnard wrote in 1699 for *Le Carnaval de Venise* bears a family resemblance to one he had penned eleven years earlier for the Théâtre Italien. At the start of *Le Divorce* Arlequin enters the stage alone, railing against his fellow actors who have all picked the very same moment to fall sick, just when the troupe needs to make money. He starts explaining to the audience that they will be reimbursed, when the heavens open and Mercure (played by Mezzetin) descends, singing. To a fragment parodied from the latest opera, he reassures Arlequin: "End your laments, may your sorrow cease. Jupiter has taken an interest in your fate and is coming to prevent you from giving any money back. I see him coming now."[2] In the prologue he wrote for the Opéra Regnard did not break the fourth wall, but the arc from disaster to *deus ex machina* is the same. In *Le*

1 See Beaucé, *Parodies d'opéra* and Le Blanc, *Avatars d'opéras*.

2 Mezzetin's first two lines come directly from the prologue of *Achille et Polixène*: "Terminez vos regrets, que votre douleur cesse: / Dans votre sort Jupiter s'intéresse, / Et vient ici revoir, dès le même moment, / Un spectacle charmant." Regnard transformed the last two lines into "Et vient pour empêcher que tu rendes l'argent. / Je le vois qui descend." (Ed. Guichemerre, 32.)

Carnaval de Venise the audience sees the interior of a theater in a state of disorder, with wood and half-built sets lying about, and carpenters ineffectually trying to pull things together. It takes intervention by the goddess Minerve to get the stage ready in time for Act 1. The resemblance between the two texts ends there, however: in *Le Divorce* Jupiter turns out to be every bit as silly as Arlequin, whereas Minerve restores dignity.

The prologue to *La Vénitienne* (1705) offers another instance of the Opéra changing the tone while borrowing from the Italian theater. This prologue, in which Momus temporarily reanimates the statues of the banished Italian comedians (see Chapter 8, pp. 223–24), comes as close as the Opéra ever did to the other Parisian stages in thematizing the rivalries among them. A scene similar to La Motte's may be found twenty years earlier in *Arlequin Jason, ou la Toison d'or comique* (1684).[3] Jason, with the help of Médée's magic, animates the statues of both the Italian and French comedians, only to hear the French troupe complain that it has lost its audience to the Italians. A gloss on this scene in the published text explains that the French troupe had recently complained to the king that the Théâtre Italien was performing in French, to which the king replied, "Then you should learn Italian." The scene, as it continues, alludes to another practice from the Italian and fair theaters, one more elusive than the parodying of texts. Médée interrupts the whining of the French troupe by conjuring up a divertissement: "all the other statues come down from the pedestals and form an *entrée de ballet*. The chaconne in [Lully's] *Amadis* is parodied. Arlequin dances and imitates Monsieur Pécour." This parody was up to the minute, *Amadis* having premiered at the Opéra in January of 1684. If the tone of Mezzetin's imitation of Mercure is anything to go by, then Arlequin's imitation of Pécour must have been played for laughs.

This *didascalie* is far from the only evidence that operatic spoofs parodied movement styles as well as texts and music. All of the possibilities are on display in Dufresny's *L'Opéra de campagne* (1692), in which the performance in a small village of Lully's *Armide* serves as part of an elaborate hoax designed to allow Octave to marry the bailiff's daughter, Thérèse. The impediment to the marriage is Thérèse's pretentious mother, Madame Prenelle (played by Mezzetin), and the solution is to distract her from her suspicions by making her the star of the performance – none other than Armide herself. *L'Opéra de campagne* provoked a response shortly thereafter from the Comédie-Française, in *L'Opéra de village* by Dancourt. Dufresny capped the series two months later, back at the Théâtre Italien, with *L'Union des deux opéras*, in which the two earlier works are personified and agree to make peace.[4]

[3] Gherardi, *Théâtre italien*, I.

[4] On these three works and their music, see Grout, "Seventeenth-century parodies," 517–23. In 1713, during the Italian troupe's banishment from Paris, *L'Opéra de campagne* was performed at the Foire Saint-Laurent, in an arrangement by Fuzelier.

Because the Hôtel de Bourgogne had the capacity for making rapid scene changes, the Italian troupe was able to parody the visual effects of the Opéra as well as its plots and music,[5] as in the following scene from the last act, when the opera finally reaches the stage. Here Arlequin is playing the role of Renaud (*L'Opéra de campagne*, III/5 and 7):

> *The stage changes and represents Armide's palace, composed of household items. In the back is a fireplace where several fowls are turning on a spit. [. . .] The orchestra plays the* sommeil *from* Armide *and Arlequin [as Renaud] seeing the spit full of meat says:*
>
> I think I see the supper of the opera cooking there. I feel more like eating than singing. So I'll sing fast.
>
> The more I observe this roast, the more I desire it.
> The spit turns slowly.
> I reluctantly forego such a succulent morsel.[6]
>
> *The orchestra returns to playing the* sommeil *and Arlequin continues* [. . .] *He throws his Roman costume and his helmet on the ground and appears only in his shirt. In this outfit he pulls out a little bed that was in the back and lies down in it. A moment later he gets up, looks everywhere under the bed, saying* "Where the deuce is the chamber pot?" *then lies down again. I forgot to point out that throughout the* sommeil *that the orchestra plays, Arlequin walks around the stage and imitates Monsieur Dumesnil, who is without doubt one of the best actors at the Opéra, and in a manner so like his that one is obliged to agree that the most famous painter in the world could not do a better job.*

This irreverent performance of *Armide* gets collapsed into the storyline, when the lovers, for whose benefit the opera is serving as a smokescreen, sink through a trap door into the room where the notary awaits them, and the hoodwinked mother of the bride, still in her role as Armide, vents her fury by destroying the stage.

Nothing this crude ever appeared on the stage of the Académie Royale de Musique, nor did the works in its repertoire respond this directly to performances in other theaters. But the operatic works of this period only make sense when considered against the backdrop of works such as this one; the Opéra was not aloof from its environment, but engaged in dialogue with it. The section that follows focuses on three framing devices that draw from the spoken theater, but that acquire their own peculiarities when placed into an entirely sung environment: operatic parodies,

[5] Moureau notes that the Théâtre Italien not only had the technical capability to produce rapid scene changes, it was not bound by the unity of place, as was the Comédie-Française. Moreover, there were no regulations against its fancy scenery; see his *Dufresny*, 124–26.

[6] "Plus j'observe ce rôt, et plus je le désire. / La broche tourne lentement. / Je m'éloigne à regret d'un morceau si friand." Gherardi, *Théâtre italien*, IV. Renaud's famous lines in *Armide* II/3, before he is lulled to sleep, are: "Plus j'observe ces lieux, et plus je les admire. / Ce fleuve coule lentement, / Et s'éloigne, à regret, d'un séjour si charmant."

dancing master scenes, and masked balls. All of them give a central role to the expressive possibilities of dance, allow the composers to expand their compositional palettes, and call attention to their own theatricality.

Operatic Parodies

Two of the Italian-inflected works written for the Opéra, both by Campra, stage an opera-within-the-opera, performed before an on-stage audience. Both occupy the functional slot of a divertissement within the larger work, but as operas in and of themselves, they also contain their own divertissements – even though one of them is Italian and should not by tradition have an internal divertissement at all. These operas offer quite different examples of the deliciously heterogeneous mixtures of French and Italian conventions that make up these "Venetian" works. Both operas have mythological librettos on ostensibly serious topics, but the performances are turned to comic effect.

The earlier of the two is found within *Le Carnaval de Venise* (1699, libretto by Regnard), a three-act ballet with a continuous plot. A French Léandre finds himself torn between two young Venetian women, but after he and Isabelle recognize their mutual affection, the two of them spend the remaining two acts trying to evade the vengeful machinations of Léonore and Rodolphe, the spurned suitors, who join forces. At the end of the third act, Léandre and Isabelle make plans to go to an opera followed by a ball, so that "the tumult and the night" will provide cover for their escape from Venice. Both take place in the same unnamed opera house, in keeping with genuine Venetian Carnival practices, where a ball sometimes followed the opera. Apparently Léandre's plan works: at the end of the ball, the two lovers are nowhere to be seen.

The opera Léandre and Isabelle attend draws upon a time-honored operatic subject, the legend of Orpheus, but treats it tongue-in-cheek. The fact that "Orfeo nell'inferi" is sung entirely in Italian gives Campra a free hand to exploit his familiarity with the Italian style from beginning to end, although he Frenchified the opera just enough to incorporate choruses and dancing. Notwithstanding the loftiness of its subject, the opera comes across as a spoof – albeit a gentle one.[7] The libretto depicts only the Underworld portions of the story and the *basso buffo* Plutone is its star. He blusters out a call to arms to his infernal followers when he realizes a human has entered his kingdom (the followers extend his eight "All'armi" with another twelve of their own, all set to harmonically static triadic figures and scurrying eighth notes – passages that recur two more times). He gives up Euridice right away, even though he thinks Orfeo is making too much of a fuss, and when Orfeo declares victory in a florid aria, he tacitly

[7] Barthélemy (*André Campra*, 102) qualifies this little opera as "neither seria, nor buffa," but it seems to me more on the buffa side, notwithstanding some affective music for both Orfeo and Euridice.

allows his followers to join in the celebrations of their own defeat, as they pick up on the words of the middle section of Orfeo's da capo aria: "laughter and song have followed pain; the Underworld has given way to the sweet charm of a pretty eyelash." After Orfeo breaks the condition Plutone had imposed and looks at Euridice, Plutone sends Orfeo away, then in a lively aria tells Euridice not to cry, as no sighs and moans will move his heart of stone.[8] In order to cheer her up, he exhorts his followers to sing, dance, and laugh (the entire text is "Si canti, si goda, / Si balli, si rida, / Non si parli di dolor, / Dove splende la face d'amor"). The Underworld gods comply; whether Euridice follows their advice is not something the sources reveal. In case it weren't obvious enough from the music and the text that this chorus is supposed to be funny, Campra's reuse of it in "Cariselli," which he dubbed a "comic divertissement" (see below, p. 51), shows that he conceived it that way.

This divertissement within *Le Carnaval de Venise* has its own two divertissements. The first follows Orfeo's victory aria and contains two dances for the Numi infernali and Spirti folletti (infernal gods and sprites), the second of which is repeated after a da capo aria by an Ombra fortunata (fortunate shade). In a standard French demonic divertissement, the dancers would have all been men, and that was probably the case here, although the sprites might have been children or perhaps even women. Even though the dance music is distinct from the vocal music, the structure of a dance heard twice on either side of a song derives from French practices, as does (in part) its musical style. The first section of the first dance ("aria") is marked adagio, but has the hallmarks of an *entrée grave*, a dance not uncommon in demonic scenes. The B section retains a meter sign of **2**, but changes tempo to presto, with running eighth notes dominating the treble and bass – another trope for demons, even if this part of the piece seems less French than the first. Whereas the first dance could have a serious character, depending on how it is played, the second dance, "Aria degli numi infernali," is in a jolly $\frac{6}{4}$ with Italianate twinges, mixing arpeggios with stepwise dotted figures. Here the infernal gods seem to be embodying the pleasures alluded to in the previous sung number. The second danced episode comes at the end, in the final chorus when Plutone and his

[8] La Laurencie, in *"L'Orfeo nell'inferni* d'André Campra" [*sic*], 132, states that this aria shows that Plutone allowed Orfeo and Euridice to be reunited: "Bref, Pluton, bon diable, et, au demeurant, fort galant homme, cède une seconde fois. Son aria vivace 'Bella non piangere' traduit sa compassion et sa bienvaillance . . . " However, no *didascalie* indicates a change of mind on Plutone's part, and at best the texts are ambiguous. In this aria Plutone alludes to "a heart of stone" that remains unmoved and that seems to be his. (The aria's full text, which does not appear in the libretto, is "Bella, non piangere, / Cessi il cordoglio. / Non si può frangere / Con pianti e gemiti / Un cor di scoglio.") The allusion to love as an antidote to sorrow in the last lines of the concluding chorus might offer support for La Laurencie, although he does not cite them. Anthony, in his introduction to the facsimile score of this opera, accepts La Laurencie's view of the ending, as does Barthélemy (*André Campra*, 102).

followers sing, dance, and laugh. The chorus, in a lively triple meter, is followed by a repeat of the "Aria degli numi infernali," which serves as the entr'acte music, but could also extend the dancing. No matter how Italian the rest of the music in this little opera sounded to its French audience, the treatment of the dances, even if abbreviated, would have seemed familiar.

If the ridiculous reversal at the very end of this piece hints at parody of French operatic practices, the opera Campra wrote into *Les Fêtes vénitiennes* makes his parodistic intentions clear. The Neapolitan hero (not French, for once) loves an opera singer and has decided to play a role in her current work in order to whisk her away from her other admirers. The opera-within-the-opera that the fictional Venetian audience watches – at the Palais Grimani, no less – turns out to be a pure French pastorale entitled the "Ballet de Flore."[9] The comic lead-up to the performance and its descent into chaos owe a good deal to operatic parodies such as *L'Opéra de campagne*. Even though its tone is much more decorous (there are no chamber pots), Danchet takes aim right from the start at the Paris Opéra, its conventions, and its performers. Already in the opening speech the masculinity of opera singers is called into question: Damire's confidant feels compelled to point out that Damire is a military hero, even if he is play-acting as Borée. Damire's justification for treading the boards is that he had fallen passionately in love with the supposedly Venetian soprano whom he saw perform the role of none other than . . . Armide. In mock-heroic language he reveals that when Léontine/Armide stood, knife poised above Renaud's prone body, "she let fall the vengeful sword from her trembling hands, but I saw in her eyes weapons still more deadly. She spared Renaud, and it was my tender heart alone that received a mortal wound."[10] The confidant offers to cast himself in the role of Ubalde, but Damire does not want to be rescued; on the contrary, he wants to rescue Armide from her life on the stage.[11] But first, she has to go through a rehearsal of her new role, Flore, during which the music master, feigning indignation that an admirer of Léontine's wants to use him as a go-between, laces his commentaries on her singing with her wealthy admirer's propositions. When the

9 Its plot has nothing to do with Lully's court ballet by the same title (1669).

10 "Le jour que sous le nom d'Armide / Des spectateurs surpris elle charma les yeux, / Cédant au plaisir qui me guide, / J'étais avec la foule accouru dans ces lieux: / Je la vis, dans le temps qu'interdite, incertaine, / A l'aspect d'un héros qui lui paraît charmant, / Elle passe en moins d'un moment / De la haine à l'amour, de l'amour à la haine: / De ses tremblantes mains tomba le fer vengeur; / Mais je vis dans ses yeux des armes plus cruelles, / Elle épargna Renaud, et mon sensible coeur / Fut le seul qui reçut des atteintes mortelles."

11 The confidant's stripped-down version of Renaud's rescue, in which only Ubalde participates (Quinault gave Renaud two rescuers) goes back to an earlier libretto of Danchet's for Campra, the entrée "Les Guerriers" from *Les Fragments de Lully* (1702), which glues together music from Lully ballets with some additions by Campra, to depict Renaud's rescue and Armide's despair.

curtain finally goes up, the admirer, Rodolphe, seats himself on the side of the stage, just as he might have done at the Palais-Royal.[12]

The "Ballet de Flore" compresses numerous pastoral clichés into its miniature framework, from its tidy beginning to its raggedy end. Flore, resting alone on a bed of flowers, calls for Zéphire; this *ariette*, which she had rehearsed earlier, is the one partial concession to Italian style. Zéphire pays Flore flowery compliments, but brushes off her concerns about his constancy and hurriedly calls upon the "inhabitants of the neighboring hamlets" to further embellish Flore's surroundings. Here the tempo of the proceedings is relaxed: the shepherds and shepherdesses, complete with musettes, perform no fewer than seven pastoral dances that are interlaced with choruses and songs, one of them by Léontine's confidante Lucie in the role of a shepherdess. The sky darkens, and Borée calls up his whirlwinds, who fly off with Flore. Zéphire calls upon Jupiter to "punish the injustice of a jealous, furious rival." Jupiter, however, fails to descend in his machine. Zéphire, baffled, looks around the stage, then breaks out of character to ask Lucie why Jupiter hasn't arrived. When Lucie tells him that Léontine has run off with Damire, Rodolphe flies into a fury and refuses to take up the role of Zéphire that the singer tries to push on him. Jupiter is no use, he says; he needs men to go to the port and block their departure.

No performances of either a *Ballet de Flore* or Lully's *Armide* ever took place at the real Palais Grimani, but Danchet and Campra were interested in satirizing their own operatic environment, not in verisimilitude. One hopes that the dancing engaged the same kind of exaggerated clichés as do the texts, but all we know is that there were nine dancers, four women and five men, with Balon and Mlle Prévost as soloists – both of them known for their abilities in a wide variety of characters. Whatever the case, the breaking of the fourth wall that characterizes the *comédie italienne* could now also happen at the Opéra, once Italy had found a home there.

Dancing Master Scenes

One comic set piece that Danchet and Campra could not resist including in *Les Fêtes vénitiennes* is the dancing master scene. All such scenes have their roots in Molière's *Bourgeois gentilhomme* (1670), where in 1/2 the music and dance teachers hired by the hapless Monsieur Jourdain spar with each other over whose art is superior. On the heels of Molière, the dancing master, with or without competition from a music teacher or another exponent of the arts, became a regular inhabitant of the French comic stage. Rizzoni has identified some three dozen scenes from French plays, parodies and opéras comiques dating from the first half of the eighteenth century in

[12] Regarding places for spectators on the stage, see La Gorce, *L'Opéra à Paris*, 66–68.

which a dancing master is made the object of ridicule; similar scenes can be found from before the turn of the century.[13] Even in the spoken theater such scenes involved movement; the dancing master, who bears a name such as M. Sautenlair, M. de l'Entrechat, or M. Trotinet, always demonstrates his abilities as he boasts about them. It would be possible to make a comparison of the extensive dance terminology alluded to in these scenes with the vocabulary Feuillet codified in *Chorégraphie* – with the caveat that terms within plays may be chosen more for their allusive value than for choreographic reasons. Because by 1710, when *Les Fêtes vénitiennes* reached the stage, there was already such a rich history of ridiculous dancing masters, it is worth taking a look at one of them, to see what Danchet and Campra might have had in the back of their minds when they set to work.

In II/II of *L'Opéra de campagne*, performed at the Théâtre Italien in 1692, Arlequin comes to Mme Prenelle in the guise of a dancing master.

Arlequin:	*[Making many bows and tours de jambes]* All of Paris agrees, Madame, that I am the best person in the world for . . . (*he does a capriole*).
Mme Prenelle:	Either appearances are deceiving, or you deserve your reputation.
Arlequin:	Anyone in the young generation, Madame, who has any aptitude for . . . (*he pirouettes*), comes to me for lessons in . . . (*entrechat*).
Mme Prenelle:	Your merit is visible in your appearance, and as soon as I laid eyes on you, I felt like dancing.
Arlequin:	People have always told me that my physiognomy inspires . . . (*he jumps*). Nothing is more in demand these days than a vigorous . . . (*he does a tour de jambe*), and one may say that dance is a universal pleasure. The great (*he does a chassé*), the lowly (*another chassé*), magistrates (*a capriole*), officers (*a capriole en avant*), everyone dances – or *should* dance, so to speak.
Mme Prenelle:	I'm the only one who doesn't know how to dance. How miserable I am!
Arlequin:	But you have all the necessary aptitudes.
Mme Prenelle:	Do you really think so, Monsieur?
Arlequin:	Walk. (*She walks.*) You have all the rudiments for making beautiful movements. All you need is to be taught.
Mme Prenelle:	If only you would take the trouble, Monsieur.
Arlequin:	People in my profession do not generally work on adult individuals.
Mme Prenelle:	Oh, I am still of a teachable age, and there is not a single young girl who is more eager than I.
Arlequin:	*[Aside]* Old horses don't do well in the riding ring. But maybe by using the spurs a bit more . . . *[To her]* Alright, Madame, let's start with your head. (*He takes hold of her head and lifts it higher.*)

13 Rizzoni, "Un représentant pittoresque." Earlier examples can be found in the works of Dancourt and of playwrights for the Théâtre Italien; Regnard, *Le Divorce* (1688), I/6–7, features Arlequin as Mr Trotenville, dancing master, and Mezzetin as a singing master.

Mme Prenelle: Aie, aie! Do you want to make me dance in the air?

Arlequin: You must elongate your neck by a good six inches. Now, for the shoulders. (*He slaps her on the shoulder.*) Turn your knees out. (*He slaps her on the knee.*) Ready, set, go! (*She dances.*) Ta ra la ra, ta ra la ra, ta ra la. And this arse, my God, this arse! (*He slaps her on the arse.*) Hold up your head. Snigger toward the boxes. Your eyes are expressing nothing? Imagine that you see your lover in the wings. Extend your arms. No! Yes! Not yet! Very good, very good! Now, give me your hand, turn! (*He makes her turn so fast that she collapses to one side, Arlequin to the other.*)

Mme Prenelle: [*Getting up*] Ah, I'm dying! (*They leave.*) [End of Act 2]

In this scene, movements of the body substitute for language in supplying humor and sexual innuendo. The dance steps mentioned can all be found in theatrical choreographies, and Evaristo Gherardi must have had real dance chops in order to put all of them across through movement alone. No information is provided about his costume, but he probably was dressed with an attempt at elegance over his still visible Arlequin outfit, and he may have held the little violin dancing masters used to supply music for their lessons. The elaborate bowing routine that opens the scene was exploited in many comic plays of the time[14] and occasionally at the Opéra, as in "La Sérénade vénitienne," when the dancing Scaramouches, who have just given the Doctor a beating, take their leave with deep bows, or in "La Comédie" in the *Ballet des Muses* (1703), where the ridiculous old man and the woman disguised as a doctor who is trying to deceive him spend a 41-bar ritournelle bowing to each other.[15] This particular scene does not quote music from familiar works, although many plays from the Italian theater do so, as when "Les Trembleurs" from Lully's *Isis* is played on a hurdy-gurdy to announce Mercury's arrival in Dufresny's *L'Union des deux opéras* (1692). But it is rich in dance allusions, and Arlequin's attempt to get Mme Prenelle to use her eyes to expressive effect is noteworthy, given that dancers of the day were generally masked and only their eyes could vary their facial expressions.

Danchet drew upon the conventions of the genre in writing his own such scene. In "Le Bal" Alamir, a prince, has put his follower Thémir in charge of the arrangements for a masked ball. Alamir and Thémir may be Polish, and they may be hosting a ball in Venice, but they are savvy enough to know they need French expertise, as Thémir insists on pointing out ("Deux maîtres renommés qu'a vu naître la France, / Doivent en préparer et les chants et la danse"). The music and dancing masters, who arrive together

[14] See, for example, Regnard's *La Coquette* 1/3. Moureau, *Dufresny*, 156–57 mentions several other plays that use "lazzi di saluti."

[15] According to the libretto, Sc. 2, "Pendant que l'on joue la ritournelle, ils [Ericine and Géronte] se font des révérences." Cf. the Marx Brothers' movie, *A Day at the Races* (1937), when Groucho, as Dr. Hackenbush – a vet pretending to be a doctor – cannot seem to break away from a cycle of bows with his new colleagues at the sanitarium.

in Scene 2, go through an elaborate and mutually flattering greeting ritual that must have been amplified by comic bowing. But the two soon turn competitive, each vaunting the superior expressive qualities of his own art. (The dancing master, whose part requires him to sing as well, was played in 1710 by one of the dancers in the troupe, Marcel. Both roles are for tenors.) Because this scene was set entirely to music, it goes beyond its model in the *Bourgeois gentilhomme* in demonstrating (as opposed to claiming) what music and dance can express. Here we get a little Cook's tour of the operatic styles of the day.

The music master opens the attack by claiming, in French-style recitative, to surpass Orpheus. The dancing master, to a gracious melody in triple time, describes the qualities of his steps; each key word is followed by a one-bar instrumental passage, during which he must illustrate his claims. It is easy to take a leaf from Arlequin's notebook and imagine that an *entrechat* might illustrate brilliance, a pirouette grace.

Dancing master: Mes pas sont autant de merveilles,
Ils sont brillants [*il danse*] et gracieux; [*il danse*]
Je sais l'art de tracer aux yeux,
Les sons [*il danse*] qui frappent les oreilles.

(My steps have just as many marvels. They are brilliant *[he dances]* and graceful *[he dances]*. I know the art of tracing before the eyes the sounds *[he dances]* that strike the ears.)

This last claim demonstrates as an article of faith the capacity of dance to translate sound into meaningful movement, claims that theorists such as de Pure and Menestrier had expressed during the late seventeenth century (see Chapter 4, p. 119ff). The music master, not to be outdone, conjures up a series of operatic clichés, starting with a storm: "Je fais siffler les vents, je soulève les flots," quoting eighteen bars of the famous *tempête* from Marais's *Alcyone*. The dancing master follows up by dancing as a whirlwind (*tourbillon*), although he gets only three measures of $\frac{6}{4}$ music, marked "Vite" in which to do so. (Since the performer has to both sing and dance, it is no wonder that his utterances are shorter than the music master's.) The back-and-forth continues, passing through the realm of sleep to music imitating, but not quoting, the *sommeil* from Act III of *Atys*; going next to the Underworld, where the dancing master transforms himself into a furious demon dancing an *entrée grave*; and returning to earth in Arcadian climes, where nightingales sing and shepherds fall in love to a bourrée and a musette.[16] In each case the dancing master puts into movement the musical realm invoked by his rival, in a miniaturized parallel to what happens inside the divertissements of a *tragédie*. It is probably no coincidence that this brief tour of divertissement *topoi* comes in five "acts." The fifth is self-referential: given the new operatic world at

[16] The operatic allusions were identified by Masson; see his "Fêtes vénitiennes," 139. All the operas Campra alluded to had been performed within the previous four years.

the Académie Royale de Musique, no survey of styles would be complete without Italy. Here the music master conjures up a "brillante saillie" in honor of Italy to a $\frac{6}{8}$ *giga*-ish passage and then, switching into Italian, launches into an aria with exaggerated roulades on the word "Volate." He gets through what looks like the A section of a da capo aria before the dancing master interrupts with "As for me, I know how to . . . ", but is interrupted in turn by Thémir, who has had enough of this vainglory. We are left wondering what the dancing master would have shown by way of Italian dancing in order to outdo the virtuosity of the aria.

This scene is a little tour de force for both performers, who have to switch characters from one moment to the next, and even though it is not within the boundaries of a divertissement in the strict sense of the word, it is akin to the choreographic set pieces for solo dancers that began to appear in operas shortly after this time (see Chapter 13). This particular scene was so successful that it found its way into programs of "fragments" (Appendix 2) and was parodied at the Foire Saint-Laurent in 1714.[17] Scene-types such as this bounced back and forth among all the theaters in Paris, high and low alike.

The Masked Ball on Stage

The entrée "L'Italie" in *L'Europe galante* not only introduced the da capo aria to the French operatic stage, it did the same for the masked ball. However, unlike the da capo aria, the staged ball had its roots in actual social practices, which were at their most visible during Carnival season. French composers began putting masked balls onto the stage only when the opening of the repertoire toward contemporary settings allowed current social practices to conform to the laws of verisimilitude; neither an Olympian god nor the king of an ancient realm would host a masked ball, but a patrician Venetian could. The first several masked balls on the French operatic stage were set in Venice, but as the repertoire broadened to include other contemporary locations, a ball might be set on the banks of the Seine. Masked balls provided a rich vehicle for entrées within opera-ballets: the disguises of the season opened up many possible storylines, the balls themselves were exploited for the tensions inherent in such social situations, and the frame of a masked ball allowed for almost any kind of dancing.

In both France and Italy, practices in the ballroom were highly codified, albeit under different codes. French writers who had visited Venice included balls in their reports, which meant that the librettists and composers at the Opéra had material to work with and the French reading public had at least some notions of how to interpret what they saw on stage. This is not to say that the creators of ballroom scenes aimed for realism, but their creations show that they depended on their audience's familiarity with current social codes.

[17] In Act III of *La Foire de Guibray* Arlequin and an Italian comedian "mock each other in imitation of the musician and dancing master in *Les Fêtes vénitiennes*." See Le Sage, *Théâtre de la foire*, I.

Balls at the French court were largely spectator events. In a formal ball, of the type held for a royal wedding, only a small proportion of those in attendance danced; the rest watched, as one couple at a time occupied the dance floor.[18] The king or the highest-ranking person present sat at the head of the room and those who had been selected to dance sat around the perimeter, the men and women in different locations, but both in order of rank. The ball opened with group dances – a suite of branles (usually four), done mostly in the round – but thereafter only one couple danced at a time. During the seventeenth century the courante was the dominant social dance, but starting in the 1660s it was gradually overtaken by the menuet, such that by the start of the new century, the courante was danced only at the most formal, tradition-laden balls. Other *danses à deux* might involve bourrées, gavottes, sarabandes, or passepieds of the type Feuillet began publishing in 1700, but the main part of a ball would consist of long strings of menuets, each danced by a single couple.[19] Occasionally menuets for four would allow more dancers to participate, and starting in the early eighteenth century, contredanses, the French version of English country dances, became a regular part of balls. In this rarefied atmosphere, the dancers had to memorize their dances in advance and pay close attention to every nuance of their steps and deportment.

Masked balls allowed for greater variety. Even though, at the court at least, a masked ball would still go through the formalized sequence of events, it might be interrupted by a group of maskers who would perform dances in accordance with their costumes. Thus a group of "Spaniards" might dance a sarabande or an *entrée espagnole*, sultanas might do a Turkish dance, and dancing *pagodes* would try to evoke an imagined China. These dances would be more theatricalized than the social dances and, if the dancers had the necessary skills, more technically challenging. Occasionally the mascarade that interrupted the masked ball would be performed entirely by professional dancers and could even have a simple storyline. The range of dance types found in masked balls was thus much broader and more akin to the operatic stage. Nonetheless, the fundamental nature of the event – performance in front of an audience – was the same in both types.

Balls in Venice set many more people in motion at a time, but to the French, Venetian dancing looked like walking. According to Saint-Didier:

> They walk two-by-two, one after the other, chatting as they go from room to room throughout the house. [. . .] There is a sort of orchestra, whose music is more sleep-inducing than dance-like. This is why [. . .] everyone considers a ball primarily as a good opportunity to explain all his feelings, with the result that everyone tries to take full advantage of the opportunity, without thinking about dancing.[20]

18 This summary is drawn from my "Ballroom dancing."

19 A collection of dance music from the court, gathered by Philidor *l'aîné* and published in 1699 (see n. 30 below), starts with a few branles and courantes, follows with English country dances, then, for 30 pages, has nothing but menuets and passepieds.

20 Saint-Didier, *La Ville*, 393–94.

But not all Venetian dancing was stately. On the banks of the canals, again according to Saint-Didier, young Venetians, mostly girls, danced the forlana to the sound of the tambourine, "throwing their feet forward and skimming their little steps with such speed and lightness, that even though they never have more than one foot in the air, it is impossible to tell which of them touches the ground at any moment."[21] Toward the end of the seventeenth century, the forlana got taken up into the Venetian ballroom, as did French *danses à deux*, especially the menuet. Balls were given not only in patrician homes, but also, on the last day of Carnival, in Venetian opera houses, where following the performance the stage and parterre would be transformed into a gigantic ballroom.[22] This too was a spectacle, with people in the boxes looking down on the costumed assembly, so in certain regards French and Italian practices were not so far apart. Ballroom scenes theatricalized what was already a spectator experience, but also provided an arena in which audience members' own muscle memory could come into play. Against this general cultural background Campra and his contemporaries exploited the material that masked balls provided in wonderfully varied ways. But they had to set up social codes that could be readable to a Parisian public, even when the ball was set in Venice.

"L'Italie" from *L'Europe galante* exploits the dissonance between the gaiety of a ball and the murderous thoughts of a protagonist. When the scene opens, Octavio reproaches Olympia for her lack of ardor, even though she has pledged herself to him. He is especially alarmed to find himself escorting her to a masked ball, where anything could happen. His fears, it turns out, are well grounded. Not only does a masked Vénitienne warn the crowds that jealousy warrants no mercy (in the da capo aria, "Ad un cuore tutto geloso, / Deve amor negar pietà"), but during the dancing, Olympia finds herself with an unknown man who pays her too much attention. Octavio follows him out, then returns to tell Olympia he has killed his rival. Olympia's fainting confirms Octavio's suspicions; he then reveals that the darkness of the night allowed the rival to escape, but she departs, leaving him vowing to kill her, her lover, and himself.

As is so often the case, the divertissement highlights the emotional world of the protagonists who watch it, but this one goes further and involves them as participants. It opens with a march; the text of the musically related chorus alludes both to the arrival of the maskers ("Tendres Amants, rassemblons-nous") and offers a warning to anyone beset by jealousy ("S'il se trouve ici des jaloux; / L'Amour ne les amène, / Que pour les tromper tous"), thus laying the groundwork for the even clearer warning about jealousy in the da capo aria that follows. The action involving Olympia and her mysterious lover takes place at the end of the divertissement.

[21] *Ibid.*, 373–74.

[22] Regarding Venetian ballroom practices, see Alm, "Operatic ballroom scenes."

Table 9-1: *L'Europe galante*, Entrée IV/2 ("L'Italie"): Octavio, Olympia.
A troupe of gallant and comic maskers enters the stage.

Heading in score	Key, meter	Paraphrase of sung text/comments
Marche des masques	D, ¢	
Le Chœur des Masques, "Tendres amants, rassemblons-nous"	D, ¢	Lovers, let us gather. Anyone suffering from jealousy should be wary. [Related to the march]
Air pour les masques	d, $\frac{12}{8}$	[binary, giga-like]
Air italien, une Femme du bal, "Ad un cuore tutto geloso"	d, $\frac{12}{8}$	Love must show no mercy to a jealous heart. [1st verse of da capo aria, related to previous piece]
Air pour les masques [repeated]	d, $\frac{12}{8}$	
La Femme du bal, "Un bel viso tutto vezzoso"		Beauty deserves fidelity. [2nd verse of da capo aria]
Première Chaconne. Rondeau	D, **3**	
Une Vénitienne déguisée, alternativement avec le chœur, "Formons d'aimables jeux"	D, **3**	Here only laughter and love are permitted. [Rondeau, related to the first chaconne]
Seconde Chaconne. Rondeau	d, **3**	
Une autre Vénitienne déguisée, alternativement avec le chœur, "Livrons-nous aux plaisirs"	d, **3**	Let us give ourselves to pleasure. [Rondeau, related to the second chaconne]
Air. Gai	D, **3**	
Une Femme du bal, "Si scherzi, si rida, / Si pensi a goder"	D, **3**	Let us laugh and enjoy ourselves. [Da capo aria, allegro; related to previous dance]

During the festivities, one of the maskers dances with Olympia and showers attention on her. When the ball is over, Octavio follows the costumed man, leaving Olympia surprised to find herself without him.

Heading in score	Key, meter	Paraphrase of sung text/comments
Forlane	D, $\frac{6}{4}$	
Menuet	D, **3**	
Forlane, repeated	D, $\frac{6}{4}$	

The outline in Table 9-1 follows the full score Ballard published in 1724. In this score the *didascalie* about the dancing, also found in the libretto but not in the earlier published scores (1697 and 1698), is located before the "Air gai," probably because this piece and the accompanying aria ("Si scherzi, si rida") were not part of the original work, but were added in 1698. I have thus moved the *didascalie* back to the place where it seems to belong. Further Italian arias were added in subsequent years, among them two composed by Marchand.[23] Long before the masked ball in *Die Fledermaus*, this ballroom scene became a site for insertion and variation.

Because the 1697 libretto does not name the dancers, we only know that, like the members of the chorus, they represented "Masques galantes et comiques," that is, there were at least two contrasting sets of characters among them. In 1706 there were eight distinguishable pairs of dancers (see the cast list in Figure 7-2, p. 215). The presence of all these matched couples does not necessarily mean that no dances were performed by groups (see in Figure 9-1 a similar scene), but it does allow for dancing that emphasizes different characters, even if the music does not suggest any particular correspondences with specific pairs. Given that everyone was in disguise for Carnival, they were all Venetians underneath their costumes, which might help explain why none of the maskers is Italian in any overt way.

A very high number of sections within this divertissement – all of the first five – intertwine dance and song in close connection. Perhaps given that so much was new about *L'Europe galante* in general and this Italian entrée in particular, Campra chose to insist on familiar structures, in order to increase the legibility of the scene for his audience – wrapping Italian music in a French package. These first five sections, which lack any standard ballroom dances, probably served as display for the various masked guests. But the sequence of song-dance pairs suddenly breaks off, just at the point where Octavio and Olympia stop watching and start participating. Two purely instrumental dances occur, neither of them connected to a vocal piece, and both of them bearing generic titles that connect them to their places of origin: forlane and menuet. The forlana (to use its Italian name) was a dance that had originated in Friuli, the region to the east of Venice; it had been described in the *Mercure galant* in 1683, so could have been known to audience members by name, although this was its first appearance on the French stage. Whether the forlane as Campra presented it bore any relation to an actual Italian model remains an open question, but in its unique musical profile (see Example 9-1) it quickly became the aural equivalent of the Place Saint-Marc.[24]

The thoroughly French menuet might seem out of place in a Venetian ballroom, but it makes perfect sense for a work performed in front of a French audience. In 1697 the menuet was the leading ballroom dance in France; everyone in the audience would have been familiar with its codes, which incorporated a choreographed courtship ritual. After a series of figures in which the single dancing couple traces several Z figures on the floor, moving from opposite corners of the room and passing each other in the center, they proceed to present their hands to each other – first the right, then the left, culminating in the presentation of both hands, just before the dance ends.

23 See Anthony, "Air and aria," 209–11.

24 For more about the forlana, see Ch. 14, pp. 422–25.

Figure 9-1: Design by Jean Berain for "Winter" from the *Ballet des Saisons*, showing a seated chorus and five pairs of dancers in individualized costumes of the *comédie italienne*.

This kind of limited physical contact seems ludicrously sedate by more recent standards, but it does encode a crescendo of emotional intensity whose conventions offer the perfect opportunity for the costumed stranger to shower attentions on Olympia. In a ballroom menuet, an over-eager presentation of the hands or a suggestively shaded shoulder might suffice for a French audience to understand why Octavio has reason to fear for his fiancée's affections. We do not know which of the dancers listed in the 1706

Example 9-1: Campra, *L'Europe galante*, "Forlana" from "L'Italie" (Paris: Ballard, 1697), 214.

libretto might have played the role of Olympia's mysterious suitor – the Frenchman seems like a good possibility – but any of the dancers could have done a ballroom menuet, and perhaps the Venetian merrymaker costumed as the Greek or even the madman would have brought more piquancy to the part. Whereas on stage a menuet could be a group dance, this one probably retained the conventions of the ballroom *danse à deux*, in order to exploit the erotic potential of its social codes to full dramatic effect.

This scene marks the first time that an aristocratic ball had been staged as part of a French opera. But Venetian opera had taken an entirely different perspective for decades. To Venetian composers and librettists it mattered little where the opera was set – it might be ancient Rome or Circe's magic island – if a party scene was needed, it somehow looked just like a Venetian ball.[25] During the 1680s and 1690s these operatic *feste di ballo* began incorporating some French dances, such as the bourrée and the menuet – in imitation of what was happening at the time in Venice's actual ballrooms. Regardless of whether Campra and La Motte knew these Venetian operatic precedents or reinvented this mixture of French and Italian practices for their own purposes, their positioning of the forlana and the menuet side-by-side in this fictional Venetian ballroom turns out to be one place in these operas where art may have imitated life.

Campra's next masked ball, which came two years later in *Le Carnaval de Venise*, had no need to involve the main characters, as it occurs at the end of the opera, after all tensions have been resolved. In fact, the two lovers, Léandre and Isabelle, who have hidden from their jealous rivals by going to see "Orfeo nell'inferi," have chosen its conclusion as their moment to escape. The succession of opera and ball would have seemed familiar to any actual Venetians, given that opera houses in Venice were used

[25] See Alm, "Operatic ballroom scenes," 350–54, and "Winged feet," 251–52 and 259–63.

during Carnival for costume balls following performances of operas.[26] However, Campra's Italian opera is followed not by a *festa di ballo*, but by a masked ball of the kind done every Carnival at the French court.

The framework for this divertissement was borrowed from Lully: personified Carnival invites everyone to enjoy indoor pleasures, since it is cold outside.[27] ("J'ouvre la porte aux jeux, aux festins, à l'amour; / A mon départ le plaisir cesse.") Because no such character ever arrives alone, he is followed by a troupe of "masks of different nations." The libretto does not reveal what countries they come from, but they are later qualified as "masques sérieux" and at least some of them must be French, since what ensues is a formal *bal paré*, complete with every one of the parts required by full court ceremonial. Since it is Carnival season, the ball is interrupted by "masques comiques," who arrive on a magnificent cart and perform dances in accordance with their costumes. This ball thus has two sections that are very distinct in their music and (presumably) in their dancing. In both sections the dancers are the center of attention; the chorus does almost nothing, except help Carnival round off the ball with sufficient pomp. Table 9-2 outlines the two parts of the ball and their frames.[28]

This ball stays so close to actual court practice that the deployment of the dancers must also have followed social norms. This means that all of the designated dancers would have participated in the four branles, but that the rest of the dances in the *bal sérieux* would have been danced one couple at a time – with a possible exception for the last menuet, since it rounds off the section. But it, too, would undoubtedly have kept the dancers in couples, unlike the branles, which were line or circle dances.[29] The dances following the branles are all canonical for a *bal réglé*, and given the date of this work, it is not surprising to see only one courante, but three menuets.

By Campra's day the branles and the courante were so old-fashioned – and apparently so unfamiliar to a musician who did not move in court circles – that he borrowed as his template dances that Lully had composed for court balls in 1665. Although over three decades old, these pieces were not published until the same year as *Le Carnaval de Venise*, in an anthology of ballroom dance music from the court. What Campra looks to have done was to open the book, take the first five dances (branle, branle gai, branle à mener, gavotte, courante), and use their rhythmic and metric profiles as a recipe. The keys may

26 *Ibid.* Starting in 1716 the Opéra also began hosting masked balls; see Semmens, *Bals publics*, 10–15.

27 See Ch. 6, p. 163ff, on Lully's *Carnaval*.

28 Table 9-2 follows the Ballard 1699 score. The manuscript score reproduced in the Pendragon facsimile, which Anthony believes dates from around 1703, lacks the suite of branles and the courante and includes a da capo aria in Italian before the forlana; see his introduction regarding the various versions.

29 This is how they are described in Arbeau's *Orchésographie* (1588). But in Louis XIV's day, according to Rameau (*Le Maître à danser*, ch. 16), the branle à mener and the gavotte were done by couples in a line, each of whom led the dance in turn. Even during the king's youth, however, the gavotte had also emerged from the suite of branles to become a dance in its own right.

Table 9-2: "Le Bal," last scene, from *Le Carnaval de Venise* (1699).
The stage shows a magnificent palace prepared for a ball. Carnival leads a troupe of maskers.

Heading	Paraphrase of sung text/ comments
[I. Introduction]	
Marche du Carnaval. Lentement	
[Recitative] Le Carnaval	In the depths of winter, I come to induce gaiety and raise everyone's spirits.
[II. Formal ball] *The maskers begin a* bal sérieux.	
[Suite of branles]	[group dances]
Branle	
Branle gai	
Branle à mener	
Gavotte	
Courante	[This and next four are probably couple dances.]
Menuet	
Bourrée	
Menuet [en] rondeau	
Repeat of first menuet	
[III. Transition]	
[Recitative, then Air] Le Carnaval	It's time for new dances, new disguises. In times of pleasure, everyone is allowed a bit of folly.
[IV. Masked ball] *A curtain is drawn to reveal* masques comiques *who arrive on a magnificent cart and mingle with the* masques sérieux.	
Chaconne	
Air des masques chinois	
Forlane	
[V. **Conclusion**]	
Carnaval and the Chorus	Let's sing and dance. The moments spent laughing are the best of all.

be different (A minor for Lully, D major and minor for Campra), but the phrasing, the number of measures, and the rhythms of the melody – no matter how idiosyncratic – are identical.[30] If Campra was so consciously modeling his ballroom scene on practices this old, then perhaps the movements of the dancers were also intended to look out of date. If so, was the satire aimed at "Venetians" aping French dancing or at the French court?

30 *Suite de danses pour les violons et hautbois, qui se jouent ordinarement aux bals chez le roi*, ed. Philidor *l'aîné* (Paris: Ballard, 1699), 2–7. Not all branles and courantes have the same structure; the very next dance in this collection is a courante with different phrasing. Campra's ballroom dances could not have resulted from coincidence. As Campra and Philidor had the same publisher, Campra might have seen the book in Ballard's shop, since he would have been working on his own score in early 1699. Incipits of Lully's branles and of the courante may be seen in *LWV* 31/1–4 and 31/8.

The spectacular arrival of new dancers also adhered to court practices. Even the disguises assumed would have fit naturally into a Carnival ball at Versailles or Marly, as would the interruption of the ball by dancers expecting to perform.[31] In Campra's "Venetian" ballroom, in the middle of what could have become an endless sequence of menuets, *masques comiques* make a spectacular entrance in a cart and "mingle while dancing with the *masques sérieux.*" The term "masques comiques" usually means characters from the *comédie italienne* – Arlequin, Scaramouche, and the like – but in this instance, it also included dancers in Chinese costumes (Figure 9-2). In this section of the ball the combination of dancers could vary; dancing by masked performers was not restricted to mixed couples. The chaconne and the forlane would probably have been the domain of the *comédie italienne* dancers – the chaconne because of its long-standing *commedia* associations and the forlane for local color. This particular chaconne is constructed in regular eight-bar couplets, but it shares melodic treatment with some of the Arlequin chaconnes, particularly near the start.

The Chinese dance marks another point of contact with the Théâtre Italien: librettist Regnard had written into his 1692 play *Les Chinois* a scene in which Mezzetin performs as a "pagode," that is, a porcelain figurine in Chinese style, often with a moveable head. In Act II, Arlequin, who is pretending to be a Chinese doctor, opens the door to a china cabinet filled with figurines. "What does that figure over there signify?" asks Roquillard. Arlequin: "It's a pagode." Roquillard: "A pagode? What's a pagode?" Arlequin: "A pagode is . . . a pagode! What the devil do you want me to say?" Roquillard: "But what is it good for? Can it do anything?" Arlequin: "It can sing. I'll show you."[32] Regnard's 1699 *pagode* doesn't sing, but it can dance; the music Campra composed shows that he wanted to particularize this character (not that the music owes anything to China). Each strain of the binary dance has two equal parts – eleven bars of $\frac{3}{2}$ moving mostly in whole and half notes in a low tessitura, followed by thirteen bars of higher and livelier material with a meter sign of **3**; the second part of each strain shows some of the musical hallmarks of the comic Arlequin-style chaconne (see Example 9-2). This idiosyncratic piece seems to have been used by Philidor *l'aîné* as a template for a Chinese dance of his own – an "entrée de la pagode" from his mascarade *Le Roi de la Chine*, which was performed at Marly in 1700 during Carnival. Philidor's dance, whose profile is identical to Campra's, down to the surface rhythms and the number of measures devoted to each meter, has a part for drum that is to be played on the repeat of each strain.[33] Perhaps Philidor got this idea from Campra as well, although Campra's score does not mention a drum. Philidor's score does bear one other useful annotation: his dance was performed by "Mr Desmoulins de l'Opéra," probably François Dumoulin, who specialized in comic roles. (His younger brother, Pierre, who is

31 See my "Ballroom dancing" regarding masked balls at the court, including the particularly spectacular 1700 Carnival season.

32 Gherardi, *Théâtre italien*, IV.

33 US-BE Ms. 455, fol. 7^{r-v}.

Figure 9-2: Jean II Berain, costume design for a Chinese drummer.

known to have danced Chinese characters from time to time, did not enter the Opéra until 1705; regarding all four brothers, see Chapter 13, p. 387ff.) Perhaps Dumoulin had danced Campra's Chinese dance in 1699 and reused the same (much applauded?) choreography a year later.[34]

[34] Destouches's *Issé*, performed at court in 1697, also has an "Air des chinois," but the music is in duple meter with a normal tessitura. Regarding Chinese characters in operatic divertissements, see Lecomte, "L'exotisme."

Example 9-2: Campra, *Le Carnaval de Venise*, "Air des masques chinois" (Paris: Ballard, 1699), 178.

Two other "Venetian" masked balls serve different dramatic purposes. The ball in the third and last act of *La Vénitienne* (1705) celebrates the union of the original set of lovers and involves a mixture of commedia characters (Arlequin, Arlequine, Spezzafer, Scaramouchette) and national types (French, Spanish, German, and Bohemian [gypsy]). But the plot that it wraps up has involved many convolutions and disguises: just at the point when the jealous Octave is about to kill his masked rival, to whom his new heart-throb Léonore has been all too clearly attracted, the unknown suitor unmasks and turns out to be his original beloved, Isabelle, who has been disguised as a man since Act 1.[35] Octave, recovering from his surprise and his near-fatal impulses, renews his expressions of love for Isabelle, while poor Léonore is devastated. The comic servants, Zerbin and Spinette, rush in with the costumed dancers, and in the midst of the masked ball, Isabelle sings a triumphant air about her success in turning infidelity back into love. But this renewed togetherness is undercut by a da capo aria in Italian about a heartless butterfly that flies where it pleases. Moreover, the dances seem almost randomly ordered. Whereas they include a mixture of French and Italian, of social and theatrical styles, they do not encompass any kind of socially sanctioned order that would represent a return to stability and balance.[36]

35 An Italian setting seems to have allowed for a somewhat different kind of gender-bending, when for some performances during the 1724 revival of *L'Europe galante*, the role of Octave, the jealous suitor in "L'Italie," was sung by Mlle Antier, "en habit de noble Vénitien." *MF* (July 1724), 1586–87. Once this particular door had been opened, more such cross-dressing ensued: two actresses at the Théâtre Français dressed as men to play a lover and his valet (*MF*, November 1724, 2242), and at the Opéra, Mlle Lambert sang the role of Atys for several performances in 1726, "applauded by the large audience that this novelty attracted." *MF* (March 1726), 578.

36 The dances include, in this order: menuet, forlana, chaconne, Isabelle's air, gigue, vocal duet by the servants related to the gigue, and branle. (This outline follows a manuscript reduced score sold by Ballard with a printed title page dated 1705: F-Pn Vm[2] 201.)

Table 9-3: *Les Fêtes vénitiennes*, "Le Bal," Scene 6.
The music and dance masters arrive with a crowd of maskers, singing and dancing, and the ball begins.

Heading in the score	Key, meter	Comments
Marche. Gai	g, **3**	Binary
Chœur, "Que les Ris, que les Jeux"	g, **3**	Related musically to *marche*
Premier Menuet	g, **3**	
Deuxième Menuet	G,**3**	No indication to repeat first menuet
Premier Passepied	g, $\frac{3}{8}$	
Deuxième Passepied	G,$\frac{3}{8}$	a3, hautbois; no indication to repeat first passepied
Air Italien (Iphise), "A l'incanto d'un bel riso"	g, **3**	Da capo aria
Air des Masques	g, **3**	Musically related to Air Italien
Premier Air Comique. Pesamment	G,**2**	
Deuxième Air Comique	G,¢	
Forlana. Rondeau	g, $\frac{6}{4}$	
Un Masque, "Le bal favorise les cœurs amoureux"	g, **2**	Binary, unrelated to the dance pieces
Premier Passepied, repeated	g, $\frac{3}{8}$	
Deuxième Passepied, repeated	G,$\frac{3}{8}$	
Premier Menuet, repeated	g, **3**	
Deuxième Menuet, repeated	G,**3**	
A section of the chorus repeated	g, **3**	

In "Le Bal" from *Les Fêtes vénitiennes* (1710) the ball proper also occurs after the plot has been resolved, but in this case the prospects for lasting happiness inspire more confidence. (A Polish prince, Alamir, has hidden his rank in order to make sure his Venetian beloved, Iphise, loves him for himself; the ball celebrates their union.) The texts of the songs reinforce the atmosphere of love, and the dances are ordered as a palindrome, in which the decorous French social dances safely enclose the unruly comic ones (see Table 9-3, which follows the 1714 Ballard score).

The libretto has no *didascalies* that track the ball's progression, but the sequence of dances conforms to the model of a masked ball interrupted by special performances. The palindromic structure calls attention to itself all the more because the sets of dances are so different from each other. The menuets and passepieds are unremittingly regular, the only exception from eight-bar phrases being the twelve bars in the B section of each menuet. The four dances in the middle, on the other hand, are all very quirky. The "Air des masques," by virtue of being musically related to a da capo aria, stands out from normative French dances. The two comic airs seem deliberately

Example 9-3: Campra, *Les Fêtes vénitiennes*, from "Le Bal" (Paris: Ballard, 1714), 65–66. (a) "Premier Air comique"; (b) "Deuxième Air comique."

(a)

(b)

clumsy (see Examples 9-3a and b.) Both are in duple meter with simple, repetitive rhythms in (mostly) square phrasing; the first is marked "heavily" and moves either in half notes with large leaps, or seesawing quarter notes. Neither modulates to the dominant at the midpoint, the harmony is ultra simple, and at the end of three out of the four strains, the melody finishes after the bass cadences, by dropping from $\hat{3}$ to $\hat{1}$ (in the remaining strain it drops from $\hat{1}$ to $\hat{5}$). The forlana has its usual ternary form, but is marked by an extraordinarily long middle section (8–24–8).

There are a few hints as to who might have danced in the contrasting parts of the ball. A *didascalie* at the start of the scene states that "the music master and dancing master come with a crowd of maskers, singing and dancing, and the ball begins"; as the ones who had been charged with the arrangements for the ball, the two masters must have made their presence felt while it was going on. The cast list of seven couples does not individualize them, but it does place at their head Marcel, who played the role of the dancing master, and Mlle Journet, the singer in the role of Iphise. (She seems to have been typecast as a dancing singer, having already played the role of Olympia in the ballroom scene in *L'Europe galante*.) She must have danced in the "serious" part of the ball; might one of the menuets have served to show off the lessons she had learned from her partner, the dancing master? As for the music master, perhaps he was the one who sang the little dance-song in the middle of the divertissement, which articulates the return from the comic dances to the passepieds and menuets.[37] At the end of the divertissement, if not also at its opening, these social

[37] The song is binary and looks like a classic dance-song (in fact, like a branle), except that there is no indication in the score that it should be played by the orchestra as well as sung. It easily could be, however, and could be danced in a circle, as a branle, to mark the return to the social dances.

dances must have been for groups. The four dances in the middle of the ball, on the other hand, would lend themselves to performances by soloists or small ensembles. For two of them – the first "Air comique" and the forlana – choreographies survive that originated during the first run of performances.[38]

Ballroom scenes, once introduced, became a topos for divertissements in works set in contemporary times. No longer did the ballroom have be Venetian; it might be outdoors in Paris, along the Cours la Reine, as in the fourth entrée of Montéclair's opera-ballet *Les Fêtes de l'été* (1716). For composer and choreographer alike, a masked ball provided a flexible framework for varied dances, that could be tied to the rest of the plot – or not, as the librettist desired. The nature of the event allowed for a huge number of dances – huge even without taking into account the possibility that some of them might have been repeated beyond what is indicated in the score: there are nine dances in the ball in *L'Europe galante*, thirteen in *Le Carnaval de Venise*, and again thirteen in *Les Fêtes vénitiennes*. The costumes worn by the guests promoted character dances; a menuet or two would anchor the ball in contemporary practices, but beyond that, almost any kind of dancing could be envisaged, from the serious to the grotesque, from patterned groups to flamboyant solos. Semi-analogous scenes in the *tragédie en musique* – the celebratory wedding scenes that conclude many operas or the village wedding – also lent themselves to expansion and variation, but did not have as broad a possible stylistic range. It is no wonder that divertissements built around masked balls proved so appealing, to creators and audiences alike.

The correspondences between the more popular theaters and the Académie Royale de Musique do not end with these three scene types, nor are they confined to divertissements. But divertissements, which since Lully's day had been defined as a "musical" realm, did offer a natural environment for the growing emphasis on soloistic display, whether of the latest Italian musical styles, irreverent set pieces, or character dances. They also provided a conceptual frame for containing the new styles, since, at the Opéra, Thalie, Momus, and their followers could not run rampant, as they could at the Théâtre Italien and at the fairs. Comic elements could be allowed onto the stage only if they were kept within bounds.

A little scene from an opéra comique by Lesage, *La Ceinture de Vénus*, performed at the Foire Saint-Germain in 1715, shows how attentively the other Parisian theaters were monitoring the Opéra's excursions into their territory. In II/3 Arlequin receives the visit of a composer who has set the same text to music in both French and Italian styles. ("Je viens de faire une chanson / Qui me paraît assez jolie. / Comme vous avez le goût bon, / Écoutez-la, je vous supplie. / Je l'ai faite également bien / En français, en

[38] See Appendix 3.

italien. / Italien, / Italien, / En français, en italien.") Arlequin enthusiastically sings along with the Italian and wrinkles up his nose at the French: "I leave that one to the bourgeoisie. The other [the Italian song] is what pleases people with titles."[39]

COMIC SIMULTANEITY

The staging of Lully's *tragédies* had as an underlying principle a single focus for the audience's attention (see Chapter 2): only within well-defined exceptions could singing and dancing happen simultaneously. The principle appears to have extended to movements within a single action: two dancers would not perform different steps and figures simultaneously, nor would a silent singer compete for attention with the one delivering the text by engaging in distracting actions.

The comic realm, however, not only allowed for more than one thing to happen at a time, it exploited simultaneity to generate laughter. In *La Coquette* by Regnard (1691), a typical *didascalie* shows "Colombine, at a little desk, folding a letter while Pierrot, behind her, performs *lazzi* of being in love."[40] When it took over character types and plots from the *comédie italienne*, the Opéra also opened itself toward this kind of staging. Toward the end of "Le Triomphe de la Folie" from *Les Fêtes vénitiennes*, a very similar sequence takes place: "While the Doctor sings with Colombine, Arlequin performs a silent scene, at the end of which Colombine gives her hand to Arlequin in defiance of the Doctor's [expressions of] love." Although the *didascalie* does not say so, the humor was probably amplified by the fact that Colombine could see Arlequin's shenanigans, whereas the Doctor remained oblivious to them throughout.

A similar example – this one involving dancers as well as singers – may be found in "La Sérénade vénitienne," one of the entrées added to *Les Fragments de Lully*, in which Éraste elopes with Léonore during a moment of inattention by her guardian. Éraste is abetted by his confidant (a singer) and three Scaramouches (dancers). The score reports that "Éraste gives a letter to one of his followers, who climbs up the Doctor's house, along with the [other] Scaramouches, in order to kidnap Léonore. During this time, Éraste and another of his followers sing the following duet."[41] All of this action must happen during the duet (whose text, in Italian, talks about how love triumphs over jealous hearts), because it is the only music available. The Doctor is so enchanted with the music that he sings along on the phrase "bring crowns of amorous myrtles," not noticing until too late what is going on behind his back. His moment of enlightenment

[39] Le Sage et d'Orneval, *Théâtre de la Foire*, I, 324. It was only one year after this play was performed that the Regent invited a new troupe of Italian players to establish themselves in Paris. Once again the Parisian theaters had to re-equilibrate.

[40] *Gherardi: Théâtre italien*, ed. Guichemerre, II, 306.

[41] This *didascalie* comes from the 1703 Ballard score, not from the *Recueil général*, which has simply "Il donne une lettre à un Scaramouche, qui escalade le balcon avec tous les autres."

was handled very cleverly by the librettist: the Doctor first hurls insults at the Scaramouches in Italian, then switches into French, all the while maintaining the rhymes and rhythms of the duet: "D'amorosi Mirthi / Portate corone. / Ahi ladri, furfanti, / Portate bastoni. O désespoir fatal! / Léonore avec mon rival!" More action ensues: "the Doctor comes down from the balcony to shut Léonore back into the house, but he is stopped by the Scaramouches, who beat him with sticks." The beating is set to an instrumental piece, thus returning to the conventional staging where only one thing happens at a time; the blows even land in time with the music.[42]

Whereas this scene involves the dancers more in miming than dancing, it does open up the question of whether it was now becoming possible for other kinds of stage business to go on while dancers were in motion, or even for dancers to engage in independent movements simultaneously. Although *didascalies* in librettos or scores are only rarely helpful, the answer appears to be a qualified yes – when the governing affect is comic and if the dramatic context makes independent simultaneous movements meaningful. In "L'Amour saltimbanque" from *Les Fêtes vénitiennes*, the French suitor and his Venetian sweetheart chat with each other during the fête, taking advantage of her chaperone's attention to the dancing. The prologue to *Le Carnaval et la Folie*, set at a feast on Mount Olympus where the gods are behaving badly, stages a choreographed scene of jealousy, set to a single instrumental piece, in which "Vénus dances with Mars [her lover], while Vulcain [her husband] mingles with them in order to observe them." A few of the engravings in Lambranzi's book of Italian-style theatrical dancing show dancers engaged in independent movements (such as when Arlequin crawls between the legs of a blind man), but more often their movements are distinct, but reciprocal, as is the case for the gondolier and his wife (Figure 8-3, p. 234). More often still, Lambranzi's dancers are shown in symmetrical arrangements, as are the various commedia characters in a scene from the *Ballet des saisons* (Figure 9-1). Nonetheless, even if the exceptions were few to the principle of a single focus and to the practice of symmetry within choreographies, the Opéra's range of staging practices had been broadened by its acceptance of practices from other theaters.

"FRAGMENTS" AS A GENRE

In 1702 a work with the title *Les Fragments de Monsieur de Lully* appeared on the stage of the Académie Royale de Musique. This was an opera-ballet, with a prologue and four independent entrées, in which Campra and Danchet borrowed pieces ("fragments") from the pre-operatic works of Lully and glued them together with new music and text.

[42] No *didascalie* so indicates, but in "La Bastonade," a duple-meter piece marked "Gravement," suggestive rests punctuate the texture at regular intervals.

In this form, the work was new to its audience, even if some of its components were familiar.[43] Before long, the application of the word "fragments" was extended to a different kind of operatic performance, one in which sections of successful works were performed together, in a "best of" manner. On such an evening the audience might see the prologue from one opera followed by three entrées, each from a different opera-ballet. This was an attractive proposition from a commercial point of view, since it meant that "new" works could be generated from past successes, but it also had implications for the dancers. With but a single exception – the *tragédie Télémaque* (1704), which Campra and Danchet constructed from pieces of post-Lully operas – the phenomenon of fragments drew from the lighter works in the repertoire, ones in which the danced divertissements were particularly extensive and where the styles of dancing included the comic. Some of the most successful individual scenes in these works thus got recycled even beyond their appearance in revivals of the work as a whole, and this prolonged their life on the stage even past the time when the creation of Italianate works fell off.

Works of this type have received very little scholarly attention. This book does not redress the historiographic imbalance, but does aim to show how widespread the phenomenon was, since the Opéra's performers devoted a fair amount of their professional activity to this kind of work. In surveying the repertoire it is easy to lose track of pieces like these, all the more since the contents of a program of fragments could vary within the same run of performances. The list in Appendix 2 is not complete, because not all such pastiches generated a libretto. To complicate matters, special performances, either for important personages or benefits for the performers, often used this kind of format.[44] These are sometimes mentioned in the *Mercure de France* or by the Parfaict brothers. The phenomenon of performing fragments of works did not end in 1733; it continued during Rameau's ascendancy and well beyond.[45] Appendix 2 conflates the two different types of "fragments," partially because the new works such as *Les Fragments de Lully* generated their own pieces that figured among the fragments on other evenings.

Appendix 2 gives only a partial picture of a larger phenomenon, which consisted of a modular approach to constructing some evenings at the Opéra. Not all of the items that contributed to programs of fragments are operatic: some are cantatas and others are purely instrumental ballets (see Chapter 13). One of these might be appended to the end of an opera, as when "Le Jaloux trompé," formerly known as "La Sérénade

[43] The only fragment Campra and Danchet borrowed from one of Lully's operatic works was the second half of the prologue to *Les Fêtes de l'Amour et de Bacchus*.

[44] See Denécheau and Serre, "Sauts, gambades."

[45] ChronOpera (http://chronopera.free.fr/), which as of this writing begins its chronology of the Opéra's performances in 1749, documents many evenings of this type. See also the *Dictionnaire encyclopédique de l'Opéra de Paris sous l'Ancien Régime* (forthcoming).

vénitienne," one of the entrées from *Les Fragments de Lully*, was performed in 1731 following *Le Carnaval et la Folie*. Even a *tragédie* might be followed by something short in a completely different character, as in 1728, when the last act of *Roland* was replaced by Lully's comic intermèdes for Molière's comedy-ballet *Monsieur de Pourceaugnac*, which had recently been performed at court.[46] This particular substitution was probably a one-off, but the rounding off of a performance with the addition of a short, independent piece was not rare and goes far beyond the skimpy list in the appendix.[47] We need to broaden our thinking to encompass this kind of performance, given how much time audiences at the Opéra spent watching mixed programs. In this regard the Opéra approached programming practices at its rival theaters, where it was common to present more than one short work on the same evening. Moreover, the phenomenon of fragments seems part of a trend during this period toward a greater emphasis on performance and performers, rather than on the work per se.

At least three of the little works that appeared both in fragments or as additions to longer works were sung entirely, or almost so, in Italian. An entire evening in Italian was not possible at the Opéra, but the fragment format offered an acceptable framework for comic bits in another language. A measure of the extent to which such works must have relied on physical comedy is that the plots are so flimsy that the best excuse for their existence lies in the performing of them. The earliest of the three is "Pourceaugnac," which was revived not only as part of Lully's *Carnaval* of 1675, but multiple times on its own between 1716 and 1741;[48] this one at least benefitted from clever texts by Molière. "Cariselli" was an entrée in the *Fragments de Lully*, where it is called a "divertissement comique." Most of its music was composed by Campra, but three of the dances come from Lully ballets.[49] The old, self-deluded Cariselli stutters his way through his opening monologue, asking Amour to explain why Vafrina scorns him, even though he is so charming and handsome ("Perchè, crudo Amore"). Three Pantalons pop up to tell him that what he needs is a new outfit. With the help of two dancing Scaramouches (also called Matassins) they dress him in a grotesque manner,

46 *MF* (May 1728), 1018–19.

47 Cyr has pointed out that Destouches's *cantate Oenone* says on its title page that it was "mise au théâtre par la même Académie en février 1716, à la suite de *L'Europe galante*." (See her edition of the *Secular Vocal Works of Elizabeth-Claude Jacquet de La Guerre* in *The Collected Works*, IV, xv.) In 1729 Lully's *Alceste* was twice followed by "Cariselli" *and Les Caractères de la danse* as a benefit for the singers; *MF* (April 1729), 7776.

48 See Ch. 6, p. 174 and Ch. 8, n. 27.

49 According to Parfaict, *Histoire*, 103, this vignette owes its origin to Lully's mockery of a stuttering Italian musician named Cariselli who appeared at court in order to challenge Lully's musical ascendancy; for a transcription of Parfaict's text, see La Laurencie, "André Campra," 159. This anecdote – reported many decades after it had supposedly taken place – seems dubious, given that most of the music of "Cariselli" is by Campra, nor is the title character a musician. Yet it must have had some currency: in 1737 a poem satirizing Rameau was entitled "Le Nouveau Cariselli" (see Sadler, "Patrons and pasquinades," 324–27).

a scene that recalls Monsieur Jourdain's outfitting in the *Bourgeois gentilhomme*. When Vafrina arrives with her lover and a troupe of masked merrymakers, she cleverly turns the ternary structure of a da capo aria, whose text is a declaration of love, to her own purposes: she sarcastically addresses the A section to Cariselli, sings the B section to her lover Garbini, and, at the return of the A section, joins with Garbini to mock Cariselli yet again.[50] On either side of her aria are dances for the maskers, who consist of a Spanish couple, a gypsy couple, Pantalon with Pantalonne, Polichinelle with a Dame Gigogne, and four Arlequins and Arlequines (probably children); they dance an "Entrée des Masques," a chaconne, canaries, and an "Air des Scaramouches." The work ends with a repeat of part of the trio sung earlier by the Pantalons.[51]

The "Professeur de folie" has a plot that is even thinner. It originated in 1703 as part of the divertissement in Act III of *Le Carnaval et la Folie* (libretto by La Motte, music by Destouches), but almost immediately was performed as a free-standing "divertissement."[52] Some adjustments were required, depending on whether it was performed within the opera or separately, but the basic situation is the same. When the curtain goes up (following an overture borrowed from *Issé*), Folie (or a Matassine, when the scene was independent of the opera) and her followers are urging (in French) everyone to laugh and be crazy. The professor enters with his followers to a lively march, then tells them (in Italian) that they can all become doctors in the arts of "allegria." He instructs, in turn, a singer (concentrating on roulades), then two dancers (their movements are set to lively arpeggios in $\frac{3}{8}$), and finally a poet (who comes up with clichéd rhymes). The chorus offers encouragement: "Sing, dance, rhyme, this is the perfection of madness" ("Cantate, ballate, rimate, / E della pazzia la perfettione"). More of each follows, in the form of two dances, one of them a chaconne, a song in French for Folie and the chorus, and a da capo aria in Italian.[53] Repeats of the chaconne and of the very first chorus draw the work to an end.

Both these works contain music that is lively and mostly Italianate, but clearly something other than the storyline kept them on the stage year after year.[54] A German visitor to Paris, Johann Friederich von Uffenbach, loved the "Professeur de folie" when he saw it in

50 In the return of the A section, Garbini doubles portions of the instrumental bass line.

51 According to the libretto, "Cariselli" was supposed to end with a chorus, "Si canti, si goda," i.e., the one sung by Plutone and his followers at the end of "Orfeo nell'inferi" (see above, p. 260). But the "Cariselli" score does not include this music, probably because, without it, no chorus is needed for a performance.

52 This discussion is based on the score published by Ballard in 1711.

53 This aria, "Si brami, si goda," is unassigned in the score and does not appear in the 1703 libretto, but in the 1706 libretto is assigned to Folie.

54 The Parfaict brothers list revivals for "Cariselli" in 1717, 1729, 1730, 1731, 1738, and 1740 and for the "Professeur de folie" in 1706, 1711, 1719, 1722, 1730, 1731, 1738, 1739, and 1748, but neither list is complete (*Dictionnaire*, II, 44–45 and 52–56).

1715.[55] Some of the credit for the work's popularity has to go to the dancers; for Uffenbach the "Professeur de Folie" was a vehicle for François Dumoulin, who specialized in comic roles.[56] More than any other works at the Paris Opéra, these two seem closest to their *comédie italienne* models in their reliance on *lazzi* and physical comedy. How far the dancers at the Paris Opera allowed themselves to adopt the freedom of movement apparent at the Théâtre Italien cannot be known, but they must have been using something other than the toney noble style. The plates in Lambranzi's book of theatrical dancing help provide a sense of the high jinks in which the dancers probably engaged.[57]

Whereas programs of fragments could include pastoral entrées or others of a more purely French character, it is striking how many of them operate in an Italian-inflected realm. They seem to have been weighted toward keeping the light-hearted parts of the repertoire before the eyes of the public, even during periods when new creations of such works were falling off.

55 Preußner, *Die musikalischen Reisen*, 144.

56 In 1703 the dancers were Balon and Subligny as the dancing couple, François Dumoulin as a Fol, with Mlle La Ferrière as a Folle, plus six male Matassins. In 1706 the roles were different: Balon and Prévost as the two dancers, François Dumoulin as Arlequin and Guyot as a female Scaramouche, plus a German couple and a French couple. Except for the two main dancers, who would have been the students in the dancing lesson, it is not obvious who would have danced where; probably the various couples took turns in the chaconne, but Dumoulin must have had a fair amount of solo time. No libretto has been located for the performance Uffenbach saw.

57 Two examples: "This buffoon does various foolish but curious *pas*, with distorted but comic jumps, which he varies as much as possible and endeavors to make still more humorous, until the air has been played three times." "Here Pantalone and his Pandora are at the ball. But since he is old, she refuses to dance with him. Finally she grips his beard, turns him round in a circle, and having done this several times, drags him off by his beard." (I, plates 38 and 42, trans. Derra de Moroda in Lambranzi, *New and Curious School*, 25–26.)

10 | The Contested Comic

The arrival in force of Italianate settings and plot lines had the effect of making the Académie Royale de Musique more hospitable to other kinds of works in a comic vein. The pastoral realm, which lent itself to both serious and burlesque treatment, provided an alternative from the urban settings of the *comédie italienne*; moreover, on the lower reaches of Olympus resided gods such as Bacchus, Pan, and Momus, who, along with their followers, could be exploited for comic potential. Village weddings – a long-standing staple of the French stage – could also be shaded to suit a librettist's or composer's desires and had the advantage of being locatable either in mythological times or in the present. Another route was to transpose Italian-style plots into contemporary French environments. The comic elements found a natural home in the divertissements, but they were not confined there. In fact, entire entrées within an opera-ballet or even entire works could be comic. But the comic remained contested, especially for full-length works, and librettists repeatedly resorted to prologues to justify its presence. By the 1720s there was a reaction in powerful places against what was seen as low humor, and the creation of new comic works slowed. Yet ones already in the repertoire continued to be revived; Appendix 1 charts the fortunes of both new works and revivals. At the end of the decade the Opéra opened itself to a different type of comedy by importing for the first time two Italian *intermezzi*. These could only go on the stage, however, when naturalized in accordance with fundamental French aesthetic principles, ones that required dancing.

DOMESTICATION

Le Carnaval et la Folie (1704)

The libretto to Destouches's *Le Carnaval et la Folie* identifies the work as a "comédie-ballet"; as Houdar de La Motte explains in the preface, he borrowed the framework from Erasmus's *In Praise of Folly*. Folly (whose parents, Wealth and Youth,[1] also figure among the *dramatis personae*) spends the better part of the opera's four acts spurning her suitor, Carnaval, until, after manipulative meddling by Momus and the endorsement of Jupiter, Vénus, Mercure, and Bacchus, the two decide to get married. In this thoroughly irreverent work three places involve the dancers in particularly interesting

[1] "Plutus, dieu des richesses" and Jeunesse.

ways. The prologue, which contains no praise at all of any earthly hero,[2] takes place during a feast of the gods, who pair up in both song and dance. The cynical tone of the texts is reinforced by a little mimed scene in which Vénus (primarily a singing role) dances with her lover Mars, while her jealous husband Vulcain spies on them (both of these dance only). On the heels of this reminder about marital infidelity, Mercure tries to entice the gods to visit earth, claiming that mortal women are eager to meet them. But only Momus, kicked out of Olympus by Jupiter for overdoing his mockery (a reference to Louis XIV's expulsion of the Théâtre Italien?), departs for the lower realms, where he chooses to meddle in Carnaval's affairs.

In the second act, as an attempt to cheer herself up, Folly calls upon her followers, who perform the Italian sketch, "Le Professeur de folie" (see Chapter 9, p. 285). This interjection of the modern world into the mythological realm bothers none of the opera's inhabitants, and it happens again, during the concluding celebrations. Here the chorus dons Carnival costumes in full view of the audience: "a troupe of various peoples comes to pay homage to Carnaval. They take masks from his hand and *marottes*[3] from the hand of Folly, then come back masked to take their places on bleachers." In a sequence that recalls the ceremonial arming of Persée before he goes off to fight Méduse (see Chapter 2, p. 62), Carnaval receives a robe covered in masks from Jupiter and Vénus, a bonnet covered with ivy and grape leaves from Bacchus, and a golden scepter topped by a masker's head from Mercure – all set to lively music in $\frac{6}{8}$ time sung in Italian and punctuated by the choral refrain, "Viva, viva, sempre viva, / Il Dio dell'allegria."[4]

The opera ends with a chorus, back in French, of the type that is common to both prologues and final celebrations – one that asks the pastoral oboes and musettes to blend their sounds with the military trumpets and drums. This chorus, however, is given a twist in the last line when Folly claims that the military instruments should resound because "Mars owes me his homage, as does Amour." This remark comes out of nowhere, as Mars has not been a presence in this opera, except for his dance with Vénus in the prologue, while the jealous Vulcain watched. Does this line aim to recuperate him from his less than heroic appearance there?[5] Or is Folly offering a

[2] An oblique allusion comes near the end of the prologue. *Momus*: "Give yourselves to pleasure; may Glory scold [*gronde*] in vain, Love is a worthier object." *Amour*: "There is a king who takes care of the world; enjoy the leisure that a mortal has made for you."

[3] A *marotte* is a little fool's head on a stick.

[4] The score describes Mercure's gift somewhat differently than the libretto: "Mercure gives [Carnaval] his caduceus and makes him *surintendant* of the festivities", which could be read as a reference to Lully, perhaps satirizing his role as *surintendant* of the king's music or acknowledging his own staging of Carnival or both.

[5] This is the trajectory found in Lully's *Psyché* (see Ch. 6, pp. 175ff): in Act II Vulcain alludes to Mars and Vénus's affair in his spat with his wife, but during the concluding divertissement in Act V the heroic side of Mars is celebrated.

critique of the current military policies of the Mars seated on the throne of France, by implying that their mixed results are due to her meddling?[6] A conclusion that invokes Mars and Amour while celebrating the marriage of Carnival and Folly cuts in many directions.[7]

Les Fragments de M. de Lully (1702)

Because it is a pastiche, this work has received very little attention, but it deserves more for the telling ways the bits and pieces have been assembled. Both the libretto and the published score name the Lully work from which each piece or sequence has been borrowed; the score is more complete, since the libretto does not make reference to the dances. The unattributed pieces were composed by Campra (see Appendix 2 for an overview of the work). With the exception of the prologue, which borrows the second part of the prologue of *Les Fêtes de l'Amour et de Bacchus*, all the Lully pieces come from his pre-operatic works and were thus between 30 and 40 years old. This means that Campra and Danchet had access to the works Lully had written with Molière as well as to Benserade's court ballets, access they exploited to mixed comic effect in "La Bergerie."

The storyline of this entrée comes from "La pastorale comique," one of the many pieces that figured at one time or another within the *Ballet des Muses* (1666). Two shepherds, Lycas and Philène, are mooning over the same shepherdess and exchange exaggerated threats: "I will strangle you, I will eat you, if you ever speak my beloved's name," sings Lycas (who in 1666 was played by Molière himself). Iris, however, has her own problems: she is in love with the absent Mirtil and so excessive is her sorrow that she expresses it via Ariadne's lament from the *Ballet de la Naissance de Vénus*, complete with its ornamental *double*, while the two shepherds eavesdrop. When they present themselves for her choice – Lycas cockily pronounces, "You have eyes; I love you. Enough said" – she rejects them both, upon which the two fall to insulting her, Lycas in speech, Philène in song ("Cœur dur!" "Tigresse!" "Inexorable!" "Inhumaine!"). The shepherds decide to kill themselves, but neither wants to go first. Just in the nick of time, another shepherd arrives to convince them that dying for love is madness.

As a conclusion to such a burlesque scene, the divertissement seems surprisingly tame. It consists of no fewer than six dance-songs for various shepherds and shepherdesses, supplemented by three independent dance pieces and rounded off by a chorus. These come from several Lully works and are held together more by key than by their

[6] This opera premiered on 3 January 1704, during the War of Spanish Succession; in November of 1703 Victor Amadeus of Savoy had switched sides away from France to join the Grand Alliance and Marlborough had invaded the Spanish Netherlands. (His defeat of the French at the battle of Blenheim was to come in August of 1704.) France had known some military successes in 1703, but it was clear already that the war would not be short.

[7] On the character of Folie in this and other operas, see Cowart, "Of women, sex, and folly."

texts, which vary in tone from the admonitory (youth is the time for love) to the coquettish. Some could lend themselves to tongue-in-cheek choreographic treatment, particularly the dance-song from the *Bourgeois gentilhomme*: "See, my Climène, the birds kissing each other under the oak? [. . .] If you want, we could be like them" (this set to overly insistent rhymes: "Qu'ils sont heureux! / Nous pouvons tous deux / Si tu le veux / Être comme eux"). But the dance pieces, including for this song, are mostly generic types – menuets, gavottes, and a bourrée. It is possible that the dances followed through on the comic spirit of the first half of the entrée, but they tend rather toward a more bucolic vision of the pastoral, and thus to reverse the balance seen in some other pastoral divertissements of serious texts inflected by comic dances. Whatever the style, the concluding chorus applauds what it has been watching: "Quel spectacle charmant, quel plaisir goûtons-nous, / Les dieux mêmes, les dieux n'en ont point de plus doux!" This self-reflexivity also concludes the nautical entrée, "Les Matelots," whose text points at the quality of the dancing: "Ouvrons tous les yeux / À l'éclat suprême / Qui brille dans ces lieux. / Quelle grâce extrême! / Quel port glorieux! / Où voit-on des dieux / Qui soient faits de même?" In its original context, this chorus expressed admiration for the god Apollon,[8] but here it sums up a sequence of jolly songs and dances by sailors: as in many of Campra's Italianate works, self-consciousness about the act of performing becomes part of the work.

Les Fêtes de Thalie (1714)

Les Fêtes de Thalie is to France as *Les Fêtes vénitiennes* is to Venice: in both opera-ballets contemporary society is filtered through a comic sensibility. This novelty provoked negative criticism, but, as the *Mercure galant* pointed out, "Many have raised their voices against *Les Fêtes de Thalie*, yet it has been playing for two months on the stage of the Académie Royale de Musique"; in fact, the work ran without interruption for 57 performances between August and December of 1714.[9] The creators of this success were both new to the Opéra. Joseph de La Font had already written several plays (his greatest prior success had been *Le Naufrage, ou la Pompe funèbre de Crispin*, written for the Comédie-Française in 1710) and Jean-Joseph Mouret, who had arrived ten years earlier from his native Avignon, was to be appointed the resident composer at the Théâtre Italien when it reopened in 1716. Although he later was to compose two *tragédies lyriques*, his talents lent themselves better to comedy; another overtly comic

[8] The chorus comes at the end of the "Jeux Pythiens" section of *Les Amants magnifiques* (1670). The role of Apollon was intended for Louis XIV, but he did not dance it; see La Gorce, *Lully*, 156–57.

[9] Cited in Viollier, *Mouret*, 46–47. Fajon believes performances continued into January and February. According to him (*L'Opéra à Paris*, 257–58), this opera was at least as successful as *Les Fêtes vénitiennes* and was not to be equaled until Rameau's *Fêtes d'Hébé* (1739).

work, *Les Amours de Ragonde*, performed at the Opéra in 1742, after his death, was an important precursor to Rameau's *Platée*.

Les Fêtes de Thalie has more conceptual unity than *Les Fêtes vénitiennes*, in that it is organized around three different stages of a woman's life: the maiden, the widow, and the wife. "La Fille" takes place in the port of Marseille, "La Veuve" in a rustic hamlet, and "La Femme" in an urban ballroom; this last is the closest in spirit to Campra's Venetian entrées. When the work was revived in 1722, Mouret added a fourth entrée, "La Provençale"; it, too, was set in Marseille and even included songs in dialect, thus nudging the investment in local color up a notch.

In a preface published not in the original libretto, but six years later in volume XI of the *Recueil général*, La Font acknowledged that he had set out to write a crossover work that borrowed from spoken comedy. His claims are exaggerated, but worth quoting in full:

> Here, I believe, is the first opera where one has seen women dressed in the French manner and confidantes who take the tone of the soubrettes of comedy. It is also the first work that hazards certain expressions appropriate for comedy that were new at the time, and even unknown on the operatic stage. At first the public was alarmed, but the theatricality that reigns from beginning to end of this ballet was found to be so amusing and playful that people came in crowds, almost grudgingly. I recognized that I was amusing the public in spite of itself, and in order to render its pleasure pure and tranquil, I hastened to write a critique of my own work, in which I attributed all its merits to the success of the music and the dance. The public was grateful for my thoughtfulness and became so friendly toward me that for 80 performances it could not resolve to abandon me. Even today it speaks of this ballet with pleasure.

Perhaps *women* had not appeared before in contemporary French dress on the stage of the Opéra (or at least not since the prologue to Lully's very first work, *Les Fêtes de l'Amour et de Bacchus*), but contemporary French *men* had been strolling through Venetian settings since 1699, as had contemporary Venetians of both sexes. The claim about the soubrettes is more persuasive; La Font's two (Doris in "La Veuve" and Dorine in "La Femme") are saucier – and in the first case, more interested in money – than any remote antecedents such as Charite in Lully's *Alceste*. As for the auto-critique, La Font did indeed write one, in the form of an additional entrée that follows up on the squabbles between the Muses of comedy and tragedy that are thematized in the prologue. La Font armed himself with the best possible weapons – humor and self-mockery – and did indeed take aim at his own texts. The prologue and the "Critique" have been described in Chapter 7, p. 205, but because Mouret's musical treatment deserves more credit than La Font gives it in his self-congratulations, the "Critique" is discussed from a different angle below.

The first entrée, "La Fille," is the most overtly comic and the most grounded in a real place, Marseille. Acaste, a sea captain, has rescued Cléon from slavery in Algiers and is now delivering him home to his wife. He is also hoping to soften the heart of the woman he has loved without return; he is counting on her mother to help his cause. Mother and daughter now arrive; Léonore, guitar in hand, declares she is only interested in pleasure, not in the slavery of marriage. Given the words she sings, the guitar she holds, and the nature of her entrance music, it is probable that Léonore enters dancing:[10]

> Rire, danser, changer, c'est mon partage, / Sans soins, sans amour, sans désirs, / Point d'hymen, point d'esclavage, / Je ne m'engage / Qu'aux seuls plaisirs.
>
> (To laugh, dance, and sing, that is my lot. Without cares, without love, without desires, no marriage, no slavery, I pledge myself only to pleasure.)

In her lovely tenor voice (Léonore's mother is played by a man) Belise urges her daughter to marry; she herself has selflessly resisted a thousand lovers these ten years that her husband has been missing, all in order to ensure her daughter's happiness. Léonore only repeats her anti-marriage refrain. Acaste, who has overheard the conversation, despairs. Belise advises him to replace Léonore with a woman who has achieved "the age of reason" – herself. Acaste gulps, but decides to play along. (Part of the humor in this scene resides in the asides whispered in various combinations among the three speakers, as they attempt to further their own interests.) Just as Belise is getting ever more affectionate, who should arrive but Cléon, leading Acaste's Algerian captives and followed by local sailors. He is horrified by his wife's betrayal, but Acaste is thrilled to have escaped Belise, and even Léonore is pleased to see that her suitor is not going to marry her mother. Cléon confers his daughter on Acaste, who expresses his gratitude by liberating his captives. The captives are ecstatic ("Chantons l'Amour") and via the intermediary of a single singing Algerian and the six Algerian dancers (all men) wish the young couple well in a strophic song and loure.[11] An unnamed girl from Marseille, however, seems to share Léonore's initial attitude toward marriage as something better avoided:

> Tout Amant / Comme le vent / Est sujet à changer, / N'en courons pas le danger. / Tel qui nous rend hommage / N'est qu'un volage, / Défions-nous / D'un vent si doux. [2nd strophe:] Sur les flots / Point de repos; / Dans l'empire amoureux / L'on n'est guere plus heureux, / Qui laisse le rivage / Court au naufrage, / C'est trop risquer / Que s'embarquer.
>
> (Every lover is like the wind, subject to change; let's not take the risk. Anyone who admires us is fickle; let's mistrust such a sweet wind. [2nd strophe:] On the waves there is no rest; in the empire of love it's just the same. Anyone who leaves the shore is heading for a shipwreck. It's too dangerous to embark.)

[10] The role was created by Mlle Poussin, who could dance at least a little, as can be seen from her role as Zélie in *Les Fêtes vénitiennes* (see Ch. 8, p. 249).

[11] In the 1720 printed score this piece is called "Air pour les captifs algériens"; in one copy (F-Pn H. 702) it is annotated "loure."

Example 10-1: Mouret, *Les Fêtes de Thalie*, "Premier Rigaudon" from "La Fille" (Paris: Ballard, 1714), 122.

No one asks Léonore whether or not she wants to marry Acaste, but the chorus seems to think she is happy and the jolly music is conventionally celebratory. Nonetheless, her compatriot's words undercut the mood and return us to Léonore's cynical perspective at the start of the entrée.

The part of the divertissement within which this song occurs, which is performed by a mixed group of sailors from Marseille, partakes of the developing conventions for a nautical divertissement in drawing parallels between the weather on the sea and the emotions within the human heart (see Chapter 12, p. 386ff). But the metaphors of shipwreck in the song performed by the girl from Marseille shade this particular divertissement toward the cynical. There are five instrumental dances: two menuets, two rigaudons, and an "Entrée des matelots" that is similar to a rigaudon in character and features a trio of flutes in its second strain. Whereas the menuet could appear in multiple contexts, the fact that this is the dance that is juxtaposed with the anti-marriage text suggests that the courtship gestures of the social dance may have been co-opted here to comic ends. The rigaudon (see Example 10-1), a dance that was new since Lully's day, had a narrower range of dramatic uses, scenes for sailors being one of them. This is not to say that all *fêtes marines* contain rigaudons, but rather that within the fluid conventions that associate character types with dance-types, sailors and rigaudons are a common pairing. The use of flutes within the "Entrée des matelots" also participates in the web of signs for the nautical, particularly for a divertissement set in Marseille, since Mouret probably aimed to imitate the *galoubet* (a type of tabor pipe, still a folk instrument in southern France), which is played together with the large drum called the *tambourin*. The dance known by metonymy as the tambourin does not figure in this particular divertissement, but at this time was in the process of becoming another common presence in *fêtes marines*. (For more regarding the confluence of the sea and the tambourin – both the instrument and the dance – see Chapter 12, p. 370.)

Whether Mouret used flutes elsewhere in this scene is uncertain, because Ballard's reduced score does not provide a complete picture of the orchestration. However, Mouret, who himself came from Provence, definitely made an effort to evoke the traditional music of his homeland in the entrée he added in 1722, "La Provençale." The sailors' songs and dances have not only a celebratory function, they help convince the ingénue that she is actually beautiful: her guardian, who wants to marry her himself, has kept her isolated and made her believe she is so ugly that no one else would have her. In their efforts to support her young suitor, the sailors couch two of their songs in Provençal – the first time this language had been heard from the stage of the Opéra. A da capo aria, sung in Italian but whose melodic style bears some kinship to a French dance-song, makes a gesture toward the *galoubet* in its obbligato parts for two *petites flûtes*. Both a menuet and a rigaudon are annotated with the word "tambourin," which here means not a dance type but a sonority: either the drum alone is expected to play along, or the little flutes and the drum together. In addition, the the table of "Airs à jouer" for this entrée reveals that "the tambourin plays with the orchestra in all of the airs of the divertissement." The dance-types Mouret chose may be common to other *fêtes marines*, but the sound world was central to his characterization of the sailors of Provence.

The other two original entrées in *Les Fêtes de Thalie* both feature divertissements that were established topoi: the village wedding and the masked ball. "La Veuve" exists in two versions, one in which the widow is torn between love for her dead husband and a new suitor, and another in which she is delighted to have the freedom to flirt as she pleases, but in both cases the village wedding is organized by a suitor attempting to get her in the mood for marriage. Like nautical divertissements, village weddings could appear in any kind of opera, shaded appropriately for their environment. But wherever they were used, most eighteenth-century village weddings featured at least two types of dancing roles: shepherds and shepherdesses on the one hand, and herdsmen or peasants (*pâtres* or *paysans*) on the other. By and large the comic peasants would be given only one or two dances within the divertissement, whereas the shepherds not only danced more, they would be supplemented by singing shepherds.

Here, however, the dancers are identified as peasants, in addition to the bridal couple and their parents. Following the entrance march, there must have been at least one duet for each of the three peasant couples; the parents' dances probably made them look out of date and ridiculous – the iconography of theatrical village elders in old-fashioned finery suggests as much. The bridal pair danced a loure – probably in a higher style, given that David Dumoulin played the groom. Among the eight instrumental dances in the 1720 score there are two pieces identified as an "Air paysan"; other dance pieces include two menuets, a musette, and a cotillon.[12] The two peasant dances are both in duple meter and share the characteristics of that style (Example 10-2; see also Chapter 12, p. 362). The high number of dances in this divertissement, sprinkled among

[12] There are numerous differences between the 1714 score – which has two supplements – and the one published in 1720; annotations in surviving copies show that many revisions to this divertissement occurred between the two publications. For the sake of simplicity, I have chosen to base my comments on the 1720 score.

Example 10-2: Mouret, *Les Fêtes de Thalie*, "Air paysan" from "La Veuve" (Paris: Ballard, 1714), 249.

the vocal pieces (including, in one version, an *ariette* for the merry widow), offers plenty of scope for variety of groupings and affects, both silly and sober.

The third entrée, "La Femme," is set at a masked ball – probably in France, but it might as well be Venice, even to the inclusion of a chaconne and a forlana. Caliste has decided to test her husband by disguising herself sufficiently to make him think she is someone else, and then making him fall in love with her disguised self.[13] She succeeds; when she unmasks, he laughs and says that Love must be watching over them. She finds it wiser to join his laughter than to reproach him.

The exposition of Caliste's plan happens before the ball starts, but it plays out against the backdrop of the ball, whose structure promotes the development of the storyline. After the chorus that serves to bring everyone on stage, Dorante (the husband) invites the unknown beauty to dance. It is unambiguous that the two of them dance a menuet; in fact, there are two menuets at this point in the score. In distinction to the masked ball in *L'Europe galante* (Chapter 9, p. 268), the *didascalies* do not hint at the emotional content of their dancing, saying merely that "Dorante opens the ball with Caliste and dances with her. The Maskers dance afterwards." The logic of the storyline, however, suggests that they would have flirted while dancing. Mlle Journet was once again cast as the dancing singer; her husband was played by Thevenard.

The troupe of costumed merrymakers then takes the stage, in a sequence of five dances that surround a comic scene in which the masked Dorine, Caliste's servant, decides to subject her own husband, Zerbin, to a similar marital test (with much less satisfactory results). Two "Airs pour les masques" and an "Air espagnol" precede their

13 Although the plot is not the same, the testing of a spouse is common to "Le Bal interrompu," an entrée added by Campra to *Les Fragments de Lully*, as are comic servants named Zerbin and Dorine. As Fajon points out (*L'Opéra à Paris*, 260), "these cruel games that ultimately have a happy ending make one think – in a curious twist – of Marivaux, whose collaborator Mouret was to become at the Théâtre Italien a few years later."

exchange, the forlane and chaconne follow it; these seem in line both with the display dances done at masked balls and with the comic scene they surround. Only three of the sixteen dancers are named in particular roles – Arlequin, Arlequine, and a *pagode* – although there must have been someone in a Spanish outfit, unless the "Air espagnol" should have been labeled "Air chinois." Wherever the *pagode* appeared, he would certainly have done a comic dance, given the character type and the dancer (Pierre Dumoulin). Arlequin and Arlequine probably danced in the chaconne, and the solo masker, danced by Mlle Prévost, may have done the forlane.[14]

On the heels of the chaconne – which, if it was danced by Arlequin and Arlequine means at the height of the zaniness – Dorante leads the still masked Caliste to the front of the stage and continues his protestations of love. After making him squirm through a series of leading questions about his marital state, she unmasks, and when he quick-wittedly says he is delighted to see his wife in the position of her own rival, she chooses to laugh along. The ball resumes, but now in a much different mode, not with carnivalesque display, but with expressions of togetherness. That, at least, is the implication of the choice of dances: two passepieds (generally group dances) and a contredanse. The contredanse (Example 10-3) was still a relative newcomer to the operatic stage, and this one is intertwined with a musically identical chorus to end both the divertissement and the entrée,[15] in the manner of the ending to an *opéra comique*. The jolly tune in time has only four bars in each strain, but could have been repeated as many times as needed to suit the figures of the choreography. It is followed by the first strophe of the chorus ("Let us amuse ourselves, the ball offers charming pleasures; everything enchants us, the sweetest pleasures gratify our desires"), a repeat of the contredanse, and, to end, the second strophe of the chorus. In the instrumental dance and on the second refrain of the chorus, all of the dancers available must have been in motion, in order to end with the requisite degree of splendor. Whereas a chorus is normal to end a work, the structure of this one, interwoven with a contredanse, must have made the audience feel as if they were at the Foire Saint-Germain rather than across the Seine in the Palais-Royal.

Whether or not such blatant structural references to practices from outside the Opéra were part of the problem, the criticisms leveled against this work led La Font to defend it in an amusing "Critique" he penned after the first two months of performances. The "Critique" returns the scene to the stage of the Opéra, where Polymnie and Thalie are in the middle of an argument over the merits of the music and the text,

[14] Here and elsewhere I have spoken as if a single set of dancers was responsible for an entire dance, but as shown in Ch. 4, the number of dancers may vary within a single dance. The eighteenth-century evidence of this practice is discussed in Ch. 14, p. 437ff.

[15] My comments are based on the 1720 score. One of the 1714 librettos has Thalie return to boast about her triumph, with a celebratory chorus in her honor in lieu of the contredanse. I have made no attempt to sort out the different layers of changes to this work.

Example 10-3: Mouret, *Les Fêtes de Thalie*, "Contredanse" from "La Femme" (Paris: Ballard, 1714), 246.

which have been attacked by the followers of Apollon and Orphée. Each denigrates the other's work and defends her own. But they are interrupted by Terpsichore, who claims that the dance is the reason for the work's success. (Her text is cited on p. 206 in Chapter 7.) Whereas Terpsichore's sketchy remarks cannot be taken as a true *ars poetica*, she does make two claims on behalf of the dance: first, that it adds luster to the texts and music (i.e., that an opera requires all three arts); and second, that dance "paints," that its creations appeal both to the eye and to the heart. In other words, Terpsichore alludes, in a stripped-down version, to the theories of aestheticians such as Menestrier. Her sisters respond by saying her art is derivative, that her designs are always based on theirs. ("Pensez-vous que votre art l'emporte sur le nôtre? / Vous qui sur nos desseins, formez toujours le vôtre?") Terpsichore ignores this remark, and instead turns to vaunting the different styles of dancing she has just put on stage. Might her failure to challenge her sisters be read as tacit acknowledgement that, at the Opéra, the libretto and music would have been created before the choreography? This particular question does not easily lend itself to dramatization inside an opera, but it is nonetheless a provocative one, particularly since opera historians have sometimes implied or stated that the choreography – or at least the requirement for dances in every act – drove the composition of the music, not the other way around. The "Critique" does not answer the question of priority, and perhaps it is unanswerable, but La Font must have meant to allude to topical disputes.

The musical choices that Mouret made in the "Critique" draw upon conventions from outside the Académie Royale de Musique. When Terpsichore taunts her sisters about how essential dance is to the success of an opera, she is behaving like a performer from the fair theaters, by setting new words to a pre-existent tune. Moreover, she does so twice: the first tune she borrows is the "Deuxième Air paysan" from the end of the village wedding in "La Veuve," and her second song, in which she praises each of her three divertissements ("my sailors," "my ball," "my shepherds"), is set to the tune danced by the Algerian slaves in "La Fille."

> Dans tous ces traits, quelle beauté!
> Admirez-en le goût, la nouveauté.
> Mes pas de deux
> Sont charmants, sont heureux;
> Ceux de mes matelots,
> Sont des plus beaux.
> Mais dans mon bal,
> Tout est original.
> Dans tous ces traits, quelle beauté!
> Admirez-en le goût, la nouveauté.
> Dans mes bergers on a pu voir,
> Et mon savoir,
> Et quel est son pouvoir.
> C'est où mon art
> Brille sans fard,
> De ce dessein
> Tout paraît divin.
> Dans tous ces traits, quelle beauté!
> Admirez-en le goût, la nouveauté.

(In all these sketches, what beauty! Admire their tastefulness, their novelty! My pas de deux are charming and cheerful; my sailor dancers are exceptionally beautiful; but in my balls, everything is original. In all these sketches, what beauty! Admire their tastefulness, their novelty! My shepherds show off my skill and its power. There my art shines without artifice; everything in this design appears divine. In all these sketches, what beauty! Admire their tastefulness, their novelty!)

In the first case Terpsichore puts words to what was, in its original location, an instrumental dance, but in the second she sets new words to a dance-song. (The

Algerian slaves' refrain was "Triomphe, Amour, de la beauté, / Qui nous rend aujourd'hui la liberté." – "Triumph, Love, over the beautiful woman who today gives us our liberty.") She also exhibits affinities with performers from the popular theaters in that, according to a *didascalie*, she dances as well as sings. It is certainly to be expected that Terpsichore would dance, but the question is to which music, as the scene has only a few untexted bars (i.e., the four-bar introduction to her second song). Whereas Terpsichore might have danced while she sang, that seems unlikely, in that even at the fair theaters, alternation of singing and dancing seems to have been the general practice.[16] Moreover, the words to these two songs matter to the "plot" of the "Critique," so would need to be delivered without the distraction of added movement. Mlle Isecq, who in 1714 was cast in the role of Terpsichore, was a dancer; this seems to have been the only opera in which she sang.[17] Terpsichore must have danced enough in this scene to validate her claims on behalf the dance. The most plausible option is that one or both of her songs were also performed instrumentally, since they began life as dances.[18]

Les Fêtes de Thalie may have aroused opposition, but it remained popular, with revivals of the whole in 1722 (when "La Provençale" was added), 1735, 1746, and 1754, and with pieces of it, especially "La Provençale," revived multiple times up until 1778. Notwithstanding the enduring success of this and other works of a comic cast, comedy on the stage of the Opéra remained contested. One comic work, *Les Amours de Mars et de Vénus* (by Campra and Danchet), was even banned after 14 performances in 1712.[19] When Fuzelier wrote the libretto for the *Ballet des âges* in 1718, he appended a defensive apologia for its comic character: "This ballet will show that I believe that Thalie has as many rights over music as does Melpomène. I will not provide a long dissertation proving that the comic genre is not incompatible with the beauties of harmony. If the *Ballet des âges* amuses the public, my enterprise is justified [. . .] I know that I risk displeasing those sad voluptuaries who love only solemn pleasures [. . .] [but] I will easily console myself from their sharpest disapproval if the public does not adopt it." Four years later, "La Provençale" provoked disapproval over language deemed too "true" by those who thought that humor should be communicated only in a

[16] See Ch. 2, n. 53, which includes examples of alternation from such theaters.

[17] According to Lecomte (private communication) the only Mlle Isecq at the Opéra was Marie-Louise, who danced there between 1710 and 1717.

[18] Such questions cannot be answered until the revisions made to the very complex musical and textual sources are sorted out. When the "Critique" was added, much of the divertissement that had ended "La Femme" migrated to the new spot, including the intertwined chorus and contredanse. The libretto printed in the *Recueil général* includes the "Critique" and does not match the 1714 libretto in several places.

[19] Parfaict, *Histoire*, II, 6, says only that "The respect owed to the wishes of sovereigns excuses us from entering into detail about this work, which was suppressed by the authorities after a small number of performances." The work aims most of its barbs at the cuckolded Vulcain.

roundabout manner, via the rhetorical figure of periphrasis (circumlocution). This attack galvanized the *Mercure de France* into defending the overt expression of the comic on the stage of the Académie Royale de Musique:

> It is said that the comic on the operatic stage requires circumlocution ("un tour periphrasé"). What prejudice! This deserves a formal response, and this author, who takes issue with this perspective, intends to publish an essay on the topic of "the comic in opera." He will first explain what the comic is in general, what its nature is, and that it is sometimes found in a word, or even a syllable, that cannot be periphrased without losing what is called the *vis comica*. After that he will turn to the first expression of the comic in opera, which is found in *Pomone* and in *Les Peines et les plaisirs de l'Amour*;[20] he will then speak of the comic that is found in the early operas of Quinault, of the periphrased comic of those that followed, and finally of the comic that is simple and without baseness that has followed the others. But to respond in advance to those who want circumlocution, the author says to them that they may want whatever they like, but that *Versibus exponi tragicis res comica non vult* ["a subject for comedy refuses to be handled in tragic verse"].[21]

Four years after this spirited defense, however, another preface reveals that the conservative forces had acquired the upper hand. As librettist Roy wrote in the preface to his opera-ballet *Les Stratagèmes de l'Amour* of 1726 (music by Destouches), "The public has decided that if this theater permits the comic, it may only be a noble type of comic, like one that reflects the character of antiquity. We have thus sought our themes in [ancient] history . . . "

It is curious that the retreat from the comic at the Opéra began right around the time that the libertine Philippe d'Orléans, regent for the five-year-old who had become king in 1715, invited a troupe of Italian comedians back to Paris. The Duc d'Orléans, an Italophile and a patron of music,[22] sought out a troupe almost as soon as Louis XIV died; the new Théâtre Italien opened its doors in May of 1716, under the leadership of Luigi Riccoboni, known by his stage name, Lélio. For its first seven years, the Italian troupe even shared the theater in the Palais-Royal with the Académie Royale de Musique, performing on alternate nights. The arrival of the new troupe changed the dynamic of the Parisian theatrical scene yet again; whether the Opéra's damping down of comedy owes anything to its return is a question that remains to be fully explored.[23] But even if the creation of works incorporating the comic became less frequent, Arlequin and his cohorts did not

[20] These pastorales were the first two works put on the stage of the Opéra, in 1671 and 1672, before Lully took over.

[21] *MF* (September 1722), 175–79. The author of this passage was probably Fuzelier, co-editor of the *Mercure* at the time. To my knowledge, he never published the announced work. The quotation in Latin comes from Horace's *Ars poetica* (89), its translation from Kraemer, *The Complete Works of Horace* (New York: The Modern Library, 1936), 400.

[22] Regarding the duke's patronage of music, see Montagnier, *Un Mécène musicien*, 36–56.

[23] Laurenti, *Valeurs morales et religieuses*, 175, places the retreat from hedonistic works, of which the comic formed a part, in the context of the collapse of John Law's financial system in 1720.

disappear; revivals kept them before the eyes of a public that had not lost its taste for humor (see Appendix 1). As late as 1730 the *Mercure* testified to the continuing appeal of one of the Italianate works, writing of the revival of *Le Carnaval et la Folie* that "the third act has always been applauded, especially the divertissement, 'Le Professeur de folie,' which always seems fresh, even though it has often been detached from this ballet in order to adorn other ones."[24]

THE REALM OF THE *HÉROÏQUE*

Following the death of Lully, an ever increasing number of works performed at the Opéra occupied a middle ground between tragedy and the frank comedy of *Les Fêtes de Thalie*. In fact, many of the works bearing the generic marker "ballet," whether they took the form of opera-ballet or had a plot worked out over several acts, were mixed in tone. After the Opéra turned away from the creation of comic works, such ballets tended to be qualified as "héroïque," a term that, as Masson explained in 1928, had broad application. Works could be dubbed "héroïque" because of "the presence of 'heroes,' divinities, spirits, mythological characters, or sometimes even historical figures. But [the designation] may also result from the nature of the action itself, if it involves violent episodes that recall the moments of crisis in classical tragedy." The "heroism" thus resides either in the characters or in the situations – or often, the two together.[25]

As is so often the case in French operatic history, the practice goes back to Lully, who called his last work, *Acis et Galatée*, a *pastorale héroïque*.[26] Over the years, a few other pastorales received the same designation: *Coronis* (1691), *Issé* (1697), and *Le Jugement de Pâris* (1718). The first ballet to be so dubbed was Fuzelier and Collin de Blamont's *Les Fêtes grecques et romaines* (1723) and many others followed. In the vast majority of cases, works qualified as "héroïque" are situated in the realm of mythology or ancient history; *Les Indes galantes* of Rameau (1735) marks a notable exception. Such works do not necessarily eschew the comic altogether, but overall the tone is more moderate than in the works set in contemporary times – discretion has replaced frankness – and, once again, it is in the divertissements where more freedom is permitted.

Les Fêtes grecques et romaines (1723)

In the long preface he published with the libretto of *Les Fêtes grecques et romaines*, Fuzelier claimed that the work:

[24] *MF* (July, 1730), 1628.

[25] As Masson points out ("Le 'ballet héroïque,'" 134–35), a work labeled "ballet héroïque" could either be an opera-ballet or have a continuous plot. In his view, some of the latter should more appropriately be called "pastorale héroïque."

[26] Lully also identified some of the dancers in *Le Triomphe de l'Amour* (1681) as "bergers héroïques."

> Is of an entirely new kind. The lyric Muse has, until the present, drawn her stories only from the chronicles of Amadis, of Ariosto, the *Metamorphoses* of Ovid, from Tasso, and other similar authors. France has only set myths to music; the more adventuresome Italy has put historical events into its operas. Scarlattis and Buononcinis have given song to the heroes that Corneille and Racine had speak. Emboldened by these examples, we have dispensed with searching through the all-too-often harvested fields of mythology and legend. We will count ourselves fortunate if we find approval in opening to librettists a path worthy of engaging the spirits of the lovers of verisimilitude.
>
> In this ballet we have assembled the best known of the fêtes of antiquity – the ones that seemed best suited to the theater and to music. We have mixed them together under the name of "Greek and Roman Fêtes," because in practice Rome took over all the gods from Athens. We have taken care to attach to these famous fêtes illustrious adventures and personages.

Fuzelier goes on to explain the choice of fêtes and of historical figures for each entrée: Alcibiades in "Les Jeux olympiques," Mark Antony and Cleopatra in "Les Bacchanales," and the Roman poet Tibullus, along with the object of some of his poems, Délie, in "Les Saturnales." Fuzelier's claim to novelty was, however, disingenuous. He himself had put the historical figures of the Roman poet Ovid and Julia, granddaughter of Augustus Caesar, on stage ten years earlier in his opera-ballet *Les Amours déguisés*. Moreover, as Pierre Mathieu de Chassiron was to point out a few years later, the historical figures in this opera behave no differently than do other operatic heroes: "The fatal necessity is imposed on them of being perpetually in love."[27] It is perhaps then no surprise that the *Mercure* made nothing special of the new work, beyond mentioning that the subjects came from history.[28] Notwithstanding Fuzelier's prognosis, French librettists did not follow the example of Italian *opera seria* in pursuing subjects from ancient history for their *tragédies en musique*. In France, the occasional foray into the realm of historical people remained the purview of ballet, where, in practice, a fête based around a figure from antiquity does not behave very differently from a fête built around a figure from the same antiquity's mythology. The main difference is that a historical work loses access to the *merveilleux*, as Fuzelier points out at the end of his preface, but as even in mythological works the *merveilleux* is not necessarily invoked in every act, the differences are less drastic than they might seem.

Fuzelier does appear to have wanted to introduce at least a modestly comic sensibility into this work. Even in the preface he points out that the first entrée, "The Olympic Games," shows Alcibiades in the role of philanderer: "This accurate portrait of the fickleness of Alcibiades will perhaps not displease the unfaithful in our own age; they will not be annoyed to find a model for themselves in respectable antiquity." Fuzelier did not choose to point out that by highlighting infidelity, he was

[27] Chassiron, *Réflexions sur les tragédies en musique* (1749), cited in Kintzler, *Poétique*, 342.

[28] *MF* (July 1723), 134–47, as quoted in Masson, "Le 'ballet héroïque,'" 136.

borrowing a well-worn theme from earlier opera-ballets. However, he did acknowledge pressure from those who did not share his view and who apparently had influence over his librettos: "As for the entrée 'Saturnalia,' we have not filled it with the comic that is authorized by the liberty of this fête. Certain respectable critics maintain that amusing situations are out of place on the operatic stage. Practice has not always upheld this opinion, but since this view favors the nobler conception, we thought it necessary to adhere to it in a libretto devoted to history."

The three entrées do maintain decorum – even Alcibiades' flightiness is couched in elevated language – but there are hints that the divertissements might have aimed for a freer tone. And even though all three divertissements come at the end of the entrée, as diegetic fêtes, each has distinguishing dramaturgical features: one of them introduces a main character for the first time, a second provides dramatic weight that is needed to round off the situation, and only the third seems primarily decorative.

In "Les Jeux olympiques" the character who arrives only at the end is Aspasie, Alcibiades' new love interest. The first four scenes lay out the feelings of the rejected Timée and the carelessness with which Alcibiades treats her. In Scene 5, Aspasie's official role is to crown Alcibiades for having won the chariot race (which took place before the opera starts), but it is also essential that she make it clear why she is now the sweetheart of the moment. (No one, not even Aspasie, hints that the relationship is likely to last.) Aspasie therefore gets to sing three songs, a high number for a main character inside a divertissement. Alcibiades responds to her first one, and a Greek woman also has a solo song, but Aspasie is the main event. This then begs the question of how her music fits with the dances, and the answer is partly textural. She does not arrive with the march that brings in the chorus and the male dancers (Greek spectators and athletes), but makes a special entrance later with her female followers during a danced rondeau whose internal couplets are attributed to a high trio (flutes on the two upper parts, violin on the functioning bass). This sonority, which characterizes her first and third songs, was becoming common during this period for some female characters. Aspasie's middle song – a simple Lullian extended binary air – is highlighted in a different way, by being surrounded by a dance for two wrestlers. The text alludes to the benefits accruing to lovers who let warriors capture the public glory, which nods in an oblique way toward her role as the person who crowned Alcibiades. After that, the attention turns away from her temporarily, during the song by the Greek woman and three dances, before she returns to center stage to sing a song that expands into the concluding chorus.

The two dances for athletes – one for two wrestlers and the other for two runners – are the only vehicles in this entrée for invoking the physicality of the Olympic games. But as Cahusac indignantly pointed out, there is a problem of verisimilitude, because the actual sporting events are already over when the curtain goes up. "In an inconceivably wrong-headed act, a match between two wrestlers as part of Olympic games that are already over was nonetheless the danced action [*action de danse*] that was performed. I must say, however, that the attraction of the moment won out over the usual judiciousness of the audience; all of Paris applauded a misinterpretation that a moment's reflection demonstrates to be absurd."[29] Cahusac's objection makes sense only if the dance was intended to represent a real wrestling match, not a ritualized combat. The libretto reveals nothing beyond the place-holding "on danse," so Cahusac's allusion to this piece as "action" at least tells us how it was perceived; presumably his remark applies equally to the foot race that occurs later in the divertissement. But a staged wrestling match is not the same as the real thing and it happens that the first ten bars of a choreography for this piece are preserved in Beauchamps-Feuillet notation – not in one of the collections of theatrical dances, but in a plate accompanying the article "Chorégraphie" in the *Encyclopédie* (Figure 10-1).[30]

The notation does not show the choreography from 1723, when it was danced by Blondy and Marcel, but from 1733, 1734, or 1741, when Dupré and Javilliers *l'aîné* filled the roles of the two wrestlers; both pairs of dancers were among the stars of their era. Pierce and Thorp have pointed out that this choreography "has many elements of an 'ordinary' dance: simple steps, such as *pas de bourrée* or *pas grave*; complicated steps, including *caprioles, assemblés battus en tournant*; and symmetrical spatial patterns, beginning and ending in mirror symmetry."[31] In other words, whatever the imitation of wrestling involved, it was done within the context of recognizable steps for the feet. Yet the commentary in the *Encyclopédie* article, which aims to explain the notational symbols in words, does confirm what Cahusac's comments suggest, that more was involved than performing the steps properly: at the point where the notation shows the two men taking hands, Goussier remarks that "the right hand of dancer A takes the left hand of the other dancer, simulating the effort that two wrestlers make in trying to overturn their adversary." This must be just one instance of the ways in which actions of the upper body inflected the notated steps. If "all of Paris applauded," and if Cahusac was moved to object to the location of this wrestling match within the opera, then the artifice involved in its performance must have made the representation of action convincing.

The music for both wrestlers and runners aims to characterize the roles and the movement: the wrestlers move to heavy half and quarter notes in regular rhythms (see Example 10-4), the runners to scalar eighth notes marked "Vite." They offer a marked contrast both to the women's dance at the start of the divertissement, during which Alcibiades was crowned, and to the two passepieds that come near the end, probably danced by the group of Greek men and women. The four athletes probably performed

[29] Cahusac, *La Danse*, III, 158–61.

[30] Goussier's article "Chorégraphie" appeared in Vol. III of the *Encyclopédie*, 367–73; the two plates were published in Vol. III of the plates.

[31] "The dances in Lully's *Persée*," par. 3.23.

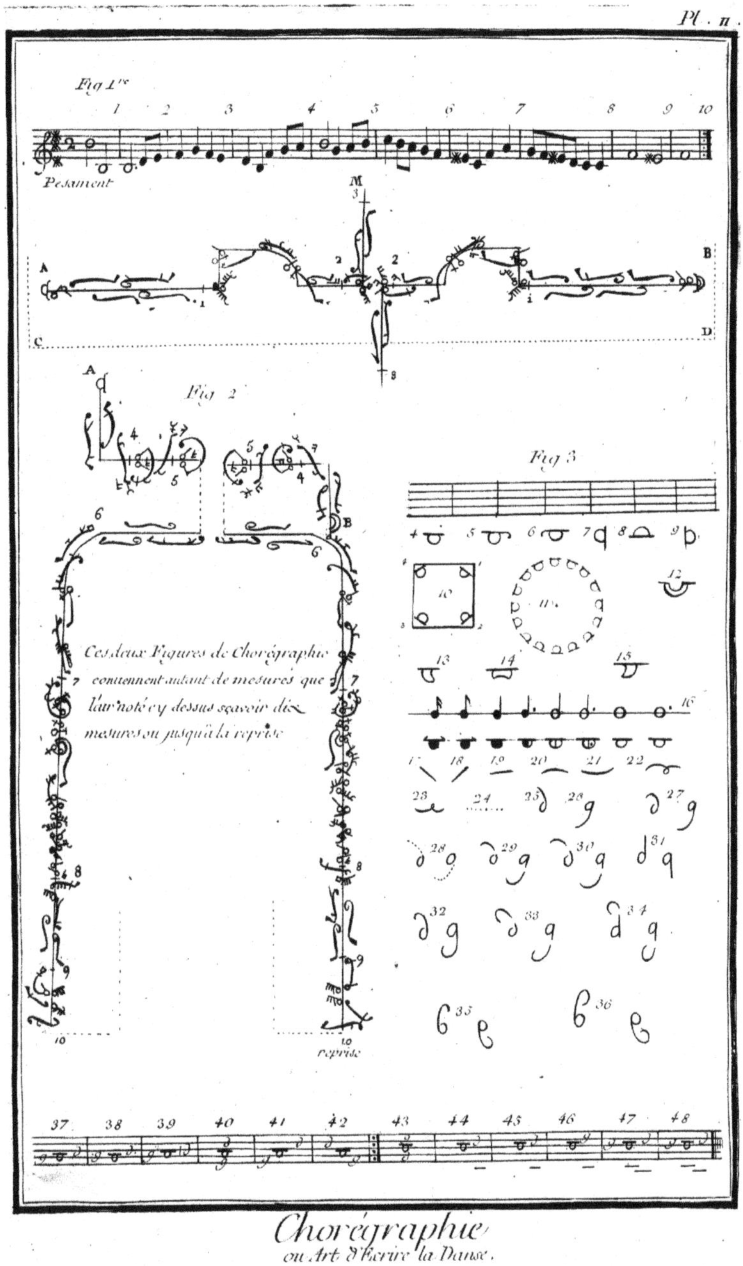

Figure 10-1: Plate from the *Encylopédie* accompanying Goussier's article "Chorégraphie." "These two figures of dance notation [figs. 1 and 2] contain as many measures as the tune notated above, that is, the ten measures of the first strain." Fig. 3 shows symbols for Favier notation.

Example 10-4: Collin de Blamont, *Les Fêtes grecques et romaines*, "Air pour les Lutteurs" (Paris: Ballard, 1723), 53.

only during their respective events; it seems unlikely that they would have participated in the celebrations honoring Alcibiades that conclude the entrée. The wrestlers' dance remained a highlight of this opera-ballet; the *Mercure* reports that when the work was revived in 1753 with one of the entrées replaced part way through the run by Rameau's *Pygmalion*, the choice of which entrée to delete was made "most probably in order to retain the dance for the wrestlers, better choreographed by M. Lani than it has ever been done before and admirably executed by Messieurs Vestris and Lyonnois."[32]

The fête invoked in the next entrée is a bacchanale, planned as part of Cleopatra's strategy to seduce Mark Antony. It is apparently no secret that Mark Antony's favorite god is Bacchus; Cleopatra understands this before she meets him. She makes a dramatic entrance on a boat floating down the river Cydnus, surrounded by Egyptians dressed as Graces, Cupids, Bacchantes, and Aegipans (the male analogue of Bacchantes), and accompanied by the sounds of alternating strings and oboes. But Mark Antony no sooner sets eyes on her than he falls in love, with a rapidity that surprises even Cleopatra. The fête is thus not needed for its original purpose, but Cleopatra decides to offer it anyhow, calling upon her followers to "finish our interrupted games," after she has coyly accepted Mark Antony's proffered love.

The decision to locate the divertissement at the end of the entrée, rather than earlier as part of the seduction, seems surprisingly undramatic. Time for a costume change cannot have been the rationale, since the dancers arrive on the boat that follows Cleopatra's. But what *is* needed is more musical weight; the dialogue, mostly in recitative, needs to be balanced by more "sung" pieces. Here again, the two main characters participate in the fête. In fact, the centerpiece of the divertissement is a duet for the two lovers and a showy *ariette* for Cleopatra ("Brillez, jouissez de la paix").[33] These two pieces are separated by a musically independent gigue, which may have been danced by the female dancer in the role of Youth.[34] Presumably because the fête

32 *MF* (August, 1753), 169.

33 This opera premiered in July of 1723. The *Mercure de France* reported in its October issue (774) that a new "cantate" had been added to the end of this divertissement for Mlle Antier in the role of Cleopatra.

34 The dancing cast consisted of la Jeunesse; a solo Aegypan, who may have served as her partner; six Bacchantes; six more Aegipans; a mixed couple of unnamed roles (probably a Bacchante and an

was intended to enhance seduction, despite being in honor of Bacchus, the Bacchantes and Aegipans are completely tame: there are no references in the text either to frenzy or to the pleasures of drink, and their music is gentle. If there was any attempt to inflect the sweetness of the atmosphere via Bacchante actions of the more usual type, the loure seems the only possible place – certainly not the menuets interwoven with the chorus "Régnez charmants Amours." In his preface Fuzelier mentioned that the Saturnalia had been tamed, and the Bacchanale seems to have suffered the same fate.

The third entrée, "Les Saturnales," involves disguises, both in the story and in the divertissement. Fuzelier explains in his preface that "the dialogues of Lucian tell us that everything may be forgiven during this indulgent holiday and that slaves may risk with impunity familiarities that would be punishable at other times of year." In the first part of the entrée he puts a reverse spin on this tradition by having the Roman poet Tibullus disguise himself as a slave, in order to woo a young relative of the rich Maecenas, Délie. This is the same basic storyline as "Le Bal" in *Les Fêtes vénitiennes*, where the Polish prince traded places with his valet to make sure he was loved for himself, only this time there are no sparring music and dance masters to liven things up. Délie figures out the ruse right away and spends the middle of the entrée making "Arcas" think she has another sweetheart, until she finally confesses that Tibulle is the one she loves. The slot occupied by the masked ball in "Le Bal" is here filled by the Saturnalia, which, since the entrée is set in the garden of Maecenas's country house, takes the form of a pastoral divertissement, complete with shepherds who sing to the sounds of their musettes, just as if they had wandered in from a French *bergerie*.

There are two hints that more may have gone on visually than the pastoral texts suggest. First, Fuzelier makes a point of explaining, both in his preface and in the *didascalie* that opens Scene 3, that Saturnalia was the "fête de la bougie," the holiday of candles. The scene therefore was spectacularly lit by candles set in freestanding candelabras and in the topiary sculptures of the on-stage garden. Candles, of course, create shadows, and one of the songs hints that the play of light and dark might have allowed for certain freedoms: "De nos boccages / Fuyez les ombrages, / Vous qui ne connaissez que l'éclat de la cour. / De nos boccages / Fuyez les ombrages, / Nous n'offrons dans nos bois de l'encens qu'à l'Amour." The second hint comes in the list of dancers, who include, in addition to fifteen shepherds and shepherdesses, four "slaves disguised in the clothes of their masters." Their presence is also underlined by a *didascalie* in the 1723 libretto (although not found in the *Recueil général*): "The shepherds and shepherdesses celebrate the age of Saturn in their dances, and the miming slaves come wearing the clothes of their masters to mingle in the fête." The master–slave role reversal must have been visible to the audience and might well have lent itself to

Aegipan), who must have danced a *pas de deux*; and two Cupids. These last were seated at Cleopatra's feet when she arrived on the boat, but may have danced as well.

comic – or even satiric – treatment, but nothing in the score or libretto indicates where the four slaves might have danced. The seven instrumental dances all have generic titles only: marche, musette, bourrée, two menuets, and two more musettes. The musettes are by definition pastoral, and the bourrée and one of the menuets are connected via musical similarities to songs by a shepherdess, so none of the dance pieces stands definitively outside the pastoral realm. (Might the slaves have used the second menuet as a vehicle for caricaturing their masters?) The casting of François Dumoulin as a soloist suggests that he was brought in to do his comic peasant routine, and such a dance (or dances) would provide a second change in tone from the prevailing celebration of an idyllic golden age. Fuzelier's preface to the libretto shows that he was chafing under the anti-comedy pressures then prevailing at the Opéra; on the surface his texts stay within narrow bounds, but they could lend themselves to nuanced interpretations. And from the dance perspective, perhaps the realization of the opera allowed for greater latitude than the texts alone suggest.

In the three entrées of *Les Fêtes grecques et romaines* the dances are framed in conventional ways and draw upon standard dance types, but in the prologue dance has an entirely different function. Because this work broke new ground (or claimed to do so) by building stories around actual historical figures, Fuzelier followed the well-worn path of justifying his procedures in a prologue featuring the Muses. A dialogue between Clio (Muse of history) and Erato (here presented as the Muse of music) quickly lays out the grounds for justifying history rather than myth as the basis for an opera. Apollon then comes to set his stamp of approval on the historical enterprise, but he stays to insist that the two sisters can't do without yet another Muse, Terpsichore. The rest of the prologue turns into a showpiece for Terpsichore, one aimed at highlighting the expressive range of the dance. The complex of works in which this innovative prologue participates is discussed in Chapter 13.

La Reine des Péris (1725)

Two years after *Les Fêtes grecques et romaines*, Fuzelier tried varying the repertoire in another direction. This time he set his story in a mythologized Near East and dubbed his new work, *La Reine des Péris*, a "comédie persane." In a sense this is a *pastorale héroïque* transported to an exotic locale, but even if the work adheres to many familiar conventions, its Persian ambience was something new.[35] (Ten years later Fuzelier was to write a "Fête persane" into *Les Indes galantes*, set to music by Rameau.) As was his

[35] Kintzler, *Poétique*, 314–16, debates whether this work should be classified as a tragedy or a *pastorale héroïque* and settles on the latter. Fuzelier's choice of a Persian theme might have been influenced by the vogue for Montesquieu's *Lettres persanes* (1721).

habit, Fuzelier wrote a preface to explain his procedure: "The public will judge, on the basis of this new work, whether the mythology of the Orient deserves a place on our stages alongside Greek and Roman mythology." His source for the Persian myths was an encyclopedic survey by Barthélemy d'Herbelot, the *Bibliothèque orientale, ou dictionnaire universel contenant tout ce qui regarde la connoissance des peuples de l'Orient*, first published in 1697. According to d'Herbelot, Fuzelier explains, Péris are good spirits; their negative counterparts are called Dives, who can be chased away "by the delicious scent of perfumes, the ordinary nourishment of the Péris." Fuzelier does not say so in his preface, but it becomes clear in the opera that both types of spirit have magical powers (Péris can fly), which means that Fuzelier's story could access the *merveilleux*. Notwithstanding his reliance on a scholarly source, Fuzelier 's treatment of geography is fluid: the main characters come from Syria, Egypt, Arabia, and the mythological Ginnistan (where the opera is set), and dancers in various divertissements are said to be Indian, Arab, Japanese, Chinese, and European. The music, composed by violinist Jacques Aubert, makes few attempts to characterize places of origin.

The storyline bears some resemblance to stories of the generous Turk, although it is a female sovereign who overcomes her internal conflicts to make a noble gesture. The queen of the Péris (who never gets a name) falls in love with the mortal Nouredin, caliph of Egypt, who has washed up on her shores. (In a comic subplot, her confidante, Selina, instantly gets involved with Nouredin's companion Ali, an Arabian prince.) The queen learns that Nouredin is still nurturing his love for Fatime, the princess of Syria, even though she has mysteriously disappeared. The queen thus tries indirect methods to win his affections, hoping that separation from the object of his love and the natural beauties of her own kingdom will overcome his memories. But a good genie rescues Fatime from the bad genie who had kidnapped her, and brings her to the queen's realm. Before realizing that the young woman is her rival, the queen promises to protect her. Bound to honor her oath, the queen resorts to magic to try to sway Nouredin's affections, but in vain. Moved at last by the pair's constancy, the queen overcomes her own desires and reunites them. The two pairs of lovers fly off in a Chinese chariot, back to Syria.

Because this is a five-act work, the divertissements have a chance to inflect the main characters in various interesting ways. The first features sailors, who are delighted to find themselves shipwrecked in such a beautiful place and whose attention to love highlights both Ali's crush on Selina and the queen's passion for Nouredin. The seven dances include two tambourins (a dance by now standard in nautical divertissements), and Ali sings a joyful *ariette*. The most interesting piece is the chorus, "Grondez Aquilons furieux," in which Italianate violin figuration represents the fury of the winds that the sailors no longer fear. In Act II Nouredin's participation in a hunt makes the queen think he is avoiding her. The hunters, led by Ali, are ignorant of the tensions, and joyously sing to the sound of the horn – this being an early instance of the use of the horn in the orchestra of the Opéra.[36] The dancers, identified in the libretto as "Chasseurs indiens," are all men. The third divertissement is designed to show off the queen's power, which is to be measured, says Selina, by her ability to provide a fête by imported European shepherds in the heart of Asia. Musically, this pastoral divertissement is indistinguishable from one set in Arcadia, with the exception of the forlane. This dance was no longer confined to Venetian settings, but it was generally given to maskers at some kind of ball (see Chapter 14, p. 424); this may be its first use in a pastoral setting. The forlane is the only dance in the divertissement that even gestures toward a world beyond France; one can only speculate as to why Fuzelier and Aubert eschewed the opportunity to feature the exotic in a divertissement that figures within the queen's realm.

One notable feature of all three of these divertissements – and of the one in Act IV – is that they have the same basic shape: entrance music followed by a chorus followed by a sequence of dances, some of them dance-songs, and often featuring a showy *ariette*, but with no further participation by the chorus after the opening. This pattern adheres even when the divertissements are framed as fêtes – which in this opera is always the case – and even when they end the act – as three out of the four of them do. The only divertissement in this entire work that is rounded off by the chorus is the one that concludes the opera – which is virtually obligatory, in that it offers the wishes of the collected Péris, as they see the four lovers off in their Chinese chariot. The diminished prominence of the chorus is striking: these divertissements have a very different inner architecture than do Lully's, even though the dancers and the choristers are still cast as members of the same group. This last marks a point of difference from some of the divertissements in the Venetian-themed works discussed above, where the dancers may have individual identities. But in both types of work, the balance between individual and group has undergone a metamorphosis: solo singing has gained in prominence at the expense of the choral. We cannot know if the danced portions of the divertissements helped redress the balance by favoring group dances over solos or *pas de deux*, but it does seem clear that the bond between chorus and dancers was decidedly weaker than it had once been.

Although it conforms to the pattern of the first three acts in regard to treatment of the chorus, the Act IV divertissement is otherwise completely different. The queen of the Péris has transported Nouredin to the Island of Inconstancy, where she hopes to make him forget Fatime. Perhaps because the queen wants so desperately to become the object of Nouredin's affections, she gives herself a starring role in the fête, by

36 Lully called for horns in the hunting scene of his comedy-ballet *La Princesse d'Élide* (1661). In "Les Jours de l'été," the second entrée in *Les Fêtes de l'été* by Montéclair (1716), horns are heard from off stage during a hunting scene; the score suggests substitute instruments, if horns are not available. Sadler ("Rameau and the orchestra," 61) reports that horns "are rarely mentioned in lists [of personnel] before 1759, and until then were normally played by supernumeraries."

Example 10-5: Aubert, *La Reine des Péris*, "Air chinois" (Paris: Boivin, 1725), 277.

singing what the score labels a "Cantate à l'honneur de l'Inconstance." At this point, Inconstancy herself makes a spectacular entrance, rising out of the sea on a chariot surmounted by a canopy carried by zephyrs. From here onwards the divertissement is pure dance; its sequence of eight instrumental dances in a row is contextualized in Chapter 13.

The last act of *La Reine des Péris* finally makes a musical nod in the direction of exoticism. After the Péris have routed the Dives, using perfume as their weapon, "the desert disappears and one sees a magnificent palace, built and decorated in Japanese style." When the Queen decides to unite the lovers, celebrations ensue, bringing together Péris, Arabs and . . . Chinese. In this relatively short divertissement of only four dances, two pieces are qualified as "Airs chinois"; the first, in particular, with its pairs of repeated eighth notes in both treble and bass (Example 10-5), aims to evoke a foreign character, albeit using a different musical vocabulary than the Chinese dance in *Le Carnaval de Venise* (Example 9-2, p. 277). The cast list in this libretto is less than precise, but probably the Chinese dancers consisted only of two men.[37] The other two dances – the entry march for the whole group and a dance-song for the Péris – were undoubtedly augmented by dancing during the concluding chorus. The two exotic dances were thus contained by conventional musical numbers whose character owes nothing to an imagined Persia. Notwithstanding the erudition to which Fuzelier had laid claim in his preface to the libretto, he did not put a fine point on cultural exactitude. The work is nonetheless interesting for the novelty of its setting and for its move in the Act IV divertissement in the direction of internal pantomime ballets.

NATURALIZING NOVELTY

In June of 1729 – more than half a century after its founding – the Académie Royale de Musique opened its stage for the first time to genuine Italian opera, sung in Italian by Italian performers. This anomalous sequence of performances was short-lived, but is

37 There are six women listed as followers of the queen, and all the men's names follow the heading of "Arabs": a soloist, six men, and two more men. These last two seem likeliest to have represented the Chinese, in that such a character dance would probably have been for one or two dancers.

noteworthy not only because it happened at all, but for the framing the Italian works received in order to naturalize them for Parisian audiences. *Serpilla e Baiocco* and *Don Micco e Lesbina* were both comic *intermezzi* performed by the same two singers, Rosa Ungarelli and Antonio Ristorini, who had been touring Europe with these works. In Italy and in other European countries where Italian opera was cultivated, the acts of each *intermezzo* would have been performed between the acts of an *opera seria*. In Paris the *intermezzo* was the main event, but since it was inconceivable for an evening at the Opéra to feature only two singers in one short work, something else had to be added. An account of the performance of *Serpilla e Baiocco* in the *Mercure de France* shows that notwithstanding the foreignness of the genre, the French aesthetic of integrating an opera and its divertissements prevailed, even if, in this instance, the mechanisms for doing so were out of the ordinary.[38]

Even before 1729 the idea of inviting Italian performers to the Opéra had been in the air. In April 1723 the *Mercure* had published a report on prospects for an Italian season later that year. Clearly the Opéra expected the novelty to draw in audiences:

> Some Italian singers from the Opera in London are set to come to Paris to give twelve performances during the course of July, in return for a large sum of money, which will be taken out of the box-office receipts. The surplus will serve as profit for the Académie Royale de Musique, which will suspend its own performances for the month. The Académie Royale de Musique will supply everything necessary for the Italians' performances: costumes, sets, choruses, ballets, instrumental music, etc. There are five people sharing the promised payment: two women, two *hautes-contre*, and one *concordant*. It is reported that the price of the tickets will go up by one third and that there will not be any free entries.[39]

The singers have been identified as leading lights of London's Royal Academy of Music: sopranos Francesca Cuzzoni and Margherita Durastanti, castrati Francesco Bernardi (Senesino) and Gaetano Berenstadt, and bass Giuseppe Boschi. They were to perform an *opera seria* by Bononcini, who was supposed to accompany them to Paris. Even though the negotiations advanced to the point where the performances were announced publicly, they never took place.[40] But it had been clear to everyone involved that an Italian *opera seria* would need to be Frenchified by the addition of dances and choruses before it could go on the stage of the Opéra. The negotiators in 1723 even chose someone for the job: Battistin Stuck, an Italian composer living in Paris, who by then had composed three operas for the Académie Royale de Musique (Chapter 12, p. 355).

[38] The account in the *Mercure* (June 1729, 1223–30 and 1401–03) provides a synopsis of both *intermezzi*, but only discusses the added divertissements for the first.

[39] *MF* (April 1723), 770–71.

[40] Regarding this failed attempt, see Lindgren, "Parisian patronage." One of the people involved in the negotiations was Luigi Riccoboni, head of the new Théâtre Italien, whose wife was the sister of Bononcini's wife.

In view of France's history of borrowing from Italian comic theater, it is not surprising that the imported operas were comic rather than serious. This was to be the case as well in the next two Italian incursions onto the stage of the Opéra: 1752–54, when performances by a visiting Italian troupe of Pergolesi's *La serva padrona* and other *intermezzi* touched off the War of the Buffoons, and again in 1778–80. But notwithstanding the more modest ambitions in 1729 over those for 1723, the same framing conditions prevailed: divertissements had to be added, performed by the members of the Opéra's own troupe. Although the *Mercure* does not spell out what was performed with *Serpilla e Baiocco*, it does suggest that the added divertissements drew from the repertoire of Italianate works that the Opéra had now been performing for three decades; in other words, just as in a French opera where the ballets were part of the work, an attempt was made to round out the evening with elements that, to the French, made sense with the *intermezzo*. On 7 June 1729 Parisian audiences were thus offered a genuine Italian opera surrounded by French interpretations of what Italian music and dance was like. The account below interleaves a shortened version of the synopsis as it appears in the *Mercure* with hypotheses about what the audience saw and heard during the divertissements.[41]

In lieu of an overture (*Serpilla e Baiocco* does not have one), the audience was treated to a performance of "sonates" – i.e., sonatas either Italian or in Italian style by a French composer, probably for the violin, and possibly performed by Jean-Pierre Guignon – or Giovanni Pietro Ghignone, to give him the name of his birth – who is mentioned as performing after Act II.

Act I: Baiocco comes home from a night of gambling, having lost everything including his sword, cloak, and watch. He knows his wife, Serpilla, will be furious, so he makes up a story about spending the night at a religious establishment and giving his possessions to the poor. She accuses him of selling them in order to gamble. He invites her to search his pockets, where she finds a deck of cards. She throws it at Baiocco's head, vowing to divorce him.

Divertissement I: a new *haute-contre*, Monsieur Dumas, sang three airs with the chorus.[42] His Venetian costume suggests that the pieces were probably drawn from the body of Venetian-themed works that had been in the Opéra's repertoire since 1697; in fact, the *Mercure* reports that the choruses were drawn from operas by Stuck and Campra, although it does not say which. In addition – and perhaps interleaved with the choruses – were solo dances by two stars of the dance troupe: one of the Dumoulin brothers (probably David) and Marie Sallé. They were probably also costumed in a Venetian manner, and although neither had performed Italian-inflected roles in the previous few years, the likely source works for their dance music – *Les Fêtes vénitiennes*, for instance – intermingle French and

[41] A more detailed exploration may be read in my article "Naturalizing novelty."

[42] Dumas had debuted in 1728 as Médor in *Roland*; *MF* (October 1728), 2283.

Italian styles to such a degree that their dancing could have featured either. One chorus by Campra that features a *haute-contre* as soloist is "Amor, amor te'l giuro a fe" from I/4 of *Le Carnaval de Venise*. It is preceded by a vénitienne (danced and then sung) and followed by a villanelle, so this unit could have offered music for the dancing as well. The divertissement was rounded off with more sonatas.

Act II: The scene is a courtroom. Baiocco has disguised himself as a magistrate, to whom Serpilla comes complaining about her husband. She is so vehement that Baiocco has difficulty hiding his anger. He has already revealed in a monologue that he is not convinced of his wife's virtue, so now as magistrate he imposes conditions for the divorce, one being that she yield to him. She is surprised, but agrees. The furious Baiocco reveals his identity; Serpilla tries to calm him, but without success. He forbids her ever to enter their house again.

Divertissement II: a similar mixture of dances and choruses prevailed as after the first act. Dumas sang airs "in a foreign language" (presumably da capo arias in Italian, of which there was a substantial supply in French opera), and Italian violinist Guignon played not only sonatas, but concertos – an Italian genre still new to France, although becoming assimilated. These concertos, however, might have been Italian imports, as Guignon had performed the "Spring" concerto from Vivaldi's *Four Seasons* at a Concert Français only a few months earlier.[43] Might it have been one of the crowd-pleasing works Guignon performed on this occasion?

The dances consisted of two solos for Mlle Camargo and a duet for Laval and Maltaire. All three had appeared together the year before in a revival of Gervais's *Hypermnestre*. Act II, Scene 4 includes a nautical divertissement in which there are two tambourins in a row, the first of which was danced as a solo by Camargo, the second as a duet for Laval and Maltaire; for the present occasion they could easily have donned gondolier costumes – all the more since the drum that gave the tambourin its name was, according to the gondolier entrée in *Les Fêtes vénitiennes*, "in use in Venice" – or, more to the point, in use in French representations of Venice. It seems plausible that Blondy, the current choreographer at the Opéra, would have taken advantage of pieces already in the troupe's repertoire. Mlle Camargo, a rising star, was known for lightness and technical virtuosity; the tambourin was to become one of her signature dances.

Act III: Serpilla, dressed as a pilgrim, is being forced to leave home, but has taken all the money she can find with her. Baiocco arrives and says he wants to kill her, but first he makes her return all the money. She begs forgiveness, arguing that he should feel ashamed that he has gambled away her dowry. He is unmoved. She then tries recalling their early love. This time he softens, but she uses gestures to let the audience know that she takes him for a fool. Their reconciliation is celebrated in a happy duet.

[43] Pierre, *Histoire du Concert Spirituel*, 237, and La Laurencie, *L'École française du violon*, 209.

Divertissement III: The *intermezzo* was rounded off with suitably comic songs and dances in the manner of the *comédie italienne.* Two of the Dumoulin brothers danced as Arlequin and Polichinelle; Mlle Roze, dressed as Arlequine, sang an *ariette* and the young Mlle Mariette danced "as her pupil in this genre." Mariette also danced a solo chaconne; it must have been of the comic variety. All these pieces might have been lifted from Campra's comic divertissement "Cariselli" (see Chapter 9, p. 284), which had been revived earlier in 1729: it contains an *ariette* for the Arlequine-like Vafrina, a role Mlle Roze had already sung;[44] dancing roles for Arlequin and Polichinelle, which had been incarnated by François and Pierre Dumoulin; and a comic chaconne.[45] Mlle Mariette, who had just joined the troupe in May, did become a soloist, dancing, for example, in the 1731 and 1740 revivals of *Les Fêtes vénitiennes* – in the latter as Arlequine. The solo dance by Monsieur Laval, which the *Mercure* does not describe, must have fit into the same theme. Although the *Mercure* does not say so, this divertissement probably ended with a rousing chorus, as was still the norm at the Opéra for any work with a happy ending.

What did the Opéra's audience make of this hybrid spectacle? The Parfaict brothers were later to claim later that "all Paris" greeted with pleasure the departure of the two "buffoons" and their replacement by Lully's *Roland.*[46] But the *Mercure* account praises both the *intermezzo* and its Franco-Italian frame, attributing the success of the former to the "precise and lively performance, notwithstanding the small amount of affinity it has with our usual operas."[47] The work garnered enough attention that, within days, the Théâtre Italien saw fit to parody *Serpilla e Baiocco*, as a scene within a play, *Les Débuts*, that made fun of aspiring actors trying out for the Italian troupe.[48] Parodying the performance was yet another way of naturalizing the work, by conceptualizing it within the normal patterns of reception.

Yet this anomalous performance also exhibits another type of reflection, one that had been visible intermittently on the Opéra's stage ever since Lully and regularly since Campra: a tonier mirroring of the already Frenchified rendering of the commedia dell'arte that Parisians knew from the Théâtre Italien and the fairs. The relationship that the Opéra established with Italy was indirect, mediated through the homegrown hybrid of the *comédie italienne.* Yet the impact of Italian theater and Italian music was crucial, in that it opened up a space for a comic realm that otherwise was kept at bay by

44 Mlle Roze sang the role of Vafrina at the premiere of "Cariselli" in 1702, but is not the singer listed for the revival in 1729.

45 The *Mercure* attributes the chaconne to "Signor Michel"; if that indicates not the choreographer but the composer, it could be Michele Mascitti, an Italian violinist living in Paris; see La Laurencie, *L'École française*, 134.

46 Parfaict, *Histoire*, II, 49–50. 47 *MF* (June 1729), 1223.

48 *MF* (July 1729), 1623–39; the text, which may be found in *Parodies du Nouveau Théâtre Italien* (Paris, 1738), IV, 183–202, bounces back and forth between Italian and French.

the rules of French classic theater. Even the low comedy of "Pourceaugnac" could be tolerated on the stage of the Opéra, provided the scatological humor resided in the mute bodes of the dancers and in texts that were not sung in French. Such a work was at the extreme remove from a *tragédie lyrique*; at the lofty Académie Royale de Musique Thalie only occasionally controlled an entire opera. Italy – especially the constructed fantasy version – could be allowed to inflect French opera, but it had to be contained. Once admitted to the circle of Muses who mattered to the management of the Opéra, Thalie could not be fully silenced, but her voice was not always heard above the din of competing interests at that complex institution.

11 | Melpomène, Muse of Tragedy

Théâtre de ma gloire, où règne l'harmonie,
Ne recevez des lois que de mon seul génie.
Mes sujets sont les rois, les héros et les dieux.
Rien ne peut égaler mes spectacles pompeux.
Théâtre de ma gloire, où règne l'harmonie,
Ne recevez des lois que de mon seul génie.
J'attendris par les sons, mes pleurs et mes soupirs.
Mes tragiques douleurs forment les vrais plaisirs.
Théâtre de ma gloire, où règne l'harmonie,
Ne recevez des loix que de mon seul génie.

Les Fêtes de Thalie, prologue

(Theater of my glory, where harmony reigns, receive your laws from my spirit alone. My subjects are kings, heroes, and gods. Nothing can equal my magnificent spectacles. Theater of my glory, where harmony reigns, receive your laws from my spirit alone. I soften hearts through sounds, my tears, and my sighs. My tragic sorrows create the truest pleasures. Theater of my glory, where harmony reigns, receive your laws from my spirit alone.)

When La Font placed these ringing alexandrines in the mouth of the Muse of tragedy, Melpomène's assertion of control over the stage of the Académie Royale de Musique cut two ways. In the prologue to a work as comic as *Les Fêtes de Thalie* La Font and Mouret may have set Melpomène up only to dethrone her, but in 1714 the *tragédie en musique* did, in fact, still reign supreme over the Opéra's stage. Notwithstanding the assaults Melpomène underwent at the hands of her sister Muses, she retained her hold on the repertoire and, crucially, her prestige. Even as the numbers of new *tragédies* began to slide – only seven premiered between 1720 and 1729 as opposed to twelve in other genres – the *tragédie en musique* remained ideologically dominant.[1]

Yet even though the model that Quinault and Lully had created together maintained its influence – not least because their operas continued to appear before the public – the move following Lully's death from a monopolistic structure to a more open one did give the institution greater flexibility. André Campra, an outsider from Aix-en-Provence, composed nineteen works for the Opéra from 1697 to 1735 – tragedies as well as ballets – several of which achieved classic status. Other composers came from

[1] Girdlestone, *La Tragédie en musique*, 268, and Fajon, *L'Opéra à Paris*, 272–75, both track the number of premieres by chronological slices. Revivals meant that the public saw more tragedies than their statistics suggest; see Lagrave, *Le Théâtre*, 346–50.

outside France, two being the Italians Théobalde Gatti and Jean-Baptiste Stuck. Composers such as Collasse and Marais, on the other hand, came up through the system, having played in the orchestra or conducted it under Lully, yet they, too, put their own stamp on the repertoire. The period between 1687 and 1733 – formerly seen as a mere transition between two great composers and covered by the teleological term "préramiste" – is starting to come into clearer focus, now that several of the operas have been performed and recorded.

The first opera to be performed after Lully's death, *Achille et Polixène*, initiated a new trend: ending the opera with the on-stage death of one of the principal characters. In fact, approximately 60 percent of the tragedies composed between 1687 and 1733 end with a death – thus excluding the possibility of ringing down the curtain with celebrations.[2] Sometimes the darkness of the storyline meant that the fifth act lacked a divertissement altogether; this was the case in Thomas Corneille's libretto for *Médée* (1694), as in La Serre's for *Pyrame et Thisbé* (1726). But more often the librettist moved the last divertissement into the interior of the act, where it acquired a different rationale.[3] Other divertissements within the opera were susceptible to shading by the prevailing gloom, even when their role was to offer a stark contrast to it. The staging of violent acts was not restricted to the Opéra; over much of this same period Prosper Jolyot de Crébillon was writing tragedies for the Comédie-Française that depicted on-stage violence and suicides. At the Opéra, this trend occurred at the same time that comedy was being allowed onto its stage.

Just as librettos underwent changes after Quinault's departure, so did composers depart from Lully's practices, the most dramatic change being the enrichment in orchestration. An increased role for instruments meant that the sound-worlds of the divertissements and the narrative portions of the opera were more similar than they had been – a case in point being the first three scenes of Act III of Campra's *Tancrède* (1702), where orchestral accompaniment of the voices gives way only rarely to the continuo. Perhaps it is for that reason that the "annonce" became an even more prominent device for alerting the audience to the start of a divertissement: an on-stage character hears the approach of someone making music – which usually takes the form of a snippet from the first instrumental piece in the divertissement – before the singing and dancing characters appear. Yet even though the main characters acquired a richer musical environment, divertissements still represented the portions of the opera where music could be allowed to attract attention for its own sake, and in these sections, too, instrumental practices evolved.

2 Laurenti, *Valeurs morales et religieuses*, 269–72, breaks down the proportions of happy to tragic endings by decade and places the distinctions within the context of changing attitudes about the gods.

3 Wood, *Music and Drama*, 248, tracks the location of fifth-act divertissements by four slices of time between 1673 and 1715.

The question of dance looms large in the historiography of this period. In his influential *French Baroque Music from Beaujoyeulx to Rameau* James Anthony declared that "Simply stated, the weakness of most *tragédies lyriques* of the *préramiste* period is their near total subordination of drama to decoration"; in support of this claim he compared the number of dance pieces in Lully's *Amadis* (13), Campra's *Tancrède* (23), and Rameau's *Dardanus* in the revival of 1744 (30).[4] His views drew upon ones expressed several decades earlier by Masson, who saw in this period a recalibration in the balance between the three essential elements in opera – poetry, music, and dance – that led to the creation of the dance-dominated opera-ballet. Wood has written that "Perhaps it was inevitable in the era of the emerging opera-ballet that the divertissement tail should come at times dangerously close to wagging the *tragédie* dog."[5] Such views have, however, been challenged by Fajon, who adopted a methodology of counting not the number of pieces, but the number of measures devoted to different components. On the basis of seven sample tragedies from Lully's *Armide* (1686) to Rebel and Francoeur's *Pyrame et Thisbé* (1726), he concluded that "contrary to the generally held opinion, the ratio between action and divertissement underwent very little modification after *Armide*." According to his quantitative method, the proportion of a work devoted to divertissement tends to hover around 46 percent, with *Armide* at 41 percent and *Pyrame et Thisbé* at 51 percent. Fajon does not say whether his count includes only notated measures or takes repeats into account, and he himself admits that this methodology provides at best a rough approximation.[6]

Such statistical approaches provide but very crude tools. First, they fail to address crucial distinctions, such as the differences in construction between the prologue and the acts of an opera or the varied treatment composers give to divertissements depending on their dramatic function. More importantly, they rest on unexamined assumptions that dances may be viewed as isolated entities, and that measuring their extent can tell us something meaningful about the qualities of a work. In working through this repertoire I have learned that there is no linear, teleological progression in the way divertissements were handled. Quinault's dramatic integration and Lully's tight musical structures did not disappear upon Lully's death; they became, though, only one possible approach. Sometimes the divertissements were all that redeemed a poor libretto, as the *Mercure* reported in 1723 about Mouret's *Pirithoüs*.[7] If not every librettist had Quinault's skill at constructing an act whose divertissement feels

4 See the revised edition, 154 and 162. 5 *Music and Drama*, 263.

6 Fajon, *L'Opéra à Paris*, 329.

7 *MF* (February 1723), 321–34: "Interest in the main scenes is lukewarm, but there is lively pleasure in the fêtes with which this opera is embellished; they are all dazzling and the satisfaction they give leaves no room for boredom." Fajon, *L'Opéra à Paris*, 311, calls the libretto "beyond doubt one of the worst ever set to music."

completely natural, a number of them did; others strove for a different kind of dramaturgy. Some of the criticisms that have been aimed at the tragedies of this long period have merit: there are, indeed, instances where divertissements seem more dutiful than thoughtful and some where choreographic display does make for imbalance. Yet others are brilliantly conceived and beautifully constructed – which may or may not mean short, as the number of dance pieces does not by itself govern effectiveness. Not infrequently, both effective and ineffective divertissements co-exist within the same work. The five tragédies examined in this chapter, each by a different composer, are not uniformly successful in their treatment of the divertissements, but show that the ideology of integrated divertissements remained in place across the period and that dance retained its power to support tragedy.

ACHILLE ET POLIXÈNE (1687)

The first opera to be performed after Lully's death was one Lully had intended to compose himself; he had, in fact, already completed the first act. Its librettist was Campistron, who had written the libretto for *Acis et Galatée*; Pascal Collasse, who stepped in to finish the music, had served as Lully's secretary since 1677. Notwithstanding the close association with the master, the opera moves some distance away from Lully's model.[8] This tragedy, which treats the period during the Trojan War when Achilles had withdrawn from battle after arguing with his commander, Agamemnon, ends with an on-stage suicide: Polixène, Priam's daughter and Achille's bride, stabs herself (on stage) with the bloody dagger with which Paris had just killed Achille (off stage). Despite the gloomy plot of this opera (or, perhaps, as a counterbalance to it), all of the divertissements are framed as fêtes and most are quite long.

In Act I, when Achille is idle after withdrawing from the war, his mother Thétis sends Vénus and her followers along every day to distract him. Diomède, one of the Greek generals, is horrified to see Achille wasting his time in this way ("Un héros doit former de plus nobles désirs"); his reaction, emitted just before the day's fête starts, suggests that the audience in the theater is intended to see the passive Achille as effeminate. Vénus's arrival, accompanied by Amour in a cloud machine, introduces a sumptuous musical world absent from the act until then. Vénus is accompanied by the Graces and Pleasures; their words both seduce Achille to pleasure ("Est-il rien de si doux / Que de vivre avec nous?") and promise him happiness in love in vague terms ("Préparez votre cœur / Au plus parfait bonheur"). The divertissement ends with an abrupt reversal: Arcas rushes in to tell Achille that Patrocle has just been killed by Hector. Achille, finally roused from his lethargy, vows revenge.

8 On the relationship of this opera and those completed by Lully, see Gaudefroy-Demombynes, "*Achille et Polyxène*."

Table 11-1: *Achille et Polixène*, 1/4–5.

Heading in score	Musical features	Paraphrase of sung text/ comments
Sc. 4: Vénus, Achille Prélude	d, **3**	Vénus appears in the air with Amour.
Vénus, "J'abandonne les cieux, je descends sur la terre"	Musically related to the prelude.	Vénus says she is coming to offer Achille solace for his unfair treatment.
Chaconne	D, **3**; 40 bars long, over ground bass	[The music to which Vénus's cloud descends to the ground and everyone gets out?]
Vénus, "Vous, Divinités aimables"	D, **3**, but without the ground	Vénus encourages her companions to cheer up Achille.
Sc. 5: Achille, les Grâces, les Plaisirs Air. Vénus et les Grâces	A, $\frac{6}{4}$; binary, with imitative entries in all 5 parts	Instrumental dance for the Graces, according to the score.
Passacaille	A, **3**; over descending ground, with middle section in a	Presumably danced by some combination(s) of Graces and Pleasures.
Une Grâce, "Grand Héros" starts extended vocal section	A, **3**; over same ground as passacaille; texture mixes solos with trios.	Singers are two Graces and one Pleasure.
Repeat of end of passacaille	A, **3**	Repeat probably begins with the return to A major.[a]

[a] No symbol in the score indicates where the repeat within the passacaille starts, but the instructions following the vocal section – "Les instruments reprennent la fin de la passacaille en bécarre"– suggest that the repeat starts at the return to the major mode. Legrand, "Chaconnes et passacailles," 126, counts 362 bars, but with a question mark.

The Vénus divertissement, which occupies two scenes, has the startling peculiarity of including both a chaconne and a passacaille (plus one other dance; see Table 11-1), but the question emerges, as in *Acis et Galatée*'s second act (see Chapter 6, pp. 195–96), as to whether the chaconne was danced:

> Vénus appears in the air with Amour; she is accompanied by the Graces and the Pleasures; the cloud that carries them descends to the bottom of the stage, they all get out and the cloud rises into the air and disappears.

This *didascalie* appears in the libretto at the start of Scene 4, just before two expository quatrains sung by Vénus, explaining that she comes to offer comfort to Achille. The relatively brief chaconne (five phrases of eight bars each) falls between her two quatrains, the second of which invites her followers to entertain Achille, thus implying that no dancing has as yet taken place. At this point there is a change of key and of scene, which means a change in the personnel on stage;[9] the music that ensues is unambiguously intended for dancing. Moreover, the air in $\frac{6}{4}$ and the passacaille offer the canonical identification between the singers and dancers who share the roles of Graces and Pleasures. Perhaps the action described at the start of Scene 4 occurs in stages, rather than all during the prelude: Vénus hovers in the air while she sings her first little recitative (13 measures), then the chaconne serves to get everyone the rest of the way down to earth and the cloud machine back into the heavens.

Arguing against this hypothesis, however, is the annotation in the 1687 libretto in the margin of both scenes 4 and 5 that "the dance in this divertissement was composed by Monsieur de Lestang." Given that the divertissement occurs over both these scenes and that there is a page turn between them in the libretto, this annotation might have a built-in redundancy. On the other hand, the repetition might be purposeful, and thus the question of the function of the chaconne remains open.

Off stage, between Acts I and II, Achille avenges Patrocle's death by killing Hector in battle, thus making the martial divertissement performed by soldiers in his honor in Act II seem natural – and thus also asserting his remasculinization. However, when the Trojan king, Priam, comes to him with Hector's widow, Andromaque, to request the return of Hector's body for burial, Achille is not moved to pity until Priam's beautiful daughter Polixène adds her pleas. The smitten Achille yields and at the end of Act II he once again resolves not to fight the Trojans.

Whereas the first two divertissements adhere to the longer end of Lully's norms (Act II has four instrumental dances), the one Collasse wrote for Act III radically exceeds them. The act even has two divertissements, the second and longer of which is awkwardly framed by the standards of Quinault. Achille requests Polixène's hand in marriage, and when Agamemnon returns Briséis to him, he is no longer interested in her. Briséis appeals to Junon, queen of the gods, for help; Junon in turn calls up Hatred, Fury, Discord, and Envy, all of them embodied by dancers, to go after the Trojans. Just as this looks to be turning into a classic demonic divertissement, it is over almost as soon as it starts, after one instrumental piece ("Air des Furies") and no singing, except by Junon. Instead, Trojan shepherds and shepherdesses arrive to celebrate the peace they believe to be imminent, thanks to Achille. Briséis cannot bear to watch festivities she attributes to Polixène's influence. Her departure means that not a single main character is on stage to watch the very long celebration that ends the act. And whereas the wedding is not mentioned explicitly in the words the shepherds sing (the negotiations are concluded in the next act), this fête seems redundant in the face of what amount to engagement celebrations that end Act IV (carried out by the Trojans with Polixène in attendance) and wedding celebrations, with the bride and groom, early in Act V.

[9] The start of Scene 4 mentions only Vénus and Achille, whereas Scene 5 has "Achille, les Grâces, les Plaisirs." Here, as in many other instances, *didascalies* name a character – Achille – who does not sing.

The Act III pastoral fête includes no fewer than six separate dance pieces – four of them in a row and independent of the vocal music – and, to end, a large chorus with instrumental interludes that were surely danced. The fête in Act IV, ordered by Priam to celebrate the peace Polixène's engagement to Achille is bringing to Troy, has fewer dance pieces but occupies at least as much time, in that it consists of a binary dance piece and a gigantic chaconne, both instrumental and vocal, that takes up 41 pages of the score. Between Acts IV and V the preparations for the wedding are made, but in the elapsed time of the opera, the festivities seem almost continuous: only seven pages of score, which contain two short scenes in which Polixène betrays her uneasiness over Cassandre's dire prophecies, separate the divertissements in Acts IV and V. The wedding fête, which Priam and Achille lead, is shorter than the previous two sets of festivities, but nonetheless involves choruses, a vocal solo, and four instrumental dances. Even for lovers of joyous song and dance, this much celebrating in a single opera seems out of all proportion to the rest of the work. Dramatically, it also seems maladroit.

The superabundance of divertissement music in *Achille et Polixène* does not characterize all the *tragédies en musique* of this generation; in fact, Collasse's next and much more successful opera, *Thétis et Pélée* (1689) balances its two long fêtes in Acts II and V with divertissements of more modest proportions in the other three acts. This equilibrium can be observed in many of the operas that followed; rarely is there a high number of dances across all five divertissements.[10] But Collasse had nonetheless established a precedent that some composers chose to follow.

MÉDÉE (1693)

By comparison even with *Thétis et Pélée*, Marc-Antoine Charpentier's opera *Médée* stays close to the Lullian model. The author of the libretto was playwright Thomas Corneille, who had collaborated with Lully on *Psyché* and *Bellérophon* and had also worked with Charpentier on the machine plays *Circé* and *L'Inconnu* (both from 1675). His experience in writing spoken tragedies is apparent in the opera's tight structure, adherence to the unity of time, carefully crafted dialogue, and unity of tone. Like Lully's *Alceste*, the libretto has classical antecedents: plays by both Euripides and Seneca, not to mention Corneille's brother Pierre's eponymous tragedy (1634). The opera centers obssessively around its heroine, who in the last two acts exacts a horrible vengeance on the wayward Jason by poisoning his new beloved, driving her father mad, killing her own two children, and destroying the city of Corinth. In this grim story the divertissements hardly divert, and even the first two, the cheerful ones, are fully anchored to the unfolding of the plot. One sign of integration is that within all four of them at least one of the main characters sings; this happens in some of Quinault's

[10] Wood comments on this balance for the period 1673–1715; see *Music and Drama*, 260.

librettos as well, but never so consistently across an entire opera. In the horrifying Act v the function of the divertissement is replaced by the spectacular finale in which Corinth is set ablaze as Médée flies off in her dragon-pulled chariot.

Before the opera opens, Jason, Médée, and their two children have taken refuge at the court of king Créon. Still earlier, Médée had betrayed her own father and murdered her brother while helping Jason win the Golden Fleece. Now the Thessalien Acaste, eager to avenge Médée's murder of his father Pelias, who had usurped Jason's father's throne, is threatening to attack Corinth for harboring them. King Créon sees Médée's presence as a liability, but the heroic Jason as an asset, and has thus encouraged Jason and his daughter Créuse to fall in love. No matter how much Jason claims he only wants Créuse to protect their children, Médée remains suspicious. Oronte, prince of Argos, arrives to offer his services in the impending war; he is hoping for Créuse's hand as a reward. Créon temporizes, putting off any decision until after the battle, in order to ensure that both Jason and Oronte will fight for Corinth. His people excitedly welcome Oronte, whose followers join them in anticipating a triumph for Glory and Love that ends Act I.

This divertissement thus occurs at a precarious moment in the opera and carries within it the tensions that have been revealed so far. It is presented as a spontaneous act by the Corinthians, who welcome Oronte's support for their cause in a rousing chorus ("Courez aux champs de Mars, volez, jeune héros"). The libretto makes it clear that the "young hero" the Corinthians welcome is Oronte, not Jason, whose uncertain position in Corinth is thus emphasized by his being sidelined by the festivities. Oronte even takes up the call himself, invoking the god of Love as his inspiration for victory; Jason, however, remains silent. The dancers among the Corinthians reinforce the military fervor by staging a mock wrestling match, set to a rondeau in triple meter whose refrains are reinforced by the trumpets. But the mood abruptly changes when Oronte's Argiens, who have not participated up to this point, perform "a galant dance." Through it we are given to see that Oronte's motivation for coming to Corinth is love, a sentiment reinforced by the duet that follows, "Quel bonheur suit la tendresse! / Heureux l'amant qui l'obtient!" This strophic song in triple meter is interwoven in Lullian fashion with a lovely sarabande. Oronte does not realize that he has a rival for Créuse in the person of Jason (nor will he until Act III); nor does he yet know that Créon is using him for his own purposes and has no intention of letting him marry Créuse. Moreover, the text of the song could apply to Jason, who is also hoping to conquer in love and who is still on stage. The dichotomy within the divertissement alerts the audience to the existence of cross-purposes by the putative allies, just before the final chorus[11] stages a show of unity: "Que

[11] In the libretto this chorus occurs only at the end of the divertissement; in the score it is performed after Oronte's air as well. It includes instrumental episodes that would certainly have invited dancing at the end of the divertissement.

d'épais bataillons sur nos rives descendent. /[. . .] / Unissons-nous en ce grand jour, / La Gloire, et l'Amour le demandent," a double chorus that pits the four-part Corinthians against a three-part solo group consisting of two Corinthians and an Argien.[12]

This opera was performed before librettos began naming the performers. As it was never revived, it is not even possible to see what the dancing cast was like later. Moreover, this libretto has few *didascalies* – a particular disappointment in the face of the very full *didascalies* of Thomas Corneille's libretto for Lully's *Bellérophon*. The one *didascalie* in the Act I divertissement that mentions the two dances shows that, in parallel with the singers, there were two different troupes, Corinthiens and Argiens. Whether either group included women seems unlikely. Not only are there no Corinthiennes or Argiennes, the vocal world is male: among the main characters only men are on stage, and the solo Corinthien and Argien who sing the vocal sarabande are both men. Assuming a fully male realm for this divertissement, it is surprising to find how much it emphasizes love; most all-male divertissements that involve human characters have more stereotypically manly rationales. This one is bookended by a wrestling match and a semi-martial chorus, but at its center lies a danced and sung paean that places the conquest of a heart above military victory. This amorous divertissement highlights Jason's and Oronte's susceptibilities and shows us already in the first act that they will be no match for Médée.

In its construction the Act I divertissement falls within the Lullian template. Its musical style is another matter, and a good deal has been written about the richness of Charpentier's compositional palette relative to Lully's.[13] For the present purposes, suffice it to say that Charpentier's Italian training lies on the surface in the second-act divertissement. By the time it starts, the audience has seen for itself that Créon, while feigning concern for Médée, is trying to get rid of her; it further knows that Oronte remains ignorant of Créon's duplicity. On the heels of Jason and Créuse's mutual declaration of love, Oronte arrives to offer Créuse a musical homage, which she manages to accept with tact, even if not with enthusiasm. Oronte tells her that the divertissement he has arranged – and which is to be performed by an Argien in the role of Amour, seconded by captives of love – speaks for him. Jason stays with Créuse to watch Oronte's homage. Throughout it he remains every bit as passive as he had been in Act I, his weakness exposed by the fact that he neither controls nor is honored by any of the divertissements in the opera.

The Act II divertissement falls into four sections. The first involves Amour's attempt to soften up Créuse both by praising her and by vaunting the pleasures of love, without naming any potential lover in particular. This section ends when he offers her his bow

[12] The voice parts of the solo group – C^3, C^4, F^4 – are the same ones assigned to Jason, Oronte, and Créon; the effect reinforces the analogy between the divertissement and the action outside it.

[13] See Cessac, *Marc-Antoine Charpentier*, and Hitchcock, *Marc-Antoine Charpentier*.

and she refuses to take it. In the face of her resistance, he says she has nothing to fear from a child. She coyly replies that whereas it is dangerous to obey Amour, it is difficult to reject him, and gets into his chariot, along with Jason and Oronte.[14] From a staging perspective, this maneuver has the virtue of getting four singers out of the way for the middle two sections of the divertissement. Since we know that this Argien dressed as Amour is functioning as Oronte's mouthpiece, the songs and dances that ensue can be seen as representing his double-barreled wooing strategy. The first group of texts aims to encourage someone who fears love – Créuse's case, Oronte erroneously believes; the next offers reassurance about a suitor's (i.e., Oronte's) sincerity and constancy. Créuse, however, might wish to hear this text as applying to Jason, who, she fears, might be tempted to return to Médée. At the end of this second song, everyone gets out of the chariot, whereupon Amour and both suitors pressure Créuse to declare her feelings. She, however, sidesteps naming anyone. The chorus assures Amour that his victory is assured.

What is particularly interesting about the central portion of this divertissement – the part performed by love's captives while Amour and the others watch – is that Charpentier chose to build it around a back-to-back chaconne and passacaille. Both are large complexes that incorporate instrumental sections, vocal solos, and choruses; the chaconne sets texts in Italian, the passacaille in French. Whereas the libretto identifies the performers in this section as "captives of different nations and both sexes," the score labels the woman who sings solos during the chaconne as "une Italienne"; the dancers in the chaconne probably would have been similarly identified, set off by their costumes from the performers in the passacaille (who are not identified in either score or libretto as to nationality). Since the divertissement is framed as a performance put on by the fake Amour, it could in theory have included any type of singing and dancing character; the choice of Italians probably served Charpentier's own musical interests. Yet even given the theatricality of this divertissement, it remains surprising to find an Italian text in a *tragédie en musique* at this point in French operatic history; the only precedents are the anomalously comic scene in Collasse's *Astrée* of two years earlier (see Chapter 8, p. 220) and the equally anomalous Italian lament in Lully's *Psyché* (1678).[15] So the question of tone emerges: does this chaconne with its Italian text allude to the *comédie italienne*, however indirectly, or is it to be taken seriously?

Examples in previous chapters have revealed the chaconne's double life: heroic, on the one hand; inflected by the *comédie italienne* on the other. Charpentier himself had composed a chaconne for Arlequin in his music for *Le Malade imaginaire* (1673).

[14] This *didascalie* comes from the libretto ("Créuse monte sur le char de l'Amour, Jason et Oronte se placent à ses côtés"). The score says that Amour places himself at Créuse's feet; it does not mention Jason and Oronte. (The score was published later than the libretto, after the opera had been put into performance.) In any case, they are available to dialogue with Amour toward the end of the scene.

[15] *Psyché* was partly recycled from Lully's eponymous *tragédie-ballet*.

However, these earlier Italianate chaconnes do not adhere to the model of French chaconnes built above a ground (or a repeating harmonic pattern), in mostly eight-bar phrases that divide into symmetrical halves, and that tend to be in a major key and start on the second beat. Rather, whereas they are also in triple meter and may occasionally allude to something that looks like a ground, they are not wedded to it, the phrase structure is unbound by any particular patterns, and they are not long. They are a genre apart and Charpentier's chaconne in *Médée* is not among their number. But nor does this chaconne sound fully French – or, more precisely, the instrumental portion of Charpentier's chaconne could pass for French, whereas the vocal section is redolent of Italy.

The chaconne opens with the instrumental section – 84 measures long, and thus of modest proportions as French chaconnes go – which is not repeated later, as it probably would have been by Lully. The vocal section, which continues from the instrumental chaconne without an intervening double bar, adheres to French practices in alternating a soloist with the chorus. The first Italianism occurs in the motto opening: an Italienne sings the first two lines of her text, listens to the bass line for two measures, and then sings her opening lines again to the same music, this time going on to the next phrase. The other most salient Italianism comes in her four-bar melisma on the last word of the quatrain – a syllable not singled out for its meaning ("has"), but for its location in the phrase; the melisma is performed twice more, the last time by soloist and chorus together. The piece thus gestures toward the virtuosic singing style for which Italy was known, where music takes precedence over text. However, "hà" does not acquire its melisma until it has already been heard once in a context where the identity of the word is clear; the Italienne delivers most of her text syllabically. French values in regard to the sung word are not sacrificed on the altar of vocal pyrotechnics and the chaconne ultimately remains a stylistic hybrid.

What might this hybridity have meant for the choreographer, Guillaume Pécour? The first question is what kind of Italian characters might have danced here. The text, for all that it invokes the sufferings love causes, particularly in its middle section, has a bouncy, hexasyllabic structure that gives the piece a carefree character.

> Chi teme d'amore
> Il grato martire,
> O non vuol gioire
> O cuore non hà.

> ("Anyone who fears the pleasing martyrdom of love, either does not want to enjoy life or has no heart.")

Charpentier's music also seems lighthearted, although not overtly comic. Perhaps not the clowns, but the *innamorati* of the *comédie italienne* would strike the right tone – the Isabelles and Léandres. In that case, the choreography – or the costumes, at the very least – would probably have been inflected by Italian elements. Moreover, the choreographer would presumably want to differentiate this dance from the passacaille to follow, not only because of the stylistic differences in the music, but because principles of contrast are fundamental to divertissement construction. The passacaille would seem to call for a different set of characters, although we cannot know, since neither the score nor the libretto provides this level of detail.

The more French passacaille is constructed to allow considerably more dancing than the chaconne. The first of its three parts is instrumental, with 48 bars in consistent eight-bar phrases that always remain in A minor. It starts on the downbeat and presumably was intended to have a slower tempo than the chaconne. Next comes a slightly longer vocal section that remains in the minor and alternates between three soloists (two sopranos and a *haute-contre*), the full chorus, and the orchestra; the two orchestral interludes were probably danced. The orchestral passacaille starts up again, but to entirely new music, this time with local tonicizations that allow for couplets on pitches other than A and with two extensions of the phrase to twelve bars. Two-thirds of the way into this section the mode changes to major, where it remains until the end of the piece.

This varied passacaille, which ends in the same key as the chaconne, acts as a climax to the divertissement within the divertissement; after this Amour modulates to a new key and opens a conversation with Créuse. It is possible that the return to A major within the passacaille marks not just a change in musical character but the place where the dancers from the chaconne would have joined their counterparts in the passacaille to form a visual, as well as aural, finale. Alternatively, the reunion of the dance troupes might have waited until the chorus that concludes both the divertissement and the act ("Ton triomphe est certain, victoire, Amour, victoire"), which alternates vocal and orchestral phrases of similar lengths in a manner that seems designed to promote the same kind of alternation of singing and dancing that Charpentier had called for in *Circé* (see Chapter 2, p. 41). The entr'acte music does not derive from repetition of a dance played earlier in the act, as was Lully's normal practice, but draws out the instrumental part of the chorus for another 27 bars, thus maintaining a unity of affect as the performers leave the stage. Yet the text of the chorus is deliberately vague: which of the two rivals is the lover who is sure to be covered in glory? The dual nature of this divertissement reinforces the ambiguity.

The two other divertissements in this opera show Médée at work. In Act III she carries out the invocations that allow her to poison the robe she plans to give Créuse, aided by Jealousy and Vengeance (singers) and by singing and dancing demons. Both the two independent binary pieces and the orchestral interludes within choruses accompany mimed action. First, the demons bring a cauldron into which they throw all the herbs Médée needs for making her poison; this action constitutes the "Premier air pour les Démons," which starts as an *entrée grave*, but changes meter and character in the second strain. After another invocation to which the Underworld replies by shaking and making groaning noises (depicted in the orchestra), Médée conjures up monsters that she then poisons, in order to test the efficacy of her concoction. The chorus repeats her words, and the *didascalie* reveals that it is during this chorus that the monsters are born and then die. After the first key phrase that the chorus sings ("Naissez, monstres, naissez . . . "), Charpentier provides several bars of atmospheric instrumental music to accompany the action; the second incantation ("Du funeste poison, par une mort soudaine, / Faites-nous voir les sûrs effets" [Show us, by a sudden death, the effects of this lethal poison]) provokes the same type of instrumental response. Now that Médée knows her poison works, she takes some from the cauldron and spreads it on the robe. This action, described in the libretto, may take place either during the "Seconde entrée des Demons" or, possibly, during the vengeance chorus that follows, which also has suggestive instrumental phrases related musically to the "Seconde entrée." In fact, all the music in this scene is so vivid that it cries out for action.

The same is true in Act IV, where Médée, having told Créon that she refuses to leave Corinth unless and until Créuse marries Oronte, proves that she, not he, is the one who wields the power. First, she turns the guards he has ordered to arrest her against each other (they come at her in a fanfare labeled "Charge," then turn to fight each other in "Les Combattants"). Next, she waves her magic wand and conjures up phantoms in the form of beautiful maidens who seduce the soldiers into abandoning Créon and following them (this involves two beautiful dance-songs for soloists and chorus). Last, she calls up Fury (Fureur) from the Underworld, who drives Créon to madness. The sequence of three scenes builds seamlessly to this terrifying climax; it serves as a powerful demonstration of how a so-called "divertissement" can act upon a main character. In the middle of the second of the dance-songs performed by the phantoms, Créon even says as much: "Par quel prodige, à moi-même contraire, / En voyant ces objets, je n'ai plus de colère?" It is rare for an operatic character who is the spectator of a divertissement to comment on the impact it is having, but here Thomas Corneille puts into words a phenomenon that we are usually left to infer.

Médée is the only opera Charpentier was able to put onto the stage of the Opéra and, difficult as it is to believe today, it had only a modest *succès d'estime* and was never revived. Given the brilliance of the music and the particularly cogent treatment of the divertissements, we can only regret that the Académie Royale de Musique never again made use of Charpentier's abilities.

TANCRÈDE (1702)

Tancrède (1702), Campra's fifth work and second *tragédie* for the Opéra, is one of several operas in this period that embrace two opposing tendencies: divertissements that adhere to the tightly constructed Lullian model alongside others that are long and diffuse. The librettist, Antoine Danchet, drew upon the same incidents in Torquato Tasso's epic *Gerusalemme liberata* that inspired Monteverdi's *Combattimento di Tancredi e Clorinda*, and, like it, Campra's opera has a tragic ending. However, the libretto eschews any overt references to Christianity and fleshes out the story with additional romantic entanglements.[16] The Saracens dominate the *dramatis personae*, who, in addition to Clorinde, the Saracen princess who dons armor and battles alongside her troops, consist of Argant, the king of Circassia, who is in love with Clorinde; Herminie, daughter of the king of Antioch, who is in love with her enemy, Tancrède; and Isménor, a powerful magician on the side of the Saracens who is in love with Herminie. Tancrède is thus the only representative of the Crusaders among the main characters; he does not even have a confidant. As a result of the imbalance among the cast, the opera takes place primarily within the realms controlled by the Saracens, which in turn has a significant impact on the divertissements. There is not, for instance, any acknowledgement of Tancrède's military prowess by his own people until Act v. In fact, Tancrède seems to operate much more without social support than most French operatic heroes.

Only two of the five divertissements take place on territory Tancrède controls, and both are mitigated in various ways. In Act ii Tancrède is shown in his own camp, engaged in an act of clemency, granting freedom to all his Saracen prisoners. Since his clemency is motivated by his love for Clorinde, who is among the prisoners, the freed Saracens are the ones who celebrate; Tancrède's soldiers watch in silence. This scene comes closest to a celebration in honor of the other "hero," the warrior princess Clorinde. She, however, rejects the exhortations of her fellow Saracens to open herself to love, since the person she secretly loves is her enemy. But she also rejects Tancrède's offer to her of freedom, as she wants it to be earned by a battle on her behalf. In Act v, the celebrations honor Tancrède's victory in the battle of the preceding night; what he learns only later is that the person he himself killed is not the Saracen leader, Argant, but Clorinde, who had deliberately put on Argant's armor before going into battle. But even without knowing what cruel news awaits him, Tancrède leaves almost as soon as the fête starts, preferring to return to the battlefield. Clorinde, who throughout the opera struggles to keep her duty to her people above her feelings of love, had rejected the divertissement in her honor after it was over; Tancrède leaves even before his gets seriously underway.

The divertissements in Acts i, iii, and iv all happen on the Saracen side and all depend on magic instigated by the sorcerer Isménor, who seems motived more by his possessive love for Herminie than by patriotic fervor. In Act i Isménor turns up just

[16] Regarding the changes the libretto underwent, see Banducci, "The libretto," in the Pendragon facsimile of the score, xvii–xx. My observations are based on the manuscript full score reproduced in this facsimile (F-Pn Vm^2 180) and on the reduced score published by Ballard in 1702.

as Argant is about to initiate a solemn ceremony in which his knights are to swear an oath on the tombs of the dead Saracen kings that they will take vengeance on Tancrède. Isménor offers his magic powers, which Argant at first rejects, then passively accepts. But first he joins his warriors in singing a prayer for divine support ("Ô Ciel! ô suprême Puissance!" I/3); its active string writing and independent solo bassoon line provide one measure of how orchestration practices had changed since Lully's death. This chorus, which could be considered either within or just preceding the divertissement, is not danced; the only dancers in this act were attached to the scene of sorcery that follows. But in at least one performance, in 1748 in Mme de Pompadour's theater inside the château of Versailles, the soldiers formed a circle in the center of the stage while they swore their oath, before returning to its sides to clear the stage for the entrance of the dancers. As Banducci has shown, this prompt note provides one of the rare pieces of eighteenth-century evidence regarding choral blocking.[17]

After the group prayer Isménor performs the first of two incantations: "Vous qui m'obéissez, remplissez mon espoir, / Montrez quel est notre pouvoir." The power is left to the dancing magicians to express, which they do in two instrumental pieces that immediately follow Isménor's order. The eight dancing magicians are all men, notwithstanding the fact that the chorus explicitly includes *magiciennes* as well.[18] The first "Air des Magiciens," in duple meter, is labeled "lent" in its first section and "fort vite" in the second;[19] the second dance, in triple meter, is musically allied with the chorus that follows, whose words exhort everyone to attack the enemies. In the episodes of its loose rondeau structure, the chorus splits between high and low voices. The *magiciennes* encourage the demons to "vanquish the courage" of their enemies by taking the form of Cupids, whereas the *magiciens* want blood and ask for the help of the Underworld. Both requests are answered inside the opera: the divertissement in Act III uses enchanted demons to try to seduce Tancrède away from battle and the male magicians get immediate satisfaction via Isménor's second incantation, which calls upon the spirits of the dead kings to rise up and inspire the warriors to vengeance. When the tombs break open, to the sound of thunder, the magicians take fright and run away. Argant pushes away Isménor's enchantments, declaring that the warriors' courage will suffice.

This divertissement has only two dances – probably involving mime – that immediately plunge the audience into the magical realm that serves as a foil to Tancrède and Clorinde's own military concerns. The same dramatic concision is apparent in Act IV, where Isménor again invokes the Underworld as he ritually prepares to kill Tancrède,

17 See p. 410 in appendix IX in the Pendragon facsimile, where Banducci has transcribed the 1748 prompt notes.

18 As of 1729, *magiciennes* joined the dancing cast.

19 The "lent" marking appears only in the manuscript score, but a slow tempo is implicit not only in the character of the music but in the change in tempo marked at the double bar in both scores.

whom he has immobilized via a powerful spell. This scene externalizes Isménor's emotions and powerfully sets up the double reversal that follows: first, Herminie's attempt to interrupt the murder when she reveals that she loves Tancrède, and, second, Clorinde's arrival, which prompts Isménor to leave Tancrède in her hands. Alone with Tancrède, Clorinde reveals that she loves him, but also resolves to continue fighting her enemies.

Concision does not characterize the other three divertissements; each, however, has provocative features. Act II takes place in Tancrède's camp, but the dances are performed by the grateful Saracen prisoners he has just freed. These include Moors, Saracens, and "Guerrières," women who, like Clorinde, have taken up arms. At least this is how the list of performers appears in the Ballard score; the libretto divides the dancers as "Mores et Sarrasins" (five men, among whom Balon was a soloist) and "Sarrasines de la Suite de Clorinde" (five women, with Subligny as soloist). The two lists are not mutually exclusive – the Saracen women could all be costumed as warriors – but, surprisingly, the second dance, an *entrée grave* in its musical style, is explicitly called "Air des Guerrières" (feminine plural) in the printed and manuscript scores. The *entrée grave* is normally a dance for men; here, apparently, the women are not only wearing male military attire, but have appropriated a masculine movement style. If its heading is accurate, this dance is a rare, if not unique, example of an *entrée grave* assigned to women.

Act III takes place in an enchanted forest where Herminie is taking advantage of Isménor's magic powers to try to induce Tancrède to love her. The divertissement (Scene 4) follows Herminie's lovely "Cessez, mes yeux, cessez de contraindre vos larmes," in which she expresses her grief over her unrequited love. This expansive ternary air, one of the best-known numbers in the opera, has a high trio texture in which Herminie is accompanied only by transverse flutes and violins, with the latter playing the functional bass. This music is not diegetic – Herminie's monologue expresses her innermost thoughts – but a similar texture returns after Tancrède has wandered into the enchanted forest, where Herminie, in order to achieve control over him, tries, in turn, flames, flying demons, groaning trees, and seductive nymphs – all of them introduced by vivid orchestral writing, while the bewildered Tancrède struggles against his fears. The eight bars of lilting high trio that finally bring the nymphs into view, and that are played on stage by a troupe of fauns, then return as the opening chorus of the divertissement, "Chantons dans ces belles retraites, / [. . .] / C'est pour l'Amour qu'elles sont faites" ("Let us sing in these beautiful retreats; they are made for love"). High sonorities recur throughout this long divertissement, in the instrumental and vocal music alike (see Table 11-2), giving it a feminine cast that seems designed both to seduce Tancrède and to recall Herminie's amorous longings. There are some breaks in the treble-oriented sound world: a sarabande with full orchestral texture is performed before and after an air sung by a Plaisir. The introduction of a real bass line here

Table 11-2: *Tancrède* III/4: Tancrède, Troupe de Bergers, de Bergères, de Faunes, et de Dryades.

Heading in score	Musical features	Paraphrase of sung text/ comments
Chœur de Bergères, "Chantons dans ces belles retraites"	C, **3**; binary	Trio of high voices (G^2, G^2, C^1) doubled – and slightly decorated – by flutes and violins
[Air] Une Dryade, "Ce n'est point le printemps qui rend ces lieux si beaux"	c, **3**; binary	Trio texture: voice (C^1), flutes (G^1), "tailles de violons et flûtes allemandes" (C^2). Not in ms. PG.
Sarabande	c, **3**; binary	a5
[Air] Un Plaisir (aka Un Silvain), "Faible raison"	c, **3**; binary	*Haute-contre*, B.C.; similar character to sarabande. Not in 1702 PR.
Sarabande, repeated	c, **3**; binary	a5
Air des Bergères. Gai	c, **3**; rondeau	a5
Deux Bergères, "L'Amour dans la vie peut seul nous charmer"	c, **3**; rondeau	Trio of two high voices (G^2, C^1) and B. C., related to "Air des Bergères." Couplets between refrains sung solo.
Air des Bergères, repeated	c, **3**; rondeau	a5
[Premier] Menuet	C, **3**; binary (8 bars per strain)	Duet for "petites flûtes" and "tailles de flûtes"
Deuxième Menuet	c, **3**; binary (8 bars per strain)	a5 "Violons"
[Air] Une Dryade, first strophe, "Nos plaisirs seront peu durables"	c, **3**; binary (8 bars per strain)	*Dessus* and B.C. In essence a sung menuet.
Deuxième Menuet, repeated	c, **3**	In ms. PG, the first menuet is the one repeated.
Une Dryade, second strophe, "Soupirons, tous nous y convie"	c, **3**	
Premier Menuet, repeated	C, **3**	In ms. PG, second and then first menuet repeated.
[Air] Une Dryade, "Règne, Amour"	C, **3**; through-composed	12-bar instrumental intro a5, vocal section varies from high duet and trio textures featuring flutes and violins to full orchestra; air leads directly into chorus.
Chœur, "Règne, Amour"	C, **3**	2 high voices (G^2) variously doubled by flutes and violins or accompanied by orchestra, interspersed with solo passages for the Dryad.

in conjunction with a complex involving a male singing character is presumably purposeful and suggests that the dancers in the sarabande were also men. (The dancers in 1702 consisted of four nymphs [female] and four Plaisirs [male].[20]) The "Air des Bergères" and the second of the two menuets are also attributed to the full orchestra.[21] The instrumental dances are all connected to vocal pieces, in typical Lullian manner, but there are four of them, each of which is repeated, thus yielding at least eight occasions for dancing (not counting the two possibly danced choruses). However, none of the individual pieces is long, and Campra's play of textures and tempos within the consistent triple meter effectively conveys the enchanted seductions of the forest.

A clumsy feature of Danchet's libretto is that Tancrède somehow disappears during the middle of the divertissement; he is on stage when it starts, but not when it ends. Herminie's first line in the following scene, "Thanks to me, Tancrède is captive in these forests," does not provide much of a clue to what may have happened, and the start of Act IV finds him still in the forest, but now in a "horrible place" within it. The writer for the *Mercure* in 1729 found this gap in the storyline sufficiently anomalous that he pointed it out: "During the fête, Tancrède disappears, supposedly attracted, despite himself, by the trap Isménor has set for him."[22] It is not possible to tell from either libretto or score how much (or how little) of the seductive singing and dancing Tancrède actually witnessed.

In Act V, on the other hand, it is clear that Tancrède leaves the stage almost as soon as the divertissement starts (just after the opening march and chorus), notwithstanding the fact that the celebrations are in his honor. He has just vanquished his arch-enemy Argant in battle – or so he thinks – and he declares his intent to bestow mercy on the Saracen troops. His soldiers, joined by the peoples of Palestine, rejoice. Tancrède, however, can find no pleasure without knowing what has become of Clorinde. His absence does not prevent his people from celebrating at length, in three more dances and a solo vocal air by a warrior happy for the return of peace. This divertissement is not long when compared with those in *Achille et Polixène*; in fact, it respects the Lullian convention of breaking off a fête before any concluding chorus when someone bearing bad news arrives. Nonetheless, it still seems misplaced when the hero it honors does not want to watch it. It is thus striking to see that it was almost immediately lengthened: by the revival of 1707, if not during the first run of performances in 1702, a loure was added between the two dances for the warriors.[23]

20 In 1748, the male dancers entered only at the start of the sarabande; the women were already on stage. See Banducci's appendix IX in the Pendragon facsimile, 413.

21 The "Air des Bergères" may have been intended for a solo woman, if a manuscript annotation in one copy of the printed score, F-Po A.60a, attributing it to Mlle Camargo, can be taken as evidence for the performance history of the piece in general. Camargo danced in this divertissement in 1729.

22 *MF* (April 1729), 769.

23 The loure appears along with the new ending to the opera, in which the dying Clorinde (rather than Argant) is carried on stage, in four separately numbered pages (labeled "Changement de la fin du

Is Campra guilty in *Tancrède* of subordinating drama to decoration, as Anthony's statistics, quoted above, imply? *Amadis*, Anthony's point of reference for Lully, is exceptionally lean at thirteen dances;[24] *Armide* makes a better comparison, not just because it has more dances (seventeen), but because the types of divertissements are more similar. Three out of the six units in the two operas have exactly the same number of dance pieces: the prologue has six in both cases, and there are only two each inside two of the acts (the *sommeil* and Haine scenes in *Armide* [II and III]; the magic and demonic scenes in *Tancrède* [I and IV]). Both of the operas' pastoral divertissements stretch out a bit (Act III in *Tancrède* has one more dance [four] than does Act IV in *Armide*), and another fête in each opera has the same relative ratio. The biggest difference in the dance count comes in the final act: *Tancrède* has four dances, which soon increased to five, whereas *Armide* has only one. That dance, however, is a gigantic passacaille, which compares in length to the five dances in *Tancrède* combined.[25] Across the opera there is thus less difference between Lully's and Campra's treatment of the dancing than the numbers alone suggest. Moreover, the differences follow a pattern: action divertissements remain lean, while the upwards creep occurs in those cast as fêtes. Here and in many other operas a balance establishes itself between divertissements where an expansive treatment of the dancing seems natural and ones where dance makes its point quickly.

The real question remains how cogently the divertissements participate in the opera as a whole. Danchet's libretto makes a point of addressing that question from within the fictional world of the opera. At the end of Act I Argant retrieves his warriors from the magic ceremonies and tells Isménor to "leave off your enchantments; our courage will suffice." In Act II Tancrède recognizes that his attempt to declare his love to Clorinde through the intermediary of her followers has failed and tells her she is free to go. Tancrède himself comments on the enchantments to which he is subjected in both Act III and Act IV, and in Act V he refuses to participate in the celebrations of his people. These framing maneuvers open themselves to varied interpretations, but they all carry weight within the opera and help the audience interpret what it has been seeing. Moreover, Campra's divertissement music fulfills its job of communicating characters effectively and may even, as in Act III, make ties to other parts of the opera. Viewing these scenes primarily through the lens of decoration does not do justice either to Danchet's texts or to Campra's music.

Cinquieme Acte") added to some copies of the Ballard score dated 1702. The new ending is reflected in the 1707 libretto.

[24] In *Amadis* there is a good deal of action performed by the dancers to instrumental music that Anthony did not count and at least one strophic song interleaved with instrumental passages that he appears also to have discounted.

[25] Ambiguities about what gets repeated make counting measures difficult.

HYPMERMNESTRE (1716)

This dark tragedy, composed by Charles-Hubert Gervais to a libretto by Joseph de La Font, was singled out for admiration from the *Mercure de France* for its divertissements, which were "perfectly introduced and part of the plot."[26] Gervais was in the circle of the Duc d'Orléans, Louis XIV's nephew, who had been named Regent for the five-year-old Louis XV after the old king died in 1715. His score stands out for its almost continuous use of the orchestra.[27] La Font had written the libretto for *Les Fêtes de Thalie* two years earlier; *Hypermnestre* was his first *tragédie en musique*, and the contrast between it and the thoroughly comic ballet could not be greater.

Like Aeschylus's *Oresteia* and other ancient tragedies that deal with the repercussions of a heinous crime into the next generations, this opera reveals the consequences of a crime committed before the opera starts: the power-hungry Danaüs's murder of Gélanor, king of Argos. Danaüs has taken the throne, but now is threatened by the military campaigns of his brother Egyptus, who has driven Danaüs's troops out of Memphis, and by the threatened rebellion of his own people, still loyal to Gélanor. Danaüs is too weak to resist militarily, so instead has reluctantly arranged to make peace by having his daughters marry Egyptus's sons, who will then, he hopes, uphold his power. The mass wedding is to take place that very day. (According to tradition Egyptus had 50 sons and Danaüs 50 daughters, as the *Mercure* explained to its readers.[28]) But Danaüs is plagued by nightmares in which the dead Gélanor seeks revenge for his death. In order to placate the ghost, Danaüs conducts a ceremony at Gélanor's tomb. Instead of feeling appeased, the ghost emerges to tell Danaüs that false regrets cannot expiate his crime; rather, the ghost predicts, "one of the sons of Egyptus will rule in your place. You spilled my blood, and he will spill yours."[29] Act I ends as Danaüs blames the gods for not stating which son represents the threat. The rest of the opera centers around Danaüs's efforts to preserve his power by inducing his daughters to murder their new husbands. Hypermnestre and her fiancé Lyncée, who had fallen in love before the opera starts, serve as the focal points; no matter what her loyalties to her

[26] The opera received a fourteen-page write-up in the *Mercure* upon its revival in 1728: "The music is widely admired and considered some of the best among modern works. The librettist surpassed himself in many places, especially the third act. The plot is as well laid out as possible for a subject that only the respect that one has for the Ancients can make tolerable. The fêtes are perfectly introduced and part of the plot." *MF* (June, 1728), 1456–57. In 1716 the *Mercure* gave little coverage to operas; the 1728 revival was the first time it devoted attention to this work.

[27] Montagnier, *Gervais*, 123, calls *Hypermnestre* a "symphonic opera," pointing out that in Act I only 14 percent of its notated measures are accompanied by continuo alone.

[28] *MF* (June, 1728), 1442.

[29] ("Un des fils d'Egyptus doit regner en ta place: / Tu fis couler mon sang, il versera le tien.") The version used in this study comes from the 1716 libretto and score, which differs from the *Recueil général*. According to Montagnier (*Gervais*, 95) this opera was performed a dozen times and then withdrawn in order to redo the last act; the new version premiered in April 1717.

father, she cannot bring herself to kill her husband. He thus escapes the slaughter of his brothers on their wedding night and leads the Egyptians in a rebellion against Danaüs, so that he and Hypermnestre can leave Argos for good. Danaüs is mortally wounded and accuses his daughter of failing to prevent his death, but the Egyptian goddess Isis, who had figured in the prologue, returns to say that Lyncée will be the new king. The stunned populace accepts.

Since in this opera the proper use of power is the contested issue, the divertissements become telling vehicles for its exploration. In Act I Danaüs's warriors help him perform the ceremony that he hopes will appease the ghost of Gélanor. In Act II a storm, which Danaüs takes as a sign that Neptune opposes him, prevents Lyncée from arriving from Egypt. After the sea calms, the sailors' celebrations amplify the joy that Hypermnestre and Lyncée experience at seeing each other and the hope for the peace to follow the weddings. In Act III Danaüs hypocritically helps the priestess of Isis lead the wedding ceremonies, only to tell Hypermnestre thereafter that her filial duty obliges her to murder her new husband. Act IV sets up another shocking reversal. On a stage lit only by the wedding torches, the young couples rejoice in their weddings until Hypermnestre emerges from her apartment, dagger in hand, aghast at the task her father has given her. In Act V choreographed battles rage; at the end of a plot this bloody, celebrations are unthinkable.

Of the five divertissements, the two controlled by Danaüs (Acts I and III) highlight his abuses of power. The two that evoke spontaneous expressions of joy (Acts II and IV) present the rising generation, the representatives of the virtuous Hypermnestre and Lyncée. The last divertissement provides the vehicle for transferring power from the corrupt king to the young hero. Three of the five (Acts I, III, and IV) also set up dramatic reversals. This Quinaultian integration on the level of the plot was, however, matched by Lullian restraint in only two of the divertissements (IV and V). But the greater scope given to instrumental dance music does not impede the dramatic coherence of this very concentrated libretto, one that respects the unities of time and action.

The first act takes place at the tomb of king Gélanor, where Danaüs performs an expiatory ceremony that he hopes will calm the spirit of his murdered predecessor – a ceremony led not by a priestly surrogate, but by Danaüs himself, who thereby becomes its focus. His "warriors make a march around Gélanor's mausoleum, to the sound of trumpets and drums, and pass flags above the tomb." The martial accompaniment, which continues throughout most of the divertissement (see Table 11-3), holds it together more than melodic or rhythmic connections. It is, however, suspended in two key places. The first is Danaüs's accompanied recitative, in which he confesses his guilt and asks the ghost to restore peace to his heart. He then reverses his approach and launches into an air in praise of Gélanor's valor and glory. The chorus repeats his sentiments, and the dance that follows introduces new music, but retains the martial orchestration. The second dance, however, introduces a complete change of mood. It

Table 11-3: Gervais, *Hypermnestre* (1716), 1/3: Danaüs, Argiens et Argiennes.

Heading in score	Musical features	Paraphrase of sung texts/ comments
Marche. Rondeau	D, **2**; with trumpets and drums on the refrain	Probably the music to which the warriors entered and passed flags over the tomb.[a]
[Récitatif], Danaüs, "Ombre d'un prince infortuné"	d, **2**; accompanied by the orchestra	Danaüs implores the spirit of Gélanor to grant him peace.
[Air], Danaüs, "Chantez, de ce héros, la valeur et la gloire"	D, **2**; orchestra includes trumpets and drums	Danaüs invokes his followers to celebrate Gélanor's memory.
Chorus, "Chantons" etc.	An extended version of Danaüs's air	Instrumental interludes allow for the possibility of dancing.
Air	D, $\frac{3}{8}$; rondeau with trumpets and drums on the refrain	Probably danced by the Argien warriors.
Sarabande	d, $\frac{3}{2}$; set as a high trio (fls, fls, vlns)	Probably danced by the Argiennes.
Gavotte. Fanfare	D, **2**; with trumpets and drums; very short, so may have been repeated	Could be either for the warriors or whole group; might involve more ceremonial gesturing.
Choeur. Vite. Prélude	F, **3**	During the prelude to the chorus, the sun disappears and the earth shakes.

[a] A parody performed at the Théâtre Italien (July 1728) used the march for that purpose: "Après cela vient une marche de Guerriers en crêpes et en longs manteaux noirs autour du mausolée de Gélanor. Après cette marche, qui se fait au son de la symphonie et des timbales, Danaüs chante le couplet suivant, sur l'air: *O reguingué*. 'Ombre d'un Prince infortuné / que j'ai moi-même assassiné . . . '"

is a tender sarabande, orchestrated as a high trio; although the score does not indicate who dances any of the instrumental pieces, this one uses musical conventions associated with women. Its minor mode makes a connection to Danaüs's expression of guilt, and its feminine cast serves, perhaps, to remind us of Hypermnestre, whose solicitousness for her father's well-being formed the thread of the preceding scene, and whose agonizings over her divided loyalties are central to the opera. Its effect, however, is contained, as it is quickly succeeded by more martial displays, then by the earthquake that presages the ghost's emergence from his tomb to predict Danaüs's death.

The Act II divertissement welcomes Lyncée's ship to the shore after a storm at sea and offers a respite from the tensions arising from Danaüs's ever-increasing preoccupations with his own survival, aptly symbolized by the stormy seas in the early part of the act. But now the waves have calmed and all is joyful; first come the sailors' celebrations, and then a love scene between Lyncée and Hypermnestre – albeit with a crowd watching, as all of the participants in the divertissement remain on stage after Lyncée debarks. The act ends when the young couple leave to join their siblings at the temple, where the wedding ceremonies are in progress.

Table 11-4: Gervais, *Hypermnestre* (1716), II/4: Hypermnestre, Matelots argiens.
Lyncée's ships are in view.

Heading in score	Key, meter	Paraphrase of sung texts/comments
Chœur des Matelots, "Venez, jeune héros, les tranquilles Zéphyrs / Ont applani pour vous le vaste sein de l'onde"	G, **2**	The chorus compares the peace on the sea that is making Lyncée's landing possible to the peace he will find on land.
Rondeau. Premier Air du Tambourin	G, $\frac{2}{4}$	Notated monophonically for *petites flûtes*; probably also accompanied by the 3 dancers playing tambourins.
Deuxième Air [du Tambourin]	G, $\frac{2}{4}$	Same instrumentation as the first.
[Recitative] Hypermnestre, *aux Peuples* "Que ne vous dois-je point"		Hypermnestre tells the people that their enthusiasm relieves her sorrows.
Air pour les Egyptiens. Rondeau	G, **3**	
Deuxième Air. Rondeau	g, **3**	Very similar to the previous dance
Air [aka *Ariette*[a]] une Argienne, "Hâte-toi de quitter les cieux, / Vole, Amour"	G, **2** [=$\frac{12}{8}$]	Asks Amour to fulfill the wishes of one who has been waiting for Neptune to bring back her lover. In da capo aria structure.
Air pour les Matelots	g, **2**	
Premier Passepied	G, $\frac{3}{8}$	
Deuxième Passepied	g, $\frac{3}{8}$	
Airs du Tambourin (both) repeated	G, $\frac{2}{4}$	
Lyncée's ship enters the harbor.		
Chœur, "Venez, jeune héros" repeated[b]	G, **2**	

[a] This piece is labeled "Air" in the score, and "Ariette" in the list of *Airs à chanter* at the front of the volume.

[b] In the 1716 libretto this chorus follows another air by the Argienne, "Doux objet," but there is no music for it in the score. The libretto in the *Recueil général* contains the texts of both vocal airs, but differently ordered within the divertissement.

The divertissement thus marks a transitional moment between Hypermnestre's fears for her fiancé's safety and the joy of his arrival, and, like the divertissement in Act I, it incorporates the words of a principal character (see Table 11-4). Gervais took advantage of this liminal moment to expand musically; there are seven instrumental dances, not counting repeats, plus an Italianate *ariette*. A *didascalie* at the start of the scene identifies the sailors as Argiens, but two of the dances are attributed to Egyptiens, which must mean sailors in the service of those of Egyptus's sons who are already on land. The *ariette* is sung by an unnamed Argienne, but alludes directly to Hypermnestre's state of uncertain anticipation.

The two tambourins are particularly interesting, not only as relatively early and somewhat quirky examples of a dance type whose use was on the rise, but because they are notated monophonically (see Example 11-1) and scored for "petites flûtes" – in imitation of the *galoubet*, the three-holed tabor pipe traditionally played with the tambourin in Provence. Gervais's score does not notate rhythms for the drums, but

Example 11-1: Gervais, *Hypermnestre* II/4, "Premier Air du tambourin. Rondeau" (Paris: Ballard, 1716), 118.

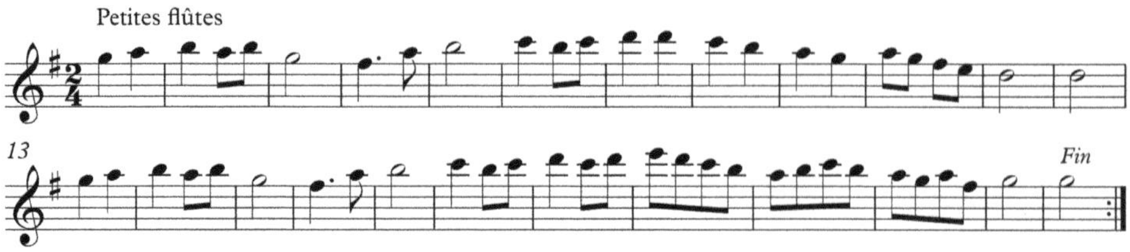

if Marais's *Alcyone* of ten years earlier can be seen as a model, then they were probably beaten on the downbeat (see Chapter 12, p. 370), presumably on-stage by the three dancers identified as "Tambourins." These two dances may have been composed by Philippe d'Orléans, Gervais's patron, as they appear in the unpublished score of his opera *Penthée* (1705). However, as Gervais apparently helped the duke on this opera, the authorship question remains open.[30]

Exceptionally, all seven of the dance pieces are independent of the vocal music – but, with the exception of the "Air pour les Matelots," they come in pairs. In the absence of help from the vocal music as to who might have danced where, the *Mercure* offers partial information for the 1728 revival: "the Dlle Camargo dances in the second 'Air de tambourin,' which draws everyone's astonishment and admiration. It is followed by a *pas de deux* by the sieurs Laval and Maltaire."[31] Camargo excelled at the rapid footwork required by tambourins; the specific mention of her performance in the second one must indicate that someone else danced the first – probably the group. This means that even if the pairing of two dances provided an aural affinity, their choreographic realization might have insisted on a visual distinction.

The divertissement in Act III comes at an emotional high point, right after the moving ceremonies during which Hypermnestre and Lyncée put their hands on the altar of Hymen to make their wedding vows. Immediately thereafter, "the doors of the temple of Isis open, and an infinity of people from Argos and the environs enter in a crowd to take part in the festivities." The chorus that follows their entrance alludes to the recent peace and wishes the young couple a loving marriage. It sets a more elevated tone than is often the case in pastoral divertissements, so it seems appropriate that the cast list identifies the dancers as Bergers and Bergères héroïques. The dance music eschews the more rustic rigaudons in favor of a loure, two gavottes, two menuets, and another instrumental dance. Yet this last piece, which was replaced after the score for Act III had been printed, suggests that Gervais did originally plan for a rustic peasant dance: the original, an "Air pour les Pâtres" in duple meter, minor mode, solid and heavy in rhythm, was replaced by one that is also in minor, but in $\frac{6}{8}$, much lighter in

[30] Montagnier, *Gervais*, 107. [31] *MF* (June, 1728), 1456.

character, and that alternates textures between strings and oboes;[32] its tone is more in keeping with the rest of the divertissement. In the event, no peasant role is listed among the dancing cast; all of the shepherds were "heroic," as they were again in the 1728 revival.[33] Perhaps this is a rare instance of a peasant dance being *removed* from an opera, rather than added.

Act III was the one that most impressed the reviewer of *Hypermnestre* at its reprise in 1728,[34] not least because of what happens after the shepherds depart. Hypermnestre, left alone with her father, swears on the same altar where she had just made her marriage vows to defend him against his enemies, only to learn he wants her to kill her husband. Act IV, however, impressed the reviewer almost as much, and in his view the composer outdid the librettist. The lighting effects probably also contributed to the success of this act: set in the gardens of the palace, it took place in penumbra, lit only by the torches carried by the newly married couples, who were all dressed in white. Exceptionally, the divertissement, identified in the libretto as an epithalamion, opens the act. Although the "young people" are not specifically identified as comprising the other 49 newly wedded couples, the chorus and dancers are clearly intended to be seen that way, in the only time in the opera any of the other sons and daughters besides Hypermnestre and Lyncée put in an appearance.

The scene is constructed around a gigantic passacaille, one rivaling the passacaille from the last act of *Armide* in intensity. It is built over a descending tetrachord, and even though it changes texture in various ways, including from instrumental to vocal, it remains in the minor mode for all of its 302 measures.[35] Since there is only one other dance in the divertissement – an entrance march – probably all thirteen dancers named in the libretto participated in the passacaille, with the configurations changing at appropriate musical moments. The dancers consisted of a female soloist (Mlle Guyot), a mixed couple (Marcel and Mlle Menés), and five each of other men and women. Here again a passacaille is associated with a female soloist, a choice that seems particularly appropriate since the focus is about to switch to Hypermnestre's agonizing choice between saving the life of her father or that of her husband. But the solo mixed couple offers a choreographic opportunity to emphasize the weddings, one supported by the texts sung during the passacaille, which highlight the union of love and marriage. In a scene that blends solemnity with tenderness, the chorus's words add a figurative sense to the torches lighting the stage: "Come, Hymen, spread your flames;

32 The replacement piece was printed in a supplement. A note in Act III instructs the reader to ignore the original piece.

33 François Dumoulin, the specialist in peasant roles, did not dance in this opera, nor in the one that immediately preceded it, *Les Fêtes de l'été*. His absence from two operas complicates the question of whether the substitution was artistic or practical.

34 *MF* (June 1728), 1446.

35 The measure count, which includes repeats, comes from Montagnier, *Gervais*, 125.

Come, Love, shoot your arrows; may you reign together forever, reign over these tender souls. [Refrain:] God of marriage, god of lovers, ah! how charming are your fires." The writer for the *Mercure* called this passacaille a masterpiece.[36]

Act v opens with Hypermnestre in a state of shock at the bloodletting she has seen; all her sisters have murdered their husbands. Even though the opera ends with the re-establishment of order, following Danaüs's death and Isis's appointment of Lyncée to rule in his place, the equilibrium is so fragile that a fête would have seemed horribly misplaced. Instead, La Font staged a battle between the Argiens and the Egyptians, with five dancers on each side, that takes place partially on and partially off stage, as Hypermnestre tries to discern who is winning and fears for the life of her husband. This scene recalls the off-stage battle in the opening act of Lully's *Thésée*, which also lets the audience hear snatches of martial music while the on-stage characters react with fear and horror. The resemblance between these two scenes increased after Act v of *Hypermnestre* was revised and the battle moved entirely off stage; in the 1728 revival no dancers figured in this act.

La Font's libretto for *Hypermnestre* recalls Quinault's tragedies – and also Thomas Corneille's libretto for *Médée* – in the seamlessness with which divertissements and storyline mesh. In a story this dark La Font's success is all the more remarkable, given the tendency during this period toward long, diegetic fêtes. The construction of the acts is so tight that Gervais could permit himself the kind of musical expansion that had become acceptable in festive divertissements and still support the dramatic intensity. But by Act iv, with horror closing in on the protagonist, Gervais became downright Lullian in his proportions.

The two creators of this opera may have operated at a higher level than did some of their contemporaries, but everyone who worked at the Opéra recognized that different kinds of divertissements had their own dramaturgy and adjusted accordingly. Yet it is clear that in some quarters dance was seen as a distraction from the drama, or even an impediment to it. This attitude found a focus in Montéclair's opera *Jephté* (1732), whose reception history reveals how much controversy dance in an opera could generate.

JEPHTÉ (1732)

As the first French opera to stage a story from the Bible, *Jephté* was highly contested – although in the end highly successful. It premiered during Lent, when the Opéra was usually closed. As the *Mercure de France* reported in its March issue (571), "the novelty of the genre had made its success seem so doubtful that no one believed the opera could be performed twice; [however,] this widely held prejudice could not stand up to the beauties of the libretto and the music." The nervousness of the authors, librettist Abbé

36 *MF* (June 1728), 1451.

Simon Joseph Pellegrin and composer Michel de Montéclair, concerned not only the use of a biblical story, but the propriety of having biblical characters dance. The lengthy justification in Pellegrin's preface, framed as a series of rhetorical questions that go through the divertissements act by act, sounds a defensive tone that allows us to infer the nature of the objections:

> It is not without trembling that I undertook to put a subject drawn from Holy Scripture onto the stage of the Académie Royale de Musique [. . .] Those who succumbed the most to the initial surprise that drives people to condemn blindly anything new or bold, made an especially big fuss about the dance [. . .] As for the ballet, which some saw as an insurmountable obstacle, I fail to understand on what grounds I should exclude it from my tragedy. Has not the art of dance existed in all times? Does it not belong to all peoples? Did not the Jewish nation devote itself to dance as much as the others? Did not David, the holiest of kings, dance before the Ark of the Lord, as do my warriors in my first act? Did not Jepthah's daughter go out to meet her father, conqueror of the Ammonites, with drums and dances? These are the words of the Holy Scripture. Can I be blamed for having used them as the basis for the fête in my second act? Could I have a firmer foundation? Could the tribes of Israel, recognizing Jepthah as their sovereign, have marked their acclamations with any greater brilliance than by the same dances that, for other peoples, have been religious ceremonies? I will say nothing about the fête in the fourth act. It includes shepherds and shepherdesses come to pay homage to their princess. What could be more natural than their pastoral dances? Moreover, we have taken care to banish all indecency, and I do not believe that the strictest censors could demand anything more.[37]

But turning a biblical story into an opera was so radical that an explanatory preface did not suffice; the justification had to become part of the work itself. This was done in the prologue by pitting Apollon and two of the Muses against Truth and the Virtues. The set is a theater, which, Apollon explains, is the sole home left to the gods of antiquity – "since the extinction of paganism," adds the *Mercure*;[38] the score even specifies that the theater in question is the Académie Royale de Musique. Apollon invites Polymnie and Terpsichore to help him amuse the mortals. People duly arrive to see the new performance, during which Vénus makes a cameo appearance and Terpsichore dances with her followers. But the lights dim on the stage, while at the same time a brightness grows in the flies. Truth, surrounded by the Virtues, descends in a Glory to the sound of beautiful music. She addresses the "seductive phantoms, the children of imposture" and tells them it is time for truth to drive away deceit. In a brief, but unambiguous show of power, she sends the mythological divinities not just away from the theater, but to the Underworld. As if they were so many demons, Apollon, the Muses, and the other gods, sink through the traps down to the bowels of the theater. Truth, the triumphant impresario, asks the Virtues to

37 Translation mine. A transcription of the entire preface with translation into English may be found in the liner notes to the recording by Les Arts Florissants (HMX 2901424.25), 21–23.

38 *MF* (March 1732), 572.

mount a new performance, one that will use the story of Jephté to both instruct and please. She tells the Virtues that they may "sweeten their severity" – i.e., use means other than the mere spoken word – but she warns them not to let "any false brilliance alter the splendor of the truth."

Thus warned, the audience must have expected a radically different kind of opera than ones governed by the gods of Olympus. What it saw did vary in some of its surface elements, both textual and musical, but it still maintained the structures and most of the conventions of the *tragédie en musique*, including the divertissement in each act. It is nonetheless clear that Pellegrin and Montéclair made a huge effort to make their opera worthy of its sacred subject and to minimize the possible objections to the act of transposing a sacred story to a secular environment.

The libretto derives from the Book of Judges, chapter 11, and tells a story familiar from Carissimi's oratorio on the same subject: the Hebrew leader Jephthah, before going off to battle the Ammonites, vows to God that if he is victorious, he will sacrifice as a burnt offering the first creature coming out of his house. Upon returning home, his daughter is the first person he sees. She accepts her fate, asking only for two months in which to bewail her lost virginity, and Jephthah duly carries out his promise. A five-act opera, however, of necessity fleshes out the lean biblical narrative. Jephté's daughter acquires a name (Iphise), a mother (Almasie), and a love interest (Ammon, the leader of the enemy Ammonites). Jephté himself has been away for so long that he does not recognize the young woman he sees. Already distressed at the idea that this young person will have to be sacrificed, he is horrified when his wife identifies her. He cannot bear to be in her presence, from which Iphise concludes that she must have done something that angers her father. When she learns that she is to be sacrificed, she accepts her fate as punishment for her guilt at loving an enemy leader and rejects Ammon's desire to rescue her. This is the state of affairs at the end of Act IV. The contested and much revised Act V is discussed below.[39]

In view of the sensitivity of asking biblical characters to dance, Pellegrin and Montéclair handled the divertissements with circumspection. Each is well anchored within the narrative and, with the exception of a single act, the number of dance pieces is restrained. In all cases the sung texts inside the divertissements maintain a tone of reverence and even allude to God. The Act I dances are embedded within a long sequence for Jephté and his warriors, who are preparing for battle. First, after a moving

[39] The source situation for *Jephté* is exceptionally complex, due to the numerous revisions. These can be seen in the various librettos, especially those published in 1732 and 1733, and in the three editions of the score. A brief overview of the different versions may be found on pp. 13–14 (26–27 in English) of the booklet accompanying the recording (see previous note). I have based my discussions primarily on the first published libretto, the separately published libretto to Act V, and the second edition of the score, while also taking into account the second libretto for 1732, the libretto for 1733, and the third edition of the score.

choral prayer, sung a cappella, and a second, madrigalesque chorus declaring that the heavens and the earth tremble before the Lord, the sacred Ark, hidden from view in a luminous cloud, descends and spreads its glory over the Israelites. The High Priest then invokes the warriors to demonstrate a "holy joy" ("sainte allégresse"); the warriors' three dances are rounded off by another prayer. The enemy is seen approaching, and Jephté makes his fatal vow to God, in exchange for victory. In response, and as a spectacular ending to the act, the Jordan River separates: "the army groups itself around Jephté to the sound of trumpets, and Jephté, at the head of the Israelites, passes the Jordan to go to combat the Ammonites."

The three instrumental dances for the Israelite warriors, of whom there were nine in 1732, one of them a soloist, are done all in a row. The first dance is marked "Majestueusement" and looks to be a musically updated version of an *entrée grave*. The next offers the contrast of a lively triple meter (marked "Gai"), and the last is a rondeau in $\frac{6}{4}$ that calls for trumpets and drums in the refrains. Even though these dances are musically independent of the vocal numbers, they can probably be seen as embodying, in order, the actions that Phinée, the High Priest, invokes in recitative upon their conclusion: "Reawaken your warlike ardor; march, run, fly, may all yield to you; disperse, like the dust, all your proud enemies." The chorus that follows prays God for His help: "Come spread disorder and fear upon the enemies of Your glory. God of combats, grant us victory; may death fly before You." Montéclair did not build into it any instrumental interludes, and as it is a dramatic double chorus, it probably depended purely on musical means for its effect. But at the end of the act, when the soldiers surround Jephté and cross the Jordan, the dancers may well have supplied – or at least led – the action.

The Act II divertissement comes on the heels of Iphise's confession to her horrified mother that she loves Ammon, their enemy. Before she can say more, Abdon arrives to announce the Israelite victory. Almasie asks her daughter to lead the celebrations, while she herself goes to the temple. Since the Bible mentions that Jephthah's daughter went out to meet him to the sound of drums (Judges 11:34), Montéclair was scrupulous to include them in his score: Scene 6 opens with a march scored for strings, *petites flûtes* and *tambourins*. The same scoring recurs later in a danced tambourin. Pellegrin supplied a suitably reverent text for the refrain of the chorus that follows the march: "O happy day! O day that the Eternal One has made!" which Montéclair set for voices without instruments, in evocation of sacred music. (The rest of this chorus alternates a larger choir plus its lively orchestral accompaniment with the a cappella refrain.) Of the three dances that follow, two are interleaved with solo airs sung by a female resident of Maspha and the chorus. Whereas the texts are not overtly religious, they are less frivolous than many of those associated with fêtes in other operas, and they focus on wishes for a lasting peace, not on love. The score does not call for any of the dances to be repeated after the vocal music, which means that the elapsed time for dancing remains relatively modest. The one and only repeat draws upon the Lullian tradition of using a previously heard piece as the entr'acte, and here it has a truly dramatic effect. After the songs and dances, a trumpet sounds and Jephté's imminent arrival is announced. As the act ends, Iphise and the others head off to meet him, to the catchy tune of the same tambourin to which they had danced only seconds before (see Example 11-2); in fact, the dancers may well have taken up their dances once again. Probably everyone leaves the stage before Jephté enters it; in other words, the audience is left to imagine the fateful meeting between father and daughter that occurs between the acts, and the divertissement continues, in a sense, out of view. On the other hand, the final *didascalie* in the act is ambiguous: "Iphise, followed by the people, goes before Jephté" ("Iphise, suivi du Peuple, va au-devant de Jephté"). A director might well be tempted to stage the encounter between the two of them, while the joyous tambourin sounds in the orchestra. Time does elapse between Acts II and III – there is a change of location – but perhaps not much, as Act III opens with the troubled Jephté meditating on the fact that he has seen the victim he has sworn to sacrifice. Whether the encounter is seen or imagined, the joyful music of the repeated tambourin makes a wrenching foil to this fateful moment.

In the course of Act III Jephté learns that the young woman he saw when returning home is his daughter. He tells his wife, Almasie, of his promise; she refuses to believe that God would demand such a sacrifice, and together they decide to consult Him to see if there is a means of avoiding Jephté's impossible choice between blasphemy and killing his only child. At that moment the Israelites arrive to declare Jephté their leader. Jephté has to hide his unhappiness while he is honored by his people; fortunately for him, the celebrations do not last long and they focus at least as much on the peace God has granted as they do on him. Following a very brief trumpet march and an invocation by the High Priest, a brilliant double chorus asks that Jephté's glory be carried to the heavens. This triple-meter piece goes on long enough and includes enough instrumental passages that it may have been partially danced. Following it comes a chaconne that has both instrumental and vocal sections. The recurring sung refrain declares that it is time for the people's fears to end, and the couplets extol the joys of peace. The choice of a chaconne, the only dance in the divertissement, was perhaps made because of its associations with heroic men, and, in fact, the dancing cast list calls for a male soloist.[40] This particular chaconne has the unusual feature of being in the minor mode, although it does conform to type in starting on beat 2. There is a section in the middle in major with trumpets and drums to highlight the military victory; the return to minor coincides with the introduction of the voices celebrating peace. The instrumental portion is not repeated after the vocal chaconne; once again Montéclair eschewed

[40] The dancers in 1732 are identified as tribal chiefs, five each of men and women, with David Dumoulin as soloist.

Example 11-2: Montéclair, *Jephté* II/6, "Tambourins" (second edition, Paris: Boivin, n.d. [1732]), 110.

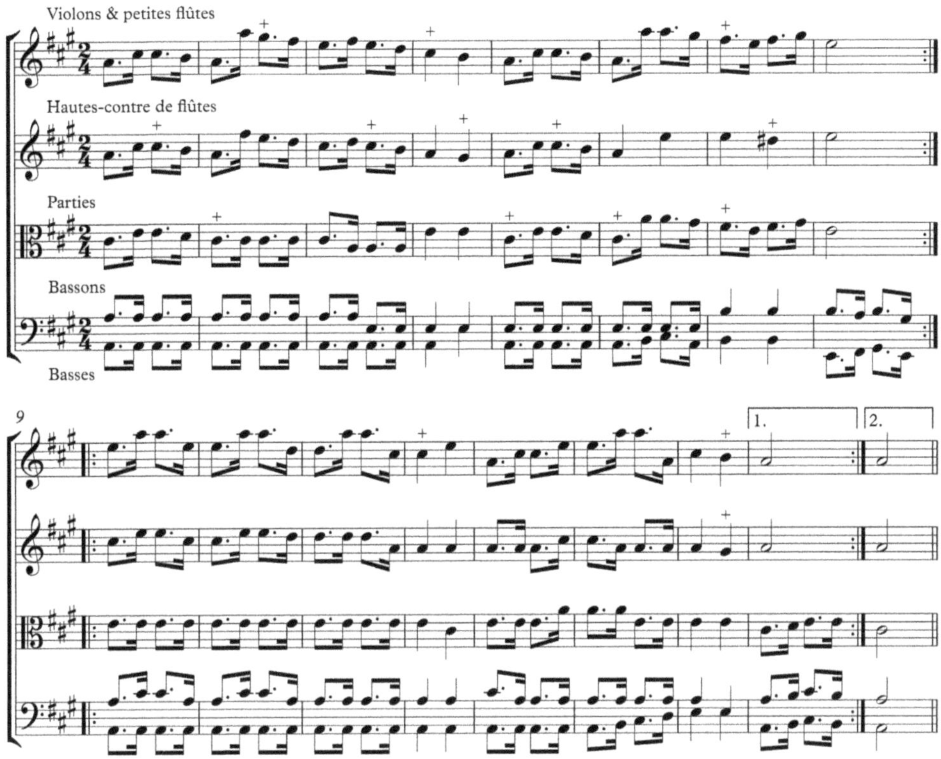

the opportunity for choreographic expansion. As a sign of the integration that this divertissement achieves within the opera, it is followed by a conversation between Phinée and Jephté, in which the High Priest reminds the new leader that God is the true ruler. His insistence on obedience to God's laws reignites Jephté's agonies, but when Phinée asks him what is wrong, he merely says that he will be faithful to the Lord and the act ends on this note.

In Act IV Iphise encounters a similar situation to that of her father. She does not yet know that she is to be sacrificed, but is nonetheless miserable because her father is avoiding her and because she feels guilty over her love for Ammon. In vain she seeks solace in the natural world, whose murmuring streams and bird calls are beautifully depicted in the orchestra. When the shepherds of the surrounding area come to honor her, she sadly greets them with the observation that they are more fortunate than she is. This divertissement – the longest in the opera and the most conventional (see Table 11-5) – is the one that Pellegrin noted he would not bother to mention because nothing was more "natural" than pastoral dances. By natural he may have meant

Table 11-5: Montéclair, *Jephté* (1732), IV/3: Iphise, Elise, Compagnes d'Iphise, Troupe de Bergers et de Bergères.
The oboes, musettes, and bassoons precede the march onto the stage.

Heading in score	Musical features	Paraphrase of sung text/ comments
Marche des Bergers. Tendrement	C, **3**, binary	
Chœur, "Nous vivons dans l'innocence"	C, **3**	Same music as the march
Première Pastourelle. Légèrement	C, **2**, ABA	Includes musettes in the orchestra
Deuxième Pastourelle	C, **2**, rondeau	Gavotte-like, trio texture with musettes, oboes, bassoons
Premier Menuet	C, **3**	Scored for strings and oboes
Deuxième Menuet	C, **3**	Scored for musette/oboe/bassoon trio
Premier Menuet repeated	C, **3**	
[Air] Une Bergère avec le Chœur, "Que tout brille en ce bocage"	C, **3**	Very similar to Pr. Menuet; orchestra includes *petits dessus de flûte*
Deuxième Menuet repeated	C, **3**	
La Bergère et le Chœur, "Des oiseaux le doux ramage"	C, **3**	Second strophe of sung menuet
[Récitatif and air] Iphise, ". . . à l'auteur de la nature / Vos chants doivent être adressés"		Iphise tells the shepherds their songs should be addressed to the Lord.
Chœur, "Que le ciel, que la terre et l'onde, / Chantent les bienfaits du Seigneur"	C, **c**	The chorus repeats Iphise's wish that heaven, earth, and sea honor the Lord's works. Orchestra scored for strings, oboes, *petites flûtes*, the latter imitating bird calls.

omnipresent; by this point in French operatic history pastoral divertissements had become a cliché. This one draws upon the conventions of the heroic pastoral genre: gentle music set to the sounds of oboes and musettes with sung texts that allude to beauties of the natural world and the innocent joys of this Arcadia's inhabitants. The *Mercure* said of this divertissement, that it is "without doubt the most graceful one in the opera and may rightfully be compared to the one in Act IV of *Roland*."[41]

Yet for all that this divertissement belongs to a recognizable genre, Pellegrin and Montéclair did make choices that distance it from the ordinary. First, the texts eschew any mention of love. Moreover, even this celebration of innocent pleasures receives a gentle reproach from Iphise, who reminds the shepherds at its end that they need to address their songs to the maker of this world, whereupon the chorus breaks into a

[41] *MF* (March 1732), 584. The musical resemblance between the opening of the two divertissements may have been cultivated by Montéclair. Both choruses (*Jepthé*'s "Nous vivons dans l'innocence" and *Roland*'s "Quand on vient dans ce boccage") have the same music as the march, are in a major mode, in triple meter, and are set homorhythmically in three-bar phrases. *Roland* had last been performed in 1728; see the outline of this divertissement in Table 12-6, p. 372.

song of thanksgiving. Second, as pastoral divertissements of this generation go, this one is relatively short, with only five dances (two of them repeated). Third, the authors avoided either of the common accretions to such divertissements: a comic dance for peasants[42] or a musically elaborate *ariette* (in other circumstances the bird-song text could have provided a prime opportunity for such a piece). Rather, they chose to remain within the old-fashioned French concept of the "natural," which here manifests itself as a tuneful – and sensitively scored – simplicity. The only musically developed piece is the concluding chorus that honors the Lord. The pastoral idyll is shattered when Iphise's mother arrives with the dreadful news that her daughter must be sacrificed in fulfillment of her father's vow.

Act v was the site of greatest contention. When the opera went on stage in February of 1732 this act had no divertissement. Instead, it built in tension through a series of confrontations between main characters (which varied among the different revisions), a shower of fire from the heavens to kill Ammon and his followers, and Iphise's confession of her guilty love, to the awful point where Phinée hands Jephté the knife. But Pellegrin could not bring himself to allow his character to die; he spared Iphise's life, through the mechanism of allowing Phinée to hear the voice of God.

> Le Dieu qui fait trembler et le ciel et la terre,
> Tel qu'au Mont Sinaï, par la voix du tonnerre,
> Va-t-il faire entendre sa loi?
> Écoutons, quel bonheur! Il me parle; il m'inspire;
> Je le vois qui suspend le trait prêt à partir;
> C'en est fait; sa colère expire;
> C'est l'ouvrage du repentir.

> (God, who makes the earth and the heavens tremble, as he did on Mount Sinai with a voice of thunder, will he announce His law? Let's listen; what happiness! He is speaking to me, inspiring me. I see him holding back the arrow ready to fly. It is over; his wrath is gone. It is the result of repentance.)

The opera ended quickly thereafter, in a brief chorus: "Ah! quels bienfaits sur nous, sa main vient de répandre! / Et que de grâces à lui rendre!" (What goodness his hand bestows upon us! What thanks we owe him!) But complaints appeared right away about this ending, which lasted for only eight performances. On 18 March a new Act v was substituted, in which Ammon's rebellion takes place on stage instead of in the wings, various other rearrangements of the events and dialogue occurred, and, most notably, a divertissement was tacked on after the chorus that had previously concluded the opera. It was introduced by Phinée, who, in words thoroughly uncharacteristic of

42 In 1732 the dancing cast consisted of four shepherds and eight shepherdesses, one of them a soloist. There were no roles for peasants, nor does any of the music lend itself to comic treatment.

his stern demeanor during the rest of the opera, invites those who live on the shores of the River Jordan to come and celebrate.

> Chantez sur ces charmantas rivages;
> Bénissez l'Éternel; célébrez ses bienfaits;
> Il bannit loin de vous la guerre et ses ravages;
> Sur son peuple fidèle il fait regner la paix.
>
> (Let us sing on these charming shores. Bless the eternal God; celebrate his goodness to us. He has banished war and its ravages far from you. He grants peace to his faithful people.)

The music for this divertissement does not appear in any of the three editions of the score, but the texts were printed in a special libretto consisting only of the new Act v. It was bookended by a chorus built on Phinée's words and had two sets of dances surrounding an *ariette*. This ending appears to have lasted for the remaining performances of 1732, but by the time the opera was revived in 1733, it had disappeared. The March 1733 issue of the *Mercure* reports (565–66):

> The fête that ended the work has been suppressed, since it had been added only to satisfy the desire of the dance enthusiasts. In place of the fête an act of thanksgiving was substituted, expressed in these four lines:
>
> "Let us consecrate the memory of the most beautiful of days. Tender vows and sweet transports, constantly renewed in our impassioned hearts, fly up like incense to the throne of the King of Glory."[43]
>
> These lines were set as a trio and this trio is sung by the three most beautiful voices at the Opéra. The chorus repeats the trio to end the work.

The three beautiful voices belonged to the singers in the roles of Iphise, Almasie, and Jephté, who in previous versions of the ending had remained silent following Iphise's miraculous deliverance. The beautiful trio Montéclair composed for them, and then expanded into a chorus, makes for a much more effective ending than the misguided divertissement must have done.

Notwithstanding all the nervousness that surrounded its creation, *Jephté* was a resounding success, revived multiple times up until 1761. Even the choreographer was praised for his sensitive treatment of the dances: "Blondy brought infinite honor upon himself in choreographing a work whose genre was unknown to his predecessors." And "as for the music," added the *Mercure*, "the greatest connoisseurs find it worthy of Lully and no one contradicts them."[44] Almost 50 years after his death, Lully remained the yardstick by which other works were judged, even if by 1732 worthiness did not require stylistic similarity. Montéclair's music stands out for the richness of its

[43] "Du plus beau de nos jours, consacrons la mémoire; / Tendres vœux, doux transports, sans cesse renaissants, / De nos cœurs enflammés, volez comme l'encens, / Jusqu'au trône du Roi de gloire."

[44] *MF* (March 1732), 587 and 571.

orchestration and his expressive treatment of instrumental timbres, not only in the dance pieces, but in the vocal airs and recitatives. The prominence accorded the chorus, which appears both inside and outside the divertissements, also distinguishes this opera. Montéclair had been playing double bass in the Opéra's orchestra since 1699 and had written one opera-ballet, *Les Fêtes de l'été* (1716), but it was only at age 65 that he composed his first and only *tragédie en musique*. The following year another seasoned composer was to make his operatic debut at the age of 50, inspired, so he claimed almost 30 years later, by Montéclair's "noble and distinguished" score. "[Rameau] recognized instantly that our [French] dramatic music was capable of a new force and new beauties. He conceived the idea of composing opera himself; he dared to be a creator. He admits no less than that *Jephté* begat *Hippolyte et Aricie*."[45] Apocryphal? Perhaps, but, given the qualities of *Jephté*, plausible.

45 *MF* (March 1761), 153. This comment appears within a review of a revival of *Jephté*. Its author does not mention that these two operas had the same librettist.

The case of *Jephté* shows how contested the role of dance could be, but the subject of an opera did not have to be biblical for dance's impact to become an issue. Two different testimonies from the early eighteenth century offer contemporary perspectives on the amount of time operas should devote to dancing. The first comes in 1705 from Lecerf de la Viéville, a defender of French opera against the Italian style:

> [Lully] did not allow as much scope for ballet as in opera nowadays, when it occupies a quarter of the time. It used to be shorter. Lully would not have been pleased to see an *entrée* repeated two or three times as happens today. He believed that to dance each *entrée* once was quite sufficient. Our *entrées*, repeated indiscriminately two or three times, greatly prolong and dull the performance (since dances, which are weak at representation and barely capable of touching the heart, necessarily dull it); perhaps this contributes to the listlessness creeping into operas these days.[1]

The Abbé Dubos, reporting in his *Critical Reflections* (1719) on the views of unnamed commentators, also saw listlessness as a problem, but offered a different diagnosis:

> The recitatives seem to have no life, and the balet airs leave us quite tranquil. They alledge as a proof of what they advance, that the representation of Lulli's operas lasts longer at present, than when they were executed under his direction; tho' they ought not to last near so long, because 'tis unusual now to repeat a great many [dance] airs, which Lulli generally played twice.[2]

What are we to make of this conflicting testimony? Dubos appears to be talking about pacing, Lecerf about superfluous repetitions, but which of them do we believe as to whether Lully performed his dance pieces twice or only once? From the testimony of the scores, we can see that individual dance pieces were often repeated by Lully as parts of larger structures (e.g., strophic dance-songs), but his successors called for such architectural repeats as well; Table 11-2 shows one such divertissement from *Tancrède*, and other pertinent examples may be seen below. Might one or both writers rather have had immediate repetition in mind – performing a dance twice in a row? If so, was Lecerf complaining about musical repetitions or about seeing the same choreography danced by the same people more than once? Or might he have been thinking of instances of several dances in a row, unattached to vocal pieces – a phenomenon rare in Lully but more

[1] Lecerf, *Comparaison*, II, 228–29; trans. Wood and Sadler, *French Baroque Opera*, 69.

[2] Dubos, *Réflexions critiques*, III, 318; trans. Nugent, III, 241; Dubos's text specifies "airs de violon."

acceptable in this period? It is frustrating not to be able to answer such basic questions, but we *can* see that Lecerf betrays a lack of interest in dance throughout his book, whereas Dubos accords it serious consideration. Given their respective attitudes, it is significant that both of them perceive something out of balance about operatic dancing since Lully – although we should be cautious in according weight to vague statements about how much better things were in the olden days. Still, if we accept the premise that there had been a change in equilibrium between the vocal and instrumental elements in the *tragédie en musique*, the likeliest places to look for what the two writers may have had in mind are those divertissements that lent themselves more easily to expansion – certain types of fêtes. There are, after all, many ways that dances can impose themselves on the attention, and repetition is only one of them.

Although neither writer says so, they may have been reacting to the infiltration of practices from other operatic genres. This chapter looks at the developing tendency for fêtes in tragedies to share content and construction with divertissements of the type found in opera-ballets. One way to get at questions of balance is to look at the divertissement topoi that went across the repertoire; another is to check what happened to Lully's operas when they were revived.

THREE DIVERTISSEMENT TYPES

Three types of fêtes – Italian-inflected scenes, pastoral divertissements, and nautical divertissements – recur so often across the repertoire as perhaps to have contributed to Lecerf's unease. None of these topoi was entirely new, but they occurred much more frequently than they had in Lully's works. All three invoke their own musicality, usually by starting with a "let's sing and dance" type of text, yet while some of these divertissements might, indeed, merit the adjective "decorative," their handling escapes simple generalizations. As always, both the inner workings and the surroundings into which a divertissement fits are crucial to understanding its functioning.

Italianisms in the *Tragédie en Musique*

The French fascination with Italy, which reached its apogee in 1710 with Campra's *Fêtes vénitiennes*, left perceptible, if sporadic, traces in the *tragédie en musique*. The nature of the highbrow genre, set in either a mythological or historical past, would seem antithetical to such a break in tone, yet we have already seen that two tragedies from the 1690s were composed with Italian songs and dances inside them: Colasse's *Astrée* and Charpentier's *Médée*. A handful of later tragedies incorporated songs in Italian from the start, and a few more had Italian arias added during revivals. In works set in Venice, naturalizing an Italian aria was not a problem, but the only way possible to do so in a tragedy, without transgressing the laws of verisimilitude, was to frame the foreign pieces as stage music, which meant locating them inside divertissements.

A naturalized Italian, Theobaldo Gatti, was the first composer to include a da capo aria in a French *tragédie en musique, Scylla.*[3] The location of the opera – ancient Greece – does not invite an Italian musical incursion, nor does the setting of the Act II divertissement, in which a sorceress conjures up demons disguised as Plaisirs.[4] This particular da capo aria seems plopped down into the middle of an otherwise French-style scene. The sentiments of its text ("Per vincer pugnando"), which invoke "your sweet glance" as a weapon in the war of love, do not conflict with the *carpe diem* advice in the choral song in French, but the aria makes no musical connections with the pieces on either side of it. It is not even clear who sings it, since no role is assigned in the score. The aria is unambiguously Italian in style – in $\frac{3}{8}$ time, preceded by a violinistic ritornello, with a motto opening and melismatic writing for the voice – but the dance that follows is a long, purely instrumental passacaille in French style; the only possible relationship between them is two different kinds of virtuosity, one vocal, the other balletic.[5] Perhaps Gatti wanted an Italian aria more than he cared about coherence; the fact that the text does not appear in the libretto suggests that the insertion was done on the composer's initiative.

La Gorce sees the inclusion of arias in Italian into tragedies as acts of "provocation," something Campra chose to avoid by confining his Italian pieces to other operatic genres.[6] Yet in 1708 Campra wrote two such arias into his tragedy *Hippodamie* – set, however, to texts in French. This is the very same year that Campra published his first book of *cantates*, a genre whose texts are in French, but whose musical style owes much to Italy. Both of the *ariettes* – as the French called Italianate da capo arias in their own language[7] – are located in divertissements, and as he had done in *L'Europe galante*, Campra took care to integrate them with the dance music: "Charmant vainqueur" in *Hippodamie* I/4 is introduced by a related dance in triple meter, and "Allez, volez" in II/5 is surrounded by a related gigue in $\frac{12}{8}$ time, a signature associated with music in Italian style. The introduction of the *ariette* broadened the formal possibilities in all types of French opera, but the phenomenon of introducing Italian arias into tragedies had not yet run its course: the following year, 1709, *Roland* and *Phaéton* of Lully, then in revival,

[3] Gatti had already published a collection of songs in Italian (Paris: Ballard, 1696).

[4] *Scylla* premiered on 16 September 1701, but shortly underwent substantial revisions; a second edition of the libretto was published for a new set of performances that started on 20 December. These remarks are based on the second edition of the libretto, which corresponds more closely to the score (Ballard, 1701). The rationale for the Act II divertissement is different in the two cases, although its sung texts and *didascalies* are the same.

[5] A choreography for the passacaille is preserved in Beauchamps-Feuillet notation; see Appendix 3.

[6] La Gorce, "Vogue et influence," 204.

[7] The term "ariette" later acquired an additional meaning in the context of opéra comique: a newly composed song in French, as opposed to a borrowed vaudeville.

were each graced with a da capo aria in Italian, as was a new tragedy, *Méléagre*.[8] Battistin Stuck was an Italian of German ancestry who had moved to France in 1705 after having already composed *opere serie*; *Méléagre* was the first of three operas for the Académie Royale de Musique. He, however, did not treat the Italian pieces in isolation: the prologue to *Méléagre* personifies both Italy and France, each country embodied by both a singer and a set of dancers. Italy says she had heard about the land governed by the renowned king and now that she is there, acknowledges that her former glories have been eclipsed. She nonetheless takes issue with France's implication of musical superiority. Apollon settles the dispute by requesting that they both join in honoring the hero; the concluding chorus invokes "the happy mingling of our sweetest harmonies."[9]

This device allowed Stuck to present an elaborate da capo aria ("Su la bella navicella di speranza") as a set piece for one of Italy's followers. Its text has nothing to do with its surroundings, but, as Campra had done before him, Stuck naturalized the aria by structuring it in a French manner, surrounding it with a gigue to which it is musically related. In an opera from two years later he and his librettist Menesson set up another extended structure that permitted the inclusion of Italian pieces. *Manto la fée* concludes with a celebratory scene that rationalizes the different nationalities as "spirits in various pleasant disguises invited by Manto" (see Table 12-1). Nominally set in Syria, this work is peopled by fairies and magicians, including Merlin; the fairy Manto falls in love with a young man, only to discover that he is her son. Even though this opera is serious and in five acts,[10] the dancers at its end, disguised as Spaniards, Chinese, and characters from the *comédie italienne*, could have stepped out of a ballroom in French fantasy Venice.

Here again a chaconne is attributed to characters from the *comédie italienne*. Moreover this particular piece shares its length with the choreographed chaconnes for Arlequin (see Chapter 14, p. 425), although it adheres more to a ground-bass than those do. However, it is surprising that this chaconne is not adjacent to the da capo Italian aria, but separated from it by a very serious passacaille[11] for Spanish characters. It

[8] Pieces in French were added as well; see Anthony, "Air and aria," 216–17. *Ariettes* have sometimes been conflated in musicological writings with the ternary monologue airs given to principal characters in tragedies (a famous example being Aricie's "Temple sacré" that opens Rameau's *Hippolyte et Aricie*). The *ariettes*, confined almost exclusively to divertissements, had a separate evolution from the monologue airs, but as French composers enriched their orchestral palettes, the two did come to share some musical features.

[9] See Porot's thesis, "Jean-Baptiste Stuck," which discusses throughout Stuck's blending of Italian and French styles; regarding this prologue, see 473–77. The music of Stuck's Italian operas does not survive.

[10] The libretto identifies *Manto la fée* not as a *tragédie*, even though it has the structural conventions of one, but simply as an "opera."

[11] A copy of the Ballard reduced score (F-Po A. 79) has numerous annotations in two hands, one of them Stuck's. This piece has no printed title, but was annotated – probably by Stuck – as a "chaconne," which would make it the third such in this divertissement, although with its slow tempo, minor mode, and descending tetrachord, it looks more like a passacaille. Regarding the annotations, see Porot, "Jean-Baptiste Stuck," 424–33.

Table 12-1: Stuck, *Manto la fée* (1711), v/5

Heading in score	Musical features	Paraphrase of sung text/ comments
Chaconne pour les Génies et les Princesses enchantées	C, **3**; built over 8-bar couplets, 48 bars	Entrance music and a dance?
[Air,] Une Princesse enchantée with chorus, "Qu'à jamais l'Amour et la Gloire / Puissent combler tous vos desirs"	C, **3**; musically related to the preceding chaconne, although not built on a ground	
Chaconne pour l'Arlequin et une Scaramouchette	C, **3**; built over a 4-bar ground (put into 8-bar couplets), 57 bars	Title suggests a comic dance for a single couple.
[Chaconne? Passacaille?] pour les Espagnols. Lentement	c, **3**; built over descending chromatic tetrachord, 97 bars	A ms. annotation in score calls this a chaconne, but musically it seems a passacaille.
Air Italien (Gai), "Lieto brilla il cor nel petto"	C, ¢; da capo, brilliant vocal writing	Attributed to a Princesse in the libretto.
Air pour les Chinois. Pesamment.	C, **2**; binary	
Deux Chinois, "Dans nos climats heureux"	C, **2**; similar in character to the preceding dance	Attributed in the libretto to two "Sauvages."
Gigue pour les mêmes. Gai	C, $^{6}_{8}$	
Chœur, "L'Amour remporte la victoire"	C, **2**; musically independent of the dances	Could involve dancing in the instrumental interludes and at end.

is still more surprising to encounter three ground-bass pieces within the same divertissement. One possible explanation is that Stuck conceived of the second and third of these pieces as a single dance with two different musical characters and two different sets of dancers. The printed score hints as much by failing to provide a double bar between them and by having the last note of the first dance overlap with the start of the second. It might even be the case that the Arlequin chaconne was repeated after the section in minor, which would put the whole complex in line with the conventions of passacailles and chaconnes that change mode in the middle. In that case, the da capo aria and the Italian dance would be adjacent rather than separated.

The phenomenon of including (or adding) arias in Italian to tragedies was of limited duration and mostly coincided with the vogue at the Opéra for things Italian around the turn of the eighteenth century, although isolated examples crop up later. In comparison to the expressive range exploited by Italian opera composers working in their native land or elsewhere in Europe, the arias in Italian that French composers built into some divertissements draw only from the cheerful end of the spectrum. The brilliant vocal style is put to the service of joy and hope, even in operas such as *Médée* with the darkest of plots. The dances allied with Italian arias – most often a chaconne or an Italianate gigue – must have conveyed the same affect. Not all composers of tragedies looked to Italy for inspiration, but enough of them did so to impact the operas both inside and outside the divertissements.[12]

Pastoral Divertissements

Whereas Italian scenes made only occasional appearances, the pastoral had been a fundamental part of French opera since its inception. Pastoral divertissements became much more numerous, however, in the works of Lully's successors, ballets and *tragédies* alike.[13] In general, the pastoral world is presented as innocent and tranquil, where fidelity in love is celebrated and the pursuit of glory holds no interest, but the details of its treatment gave it a broad range of expressive possibilities.[14] Since pastoral divertissements figure among those in which the participants are conceived as singers and dancers by nature, they lent themselves particularly well to choreographic expansion. (This section deals only with pastoral divertissements in the *tragédie en musique*, but many of the points apply to other genres as well.)

On a purely functional level, the character types that people pastoral realms are not always easy to separate. Whereas shepherds and shepherdesses put in frequent appearances, they may be supplemented or replaced by demi-gods such as fauns and various types of nymphs, who in turn may be found in the company of river gods, Pleasures, or the Muses. Sometimes the shepherds may not be what they seem, but are conjured up by a magician and may even be demons in disguise. The inhabitants of the enchanted isle in Act IV of Lully's *Thésée* serve the sorceress Médée: their songs are not as innocent as they appear. Some shepherds seem firmly anchored in the real world, whereas others inhabit an idealized Arcadian realm. Destouches's *Callirhoé* (1713) has two pastoral divertissements: Act III involvies satyrs and dryads, followers of the god Pan, while Act IV has shepherds and shepherdesses. In other pastoral settings, humans and demi-gods appear side by side. The slippage between character types makes it difficult to perform as seemingly simple a task as counting the pastoral divertissements. As a general trend, nymphs and fauns are likelier to be found in the earlier part of this period and cede more to human pastoral types as time goes on, even though most tragedies remain based in mythology, where demi-gods could reasonably put in an appearance.

[12] Fajon, *L'Opéra à Paris*, returns throughout his book to the ever-increasing mingling of the two national traditions in the works of some composers, most notably Campra, Stuck, Gervais, the team of Rebel and Francoeur, and, on the horizon, Rameau.

[13] For one measure of the increase, see Wood's statistics regarding character types in divertissements (*Music and Drama*, 249).

[14] For insights into the pastoral ethos as expressed in opera of this period, see Laurenti, *Valeurs morales et religieuses*, esp. 100–06 and 121–27.

Table 12-2: Gatti, *Scylla* (1701), IV/3: Nisus, chœur et troupe de Bergers et de Bergères

Heading in score	Musical features	Paraphrase of sung text/comments
Menuet	G,**3**	Binary, full length (16 bars), but functions as an *annonce*.
[Récitatif], Artémidor and Capis, "Mais j'entends d'aimables concerts"		Artémidor hears the shepherds approaching. Capis finds the music infuriating and leaves the shepherds to their "imaginary good."
Chœur, "La paix va paraître ici bas"	G,**3**	Chorus of shepherds urges all to enjoy the pleasures of peace.
Entrée	g, **3**	
Loure	g, $\frac{6}{4}$	
Bergère égyptienne, "Viens, Amour"	g, $\frac{6}{4}$; similar to the loure	Urges Amour to rule even over those who despise him.
Premier Rigaudon	G,**2**	
Deuxième Rigaudon	g, **2**	
Menuet, repeated	G,**3**	Same menuet as above.
Deuxième Menuet	g, **3**	
Chœur, "La paix," repeated	G,**3**	Includes oboe trios that could be danced.

Even for Lully the pastoral offered an opportunity for musical expansion: whereas he tended to write only two or three dances into his divertissements, the fourth act of *Thésée* has four dance-songs, all of them strophic, which means that there are eight possible places in which to dance. Lully's constant interleaving of song and dance keeps attention on the words, but this cumulative divertissement is still quite long. Later composers tended not to be quite so systematic in integrating the dance with the vocal music, even though the basic model remained in place.[15] A case in point is the pastoral fête from Gatti's *Scylla* (Table 12-2), which has six instrumental dances and relatively little vocal music.[16] Yet an attentive listener would notice that all the pieces have the same tonic, the menuets have affinities with the chorus, the loure has a vocal analogue, and only the rigaudons and the entrée are unanchored by something with a text. Lully's underlying principles have been stretched only a bit.

The pastoral divertissement in Stuck's *Méléagre* (1709) is considerably more diffuse.[17] Unlike the one from *Scylla*, which seems both arbitrarily introduced and unnecessary to

15 In the pastoral divertissement in *Tancrède* III (Table 11-2, p. 333), the four dances do have at least some connection to the vocal music.

16 Regarding the sources for *Scylla*, see n. 4.

17 Even though this opera was not revived, Jolly made major revisions to his libretto after the premiere. It is the revised version that is printed in vol. X of the *Recueil général* (1714). The notes here are based on the 1709 libretto and score.

the plot, this divertissement serves a crucial turning point. The title character, son of the queen of Calydon, has just killed a monster sent by the goddess Diane that had been ravaging his country. The celebrations in his honor only make him wonder what good glory does him, if the woman he loves, Atalante, seeks to avoid him; she, it turns out, had wanted the glory of killing the monster herself. He encounters her in the forest, after she has argued with his violently jealous rival, Méléagre's uncle. Reluctantly and hesitantly, she overcomes what she had perceived as Méléagre's theft of her glory and admits she loves him. She then calls upon a rustic troupe to honor the hero and share her joy. But their happiness does not last. The rival alerts the still angry Diane, who, through occult ceremonies involving the three Fates, sets up Méléagre's unconscious mother to bring about the death of her son. In the middle of his wedding festivities, Méléagre feels as if he is consumed by fire. As she watches her son die, his delirious mother realizes that the Fates had put the fatal torch into her hands. Atalante's declaration that she will not outlive Méléagre ends the opera.

In this grim story, the Act III divertissement provides the only moment of unadulterated joy. The first divertissement features a religious ceremony that attempts to appease Diane; the second honors the unhappy hero; the fourth shows the three Fates conspiring against Méléagre; and the celebrations in the last act are overshadowed by the unfolding catastrophe. Three of the five have a tight, Lullian construction; only the divertissements in Acts II and III, both fêtes, have more than three dances. Coming as it does during the only moment in the opera in which happiness appears realizable, this divertissement not only celebrates the love of Atalante and Méléagre – the faun and dryad even share their voice parts – but offers an expansive view of the beauties of the pastoral world, which serves as a respite from the tensions the characters are facing (see the outline in Table 12-3).

This scene shows that even if pastoral divertissements were becoming a staple, a resourceful composer could do unusual things with the music. *Méléagre* is the opera in which Italy and France confront each other in the prologue, and in this scene, Stuck composed exceptionally vivid music. (He also adhered to his Italian habits in preferring the time signature $\frac{3}{4}$ to the French **3**.) In this divertissement he picked up several opportunities offered to him by the text to engage in word painting: orchestral echos in the first chorus following the words "Echo, répondez-nous," and, in the Faune's air, illustrations of the "profound peace" by a hurdy-gurdy effect and of the "little birds" with chirpings by the flutes; in the duet, the declarations of love grow in intensity via the ever-expanding melismas on the word "chaine," which eventually turn into a descending sequence. These last two numbers highlight the phenomenon of elaborate vocal pieces that was gaining momentum inside divertissements – the pastoral being a particularly welcoming realm for such interventions. Often these take the form of *ariettes* in da capo form, but Stuck's Italianisms here are more madrigalistic than formal. His innovations are not confined to the vocal pieces. Even before the voices enter, the

Table 12-3: Stuck, *Méléagre* (1709), III/6: Atalante, Méléagre, une Dryade, un Faune, Choeurs de Divinités champêtres, de Bergers et de Bergères.
The divinities form into a march.

Heading in score	Musical features	Paraphrase of sung text/ comments
Marche. Pesamment	C, $\frac{6}{4}$	Features several changes of texture among strings and winds in various combinations.
Premier Menuet	C, $\frac{3}{4}$	Also changes texture.
Deuxième Menuet	c, $\frac{3}{4}$	Trio for flutes and basse.
Chœur de Bergers, "Que nos craintes finissent"	C, $\frac{3}{4}$	Shepherds call for Echo to respond and the orchestra obliges.
Air pour les Paysans	G, **2**	See Examples 12-2, p. 362.
Gigue	g, $\frac{6}{8}$	Irregular phrase structure.
Air. Le Faune, "Nous vivrons désormais dans une paix profonde"	F, $\frac{3}{4}$; Lentement	Word painting of peace, rivers, and birds.
Duo, Dryade and Faune, "Les soins et les peines"	B♭, $\frac{6}{8}$; Gracieusement	Melismas on "chaine" grow in length at each iteration.
Air	B♭, **2**	Phrases echoed between violins and oboes.
Duo, Dryade and Faune, with Chorus, "Chantez, Bergers"	B♭, $\frac{3}{8}$	Alternates duet and chorus; also includes instrumental interludes.

dance pieces, particularly the march, present several different instrumental textures, perhaps by way of differentiating among the various demi-gods and humans. The opening gambit of three dances in a row is uncommon and in this instance seems to offer a non-verbal form of expression, via dancing surrogates, to the two lovers who have been unable to speak openly to each other until the end of the preceding scene. Also unusual is the disjunction between the vocal pieces and the dances, none of which are paired with each other, and which include a startlingly disparate range of keys – four pitch levels, two of which change mode. Yet the idea of the echo – or of voices and instruments responding to each other, even when the repeat is not literal – holds together a divertissement that takes a remarkably fresh musical approach overall.

Only one dance in this divertissement identifies the performers: the "Air pour les Paysans." This points to a casting distinction that was becoming more common between two types of rustic characters: *bergers* (shepherds) on the one hand, and, on the other, *pâtres* or *paysans* (herdsmen or peasants; the two terms appear to be used interchangeably). This juxtaposition can be found as early as 1674 in Lully's *Alceste* and again in *Roland* in 1685, but it picked up momentum after the turn of the century, when one of the dancers in the troupe, François Dumoulin, began to make a specialty out of peasant roles. An engraving of him in peasant mode (Figure 12-1) shows him clad in an outmoded and dilapidated style, with a wispy beard and ridiculous hat, his left hand

Figure 12-1: "Dumoulin in peasant costume dancing at the Opéra."

held awkwardly above his head. His name appears in libretto after libretto as a solo peasant, starting from Act IV of *Scylla* in 1701, always in divertissements where shepherds are also featured – and sometimes other *pâtres* and *pastourelles* in group roles;[18] see the cast lists in Figures 12-2 (Act IV) and 7-2 (Seconde Entrée). Relying on dancing bodies allowed the creators of these operas to sandwich humor into otherwise serious

[18] The terminology for such distinctions was not always consistent. In the 1712 revival of *Achille et Polixène*, for example, the cast for Act II was listed as *pâtres, pastourelles, paysans, paysannes*, and a single *pâtre* (F. Dumoulin), whereas the start of the scene calls for "une troupe de Bergers et de Bergères."

Example 12-1: Lully, *Roland* IV/3, "Entrée de Pâtres, de Pastourelles, de Bergers et de Bergères" (Paris: Ballard, 1685), 246.

Example 12-2: Stuck, *Méléagre* III/6, "Air pour les Paysans" (Paris: Ballard, 1709), 272.

works; earthiness could undercut the nostalgia for an idealized world expressed in the shepherds' songs.

The advantage of the *Méléagre* score is that it identifies which piece was danced by the peasant characters, as does the score for Lully's *Roland*. Both pieces (see Examples 12-1 and 12-2) are in duple meter with a single anacrusis and have simple, repetitive melodies that move mostly in notes of equal value. (For another peasant dance, see Example 10-2, p. 295.) With these characteristics in mind, it becomes possible to propose other likely pieces for peasants in scores where the dances are unattributed: the *Scylla* divertissement outlined above (Table 12-2) had a role for François Dumoulin as a solo peasant, along with other *paysans* and *paysannes*; the two rigaudons seem the likeliest spots for them to have danced. *Scylla* calls for group peasants, but often a cast list names only one or two.

Marais's opera *Sémélé*, which premiered in 1709, just before *Méléagre*, carries the peasant shenanigans to an extreme. Even though this tragedy ends with a conflagration that destroys the king's palace and almost kills the title character, it does not eschew humor. In fact, La Motte, seems to have cast his eye back to the comic subplots of Lully's earliest tragedies, *Cadmus* and *Alceste*. The story centers around Jupiter's infatuation with the mortal Sémélé; he disguises himself under the name of Idas, so that she will love him for himself. In his excursions to earth he is accompanied by

Mercure, also in disguise, who carries out a flirtation with Dorine, Sémélé's confidante, which acts as a running comic commentary on the loves of the nobler characters.[19] Acts II and IV contain parallel acts of revelation on the part of the two gods to their respective sweethearts, each of which provokes a complementary divertissement.

In Act II Jupiter reveals his true identity to Sémélé in order to prevent her from obeying her father's order that she marry another. Sémélé welcomes the revelation, which both satisfies her love and will bring her glory. Jupiter conjures up a brilliant fête in her honor, which consists of two extraordinary pieces: a chorus laced with bird calls and a long instrumental chaconne, whose startling changes of character seem designed to allow the dancers to display multiple facets of Jupiter's powers.[20] (The dancing cast in 1709 – identified as fauns and nymphs – involved a male soloist plus six men and women, some of whom were stars themselves and likely to have danced in small groups.) Act IV performs a comic reversal on this scene. When Mercure reveals his identity to Dorine, she instantly loses interest: "If you are a god, I love you less for it [. . .] Too much inequality [in social station] annoys me." ("Si vous êtes un dieu, je vous en aime moins [. . .] Trop d'inégalité me gêne.") Nor does she believe for an instant that Mercure will be any more faithful than his master Jupiter ever is. But she does stay to watch the pastoral fête Jupiter has ordered Mercure to arrange for Sémélé's pleasure.

At a wave of Mercure's hand the scene changes from a grotto to a hamlet. The shepherds' texts present orthodox examples of an idealized Arcadia ("Here everyone vows never to change affections"), except for the fact that the expressions of fidelity come so swiftly on the heels of Mercure's sweet talk to Dorine that they seem to be sung with a knowing wink. Something still more surprising is hiding in the cast list (Figure 12-2): the hamlet Mercure conjures up is not in Arcadia but in rural France; it supplies not only the obligatory peasants, but a bailiff and a tax collector. The intrusion of contemporary farce into the mythological may not surprise in *comédie-italienne*-inflected works, but inside a tragedy it startles.[21] Even Jupiter seems embarrassed by the coarseness of the scene and apologizes to Sémélé: "These festivities do not measure up to my lofty grandeur, but I am purposefully withholding it from you now. Wanting to be loved for myself, I am hiding the god from you; behold only your lover."

[19] Laurenti, *Valeurs morales et religieuses*, 263–64, points out that in the *tragédie en musique* Mercure always represents "a transposition of the comic servant into the heroic realm."

[20] This chaconne has an exceptionally varied orchestration that even gives the melody to the *basses de violon* for one couplet and, still more surprisingly, twice changes in and out of duple meter, while still respecting the repeated four-bar phrases that characterize chaconnes. At one point the upper part plays in $\frac{6}{8}$, the lower in cut time.

[21] Later in the century some of the dances in this particular divertissement were added to the pastoral Act I divertissement of Lully's *Acis et Galatée*, another work with a mixed tone (see Ch. 6, p. 192ff). This addition had happened by the revival of 1744, if not before; see Denécheau, "Les opéras de Lully remaniés," table 4.

xij DIVERTISSEMENTS.

QUATRIÉME ACTE.

BERGERS.
Meſſieurs Dangeville-L., Pecourt, & François.
BERGERES.
Mademoiſelle Prevoſt,
Meſdemoiſelles Douville, Menés, & Caré.

PASTRES.
Meſſieurs Dangeville-C., Pieret, & Dubreüil.

PASTOURELLES.
Meſdemoiſelles Lemaire, Dufrênne, & Mangot.

UN BERGER.	Monſieur D-Dumoulin.
UNE BERGERE.	Mademoiſelle Guyot.
UN BAILLY.	Monſieur Ferand.
LA BAILLIVE.	Mademoiſelle Chaillou.
UN PROCUREUR FISCALLE.	Mr Marcelle-L.
SA FEMME.	Mademoiſelle Lacroix.
PAYSAN.	Monſieur F-Dumoulin.

CINQUIÉME ACTE.

THEBAINS.
Monſieur Dangeville-L.
Meſſieurs Germain, Dumoulin-L., Ferand, Blondy,
Marcelle-L., & Javillier.
THEBAINES.
Meſdemoiſelles Prevoſt, & Guyot.
Meſdemoiſelles Chaillou, Milot, Menés, Lemaire,
Mangot & Douville.

SEMELE',

Figure 12-2: Part of the cast list from the libretto of *Sémélé* (1709).

This divertissement, which already invokes both Arcadian and comic registers, is further enriched by drawing upon the conventions of the village wedding,[22] with two of the leading dancers at the Opéra, Mlle Guyot and David Dumoulin, in the roles of bride and groom (identified in the cast list as shepherd and shepherdess). There are no fewer than twenty dancers, who fall into three categories: shepherds and

[22] Act IV of Lully's *Roland* marks the first village wedding at the Opéra, but the topic was common in many theatrical genres. The cast list for the second entrée of Collasse's *Ballet des saisons* – especially as listed for the 1700 revival – looks quite similar to the one in *Sémélé*, complete with the bailiff.

shepherdesses; the rustic *pâtres* or peasants; and the other comic characters, the bailiff and the tax collector, each with a wife. Those who danced solos or in couples look to have included Mlle Prévost, another star of the troupe, who represents an additional shepherdess in an otherwise standard group of three. The mixed tone that characterizes *Sémélé* did not come out of nowhere; it was anticipated in the prologue, where Bacchus, "the god who troubles the mind," was honored by none other than Apollon. But even if this particular divertissement flirts with farce, the phenomenon of introducing a comic or even irreverent note into *tragédies en musique* via the dancing body was common to many pastoral divertissements. The developing musical conventions for peasant characters provide one means of tracking this phenomenon; the cast lists in the librettos furnish another.

So to which music might these characters have danced? The score provides a good deal of dance music (see Table 12-4), but the headings do not answer the question. Marais insisted upon the rusticity of this fête by building all the instrumental dances above a drone assigned to the bassoons, in imitation, he says at the start of the first piece, of the bagpipe. The divertissement almost certainly had additional instrumental dances: two Pécour choreographies said to have been danced in *Sémélé* were published by Gaudrau in 1713. Given that this opera was not revived, the two dances must have figured in the original run of performances. Both are for the same couple, David Dumoulin and Mlle Guyot (the solo Berger and Bergère above[23]), and Marais published the music for one of them, a musette, in his *Pièces de viole,* Book 3 (1711).[24] A plausible location for them could be in the vicinity of the song/chorus, "Ici chacun s'engage," following which the character change in the music suggests that the peasants take the stage. The passepied, which often closes a divertissement, provides an opportunity for a large group dance.

The word "musette" appears four times in Marais's score: the first two times it alludes to members of the bagpipe family, but the two mentions toward the end reveal the slippage that was happening in usage from instrument to dance type. Whereas it is possible that the piece headed "Hautbois pour les mêmes" (Figure 12-3) and the passepied also called for the musettes to play, when Marais published his third book of *Pièces de violes* in 1711 the "musette" that probably originated in this divertissement was now attributed to a string instrument. Regardless of their instrumentation, musettes are characterized by a drone; they may be in any meter. According to Fajon, their first appearance in a *tragédie en musique* was in the prologue to Campra's *Hippodamie* (1708)[25]; by then they had also played a menuet in the pastoral entrée of the

[23] See Appendix 3.

[24] The "Muzette," piece 105, is in $\frac{6}{8}$ and in G major, with a rondeau structure. A source for the other piece, also in G major, but in duple meter, has not yet been located.

[25] Fajon, *L'Opéra à Paris*, 212–13. Musettes are, however, mentioned in sung texts well before this time – e.g. the prologue to *Thésée* (1675), where Mars sings "Que les hautbois, que les musettes /

Table 12-4: Marais, *Sémélé* (1709), IV/2: Jupiter, Sémélé, Mercure, Dorine, Chœur de Bergers et de Bergères.

Heading in score	Musical features	Paraphrase of sung texts/comments
Marche pour les Bergers	g, **2**; tonic drone	Binary, played "2 fois"; melody assigned to violins and 2 musettes, with "bassons imitant la cornemuse."
Chœur, "Venez, tendres Bergers"	g, **3**	Dialogue between high duet (shepherdesses) and low trio (shepherds).
[Récitatif and air] Jupiter, "Que ma gloire"	G, **3**	Jupiter apologises for the humble festivities, but says he does not want to appear as a god.
2 Menuets	g, **3**; tonic drone	First menuet played by strings, second by oboes and musettes. Both in 4-bar phrases.
Un Berger ou une Bergère, "Ici chacun s'engage / Pour ne jamais changer"	G, **3**	Alternates soloist(s) and chorus; set in consistent 3-bar phrases. Strophic. Might also have been played as instrumental dance between the two strophes.[a]
Air pour les mêmes	G, $\frac{4}{8}$; tonic or dominant drone	"Fort gai"
Deux Bergères avec le choeur, "Amoureux oiseaux, célébrez le retour de Flore"	G, $\frac{4}{8}$; tonic or dominant drone	"Un peu plus lent." Similar in character to preceding dance. Duet alternates with the chorus.
Hautbois pour les mêmes. Musette [Fig. 12-3]	G, $\frac{4}{8}$; tonic or dominant drone	"Gai." Same music as the vocal duet, played by two oboes and basse de violon, with bassoons providing the drone.
[Second strophe of duet/chorus]	G, $\frac{4}{8}$	Second strophe appears in libretto only.
[Hautbois repeated[b]]	G, $\frac{4}{8}$	
Passepied. Musette	G, $\frac{3}{8}$; tonic drone	

[a] This kind of alternation was standard practice in Lully's operas; see Ch. 2, p. 46ff.

[b] The presence in the libretto of a second strophe suggests that the musically identical instrumental piece ("Hautbois") would have been repeated thereafter, as was the norm with strophic structures.

same composer's *Ballet des Muses* (1703). The musette sonority, whether played on the instrument itself or imitated by other members of the orchestra, was to remain a marker of the pastoral on the operatic stage.

As for purely choreographic markers of the pastoral, the only dance type that appears in all six pastoral divertissements mentioned in this chapter is the menuet.

L'emportent sur les trompettes / Et les tambours." ("May the oboes and musettes take precedence over the trumpets and drums.") The libretto says that "rustic instruments" (*instruments champêtres*) play while Mars descends.

Figure 12-3: Musette for oboes and bassoons from the pastoral divertissement in *Sémélé*.

Other dance types found at least once include the loure, gigue, rigaudon, and passepied, plus many "airs" and "entrées" in a variety of meters that do not adhere to any generic type. The rigaudon, a dance that was new at the end of Lully's life, is in a lively duple meter; like the bourrée, it has an anacrusis, but its first full bar often consists of two half notes, giving it a sturdier sound (see Example 12-3).

This list is not complete; a look at other pastoral divertissements would find bourrées and gavottes, inter alia,[26] and given that pastoral characters almost always acknowledge the fact that they are making music, many such scenes open with a march, which could be in either duple or triple meter. A chaconne appears in the Act II divertissement in *Sémélé*, an exception probably explainable by the character types – demi-gods (nymphs and fauns) rather than humans. A sarabande, another rare dance in a pastoral scene, can be found in Act III of *Tancrède*, probably due to the enchantments. So whereas a systematic study of pastoral dance types in French opera would undoubtedly turn up more identifiable trends, it is clear that the choice of dances is broad, but shaded by the tone of a divertissement, the characters within it, and the context

[26] Thorp's list of dances seen as pastoral, based on European and English sources between 1704 and 1732, includes the rigaudon, passepied, gavotte, loure, and musette. See "And the peasants came too."

Example 12-3: Gatti, *Scylla* IV/2, "Premier Rigaudon" (Paris: Baussen, 1701), 160.

surrounding it. The situation seems analogous to the way step-vocabulary functions within any particular choreography: the entire lexicon is available, but generic conventions favor certain choices over others.

Nautical Divertissements

Whereas a handful of sailors may be found in Lully's works (*Alceste* I/7 and *Persée* IV/7) and in those of his immediate successors (e.g., *Ariane et Bacchus* [1696] II/6), it was in the first decade of the eighteenth century that the *fête marine* came into its own. In both tragedies and ballets it is framed as a celebration of love, whose sung texts draw parallels between the weather on the sea and the emotions within the human heart. The *locus classicus* is III/3 of Marais's tragedy *Alcyone* (1706), two excerpts from which may serve to convey the tone: "Quelque vent qui gronde, / L'Amour calme l'onde" and "Mettons à la voile: / Nous avons pour étoile / Le flambeau de l'Amour." ("No matter which wind rumbles, love calms the waters" and "Let's set sail; we have love's torch as our lodestar.") Because love is the governing emotion, the singing and dancing cast always requires both *matelots* and *matelottes* or *mariniers* and *marinières*. The relationship between these characters and the actual sea is about the same as that between pastoral characters and real sheep; in fact, this type of divertissement is akin in character and function to ones that take place in the pastoral realm – a kind of marine pastoral, so to speak.[27] In *Alcyone* the person who hears the sailors coming even

[27] Wood includes sailors among pastoral characters (*Music and Drama*, 248). Laurenti points out that sailors are sometimes used to allude to the world of commerce and to France's maritime trade, including with her colonies in the New World. The references had to be oblique: "the risk was to fall into a technical realism in poor taste, and, moreover, allusion to bourgeois preoccupations with money was barely allowable in the aristocratic setting of the Opéra." (*Valeurs morales et religieuses*, 138, and, on the theme of embarking, 112–17 and 166–70.)

Figure 12-4: Jean Berain, sailors dancing around a mast and seated oboists, probably in *Philomèle* (1705). (Photo by the Archives Nationales)

announces the approach of a "rustique fête."[28] Nautical divertissements, however, invoke an element of risk: in order to reach the port, the sailor has first to embark and risk the danger of storms. Frequently, as in *Alcyone*, the confidence in a fortunate outcome is undercut by subsequent events.

Like its pastoral analogue, a nautical divertissement has two possible sets of characters: demi-gods – tritons and water nymphs – and, more frequently, human sailors (Figure 12-4). The nautical divertissement in *Alcyone* belongs squarely to the human realm. The sea is a central theme in the opera: Alcyone's husband, Céix, is obliged by the machinations of a magician to take a sea voyage to consult Apollon (he departs in Act III); he drowns in a storm (depicted in Act IV); and Alcyone discovers his body

[28] These words are found in the score; the libretto lacks the word "rustique."

Table 12-5: Marais, *Alcyone* (1706), III/3: Pélée, le Chef des Matelots, Troupe de Matelots.

Heading in score	Key, meter	Paraphrase of sung texts/comments
Marche pour les matelots	e, $\frac{6}{8}$	Drum plays on downbeat of each bar.
Chœur, "Régnez, Zéphyrs, sur la liquide plaine"	e, **3**	Expresses wish that Aeolus keep the violent winds in check.
Un Matelot, "Toi qui tiens dans tes mains"	e, **3**	An appeal to Neptune for favorable winds.
Marche, repeated	e, $\frac{6}{8}$	
Une Matelotte, "Amants malheureux"	e, $\frac{6}{8}$	Says that love calms the waves. Set to the tune of the march.
Deuxième Air des Matelots	e, **2**	Drum plays on downbeat of each bar.
Deuxième Matelotte, "Pourquoi craignons-nous?	e, $\frac{6}{8}$	In love, pleasure follows sighs.
Troisième Air des Matelots	e, $\frac{4}{8}$	Drum plays on downbeat of each bar.
Chœur, "Régnez," partially repeated	e, **3**	

floating in the water, before she attempts suicide and Neptune transforms the two into aquatic birds (Act V).[29] Marais's vivid orchestral writing for the storm created a sensation; it was imitated – and parodied – by many other composers.[30] But before Céix boards his vessel, the sailors appeal to Neptune to send them favorable winds (Table 12-5). Soon, however, the sailors slip into the rhetoric of love, and the remaining music of this divertissement features a series of catchy tunes – particularly the march, which English speakers may know as the carol "Masters in this hall."[31]

The dancers included, in addition to four each of *matelots* and *matelottes*, four *joueurs de tambourins*, probably playing the tall tabor often called the *tambourin de Provence* on account of its place of origin. *Alcyone* is the first French opera to call unambiguously for this kind of drum: the score indicates drum strokes on the downbeats of all three dances in this divertissement.[32] In 1706 the term "tambourin" did not yet indicate a dance type; as with the musette, the dance acquired its name gradually, by metonymy. In *Alcyone* the drum does not appear to be accompanied by a *petite flûte*, as was to become common later – an association that also derives from Provence.[33] Another point of separation lies in the different meters each dance has, whereas the tambourins that lay

[29] The transformation into birds (halcyons) comes from Ovid's *Metamorphoses*.

[30] See La Gorce, "Tempêtes." On Marais's exceptional orchestral effects, see Cyr, "*Basses* and *basse continue*." For one parody, see Ch. 9, p. 265.

[31] This tune served as the basis for three notated choreographies and a contredanse, "La Matelotte," published by Feuillet in a collection of contredanses from the same year as the opera. La Gorce notes that the tune sounds as if it might be of popular origin; see his liner notes to the recording directed by Minkowski (Musifrance 2292-45522-2, 1990), 17.

[32] In order to save space, the engraver notated only four bars of drumbeats at the end of each dance.

[33] See Ch. 10, pp. 293–94 regarding Mouret's "La Provençale."

in the future were usually in a quick duple time. (The "Troisième Air" comes closest in character to later tambourins.) The tambourin (both drum and dance) was to figure in many future nautical divertissements, although it was by no means confined to such scenes. Its watery associations extended to Venice: an engraving for Campra's opera-ballet *Le Carnaval de Venise* (1699) depicts a Venetian gondolier playing the fife and tambourin, and the libretto for the "Fête des barqueroles" from his *Fêtes vénitiennes* (1710) explains that tambourins "are in use in Venice."

Three other dance types that were to figure often in nautical divertissements are the rigaudon, menuet, and passepied – these three, unlike the tambourin, marking a point of contact with the pastoral realm. As with the pastoral, many of the dances in nautical divertissements aim to characterize the dancers without adhering to a specific dance type.

LULLY REVIVALS

The trends visible in newly composed divertissements impacted Lully operas when they were revived. Notwithstanding the fact that new operas premiered every year, the company relied on revivals of the master's works to shore up the institution's finances.[34] However, Lully's operas underwent modifications when they were revived – both cuts and additions. The most massive changes took place under the aesthetic pressures launched by the War of the Buffoons; Rosow has documented that the most extensive modifications to *Armide* were done by Francoeur and Rebel in 1761.[35] But even shortly after Lully's death, his successors began tinkering with his tragedies, particularly the divertissements.

Armide's Act IV is one of the spots that accrued more dance music over the years. Two knights come looking for Renaud in order to free him from Armide's clutches. She, however, tries to sidetrack them by transforming demons into images of their own beloveds, who attempt to seduce each knight in turn. As Lully composed it, the divertissement had only three instrumental pieces: an "Air" that served as entrance music for the disguised demons, and, between vocal solos and choruses, a gavotte and a canarie. For the 1697 revival a new dance was added, a rondeau borrowed from the ballet music Lully had composed in 1660 to accompany Cavalli's opera *Xerxès*.[36] In *Armide* it followed the canarie and was dubbed a contredanse (see Chapter 14, p. 434ff, on operatic contredanses). The divertissement now had three instrumental dances in a

34 According to Lagrave, *Le Théâtre*, 346, of the 39 operas revived between 1715 and 1750, fourteen were by Lully, seven by Campra, six by Destouches, two each by Desmarest and Mouret, and one each by several more composers.

35 Rosow, "How eighteenth-century Parisians heard Lully's operas," esp. 228–36. For an overview of the changes made to Lully's operas after his death, see Schneider, *Rezeption*, 75–100.

36 *LWV* 12/3; in its original context the dance is for Basques.

Table 12-6: The Act IV divertissement from *Roland* as performed in 1690.
Titles of the new pieces are indicated in bold.

Musical Unit	Key, meter	Comments
Marche	C, **3**	Rondeau, 3-bar phrases, alternates strings and oboes
Chœur, "Quand on vient dans ce boccage"	C, **3**	Chorus of shepherds; same music as march
Menuet	C, **3**	
Hautbois	C, **3**	
Entrée de Pâtres, de Pastourelles, de Bergers et de Bergères	C, $\frac{4}{8}$	"Fort gay"
[Duo,] Un Pâtre, et une Pastourelle, "Vivez en paix, Amants"	C, $\frac{4}{8}$	Musically similar to the Entrée de Pâtres
La Mariée	G, ¢	Borrowed from Lully's ballet *Les Noces de Village*
Rondeau	G, **3** (following scene is in g)	Borrowed from Lully's *Plaisirs de l'île enchantée*

row – rare for Lully – and in 1713 yet another dance was added, this time a menuet, also borrowed from an earlier work by Lully.[37] The 1703 libretto is the first to have a cast list; the dancers that year involved Balon and Mlle Subligny, listed together and presumably dancing a duet, four additional couples, plus François Dumoulin as a *pâtre*. On one level a comic peasant seems an odd choice for a divertissement aimed at seducing a knight away from duty, but perhaps he was added to appease those critics who saw this act as "too moral."[38] Or perhaps François Dumoulin's peasant routine had simply become an expected component of pastoral divertissements; he figured in the 1713 cast as well.

The village wedding scene of *Roland* also underwent expansion, from as early as 1690, when two dances were borrowed from earlier works by Lully (see Table 12-6).[39] This divertissement falls in the middle of the act as one stage in the process by which the military hero Roland learns that the woman he loves, Angélique, queen of Cathay, has eloped with the low-born Médor, a discovery that drives him to madness.[40] In Lully's day the divertissement had four dances and two vocal numbers; the two pieces added in 1690 were placed at the end, where the fact that they were in G major helped smooth the transition into the following scene in G minor.

The choice of the first borrowing may have been governed by its attribution to the same type of character – a rustic bride and groom – as it had in its original context. In

37 *Ballet royal de Flore* (1669), *LWV* 40/39. Regarding these changes, see Rosow, "How eighteenth-century Parisians," 217–19.

38 *Ibid.*, 214–15.

39 Regarding the dating of the insertion, see my article "*La Mariée*," 247–49.

40 See my "Reading *Roland*," pars. 7.1–7.10.

Les Noces de Village (1663), called a "mascarade ridicule" in its libretto, all the female roles, including the bride and the midwife, were danced by men; the ballet comes to a chaotic conclusion when thieving gypsies get into a fight with the forces of the law and four young men attempt to kidnap the bride. Could this deliberately ridiculous scenario have left any traces when the dance for the bride and groom was inserted into *Roland*? Lully had already chosen a mixed tone for this divertissement, by juxtaposing Arcadian shepherds with rustic peasants – danced in 1705 (year of the first cast list), by the inevitable François Dumoulin and his younger brother Pierre. But a dance for a bride and groom could lend itself to a variety of interpretations. In this instance a choreography by Pécour set to this music exists, but it was published in 1700 in a collection of ball dances, with the suggestive title "La Mariée" (the bride).[41] There is no way of knowing whether this choreography is the same one that Pécour set for the revival of 1690, but the quirkiness of both the music and the dancers' movements makes a theatrical origin plausible.[42] The choreography draws upon an orthodox step vocabulary, but uses it in ways that, when considered alongside the two dancers' relationships in space, permits a reading of the dance as a mixture of grace and awkwardness.[43]

The Act IV divertissements in both *Armide* and *Roland* went on to acquire dances by other composers as they were revived again and again (for *Roland* see Table 12-7 below), but the practice visible in the early revivals of expanding by borrowing from Lully's own works is noteworthy. Another such example can be seen in *Thésée*, where a piece from Lully's ballet music for *Xerxès* (LWV 12/13), was added as a dance for a solo man, probably to the prologue during the revival of 1707–08.[44] This phenomenon fits into a larger pattern: during the first decade and a half following Lully's death his works were repeatedly mined and reformulated for new performances. For both the *Ballet des saisons* (1695) and *La Naissance de Vénus* (1696) Collasse borrowed heavily from Lully's ballets and comedy-ballets, which he stitched together with music of his own. The scores even indicate which pieces can be attributed to the deceased master.[45] In 1702 Campra went through a similar process in putting together his pastiche *Les Fragments de Lully* (see Chapter 10, pp. 289–90).

Lully's music remained an important source for borrowings even as late as the 1760s, but more and more, the divertissements in his tragedies were embellished by pieces

[41] This choreography was republished a number of times, the latest being in 1765.

[42] For a fuller airing of the evidence, see my article "*La Mariée*," 249–54. The music has a highly unusual phrase structure: a sequence of 5, 4, and 5 bars in the first strain, and of 7 plus 5 in the second.

[43] This divertissement, which artist Charles-Antoine Coypel represented in one of his paintings of theatrical scenes, was the centerpiece of an experimental workshop at the conference *Le Tableau et la scène* in Nantes, France, May 2011. See, in the conference proceedings, Hazebroucq, "Les danses de l'Acte IV de *Roland*."

[44] See Appendix 3.

[45] The 1695 score of *Le Ballet des saisons* contains only the pieces Collasse composed, but the 1700 score includes those by Lully as well.

Table 12-7: The Act IV divertissement from *Roland* as transmitted by manuscript annotations in two Ballard scores (FPo A.17.a^{I} et A17.a^{2}).
Titles in bold indicate pieces added after Lully's death.

Musical Unit	Key, meter	Attribution
Marche	C, **3**	Lully, *Roland*
Chœur, "Quand on vient dans ce boccage"	C, **3**	Lully, *Roland*
Musette	C, **3**	Source unidentified
Air gay	C, **2**	Source unidentified
Menuet	C, **3**	Lully, *Roland*
Hautbois	C, **3**	Lully, *Roland*
Entrée de Pâtres, de Pastourelles, de Bergers et de Bergères	C, $\frac{4}{8}$	Lully, *Roland*
[Duo,] Un Pâtre, et une Pastourelle, "Vivez en paix, Amants"	C, $\frac{4}{8}$	Lully, *Roland* (this duet is crossed out in both scores)
Mineur	c, $\frac{2}{4}$	Mouret, *Pirithoüs* V (1723) (rigaudon)
Entrée de Pâtres, repeated	C, $\frac{4}{8}$	Lully, *Roland*, but repeat came later
La Mariée	G, ¢	Lully, *Les Noces de Village*; added to *Roland* in 1690
Rondeau	G, **3**	Lully, *Les Plaisirs de l'île enchantée*; added to *Roland* in 1690

written well after his death. Marais's *Sémélé*, which was never revived, served as the source for several; the chaconne in particular turned up in *Persée* in 1747, *Atys* in 1753, and *Thésée* in 1754; pieces by Leclair and Rameau were added to divertissements in *Thésée* in 1765–67.[46] Many Lully scores preserved in libraries in Paris and Versailles contain collettes onto which have been copied pieces taken from other operas, often in more than one hand. The surviving Lully scores must preserve only a portion of the actual practice of expansion, and Table 12-7 may serve as an example: it shows subsequent additions made to Act IV of *Roland*, as preserved in two scores and a set of parts housed in the Bibliothèque de l'Opéra. These belonged to the Marquis de La Salle and were intended for his private use, but they probably represent what was performed at the Opéra in the 1750s, when Rebel and Francoeur were heading the institution. Given its date of 1723, the piece from Mouret's *Pirithoüs*[47] could have been added at any revival thereafter (1727, 1743, or 1755), whereas the two unidentified pieces are later in style and probably date from Rebel and Francoeur's period.

At some time during this process of tinkering the vocal duet was deleted, leaving nine instrumental dances in a row. This emphasis on dancing at the expense of singing accords with the changes over time in the dancing cast, whose names and roles are known (see Table 12-8). Not only did the number of dancers tend to increase, the

[46] See Denécheau, "Les opéras de Lully remaniés."
[47] Borrowing identified by Denécheau, *ibid.*, table 6.

Table 12-8: Transformations in the dancing cast of *Roland*'s Act IV divertissement. Roles added since the previous revival are shown in bold.

Year of revival	No. of dancers	Roles
1705	14	le Marié, la Mariée 2 Pâtres, 2 Paysannes 4 Bergers, 4 Bergères
1709	21	le Marié, la Mariée **le Père, la Mère, son fils Jannot** 5 Pâtres, 3 Paysannes 4 Bergers, 4 Bergères
1716	16	le Marié, la Mariée le Père et la Mère du Marié **le Père et la Mère de la Mariée** 2 Paysans 4 Bergers, 4 Bergères
1727 and 1728	17	le Marié, la Mariée le Père du Marié, la Mère du Marié le Père de la Mariée, la Mère de la Mariée **la Sœur de la Mariée** 2 Pâtres 4 Bergers, 4 Bergères
1743	18	le Marié, la Mariée le Père du Marié, la Mère du Marié le Père de la Mariée, la Mère de la Mariée la Sœur des Mariés, **le Frère des Mariés** 2 Pâtres 4 Bergers, 4 Bergères 7 Bergers jouant des instruments
1755	20	le Marié, la Mariée les Pères et Mères des Mariés les **2 Frères et 2 Sœurs** des Mariés **un Berger, une Bergère** 4 Bergers, 4 Bergères 7 Bergers jouant des instruments

number of roles for various relatives of the bride and groom expanded to include fathers and mothers, sisters and brothers. When the names of the performers are taken into account, it becomes apparent that more solos and couple dances were being added. In 1727, for example, the new role of sister of the bride was danced by Mlle Camargo and in 1709 Jannot, a brother, was probably given a comic cast by Marcel, who subsequently appeared in *Les Fêtes vénitiennes* as the boastful dancing master.[48] In fact, the appearance of multiple relatives among the wedding guests recalls blatantly

[48] A full list of the dancers in revivals may be found in my "'Roland apprenant l'infidélité d'Angélique'."

comic works from the Opéra's repertoire: the wedding in "La Comédie" of Campra's *Ballet des Muses* (1703) involved the parents of both the bride and groom, five couples of relatives, multiple children, and domestic servants. The village wedding in "La Veuve" from *Les Fêtes de Thalie* (see Chapter 10, p. 294) had only twelve dancers, but its roles are very similar to those in the 1716 revival of *Roland* of only two years later, and some of the group dancers were even the same people. Perhaps the spirit of these comic divertissements and the one in *Roland* as it was performed over the years was not so different.

In a study of Lully's *Alceste*, where the changes in the dancing personnel over revivals up to 1739 are less dramatic than the ones cited here, Thorp has provocatively hypothesized that "the more the dancing characters change between different productions, the more likely it is that their general characterization and influence upon the storyline remains vague or peripheral."[49] She does not raise the issue of possible musical additions, but this kind of loosening of the musical structure could be construed as supporting a slightly reformulated version of her point, one that allows for added characters to take the internal storyline of the divertissement in new directions, but to attenuate its connections to the surrounding scenes. The highlighting of more and more star dancers would also serve to draw attention away from larger plot and toward the act of performing. Such divertissements do open themselves to criticisms that the dancing exceeded its proper proportions.[50]

Two other types of expansion are discernible in Lully revivals: first, some of the divertissements to which Lully and Quinault had assigned only male roles acquired female dancers; and second, a few acts that had originally lacked a danced divertissement acquired one. The dance troupe was entirely male until 1681, but once women joined, the number of female roles increased, even though quite a number of divertissements remained the preserve of male dancers only (see Chapter 3, p. 102). In the eighteenth century several of these were modified to include women: the dancing Africains in Act I of Lully's first tragedy, *Cadmus et Hermione*, began to include Africaines as of 1711, and in 1737 for the first time the statues brought to life in Act II were female as well as male. The dreams who reveal Cybèle's love to Atys in Act III of the eponymous opera were all male through the revival of 1699, but by 1708 the sweet dreams began to include women, whereas the nightmares remained male in perpetuity. Even the inhabitants of the Underworld might become mixed: the Divinités infernales in Act IV of *Proserpine* were still male as late as 1699, but included women in the revivals of 1715, 1727, and 1741. In at least some of these cases, new music must have been provided to characterize the female dancers, or to allow for the two groups to dance together.

49 Thorp, "Dance in Lully's *Alceste*," 87–88.

50 According to Anthony, *French Baroque Music*, 147, a score for *Alceste* marked up for performances (F-Po A.5a) shows that in 1754 the concluding chorus was replaced by a sarabande, musette, march, *ariette*, and chaconne. The shift from ending a tragedy with instrumental dances instead of a chorus did not happen until well into Rameau's period; see my "Comment terminer un opéra?"

The other phenomenon – the addition of an entirely new divertissement – may reflect the increasing appeal of the pastoral realm. As Lully and Quinault envisaged *Bellérophon* in 1679, Act IV staged a spectacular battle scene by way of a divertissement: the hero, mounted on the flying horse Pegasus, makes several passes through the air, then swoops down from the skies to kill the Chimera.[51] However, by 1705 a divertissement had been added, one whose libretto provides a line-up that looks very much like the cast lists for the pastoral divertissements already discussed: a shepherd and shepherdess danced by stars of the troupe, plus several additional shepherds and peasants (including François Dumoulin as a soloist). No music has as yet turned up for this divertissement, but it probably occurred at the end of the act by way of celebration for Bellérophon's victory.[52] Similarly, *Psyché*, which had lacked a divertissement in Act III, acquired one in 1703, performed by Youth and her followers.

Revivals did not inevitably produce expansions; Rosow has shown that the Act II divertissement of *Armide* was shortened during the 1746 revival.[53] Until careful longitudinal studies make it possible to date the additions and deletions to more operas – not just Lully's – conclusions about the editing of the divertissements must remain tentative. Yet as the eighteenth century progressed there does seem to have been a trend toward making Lully's operas conform to the growing taste for sequences of dance pieces that were less grounded by songs or choruses. The divertissement structures that Lully had so tightly controlled became more diffuse and, as time went on, audience members were likely to hear music that sounded quite different from Lully's own among the mix. Commentators such as Noverre, who make scathing remarks about the dance in Lully's operas, may not have known his divertissements in anything like their original form.

[51] The 1679 score contains no dance music in Act IV and the libretto for the 1680 court performances lists no dancers for this act, although it provides them for all the others.

[52] An analogous structure from a later Lully opera, *Persée* (1682), could have provided a model: the hero's rescue of Andromède from the sea monster early in Act IV provokes rapturous public celebrations at its end.

[53] Rosow, "How eighteenth-century Parisians," 226.

Non, ce n'est pas assez de vos charmants concerts,
Une Muse vous manque encore.
Croyez-vous réunir les suffrages divers
Sans le secours de Terpsichore?

Apollon to the Muses in the prologue to *Les Fêtes grecques et romaines*

(No, your charming concerts do not suffice; you are missing one of the Muses. Do you believe you can win favor without Terpsichore's help?)

By the 1720s the balance of power among the Muses had shifted. Melpomène retained her prestige, even as premieres of tragedies declined in number; Thalie's day had peaked, although her most beloved creations remained on the stage; Terpsichore's star was in the ascendant. More and more she herself stepped onto the stage, confirming in her own person not only dance's status, but its expressivity. Her influence even gave rise to long dance sequences independent of any particular opera – a startling break with the Opéra's practices. Composers responded by enfolding her into their works; whereas Terpsichore's cameo role in the *Critique des Fêtes de Thalie* (1714) had cast her as both singer and dancer, the entire prologue of *Les Fêtes grecques et romaines* (1723) was built around her expressive dancing. Innovative developments appeared primarily in opera-ballets and other light genres, but Terpsichore's impact was felt across the repertoire.

THE DANCE TROUPE DURING THE EARLY EIGHTEENTH CENTURY

Only during Campra's early years composing for the Opéra are there finally personnel records for the troupe. Pierre Beauchamps retired upon Lully's death in 1687 and was replaced by Guillaume-Louis Pécour, after a brief period in which Pécour shared choreographic duties with Lestang.[1] Like his former mentor, Pécour did not give up dancing when he assumed his new role; in 1695, reported Louis Ladvocat, "Many people came to see the *Ballet des saisons* and simply cannot wait to come again;

[1] A printed annotation in the 1687 libretto for *Achille et Polixène* indicates that the divertissement in 1/4–5 was choreographed by Lestang. The preface to the *Recueil général* reports that both Pécour and Lestang choreographed *Thétis et Pélée* (1689), but that thereafter Pécour worked alone.

yesterday, the situation was extreme, people doubling up in the first and second boxes, people suffocating in the pit, and they were one on top of the other in the gods – and all because Pécour danced a Spanish sarabande."[2] Pécour probably stopped dancing in 1702, at the age of 46, after 31 years on the stage.[3] He remained the troupe's choreographer until his death in 1729, although toward the end of his life he sometimes handed over his responsibilities, as occasional notices in the *Mercure de France* indicate: "The dances, composed by the Sieur Blondy instead of by Pécour, who was ill, were very well executed."[4]

Michel Blondy, who had learned dancing from his uncle, Pierre Beauchamps, and had been in the troupe since around 1691, took over when Pécour died. In his prime Blondy was considered to be "the best dancer in Europe for *la danse haute*, entrées of Furies, and other character dances"[5]; he was around 53 when he assumed his official new position and died ten years later, in 1739. On paper, if not in its day-to-day operations, the dance troupe thus had only three choreographers over the first 60 years of its existence.

Personnel and Staffing

This remarkable stability can also be discerned in personnel lists from 1704, 1713, and 1718.[6] This information can be checked against the cast lists in the librettos sold at the door of the Opéra, which, as of 31 July 1699 (a revival of *Proserpine*), started identifying the singers and dancers; henceforth the librettos served simultaneously as programs of a sort,[7] although these cast lists were not updated to reflect substitutions. Lists may, however, mask a number of individuals under a single family name; sometimes the listings append a qualification such as "the elder" (*l'aîné/l'aînée*) or "the younger" (*le cadet/la cadette*) to the family name, but not consistently. Nonetheless, these two types of document remain precious: the first provides an overview of the membership and hierarchies of the troupe, whereas the second allows us to glimpse the dancers in their roles.

2 Cited in La Gorce, "Pecour," 10; see 19–22 for Pécour's dancing roles.

3 Pécour's obituary (*MF*, April, 1729, 777) claims that he had not danced in 30 years. Between 1706 and 1710, and again from 1715 to 1718 the name Pécour appears in librettos, as a member of groups. The likely candidate is Georges Ernest Pécour, whose relationship to Guillaume-Louis is unknown; see La Gorce, "Pecour," 14–16.

4 *MF* (July 1721), 8.

5 Parfaict, *Histoire*, 1, 84. On Blondy's career, see Lecomte, "Un danseur d'exception."

6 The 1704 list derives from a notarial document published by La Gorce: "L'ARM en 1704." The second list comes from an appendix to the rules drawn up in January 1713 to govern the Opéra (F-Pan AJ13/1); its list of dancers has been published by Lecomte in "Danseuses and danseurs," 143, table 3. The 1718 list comes from Boindin, *Lettres historiques*, 112–18.

7 Lecomte has mined the data on performers from 1699 to 1733 in an unpublished catalogue and a series of articles; see the Bibliography.

Table 13-1 presents the three personnel lists, with the spelling of names standardized. In 1704 the troupe appears to have included 21 dancers, eleven men, ten women; during the next decade the numbers are only slightly higher: twelve men and ten women in 1713, thirteen men and twelve women in 1718. However, when these rosters are compared with the names derived from librettos for the same year, it becomes apparent that they are incomplete. Whereas all the people named in the table did, in fact, dance during the respective year, so did several more. Table 13-2 lists these additional dancers, some (but not all) of whom appear to have been regular members of the troupe. The 1718 list, for example, mentions only one Dangeville, whereas the librettos include two brothers, both of whom were in the troupe in 1704. Marcel's name is not on the 1704 list, but he danced in all six of the productions that year; on the other hand, it is possible that these are not the same person, since librettos in 1718 mention an elder and a younger Marcel. The absence of Mlle Menés from the 1718 list looks to be an oversight, as she appears regularly in librettos over 21 seasons, from 1708 until 1728. The following tables represent snapshots of the troupe at three different moments and cannot be seen as complete lists of membership during the first two decades of the eighteenth century.[8]

Table 13-2 hints at two phenomena revealed in greater detail by Lecomte's studies of the cast lists: first, that the Opéra supplemented its regular employees by dancers from outside; and second, that choristers might occasionally dance. Mlles Guillet and Basset are listed in the chorus for the entire 1704 season, but a Mlle Guillet danced in the first two operas of the year, Mlle Basset in a later one – always in groups and in only one or two divertissements. Whereas it is possible that the dancers and singers are different people, it seems likelier that these two singers had sufficient dance training to fill in when needed. But if the reasonably frequent appearance of dancers from outside the troupe is any indication, the demand for supplementary dancers was greater than the chorus alone could supply. Some of the extras danced in a single work (e.g., Mlle Blin in the 1704 revival of *Acis et Galatée*), while others appeared for several years, such as Monsieur and Mlle Rameau, who danced in various works from 1711 to 1717 and from 1712 to 1717 respectively.[9] Some dancers came and went: "Duval" danced in 1704, 1710–16, 1718, and 1721–25. Extra dancers may have been hired when there were special roles to fill. Six of the dancers in 1704 were probably children, needed to perform as the followers of Youth in *Le Carnaval et la Folie* and four among them as Cupids in *Télémaque*; these are "la petite

[8] Dancers other than the ones named in these tables appear in the collections of Pécour's theatrical dances published in 1704 (Chevrier [Cherrier], Piffetot, and Philbois) and 1713 (Klin and Mlle Chaillou); see Ch. 14, p. 411 for more on these two collections. Dechars is named in Parfaict, *Dictionnaire*, as having danced Polichinelle in the *Ballet des Saisons* (probably in 1695) before moving to Brussels.

[9] Lecomte believes that this was probably not Pierre Rameau, author of *Le Maître à danser*, since none of the known documents about the latter mention any service at the ARM; see "The female ballet troupe," 102 and 119n.

Rochecour," and Messieurs Pierret, Gillet, La Porte, Duval, and Sallé. One of them, Pierret, eventually joined the troupe, as his name figures in the two later lists.[10] Hiring outsiders was also a recruitment device. The 1714 regulations state that "the singers, dancers, and orchestral musicians may only be engaged after having demonstrated their abilities in several performances and having earned the approbation of the public" (article 18).

It is not hard to understand why the troupe needed to supplement its ranks. Lecomte's statistical analyses show that a four-divertissement work (one with a prologue and three acts), such as Lully's *Acis et Galatée*, might have a "mere" 40 dancing roles in the 1704 revival, but that for longer works a number as high as 75 or 80 was not uncommon.[11] Campra's *Hippodamie*, a *tragédie* with five acts and a prologue, called for 87 dancing roles at its premiere in 1708, 61 male and 26 female. In order for the eleven or twelve men of the company to fill all 61, each would have had to dance in all six divertissements, but the task becomes impossible given the uneveness in role-distribution across the opera: the prologue has fifteen male roles, Act IV has thirteen. In fact, 22 different men danced in *Hippodamie*, and even so several of them figured in four or five divertissements. During that same year the 58 male roles required by the revival of *Atys* were also danced by 22 men, the 57 male roles in *Thétis et Pelée* by 18 men. (The mind boggles at the thought of 75 or so costumes per opera for the dancers alone, even if demons or shepherds could wear the same outfit in more than one work.) Presumably if the pressures had been great enough, Pécour could have cut back on the number of dancers per divertissement, but at least through 1725 the number of dancers on stage consistently exceeded the number officially in the troupe. A system must have been in place to support both regulars and extras.[12]

The continuing presence of extra dancers notwithstanding, the membership of the core troupe remained remarkably stable. Pécour was employed there for a stunning 57 years, as a member of the original dance troupe and then as its choreographer. Other names that appear on all three membership lists include Dangeville *l'aîné*, two of the four Dumoulin brothers, Javilliers, and Mlle Prévost. Several others either were dancing for the troupe even when not named on every list, or appear on two out of the three. The *Mercure de France* takes it for granted that the names of the leading dancers are familiar to its readership.

Two sets of regulations governing the running of the Opéra, from 1713 and 1714, provide glimpses into the dancers' working conditions. Article 22 of the 1714 rules stipulates that all performers, singers and dancers alike, are obliged to accept the roles

10 Lecomte's *Catalogue* shows that Pierret danced 1703–06 and 1708–28.

11 See Lecomte, "Danseuses and danseurs," figure 12. By "dancing roles" is meant the sum for the entire opera of the number of dancers required in each of the acts.

12 The Opéra was, however, in perpetual financial difficulty; see La Gorce, *L'Opéra à Paris, passim*.

Table 13-1: Members of the troupe of the Opéra as listed in documents from 1704, 1713, and 1718, arranged to show longevity.
Asterisks indicate family names that also appeared in Lully's troupe (see Chapter 3, p. 98).

1704	1713	1718
Pécour*	Pécour	Pécour
Dancers, male (11)	(12)	(13)
Balon		
Bouteville*		
Dangeville *le cadet*		
Lesvesque		
Germain*	Germain	
Blondy	Blondy	Blondy
Dangeville *l'aîné*	Dangeville [*l'aîné*?][a]	Dangeville [*l'aîné*]
Dumoulin	Dumoulin	Dumoulin
Dumoulin C. L.é [*sic.*]	Dumoulin	Dumoulin
Ferrand	[cf. Table 13-2]	Ferrand
Javilliers	Javilliers	Javilliers
[cf. Table 13-2]	Marcel	Marcel
	Gaudrau	
	Guyot	Guyot
	Dumoulin	Dumoulin
	Dumoulin	[Dumoulin[b]]
	Pierret	Pierret
		Dupré
		Laval
		Maltaire (Malter)
Dancers, female (10)	(10)	(12)
Dangeville		
Du Plessis		
Le Fevre		
Noisy		
Subligny		
Tissard		
Victoire		
La Ferrière	[cf. Table 13-2]	La Ferrière
Prévost	Prévost	Prévost
Rose		Rose[c]
	Fleury	
	Isecq	
	Nadal	
	Guyot	Guyot
	Haran	Haran
	Lemaire	Lemaire
	Le Roy	Le Roy
	Mangot	Mangot
	Menés	[cf. Table 13-2]
		Dupré
		Duval
		Emilie
		Le Roy *la cadette*

[a] According to Lecomte (personal communication), both Dangevilles were away from the Opéra in 1710. The elder Dangeville returned in 1711 and remained until at least 1733; his younger brother danced there again only between 1712 and 1714.

[b] Boindin's list includes "les trois Dumoulin," but in fact all four brothers were dancing at the Opéra for years on either side of this date; see below, p. 387.

[c] A Mlle Rose appeared in librettos from 1700–04, 1706–08, 1712, 1716, 1718–19; whether this is a single person or more than one is unclear; see Lecomte, "The female ballet troupe," 101.

Table 13-2: Dancers listed in librettos as having performed at the Opéra in the years 1704, 1713, and 1718, beyond those in Table 13-1.

1704	1713	1718
Dancers, male (10)	(5)	(4)
*Dumirail	Dangeville [*le cadet*?[a]]	Duval
Duval	Duflot	Landais
Fauveau[b]	Duval	Marcel (*l'aîné* and *le cadet*)
Gillet	Ferrand	Pecourt[c]
Landais	Rameau	
La Porte		
Lavigne		
Marcel		
Pierret		
Sallé		
Dancers, female (9)	(6)	(4)
Bassecour	Corbiere	Brunel
Basset	Dimanche *l'aînée*	Châteauvieux
Bertin	Dimanche *la cadette*	Corail
Blin	Duval	Menés
Boulogne	La Ferrière	
Guillet	Rameau	
Le Comte		
Morancour		
La petite Rochecour		

[a] Both brothers appear in some of the same operas in 1713.
[b] According to Boindin, *Lettres historiques*, 119, Fauveau was the dancing master to the women in the troupe. Boindin does not list a dancing master to the men.
[c] Probably Georges Ernest Pécour; see above, n. 3.

assigned to them, under penalty of a fine, or, upon repeated offence, dismissal. The ballet master (Pécour during this period) is authorized to make the asssignments of the roles; either he or his assistant (the *maître des salles*) will attend all rehearsals to make sure that the dances are performed "in the style in which they were choreographed" (article 29). Performers are forbidden to appear on stage wearing something other than the correct costume for the role; they must be dressed and ready to go fifteen minutes before the performance starts (articles 32–33). Performers are not allowed to arrange for a substitute without prior permission from the Inspecteur (article 33). Performers will become eligible for a pension after fifteen years of service, if they are too old or otherwise unable to perform their duties; if they are disabled in the service of the Opéra, they become eligible for a pension immediately (articles 40–41).[13]

Even though by 1704 the numbers of men and women in the dance troupe were almost equal and were to remain so, there were nonetheless more dancing roles for

[13] See Durey de Noinville, *Histoire*, 108–18 for the 1713 rules, and 125–46 for those from 1714.

men than women.[14] The continued assignment of grotesque female roles such as sorceresses to men offers a partial explanation, but it is still striking that ballet in this period was an art in which men predominated. The emergence of female stars was, however, beginning to tip the balance.

The Stars of the Troupe

Not all dancers had equal status, and their salaries rewarded the hierarchy among them implicit in the librettos.[15] In 1704 M. Balon and Mlle Subligny were clearly the premier dancers, as gauged both by their earning power and their prominence as soloists. Claude Balon (1676–*c.* 1739) had entered the troupe in 1691 when he was only fifteen[16]; already by 1688 he had danced at court in Lorenzoni's *Orontée*. Balon is often depicted as exemplifying the noble style (see Figure 3-2). According to Bonin, "whoever has seen him can only be astounded at the summit achieved by human speed, as illustrated by Balon with his feet, with incredible skill"; Bonin further claimed that Balon "excelled in gigues and entrées."[17] Pierre Rameau said that he "was possessed of infinite grace and exceptional lightness."[18] Balon danced comic as well as serious roles; another engraving shows him in the costume of a madman. He retired from the Opéra in 1710.

Marie Thérèse Perdou de Subligny (1666–1736) was a member of the troupe by 1687, when the Swedish architect Tessin praised her dancing,[19] and retired in 1705. Her value to the troupe can be measured by her salary, which in 1704 was over twice as high as the next woman in the hierarchy.[20] Some of her solo roles include a gypsy in *Marthésie* IV (1699); one of the three Graces in Act V of the same opera; the goddess Diane in the prologue to *Canente* (1700); the lead shepherdess in *Acis et Galatée* I (revival of 1702); a Scaramouchette in *Psyché* V (revival of 1703); and the bride in the village wedding in *Roland* IV (revival of 1705). This sample alone shows her fluency in several different styles. During the winter of 1701 Subligny performed in London for several weeks (following Balon's example of two years earlier); two of Pécour's notated choreographies for her appear to date from that trip.[21] Although Balon and Subligny danced more

[14] Lecomte, "The female ballet troupe," esp. figure 4.5.

[15] For salary listings from 1704 and 1713, see Lecomte, "Danseuses and danseurs," 143, table 3, and "The female ballet troupe," 115–16; see also La Gorce, "L'ARM en 1704," 174–76, which gives the salaries for both singers and dancers. The singers in the chorus were paid on approximately the same level as the lowest-paid members of the dance troupe, whereas the singers in the principal roles earned consiberably more than the solo dancers.

[16] Parfaict, *Histoire*, 84. [17] Bonin, *Die neueste Art*, 75 and 165.

[18] Rameau, *Le Maître à danser*, xiv.

[19] Cited in Wood and Sadler, *French Baroque Opera*, 126. Parfaict, *Histoire* I, 73, says only that she entered the troupe "toward 1690" and that she retired in 1705, which can be confirmed by the librettos (Lecomte, *Catalogue*).

[20] See La Gorce, "L'ARM en 1704," 176. [21] Thorp, "Mlle Subligny in London."

often than not as soloists or as part of a solo couple (generally together), each appears to have sometimes performed as part of a group. In 1699, for example, both of them are listed in *Atys* III as among the twelve Songes funestes. On the other hand, such listings may mask solos or duets. In Act III of *Omphale* (1701) the two appear among the ten Grecs and Grecques, but in 1704 Feuillet published a duet choreography for them from this divertissement. In fact, ten of their duets are preserved in Beauchamps-Feuillet notation (see Chapter 14, p. 413).

Next in the salary hierarchy for 1704, and all at the same level, come Michel Blondy, Louis Bouteville, François Dumoulin, and Antoine Germain. Three women – Michelle Dangeville, Mlle Rose, and Mlle Victoire – appear to be on an equal level with each other, although they earn slightly less than the four men. Françoise Prévost (*c.* 1680–1741), who was to have a long and brilliant career (1695–1730),[22] did not become a soloist until after Mlle Subligny retired in 1705. Pierre Rameau compared her to Proteus, because she could "assume all manner of forms at will."[23] Her skill at acting while dancing was cultivated in a series of choreographed *symphonies* by Jean-Féry Rebel and inside operas in roles such as Inconstancy in *La Reine des Péris* (see below). Her achievements marked a major turning point in the stature of women dancers, who up until this point had been subordinate in prestige to the men.

Another future soloist, Marie-Catherine Guyot, began dancing at the Opéra in 1705 and remained until 1722. In 1713 she and Prévost were the two highest-paid women and they also danced together: no fewer than five of their duets were notated by Gaudrau (see Chapter 14, p. 413). Mlle Menés, who along with Mlles Lemaire, Isecq, and Haran occupied the next tier in the salary structure, also appeared frequently as a soloist.[24] By 1713 Balon and Bouteville had retired; now Michel Blondy and François Dumoulin shared the top salary slot among the men, with Germain, Marcel, and two more of the Dumoulin brothers, David and Pierre, slightly below them. The 1718 list does not give salaries, but the librettos show that Prévost, Guyot, and Menés continued to lead the women, whereas Blondy, Marcel, and the Dumoulin brothers remained as featured dancers, along with three new men, Maltaire, Laval, and Dupré (Louis, the future "grand Dupré"), who were headed for major careers.

Toward the end of her career, Mlle Prévost presented three young students to the public: Mlle Richalet in 1723, Marie Anne Cupis de Camargo in 1726, and Marie Sallé in 1727. It is possible to pinpoint the dates of these debuts because the *Mercure* had begun reporting them – a notable shift in the public attention accorded to dancers. The *Mercure* did not limit its attention to the Opéra; in the same issue (September 1723) that it featured Richalet's debut, it also reported on two children who danced for the first

22 See Astier, "Françoise Prévost"; its appendix lists her known roles.
23 Rameau, *Le Maître à danser*, xv.
24 Regarding Menés's partners, see Lecomte, "The female ballet troupe," 112–13.

time at the Comédie-Française. Richalet remained in the troupe for ten years, but did not reach the same heights as Prévost's other two students. Camargo debuted in May; by August she was earning so much applause that a performance of *Le Jugement de Pâris* was interrupted.[25] One month later Marie Sallé danced for the first time at the Opéra, replacing Mlle Prévost, who was ill. Before long the teacher and her two students were dancing in the same operas, although not necessarily in the same divertissements. A newcomer from the provinces, Mlle Mariette, debuted in June 1729; the *Mercure* found sufficient merit in her dancing to rank her just behind the other three and exclaimed over the superabundance of talent that had so recently emerged.[26] Prévost, who had been on the stage for at least 35 years, retired in 1730.

Much has been written about Camargo and still more about Sallé.[27] Laudatory verses by Voltaire, published in the *Mercure* in January 1732, have done much to crystallize notions of their styles:

> Ah, Camargo que vous êtes brillante!
> Mais que Sallé, grands Dieux, est ravissante !
> Que vos pas sont légers et que les siens sont doux!
> Elle est inimitable et vous êtes nouvelle:
> Les Nymphes sautent comme vous,
> Mais les Grâces dansent comme elle.
>
> ("Oh Camargo, how brilliant you are, / But Sallé, great gods, is ravishing! / How light are your steps, but how gentle are hers! She is inimitable, while you are novel. / The Nymphs leap like you, / but the Graces dance like her."[28])

Camargo's technical brilliance allowed her to do *entrechats* and other *cabrioles* that had formerly been the province of men;[29] her ability to dance like a man was not admired by traditionalists. Sallé had a more lyrical style; she has enjoyed a reputation as a dance reformer from her performances in England and from some of her roles in Rameau operas. Historiography has emphasized their differences, yet a comparison of their repertoires shows a fair degree of overlap. Whereas Camargo was much likelier to be cast as a sailor, where she danced lively tambourins and rigaudons, the two not only

[25] *MF* (May 1726), 1003, and (August 1727), 1869–70. [26] *MF* (June 1729), 1221–22.

[27] Both appear in virtually every dance history that covers this period. Book-length biographies were published early in the twentieth century: Letainturier-Fradin, *La Camargo*; Dacier, *Une Danseuse de l'Opéra*, which includes a list of (almost) all of Sallé's roles. For Camargo's roles, not to mention numerous anecdotes about her, see Compardon, *L'Académie Royale de Musique*. For more recent work on Sallé see articles by McCleave listed in the bibliography (mostly concerning her career in England), the articles on both by Astier in the *International Encyclopedia of Dance*, and Laurenti (ed.), *Marie Sallé*.

[28] Trans. (with one modification) by Guest, *The Paris Opéra Ballet*, 19.

[29] Even the engraving based on the portrait of Camargo by Lancret alludes to this claim in its accompanying quatrain: "Fidèle aux loix de la cadence / Je forme, au gré de l'art, les pas les plus hardis; / Originale dans ma danse / Je puis le disputer aux Balons, aux Blondis."

had many role-types in common, one was not infrequently cast during revivals in a role the other had created.[30] Although the two debuted within a year of each other, they only overlapped at the Opéra between September 1727 and the end of 1732, with a gap of several months in 1730–31 while Sallé was in England. In December 1732 Sallé left again for England and when she returned in 1735, Camargo had just withdrawn for what turned out to be seven years. By the time she decided to return, in 1742, Sallé had retired. Camargo herself retired in 1751. Both of them were in the troupe long enough to make important contributions to Rameau's operas.

Sallé and Camargo were not always exempt from dancing in groups – or so the librettos suggest – but they were more likely to appear in solos, *pas de deux*, or *pas de trois*. They generally danced no more than once or twice per opera, in distinction to the men in the troupe, who were called upon to fill more roles.

A Case Study: The Dumoulin Brothers

The extraordinarily long careers of the four Dumoulin brothers prove instructive as to the range of roles and degree of specialization expected from dancers. Henri Dumoulin joined the troupe in 1695, according to the Parfaict brothers[31], who also report that he was the product of his mother's first marriage and took his stepfather's name when his mother remarried. Certainly he was appearing regularly by 1699, when the first librettos with names were published. His half-brother François joined the troupe in 1700, according to Parfaict, but his name starts appearing as of 29 November 1699 in Destouches's *Marthésie*. From then on the librettos distinguish between Dumoulin *l'aîné* or Dumoulin-L for the elder brother, and Dumoulin *le cadet* or Dumoulin-C for the younger. When Pierre joined, as of the premiere of Campra's *Alcine* on 15 January 1705, he was referred to as "Dumoulin le jeune," but when David arrived shortly thereafter (18 February 1706 in Marais's *Alcyone*), a new system of nomenclature appeared (most of the time – the librettos are not completely consistent) that gave each his first initial: F-Dumoulin, etc. (see all four brothers in Figure 7-2, p. 215, the second entrée). The brothers must have come from remarkably healthy stock: Henri danced at the Opéra until 1730, shortly before his death (a 35-year career), François for an astonishing 49 years until his retirement in 1748, Pierre also until 1748 (43 years), and David until 1751, for 46 years.[32] Even if, like Balon, they were adolescents when they began to dance professionally, they performed beyond an age when many dancers today retire. It is striking that all four danced in all the

[30] See Lecomte and Harris-Warrick, "L'opposition Sallé–Camargo," 49–64.

[31] All references to Parfaict allude to their *Dictionnaire*, II, 349–50.

[32] The terminal dates for the three younger brothers come from Parfaict, but they are corroborated by the Rameau libretto catalogue, 337–38, except that David's last role in a Rameau opera took place in 1749.

operas, year in and year out, at least through 1711;[33] they apparently did not take leaves to go dance abroad, as did some of their comrades in the troupe.

The variety of the brothers' roles shows they had a broad training that taught them the movement vocabulary for many different character types. In the *Fragments de Lully* (1702) François danced as a warrior in the prologue, a sailor in the first entrée, and as Polichinelle, with Dame Gigogne as his partner, in the *divertissement comique* – that is, in styles ranging from the noble to the comic and including what would later be called *demi-caractère*. In the 1713 revival of Lully's *Psyché*, Pierre danced in the prologue as a follower of the goddess Flore, in Act II as one of Vulcain's blacksmiths, in Act IV as a demon, and in Act V as a follower of Apollon. It is not uncommon to find two or more brothers dancing in the same group. One even wonders if each brother was not at least partially responsible for training his younger sibling: in his early performances the latest newcomer always dances with one of his older brothers. For example, in *Alcyone* (1706) Pierre and David, the two newest, appear only in roles that either Henri or François is also dancing; in 1710 all four danced as Forgerons in *Persée*. By and large, out of the six opportunities for dancing in a *tragédie* or the four to five in a ballet, each member of the Dumoulin clan could expect to dance in three or four.[34]

Notwithstanding the breadth of their abilities, the brothers did have distinct profiles. Each sometimes danced as a soloist, but François and David featured alone or in a solo couple much more often than the other two (see, in Figure 12-2, p. 364, assignments for three of the brothers). François clearly had comic abilities. According to Parfaict, "He is the one who adopted the role of Arlequin, whose entrées he danced in the ballets at the Académie." This can be verified; as of 1700 in the *Ballet des Saisons* he is dancing as Arlequin, a role he was to fill many times over the years. He also performed other roles from the *comédie italienne*, such as Polichinelle, but even more frequently he had another standard shtick, as a *pâtre* or *paysan*.[35] Often, but not always, these appear to be solo roles. An engraving of François as a peasant gives him clothes that look both out of date and tattered; he is wearing a beard in an era when they were out of fashion, and his arms are over his head in a gesture exceeding the boundaries of the noble style (see Figure 12-1). Whether for these specialized roles or for the quality of his dancing in general, he was the most highly paid of the brothers in 1713, earning the same amount as Blondy at the top of the scale. We know he was a tenor, because he assumed one singing role, that of Arlequin/Diogenes in one of the entrées from Campra's *Fêtes vénitiennes*.

[33] My inventory of their roles goes through 1711. The only possible absence is for François, whose name does not appear in the 1703 libretto for *Persée*, which, however, lacks the cast for Act V.

[34] According to Lecomte, the average woman danced three times per opera; see "The female ballet troupe," 115.

[35] On dances for peasants, see Chs. 12, p. 360 and 14, p. 427.

David Dumoulin excelled in the noble style. He is frequently featured as a soloist or as half of a solo couple – at least once per opera – in roles such as a heroic shepherd, a Songe agréable, or the follower of a god. Parfaict says that he performed "the leading entrées, and slow and serious dances." Whereas early in his career he generally danced in four of the six divertissements in a typical opera, in 1711 and 1712 he appeared only once or twice per work, always at least once as a soloist. It would be tempting to conclude that his star-power exempted him from some appearances in group dances, except for the fact that in 1713 the number of his roles rose again. He also danced frequently in *pas de deux*, especially with Mlle Guyot and, after 1710, when Balon retired, with Mlle Prévost.[36] According to Pierre Rameau, David Dumoulin was the one "who most resembled Balon and who consoled the public in some measure for his loss."[37] Noverre wrote the following appreciation of him in 1760:

> Nobody has yet succeeded to Mr Dumoulin. He danced his *pas de deux* with a superiority difficult to emulate; always tender, always graceful, be he a butterfly or a zephyr; at times inconstant, at others faithful, but always expressing new feelings, he could portray all the aspects of sensuous and tender love.[38]

Henri, like David, tended to be cast often, although not exclusively, in noble-style roles, but rarely as a soloist. When he was featured, it was almost always with a female partner, as the lead couple among a larger group of dancers. In the 1713 revival of *Armide*, for instance, he danced with Mlle Menés among the people of Damascus, along with a group consisting of four men and four women, but that also featured a male soloist. In addition to his engagements at the Opéra, he moonlighted at the fair theaters; according to Parfaict, he choreographed for the Opéra Comique between 1714 and 1719.[39]

Pierre was a utility dancer, who adopted all kinds of roles. The Parfaicts' claim that he performed Scaramouche and Pierrot and "other character dances" is confirmed for his occasional solo appearances, but he mostly appeared in groups.

The early careers of the Dumoulin brothers exhibit two tendencies that hold for other dancers of this period as well. First, their training equipped them to dance a wide spectrum of styles and characters; whereas some dancers developed specializations, none were confined to them. Second, even highly paid soloists were expected to participate in group dances upon occasion. This tendency is harder to discern on the basis of role attributions alone, and it may be one that diminished with time. Certainly, once Mlle Prévost was an established star, she seems to have danced primarily solos or

[36] See Lecomte, "Danseuses and danseurs," 138. [37] Rameau, *Le Maître à danser*, xiv.

[38] As cited in Astier, "Dumoulin Brothers," *International Encyclopedia of Dance*.

[39] A footnote in the preface to Le Sage, *Théâtre de la foire* (1737) confirms that Dumoulin *l'ainé* was *maître de ballet* at the Opéra Comique, but provides no dates.

duets. Still, the kind of highlighting of individual dancers seen later in the century existed in a milder form in this period.

Crossovers

Among the dancers at the Opéra, many either began their careers in other theaters or devoted part of their activities to them. Marie Sallé was born into an extended family of itinerant performers and started dancing at a young age at the Parisian fairs, in the provinces, and in London;[40] her apprenticeship has often been seen as nurturing the acting abilities she was to demonstrate later at the Opéra. Similarly, Mlle Corail danced at the fairs starting in 1713, before joining the troupe in 1718;[41] other prominent dancers who came from the fairs included Mlles de Lisle and Menés.[42] And just as playwrights and composers circulated among the various Parisian theaters – Fuzelier being the most connected – so did choreographers. Henri Dumoulin choreographed for the fairs between 1714 and 1719; his colleague Antoine-François Dangeville, who came from a family of actors, choreographed "for several years" at the Comédie Française during the 1720s[43].

The circulation of creative artists among rival theaters has two important implications for theatrical dancing. First, dancers and choreographers must have been vectors for some of the borrowings that worked their way onto the stage of the Opéra. Second, the fact that dancers could perform on such different stages means that they all shared a basic dance technique. Each theater undoubtedly cultivated its own movement styles and the surviving choreographies provide a partial glimpse of the range of possibilities (see Chapter 14). Arlequin and his cohort may have deliberately trangressed stylistic conventions, but, no matter on which stage they danced, they relied on a common technique with the dancers from the Opéra.

LES CARACTÈRES DE LA DANSE AND ITS OFFSPRING

In 1715 violinist Jean-Féry Rebel published a sequence of fourteen linked movements, most of them generic dances, that he entitled *Les Caractères de la danse*. Whether he conceived the work from the start for Françoise Prévost is not known, but by 1721, if not before, she had turned it into an exhibition piece for herself; it was quickly adopted by other dancers.[44] The work has two major claims to novelty. First, it was generally performed as an extended solo (eight to nine minutes) that requires the dancer to

[40] See LMC 8120, a choreography by Tomlinson danced by Sallé and her brother, "the two French children," in Lincoln's Inn Fields.

[41] Parfaict, *Dictionnaire*, II, 172. [42] Parfaict, *Mémoires*, vii.

[43] Parfaict, *Dictionnaire*, II, 247 and 350; *MF* (September 1722), 175; (September 1723), 576.

[44] On its performance history, the classic work remains Aubry and Dacier, *Les Caractères de la danse* (1904); see, more recently, Lalonger, "Rebel's *Les Caractères*."

change style every few seconds – from a sarabande to a gigue to a rigaudon, in one section – and thus demands an ability both to inhabit different styles convincingly and to alter them in the blink of an eye. This is a very different type of contrast from the familiar pattern of two contrasting dances in a row for the same set of characters. Second, Rebel's sequence of purely instrumental movements had an identity independent of any opera. Even if the concept of the "fragment" had opened the way to evenings composed of disparate elements, a dance sequence without vocal music and unattached to a larger work was something new.

Rebel himself composed at least five such "symphonies" for the Opéra between 1711 and 1737, all of them admired and imitated.[45] *Les Caractères de la danse*, however, not only had the widest distribution, it generated a new type of divertissement within operas, one organized around a star female performer – Prévost in the first instance, later her students Sallé and Camargo. The best-known of the operatic offspring is the "Ballet des Fleurs" from Rameau's *Indes galantes* (1735), conceived for Sallé; Rameau, however, does not deserve the credit he is often accorded for the creation of this type of work. His librettist for *Les Indes galantes*, Fuzelier, played a key role in the evolution from Rebel's freestanding ballets to integrated operatic divertissements.

The *Symphonies* of Jean-Féry Rebel

When Rebel composed his first *symphonie, Caprice*, in 1711, the *Mercure de France* had not yet begun to cover theatrical performances in a regular way, and nothing is known about the circumstances surrounding its creation. That it was, in fact, danced and not just played comes from an unexpected source – a police report. Following a visit to the Foire Saint-Laurent in August of that year to check whether its performers were obeying regulations, the report's author wrote that the current play, *Arlequin à la guinguette*, ended with "the new dance *Caprice* from the Opéra, which is currently playing, and which Arlequin danced while mimicking Mlle Prévost, who dances it at the Opéra."[46] That *Caprice* was choreographed is eye-opening, because the work consists not of French dances, but of two through-composed movements in a violinistic Italian style, marked Gravement and Vivement (Example 13-1). We thus know that as early as 1711 Prévost was dancing to music far removed in style from the usual dances at the Opéra. Twelve years later, in 1723, Bonnet cited "la danse du Caprice par la Prévost" among examples of the "perfection" that French theatrical dancing had attained.[47]

[45] See Cessac, *Rebel*, 79–122.

[46] Quoted in Campardon, *Spectacles de la foire*, 1, 92–93. According to Parfaict, *Mémoires*, 1, 118, the Arlequin was an Englishman named Baxter, who dressed as a woman to imitate Prévost.

[47] Bonnet, *Histoire générale*, 69. Nemeitz, *Séjour de Paris* (1727), 352, also reported that *Caprice* and *Les Caractères des danses* [sic] had been vehicles for Prévost. It is possible that Rebel's *Boutade* (1712) was assimilated into *Caprice*; see Cessac, *Rebel*, 84–85.

Example 13-1: Jean-Féry Rebel, *Caprice*. (a) "Gravement"; (b) "Vivement."

(a)

(b)

In light of this early association between dancer and composer, it seems probable that when Rebel published *Les Caractères de la danse* four years later, it was written with Prévost's abilities in mind – even if a firm connection between Prévost and this work can be established only in 1721, when the *Mercure* identified the "inimitable danseuse" who had made the work's reputation.[48] No choreography exists for any of Rebel's symphonies, leaving open the question of whether, given their titles (see Table 13-3), all fourteen movements were danced.

The generic dances range in length from seven to thirty-six bars, some of them amounting to the A section of a binary piece and ending on the dominant; the two sections of the *sonate* are relatively long and decidedly violinistic. Some of the recent dancers who have choreographed *Les Caractères de la danse* have concluded that the prelude and the *sonate* were not intended for dancing, even though it seems peculiar to end the work with the dancer either absent or standing still. The case of *Caprice* may answer the question; if Prévost was dancing to through-composed Italian-style movements as early as 1711, then surely a "sonate" would not have deterred her a few years later. It is worth remembering that in 1710, in "Les Devins de la Place Saint-Marc" from

[48] *MF* (June-July 1721), 1, 64. However, given that, according to the title page, the score was sold "at the door of the Opéra," the work must have been familiar to the Opéra's audience by 1715.

Table 13-3: Structure of *Les Caractères de la danse*.
Each movement ends on the tonic, unless otherwise indicated.

Heading in score	Meter, Key	Number of bars
Prélude	¢, D (ends on V)	14
Courante	$\frac{3}{2}$, D (ends on V)	‖: 7 :‖
Menuet	**3**, D (ends on V)	16
Bourrée	**2**, D	22
Chaconne	**3**, D	36
Sarabande	$\frac{3}{2}$, d (ends on V)	8
Gigue	$\frac{6}{4}$, d	20
Rigaudon	**2**, d (ends on V)	16
Passepied	**3**, d	28
Gavotte	¢, d	22
Sonate (Fort et vite)	**3**, D	29 [ABB′]
Loure	$\frac{6}{4}$, D (ends on V)	7
Musette	$\frac{6}{8}$, D	‖: 7 :‖ 23
Sonate	**3**, b → D	50

Campra's *Fêtes vénitiennes*, Zélie had danced during the ritornelli that follow Italian-style *ariettes* (see Table 8-3, p. 251).

Yet when in 1721 the *Mercure* published a parody of *Les Caractères de la danse* – that is, a set of verses designed to fit the melody – it included no verses for the *sonates*, a lack that to some has also suggested that these movements were not danced.[49] This view ties into a larger interpretive position, one that accepts the parody as evidence of what each movement represented, on the grounds of a suggestive sentence in the *Mercure*: "The author has expressed in these verses what the inimitable dancer who made the reputation of this lovely caprice expressed through her attitudes and steps, always brilliant and always varied."[50] Each little poem, one for each dance, paints a miniature first-person portrait of a different individual in the throes of love, from the old man enraputured with a girl much too young for him (courante) to a happy shepherdess (musette). The French-style prelude receives an introductory text in which Love exhorts mortals to make wishes. Did Prévost's dance tell a series of little stories?

It is important to note that the verses were written after the fact and that their rhythms and rhymes had to fit the music; these constraints mean that some of the pieces provide more scope for verbal development than do others (the musette has thirty lines of verse, the loure seven). The practice of adding words to pre-existent instrumental music was long-standing – the *Mercure* often published texts adapted to instrumental pieces by

49 This is Aubry and Dacier's view (n. 44); they do not mention the precedent offered by *Caprice*. Lalonger also takes it for granted that the prelude and the sonates are not danced.

50 *MF* (June–July 1721), 64–72; transcribed by Lalonger, "Rebel's *Les Caractères*," 121–23.

composers such as Marais – and is related to the theatrical use of vaudevilles, where new words were set to both vocal and instrumental tunes. The anonymous versifier for *Les Caractères de la danse* was participating in a broad-based cultural phenomenon; in fact, the words were published at least twice with the music, in 1730 and again a few years later.[51] The *sonates*, with their large leaps and runs of sixteenth notes, are too violinistic to lend themselves to being sung; their musical profile alone suffices to explain why they were not given a text in any of the three publications.

But the question remains as to whether the verses have any connection to what Prévost did on stage. The overall frame of reference does seem theatrical. Over half the texts – bourrée, sarabande, gigue, passepied, gavotte, and musette – evoke the pastoral world, either by referring to the lover as a shepherd or shepherdess, or by calling the lover a standard pastoral name such as Thémire. Of these six, the speaker is a woman in five – only the sarabande has a male persona – and for four of the six their love is unrequited. The woman in the musette, however, wishes only to thank Love, and the lively singer of the gigue sounds like the daughter in the first entrée of *Les Fêtes de Thalie*, wanting only to sing and dance. The other five poems come from the comic realm and four of the speakers are men. In the one exception – the menuet – a twelve-year-old girl experiencing the first stirrings of love wishes that her "mean Mommy" will fall asleep when her lover comes. The other texts belong to the low comedy associated with the fair theaters or Théâtre Italien. The speaker of the courante text is a Pantalon type, the old man who lusts after a young girl, despite her derision ("De mon ardeur / Elle ne fait que rire"). The chaconne represents a young fop, proud of his powdered wig, his big blue eyes, and his full mouth of teeth, but worried because, for reasons he can't fathom, people make fun of him. The rigaudon portrays a self-satisfied man who uses his money as the route to a woman's heart, but asks Love to get rid of the abbé who has a deeper purse. The loure is a drinking song.

Whether or not these little poems have anything to say about Mlle Prévost's performance, they do underscore what the construction of the music already suggests: that the point is to challenge the dancer's ability to crystallize a characterization almost instantly and then to switch to something completely different. Even if the first two movements did require Prévost to transform herself from a randy old man into the young object of his affections, what really mattered is that she had to change character in the time of a dotted quarter note. Moreover, she had to evolve through her multiple roles without the help of costume changes. This work does not challenge the aesthetic principle that makes dancers responsible for communicating the affect of the music (see Chapter 4, p. 119ff) – rather, it reinforces it – but it does turn its practice into a virtuosic *tour de force*. By the middle of the 1720s *Les Caractères de la danse* had become a signature piece for young

[51] In *Les Parodies nouvelles et les vaudevilles inconnus* (Paris: Ballard, 1730) and *Recueils d'airs de contredanses* (Paris: Mme Boivin, n.d.), both cited by Cessac, *Rebel*, 96.

female dancers. Mlle Camargo, a student of Mlle Prévost, danced it for her debut at the Opéra in 1726, and many times thereafter. In 1729 Mlle Sallé danced it as a *pas de deux* with Antoine Laval; she took the piece with her to London in 1731 and again in 1734. Dancers on other stages performed the work as well, each performer making the work her own.[52]

Rebel's third *symphonie, La Fantaisie*, which did have a story to tell, drew a particularly fulsome report from the *Mercure* in 1729:

> The Académie Royale de Musique reopened on Monday the second of this month with the opera *Tancrède*, ended by the *pas de trois*, danced by Mr Blondy, leading dancer and choreographer for the Opéra, by Mr Dumoulin the young [Pierre], and by Mlle Camargo. This famous *pas*, or rather, this ballet for three, the performance of which must be viewed as the triumph of dance in general and of almost all the characters in particular, represents a jealous teacher and two students. It is danced to an excellent piece of music by Rebel *le père*, composer for the king's chamber and music master at the Académie Royale.[53]

The Parfaict brothers, paraphrasing the *Mercure*, added that "the same subject reappeared at this theater in 1752 under the title *Le Maître de musique*, Italian intermezzo in two acts."[54] *Il maestro de musica* also has three characters: an aspiring young singer finds herself navigating between her teacher, who thinks she needs more lessons, and the impresario trying to lure her onto the stage. In the *pas de trois* the jealous teacher – presumably a dancing master – must have been the role for Blondy, who was in his 50s, with the young Camargo and Dumoulin as the two students. Both the general subject of a jealous teacher and the analogy to an *opera buffa* suggest that this little ballet had a comic tone. Rebel supplied an Italian-style movement (Grave, 15 bars in $\frac{3}{2}$ meter) and dance pieces in disparate styles (chaconne, loure, tambourin, a return to the chaconne). The tambourin might have been intended for Camargo, who specialized in this dance; the previous year the *Mercure* had praised her for one she danced in the second act of *Hypermnestre* "to everyone's astonishment and delight."[55] Like *Les Caractères de la danse*, the *Fantaisie* was performed numerous times at the Opéra.

Les Plaisirs champêtres premiered on 19 September 1734, following a performance of *Acis et Galatée* – an appropriate addition to a pastoral opera. The *Mercure* reports only that "one has hardly seen any pieces better characterized or more piquant," but does reveal that it was choreographed by Blondy for six dancers: Mlles Camargo and Mariette, plus Dumoulin (which brother is not stated), Dupré, Maltaire, and Javilliers.[56] The unequal number of men and women suggests that there may have been some kind of story, or a

[52] *MF* (May 1726), 1003; (February 1729), 335; (June 1729), 1221–22. Aubry and Dacier, *Les Caractères de la danse*, 16–24, trace the performance histories of the work and its offshoots, such as *Les Nouveaux Caractères de la danse* by Grandval.

[53] *MF* (May 1729), 987–88. The previous month the *Mercure* had named Laval as the third performer and said that the *pas de trois* was "extrêmement applaudi." *MF* (April 1729), 776.

[54] Parfaict, *Dictionnaire*, v, 350–51. [55] *MF* (June1728), 1456.

[56] *MF* (September 1734), 2053–54.

set of little vignettes. In any case, a distribution of two women and four men seems to have been fundamental to the work's identity. Not only was it generally referred to thereafter as "the *pas de six*" rather than by its title, but when it was parodied on the stage of the Théâtre Italien a few months later, the same distribution was retained, translated into commedia roles: Arlequin and Arlequine, Pierrot and Pierrette, Polichinelle and a peasant in wooden shoes.[57]

Rebel's last *symphonie, Les Éléments* (1737), has achieved notoriety due to its dissonant portrayal of chaos, "the confusion that reigned among the elements before the moment in which [. . .] they took the place assigned to them in the order of Nature." In the same preface to his published score, Rebel called this section the "introduction," which suggests that it was not danced. The rest, however, was: "The elements painted by dance and music seemed to me open to an agreeable variety, both in relation to the different genres of music, and to the costumes and steps of the dancers." How the dancers moved in depicting earth, air, fire, and water is a question neither Rebel nor other writers address; the *Mercure* reveals only that *Les Éléments* was treated as a *pas de six*, like the *Plaisirs champêtres* of three years earlier, and with almost the same cast: Mlles Sallé and Mariette, plus Dumoulin, Dupré, Maltaire, and Javilliers.[58] Whether or not the dancing style matched the radicality of the music, it must have looked very different from what Prévost had done in *Caprice* 26 years earlier.

Rebel's *symphonies* appear to have been performed primarily on special occasions, such as the closing of the season or the performances for the *capitation*, when the performers received the bulk of the box-office.[59] One such program included:

- "Le Professeur de folie" from *Le Carnaval et la Folie*;
- "La Turquie" from *L'Europe galante*, which concluded with the cantate *Zéphire et Flore* by Bourgeois;
- the scene involving the singing and dancing masters from *Les Fêtes vénitiennes*, concluded with *Les Caractères de la danse*, performed by Mlle Prévost;
- "La Provençale" from *Les Fêtes de Thalie*.[60]

In this case *Les Caractères de la danse* was worked into a scene where it fit; this may have been the case for *Caprice* in 1711 when the opera on the boards – probably *Les Fêtes vénitiennes*[61] – could have incorporated an Italian-style dance sequence in any number of places. But sometimes Rebel's *symphonies* were performed in conjunction with a

57 *MF* (February 1735), 364. "This figured and very well characterized dance was performed perfectly by the actors in the troupe [. . .] the tunes were parodied from those written for the *pas de six* at the Opéra."

58 *MF* (October 1737), 2266. This is a completely different work from the ballet *Les Éléments* composed for Louis XV by Lalande in 1721 and expanded for the Opéra in 1725 by Destouches.

59 For this type of performance, see Denécheau and Serre, "Sauts, gambades."

60 *MF* (April 1726), 805.

61 Ducrot, "Les représentations"; the next opera, *Cadmus et Hermione*, did not open until after the *Mercure*'s report had been written.

full-length opera, often at its end, as in 1734 when *Les Plaisirs champêtres* followed Lully's *Acis et Galatée*. This opera ends with celebrations, but *Tancrède*'s tragic conclusion was also followed by a danced *symphonie* on several dates in the same year.[62] Even if audiences conceived such special performances differently than they did the rest of the season, they had been introduced to the idea of concluding an evening at the opera with dancing rather than a chorus – a practice that was to become more common in the Rameau era.[63]

Rebel's innovative *symphonies* provided an additional artistic outlet for the star dancers of the troupe, and the dancers' public profiles received an important boost when the *Mercure* increased its attention to the arts, starting with the very issue that included the verses set to *Les Caractères de la danse*. The new editors, among them the prolific playwright and librettist Louis Fuzelier, committed themselves to establishing a section dedicated to the theater, which would cover "novelties from the Comédie-Française, the Opéra, the Comédie-Italienne, plays and entertainments from the [Jesuit] colleges, and other popular spectacles given during the fairs under the name of Opéra-Comique [. . .] plus various spectacles from the provinces and abroad."[64] Even though Fuzelier left the *Mercure* in 1724,[65] the coverage of the theatrical scene initiated in 1721 remained a regular part of each monthly issue. His journalism was undoubtedly enriched by his insider's perspective on theatrical life, and his librettos show him paying close attention to the performances he covered – *Les Caractères de la danse* in particular.

Operatic Incarnations

Even though Rebel's choreographic *symphonies* were conceived outside of an operatic framework, the aesthetic principle that integrated music and dance still held sway. One measure of its tenacity was the subsequent practice of folding *Caractères de la danse*-like scenes into operatic divertissements – the result, in its early instances, of an artistic alliance between Fuzelier and Prévost.

The first is found in the prologue to *Les Fêtes grecques et romaines* by Collin de Blamont (1723). After Clio and Erato justify basing a ballet on ancient history (see Chapter 10, p. 308), Apollon insists, in the verses quoted at the start of this chapter, that yet another Muse is essential – Terpsichore. Fuzelier had already demonstrated his partiality for dance in three earlier librettos,[66] but here he developed a new

62 *MF* (April 1729), 776 and (May 1729), 987–88.

63 See my "Comment terminer un opéra?"

64 *MF* (June–July 1721), v–xii (statement about the new editorial policies) and 131–32 (introduction to the new section, "Spectacles"). The other two editors were Charles Dufresny, who had been at the helm for several years, and Antoine de La Roque; see Trott, "Louis Fuzelier et le théâtre," 615. This issue also introduced a shorter title, *Le Mercure*; it became *Le Mercure de France* in 1724.

65 Fuzelier had another stint as co-editor from 1744 to 1752.

66 *Les Amours déguisés* (ballet, 1713), *Arion* (tragedy, 1714) and the *Ballet des âges* (1718); Anthony (*French Baroque Music*, 175) accused the last of a "reckless proliferation of dances."

construction for featuring the troupe's reigning Terpsichore, Mlle Prévost. Normally it is a singer who has followers, but the Muse of the dance "enters at the head of her pupils, who are variously clothed and characterized"; her entourage included a Chef de la danse (Blondy) and twelve followers (one mixed couple, four men, and six women). The singing chorus is cast as pupils of Erato. The long divertissement – occupying over 50 pages in the reduced score – falls into two parts (see Table 13-4); the first has a classic mixture of songs, choruses, and dances, while the innovative second part highlights Terpsichore.

Part I features Terpsichore's followers. The chaconne's length and musical variety suggest that the personnel varied – possibly incorporating solos for Terpsichore and the Chef de la danse, along with various combinations of her "variously characterized" followers. The text addressed to beautiful young women is associated with the sarabande, which may thus have accommodated a group of female dancers. The featured couple could have danced anywhere in part I. The chorus that rounds it off was clearly danced, given its alternating instrumental passages and its key line, "Ranimons nos pas et nos voix." A score marked up for a revival (probably of either 1753 or 1762)[67] bears the annotations "Danse" for the first three instrumental passages, "Danse / les femmes" in the fourth, and "Danse / les hommes" when the text is sung for the last time (see Figure 13-1).

The *didascalie* that introduces part II calls what follows a "cantate." Like the *cantates* inside *Les Fêtes vénitiennes* (see Chapter 8, pp. 251–53), it features a soloist, but here the "arias" are danced and the commentary by Erato and Apollon fills the slot normally occupied by recitative. In fact, the *didascalie* says that Terpsichore "expresses" the instrumental pieces and the songs "through her varied steps and *attitudes*" – a formulation that is almost identical to what the *Mercure* said about Prévost's dancing in the *Les Caractères de la danse*. The attribution "pour Terpsichore" suggests that Prévost danced the three "arias" alone. In the vocal sections Erato and Apollon provide a kind of running commentary on her dancing, which alternates and even overlaps with their words – not on her movements, but on the affect they project. The first commentary is quite general and the music bourée-like.

Apollon et Erato: Quelle danse vive et légère!
Les Jeux, les Ris vous suivent tous;
Muse brillante, auprès de vous
On voit plus d'Amours qu'à Cythère.

(What lively, light dancing! Pleasure and laughter follow you. Brilliant Muse, there are more Cupids near you than on Cythera.)

[67] F-Po A.197a. See Ch. 7, p. 212 about the status of such scores.

Table 13-4: *Les Fêtes grecques et romaines*, Prologue, Scene 2.
Sections entirely sung are in white, entirely danced light gray, mixed singing and dancing dark gray.

Heading in score	Musical features	Paraphrase of sung text/ comments
	[Part I]	
[Trio] Clio, Erato, Apollon, "Charmante Muse de la danse"	G, **3**	"Charming Muse of the dance, the fêtes that you adorn will triumph forever."
Chaconne	G, **3**; section in minor, 248m.	Many changes of character and dynamics.
Sarabande	g, **3**; binary	Danced by the six women?
Air, [Suivant d'Apollon], "Jeunes beautés"[a]	g, **3**; binary, almost identical to sarabande	Exhorts "young beauties" to sing and dance.
Premier Rigaudon	g, ¢; binary	
Deuxième Rigaudon	G, ¢; for oboes and bassoons	
[Air] Apollon, "Retracez aujourd'hui les plus aimables fêtes"	B♭, **3**; binary	Apollon alludes to the ancient heroes to appear later in the opera.
Chœur des Elèves de Terpsichore et d'Erato, "A des emplois nouveaux, Apollon nous appelle"	B♭, **2**	The pupils say that Apollon has given them a new function; in obeying they will both sing and dance.
	***Cantate* [Part II]**	
Erato and Apollon sing the praises of Terpsichore in a cantate, *and the Muse of the dance expresses [the* cantate*'s] instrumental pieces and songs through her varied steps and* attitudes.		
Gigue, pour Terpsichore	B♭, $\frac{6}{8}$; binary	Terpsichore dances.
[Duo] Erato, Apollon, "Quelle danse vive et légère!"	B♭, **2**	Their comments are interspersed with instrumental phrases during which Terpsichore dances.
Air, pour Terpsichore. Rondeau	B♭, **3**; rondeau, for flutes with violins on the "bass"	Terpsichore dances.
[Duo] Erato, Apollon, "Vous peignez à nos yeux les transports des amants"	Varies in key, meter, and affect [see Example 13-2]	The sung phrases are interspersed with affective and varied instrumental phrases during which Terpsichore dances.
Menuet, pour Terpsichore. Rondeau	B♭, **3**; rondeau, for flutes with violins on the "bass"	Terpsichore dances.
[Duo] Erato, Apollon, plus Choeur, "Quelle danse vive et légère!"	Shortened repeat of earlier duo, which becomes a chorus with the same text.	Instrumental phrases and chorus probably danced by Terpsichore and the group.

[a] The text of this air appears in neither the 1723 or 1733 libretto and the singer (a *haute contre*) is not identified in the printed score, except by a handwritten annotation in F-Po A.107a.

Figure 13-1: The end of the chorus "À des emplois nouveaux" in the prologue to *Les Fêtes grecques et romaines*; reduced score (1723) annotated (in the 1750s or 1760s) as to the dancing. (Photo BnF)

The second, which follows the gentle rondeau for Terpsichore, is constructed as a dialogue between the words of Erato and Apollon on the one hand, and the movements of Terpsichore on the other (see Example 13-2). The few operatic antecedents for such short-breathed exchanges between song and dance are comic: the dancing lesson in the "Professeur de folie" or the boasting dancing master in *Les Fêtes vénitiennes*; here, however, the commentary comes from two on-stage admirers, who usually announce the sentiment that the dance paints, but sometimes react to it. As did *Les Caractères de la danse*, this sequence put Mlle Prévost's ability to inhabit one affect after another on display. The last line sung by Erato and Apollon, "all your steps are feelings," makes two key points: it insists on what the *cantate*'s *didascalie* had already stated – that Terpsichore derives her expressivity from her steps and *attitudes* rather than from gestures – and that her dancing aims to express not characters, but feelings.

Example 13-2: Collin de Blamont, *Les Fêtes grecques et romaines* prologue, sung dialogue with danced interjections by Terpsichore (Paris: Ballard, 1723), lxxviii–lxxx. Erato and Apollon: "Before our eyes you paint the transports of lovers. / The tender attentions, the flattering hope, / jealous despair, / cruel revenge; / all your steps are feelings." (The source, a reduced score, does not show either the full instrumentation or the B.C. that would have accompanied the singers.)

Fuzelier wrote later that the sequence came close to being suppressed:[68]

> This ballet [of Terpsichore], which has been applauded ever since its birth, was almost rejected at the dress rehearsal, and Mlle Prévost, who was responsible for its success, almost succumbed to erroneous criticism . . . but let us pass over the details of an incident that does no honor to the discernment of the critics of those days; let us rather say that this wonderful ballet has been performed since then to universal applause by Mlle Camargo, Mlle Barbarine, and the young Mlle Cauchois.[69]

This sequence's intermingling of solo singing and dancing impressed Cahusac, who singled it out as "a kind of noble pantomime."[70] The novelty is not that the prologue featured a star dancer, but that it focused so exclusively on her, elevating her to the status of a Muse by deliberately conflating the performer and the role. The only music in the entire sequence outlined in Table 13-4 that is not dedicated to Terpsichore is Apollon's little air setting up the rest of the opera. Even the chorus that ends the prologue honors not the king, but the Muse of the dance.[71] Handel, inspired by this prologue, composed a similar scene of his own for Marie Sallé in *Terpsichore* (1734).[72]

In 1725 Mlle Prévost featured in another extended dance scene, this one within Act IV of *La Reine des Péris*, a five-act "Persian comedy" by violinist Jacques Aubert, who had previously composed for the fairs, and, once again, Fuzelier. Péris, the libretto's preface explains, are benevolent genies, "whose goodness equals their beauty." Their queen's goodness is put to the test when she falls in love with Nouredin, Caliph of Egypt, who himself is enamoured of the princess of Syria. In a vain attempt to drive them apart, the jealous queen transports Nouredin to the Island of Inconstancy. Even she recognizes the irony of trying to induce fidelity to *her* by making infidelity attractive, but she nonetheless calls a personified Inconstancy to her aid. A gavotte-like march brings Inconstancy's followers – unfaithful people of different nations – onto the stage, but the arrival of Inconstancy herself is delayed until after a chorus and a "cantate à l'honneur de l'Inconstance" (an accompanied recitative and an air that is a cross between a rondeau and an *ariette*). Next, in what must have been a spectacular piece of stagecraft, one designed to focus all attention on Mlle Prévost, "Inconstancy emerges from the sea, seated in a lovely chariot that is surmounted by a canopy supported by Zephyrs." From here onwards the divertissement is pure dance; no songs interrupt its eight

68 [Fuzelier], "Neuvième suite des Réflexions sur les ballets," *MF* (February 1746), 153–57. This series of articles was published while Fuzelier was co-editing the *Mercure* for the second time.

69 Camargo danced the role in 1733 and 1734; Barbarina Campanini, a visiting Italian virtuouso, in 1741; Mlle Puvigné in 1753; Mlle Allard in 1762; and Mlle Guimard in 1770.

70 Cahusac, "Ballet aux chansons," *Encyclopédie*, II, 46.

71 In 1723 Louis XV was only thirteen years old. This prologue does not mention him at all and only obliquely hints that the ancient heroes have contemporary analogues.

72 See McCleave, *Dance in Handel's London Operas*, 149–61.

Table 13-5: Aubert, *La Reine des Péris* (1725), IV/4.
Inconstancy dances and demonstrates her character, both through the variety of her steps and dances and through those of the dancers of different nations whom she chooses in turn.

Heading in Score	Musical characteristics
Prélude	e, **2**; through-composed
Sarabande	e, **3**; binary
Menuet	e, **3**; binary, scored for high instruments
Loure	E; binary; A section = Loure in $\frac{6}{4}$; B section = Gay in **2**
Air gay	e, $\frac{2}{4}$; binary
Cotillon	E, **2**; binary; gavotte-like, built over an immutable tonic pedal
Air du Zéphyr et de l'Inconstance	G, **3**; binary, with frequent changes of character and dynamics
Cotillon	G, **2**; gavotte-like, built above pedal tones

instrumental pieces. The music evokes fickleness by changing character from piece to piece; the loure even changes meter and tempo in the middle.

The headings in the score provide little help as to who danced where. Beyond Mlle Prévost, the cast included David Dumoulin as Zéphyr, plus three each of male and female followers of Inconstancy – the relatively small size of the group further serving to heighten the focus on the soloist. The prelude must have accompanied Inconstancy's arrival, and the two cotillons were probably group dances. These bookend the most interesting piece of the sequence and the only one to indicate who is dancing: the "Air du Zéphyr et de l'Inconstance." The queen's *ariette* had urged lovers to model their behavior on "fickle Zéphyr"; the adjective presumably extended to Dumoulin's movement-style. The music of the *pas de deux* alternates two contrasting characters: rushing sixteenth notes marked "fort" and gentle triplets scored for treble instruments, marked "doux" (Example 13-3). The score suggests sexual stereotyping: the aggressive passages for Zéphyr, the soft ones for Inconstancy. The piece ends with four bars of the gentle triplets; as is appropriate in a sequence about faithlessness, the two dancers end separately. The second cotillon ends the act; the *Mercure* called the sequence a "tableau vivant."[73]

The queen's stratagem fails to alter Nouredin's affections; in fact, he does not even watch Inconstancy dance ("Nouredin, lost in his own thoughts, withdraws when Inconstancy appears"). The true audience for this spectacular is thus revealed to be the Parisian public, and even though *La Reine des Péris* failed to generate any revivals in Paris, this particular scene was imitated in John Rich's theater in Lincoln's Inn Fields the following year, with Marie Sallé in the starring role of Flora, representing an Inconstant.[74] The English imitation has the virtue of specifying the "dancers of different

[73] *MF* (April 1725), 798.

[74] In the pantomime *Apollo and Daphne*, scenario by Lewis Theobald, music by John Ernest Galliard, first performed in January 1726; the connections are reported in my unpublished "French dance music."

Example 13-3: Aubert, *La Reine des Péris* IV/4, "Air du Zéphyr et de l'Inconstance" (Paris: Boivin, 1725), 230.

nations" who are unidentified in Fuzelier's libretto: one couple each from Spain, Poland, and France. All three seem plausible for the original work as well – the French and Spaniards on account of familiar operatic stereotypes, and Poles because the young Louis XV was about to marry a Polish princess, Maria Leszczinska. We can only speculate as to where the couples might have danced (the French to the menuet, the Spanish to the sarabande, taking turns in both with Mlle Prévost?). Whatever the case, this sequence not only reflects the impact that Rebel's symphonies were having inside operas, but shows that the "Ballet des Fleurs," which Rameau and Fuzelier inserted ten years later into another Persian-themed work, the "Fête persane" in *Les Indes galantes*, was not as innovative as it has been portrayed. Prévost appears to deserve some of the credit for introducing pantomime ballets to the Opéra that has generally been accorded to Sallé.[75]

Fuzelier was not, however, the only librettist who constructed special dance scenes into his operas, and now that Prévost was nearing the end of her career, her best pupils began to feature in divertissements of this type. *La Princesse d'Élide* (1728) a *ballet héroïque* by another experienced librettist, Pellegrin, set to music by the newcomer Villeneuve, makes the allegory of the Muses explicit by setting the prologue on the stage of the Opéra. Terpsichore and her pupils dominate the stage; in a danced and sung dialogue reminiscent of the prologue to *Les Fêtes grecques et romaines*, she exhorts them to invoke

[75] Astier's "Françoise Prévost" helps redress the historiographic balance.

Example 13-4: Villeneuve, *La Princesse d'Élide* prologue, the second of two airs for Terpsichore's pupil (Paris: Ballard, 1728), xviii.

Mars (trumpets sound), then Love (musettes). She then turns to a pupil: "And you, charming nymph, who are trained in all the steps thanks to my attentions, begin!" It is hard not to hear the singing Terpsichore as the mouthpiece for Mlle Prévost herself; her own pupil, Mlle Camargo, immediately dances two consecutive airs, both of which alternate characters throughout (see Example 13-4). The *Mercure* called her solos "a school for dancing" ("une école de danses").[76]

The next year Camargo was herself cast as Terpsichore, complete with pupils of her own, in the third entrée, "Melpomène et Linus," from *Les Amours des déesses*. Fuzelier knew that he was on shaky ground depicting a Muse in love, even if Linus was a poet ("the inventor of the elegy"),[77] but a setting on the banks of the Permesse allowed him to invite the other eight Muses to the wedding celebrations that conclude the entrée. The divertissement has a double structure, one section for most of the sisters and a second, longer one, for Terpsichore, who is granted a separate entrance: "Terpsichore, represented by Mlle Camargo accompanied by her two most illustrious pupils, performed by Mlles Sallé and Mariette and followed by serious and *galant* maskers, ends the divertissement by a *pas de trois*, which does honor to the inventiveness of the Sieur Blondy and the talents of these skillful *danseuses*."[78] Only one vocal piece – an *ariette* for Melpomène – interrupts the dancing, which concludes with two menuets, an air en rondeau, and a chaconne; there is no concluding chorus.

The dance-driven divertissements that follow in the wake of *Les Caractères de la danse* do not all have the same shape, nor do they figure in all the ballets of this period, but it is clear that some of the people attached to the complex organism of the Opéra worked to promote structures that offered more separation between dancing and the sung word. The librettists and composers most instrumental in these developments did not restrict their activities to the Opéra, but worked at the fair theaters, Théâtre Italien, or Comédie-Française as well. They must have constituted a community of interest with certain star dancers – who, notwithstanding the remark just quoted from the *Mercure*, probably had a hand in the choreography (see Chapter 14, p. 421). Changes across the

[76] *MF* (August 1728), 1841–42. [77] Fuzelier justified this storyline in the libretto's preface.
[78] *MF* (August 1729), 1840.

repertoire were sporadic and uneven, but two threads run through them: a greater number of musical structures that allowed for contrast on a local level; and an expanded interest in dance's capacity to paint emotions.

Shared Practices

Whereas Rebel's *symphonies* allowed for changes of character by juxtaposing dance pieces, a suppler option was to build contrasts into a single piece. The phenomenon is easiest to track in the music Mouret wrote for the Théâtre Italien between 1717 and 1737, much of which he published and some of which he annotated as to who was dancing. The incidental music for *L'Audience* (1725) features groups of dancers representing different theaters of Paris, all to a single piece in four sections: the French comedians (duple meter, "noblement"), the Italian comedians (in $\frac{12}{8}$, "gracieusement"), the *forains* (in C, "gai") and the judgment by Apollon (in C, "lentement"). *Le Triomphe de la Folie* (1723) includes an air for "blind people being led by Cupids who play tricks on them" (Example 13-5), in which the dancing personnel changes quickly and often.

Example 13-5: Mouret, *Le Triomphe de la Folie*, "Air pour des Aveugles conduits par des Amours qui leur font des niches," *Divertissements du Nouveau Théâtre Italien*, III, 238.

At the Opéra, musical dialogue within a single piece has some precedents in Lully's works (see, in Chapter 4, Example 4-1 and p. 117), but it wasn't until the eighteenth century that such pieces gained purchase. The rondeau, whose structure lends itself to contrasts, provided a useful mechanism, one Campra exploited in the prologue to the *Ballet des âges* (1718) by giving radically different profiles to the refrain and the couplets: the refrain is in duple meter marked "vite" with a violinistic style, the couplets in a gentle triple meter attributed to flutes. A *didascalie* in Fuzelier's libretto explains the action: "The followers of Time, enemies of pleasure, pursue the followers of Hébé, whose dances depict the insouciance of the youths who renew their pleasures as many times as they are interrupted." In other scores, however, the changes in the musical writing happen more rapidly, within a strain, as for Inconstance and Zéphyr (Example 13-3). When the characters are more in accord, the musical distinction may be more subtle. In the first entrée of Pellegrin and Montéclair's *Fêtes de l'été* (1716), the score of the dialogue between a shepherd and shepherdess (Example 13-6) does not indicate which character dances to the oboes, which to the violins, but as the lines swap instruments upon repeat of the opening phrase, either dancer could take the lead. One initiates, the other responds, and by measure 7 they are dancing together, with a little flirtatious exchange in mm. 13–16 before the sequence starts again in m. 18. In this piece a literal correspondence between instrumental line and individual dancer works. Does, then, the musical writing tell the dancers when to move and when to stay still?

In the *Ballet des âges*, the two groups could reasonably dance in alternation; the followers of Time could threaten and menace, and then stop while the followers of

Example 13-6: Montéclair, *Les Fêtes de l'été*, "Air en dialogue pour un Berger et pour une Bergère" (second edition, Paris: Ballard, 1716), 41–42.

Hébé frolic. In a dance about faithlessness, Inconstance and Zéphyr have no reason to dance simultaneously. Mouret's blind people and his Cupids have strongly characterized music that suggests independence of movement, not togetherness. Moreover, this kind of alternation adheres to aesthetic principles familiar from the alternation between singing and dancing that undergirds the construction of divertissements. Yet it could be argued that there is reciprocity between the sets of characters. When the Cupids play tricks, wouldn't the blind people react? Don't the followers of Hébé run away when the followers of Time pursue them? Thirty years earlier Menestrier had allowed for dancers to engage in different movements provided they were reciprocal, as when one swordsman strikes a blow that the other parries.[79] Could these dances be an extension on a structural scale of that phenomenon? Could the notion of comic simultaneity evoked in Chapter 9 override musical distinctions? Or are these dances rather instances of an aesthetic that places activities consecutively, within distinct time frames, but expects the audience to interpret them as simultaneous?[80]

Even in the absence of unambiguous answers, it does seem that pieces constructed around contrasting musical ideas imply a more literal connection between different modes of expression than we easily accept today. If so, it behooves us to pay close attention to the music for clues to the choreography. (Sensitive listening to ballet music is a skill historians and performers alike need to develop.) A related question that emerges, both from this type of piece and from more extended dance sequences, is the extent to which they may (or may not) progress. Do the tricks the Cupids play culminate in some kind of resolution? Do the eight consecutive dances in *La Reine des Péris* construct an argument sufficient to sway Nouredin's affections? Do any of the works discussed in this chapter cross into the realm of pantomime ballet?

Probably not. All these cases, even Mouret's dance, seem to respect the time-honored representation of characters more than they do the development of situations. This observation applies as much to *Les Caractères de la danse* as it does to the followers of Time and Hébé. The duet between Inconstance and Zéphyr expresses – several times over – stereotypes of zephyr-ness and feminine sweetness. The overall sequence of which this dance is a part seems more to invoke different takes on infidelity than it does a story. Yet it may be that Fuzelier had high aspirations, but that Aubert was not up to the task; the libretto of this opera is more interesting than its music. A decade later Rameau's expressive dance music for *Les Indes galantes*, set to another libretto by Fuzelier, edged ballet closer to narration.[81]

We should not discount the impact the more popular theaters may have had on the Opéra in ways not yet fully recognized. The linking together of several dances owes at least as much to a governing concept as it does to display, and the dancers' performances

[79] Ch. 3, p. 89. [80] See Ch. 2, p. 55.

[81] The ballet for Inconstance looks like a warm-up for the "Ballet des fleurs" in the Persian entrée.

may have been nuanced in expressive ways to which we have little access. By the end of the 1720s, the *forains* were beginning to perform ballets "without the help of words," such as one depicting love and jealousy among people of different nations in a Dutch cabaret.[82] It may well have consisted of a series of character dances and perhaps even a song or two.[83] By 1734, however, François Riccoboni's *Pygmalion*, choreographed for the Théâtre Italien, conveyed primarily through dance a compact setting of the sculptor's infatuation with his statue and her animation by Amour; Mouret's music depicts both key moments in the story and the emotions they provoke.[84] Crossover artists gave the Académie Royale de Musique professional connections with its competitors; its enlarged palette of divertissement types looks like a response to those ties.

"TOUS VOS PAS SONT DES SENTIMENTS"

In the first third of the eighteenth century Terpsichore's presence on the stage of the Opéra was both symbolic and real. The symbiosis between dancer and role, expertly cultivated by Mlle Prévost, afforded women a growing professional prominence that simultaneously allowed for new kinds of dancing roles. Certain librettists and composers took advantage of the flexible structures of opera-ballets and pastorales to pursue innovations in the dramatic functions attributed to dance. Terpsichore's symbolic presence signaled an increase across genres in the amount of time devoted to dancing – notwithstanding the many exceptions – and, moreover, allowed for longer sequences of dance music that was less connected to sung texts than what Lully and Quinault had established. Her combined influence produced varied, and even contradictory, results, two of which Fuzelier encapsulated twenty years later while looking back at the prologue he had penned for *Les Fêtes grecques et romaines*:

> This praise offered to Terpsichore [by Erato and Apollon] should be a lesson to her disciples, whose dancing, bereft of order and expression, is often only a web of steps inspired by whim, without any connection to the role of the dancer who executes them.[85]

[82] *MF* (July 1729), 1660–62.

[83] Singing seems to figure in the "ballet pantomime" *La Noce anglaise*, performed at the Opéra-Comique in 1729; *MF* (August 1729), 1844–46. There is a sizeable literature on the history of pantomime ballet, but no study yet of its music. For a recent overview of developments in France and England, see Lada-Richards, "Dead but not extinct."

[84] This ballet is not the same *Pygmalion* performed in London by Marie Sallé three months earlier and may even have been a parody of it; Sallé's performance – known primarily from a description in the *Mercure* (April 1734, 770–72) – does not map onto Mouret's score. Riccoboni's *Pygmalion* was reconstructed by Catherine Turocy for performance by the New York Baroque Dance Company at Cornell University in 2007.

[85] [Fuzelier], "Neuvième suite des Réflexions sur les ballets," *MF* (February 1746), 153–57. This series of articles (see Rubellin, "Écrire") was published while Fuzelier was co-editing the *Mercure* for the second time.

Operatic parodists – Fuzelier among them – often mocked what they portrayed as expressionless technical display, not that their own theaters eschewed virtuoso dancing. Fuzelier's belief in the power of dance-steps to convey not just characters but feelings was eloquently expressed by "Monsieur le Roy," almost certainly Pierre-Charles Roy, himself a librettist, in an "Ode de la danse" published in the same year as *Les Fêtes grecques et romaines*.[86] The heading for this section of the ode is "Danses de caractère"; at the Opéra the old aesthetic and the new existed side-by-side:

Tout ce que la langue exprime
Saisit lentement l'esprit;
Par la danse tout s'anime,
En un instant tout est dit;
Ses gestes, ses pas agiles,
Ses caractères mobiles
Décrivent nos sentiments;
Et ces vivantes peintures
Changent d'autant de figures
Que le cœur de movements.

(Everything the tongue expresses takes hold of the mind gradually; with dance everything is said in an instant. Its gestures, agile steps, and varied motions describe our feelings, and these vivid paintings change shapes as often as do the movements of the human heart.)

[86] Published in Bonnet, *Histoire générale* (1723), 138–45; Bonnet said that the ode had won a prize from the Académie Française in 1714. Roy wrote the librettos for *Philomèle, Callirhoé,* and *Les Éléments*, inter alia.

14 | In the Traces of Terpsichore

Vous, qui tracez aux yeux une vive peinture,
Des sentiments les plus secrets,
Faites briller les plus beaux traits,
Que l'art ingénieux ajoute à la nature.

La Princesse d'Élide, prologue

(You who trace before the eyes a vivid painting of the most secret sentiments, display the most beautiful features that ingenious art adds to nature.)

Terpsichore did not have dance notation in mind when she sang these words to her followers, but it is thanks to traces left by ink on paper that the "ingenious art" of early eighteenth-century ballet has been preserved. This chapter explores what can be learned about the practices of operatic dance on the basis of the notated theatrical choreographies. Two contrasting case studies from the stage of the Opéra illustrate the benefits and limitations of close readings of these notations; next, a broader range of notations is mined for what it reveals about the practices of some of the dance types found in operas of this generation. Since almost none of the theatrical notations is for more than two dancers, the chapter then turns toward other types of evidence for help in resolving, for this later period, practical issues that could help us envisage how such scenes looked on stage.

NOTATED CHOREOGRAPHIES "DANSÉES À L'OPÉRA"

Of the approximately 350 choreographies preserved in Beauchamps-Feuillet notation, over 100 are theatrical in style; among these are 47 dances whose headings indicate that they were danced at the Opéra. All 47 were composed by Pécour and published in one of two collections: the first, from 1704 and notated by Feuillet, has 24 dances; the second, undated but probably published late in 1713, and notated by Michel Gaudrau, has 23. Between them the two collections preserve eighteen additional theatrical dances (eleven in 1704, seven in Gaudrau), some of them for dancers at the Opéra or set to music that was in its repertoire; a few titles say that the choreography was "non dansé à l'Opéra." Various sources from both France and England preserve additional theatrical dances, and this broader repertoire extends our understanding of theatrical styles;[1] new sources continue to come to light. Information about the notations, their music, and

[1] The largest English collection was published *c.* 1725 by Anthony L'Abbé, a former member of the troupe of the Opéra who had moved to London.

their sources may be found in two catalogues, one by Little and Marsh, the other by Lancelot (see Chapter 3, n. 3).

The 47 choreographies come from 24 different works: fifteen tragedies (accounting for 30 of the dances); four *pastorales héroïques* or other works with a continuous storyline (five dances); and five opera-ballets (twelve dances). The criteria for inclusion in these collections are not known, but the repertoire does favor serious works.[2] The number of notations per opera ranges from one to four: the three operas with four are Lully's *Persée*; Campra's *Tancrède*; and Campra's *Fêtes vénitiennes*. In the cases of *Persée* and *Tancrède*, the choreographies are associated with different revivals, something that emerges from checking the dancers' names against cast lists in the librettos. The choreographies originated over a twenty-year period, from 1693 (*Alcide*) to 1713 (*Ballet des Amours déguisés*), although the music may have been composed earlier; all eleven dances set to music by Lully (from five operas) come from revivals. Appendix 3 identifies the source of each dance and describes its dramatic context.

The dancers named in the choreographies (see Table 14-1) are most often prominent members of the troupe, but some do not appear in any of the rosters. Chevrier (Cherrier), whose three dances all date from the 1690s, mostly worked abroad, including in London.[3] Piffetot was murdered in 1698,[4] Philbois is known only from the 1701 libretto for *Scylla*, and Klin (Clin, Klein) appears only in two other operas and one ballet at a Jesuit theater.[5] For those whose names feature repeatedly, these dances reveal the existence of regular partnerships (Balon and Subligny or Prévost and Guyot) and, more importantly, allow us to evaluate the qualities of individual dancers; to date, Mlle Guyot's dancing has received the most study.[6]

How trustworthy are these notations? Certainly the exclusive focus on solos and duets distorts our view of practices on stage; moreover, problems may emerge from the process of trying to think a particular choreography back into its original context (see Case Study 1 below). On the other hand, the librettos confirm, with few exceptions, that the dancers named in the choreographies did appear in the pertinent divertissements.[7] Feuillet claimed in his 1704 preface that it required "immense effort and diligence to collect the dances and to engrave them with as much precision as they are here." After Feuillet died, in 1711, Pécour acquired his own privilege for publishing dances, but soon ceded it to Michel

[2] The collections were compiled before the creation of new tragedies began to decline.

[3] Bonin, 76; Goff, *The Incomparable Hester Santlow*, 4–5. [4] Ladvocat, *Lettres*, XXVIII.

[5] Lecomte, personal communication.

[6] On Guyot's solos, see Thorp, "The notion of grace"; Colonna, "The 'Demoiselle' behind the score"; and Whitley-Bauguess, "An eighteenth-century dance reconstruction." On her duets, see Goff, "Masks and disguises."

[7] See Appendix 3 and Laurenti, "Les structures de distribution."

Table 14-1: Choreographies by Pécour "dansées à l'Opéra" in the collections published by Feuillet and Gaudrau.

Feuillet (1704)		Gaudrau ([1713])	
Mixed couple: 26 dances			
9	Balon and Subligny	1	Balon and Subligny
2	Dumirail and Victoire		
1	Blondy and Victoire		
1	Dumoulin *l'aîné* [Henri] and Victoire		
2	Dumoulin *l'aîné* and Dangeville		
		3	Dumoulin *l'aîné* and Chaillou
		2	F. Dumoulin and Guyot
		5	D. Dumoulin and Guyot
Two men: 9 dances			
3	Piffetot and Chevrier		
1	Blondy and Philbois		
1	L'Eveque and Dangeville		
		3	Blondy and Marcel
		1	Marcel and Gaudrau
Two women: 6 dances			
1	Victoire and Dangeville		
		5	Prévost and Guyot
Solo woman: 5 dances			
2	Subligny		
1	Victoire		
		2	Guyot
Solo man: 1 dance			
1	Klin		

Gaudrau, who had joined the troupe in 1708 at the age of sixteen.[8] Gaudrau's collection includes two dances from the very first work in which he performed. In fact, all but four of Gaudrau's choreographies come from works in which he himself danced, sometimes in the same act or entrée. His insider status inspires confidence.[9]

Generic dance-types account for fewer than half of the notations; most are identified by character type ("Entrée pour un Berger et une Bergère"). These run the gamut from the noble to the galant: followers of various gods; supernatural beings; ancient peoples (Greeks, Scythes, and even Bacchantes); shepherds and nymphs; sailors; and guests at masked balls. Only this last group engages with the comic, most overtly in the "Air

[8] Astier, "Michel Gaudrau."

[9] That said, dancers continue to debate not only what the choreographies in both collections represent, but why the theatrical dances were published at all, since the market must have been much smaller than for the ballroom dances.

comique" from *Les Fêtes vénitiennes* (see Chapter 9, p. 279). One distinction overrides character types: the gender of the dancers. Dances for men feature technically challenging movements involving *cabrioles*, beaten steps, leaps, multiple pirouettes, and feats of balance; many steps can be interpreted as a basic step-unit with ornamentation – a *contretemps* that is beaten in the air, for example. The dances for women engage a less technical step vocabulary; they do not eschew pirouettes, beats, or jumps and their footwork often requires speed and agility, but they remain closer to the ground and their choreographic ornaments are more nuanced. In couple dances the men and women usually do the same steps and figures in unison, which means that dances for a mixed couple remain within boundaries of technical norms for women. The next generation of female dancers began to adopt some aspects of male technique, but the extant notations do not preserve these developments.

Identifying the dancing roles for any choreography offers a point of departure, but understanding the dramatic context is crucial. The two Bacchantes in *Philomèle* dance at a turning point from serenity to violence; performers of Pécour's choreography need to decide in what light to interpret the notated movements. The Divinités infernales in *Persée* may come from the Underworld, but they are not demons – rather, they are on the side of the hero and have dignity in their carriage (see below). On the other hand, the cyclopes from *Acis et Galatée*, who are presented in the libretto as inopportune or even grotesque (see Chapter 6, pp. 196–97), mix self-control with moments of awkwardness – through orthodox steps put into unusual spatial relationships, unexpected step sequences, or when the steps play against the music. The two aim to dance in a high style – they are trying to impress Galatée, after all – but don't quite manage to achieve it.[10]

The pastoral dances, which represent about a quarter of this corpus, inhabit an entirely different movement world. Since most include women, they make fewer technical demands; they also exhibit an emphasis on the relationship between the two dancers, as is appropriate for a realm governed by love. Yet even here there are stylistic distinctions: surviving musette choreographies feature gentle pulsing movements combined with quarter turns in places that do not appear in the other dances for shepherds.

The two case studies – chosen for their contrast – illustrate some of what can be learned about expression and characterization when dance notations are read alongside librettos and scores. Whereas the nature of Beauchamps-Feuillet notation orients analysis toward the steps, Pierce observes that "it's not so much the steps themselves that define the character as their arrangement in sequence and space."[11] Hazebroucq points out that the choice and succession of steps, even when seemingly abstract, reveal

[10] I thank Ken Pierce and Hubert Hazebroucq for these insights. [11] Email, 1 Nov. 2009.

an intention that lends itself to interpretation.[12] It is in the process of reconstructing and performing these dances that dancer-researchers are learning to decode the nuances of choreographic characterization.

Case Study 1: "Entrée de deux hommes dansée par Messieurs Marcel et Gaudrau à l'opéra de *Persée*"

This male duet has the distinction of being one in which the notator himself danced.[13] It dates from the 1710 revival of Lully's *Persée* – from the sequence in Act II in which different divinities arm Persée for his battle with Méduse. The cyclopes have brought him a sword and winged shoes, the warrior nymphs a shield; now the Divinités infernales rise from the Underworld to bring him Pluton's helmet (see Table 2-10, p. 62 for an outline of the entire divertissement). Each group remains on stage when the next arrives, and as the three groups must have been costumed differently, the cumulation of five solo singers, thirteen dancers, and a chorus must have made an impressive tableau. The entire sequence is serious and ceremonial, one that highlights Persée's heroism and the dangers he faces.

Each group of demi-gods dances twice, once on either side of a song that explains the gift. The singing Underworld divinity is a bass; his air does not use the same music as the dance but shares its affect, and, like the dance, is marked "Gravement." Its text alludes to the invisibility that the helmet confers, as well as offering a maxim on effective leadership.

[Recitative:] Ce casque vous est présenté
Au nom du souverain de l'empire des ombres.
Au milieu du péril, pour votre sûreté,
Il répandra sur vous l'épaisse obscurité
Qui règne en nos demeures sombres.

[Air:] Ce don mystérieux doit apprendre aux humains
Comme on peut s'assurer d'un succès favorable;
Il faut cacher de grands desseins
Sous un secret impénétrable.

(This helmet is presented to you in the name of the sovereign of the Underworld. In times of danger it will confer upon you the protective obscurity that reigns in our dark home. [Air:] This mysterious gift will teach humans how to achieve a favorable outcome; it is necessary to hide great plans inside an impenetrable secret.)

12 "De la danse comme geste." See Ch. 4, p. 120 on Dubos's claim that dancers in his day recognized sixteen character types.

13 Gaudrau, part 2, 91–94: LMC 2940, FL/1713.2/34

The notation occupies four figures, each corresponding to one strain of the music, played AABB. The $\frac{6}{4}$ time signature could accommodate either one or two step-units per measure, but here there are two, whose degree of complexity would impose a slow tempo even if the score were not marked "Gravement." The choreography is through-composed; the difference in length between the two strains (five bars in A, eight in B) makes the notation of the B sections very dense. To make the correspondence between music and steps easier to discern, Gaudrau added dotted barlines to the musical staff; thus in Figure 14-1 (the first A section) both music and dance have ten "measures," each corresponding to one step-unit.

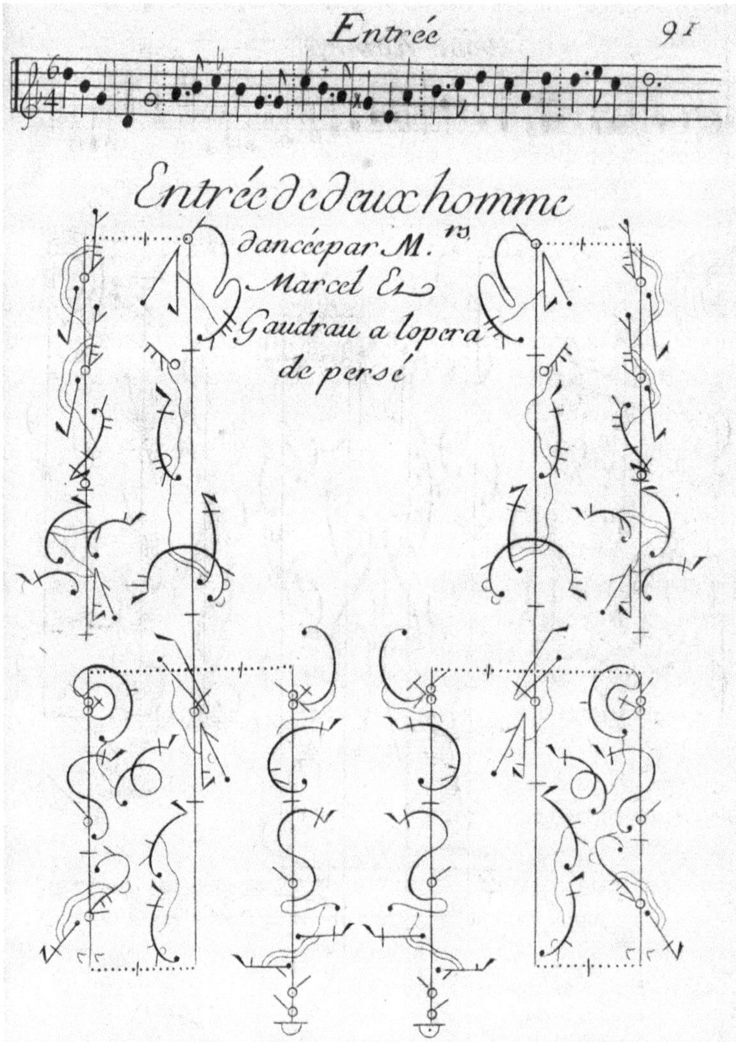

Figure 14-1: Pécour, "Entrée for two men danced by Messieurs Marcel and Gaudrau in *Persée*" (Gaudrau, part II, 91).

The dance begins with each dancer balanced on the outside foot and gesturing with the other for nine beats – a challenging opening that foregrounds the power and stability of the divinities even before they begin moving downstage. Once they do, the footwork remains ornamented with *ronds de jambe* and beats, which lend themselves to nuancing via subtle inflections in the timing of the ornaments. But whereas the footwork is complex, the figures are simple. For much of the dance the men remain side-by-side, facing front, moving forward and back each along his own axis. Every page does, however, require each dancer to make at least one turn around himself, mostly with sprung pirouettes; the longest such sequence is in the third figure. These passages do put the two briefly into eye-contact with each other and intersperse bursts of animation into their movements. The dancers never revolve around each other, but they do swap sides during the repeat of the A section and return to their original orientation during the first B. The result of the spatial orientation and figural simplicity is that the entire dance is in mirror symmetry; the two dancers face front much more than they do each other. Overall, the dance connotes self-control and self-presentation, with, according to Pierce and Thorp, "a careful choice of steps – sudden drops, turns, brushes, and so on – to evoke [the divinities'] subterranean and immortal origins."[14] According to Astier's summary of the four notated duets that involve Marcel, "dances such as these require an impeccable control of the body, an unfailing sense of direction together with strength, speed and precision."[15]

It is impossible to know whether this choreography was the one preceding or following the vocal air, but we can be certain that the other iteration of the music accompanied a different choreography. The 1710 libretto identifies four Divinités infernales, none of them set off as soloist, although one was Blondy, the highest-paid dancer in the troupe; perhaps he featured in another duet. Still, the four must have danced together, so either the other iteration involved the whole group, or the existing choreography only communicates two of the four parts. Pierce and Thorp have speculated that the dance might have been "cloned . . . to form a group dance."[16] This is not a process that would work for every choreography, but a few small adjustments would allow this one to be danced by four. Other questions concern the presentation of the helmet – whether the singer or a dancer carried it onto the stage, when it might have been presented to Persée (during the recitative, perhaps?), or even whether he received it into his own hands or merely acknowledged the gift. All that can be

[14] "The dances in Lully's *Persée*," par. 3.18. I thank Pierce and Thorp for additional conversation about this choreography.

[15] "François Marcel," 13. [16] "The dances in Lully's *Persée*," par. 4.5.

known is that this choreography does not include any such transaction; however the helmet was presented, it happened elsewhere in the scene.

Case Study 2: "Entrée de deux femmes dansée par Mlle Prévost et Mlle Guyot aux *Fêtes vénitiennes*"

Campra's enormously popular opera-ballet consists of a series of vignettes set in Venice during Carnival season; "L'Amour saltimbanque" was one of its original entrées and among the most frequently performed. This choreography[17] might have derived either from the premiere in 1710 or the 1712 revival; Prévost and Guyot danced in both. In this divertissement, Amour, disguised as a street performer, arrives in the Place Saint-Marc with a troupe of thirteen dancing merrymakers, variously costumed as commedia masques, peasants, Spaniards, and old folks. In a series of three airs interspersed with dances, he vaunts his powers, ending with a cynical statement that fidelity is no longer in fashion. This dance follows Amour's second song, a rondeau in an Italianate style, to which it is musically connected.

Effet admirable
De mon savoir;
Tout devient aimable
Par mon pouvoir.

La jeunesse en est plus brillante,
La vieillesse moins pesante,
La laideur se perd par mon fard,
La beauté paraît plus touchante
Avec le secours de mon art.

Effet admirable, etc.

Au plus timide cœur je donne du courage,
J'anime le plus indolent,
J'adoucis une âme sauvage,
Je rends vif l'esprit le plus lent.

Effet admirable, etc.

("Oh wondrous effect of my knowledge: everything becomes lovable thanks to my power. With my help youth is more brilliant, old age less burdensome, ugliness repaired, beauty more touching. I give courage to the most timid, arouse the laziest, soften the hardest, and make the dullest spirit lively.")

[17] Gaudrau, part 2, 64–66; LMC 2900, FL/1713.2/26

Ambiguity exists as to who danced here: a manuscript full score (F-Po A.78a) calls this piece "Air des Espagnoles," whereas the printed reduced scores of 1710 and 1714 label it "Air des Polichinelles." According to the libretto, Prévost and Guyot danced as Espagnolettes; a dance for Polichinelles would have been assigned to men. But with the divertissement structured as it is, any among Amour's troupe could have danced; the text of the song does not restrict the possibilities, nor does the Italianate music, which is a far cry from the sarabandes or loures usually accorded to Spanish characters. These Espagnolettes are, however, Venetians in Carnival costumes. Perhaps this choreography has more piquancy if we imagine Polichinelles as subtly inflecting their movements.

Gaudrau's transcription of the melody line (see Figure 14-2) augments the note values and breaks the measures in half from what is in the scores (cf. Example 8-4, p. 254). In his system this binary piece has 10 bars in the A section, 24 in the B, for a total of 68 with the repeats; Gaudrau manages to squeeze them all onto three pages. It helps that the dancers have only one step-unit per bar, as is standard for quick dances in duple meter. The step vocabulary privileges hops, springs, and *pas tombés*; it is hard to find more than one step-unit in a row that lacks a sign for leaving the ground. According to Goff, the steps have "a wide dynamic range, from the flowing *tems de courante* to an explosive *pas composé* comprising a *pas assemblé*, a *pas tombé*, and a *saut* (the whole performed in one bar of music and incorporating a full turn)."[18] The springs may be modest, but overall the dancers' movements are lively and bouncy.

Unlike the Divinités infernales, these dancers have a strong connection to each other, visible most obviously in their circling figures in the B sections. When the dancers face forward, it is rarely for long; in fact, their first movement is a quick quarter turn toward each other. The connection nonetheless has a strong element of play that is fostered by the rapid changes in orientation between facing front and facing each other, particularly in the A sections. A playful echo passage in the first B section has one dancer stand still while the other moves away on a diagonal, only to jump around towards her partner; the second then repeats the maneuver, which brings them back face-to-face. Another echo occurs in the second B, in which the dancers also change from facing away to facing toward each other. The two cross paths several times and even end on opposite sides from where they started – a highly unusual conclusion, even for the theater. Goff finds this "the most complex of Pecour's notated duets for Guyot and Prévost. It is lively and teasing, with light and sophisticated comedy rather than the broader commedia dell'arte comic style." She goes on to speculate as to whether more levels of meaning could be read into the

[18] "Masks and disguises," 27.

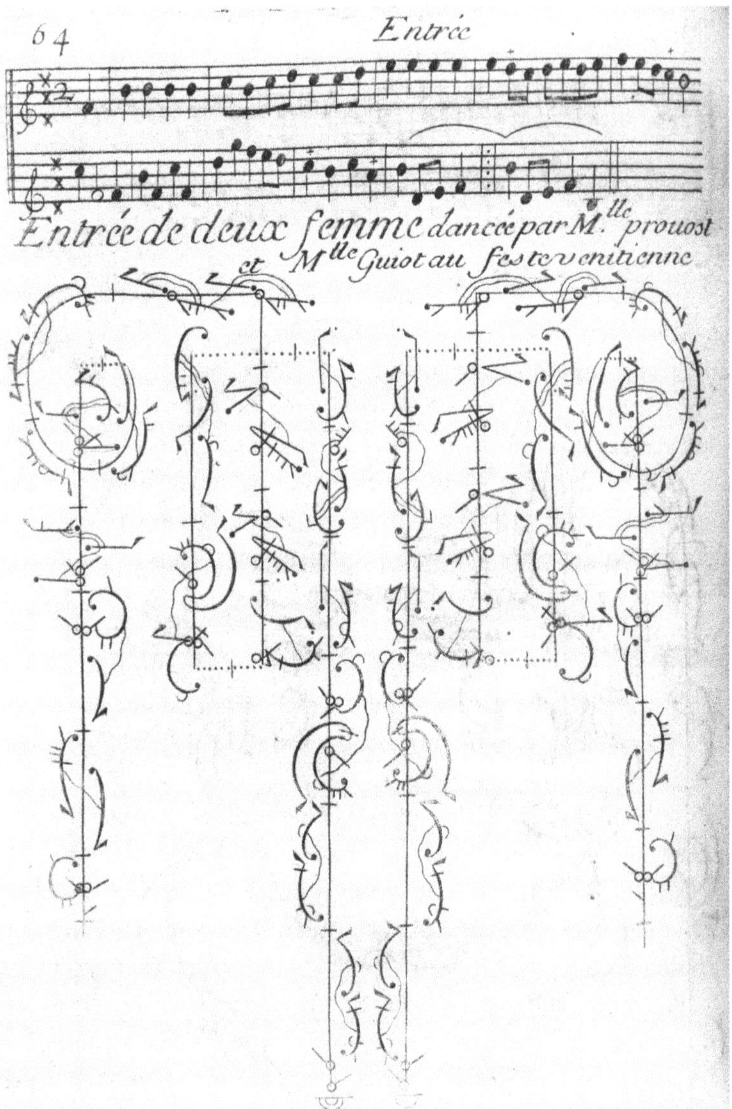

Figure 14-2: Pécour, "Entrée for two women danced by Mlle Prévost and Mlle Guyot in *Les Fêtes vénitiennes*" (Gaudrau, part II, 64).

notation.[19] A sparkle inheres in the choreography and its music; might Amour's words – juxtaposed against the violin obbligato that outlines the same melodic figures as the dance – authorize keeping an eye out for potential elements of hucksterism in the choreography?

19 *Ibid.*, 28.

SOLOISTS AS CHOREOGRAPHERS

During Pécour's 42-year-long tenure as *maître de ballet* at the Opéra, the *Mercure* often complimented him on his choreography in articles that imply he was responsible for all the dances in a work: "The ballet in general, composed as always by the inimitable Pécour, is enchanting, and the individual dances are very well characterized and artfully distributed."[20] Yet Table 14-1 reveals a striking imbalance in the distribution of solo dances among the choreographies that originated at the Opéra: five for women – all of them stars – and only one for a man, the obscure Klin. There is not a single solo notated for any of the highly paid dancers such as Balon, Blondy, François Dumoulin or his brother David.[21] Similarly, the only two places left unnotated in *Le Mariage de la grosse Cathos* are where a male soloist danced.[22] Might individual dancers have been responsible for their own solos?

Several men in the troupe are known to have choreographed: Blondy took over Pécour's position in 1729 and even before then choreographed when Pécour was ill; Henri Dumoulin choreographed for the fairs; François Dangeville did so for the Comédie-Française.[23] Yet the most direct testimony as to who choreographed for the soloists alludes to both sexes. According to the Parfaict brothers, writing about Mlle La Fontaine, who debuted in 1681, "In a short time she so far surpassed her comrades that she was judged capable not only of dancing alone, but of composing her own entrées, as did Pécour and Lestang *le cadet*."[24] Another woman who must have earned this right is Mlle Prévost, whose bona fides as choreographer for *Les Caractères de la danse* have never been questioned. Furthermore, the *Mercure* hints at her choreographic abilities in some of its reviews: "The Opéra is continuing its performances of the *Ballet des Éléments*, in which Mlle Prévost often attracts admiration by a new entrée, much to the appreciation of the public."[25] It is hard to imagine that Sallé and Camargo did not also control their own solo entrées.

The statistics in Table 14-1 suggest two further distinctions: first, that whereas the male soloists look to have choreographed for themselves, some of the women may not have done so. Mlle Subligny even went to England with solos made for her by Pécour. Second, soloists of both sexes, including Balon, Blondy, various Dumoulins, and Mlle Prévost, all danced at least some duets choreographed by Pécour, so the absence of

[20] *MF* (June 1725), 1210, re *Les Éléments*.

[21] The 1704 collection has eight unattributed male solos, most of which say "non dansée à l'Opéra"; Gaudrau has two.

[22] HW&M, 48. [23] See Ch. 13, p. 390.

[24] *Histoire*, 48–49. De Pure suggests as much about court ballets: "Moreover, a solo entrée does not run the risks of an entrée for several dancers, for there one is free, without having to depend on anyone else, and needs only one's feet and ears. [. . .] In a group dance, on the other hand, memory counts as much as does skill." *Idée*, 240–41.

[25] *MF* (July 1725), 1656.

solos for them must not mean that they did not want to cooperate with a notator. Occasional reports in the *Mercure* also show the *maître de ballet* in charge of dances for small ensembles, as when it credits Blondy with choreographing a *pas de trois* for Mlles Camargo, Sallé, and Mariette at the end of *Les Amours des déesses* (1729).[26] We are left with the impression that dances for two or more remained the responsibility of the principal choreographer, no matter the star power of the dancers.

DANCE TYPES, NEW OR NEWLY CHARACTERIZED

The expansion of the repertoire following Lully's death promoted the development of new divertissement types (e.g., masked balls) or a shift in emphasis within existing ones (the pastoral). The extant notations offer a point of entry into the new choreographic developments and help us discern the features of already known types, although in both cases it is necessary to look beyond the body of dances from the stage of the Opéra. The following sections take stock of the particularities of some fundamental dance types, including ones defined by the nature of the dancing role.

"Venetian" Dances

In the fantasy Venice that first appeared on the stage of the Opéra in 1697, the forlane was its choreographic emblem. A dance called the forlana did exist in Friuli, the region to the east of Venice; French readers might have been familiar with the account of it in Saint-Didier's best-selling book about Venice (1680) or the article by Chassebras de Cramailles in the *Mercure galant* in 1683, which spoke of the dance's "marvelous speed and lightness."[27] But authenticity did not concern Campra, who seems to have developed his own musical template for the forlane, one to which he remained wedded in his several Venetian works (see Example 9-1, p. 272, the forlane from *L'Europe galante*).[28] Its hallmarks are:

- $\frac{6}{4}$ meter;
- two-bar repeated phrases, resulting in strains of multiples of four bars;
- ABA form, with A having eight bars and B usually 32 (sometimes 24);
- gigue rhythms in the odd-numbered bars and a long-short-long rhythm in the even-numbered bars, often on repeated pitches, yielding a typical rhythmic profile: 

[26] *MF* (August 1729), 1840. Blondy also choreographed Rebel's *Fantaisie* (three dancers) and his *Plaisirs champêtres* (six); see Ch. 13, p. 395.

[27] For Saint-Didier, see Ch. 8, p. 225; also see 53–54 in the April 1683 issue of the *Mercure*.

[28] The minimal musical traces of the Friulian forlana do not resemble Campra's forlane, nor does either "furlana" tune in Lambranzi (II, plates 5 and 6; see Ch. 8, n. 28 and Fig. 8-3). Much of this section is based on C. G. Marsh's unpublished paper "Dancing Venice" and on subsequent conversations.

Campra's forlane may derive from his mining of Lully's early works. We have already observed Campra modeling his own branles on ones by Lully (see Chapter 9, p. 274) and in 1702 he was to compile *Les Fragments de Lully*, a pastiche into which he mingled some pieces of his own. His possible forlane model – a piece from the ballet accompanying Cavalli's opera *Xerxès* (1660) that had been added to the fourth act of *Armide* in 1697[29] – shares the rhythmic and melodic features of his forlane and differs only in that it is a full rondeau whose interior couplets are not so disproportionally long. However Campra derived it, his forlane looks like no other dance of the period: the insistent rhythms, repeated pitches, very square phrases, and lopsided ternary structure all separate it from other dances in $\frac{6}{4}$ such as the loure or gigue.

Among the choreographies danced at the Opéra there are two forlanes (see Appendix 3), both set to music by Campra: one for a solo woman from "Le Bal" in *Le Carnaval de Venise*; and one for two women from "La Sérénade vénitienne," an entrée added to *Les Fragments de Lully* and also set during a masked ball. These two dances – like all forlane choreographies – have one step-unit across each six-beat bar, which means that most steps adopt either an 𝅗𝅥 ♩ 𝅗𝅥. or 𝅗𝅥. 𝅗𝅥. rhythm; even if the tempo is brisk, the pacing feels relaxed. The step vocabulary stays within the norms for women's dances and favors steps with little hops or jumps (e.g., *contretemps*, *pas de sissonne*, *chassés*, and *pas de rigaudon*). The two- and four-bar phrases are respected in the dance without being slavishly imitated; the first page of the forlane for two women, for example, organizes the steps into two four-bar phrases, whereas the music repeats in groups of two bars. Within phrases the variety of steps is thus greater than the musical variety, but in both parameters clarity governs the structures; in the solo dance the return to the A music, eight bars before the end of the dance, is marked by a dramatic *pas tombé* into fifth position in *plié*, which is surrounded by half-turn pirouettes with the dancer's back to the audience. The duet alternates downstage figures with ones in which the dancers face each other in profile. In the solo the dancer's changes of direction, particularly when she moves into and out of a 45-degree angle, could be read as coquettish. Both dances are lovely and have a gently rustic character (see Figure 14-3), but they are not sufficiently flashy to owe anything beyond their name to the Friulian forlana. Like Campra, Pécour chose to evoke the foreign via a modest variant on the familiar.

A few other compound duple dances appear occasionally in Italian settings: the vénitienne, villanelle, and saltarelle all figure in *Le Carnaval de Venise*, with individual instances in a handful of other works. A dance labeled "sicilienne" is found in "Le Triomphe de la Folie" from *Les Fêtes vénitiennes*, although it looks more like a saltarelle than the siciliano as composed by Italians. Attempts at local

[29] Rosow, "How eighteenth-century Parisians," 218–19.

Figure 14-3: "Daughter of a gondolier dancing the furlana at the Opéra in *Le Carnaval de Venise*." (Photo BnF)

color were more symbolic than systematic; it sufficed to drop an "Italian" dance into a scene that was otherwise very French in its construction. The gondoliers in *Le Carnaval de Venise* III/4 do dance a saltarelle, but spend more time on gavottes and rigaudons.

After almost two decades on the operatic stage, the forlane escaped Venice. At first it remained within the realm of masked balls, as in "La Femme" of *Les Fêtes de Thalie* (1714), or in the fourth entrée of *Les Fêtes de l'été* (1716), which is set on the Cours la Reine in Paris. By 1725, however, it appears in *La Reine des Péris* in a pastoral divertissement, danced in Persia by European shepherds; in *Les Amours des dieux* (1727) it is even danced by warriors.

In all of these works the music retains compound duple meter, but departs from Campra's formal structure: Mouret's forlane is a classic ABACA rondeau, entirely in eight-bar phrases, whereas the others are binary. But even as it evolved, the forlane remained the property of the opera-ballet; it never entered the *tragédie en musique*.

Dances for Arlequin

Of all the commedia characters who danced across the French stage, the only one who left traces in Beauchamps-Feuillet notation is Arlequin.[30] The three extant choreographies are all chaconnes, and whereas the divertissements involving commedia characters (see Appendix 1) include a wide variety of dance-types, enough chaconnes figure among them to make it clear that a sub-genre of comic chaconnes existed in this period.[31] The music for the chaconne from Lully's *Bourgeois gentilhomme* by way of *Le Carnaval*, to which two of the choreographies are set, does not conform to the chaconne's familiar template, being short, irregular in phrasing, and quirky in its melodies (see Chapter 6, p. 167, and Example 6-2). The third is set to a chaconne written by Charpentier for *Le Malade imaginaire*; like Lully's dance it has only 56 measures and peculiar turns of phrase.[32] Chaconnes for commedia characters from eighteenth-century scores are generally more orthodox, but still exhibit comic characteristics.[33]

The three Arlequin dances are by different choreographers: anonymous, but possibly Feuillet; La Montagne, who worked primarily at the Comédie-Française; and Le Roussau, a French choreographer working in England.[34] La Montagne is identified in a document from 1688 as "danseur ordinaire de l'Opéra," but nothing in the notations connects any of these chaconnes to performance there. However, the dances are similar enough to suggest that the unusual movement vocabulary for Arlequin was a trope that would have been recognizable in various theaters.[35]

30 Lambranzi (1716) includes dances for Arlequin, Arlequine, Polichinelle, Scaramouche, and other comic characters, but his engravings and commentary do not allow for precise reconstruction; see Figs. 8-2 and 8-3.

31 Chaconnes danced by "comic masks" may be found, inter alia, in "L'Italie" from *L'Europe galante*; "Le Bal" from *Le Carnaval de Venise*; the prologue of *La Vénitienne*; "L'Amour saltimbanque" from *Les Fêtes vénitiennes; Manto la Fée* v; "La Femme" from *Les Fêtes de Thalie*; and the last entrée of *Le Ballet des âges*.

32 The chaconne for Arlequin in Lambranzi also has 56 bars, and the one in *Astrée* v has 57. Given the irregularity of the music in all these dances, such consistency begs for explanation. Regarding how the Harlequin chaconnes by Lully and Charpentier were created and reused, see Laurenti, "Le contexte des danses d'Arlequin."

33 On the music of the Arlequin chaconnes, see Porot, "Les ressorts."

34 La Montagne survives in one copy (LMC 1880; FL/Ms05.1/07), the others in two each: Anonymous/Feuillet in LMC 2760; FL/Ms05.2/01 and in FL/Ms05.2/pièce 1 (private collection); and Le Roussau in LMC 1980; FL/Ms13.1/09 and FL/1728.3s. All except the one owned privately are reproduced in *Arlequin danseur*, 38–72. Regarding the two known choreographers, see Lecomte, "Pierre de La Montagne," and Thorp, *F. Le Roussau*, 3–10.

35 See Lalonger, "Les chaconnes d'Arlequin"; and Colonna, "Les chaconnes d'Arlequin."

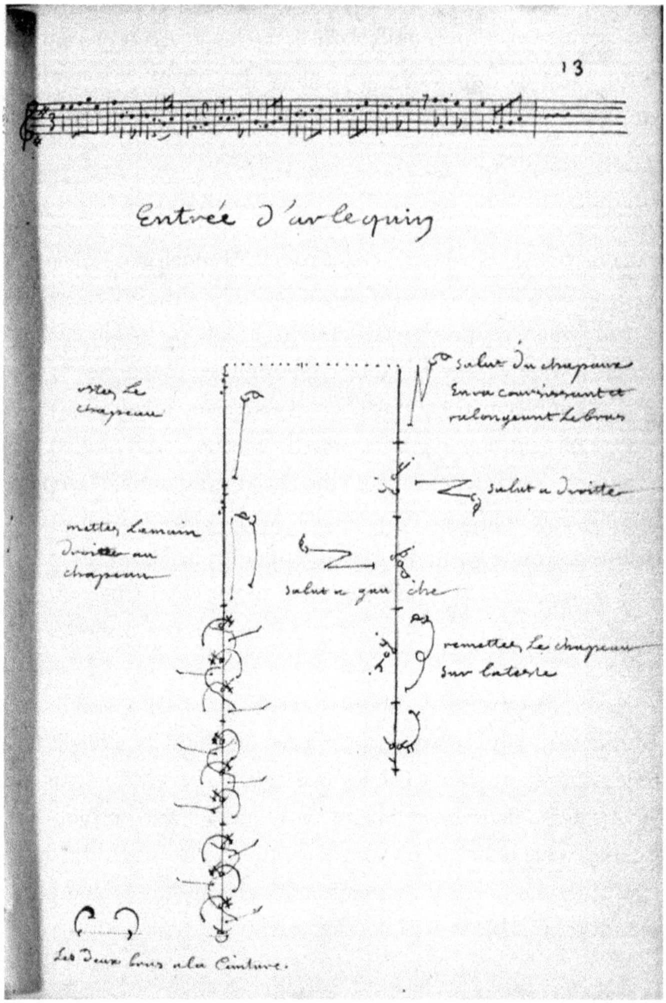

Figure 14-4: This page, from the "Entrée d'Arlequin" probably by Feuillet, includes instructions about placing the hands on the waist, removing the hat, making gestures of greeting, then putting the hat back on. (Photo BnF)

One measure of how much the Arlequin style depended on the whole body is that all three of the choreographers felt compelled to supplement the notation with verbal instructions or drawings (see Figure 14-4). Le Roussau even provided a little drawing of Arlequin in his motley costume with mask and slapstick on every page. All three dances open with Arlequin presenting himself to the audience and then doffing his hat in an elaborate bow – a breaking of the fourth wall not seen in other notated dances, but consistent with the self-consciousness that marks the comic works of the early eighteenth century. After the bow the three dances go their own ways, but all use at least some of the following unusual sequences, which are assembled in a collage-like manner: running in little steps around in a circle; repeated *échappés* or *saillies*, that is, jumps into an open second or fourth position on both feet; jumping sideways or back and forth with the feet together and sometimes even parallel; false positions of the feet; and choreographic accentuation on unexpected parts of the measure. The upper-body movements are just as unorthodox: Arlequin fiddles with his hat, looks back and forth and even over his shoulder, puts his hands on his waist, and circles his entire arm.[36] Le Roussau's dance ends with Arlequin running off stage, his back to the audience; Feuillet has him leap upstage, also facing away. From beginning to end, comic transgressions against the noble style mark these choreographies.

This does not mean, however, that dances such as these go too far for the Opéra. These choreographies may aim to provoke laughter, but they remain within acceptable bounds of taste, whereas at other Parisian theaters Arlequin might make salacious jokes with his body: according to a 1710 police report from the Foire Saint-Germain, "In order to make the audience laugh, Arlequin and Pierrot engage in gestures and postures that are indecent and scandalous."[37] These toned-down choreographies help give us a measure of the continuum between noble and grotesque styles at the Opéra; the heroic *entrée grave* stands at one end, Arlequin's antics at the other. Yet even if the expressive spectrum had a shorter comic end at the Opéra than at the fairs, these choreographies confirm that the same kind of self-parody that characterized the popular theaters and that had even made its way onto the stage of the Opéra in the years around 1700 had a choreographic analogue.

Peasant Dances

As pastoral divertissements multiplied, so did dances at the comic end of the spectrum (see Chapter 12, p. 360, and Figure 12-1). The music for peasant dances is in a lively duple meter, with or without upbeat, in simple, repetitive rhythms, and the phrasing, while not always square, is nonetheless straightforward (see Examples 10-2, p. 295, 12-1, and 12-2). Of the five choreographies for peasant characters, none has any known connections with the Opéra; only one involves a woman.[38]

36 These elements lasted a long time: in 1740 a newcomer to the Comédie-Française danced a chaconne in the role of Arlequine with "les petites singeries du chapeau, de la tête, etc. " *MF* (June 1740), 1196.

37 Cited in Campardon, *Spectacles de la Foire*, II, 299.

38 "Entrée de paysan" (LMC 3040, FL/Ms05.1/06); "Entrée de paysan de Mr Feuillet" (LMC 3060, FL/Ms05.1/05); "Madelon friquet payhisans" (LMC 5320, FL/Ms17.1.03); "Entry for Two French Country Men" (LMC 4130, FL/ Ms13.1/08); "La Paysanne" (LMC 6800; FL/1713.2/22). Gaudrau includes two dances attributed to a *pâtre* and *pastourelle*, but in one case (from *Fêtes vénitiennes*) the role attribution does not match the libretto, and in the other, the same two dancers are identified as *berger* and *bergère* in another choreography from the same act of *Sémélé*; see Appendix 3.

The choreographies employ a common movement vocabulary that departs significantly from dances in the noble style and even has points in common with the Arlequin chaconnes.[39] Thorp identifies the following steps as characteristic of the comic or rustic elements (all being interspersed with a more orthodox step vocabulary): sequences of "*demi-contretemps* incorporating a beat"; "repeated hops on one foot, or from foot to foot"; "falls into second position (feet apart) followed by a jump to bring the feet together"; and "unusual combinations of stamps, hops, shuffles, and steps onto flat foot, heel or toe." According to Hazebroucq, almost every measure in the three male solos contains some kind of hop or jump, except for movements involving foot stamps, special arm positions (hands behind the back), or other unusual step sequences, such as parodic variants on the *pas de rigaudon*. In his view, the peasant demonstrates "an inability to elaborate complex step sequences [. . .] displaying naïve joy without artifice or refinement," and sometimes even tipping into clumsiness. Thorp points out that in the choreography for a mixed couple, the woman keeps getting on the wrong foot, "and it is possible to interpret the whole dance as a series of jokes on the concept of symmetry." Lambranzi shows his peasant bent at the waist, supported on a flat foot with the other heel on the ground, the toe in the air (Figure 14-5). These choreographies validate Bonnet's assertion that "a peasant dance must be uncouth and rustic."[40]

Dances for shepherd and shepherdess, on the other hand, are not strongly characterized, even though their music exhibits greater metrical variety. One step, "a repeated bend and rise while turning the body slightly," occurs in three pastoral dances (two musettes and a branle),[41] but otherwise they generally share movement vocabulary with dances for other benign characters expressing joy and love.[42]

Entrée grave

The *entrée grave* stands at the opposite end of the expressive continuum from the comic dances; its technical virtuosity conveys strength and control. It is the only dance-type that seems to have been reserved exclusively for men;[43] within the *tragédie en musique* it is used for powerful beings. It is in duple meter (see Example 2-3) and its two, technically demanding step-units per bar impose a slow tempo. Whereas all other dance-types, including those called "Air" or "Entrée," can be, and often are, paired with a vocal piece of similar character, the jagged rhythms of the *entrée grave* are peculiar to

[39] This account relies upon Thorp, "Serious, comic and grotesque"; Hazebroucq, "Les danses de l'acte IV de *Roland*," esp. 109–15; Pierce, "Shepherd and shepherdess dances"; and Tomko, "Positioning peasants."

[40] *Histoire générale*, 63. [41] Pierce, "Shepherd and shepherdess dances," 7.

[42] *Ibid.*, table 2, listing choreographies for pastoral characters; Hazebroucq, "Les danses de l'acte IV de *Roland*."

[43] *Tancrède* has an *entrée grave* that might have been assigned to *guerrières*; see Ch. 11, p. 332.

Figure 14-5: A dancing peasant. Lambranzi, *Neue und curieuse theatrialische Tantz-Schul* (1716).

instrumental music and do not get sung. This means the dance has to get its meaning across through music and movement alone, without the help of words.

There are no extant *entrée grave* choreographies said to have been danced at the Opéra, but Pécour's "Entrée d'Apollon," published by Feuillet in 1704, may be taken as representative (Figure 14-6). The music comes from Lully's *Triomphe de l'Amour* (Example 6-8), where it was, indeed, attributed to Apollon. Another male solo to the same music was choreographed by Feuillet and published in 1700; it differs in many particularities, but shares overall features with Pécour's.[44] In their focus on footwork, both have points in common with the dance for two men discussed in Case Study 1.

[44] LMC 2720, FL/1700.1/14 and LMC 2740, FL/1704.1/30. The two are compared in Pierce's unpublished paper "Choreographic approaches"; my account relies upon his analysis. On both dances, see also Barros, *Dance as a Discourse*, 103–35.

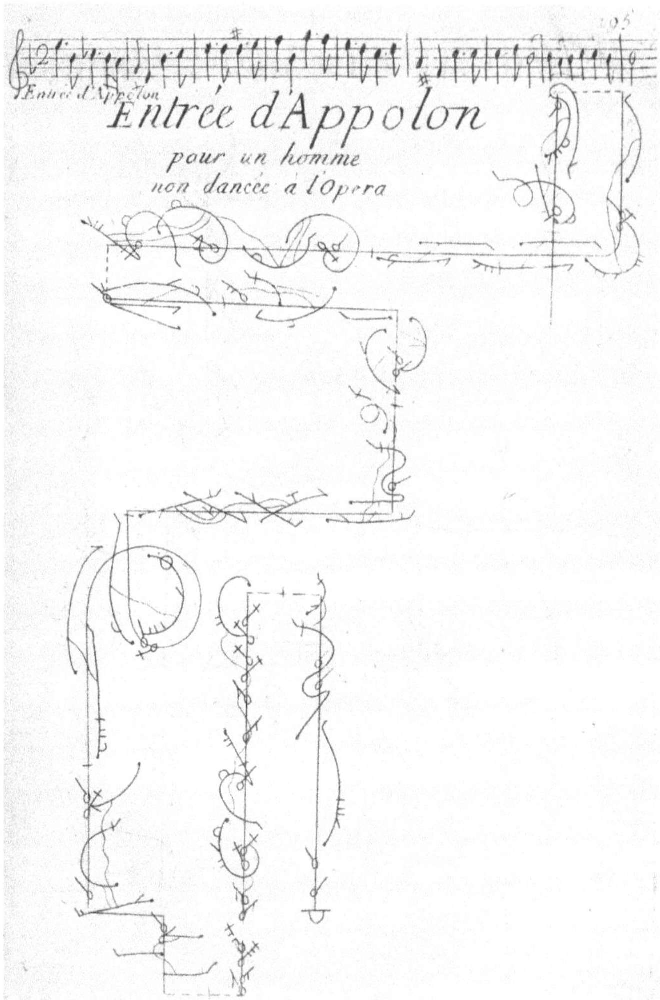

Figure 14-6: Pécour, "Entrée d'Apollon for a man, not danced at the Opéra." (Feuillet 1704, 195.)

In Pécour's "Entrée d'Apollon" the steps are difficult and highly ornamented, while the figures keep the dancer mainly moving forward and back, with only occasional excursions to the sides. There are almost no curves in the paths of the dancer, whose body mostly faces forward; sequences that change orientation do so only briefly. The first bar involves beats behind and in front of the supporting leg; the second ornaments a full-circle turn with *entrechats*; the third offers a bit of respite; and the fourth has the dancer take off backwards into a *cabriole* with a full circle turn – all this before the midway point of the first A section. Recurring steps include *cabrioles, entrechats* beaten pirouettes, other ornamental beats, *ronds de jambe*, and many forms of rotation. Notwithstanding their complexity, the steps form phrases that complement the music, which is quite irregular: nine bars in the A section, nineteen in B, of which the last seven mark a slow descent down the octave, repeated as a *petite reprise*. During this coda, the dancer performs a flurry of beats, until he slowly retreats upstage on the cadential note.

In this thrilling choreography Hazebroucq notes successions of power, skill, and elegance; variety in the subtle modulation of effects within an overriding rationality; and, at its end, a brilliant outburst that nonetheless expresses lightness and clarity. The equilibrium required "evokes control, self-mastery, and especially the possibility of escaping the constraints of walking and of gravity; it thus represents the grace to transcend the human condition and applies perfectly to the incarnation of a divinity."[45]

Menuet

Much is known about the ballroom menuet; treatises on into the nineteenth century saw its practice as essential for persons of good breeding. On the operatic stage some dramatic situations would make a ballroom-style menuet virtually essential – as when a main character dances at a masked ball (see Chapter 9, p. 272 and p. 279) – but the menuet's theatrical usages are sufficiently broad to raise the question of how it was choreographed in other types of scenes. The menuet could appear in any part of a tragedy or opera-ballet, even if, in this era, it was particularly welcome in pastoral or nautical divertissements.[46] Two choreographies "danced at the Opéra" offer guidance as to how the theatrical menuet compared to its social counterpart.[47] Both are for a mixed couple, although on stage the menuet could be assigned to other combinations of dancers or even to a group.

The settings for both dances are mythological, although one comes from an opera-ballet, the other from a tragedy. In "Le Triomphe de Vénus," an entrée with music of his own that Campra added to *Les Fragments de Lully*, the scene is a beautiful garden where the Pleasures and Graces are honoring Vénus. After a brief sequence that puts them face-to-face, the two dancers do nothing but menuet steps (steps of two and three movements and *contretemps de menuet*), plus the occasional *balancé*, albeit with a few slight exceptions to ballroom practices, such as *contretemps* going backwards. The figures do not use the classic S or Z paths, nor is there a presentation of hands, but the dancers spend much of the dance circling each other. Even when at the start of the second B section the dancers do a figure in which one advances while the other, facing,

45 Hazebroucq, "De la danse comme geste."

46 I observed in Ch. 3, p. 94 that in Lully's operas menuets appeared more frequently in prologues than in other acts; in Campra's day, however, menuets appear across an opera, usually in pairs.

47 Both come from the 1704 collection: LMC 4400, FL/1704.1/09 (Omphale) and LMC 5540, FL/1704.1/07 (Fragments). See Appendix 3 for their contexts.

retreats, before the roles are reversed, their focus remains on each other. Members of the audience would surely have identified this dance as a menuet.

The *Omphale* menuet also takes place in a garden, danced by a Greek couple. But here a menuet skeleton is overlaid with other movements. Except in bars 3 to 8, where the woman does menuet steps around the man while he pirouettes, there are very few classic menuet steps. There are, however, two-bar sequences that look like subtle variants on six-beat steps: two *coupés* of different types in lieu of a menuet step of three movements, or a distant relative of the *contretemps de menuet* that incorporates a *pas tombé*. These variations tend to come in pairs or even in a sequence of three – repetition of steps being a feature of the ballroom menuet – and as in the first dance, *balancés* across two bars either set up a new sequence or punctuate a phrase. Nonetheless, distance from the ballroom menuet manifests itself not only in the steps, but in the figures. The tracks tend to sketch squares, and while the dancers sometimes face each other, they also pass back-to-back. Toward the end there are two consecutive echo figures – not a feature of ballroom menuets, even if each dancer does move across six beats. In its reinterpretation of the menuet, this dance is considerably more subtle than the other; whether it even remained legible as a menuet is an open question. Two solo menuets, neither danced at the Opéra, also blur the choreographic boundaries of the genre.[48]

The two operatic choreographies were published in 1704, early enough in the century to make us wonder what theatrical menuets looked like ten or twenty years later, especially ones for shepherds or sailors. The menuet for the painter and his wife in the Ferrère manuscript (1782) makes use of the occasional menuet step, so perhaps that is a hint that some basic elements remained as points of reference. But even this small sample shows that, on stage, the menuet was not fixed in either its steps or figures; like any other dance, it was susceptible to choreographic creativity.

Passepied

Passepieds, of which there are many in all types of opera, could be danced by a soloist or a couple,[49] but seem to have been performed primarily by groups. One testimony comes from Bonin (1711), who says that theatrical passepieds are danced not as in the ballroom, but by four, eight, or even more people.[50] Moreover, passepieds tend to come at the end of a divertissement, where a group dance would be expected. In fact, the passepied that concludes an *intermède* done at court in 1720 is annotated "tous les danseurs."[51]

[48] One is a male solo attributed to Balon (LMC 5700, FL/Ms.17.1/36), the other a solo for Hester Santlow by L'Abbé (LMC 5780, FL/1725.1/03).

[49] *E.g.*, Sallé danced a passepied in a revival of *Les Fêtes vénitiennes; MF* (August 1731), 1991.

[50] *Die neueste Art*, 187. [51] Score of *L'Inconnu*; see below, p. 440.

Only one theatrical group choreography is known – in *Le Mariage de la grosse Cathos* (Versailles, 1688), where it does round off the instrumental dances in the divertissement.[52] The eight dancers consist of four men and four women, but they are not treated as couples; rather they function as groups of either eight or four, who kaleidoscope through circling figures. The steps consist only of menuet steps and *contretemps de menuet*; the interest of the dance lies in its floor patterns. One section, for nine dancers, even snakes in a line around the stage.[53]

It seems unlikely that the eighteenth-century operatic passepied would have restricted itself to steps in the menuet family, even if its movements continued to be read as a figural type of running. Perhaps even the translational symmetry that characterizes the ballroom passepied – the partners are not only on the same foot but move together around the space – was retained in the theater. At the very least the dance's vivacity must have made it an appealing choice for ending a joyous fête.

Tambourin

In the beginning the tambourin was a drum. On the operatic stage it was played by characters who make their living from the water – either gondoliers or sailors – who danced to pieces in various meters; the three "Airs des matelots" in Marais's *Alcyone* (1706) are in $\frac{6}{8}$, **2**, and $\frac{4}{8}$.[54] By metonomy the word gradually became the name of a dance, still associated with sailors; in the intermediate stages a piece might be labeled "Premier Air des tambourins" (*Hypermnestre*, 1716) or "Menuet. Tambourin" ("La Provençale," 1722), where the word evokes the drum or the drummer as much as a dance-type. Some scores include the drum part or at least mention it; some may specify that the melody line is to be played by *petites flûtes*, in imitation of the three-holed pipe played by the same person beating the tambourin in traditional usages (Example 11-1). During the 1720s the music acquired its familiar profile: $\frac{2}{4}$ meter with a tempo marking of "très vite," a simple melody largely in eighth notes with turning sixteenth-note figures, and, often, a rhythmic tonic pedal (Example 11-2 exhibits most of these features). Mlle Camargo, who joined the troupe in 1726, earned a reputation for dancing the tambourin with "brilliant vivacity."[55]

No theatrical choreographies exist for the tambourin from the first half of the eighteenth century. There are, however, two tambourins in the Ferrère manuscript (1782), both virtuoso male solos.[56] One involves the dancer in fancy maneuvers with a

[52] See Ch. 4, p.109.

[53] Marsh ("In search of the passepied") has pointed out that a common figure in ballroom passepieds involves the couple holding inside hands and traveling sideways, as if part of a line dance.

[54] Ch 12; see also Chs. 10 and 11. Sometimes dancers are identified in cast lists as "tambourins"– presumably drummers.

[55] E.g., *MF* (February 1732), 373.

[56] Marsh and Harris-Warrick, "Putting together a pantomime ballet", 194–95 and 255.

tambourine (not something mentioned in reports of operatic tambourins). The "tambourin sérieux" comes from the second *intermède* for the play *L'Embarras de richesses*, set to a piece borrowed from Rameau and attributed to a "galant peasant." It involves lively jumps and technically challenging movements such as multiple pirouettes, double *ronds de jambe*, *brisés*, beats, and *entrechats*; its style is considerably later than Pécour's, especially in its predilection for repeating steps several times in a row.[57] Whereas the vivacity and speed demanded by this choreography are consistent with the technically demanding style for which Camargo was famous, the step sequences are the product of a different era.

Tambourins were not exclusively solo dances, but could be danced by couples as well.[58] When they occur at the end of a divertissement, as at the conclusion to "L'Aurore et Céphale" from *Les Amours des déesses* (1729), they were undoubtedly danced by a group.

Contredanse

The contredanse, an offspring of the English country dance with a decidedly French accent, had spectacular success in the eighteenth-century ballroom; the hundreds of dances published from 1706 onwards show us what it looked like in a social environment. For the theatrical contredanse, however, it is difficult to ascertain – especially in the early decades of the century – how the term and the choreographic practices mapped onto each other. Eventually the *contredanse générale* – a dance for the entire cast – became the standard way to end a performance at the fairs or the Théâtre Italien, a practice that even spread to the Opéra in the era of Rameau. In its early days, however, the theatrical contredanse is elusive.

The ballroom contredanse was introduced into the French court from England in 1684; the two manuscripts that dancing master André Lorin offered to the king show that he had adapted longways country dances by adding French footwork to the English figures.[59] The first publication, Feuillet's 1706 *Recueil de contredanses mises en chorégraphie*, includes 32 longways dances for an indeterminate number of couples – some of them arrangements of English dances, others composed in France. There is no predominant meter or rhythmic pattern and the tune is repeated as many times as necessary for each couple to work through all the figures. Its cousin, the cotillon (later known as the *contredanse française*), arranged two or four couples in a square or a circle and used similar figures.[60] How rapidly contredanses spread beyond court circles is

57 The information about this choreography comes from Guillaume Jablonka (personal communication).

58 *MF* (December 1735), 2719 and (October 1736), 2338.

59 HW&M, 85. For a history of the ballroom contredanse, see Guilcher, *La Contredanse*.

60 The first notated cotillon was published by Feuillet in 1705; see Guilcher, *ibid.*, 72ff.

unclear; in his 1706 collection Feuillet went to great pains to instruct those encountering the dances for the first time, and his publication undoubtedly helped make them known. The timing of its diffusion matters for the theatrical contredanse, in that pieces labeled "contredanse" began to appear in operatic scores during this intermediate period. The question is whether the term alone is sufficient to indicate that something like the ballroom contredanse was performed then on the stage of the Opéra.

1697 marks the first appearances of the "contredanse" in opera scores, at the end of the prologue of La Coste's *Aricie* and in a piece added to the fourth act of Lully's *Armide* when it was revived that year.[61] Other early examples are found in *Les Fragments de Lully* (in an entrée by Campra), the *Ballet des Muses* (1703), *Bradamante* (1707), *Hippodamie* (1708), and *Les Fêtes vénitiennes* (1710). These dances tend to come toward the end of their divertissements, thus increasing the likelihood that they were danced by groups; more than half of them, however, originate in works based in mythology or chivalry, where a dance imported from the contemporary ballroom would seem out of place. (The dance in *Hippodamie* is attributed to the Peoples of Phyrgia, the one in *Bradamante* to Arcadian shepherds.) Moreover, the only "contredanse" in Beauchamps-Feuillet notation said to have been danced at the Opéra is for a mixed couple and makes no reference whatsoever to the kinds of figures seen in ballroom contredanses (LMC 2180; FL/1704.1/20); the *Tancrède* score (v/3) calls it a gigue, and its phrasing is irregular. Two other contredanses for a couple in Beauchamps-Feuillet notation (neither for the stage) fail to show any choreographic affinity with the ballroom contredanse. Taken together, these data suggest that the word had two choreographic meanings at the turn of the eighteenth century. The gigue connection is suggestive: excepting the dance in *Bradamante*, all the contredanses in early scores or notated a2 in choreographies are in $\frac{6}{4}$ time and some of them are musically complex. Perhaps during the two decades when the English-style contredanse was gaining traction in the ballroom, the word also had a more general sense as a lively gigue-like dance that could be performed on stage by varied numbers of dancers without reference to ballroom practices.[62]

A turning point came in *Les Fêtes de Thalie*, a comic work by La Font and Mouret set in contemporary France. By 1714 the contredanse was sufficiently well established in the ballroom that a theatrical choreographer could draw upon its social resonance for dramatic purposes. In addition, the vaudeville finales that often concluded plays at the fairs and other Parisian spoken theaters had begun intertwining strophic songs with

[61] Rosow, "How eighteenth-century Parisians," 218–19; this is the same piece that may have served as a musical model for Campra's forlane (see above, p. 423).

[62] A curious point is that all the pre-1714 operas with identifiable contredanses were composed either by La Coste or Campra.

dances; insofar as it is possible to tell, these often shared the same tune.[63] La Font's own *Le Naufrage, ou la Pompe funèbre de Crispin*, written for the Comédie-Française in 1710, had ended in such a manner; in his preface to *Les Fêtes de Thalie* La Font declared that he had drawn upon practices from comedy that were heretofore unknown on the operatic stage. Mouret unambiguously looked outside the Opéra in constructing his finale: the masked ball that closes the last entrée, "La Femme," ends with a jolly, very simple tune that has only four bars in each of the two strains and is interwoven with the strophes of a chorus set to the same music (see Example 10-3). Despite being in compound duple meter, it has none of the complexities of the earlier gigue-like contredanses and is so short that it must have been repeated multiple times. This is the first opera score where the music looks like a group contredanse and where the dramatic context seems to call for one.[64]

With this development contredanses disappeared from tragedies, not to return until 1749, in Rameau's *Zoroastre*. They became regular features, however, of opera-ballets, usually in ballroom scenes and usually at or toward the end of the divertissement; the libretto of *Le Ballet des âges* (1718) reveals that in the first entrée "the ball ends with contredanses." Once the contredanse became a marker for real dancing, its meters expanded beyond $\frac{6}{4}$; some contredanses look like gavottes. More and more it makes sense to imagine that the choreography would have alluded to figures familiar from the ballroom, although surely more theatricalized.

The only notated theatrical contredanses come in the Ferrère manuscript, from much later in the century and from a tradition akin to the fair theaters, but reveal something already implicit in the contredanse from *Les Fêtes de Thalie* – that the dance may be much longer than the music suggests.[65] In one instance sixteen notated bars of music become 144 bars of dance. Across this length – which is through-choreographed – the emphasis is on creating interesting and constantly shifting floor patterns; some patterns may relate to contemporary social contredanses, but most are more elaborate. Not surprisingly for presentation on stage, the figures tend to be oriented toward the audience, not inward toward the other dancers. Because Ferrère's contredanses generally conclude pantomime ballets, they involve the entire group, but the number of dancers may vary from phrase to phrase. Even the soloists join in, usually entering the dance about halfway through to perform a short passage before the group returns. Their step vocabulary is flashier, but in some of the dances even the group may get

[63] The musical sources for spoken plays are incomplete and it is not yet possible to pin firm dates onto early appearances of the contredanse at the fairs. For the period around 1718, see Porot, "Watteau au spectacle," esp. 244–45.

[64] The revised version of the second entrée, "La Veuve coquette," includes a cotillon (aka "Deuxième Air paysan"); this brief tune (twelve bars) was choreographed as a ballroom cotillon and published by Dezais, successor to Feuillet, in the *XIV*[e] *Recueil de danses pour l'année 1716* [1716]. As the "Cotillon de Thalie," the tune became a vaudeville.

[65] Marsh and Harris-Warrick, "Putting together a pantomime ballet," 273–76.

challenging steps. Whereas the details of Ferrère's dances belong to a later period, the general principles – multiple repeats of short pieces of music; inventive floor patterns with some reference to ballroom practices; orientation of the dancers toward the audience; and possibly even passages for soloists – seem plausible for the Opéra around the 1720s.

WHO DANCES WHERE

The most basic of the conventions Lully and Quinault established – the alternation of singing and dancing – continued into the generations that followed. Some scores provide specific instructions to that effect, as in the prologue to *Les Fêtes de l'été* (1716), where "the violins and flutes play this sarabande before it is sung." More frequently librettos follow the text of a vocal piece with a laconic "on danse" or "le divertissement continue." This particular convention held across theaters, even ones where the same performers both sang and danced. A 1710 police report from one of the fair theaters, which was parodying *Alceste*, reported that "we noticed that the singers, after having sung together, sang duets or other airs accompanied by the orchestra, and then danced two by two, or four together or still more, different dances to the sounds of the same instruments."[66]

The groupings of dancers, however, expanded to include more combinations. Whereas groups of four or eight remain frequent, groups of six become more numerous.[67] The tragedy *Théonoé* (1715) shows both the older and the newer practices: dancers in groups of six in Acts II and V, with groups of four or eight in Acts I and III. Act IV has both: one group of four, another of six. Choreographies for six probably used the space differently than did dances for eight, with three dancers on either side of the center line, thus requiring different kinds of symmetrical patterns. This may have been the case in "Les Sérénades et les joueurs" from *Les Fêtes vénitiennes*, which in 1710 had three each of Espagnols and Espagnolettes, and three more each of Biscayens and Biscayennes. *Aréthuse* (1701) includes a sequence for the four corners of the world, each of which is represented by two men and a woman. Other odd numbers of dancers appear in groups as well, as in the last act of *Hypermnestre* (1716), which has two groups of five warriors in combat with each other. Groups of five may show up in co-operative contexts, as when five each of masked men and women appear at a ball in *Les Fêtes de l'été*; all ten probably dance together at least once. A perplexing situation is found when one of the groups also has a solo dancer attached. Act IV in *Bradamante* (1707) calls for five undifferentiated shepherds, but four shepherdesses plus one shepherdess soloist. There seem to be three possibilities for the group dances: one of the shepherds was also

66 Cited in Campardon, *Spectacles de la foire*, I, 6–7.
67 For Lully's practices, see Chapter 4, pp. 105–06.

a soloist, leaving eight for the group; the solo sherpherdess joined the group for a dance of ten; or the men and women really did form a group of nine. The solution may not be clear, but librettos of this era list so many groups that do not come in multiples of four that there must have been more variety in the spatial arrangements for the *corps de ballet* than in Lully's day.

Another dramatic change is that soloists now dance in virtually every act; it is rare for there not to be at least one name set off on a separate line from the others in the cast list. Soloists appear across the opera, regardless of character type, and in tragedies as well as ballets. Reports in the *Mercure* sometimes even indicate that a single soloist might dance alone more than once per act, as in *Médée et Jason* (revival of 1727), where Mlle Prévost danced "several entrées" in Act III and Mlle Camargo two as a matelotte in Act IV.[68] The arrangement of names in librettos also suggests frequent duets performed by the leading dancers (see in Figure 12-2 the listing in Act V for Mlles Prévost and Guyot) and, particularly toward the end of the period, a growing number of *pas de trois*. Sometimes such combinations are suggested by the presentation of names in a libretto, as in the 1731 revival of *Callirhoé*, where in Act II the *sacrificateurs* are presented as one soloist, a group of three, and a group of six. However, the libretto may not tell the full story; the *Mercure* admired a *pas de trois* danced by David Dumoulin, Camargo and Sallé in Act IV of the same revival,[69] whereas the layout in the libretto suggests a solo for him and a duet for the women. The existence of a *pas de trois* does not preclude the other two possibilities, and, exceptionally, it is possible to identify the music for the duet: the "Premier Air des Bergers (Gracieusement)", for which a choreography for two women from the 1712 premiere is transmitted by Gaudrau (see Appendix 3). This is not to say that fifteen years later the same choreography was necessarily used, but that there seems to have been a continuity across revivals in the role assignments and characterizations that the extant operatic choreographies allow us to glimpse.

It is a shame that no *pas de trois* choreographies exist from this era to supply models of how symmetry was treated; the two in the Ferrère manuscript are not only later (1782), they both involve pantomime. In their danced sections, the person who is identifiably different from the other two dances in the middle, doing either different steps or different floor patterns. Yet mirror-image symmetry remains the guiding principle. Parallel motion for all three dancers occurs in only one two-bar passage – a tiny fraction of the two dances.[70]

Greater variety in the configurations of the dancers is not surprising in an era when the amount of dancing in operas was increasing. A libretto such as Fuzelier's for the *Ballet des âges* (1718) calls attention to the staging of the varied groups in its long masked ball – a type of scene that could embrace any

[68] *MF* (May 1727), 985–86. [69] *MF* (January 1732), 146.

[70] See Marsh and Harris-Warrick, "Putting together a pantomime ballet," 269–72.

sequence desired. This one, which ends the first entrée ("La Jeunesse"), is set outdoors at the Foire de Bezons near Paris. It opens with a march that brings in a group of maskers consisting of a chorus, who sit down around the trees, and twelve dancers in three groups of four. After they sing and dance, new maskers make a dramatic arrival by boat – three in one group, four in the other, all of them principal dancers. (Seven years later, in Act IV of *La Reine des Péris*, Fuzelier was again to withhold the arrival of the soloist until the middle of the divertissement; see Chapter 13, p. 402.) The overall trajectory of these two sections thus appears to move from group dances to solos and small ensembles, performed in front of the on-stage audience. Unfortunately, eighteenth-century scores are no more informative than were Lully's as to which characters dance to each piece. If anything, they are less so, because of the greater number of generic dances, where the score simply says "Sarabande" or "Rigaudon." (A glance through the tables in Part II will reveal how rarely dances are attributed to specific characters.)

It was during this period that composers began to put two dances of the same type back-to-back – menuets, passepieds, and rigaudons being the most frequently paired. The earlier scores do not indicate that the first would be repeated after the second in a large ternary shape; in fact, either there is no indication for either dance to be repeated, or there is variety in the patterns, as in *Tancrède* III/4, where two consecutive menuets are repeated in reverse order only after interleaved strophes of a song (see Table 11-2). The score of *Manto la fée* (1711) was printed without repeat indication following the two consecutive passepieds in Act II, but an annotation in Stuck's hand[71] calls for repetition of the first. By the time of *Jephté* (1732), repetition of the first dance after the second had become conventional, but even in IV/3 the second menuet is played again, after a song (see Table 11-5). Another kind of extension, visible in only a few scores, is when a note indicates that a piece should be played twice in a row, as in "La Provençale" from *Les Fêtes de Thalie* (score, p. 63): "On joue deux fois le menuet." A few theatrical choreographies require the music to be played twice through to accommodate the dance, or exhibit varied patterns of repetition (see Chapter 4, p. 132).

These elusive variants in the amount of music a divertissement may contain are not surprising in a theatrical art, but do complicate our thinking about how dancers might have been distributed. The default assumption, one most writers today tacitly accept, is that one dance requires one and only one set of characters who dance throughout; such an inference follows from the choreographies in Beauchamps-Feuillet notation, almost all of which behave this way.

[71] See Porot, "Jean-Baptiste Stuck," 424–33.

But there is even more evidence in this period than there was in Lully's day for two other ways of assigning dancers: first, within a single piece, the configuration of dancers might change at structural points; second, a dance piece could acquire a second set of dancers when it was repeated. In Chapter 13 we encountered instances where opposing groups of dancers could be set into dialogue (p. 406ff), supported by strong musical distinctions. Cahusac reports in the *Encyclopédie* on how internal repetitions could also lend themselves to choreographic variation:

> Entrée (Dance). An instrumental piece to which, in the act of an opera, the dancers enter the stage. This term also applies to the dance itself that is performed. It is normally the group dancers [*chœurs de danse*] who appear to this music; it is for this reason that they are called "corps d'entrée." They dance the A section ["un commencement"[72]]; a solo dancer, male or female, dances another A and a B ["une fin"], and the group performs the last B.[73]

In this instance the soloist is enfolded within a single piece that also involves the group. The "Ballet de neuf danseurs" (Table 4-2) shows that other binary pieces besides entrance marches could receive similar treatment. Another source provides a concrete example of the choreographic variety possible when the entire piece of music repeats.

L'Inconnu, a 1675 play by Thomas Corneille, received new *intermèdes* by Lalande in 1720, when it was performed at court for the ten-year-old Louis XV. In an attempt to revive the *ballet de cour*, three of its five *intermèdes* were danced by the king and young noblemen; the other two, however – a pastoral divertissement and a village wedding – were choreographed by Balon for members of the Opéra's troupe. Lalande's two published scores – one with the vocal music, the other with the dances – identify the performers of each piece, down to changes in personnel when the music repeats.[74] A special performance of this type, whose two *intermèdes* involved only seven and twelve dancers respectively – the cream of the troupe – cannot be taken as representative of performances in the Palais-Royal. Still, the variety on display may reflect operatic practices. Eight years later *L'Inconnu* was repeated at court with new music, most of it by Collin de Blamont. This time all the dancers came from the Opéra, with choreography again by

72 "Entrée," *Encyclopédie*, v (1755), 730. That "beginning" and "end" indicate the sections of binary pieces can be seen in several scores, annotated in the mid-eighteenth century, with instructions such as "deux commencements, une fin." Cahusac's second definition within this article allows for free-standing solo dances: "Each dance that a *danseur* or *danseuse* performs is also called an entrée. It also is given the name pas."

73 *Encyclopédie*, v (1755), 730.

74 *L'Inconnu, premier ballet dansé par Sa Majesté* (includes the vocal airs and cast lists) and *Airs de violon de L'Inconnu*, both published by Ballard in 1720. For more about this work, see Sawkins, *A Thematic Catalogue of the Works of Michel-Richard de Lalande*, 557–59.

Balon. The long report in the *Mercure*[75] is less precise than the 1720 scores, but it confirms practices seen in the earlier performances.

- The same piece may be done twice in a row, with different dancers.
- In such cases, the change may be from group to soloist(s), from soloist(s) to group, or from soloist(s) to soloist(s). For example, the "Air de paysan" in the 1720 pastoral *intermède* was danced first by Dumoulin alone, then by the remaining six dancers. In the fifth *intermède* in 1728 – a village wedding – a bourrée was danced first by the bride and a vicomte, then a second time by a village woman, "in an original manner."
- In the one instance of a strophic dance-song (from the third *intermède* in 1728), the two iterations of the dance change personnel: before the first strophe of its sung analogue, the sarabande was danced by "several," then, before the second strophe, danced as a solo by Mlle Prévost.
- Another situation involved performing two pieces in a row by the same personnel, then the same two pieces with different personnel, as when Mlle Prévost danced a musette and passepied that were subsequently danced by Marcel and Mlle Menés.
- The *intermèdes* open and close with group dances.[76]

The practice of alternating soloists and groups also characterizes the choreography of the longest dances done on stage – chaconnes and their less-frequent relatives, the passacailles. The twenty chaconne and passacaille choreographies in Beauchamps-Feuillet notation might seem to contest this assertion, in that they are all notated for either a soloist or a couple who dance the entire piece, even when the dance is as long as 209 measures.[77] But of these only two come from the stage of the Opéra, both from the very beginning of the eighteenth century.[78] The variability in the groupings of dancers applies both to chaconnes in the noble style and those danced by comic, usually Italian characters. Where musical evidence exists, it shows that changes in dancing personnel correspond with points of articulation in the music, such as changes in mode, texture, or affect.

Louis Bonin, French born and trained, who spent his professional life in Germany, and Gennaro Magri, an Italian *grottesco* with an international career, reported the same basic outlines for a chaconne choreography, even though their books were published 67 years apart in different countries: a chaconne begins with the whole group minus the soloist (who waits upstage, according to Bonin); the soloist takes over after 24 or so bars and dances an equivalent amount (this number from Magri), while the group dancers remain still. The number of alternations between group and soloist is a function of the

[75] *MF* (December 1728), 2931–38.

[76] This is the case in 1720 and for the openings of the 1728 *intermèdes*, but the endings of some of the latter are ambiguous.

[77] "Passacaglia of Venus and Adonis" by L'Abbé.

[78] The passacaille for a solo woman from *Scylla* and the passacaille for a man and a woman from *Persée*.

length of the piece, and Bonin adds that subgroups from within the whole may also form and the soloist may dance with a partner.[79] Undated annotations in the *Ballet des Sens* by Mouret (1732) outline this very type of alternation: over the chaconne's 228 bars, the group dances at the beginning, in the middle, and at the end, each time for around 50 bars; the soloist dances for around 40 bars during each of his intervening solos.[80] Reports in the *Mercure* about dancing at the Opéra tend to focus on the soloists. In *Les Amours des dieux* II/9 "Blondy dances a warlike chaconne with steps and attitudes that perfectly express the joy and pride of a conquering hero . . . "[81] Yet a look at the score suggests this was not a solo throughout: the chaconne has 313 measures and alternates a military affect with calmer passages; the cast list for this divertissement involved two other soloists and a dozen more group dancers. Annotations in a manuscript score for the chaconne from Rameau's *Dardanus*, probably dating from 1744, indicate where another famous soloist, Louis Dupré, danced; as in the *Ballet des Sens*, he had two solo passages, each between 40 and 45 bars long.[82] The chaconne that concludes Mozart's *Idomeneo* (1781) follows the same pattern in its three different annotations as to the dancers: "pour le ballet," "pas de deux," and "pas seul"; the group begins, ends, and alternates with the soloist and the couple.[83] A similar testimonial comes from a policeman visiting the Foire Saint-Germain in 1721:

> The last act ended with the dance of a chaconne. The aforesaid actors and actrices started it altogether, then continued by four, then two, then one alone, costumed as a hump-backed peasant, then finished together, all to the sound of the aforementioned instruments that in the entr'actes never stopped playing different pieces of music, having in front of them notated pages.[84]

The length and potential for musical contrasts made chaconnes susceptible to dramatic treatment; testimonials to this practice start in the 1720s. A comic chaconne performed at the Théâtre Italien in 1729 has annotations printed into the score that hint at a sketchy story.[85] At least five dancers were needed; the annotations suggest that everyone, including the soloists, danced at the beginning and the end (Table 14-2).

79 Bonin, *Die neueste Art*, 185–88; and Magri, *Trattato*, I, 104–05, the latter quoted in Goff, "Steps, gestures," 208–10.

80 The annotations, in pencil, are found in a copy of the published *partition réduite* (F-Po A.125a) in Sc. 8 of the first entrée, "L'Odorat."

81 *MF* (September 1727), 2081.

82 See the score in the Appendix to Rameau, *Œuvres complètes*, X, 81–87 and Malherbe's preface to the edition, cxvi.

83 *Neue Mozart Ausgabe*, II/5/11, 2, 495–531.

84 Campardon, *Spectacles de la Foire*, I, 16.

85 For other instances of chaconnes used in comic contexts, see Ch. 6, Ch. 8, Ch. 9, Ch. 10, Ch. 11, Ch. 12, and Ch. 13.

Table 14-2: Outline of the "Chaconne comique" from Mouret, IV. *Recueil des Divertissements du Nouveau Théâtre Italien*, 247–54. The annotations are printed into the score.

Bars	No. of bars	Annotation
1–56	56	All the pantomimes
57–100	44	Arlequin and Arlequine
101–20	20	Swiss man, who chases Arlequin
121–44	24	Swiss woman, weeping
145–60	16	Excuses by the Swiss man
161–68	8	Reconciliation
169–76	8	Polichinelle's jealousy
177–94	18	His despair
195–219	25	All the pantomimes

A narrative chaconne from the Opéra may be found in the entrée "La Bergerie" of the opera-ballet *Les Romans* (1736) with music by Niel (score, p. 53):

> During the chaconne Fortune appears, richly dressed and dancing with her magnificent retinue. The shepherds, attracted by her splendor, follow her and allow themselves to be bound by golden chains. The shepherdesses, alarmed, come tenderly to disengage them and enchain them instead with garlands of flowers. The goddess, annoyed by her lack of success, leaves. The happy shepherds continue their dances.

Such indications may be intermittent, but do suggest that other chaconnes may lend themselves to dramatic (not necessarily narrative) treatment, particularly when the music suggests strong contrasts. The chaconne from Act II of Marais's *Sémélé* (1709) is exceptionally vivid; it is not surprising that it was inserted into revivals of operas by other composers in the middle of the eighteenth century, when *ballets figurés* had become accepted on the stage of the Opéra.[86]

THE MUSES' ENTENTE

By the start of the 1730s the Muses were no longer in open competition, even if the balance among them varied from work to work. The works governed by Melpomène could follow a Lullian model or might exhibit features that brought them closer to ballets or pastorales. Thalie, after her exuberant early years at the Opéra, had toned down the humor, and Terpsichore made her expanded presence felt in both time-worn and innovative ways. The attention the *Mercure* now accorded to theatrical spectacles

[86] This chaconne was worked into Lully's *Persée* in 1747 and his *Thésée* in 1754; see Denécheau, "Les opéras de Lully remaniés," 10. The topic of *ballets figurés* is addressed in the forthcoming sequel to this book.

offers a means of assessing the equilibrium that prevailed within and between works during what, in retrospect, can be seen as a sensitive moment in the institution's history – the period just before Rameau's operatic debut. The following summary of the Opéra's repertoire from 1731 to 1733 draws upon the librettos published for each opera and upon the "Spectacles" sections of the *Mercure*.

January and February 1731 saw the continued revival of Lully's *Phaéton* that had begun in late December. This *tragédie en musique* had not been seen since 1721 and was greatly admired; the new décors by Servandoni were particularly pleasing. Already in 1721, the divertissement in Act IV, set in the palace of the Sun, had been reconfigured away from Spring and his followers to include vignettes for four mythological couples, each representing a season – Zéphyr and Flore, Vertumne and Cérès, Bacchus and Arianne, Borée and Orythie. This must have required more dance pieces than Lully's original two (see Table 2-6). The January issue of the *Mercure* devoted a long paragraph to the engraving of Lancret's portrait of Mlle Camargo, now available for purchase. The Opéra also offered a few performances of *Le Carnaval et la Folie*, with the ever popular "Professeur de Folie" in Act III; on 18 January "Le Jaloux trompé," a reworking of "La Sérénade vénitienne" from *Les Fragments de Lully*, was attached to its end. During February, on the last two days of Carnival, "Cariselli" and "Pourceaugnac," "works particularly appropriate to the season," were appended. In early March two special performances of Lully's *Thésée* closed the winter season; following each, Camargo danced *Les Caractères de la danse*.

When the Opéra reopened in April, it was with a revival of Campra's *Idoménée*, which generated no commentary in the *Mercure*. In May the first premiere of the year took place – the *pastorale héroïque, Endymion*, with music by Collin de Blamont; the *Mercure* provided a synopsis but had nothing to say about the dancing. (*Endymion* was never revived.) The May issue of the *Mercure* reported on the spectacular success Marie Sallé was having in London, and imparted the news that she would be returning to Paris in July. June brought a revival of *Les Fêtes vénitiennes*, last seen in 1721, that was so successful, it ran on into the fall. The *Mercure* singled out Blondy's choreography for praise and mentioned that the dance scene that concludes "Le Bal" was particularly applauded. In August Sallé did indeed make her welcome return, dancing a musette, a passepied, and a *pas de deux* with Dupré in *Les Fêtes vénitiennes*. In September, *Phaéton* returned, and in October Lully's *Amadis*, which had not been seen for thirteen years; it continued successfully into November. Camargo did not dance in its early performances, but in November she danced two "airs" in Act IV; these must have been add-ons, given that the original divertissement only had two menuets. "This excellent *danseuse* wanted, no doubt, to share in the success of this opera," opined the *Mercure*. During this same month, the entrée "L'Opéra" was added to the ongoing revival of *Les Fêtes vénitiennes*. Both Sallé and Camargo were now dancing in this work, much to the delight of the public. Nothing new was performed in December, but the parody of

Amadis at the Théâtre Italien mocked the hero for taking a dancer for Oriane in Act IV and parodied the chaconne in Act V.

This overview of 1731 shows a balance between Melpomène and Thalie, but also that the year relied on revivals; there was only one – unsuccessful – new work. In 1732 the balance shifted: *tragédies* dominated the repertoire, only one of them – *Isis* – by Lully. Two were new: *Jephté* was a huge success, *Biblis* a failure. The only ballet performed that year – the *Ballet des Sens* – was also new; it went on to enjoy two revivals. *Jephté* continued its run on into 1733, following a revival of *Omphale*. The *Empire de l'Amour*, a new opera-ballet – also a success – was followed by the reliable *Fêtes grecques et romaines*. Rameau's *Hippolyte et Aricie*, which premiered in October, thus emerged from a period when the *tragédie en musique* had some momentum. But the overview also highlights Terpsichore's impact inside operas. The divertissements in the Lully revivals look to have expanded and the big hits of 1731 – *Le Carnaval et la Folie* and *Les Fêtes vénitiennes* – had always owed a good portion of their success to the dancing. The *Mercure*'s glowing coverage of the star dancers – especially of Camargo and Sallé – extends beyond their performances at the Opéra. It was in January of 1732 that the success of the revived *Callirhoé* provoked the *Mercure* into publishing two poems comparing the two *danseuses* (see Voltaire's verse in Chapter 13, p. 386). Even the parodies at other theaters make hay of the dancing at the Opéra.

Opera historiography, victim of its own prejudices, has painted all the dancing on the stage of the Opéra with the same brush. Yet variety characterizes the dramatic valence of the dancing as much as it does the choice of repertoire. Concepts of genre continue to distinguish most divertissements in tragedies from ones in opera-ballets or pastorales, but cross-genre influences – from both within the Opéra and from other theaters – mean that every work struck its own balance of elements. Even if ways had been developed to allow for independent *cantates* or danced *symphonies* to figure as part of an evening at the Académie Royale de Musique, the institution's core values concerning the integration of the arts remained in place. Moreover, principles of verisimilitude allowed for a whole range of ways for dance to participate as one element among many in the drama. The choices that the Opéra's creators made reveal a gamut of aesthetic agendas, many of them productive of masterpieces, whose full qualities only become recognizable when the entire opera, divertissements and all, is taken into consideration. We may no longer be able to see the spectacle in all its reality with our own eyes, but we can at the very least honor its riches.

Epilogue

In 1735 Campra, who had not composed a new opera since 1718, wrote one last *tragédie en musique*. He had not been absent from the Académie Royale de Musique; over the intervening years works of his had been revived many times and he had been named its *Inspecteur* in 1730. Nonetheless, *Achille et Déidamie*, written with his long-time librettist Danchet, is often seen as a response to *Hippolyte et Aricie*, even though the work was well underway over a year earlier.[1] The opera's failure after only eight performances has been blamed on its divertissements ever since the Commissaire Dubuisson's biting critique from March 1735:[2]

> The Opéra has just given *Achille et Déidame*. [...] What I would like to tell you about the libretto is that the subject is so drowned by the divertissements that no one has wanted to honor the work with the name of tragedy and the author will have to settle for that of pastorale. All that would be required would be to not kill off Déidamie, and, in truth, that would be one less stupidity. As for the music, one hears and loses Campra in turn. But isn't it quite something for an octogenarian to have people sometimes say, "there he is"?

The vivid and much-cited key phrase has become a shorthand for decrying what had supposedly gone wrong in the *tragédie en musique* in the eighteenth century – a radical increase in the number of dances under the influence of the opera-ballet. But does that reframing of Dubuisson's critique have merit? It happens that *Achille et Déidamie* has exactly the same number of dances as *Tancrède*, written in 1702. What, then, can this opera tell us about the status of dance in tragedies in 1735?

Even before the singing starts Danchet's prologue asserts old-fashioned values by locating laurel-crowned statues of Lully and Quinault at the foot of Mount Parnassus above monuments to the goddess of Harmony and the Muse Erato. The other Muses, along with the Graces and Pleasures, are arranged around them. Erato is even shown enchaining Satire – a statement by Campra and Danchet that their own comic works have nothing in common with this one? Glory, Melpomène, and Love all pay homage

[1] According to Argenson's first report about this opera, Danchet's libretto was already finished and the music in progress by July 1732. (II, 455–56)

[2] Letter to the Marquis de Caumont, quoted by Barthélemy, *Campra* (revised ed., 276–77) and cited by Anthony in several publications. Pintiaux's "Achille et Déidamie," which provides a much fuller consideration of this opera's failings, nevertheless reports (p. 221) that, when compared with Campra's earlier tragedies, especially *Tancrède* and *Idoménée*, "*Achille et Déidamie* may seem like a pretext for dances."

to the two creators of French opera. But just when it appears the aesthetic clock has been turned back several decades, Amour seeks out Terpsichore from among her sisters and leads her to the front of the stage. Terpsichore responds to the compliments Amour, Glory, and Melpomène pay her by dancing a 94-bar sequence in eight sections that changes character every few measures – a challenging showpiece for the much-admired Mlle Camargo in yet another operatic spin-off from *Les Caractères de la danse*. A chorus may round off the prologue, but the audience is left with Terpsichore and the Graces before their eyes.

Lully and Quinault did indeed forge an alliance between Melpomène and Amour, and no one could take issue with Glory when she asserts the pair's centrality to French opera. They never, however, constructed a scene anything like the one for Terpsichore, and by including it Danchet and Campra were paying barely veiled tribute to Fuzelier and Collin de Blamont, who had featured Terpsichore in just such a starring role in the prologue to *Les Fêtes grecques et romaines*, a work revived in 1733 and 1734. The audience in the Palais-Royal in 1735 might well have been perplexed after they watched this bifurcated prologue: would the divertissements in the rest of the opera exhibit Quinaultian restraint or Fuzelierian abandon?

Campra, who had written in many more styles than any other composer in his environment, chose conservatism. Danchet, however, had apparently forgotten how to construct a coherent plot. *Achille et Déidamie* recounts the goddess Thétis's attempt to shield her son from the death in battle predicted for him. Achille has been raised on the island of Scyros as a shepherd, unaware of his parentage. Ulisse's ruses succeed in locating him, and after Achille agonizes over leaving the princess with whom he has fallen in love, he departs with Ulisse for Troy. At the premiere of the opera Déidamie killed herself, but Danchet quickly rewrote the libretto to let her survive, weeping over Achille's departure.

The divertissements in Acts I through III, all of them fêtes, come into being through flimsy contrivances that deprive them of the opportunity to engage meaningfully with the storyline. In Act I Thétis tries to convince the restless Achille to stay on Scyros by showing him the happy tritons and nereids who happen by. The Act II divertissement, in honor of Diane, follows Déidamie's reluctant admission of loving the lowly shepherd "Polemon"; its rationale seems to be that they met while hunting. The third act has somewhat more cogency in that Achille / Polemon himself leads a ceremony at the temple of Love, following which he discovers the weapons that Ulisse has left on the altar; his preference for them over garlands of flowers reveals to Ulisse which shepherd is Achille. A generous reading might see all three as depicting the effeminate state in which Achille finds himself thanks to his mother, a point that does not need to be made three times. Danchet seems to be ticking the boxes on time-worn varieties of happy divertissements: old-fashioned nautical (the kind with demi-gods), hunting, and pastoral.

In between Acts III and IV Ulisse reveals to Achille his true identity (another weakness of the libretto is that this moment of discovery does not take place on stage), but his elevation in status does finally provide the divertissements with greater purchase. In Act IV Achille's own people, the Thessaliens, aclaim him their king. This kind of framework has echoes of Quinaultian celebrations of the hierarchy, although it does spin off into celebratory dances for sailors. Act V again draws upon Lullian traditions, by having the gods arm Achille before he goes off to battle, just as had happened in *Persée*'s Act II, even to similar music. Moreover this divertissement has only two dances; it is downright Lullian in its proportions. In fact, throughout the opera Campra was attentive to Lullian practices – that is, to the expanded version of Lullian practices he had adopted in his tragedies from the start. The dances are interwoven with vocal music and the only places multiple dances appear in a row are when there are two of the same type followed by a repeat of the first; even some of these are integrated with dance-songs. Campra eschewed the accretions found in some other tragedies: there are no comic peasants, even though the pastoral contexts could have made them plausible, nor are there any commedia masks, as there were to be in Act IV of the next tragedy mounted at the Opéra, *Scanderberg*. Fewer than half of the dances are generic types, and all of them are well characterized. Campra's dance music does not sound like Lully's, but it does sound French; the only Italianisms come in the *ariettes* that figure in three divertissements, a type of Italianism that had been part of Campra's arsenal since 1708 (*Hippodamie*). There are several substantial choruses, and if a response to *Hippolyte et Aricie* is to be found in this opera, it is in the hunting chorus in Act II.

Only Act IV has practices possibly attributable to the opera-ballet. The "Air pyrrhique," a martial dance that asserts Achille's newly recognized warrior status, was probably performed by the two men listed as a pair among the dancing Thessaliens. Its likely antecedent is the dance for two wrestlers from *Les Fêtes grecques et romaines*, a much applauded choreography (see Chapter 10, p. 304). Another moment comes at the start of the same divertissement. The Thessaliens, who have just learned that they have a king, need encouragement from Ulisse to approach Achille. Campra wrote for them a jolly dance in duple meter that could have served as the opening march, except for the fact that he broke it into four sections, which he interspersed with encouraging words from Ulisse, sung in recitative, that give us a sense of the action: [dance phrase]; "See the hero to whom the gods have submitted you"; [dance phrase]; "Show him your love; approach without hesitation"; [dance phrase]; "It is only to your enemies that he should inspire fear"; [cadence of the dance]. This kind of progressive group action seems like something Fuzelier might have designed, and, in fact, Campra had worked with Fuzelier in the *Ballet des âges* (1718; revived 1724), where, in the prologue there is a danced dialogue between two different groups (see Chapter 13, p. 407). But the only spot in the entire opera that unambiguously crosses the boundary between *tragédie en musique* and opera-ballet comes in the prologue, in the sequence of showy dances for

Terpsichore, whose eight sections gave Mlle Camargo the opportunity to project military affects on the one hand and various shades of love, from joy to sighs – dance moves ratified by the chorus: "Brilliant Glory, tender Love, triumph in turn."

When the whole opera is taken into account, it becomes clear that Glory's statement that Terpsichore is essential serves only to set up Camargo's performance in the prologue. The remaining divertissements are within the norms for this period; some are downright conservative. Soloists did dance within every act, but that kind of distribution had long since become conventional and Campra balanced short divertissements against long ones, just as he had in *Tancrede*. If the divertissements appear oversized, it is because Danchet failed to integrate them. The *Mercure* said nothing at all about the divertissements, but was uncharacteristically blunt about the choice of subject: "not even Apollon could have made it interesting."[3] If a showpiece for Camargo failed to sell tickets, then the problem did not lie in excessive attention to dancing. The fact that recent commentators have been quick to blame the divertissements says more about pre-conceived notions than it does about this opera.

Lully and Quinault had envisaged a central but circumscribed role for dance in their operas, one of its merits being that it allowed for musical and visual sumptuousnous in an otherwise sober art modelled on spoken tragedy. With dance as a core element, French opera developed in ways Italian opera did not; it cultivated an emphasis on groups, who not only gave the protagonists a meaningful social context, but by analogy and contrast could nuance the audience's understanding of the individual characters. Over time and with the infusion of new types of opera, the range of possible relationships among singing and dancing characters expanded, even while concerns with verisimilitude remained fundamental; divertissements had to make sense and what happened within them needed to cohere. Social relationships – the domain of librettist, composer, and choreographer alike – remained fundamental. If our impulse today is to perceive an abundance of dance music as antithetical to drama, it is because we have absorbed other kinds of values over the centuries of opera's development. Once we look and listen, we discover a vast dramatic repertoire, richly deserving of study and performance.

[3] *MF* (March 1735), 546.

Appendix 1 Works Performed at the Académie Royale de Musique, 1695–1732, in Which the Impact of the *Comédie Italienne* Can Be Seen

1695: *Le Ballet des saisons*. Libretto by Pic; music excerpted from ballets and comedy-ballets of J.-B. Lully, arranged and supplemented by Collasse. Opera-ballet: prologue and 4 entrées, each representing one season.

At the end of the fourth entrée, "L'Hiver" (Winter), Apollon appears with Momus to set up a final celebration uniting all four seasons with Les Jeux and Les Plaisirs. The dancing followers of Momus are not identified, but included Arlequin, Arlequine, Pantalons, Polichinelles, and Scaramouches.[1]

1697: *L'Europe galante*. Libretto by La Motte; music by Campra. Opera-ballet with 5 entrées: [Prologue]; "La France"; "L'Espagne"; "L'Italie"; "La Turquie."

This work mixes traditional genres (mythological prologue; a pastorale for "La France") with entrées set in "real" places with contemporary people: a public square in Spain; a ballroom in Italy; a seraglio in Turkey. The Italian entrée borrows character names (Octavio, Olimpia) and situations from the *comédie italienne*, although the plot is not comic.

1698: *Les Fêtes galantes*. Libretto by Duché; music by Desmarest. Ballet: prologue and 3 acts.

The Neapolitan setting for the work (the heroine is queen of Naples, her suitors princes of Sicily, Tuscany, and Persia) allows for arias in Italian in all three divertissements; the third also has dances for Neapolitans costumed for a masked ball.

1699: *Le Carnaval de Venise*. Libretto by Regnard; music by Campra. Ballet: prologue and 3 acts. Last act extended by 2 divertissements: a little opera in Italian, "Orfeo nell'inferi" and a masked ball ("Le Bal").

The main singing characters, one French and three Venetians, belong to the realm of the *innamorati*; the only Italian "masques comiques" appear as dancers in the ball. There is a good deal of Venetian local color, but filtered through French sensibilities. Regnard, who had visited Venice for Carnival in 1678, had already written a number of plays for the Théâtre Italien between 1688 and 1694; this was his only libretto for the Opéra.

1700: revival of *Le Ballet des saisons* (1695)

In this revival the Italian element may have increased: Momus's dancing followers are said to include Arlequine, two Arlequins, two Scaramouchettes, an Allemande, an Allemand,

[1] See Fig. 9–1, p. 271. Information about the dancing roles comes from an attendee at the 1695 performances: see Ladvocat, *Lettres*, 52 and 56–58. Ladvocat remarked upon the novelty of the dances.

Polichinelle, and two little Polichinelles. Two Italian songs were added to the concluding scenes, but were assigned to an Espagnol and an Espagnolette.[2]

1700: revival of *Le Carnaval* (1675). Libretto a pastiche of texts by Benserade and Molière; music by J.-B. Lully. Mascarade: variable number of entrées.

In this revival nine entrées were performed, three of which were sung, all or in part, in Italian. Italianate dancing roles included Polichinelles, Arlequin, Trivelins, Scaramouches, and Matassins.

1702: *Les Fragments de M. de Lully*. Libretto arranged by Danchet; music arranged and supplemented by Campra, on the basis of borrowings from the works of Lully. Opera-ballet: prologue and 4 entrées at the premiere, with 4 others added or used as replacements during the run of performances.

Two entrées take their plots from the *comédie italienne*: in "La Sérénade vénitienne" the Docteur, old and stuttering, wants to marry his young ward, Léonore. Her lover, Eraste, arranges her escape from her balcony with the help of three Scaramouches (dancers), who beat and mock the Docteur amid general rejoicing. "Cariselli," a *divertissement comique*, was sung entirely in Italian. Both also use other commedia masques in dancing roles.

1703: *Ballet des Muses*. Libretto by Danchet; music by Campra. Opera-ballet: prologue and 4 entrées.

After a prologue starring Momus and a chorus of Muses and climaxing in the arrival of Apollon, the four entrées portray the genres of pastoral, satire, tragedy, and comedy. "La Comédie," its setting in ancient Athens notwithstanding, has a comic plot in the manner of the *comédie italienne*, in which a young girl disguises herself as a doctor in order to outwit the old man her father wants her to marry.[3] The successful outcome is celebrated in both a French-style wedding scene and a sung *divertissement italien*.

1703: Revival of Lully's tragedy *Psyché* (1678)

This opera, based on Lully and Molière's *tragédie-ballet* of 1671, has a concluding divertissement involving characters from the *comédie italienne* (Arlequin, Scaramouchette, Trivelins).

1704: *Le Carnaval et la Folie*. Libretto by La Motte; music by Destouches. *Comédie-ballet* (so labeled in the libretto): prologue and 4 acts.

[2] The observations offered here are tentative. The incomplete and conflicting source situation for the *Ballet des saisons* makes it hard to tell how many *comédie italienne* characters figured in the 1695 production and to what music, whereas in the 1700 revival there were clearly several. (The 1695 score contains only the music Collasse contributed to this pastiche; the 1700 score includes the music of Lully, but presumably what was used in 1700, which may not have been the same as in 1695. To complicate matters, the 1700 libretto and the 1700 score have many points of difference.)

[3] According to Anthony, this entrée is "an improbable pastiche made up of elements from Molière's *Amour médecin* and an episode described in Plutarch's lives." *French Baroque Music*, 172.

This work is more French than Italian overall – except that it is hard to conceive of such an opera, in which the personified Carnaval falls in love with Folly and desperately seeks to marry her, as being created at the Opéra outside the Italian-friendly ambience of this period. Moreover, Act III incorporates a little scene called "Le Professeur de folie," framed as a spectacle watched by Momus and Folly and sung mostly in Italian, in which the professor instructs a musician, two dancers, and a poet in the "arte d'allegria." In Act IV, when Folly decides to marry Carnaval, the gods offer their gifts to the bridegroom in little Italian songs with a choral refrain: "Viva, viva, sempre viva, / Il dio dell'allegria."

1705: *La Vénitienne*. Libretto by La Motte; music by La Barre. *Comédie-ballet*: prologue and 3 acts.

In the prologue Momus alludes to the expulsion of the Italian troupe and invites them back for the duration of this work, under the control of Euterpe, "Muse de la musique." In a plot reminiscent of the *comédie italienne*, three *innamorati*, Isabelle, Léonore, and Octave, work out their amourous intrigues with the help of two wily servants, Zerbin and Spinette. The *troupe de masques* that joins in the final celebrations includes Arlequin, Arlequine, Spezzafer, Scaramouchette, and Polichinelle, along with people of different nations, all in dancing roles.

1706: revival of *L'Europe galante* (1697)

1706: "Le Professeur de folie" added to the end of the revival of Lully's *Les Fêtes de l'Amour et de Bacchus* (1672)

1707: revival of the *Ballet des saisons* (1695)

1708: revival of *Les Fragments de M. de Lully* (1702)

This revival did not include either "Cariselli" or the "Sérénade vénitienne." However, the "Fête marine" added an aria in Italian, and the "Bal interrompu" now implied a Venetian setting and had a new comic scene in Italian.

1710: *Les Fêtes vénitiennes*. Libretto by Danchet; music by Campra. Opera-ballet: prologue and multiple entrées.

This enormously popular opera-ballet underwent numerous revisions and substitutions even within its first run of performances, by the end of which there were two versions of the prologue and eight possible entrées, all of them set in Venice, and many in familiar spots such as the Piazza San Marco. In most of the entrées, the main characters are young *innamorati*, but in one, "Le Triomphe de la folie," the main singing characters are Arlequin (in the role of the philosopher Diogenes), Colombine, and the Doctor.

1711: *Les Nouveaux Fragments*, a pastiche of entrées from the *Ballet des Muses*, *Le Carnaval et la Folie*, and *La Vénitienne*.

1711: *Manto la fée*. Libretto by Menesson; music by Stuck. Opera (so labeled in the libretto): prologue and 5 acts.

This opera is set in the realm of the fairies, but the concluding divertissement calls upon spirits "in agreeable disguises," two of whom are Arlequine and Scaramouchette, who dance a chaconne. There is also a da capo aria in Italian.

1712: Revivals of the *Ballet des saisons* (1695) and of *Les Fêtes vénitiennes* (1710).

1712: *Les Amours de Mars et de Vénus*. Libretto by Danchet; music by Campra. Ballet: prologue and 3 acts.

The mythological subject notwithstanding, Momus appears at the end of the work to celebrate the reconciliation of Vénus and Vulcain with a *troupe comique* made up of Arlequin, Pantalon, Mezzetin, Scaramouche, le Docteur, Pierrot, Polichinelle, and other comic characters.

1713: revival of Lully's *Psyché* (1678)

1714: *Les Fêtes de Thalie*. Libretto by La Font; music by Mouret. Opera-ballet: prologue, 3 entrées, and epilogue.

The Muse of Comedy, Thalie, does indeed reign over this entire opera-ballet, whose spirit is much more French than Italian. Nonetheless, the familiar Italian masques (dancers) make an appearance in the third entrée, which is set during a masked ball.

1715: *Les Plaisirs de la paix*. Libretto by Ménesson; music by Bourgeois. Opera-ballet: prologue and 3 entrées, with *intermèdes* between entrées.

The tone of this work is decidedly comic (including a drunken "Fête bacchique" in the second entrée), but the Italian elements are primarily decorative: the first entrée, "L'Assemblée," includes a little courtship scene sung in Italian as an entertainment by Isabella and Valerio, and the entire work is rounded off with the apppearance of Carnaval and a troupe of masques, both serious and comic (i.e., Arlequin et al.).

1715: revival of *L'Europe galante* (1697)

Performances were cut short by the death of Louis XIV on 1 September.

1716: *Les Fêtes de l'été*. Libretto by Pellegrin; music by Montéclair. Opera-ballet: prologue and 3 entrées, to which one added later.

Each entrée represents a time of the day. Despite being set on the banks of the Seine, "Les Soirées" has a *comédie italienne*-esque plot involving the machinations of a young couple and their respective servants in order to avoid her marriage to her old tutor. "Les Nuits," set at a masked ball on the Cours la Reine in Paris, has a plot familiar from masked balls set in Venice, not to mention the obligatory *troupe de masques*.

1717: *Fragments* from previously performed ballets, including the "Sérénade vénitienne" and "Cariselli."

1718: *Ballet des âges*. Libretto by Fuzelier; music by Campra. Opera-ballet: prologue and 3 entrées.

A preface in the libretto argues the rights of Thalie, the Muse of Comedy, to appear on this particular stage, and an Italian tint colors much of the work, especially the third and last entrée, "La Vieillesse," which is set in Padua. In a summarizing scene at the end, Italian masques (Arlequin et al.) celebrate the "Triomphe de la folie" in an Italian song and a French chorus. The first entrée has a *comédie-italienne*-style plot, including a comic nurse sung by a man and many disguises, even though it is set on the banks of the Seine.

1719: revival of *Le Carnaval et la Folie* (1704).

1719: *Les Plaisirs de la campagne*. Libretto by Pelegrin-Barbier; music by Bertin. Opera-ballet: prologue and 3 entrées.

Each entrée represents a different outdoor recreation: fishing, the harvest, and the hunt. In the first, the shipwrecked hero disguises himself as an Italian fisherman and sings an aria in Italian in order to win back his beloved.

1721: revival of *Les Fêtes vénitiennes* (1710).

1722: revival of the *Ballet des saisons* (1707); revival of *Les Fêtes de Thalie* (1714), with a new entrée, "La Provençale."

1724: revival of *L'Europe galante* (1697); revival of *Ballet des âges* (1718).

1725: revival of *Les Fêtes de l'été* (1716).

1726: *Le Ballet sans titre*: fragments including "la Fille" from *Les Fêtes de Thalie*; part of the *Ballet des Muses*; and part of *La Vénitienne*.

1728: *La Princesse d'Élide*. Libretto by Pellegrin; music by Villeneuve. *Ballet héroïque*: prologue and 3 acts.

Although set in a mythological realm, the concluding celebratory divertissement includes "a troupe of Argiens representing ancient mimes, in more modern character," one of whom is Arlequin. "Cariselli" was added to performances of this work in 1729.

1729: *Serpilla e Baiocco* aka *Le Mari joueur et la femme bigotte*, aka *Il marito giocatore e la moglie bacchettona* (1715). Libretto by Salvi; music by Orlandini. *Intermezzo*: 3 acts.

This first Italian opera put on the stage of the Académie Royale de Musique was performed by Rosa Ungarelli and Antonio Ristorini and was followed a week later by another *intermezzo*, *Don Micco e Lesbina*, done by the same two singers. The *intermezzi* were performed with danced and sung divertissements provided by members of the Opéra's troupe, consisting of excerpts from French operas, with an emphasis on ones with an Italian connection. These were the only two Italian operas to be performed at the Opéra until *La serva padrona* in 1752.

1729: *Les Nouveaux Fragments*, drawn from works by Campra and Danchet, including "Les Sérénades et les joueurs" from *Les Fêtes vénitiennes*.

1729: *Les Amours des déesses*. Libretto by Fuzelier; music by Quinault. Opera-ballet: prologue and 3 entrées.

Mezzetin and Mezzetine squeeze into the end of the work.

1730: fragments that include "Pourceaugnac" and "Cariselli."

1730: revival of *Le Carnaval et la Folie* (1704), including "Le Professeur de folie."

1731: "Le Jaloux trompé" (aka "La Sérénade vénitienne") added to *Le Carnaval et la Folie*.

1731: revival of *Les Fêtes vénitiennes* (1710).

Appendix 2 A Partial List of Performances Consisting of "Fragments," 1702–1732[1]

1702: *Les Fragments de M. de Lully*

(The score published by Ballard in 1702 identifies which pieces were taken from which Lully works [for an index, see LWV 79]; the rest were composed by Campra.)

Prologue: from *Les Fêtes de l'Amour et de Bacchus* (Lully)
Première Entrée, "La Fête marine": largely, but not exclusively, excerpts from Lully
Seconde Entrée, "Les Guerriers": largely excerpts from Lully
Troisième Entrée, "La Bergerie": largely excerpts from Lully
Quatrième Entrée, "Les Bohémiens": largely excerpts from Lully
Divertissement comique, "Cariselli": mostly by Campra
Added entrées: all by Campra
"Le Triomphe de Vénus"
"La Sérénade vénitienne"
"Le Bal interrompu"

(The entrées were combined in different ways on different evenings. One libretto includes the prologue, "La Fête marine," "La Bergerie," "Les Bohémiens," and "Cariselli." Another has the same first three parts, then "Le Bal interrompu," "La Sérénade vénitienne," and "Cariselli.")

1704: *Télémaque, tragédie, Fragments des modernes.*

1706: "Le Professeur de folie," from *Le Carnaval et la Folie* (1704), performed after *Les Fêtes de l'Amour et de Bacchus.*

1708: Revival of *Les Fragments de M. de Lully*

Prologue from *Le Temple de la paix*; "La Fête marine" (with changes); "La Bergerie"; "Les Bohémiens"; "Le Bal interrompu" (expanded).

1711: *Les Nouveaux Fragments*

Prologue from *Le Triomphe de l'Amour*; "La Pastorale" from the *Ballet des Muses;* part of Act III of *Le Carnaval et la Folie*; Act III of *La Vénitienne.*

1717: [*Fragments*]

Prologue from *La Grotte de Versailles*; "La Sérénade vénitienne" from *Les Fragments de M. de Lully*; "L'Amour médecin" from *Ballet des Muses*; "Le Bal interrompu;" and "Cariselli," both from *Les Fragments de M. de Lully.*

[1] Unless otherwise noted, this information comes from the article "Fragments" in Parfaict, *Dictionnaire*, II, 635–42 and from librettos in F-Po.

1722: [*Fragments*][2]
Cantate of *Démocrite et Héroclite* by Stuck; "Pourceaugnac" by Lully; *cantate* of *Silène et Bacchus* by Campra; "Le Professeur de folie" from *Le Carnaval et la Folie*; "Le Bal" from *Les Fêtes vénitiennes*; an *ariette* in Italian.

1726: *Le Ballet des ballets*[3]
"Le Professeur de folie" from *Le Carnaval et la Folie*; "La Turquie" from *L'Europe galante; cantate* of *Zéphyre et Flore* (Bourgeois); the scene of the dance and music masters from "Le Bal" in *Les Fêtes vénitiennes;* "Les Caractères de la dance," performed by Mlle Prévost; "La Provençale" from *Les Fêtes de Thalie.*

1726: *Le Ballet sans titre*
Prologue from *Méléagre*; "La Fille" from *Les Fêtes de Thalie*; "La Comédie" from the *Ballet des Muses*; and Act III of *La Vénitienne.*

1729: *Les Nouveaux Fragments*
Prologue from *Les Amours de Mars et de Vénus*; "La Fête marine" from *Les Fêtes vénitiennes*; "La Pastorale" from the *Ballet des Muses*; "Les Sérénades et les joueurs" from *Les Fêtes vénitiennes.*

1730: [*Fragments*][4]
Prologue from *Les Amours de Mars et de Vénus*; "La Pastorale héroïque";[5] "Pourceaugnac"; "Cariselli."

1730: Revival of *Télémaque* (1704).

[2] This set of pieces was done several times by a small group of performers at the Opéra, while the rest were in various châteaux performing during the festivities surrounding Louis XV's coronation. *MF* (November 1722), II, 156–58.

[3] *MF* (April 1726), 805, and Parfaict, *Dictionnaire*, I, 366–67. [4] *MF* (February 1730), 376.

[5] A one-act work by François Rebel, set to a libretto by La Serre, written in 1730 to honor the birth of the Dauphin and first appended to Campra's *Hésione*.

BIBLIOGRAPHY

SEVENTEENTH- AND EIGHTEENTH-CENTURY SOURCES

Argenson, Marquis de Paulmy d'. *Notices sur les œuvres de théâtre*. 2 vols. Ed. Henri Lagrave. Geneva, 1966.

Beffara, Louis-François. *Dictionnaire de l'Académie royale de musique (1783–1784)*. F-Po Rés. 602.

Boindin, Nicolas. *Lettres historiques sur tous les spectacles de Paris*. Paris, 1719.

Bonin, Louis. *Die neueste Art zur galanten und theatralischen Tanz-Kunst*. Frankfurt, Leipzig, 1711. Rpt. Berlin: Edition Hentrich, 1996.

Bonnet, Jacques. *Histoire générale de la danse sacrée et profane*. Paris, 1723. Rpt. Geneva: Slatkine, 1969.

Cahusac, Louis de. *La Danse ancienne et moderne ou Traité historique de la danse*. The Hague, 1754. Rpt. Geneva: Slatkine, 1971. Ed. Nathalie Lecomte, Laura Naudeix, and Jean-Noël Laurenti. Paris: Éditions Desjonquères / Centre National de la Danse, 2004.

Dictionnaire de l'Académie française. Paris, 1694.

Dubos, Jean-Baptiste. *Réflexions critiques sur la poésie et sur la peinture* (Paris: Mariette, 1719). Trans. Thomas Nugent as *Critical Reflections on Poetry, Painting, and Music, with an Inquiry into the Rise and Progress of the Theatrical Entertainments of the Ancients*. 5th ed. London, 1748.

Durey de Noinville, Jacques Bernard. *Histoire du théâtre de l'opéra en France depuis l'établissement de l'Académie Royale de Musique jusqu'à présent*. Paris: Barthou, 1753.

Encyclopédie, ou Dictionnaire raisonné des sciences, des arts, et des métiers. Ed. Denis Diderot and Jean Le Rond d'Alembert. Paris: Briasson & Durand, 1751–80.

Ferrère, Auguste. *Partition et chorégraphie* (1782). F-Po Rés. 68.

Feuillet, Raoul Anger. *Chorégraphie, ou l'art de décrire la danse*. Paris, 1700. Rpt. New York: Broude Bros., 1968.

Feuillet, Raoul Anger (ed.). *Recueil de dances contenant un très grand nombre des meilleurs entrées de ballet de Monsieur Pécour et recueillies et mises au jour par Monsieur Feuillet*. Paris, 1704. Rpt. Westmead: Gregg International, 1972.

Furetière, Antoine. *Dictionnaire universel*. The Hague and Rotterdam, 1690.

Gaudrau, Michel (ed.). *Nouveau recueil de danse de bal et celle de ballet contenant un très grand nombre des meilleures entrées de ballet de Monsieur Pécour et recueillies et mises au jour par Monsieur Gaudrau*. Paris, [1713].

[Gherardi, Evariste.] *Le Théâtre italien de Gherardi, ou le recueil général de toutes les comédies et scènes françaises jouées par les comédiens italiens du roi*. Amsterdam, 1701. 6 vols. Rpt. of 1741 edition, Geneva: Slatkine, 1969. Excerpts ed. Charles Mazouer as *Le Théâtre italien*. Paris: Société des Textes Français Modernes, 1994.

L'Abbé, Anthony. *A New Collection of Dances*. London: *c*. 1725. Rpt. introduced by Carol G. Marsh. London: Stainer & Bell, 1991.

Ladvocat, Louis. *Lettres sur l'opéra à l'abbé Dubos*. Ed. Jérôme de La Gorce. Paris: Cicero, 1993.

Lambranzi, Gregorio. *Neue und curieuse theatrialische Tantz-Schul*. Nuremberg, 1716. Trans. Derra de Moroda and ed. Cyril W. Beaumont as *New and Curious School of Theatrical Dancing*. New York: Dance Horizons, 1966.

Lecerf de la Viéville, Jean-Laurent. *Comparaison de la musique italienne et de la musique française*. Paris, 1704–1706. Rpt. of Brussels edition, Geneva: Minkoff, 1972.

Le Roussau, F. *A Collection of New Ball- and Stage Dances, 1720*. GB-Eu Ms. LA. III/673. Facsimile with notes by Jennifer Thorp. Lulu.com, 2008.

Le Sage, Alain René and J.-P. d'Orneval. *Le Théâtre de la foire, ou l'opéra-comique*. 9 vols. Paris, 1721–1737.

Lorin, André. *Livre de contredanse*. F-Pn ms. fr. 1697. Facsimile ed. Julia Sutton as *Dances for the Sun King*. Annapolis, MD: Colonial Music Institute, 2008.

Magri, Gennaro. *Trattato teorico-prattico di ballo*. Naples, 1779. Trans. Mary Skeaping as *Theoretical and Practical Treatise on Dancing*. London: Dance Books, 1988.

Menestrier, Claude-François. *Des Ballets anciens et modernes selon les règles du théâtre*. Paris, 1682. Rpt. Geneva: Minkoff, 1972 and 1984.

Mercure de France. Paris, 1724–1791. Rpt. Geneva: Slatkine, 1974.

Mercure galant (aka *Nouveau Mercure galant; Nouveau Mercure; Le Mercure)*. Paris 1677–1723.

Montéclair, Michel Pignolet de. *Principes de musique*. Paris, [1736].

Nemeitz, Joachim Christophe. *Séjour de Paris, c'est-à-dire, Instructions fidèles pour les voyageurs de condition*. 2nd ed. Leiden, 1727.

Noverre, Jean-Georges. *Lettres sur la danse et sur les ballets*. Lyon, 1760. Rpt. of 1760 Stuttgart edition, New York: Broude Brothers, 1967.

Parfaict, Claude and François. *Dictionnaire des théâtres de Paris*. Paris, 1756. Rpt. of 1770 ed., Geneva: Slatkine, 1967.

Histoire de l'Académie Royale de Musique (1741). F-Pn (Manuscrits) fonds fr. nouv. acq. 6532.

Mémoires pour servir à l'histoire des spectacles de la foire. Paris, 1743.

Parodies du Nouveau Théâtre Italien. 4 vols. Paris, 1738.

Pécour, Guillaume-Louis; see Feuillet (ed.) and Gaudrau (ed.).

Pure, Michel de. *Idée des spectacles anciens et nouveaux*. Paris, 1668. Rpt. Geneva: Minkoff, 1972 and 1985.

Raguenet, François. *Parallèle des Italiens et des Français en ce qui regarde la musique et les opéra*. Paris, 1702.

Rameau, Pierre. *Le Maître à danser*. Paris, 1725. Rpt. New York: Broude Brothers, 1967. Trans. J. Essex as *The Dancing Master*. London, 1728. Also trans. Cyril W. Beaumont as *The Dancing Master*. London: Beaumont, 1931; rpt. Alton: Dance Books, 2003.

Règles pour faire des ballets. Ms, 195p. F-Po C. 4844.

Regnard, Jean-François. *Les Comédies italiennes de J. F. Regnard*, republished in *Évariste Gherardi: Le Théâtre italien*, vol. 2. Ed. Roger Guichemerre. Paris: Société des Textes Français Modernes, 1996.

Saint-Didier, Alexandre-Toussaint Limojon de. *La Ville et la république de Venise*. 4th ed. The Hague, 1685.

Saint-Hubert, Monsieur de. *La Manière de composer et faire réussir les ballets*. Paris, 1641.

Saint-Lambert, Monsieur de. *Les Principes du clavecin*. Paris, 1702. Trans. R. Harris-Warrick. Cambridge University Press, 1984.
Saint-Mard, Rémond de. *Réflexions sur l'opéra*. The Hague, 1741.
Tomlinson, Kellom. *The Art of Dancing*. London, 1735. Rpt. Farnborough: Gregg International, 1970.

SCORES AND LIBRETTOS

Individual scores and librettos, whether from the seventeenth and eighteenth centuries or in modern editions, are mentioned in the relevant chapters. Three important collected series were consulted.

Lully, Jean-Baptiste. *Œuvres complètes*. General editor Henry Prunières. Paris: Éditions de la Revue Musicale, 1930–39. Rpt. New York: Broude Brothers, 1966. Three of the ten volumes include operas: *Cadmus et Hermione, Alceste, Amadis*.
Lully, Jean-Baptiste. *Œuvres complètes*. General editors Jérôme de La Gorce and Herbert Schneider. Hildesheim: Olms, 2001–
Series I (Ballets et mascarades), VI: *Ballet des Saisons, Les Amours déguisez, Ballet royal de Flore* (2001)
Series II (Comédies-ballets et autres divertissements), IV: *Monsieur de Pourceaugnac, Le Bourgeois Gentilhomme* (2006); VI: *Psyché* (2007)
Series III (Opéras), IV: *Thésée* (2010); VI: *Isis* (2014); XIV: *Armide* (2003).
Recueil général des opéra représentés par l'Académie Royale de Musique depuis son établissement. 16 vols. Paris: Ballard, 1703–1746. Rpt. Geneva: Slatkine, 1971. For Quinault's librettos, see also Norman (ed.).

SOURCES SINCE 1800

Abbreviations

ACRAS	Association pour un Centre de Recherche sur les Arts du Spectacle aux 17e et 18e Siècles
COJ	*Cambridge Opera Journal*
EM	*Early Music*
JAMS	*Journal of the American Musicological Society*
JSCM	*Journal of Seventeenth-Century Music* (online, open access)
ML	*Music and Letters*
PRMA	*Proceedings of the Royal Musical Association*
RdM	*Revue de musicologie*
RMFC	*Recherches sur la musique française classique*
SDHS	Society of Dance History Scholars

Alm, Irene. "Operatic ballroom scenes and the arrival of French social dance in Venice." *Studi musicali* 25 (1996): 345–71.
"Winged feet and mute eloquence: Dance in seventeenth-century Venetian opera." *COJ* 15.3 (2003): 216–80.

Andrijeski, Julie. "The elusive loure." *Proceedings of the 21st Annual Conference of SDHS* (University of Oregon, 1998): 295–300.

Anthony, James R. "Air and aria added to French opera from the death of Lully to 1720." *RdM* 77.2 (1991): 201–19.

French Baroque Music from Beaujoyeulx to Rameau. Revised and expanded ed. Portland, OR: Amadeus Press, 1997.

"The French opera-ballet in the early 18th century: Problems of definition and classification." *JAMS* 18.2 (1965): 197–206.

"Printed editions of André Campra's *L'Europe galante*." *Musical Quarterly* 56.1 (1970): 54–73.

Antoine, Michel. "Les Magny: Danseurs du roi de France et du duc de Lorraine." *Annales de l'est* 5e série, 10e année.1 (1959): 1–22.

Astier, Régine. "François Marcel and the art of teaching dance in the eighteenth century." *Dance Research* 2.2 (1984): 11–23.

"Françoise Prévost: The unauthorized biography." In Brooks (ed.), *Women's Work*, 123–59.

"Louis XIV, 'Premier danseur'." *Sun King: The Ascendancy of French Culture during the Reign of Louis XIV*. Ed. David Lee Rubin. Washington: Folger Books, 1992. 73–102.

"Michel Gaudrau: Un danseur presque ordinaire." *Les Goûts-réünis, numéro spécial: La Danse baroque* (1982): 59–66.

"Pierre Beauchamps and the *ballets de collège*." *Dance Chronicle* 6.2 (1983): 138–63.

"La vie quotidienne." *Les Goûts réunis, numéro spécial: La Danse baroque* (1982): 30–39.

Aubry, Pierre and Emile Dacier. *Les Caractères de la Danse: Histoire d'un divertissement pendant la première moitié du XVIIIe siècle*. Paris: Champion, 1905.

Auld, Louis E. "'Dealing in shepherds': The pastoral ploy in nascent French opera." *French Musical Thought, 1600–1800*. Ed. Georgia Cowart. Ann Arbor: UMI Research Press, 1989. 53–79.

Banducci, Antonia. "Staging a *tragédie en musique*: A 1748 promptbook of Campra's *Tancrède*." *EM* 21.2 (1993): 180–90.

"Staging and its dramatic effect in French baroque opera: Evidence from prompt notes." *Eighteenth-Century Music* 1.1 (2004): 5–28.

Barros, Ricardo. *Dance as a Discourse: The Rhetorical Expression of the Passions in French Baroque Dance*. Saarbrücken: Lambert, 2010.

Barthélemy, Maurice. *André Campra (1660–1744): Étude biographique et musicologique*. Arles: Actes Sud, 1995. Revised and expanded ed. of *André Campra: Sa vie et son œuvre* (1957).

Métamorphoses de l'opéra français au siècle des Lumières. Arles: Actes Sud, 1990.

"L'opéra-comique des origines à la Querelle des Bouffons." *L'Opéra-comique en France au XVIIIe siècle*. Ed. Philippe Vendrix. Liège: Mardaga, 1992. 9–78.

Beaucé, Pauline. *Parodies d'opéra au siècle des Lumières: Évolution d'un genre comique*. Rennes: Presses Universitaires de Rennes, 2013.

Beaussant, Philippe. *Lully ou le musicien du Soleil*. Paris: Gallimard, 1992.

Betzwieser, Thomas. *Exotismus und "Türkenoper" in der französischen Musik des Ancien Régime*. Laaber: Laaber-Verlag, 1993.

"Musical setting and scenic movement: Chorus and *chœur dansé* in eighteenth-century Parisian opera." *COJ* 12.1 (2000): 1–28.

Bloechl, Olivia. *Native American Song at the Frontiers of Early Modern Music*. Cambridge University Press, 2008.

Bourqui, Claude. *Les Sources de Molière*. Paris: Sedes, 1999.

Brooks, Lynn Matluck (ed.) *Women's Work: Making Dance in Europe before 1800*. Madison: University of Wisconsin Press, 2007.

Burgess, Geoffrey. "The chaconne and the representation of sovereign power in Lully's *Amadis* (1684) and Charpentier's *Médée* (1693)." In McCleave (ed.), *Dance and Music*, 81–104.

"Revisiting *Atys*: Reflections on Les Arts Florissants' production." *EM* 34.3 (2006): 465–78.

Burke, Peter. *The Fabrication of Louis XIV*. New Haven, CT and London: Yale University Press, 1992.

Campardon, Emile. *L'Académie Royale de Musique au XVIIIe siècle*. 2 vols. Paris: Berger-Levrault, 1884.

Les Spectacles de la foire. 2 vols. Paris: Berger-Levrault, 1877.

Cessac, Catherine. *Jean-Féry Rebel (1666–1747): Musicien des Éléments*. Paris: CNRS, 2007.

Marc-Antoine Charpentier. Paris: Fayard, 1988. Trans. E. Thomas Glasow. Portland, OR: Amadeus, 1995.

"Marc-Antoine Charpentier et les pièces à machines." *Littératures classiques* 21 (1994): 118–21.

Cessac, Catherine (ed.) *Itinéraires d'André Campra: D'Aix à Versailles, de l'Église à l'Opéra (1660–1744)*. Wavre., Belgium: Mardaga, 2012.

Charlton, David. *Opera in the Age of Rousseau: Music, Confrontation, Realism*. Cambridge University Press, 2013.

Christout, Marie-Françoise. *Le Ballet de cour de Louis XIV, 1643–1672*. Paris: A. et J. Picard, 1967.

Coeyman, Barbara. "Theatres for opera and ballet during the reigns of Louis XIV and Louis XV." *EM* 18.1 (1990): 22–37.

"Walking through Lully's opera theatre in the Palais Royal." In Heyer (ed.), *Lully Studies*, 216–42.

Colonna, Deda Cristina. "Les Chaconnes d'Arlequin." *Aspetti della cultura di danza nell'Europa del Settecento*. Ed. Fabio Mòllica. Bologna: Libri della Società di Danza, 2001. 41–56.

"The 'Demoiselle' behind the score: A tentative technical portrait of Mlle Guiot as she appears in the choreographies bearing her name in the Pécour-Gaudrau collection." Proceedings of the second Rothenfelser Tanzsymposium (2008): *Vom Schäfferidyll zur Revolution: Europäische Tanzkultur im 18. Jahrhundert*. Freiburg: Fa-gisis Musik- und Tanzedition, 2008. 39–51.

Cornic, Sylvain. "*Ad limina templi Polymniae*: Les fonctions du prologue d'opéra chez Quinault." *Recherches des jeunes dix-septiémistes: Actes du Ve colloque du Centre International de Rencontres sur le XVIIe siècle*. Ed. Charles Mazouer. Bordeaux: Université Michel de Montaigne–Bordeaux III; Gunter Narr Verlag, 1999. 47–62.

Couvreur, Manuel. *Jean-Baptiste Lully: Musique et dramaturgie au service du prince*. Brussels: Marc Vokar, 1992.

Cowart, Georgia. "Carnival in Venice or protest in Paris? Louis XIV and the politics of subversion at the Paris Opéra." *JAMS* 54.2 (2001): 265–302.

"Of women, sex and folly: Opera under the Old Regime." *COJ* 6.3 (1994): 205–20.

The Triumph of Pleasure: Louis XIV and the Politics of Spectacle. University of Chicago Press, 2008.

Cyr, Mary. "Basses and *basse continue* in the orchestra of the Paris Opéra 1700–1764." *EM* 10.2 (1982): 155–70.

"The dramatic role of the chorus in French opera: Evidence for the use of gesture, 1670–1770." *Opera and the Enlightenment*. Ed. Thomas Bauman and Marita Petzoldt McClymonds. Cambridge University Press, 1995. 105–18.

Dacier, Emile. *Une Danseuse de l'Opéra sous Louis XV: Mlle Sallé (1707–1756)*. Paris: Plon, 1909.

Dartois-Lapeyre, Françoise. "Danser à l'Académie royale de musique et à la Comédie-Française au XVIIIe siècle." *L'Opéra de Paris, la Comédie-Française et l'Opéra-Comique: Approches comparées (1669–2010)*. Ed. Denis Herlin, Sabine Chaouche, and Solveig Serre. Paris: École des Chartes, 2012. 281–302.

"*Les Fêtes vénitiennes* et leurs reprises: Un cas atypique." In Cessac (ed.), *Itinérairies d'André Campra*, 123–36.

Denécheau, Pascal. "Les opéras de Lully remaniés par Rebel et Francoeur entre 1744 et 1767: Héritage ou modernité?" *La Notion d'héritage dans l'histoire de la musique*. Ed. Cécile Davy-Rigaux. Paris: Éditions électroniques de l'IReMus, collections "Séminaires": forthcoming.

"Thésée de Lully et Quinault, histoire d'un opéra: Étude de l'œuvre de sa création à sa dernière reprise sous l'Ancien Régime (1675–1779)." Unpublished Ph.D. dissertation, Université de Paris IV / Universität des Saarlandes, 2006.

Denécheau, Pascal and Solveig Serre. "Sauts, gambades et monnaie de singe: Les représentations pour la capitation du personnel de l'Opéra sous l'Ancien Régime." *RdM* 97.1 (2011): 35–60.

Ducrot, Ariane. "Les représentations de l'Académie royale de musique à Paris au temps de Louis XIV (1671–1715)." *RMFC* 10 (1970): 19–55.

Duron, Jean (ed.) *Cadmus et Hermione (1673) de Jean-Baptiste Lully et Philippe Quinault: Livret, études et commentaires*. Wavre, Belgium: Mardaga, 2008.

Le Carnaval de Venise d'André Campra et Jean-François Regnard: Livret, études et commentaires. Wavre, Belgium: Mardaga, 2010.

Ellis, Meredith. "The dances of J.-B. Lully (1632–1687)." Unpublished Ph.D. dissertation, Stanford University, 1967.

"Inventory of the dances of Jean-Baptiste Lully." *RMFC* 9 (1969): 21–55.

See also Little, Meredith Ellis.

Eppelsheim, Jürgen. *Das Orchester in den Werken Jean-Baptiste Lullys*. Tützing: Hans Schneider, 1961.

Fader, Don. "The 'Cabale du Dauphin,' Campra, and Italian comedy: The courtly politics of French musical patronage around 1700." *ML* 86.3 (2005): 380–413.

Fairfax, Edmund. *The Styles of Eighteenth-Century Ballet*. Lanham, MD: Scarecrow, 2003.

Fajon, Robert. *L'Opéra à Paris du Roi Soleil à Louis le Bien-Aimé*. Geneva: Slatkine, 1984.

Gaudefroy-Demombynes, Géraldine. "*Achille et Polyxène*: The Trojan war and a plea for peace at the Académie royale de musique." *EM* 43.3 (2015): 397–415.

Girdlestone, Cuthbert M. *La Tragédie en musique (1673–1750) considérée comme genre littéraire*. Geneva: Droz, 1972.

Goff, Moira. *The Incomparable Hester Santlow: A Dancer-Actress on the Georgian Stage*. Aldershot: Ashgate, 2007.

"Masks and disguises: Guyot, Prévost, Pécour and duets for female dancers." In Okamoto (ed.), *Structures and Metaphors*, 21–39.

"Steps, gestures, and expressive dancing: Magri, Ferrère, and John Weaver." In Harris-Warrick and Brown (eds.), *The Grotesque Dancer*, 199–230.

"Surprising monsters: The first female professional dancers." *Proceedings of Terpsichore 1450–1900: International Dance Conference*. Ed. Barbara Ravelhofers. Ghent: Institute for Historical Dance Practice, 2000. 179–87.

Gros, Etienne. *Philippe Quinault: Sa vie et son oeuvre*. Paris: Honoré Champion, 1926.

Grout, Donald Jay. "The music of the Italian theatre at Paris, 1682–97." *Papers of the American Musicological Society* (1941): 158–70.

"Seventeenth-century parodies of French opera." *Musical Quarterly* 27 (1941): 211–19 and 514–26.

Guest, Ivor. *The Paris Opéra Ballet*. Alton, Hampshire: Dance Books, 2006.

Guilcher, Jean-Michel. *La Contredanse et les renouvellements de la danse française*. Paris: Mouton, 1969. New edition: *La Contredanse: Un tournant dans l'histoire française de la danse*. Brussels: Complexe, 2003.

Guillo, Laurent. "L'édition musicale française avant et après Lully." *L'Invention des genres lyriques français et leur redécouverte au XIXe siècle*. Ed. Agnès Terrier and Alexandre Dratwicki. Lyon: Symétrie, 2010. 79–98.

Hansell, Kathleen K. "Theatrical ballet and Italian opera." *Opera on Stage. History of Italian Opera*, Part II. Ed. Lorenzo Bianconi and Giorgio Pestelli. Chicago and London: University of Chicago Press, 2002. 177–308.

Harris-Warrick, Rebecca. "Ballet, pantomime, and the sung word in the operas of Rameau." *Coll'astuzia, col giudizio: Essays in Honor of Neal Zaslaw*. Ed. Cliff Eisen. Ann Arbor: Steglein, 2009. 31–61.

"Le bal masqué selon Campra." In Cessac (ed.), *Itinéraires d'André Campra*, 181–91.

"Ballroom dancing at the court of Louis XIV." *EM* 14.1 (1986): 41–49.

"Le comique sur la scène de l'Académie Royale de Musique à l'époque de Campra." In Duron (ed.), *Le Carnaval de Venise*, 61–78.

"Comment terminer un opéra?" *Jean-Philippe Rameau: Entre Art et Science*. Ed. Sylvie Bouissou. Paris: École des Chartes, 2016.

"Contexts for choreographies: Notated dances set to the music of Jean-Baptiste Lully." In La Gorce and Schneider (eds.), *Jean-Baptiste Lully*, 433–55.

"Dance and representation in the operas of Lully." *'L'Esprit Français' und die Musik Europas (Festschrift in honor of Herbert Schneider)*. Ed. Michelle Biget-Mainfroy and Rainer Schmusch. Hildesheim: Olms, 2007. 208–18.

"La danse dans *Cadmus et Hermione*." In Duron (ed.), *Cadmus et Hermione*, 231–50.

"A few thoughts on Lully's *hautbois*." *EM* 18.1 (1990): 97–106.

"French dance music on the London stage in the time of John Rich." Unpublished paper given at the conference *John Rich and the 18th-Century London Stage*. London, 2008.

"Louis XIV et la danse." *Le Prince et la musique: Les passions musicales de Louis XIV*. Ed. Jean Duron. Wavre, Belgium: Mardaga, 2009. 117–36.

"Lully's on-stage societies." *Opera and Society in Italy and France from Monteverdi to Bourdieu*. Ed. Jane F. Fulcher, Victoria Johnson, and Thomas Ertman. Cambridge University Press, 2007. 53–71.

"Magnificence in motion: Stage musicians in Lully's ballets and operas." *COJ* 6.3 (1994): 189–203.

"La Mariée: The history of a French court dance." In Heyer (ed.), *Jean-Baptiste Lully*, 239–58.

"Naturalizing novelty: Italian opera as Parisian audiences saw it in 1729." *"Virtute et arte del danzare": Contributi di storia della danza in onore di Barbara Sparti*. Ed. Alessandro Pontremoli. Rome: Aracne Editrice, 2011. 165–79.

"The phrase structures of Lully's dance music." In Heyer (ed.), *Lully Studies*, 32–56.

"Reading *Roland*." *JSCM* 16 (2010).

"Recovering the Lullian divertissement." In McCleave (ed.), *Dance and Music*, 55–80. Rpt. in *Studies in Seventeenth-Century Opera*. Ed. Beth Glixon. Farnham: Ashgate, 2010. 333–58.

"'Roland apprenant l'infidélité d'Angélique': Les différentes versions de l'acte IV de *Roland* au fil des reprises." In Laurenti (ed.), *Le Tableau et la scène*, 99–107.

"Staging Venice." *COJ* 15.3 (2003): 297–316.

Harris-Warrick, Rebecca and Bruce Alan Brown (eds.). *The Grotesque Dancer on the Eighteenth-Century Stage: Gennaro Magri and his World*. Madison: University of Wisconsin Press, 2005.

Harris-Warrick, Rebecca and Carol G. Marsh. *Musical Theatre at the Court of Louis XIV: Le Mariage de la Grosse Cathos*. Cambridge University Press, 1994.

Hazebroucq, Hubert. "De la danse comme geste au début du XVIIIe siècle: Ou, de la signification des danses virtuoses abstraites." Unpublished paper given at the conference *Gesture on the French Stage, 1675–1800* (Utrecht, NL, August 2010).

"Les danses de l'acte IV de *Roland*: Questions de reconstruction et d'interprétation." In Laurenti (ed.), *Le Tableau et la scène*, 108–22.

Heyer, John Hadju (ed.). *Jean-Baptiste Lully and the Music of the French Baroque: Essays in Honor of James R. Anthony*. Cambridge University Press, 1989.

Lully Studies. Cambridge University Press, 2000.

Hilton, Wendy. *Dance of Court and Theater: The French Noble Style 1690–1725*. Princeton: Princeton Book Company, 1981. Expanded reprint, *Dance and Music of Court and Theater: Selected Writings of Wendy Hilton*. Stuyvesant, NY: Pendragon Press, 1997.

"Dances to music by Jean-Baptiste Lully." *EM* 14.1 (1986): 51–63.

Hitchcock, H. Wiley. *Les Œuvres de Marc-Antoine Charpentier: Catalogue raisonné*. Paris: Picard, 1982.

Marc-Antoine Charpentier. Oxford University Press, 1990.

Howard, Patricia. "The influence of the Précieuses on content and structure in Quinault's and Lully's *tragédies lyriques*." *Acta Musicologica* 63 (1991): 57–72.

Hunter, Mary. "The *alla turca* style in the late eighteenth century: race and gender in the symphony and the seraglio." *The Exotic in Western Music*. Ed. Jonathan Bellman. Boston: Northeastern University Press, 1998. 43–73.

The International Encyclopedia of Dance. Ed. Selma Jeanne Cohen and Dance Perspectives Foundation. Oxford University Press, 1998.

Kintzler, Catherine. *Poétique de l'opéra français de Corneille à Rousseau*. Culture et société. [Paris]: Minerve, 1991.

"Representations of 'le peuple' in French opera, 1673–1764." *Opera and Society in Italy and France from Monteverdi to Bourdieu*. Ed. Jane F. Fulcher, Victoria Johnson, and Thomas Ertman. Cambridge University Press, 2007. 72–86.

"La tragédie lyrique et le double défi d'un théâtre classique." *La Tragédie lyrique*. Carnets du Théâtre des Champs-Elysées. Paris: Cicero, 1991. 51–63.

La Gorce, Jérôme de. "L'Académie Royale de Musique en 1704, d'après des documents inédits conservés dans les archives notariales." *RdM* 65.2 (1979): 160–91.

Berain: Dessinateur du Roi-Soleil. Paris: Éditions Herscher, 1986.

"De l'opéra-ballet aux fragments." *XVIIe Siècle* 198 (1998): 37–50.

Féeries d'opéra: Décors, machines et costumes en France, 1645–1765. Paris: Éditions du patrimoine, 1997.

"Guillaume-Louis Pecour: A biographical essay." *Dance Research* 8.2 (1990): 3–26.

Jean-Baptiste Lully. Paris: Fayard, 2002.

"Lully's first opera: A rediscovered poster for *Les Fêtes de l'Amour et de Bacchus*." *EM* 15.3 (1987): 308–14.

L'Opéra à Paris au temps de Louis XIV. Paris: Éditions Desjonquères, 1992.

"L'orchestre de l'Opéra et son évolution de Campra à Rameau." *RdM* 76.1 (1990): 23–43.

"Some notes on Lully's orchestra." In Heyer (ed.), *Jean-Baptiste Lully*, 99–112.

"Tempêtes et tremblements de terre dans l'opéra français sous le règne de Louis XIV." *Le Mouvement en musique à l'époque baroque*. Ed. Hervé Lacombe. Metz: Éditions Serpenoise, 1996. 171–88.

"Vogue et influence de l'air italien dans l'opéra français autour de 1700." *Studi Musicali* 25.1–2 (1996): 197–207.

La Gorce, Jérôme de (ed.) *Menus Plaisirs du roi: Inventaire des œuvres d'art graphique des Recueils des Menus Plaisirs des Archives nationales (CP/O/1/3238 à 3242/C)*. In ARCHIM, online database, Paris: Archives nationales, 2010–2011. http://www.culture.gouv.fr/documentation/archim/menus-plaisirs.html

La Gorce, Jérôme de and Herbert Schneider (eds.) *Jean-Baptiste Lully (1632–1687), Actes du Colloque/Kongreßbericht, Saint-Germain-en-Laye–Heidelberg 1987*. Laaber: Laaber-Verlag, 1990.

Quellenstudien zu Jean-Baptiste Lully: Hommage à Lionel Sawkins. Hildesheim: Olms Verlag, 1999.

La Laurencie, Lionel de. "André Campra, musicien profane." *L'Année musicale* 3 (1913): 153–205.

L'École française du violon de Lully à Viotti. 2 vols. Paris: Librairie Delagrave, 1922.

"*L'Orfeo nell'inferni* d'André Campra." *Revue de Musicologie* 9 (1928): 129–33.

Lada-Richards, Ismene. "Dead but not extinct: On reinventing pantomime dancing in eighteenth-century England and France." *The Ancient Dancer in the Modern World: Responses to Greek and Roman Dance*. Ed. Fiona Macintosh. Oxford University Press, 2010. 19–38.

Lagrave, Henri. *Le Théâtre et le public à Paris de 1715 à 1750*. Paris: Klinksieck, 1972.

Lajarte, Théodore. *Bibliothèque musicale du théâtre de l'Opéra: Catalogue historique, chronologique, anecdotique*. Paris: Librairie des Bibliophiles, 1878. Rpt. Hildesheim: Olms, 1969.

Lalonger, Edith. "Les chaconnes d'Arlequin conservées en notation Feuillet." In Laurenti (ed.), *Arlequin danseur*, 13–17.

"J. F. Rebel's *Les Caractères de la danse*: Interpretative choices and their relationship to dance research." In McCleave (ed.), *Dance and Music*, 105–23.

Lancelot, Francine. *La Belle Dance: Catalogue raisonné fait en l'an 1995*. Paris: Van Dieren Éditeur, 1996.

Laurenti, Jean-Noël. "Les structures de distribution dans les danses de théâtre à travers les recueils de Feuillet 1704 et Gaudrau." *Tanz und Bewegung in der barocken Oper: Kongreßbericht Salzburg 1994*. Ed. Sibylle Dahms and Stephanie Schroedter. Innsbruck and Vienna: Studien Verlag, 1996. 45–63.

Valeurs morales et religieuses sur la scène de l'Académie royale de musique (1669–1737). Geneva: Librairie Droz, 2002.

"Le contexte des danses d'Arlequin dans les comédies-ballets de Molière." In Laurenti (ed.), *Arlequin danseur*, 78–83.

Laurenti, Jean-Noël. (ed.) *Arlequin danseur au tournant du XVIIIe siècle*. Annales de l'ACRAS 1 (2005).

Marie Sallé, danseuse du XVIIIe siècle: Esquisses pour un nouveau portrait. Annales de l'ACRAS 3 (2008).

Le Tableau et la scène: Peinture et mise en scène du répertoire héroïque dans la première moitié du XVIIIe siècle; Autour des figures des Coypel. Annales de l'ACRAS 5 (2013).

Le Blanc, Judith. *Avatars d'opéra: Parodies et circulation des airs chantés sur les scènes parisiennes*. Paris: Classiques Garnier, 2014.

"L'opéra en mineur: Le cas de Fuzelier et de l'autoparodie." *Écrire en mineur au XVIIIe siècle*. Ed. Christelle Bahier-Porte and Régine Jomand-Baudry. Paris: Desjonquères, 2009. 415–36.

Lecomte, Nathalie. "Un danseur d'exception sur les tréteaux de Louis-le-Grand: Michel Blondy (1676?–1739)." *La Chair et le verbe: Les jésuites de France au XVIIIe siècle et l'image*. Ed. Edith Flamarion. Paris: Presses Sorbonne Nouvelle, 2008. 135–57.

"Danseuses and danseurs at the Opéra de Paris (1700–1725) according to the cast lists in the libretto-programs." *Dance Discourses: Key Words in Dance Research*. Ed. Susanne Franco and Marina Nordera. Abingdon and New York: Routledge, 2007. 131–52.

"L'exotisme dans le ballet: Les chinoiseries au XVIIIe siècle." *La Recherche en danse* 3 (1984): 29–41.

"The female ballet troupe of the Paris Opéra from 1700 to 1725." In Brooks (ed.), *Women's Work*, 99–122.

"Un maître à danser à la cour de Sceaux: Claude Balon." *La Duchesse du Maine (1676–1753): Une mécène à la croisée des arts et des siècles*. Ed. Catherine Cessac and Manuel Couvreur. Brussels: Éditions de l'Université de Bruxelles, 2003. 127–36.

"Pierre de La Montagne." In Laurenti (ed.), *Arlequin danseur*, 73–74.

Lecomte, Nathalie and Jérôme de La Gorce. Unpublished catalogue, *La Troupe de l'Opéra d'après les distributions des livrets (1699–1733)*.

Lecomte, Nathalie and Rebecca Harris-Warrick. "L'opposition Sallé–Camargo: Réalité ou fantasme?" In Laurenti (ed.), *Marie Sallé*, 49–64.

Legrand, Raphaëlle. "L'âge du ballet: Cartographie des divertissements et écriture de la danse dans les opéras d'André Campra." In Cessac (ed.), *Itinéraires d'André Campra*, 297–308.

"Chaconnes et passacailles dansées dans l'opéra français: Des airs de mouvement." *Le Mouvement en musique à l'époque baroque*. Ed. Hervé Lacombe. Metz: Éditions Serpinoise, 1996. 157–70.

Lesure, François. *L'Opéra classique français: XVIIe et XVIIIe siècles*. Geneva: Minkoff, 1972.

Letainturier-Fradin, Gabriel. *La Camargo, 1710–1770*. Paris: Flammarion, 1908? Rpt. Geneva: Minkoff, 1973.

Lindgren, Lowell. "Parisian patronage of performers from the Royal Academy of Musick (1719–28)." *ML* 58.1 (1977): 4–28.

Little, Meredith Ellis. "Problems of repetition and continuity in the dance music of Lully's *Ballet des Arts*." In La Gorce and Schneider (eds.), *Jean-Baptiste Lully*, 423–32.

See also Ellis, Meredith.

Little, Meredith Ellis and Carol G. Marsh. *La Danse Noble: An Inventory of Dances and Sources*. Williamstown, MA: Broude Brothers, 1992.

Locke, Ralph P. *Musical Exoticism: Images and Reflections*. Cambridge University Press, 2009.

Marsh, Carol G. "Dancing Venice: The forlana in France." Unpublished paper given at the annual conference of the Society for Seventeenth-Century Music (Princeton University, 2002).

"In search of the passepied." Unpublished paper given at the 24th annual conference of SDHS (Goucher College, 2001).

"Regular and irregular figures: Symmetry in baroque dance choreographies." Unpublished paper given at the annual conference of the Society for Seventeenth-Century Music (Wellesley College, 1996).

Marsh, Carol G. and Hubert Hazebroucq. "Revisiting the male solo choreography: A new source." (forthcoming).

Marsh, Carol G. and Rebecca Harris-Warrick. "Putting together a pantomime ballet." In Harris-Warrick and Brown (eds.), *The Grotesque Dancer*, 231–78.

Masson, Paul-Marie. "Le 'ballet héroïque.'" *Revue musicale* 9.8 (1928): 132–54.

"'Les Fêtes Vénitiennes' de Campra (1710)." *RdM* 13 (1932): 127–46 and 214–26.

L'Opéra de Rameau. Paris: Henri Laurens, 1930.

Mazouer, Charles. "Les Comédiens italiens dans les ballets au temps de Mazarin." *La France et l'Italie au temps de Mazarin*. Ed. J. Serroy. Grenoble: Presses Universitaires de Grenoble, 1986. 319–29.

McCleave, Sarah. *Dance in Handel's London Operas*. University of Rochester Press, 2013.

"Marie Sallé and the development of the *ballet en action*." *Musique et geste en France de Lully à la Révolution: Études sur la musique, le théâtre et la danse*. Ed. Jacqueline Waeber. Berne: Peter Lang, 2009. 175–95.

"Marie Sallé, a wise professional woman of influence." In Brooks (ed.), *Women's Work*, 160–82.

McCleave, Sarah (ed.). *Dance and Music in French Baroque Theatre: Sources and Intepretations*. London: King's College, 1998.

Montagnier, Jean-Paul. *Charles-Hubert Gervais: Un musicien au service du Régent et de Louis XV*. Paris: CNRS Editions, 2001.

Un Mécène musicien: Philippe d'Orléans, Régent (1674–1723). France: Zurfluh, 1996.

Moureau, François. *De Gherardi à Watteau: Présence d'Arlequin sous Louis XIV*. Paris: Klincksieck, 1992.

Dufresny, auteur dramatique (1657–1724). Paris: Klincksieck, 1979.

Naudeix, Laura. *Dramaturgie de la tragédie en musique (1673–1764)*. Paris: Honoré Champion, 2004.

Norman, Buford. *Touched by the Graces: The Libretti of Philippe Quinault in the Context of French Classicism*. Birmingham, AL: Summa Publications, 2001.

Norman, Buford (ed.). *Philippe Quinault, Livrets d'opéra*. 2 vols. Toulouse: Société de littératures classiques, 1999.

Okamoto, Kimiko (ed.). *Structures and Metaphors in Baroque Dance: Proceedings of the Conference at the University of Surrey Roehampton, March 31, 2001*. London: Center for Dance Research, University of Surrey Roehampton, 2001.

Pierce, Ken. "Choreographic approaches to the role of Apollo in the early 18th century." Unpublished paper given at *Roi Soleil and Soleil Dieu*, Fifth Annual Oxford Dance Symposium (March 2003).

"Choreographic structure in baroque dance." *Dance, Spectacle, and the Body Politick, 1250–1750*. Ed. Jennifer Nevile. Bloomington and Indianapolis: Indiana University Press, 2008. 182–208.

"Choreographic structures in dances by Feuillet." *Proceedings of the 25th Annual Conference of SDHS* (Temple University, 2002): 96–106.

"Dance notation systems in late 17th-century France." *EM* 26.2 (1998): 286–99.

"Dance vocabulary in the early 18th century as seen through Feuillet's step tables." *Proceedings of the 20th Annual Conference of SDHS* (Barnard College, 1997): 227–36.

"Shepherd and shepherdess dances on the French stage in the early 18th century." *Proceedings of the 28th Annual Conference of SDHS* (Northwestern University, 2005): 123–34.

Pierce, Ken and Jennifer Thorp. "The dances in Lully's *Persée*." *JSCM* 10.1 (2004).

Pierre, Constant. *Histoire du Concert Spirituel 1725–1790*. Paris: Société Française de Musicologie, 1975.

Pintiaux, Benjamin. "*Achille et Déidamie* (1735): Campra 'dans l'âge où l'on radote'?" In Cessac (ed.), *Itinéraires d'André Campra*, 215–26.

Porot, Bertrand. "Jean-Baptiste Stuck (1680–1755) et la réunion des goûts en France au seuil du XVIIIe siècle en France." Unpublished Ph.D. thesis, Université de Tours, 2001.

"Les ressorts du comique musical: Les chaconnes d'Arlequin au tournant du XVIIIe siècle. In Laurenti (ed.), *Arlequin danseur*, 120–30.

"Watteau au spectacle: La danse sur les scènes parisiennes (1702–1721)." *Watteau au confluent des arts esthétiques de la grâce*. Rennes: Presses Universitaires de Rennes, 2014. 237–55.

Powell, John. "Pierre Beauchamps, choreographer to Molière's Troupe du Roy." *ML* 76.2 (1995): 168–86.

Music and Theatre in France 1600–1680. Oxford University Press, 2000.

Preußner, Eberhard. *Die musikalischen Reisen des Herrn von Uffenbach*. Kassel and Basel: Bärenreiter, 1949.

Quéro, Dominique. *Momus philosophe: Recherches sur une figure littéraire du XVIIIe siècle*. Paris: Honoré Champion, 1995.

Rizzoni, Nathalie. "Un représentant pittoresque de Terpsichore: Le maître à danser dans le théâtre français de la première moitié du XVIIIe siècle." *Sociopoétique de la danse*. Ed. Alain Montandon. Paris: Anthropos, 1998. 207–22.

Rosand, Ellen. *Opera in Seventeenth-Century Venice: The Creation of a Genre*. Berkeley and Los Angeles: University of California Press, 1991.

Rosow, Lois. "The descending minor tetrachord in France: An emblem expanded." *New Perspectives on Marc-Antoine Charpentier*. Ed. Shirley Thompson. Farnham: Ashgate, 2010. 63–87.

"From Destouches to Berton: Editorial responsibility at the Paris Opéra." *JAMS* 40.2 (1987): 285–309.

"How eighteenth-century Parisians heard Lully's operas: The case of *Armide*'s fourth act." In Heyer (ed.), *Jean-Baptiste Lully*, 213–37.

"Lully's musical architecture: Act IV of *Persée*." *JSCM* 10.1 (2004).

"Making connections: Thoughts on Lully's entr'actes." *EM* 21.2 (1993): 231–38.

"Paris Opéra orchestration, 1686–1713: Deciphering the code in the orchestral parts." In McCleave (ed.), *Dance and Music*, 33–53.

"Performing a choral dialogue by Lully." *EM* 15.3 (1987): 325–35.

"The principal sources for Lully's *Armide*." In La Gorce and Schneider (eds.), *Quellenstudien*, 248–63.

Rubellin, Françoise. "Écrire pour tous les théâtres: Le cas singulier de Louis Fuzelier." *L'Opéra de Paris, la Comédie-Française et l'Opéra-Comique: Approches comparées (1669–2010)*. Ed. Denis Herlin, Sabine Chaouche, and Solveig Serre. Paris: École des Chartes, 2012. 267–79.

Sadie, Julie Anne. "Paris and Versailles." *The Late Baroque Era from the 1680s to 1740*. Ed. George J. Buelow. Englewood Cliffs, NJ: Prentice Hall, 1993. 129–89.

Sadler, Graham. "The *basse continue* in Lully's operas: Evidence old and new." In La Gorce and Schneider (eds.), *Quellenstudien*, 382–97.

"Patrons and pasquinades: Rameau in the 1730s." *Journal of the Royal Musical Association* 113 (1988): 314–37.

"Rameau and the orchestra." *PRMA* 108 (1981–82): 47–68.

Sakhnovskaia, Anastassia. "Sur les traces des Italiens à la foire pendant les années de disgrâce (1697–1716)." Paper presented at the 2004 CESAR Conference: http://cesar.org.uk/cesar2/conferences/cesar_conference_june_2004/sakhnov_paper.html

Sawkins, Lionel. *A Thematic Catalogue of the Works of Michel-Richard de Lalande (1657–1726)*. Oxford University Press, 2005.

Schneider, Herbert. "Canevas als Terminus der lyrischen Dichtung." *Archiv für Musikwissenschaft* 42.2 (1985): 87–101.

Chronologisch-thematisches Verzeichnis sämtlicher Werke von Jean-Baptiste Lully (LWV). Tutzing: Hans Schneider, 1981.

Die Rezeption der Opern Lullys im Frankreich des Ancien Régime. Tutzing: Hans Schneider, 1982.

Schroedter, Stephanie. *Vom "Affect" zur "Action": Quellenstudien zur Poetik der Tanzkunst vom späten Ballet de Cour bis zum frühen Ballet en Action*. Würzburg: Königshausen & Neumann, 2004.

Schwartz, Judith L. and Christena L. Schlundt. *French Court Dance and Dance Music: A Guide to Primary Source Writings, 1643–1789*. Stuyvesant, NY: Pendragon Press, 1987.

Scott, Virginia. *The Commedia dell'Arte in Paris, 1644–1697*. Charlottesville: University Press of Virginia, 1980.

Semmens, Richard. *The Bals Publics at the Paris Opera in the Eighteenth Century*. Hillsdale, NY: Pendragon Press, 2004.

Tanguy, Camille. "*Le Carnaval de Venise*: L'imaginaire renouvelé de Regnard et Campra." *Le Carnaval de Venise: Livret de 1699*. Paris: Editions de l'Académie Desprez, 2007. 7–47.

Thorp, Jennifer. "And the peasants came too: Pastoral themes in entr'acte dances on the London stage." Unpublished paper given at *Dance and the Pastoral*: Seventh Annual Oxford Dance Symposium (April 2005).

"Dance in Lully's *Alceste*." *Ancient Drama in Music for the Modern Stage*. Ed. Peter Brown and Suzana Ograjensek. Oxford University Press, 2010. 85–95.

"Mademoiselle Subligny in London." Unpublished paper given at the Ninth Annual Oxford Dance Symposium (May, 2007).

"The notion of grace in the early eighteenth century: Mademoiselle Guiot's dances in Lully's *Atys*." *Sur quel pied danser: Danse et littérature*. Ed. Edward Nye, Hélène Stafford, and Michael Freeman. Amsterdam and New York: Rodopi, 2005. 91–106.

"Serious and comic in the work of F. Le Roussau, 1720." In Okamoto (ed.), *Structures and Metaphors*, 10–20.

"Servile bodies? The status of the professional dancer in the late seventeenth and early eighteenth centuries." *The Ancient Dancer in the Modern World: Responses to Greek and Roman Dance*. Ed. Fiona Macintosh. Oxford University Press, 2010. 169–87.

Thorp, Jennifer and Ken Pierce. "Taste and ingenuity: Three English chaconnes of the early eighteenth century." *Historical Dance* 3.3 (1994): 3–16.

Tomko, Linda. "Framing Turkish dances." *Music in Art* 36.1–2 (2011): 131–59.

"Positioning peasants." In Okamoto (ed.), *Structures and Metaphors*, 1–9.

Trott, David. "Louis Fuzelier et le théâtre: Vers un état présent." *Revue d'Histoire Littéraire de la France* 83.4 (1983): 604–17.

Tunley, David. *The Eighteenth-Century French Cantata*. 2nd ed. Oxford and New York: Clarendon Press, 1997.

Viollier, Renée. *Jean-Joseph Mouret: Le Musicien des Grâces, 1682–1738*. Paris: Librairie Fleury, 1950.

Whaples, Miriam K. "Early exoticism revisited." *The Exotic in Western Music*. Ed. Jonathan Bellman. Boston: Northeastern University Press, 1998. 3–25.

"Exoticism in dramatic music, 1600–1800." Unpublished Ph.D. thesis. Indiana University, 1958.

Whitley-Bauguess, Paige. "An eighteenth-century dance reconstruction: Performance by Mlle Guyot." *Dance Notation Journal* 5.1 (1987): 11–24.

"Reading baroque dance notation." *BaroqueDance.com* (2010): http://www.baroquedance.com/research/dancenotation.htm#readingfeuillet

"The search for Mlle Guyot." *Proceedings of the 11th Annual Conference of SDHS* (North Carolina School of the Arts, 1988). 32–67.

Witherell, Anne. *Louis Pécour's 1700 Recueil de dances*. Ann Arbor: UMI Research Press, 1983.

Wood, Caroline. *Music and Drama in the Tragédie en Musique, 1673–1715: Jean-Baptiste Lully and his Successors*. New York and London: Garland, 1996.
"Orchestra and spectacle in the *tragédie en musique* 1673–1715: Oracle, *sommeil* and *tempête*." *PRMA* 108 (1981–82): 25–46.
Wood, Caroline and Graham Sadler (eds.). *French Baroque Opera: A Reader*. Aldershot: Ashgate, 2000.
Zaslaw, Neal. "Lully's orchestra." In La Gorce and Schneider (eds.), *Jean-Baptiste Lully*, 539–79.

INDEX OF PEOPLE AND TERMS

Individuals indexed by family name only are dancers whose first names are unknown. Composers and librettists are indexed here if their contributions are discussed, but not when they are mentioned only as the author of a particular work, for which see the Index of Works. Appendix 3 is online at www.cambridge.org/9781107137899

A number in bold refers to a figure; a number in italics refers to a music example.

INDEX OF WORKS

This index includes those works mentioned in this study that were performed on the stage of the Académie Royale de Musique; it is not, however, a complete list of the institution's repertoire. Selected works from other theaters (plays, court ballets, etc.) are listed here as relevant, but this index does not include all such works mentioned in the text.

A number in bold refers to a figure; a number in italics refers to a music example. Appendix 3 is online at www.cambridge.org/9781107137899

For EU product safety concerns, contact us at Calle de José Abascal, 56–1°, 28003 Madrid, Spain or eugpsr@cambridge.org.

www.ingramcontent.com/pod-product-compliance
Ingram Content Group UK Ltd.
Pitfield, Milton Keynes, MK11 3LW, UK
UKHW061109121125
464974UK00009B/318